When the Body Is the Target

Self-Harm, Pain, and Traumatic Attachments

SHARON KLAYMAN FARBER, PH.D.

JASON ARONSON INC.
Northvale, New Jersey
London

This book was set in 10 pt. Goudy by Alpha Graphics of Pittsfield, NH, and printed and bound by Book-mart Press, Inc. of North Bergen, NJ.

Library of Congress Cataloging-in-Publication Data

Farber, Sharon Klayman.
    When the body is the target : self-harm, pain, and traumatic attachments / Sharon Klayman Farber.
        p. cm.
    Includes bibliographical references and index.
    ISBN 0-7657-0256-8
    1. Self-mutilation.   2. Self-injurious behavior.   3. Eating disorders.   4. Bulimia
    5. Anorexia nervosa.   I. Title.

RC552.S4 F36 2000
616.85'82—dc21   99-055414

Printed in the United States of America on acid-free paper. For information and catalog write to Jason Aronson Inc., 230 Livingston Street, Northvale, NJ 07647-1726, or visit our website: www.aronson.com

Contents

Part II
Neglect, Violence, and Traumatic Attachments

Part IV
Clinical Implications

This book is dedicated to my husband, Stuart, and my son, David, both of whom have taught me so much about attachment and love.

This book is dedicated to my patients and the courageous people who participated in my study, for allowing me the privilege of entering their lives and teaching me so much. To all who struggle with self-harm, I wish you hope, health, and healing.

This book is dedicated as well to the memory of Kathy, who left this world far too soon.

Preface: Genesis

This book had its beginnings in the curiosity and passion that power the wish to understand concepts, people, and connections. My interest in self-harm began a long time ago, in a creative writing class in high school, where I learned about the process of stream of consciousness, the technique used by many writers of fiction and poetry, of whom James Joyce is probably the best-known example. The class was given the assignment of writing that way, allowing our minds to wander wherever they wanted, not censoring anything that we might ordinarily censor. I began to write in that mode, which I came to know later was akin to the process of free association. I was astounded and intrigued at what I wrote. It was primitive, strange, and so different from what my usually logical mind produced. I wanted to understand it.

A few years later when I was an English major in college and had begun my own psychoanalysis, I stumbled upon Georg Groddeck's *The Book of the It* (1923), which was very exciting because it linked free association with the mystery of the mind–body relationship. Groddeck, I soon discovered, was regarded by some as the father of psychosomatics, an eccentric angel, and a genius. He was regarded at the same time by others as a "wild analyst," a lunatic, a terrible embarrassment to psychoanalysis. Many of his ideas were wild and irresponsible, provoking a number of his colleagues to wash their hands of him. Nevertheless, I thought his ideas were exciting and brilliant.

I have been interested for a long time in understanding the mysterious, and certainly mental illness is very mysterious. After college I worked in the recreation therapy department of Gracie Square Hospital, a small private psychiatric

hospital with locked wards. It was an unsettling experience, shaking up my notions of normality and abnormality. That first week I saw a young woman my age
in restraints in a "quiet room," and was shocked to recognize her as one of my
college classmates. I barely knew her, but she had seemed normal. I began to
question what normal was.

The first week I did not have a set of keys to unlock the ward doors and had
to depend on other staff members to let me in and out. Initially it was just a nui-
sance but then, to my astonishment, it became a problem. I had introduced myself to a nurse and asked her to unlock the door for me. There was an unsettling
pause and I realized that she did not believe that I was a new employee. She spoke
to me in the well-intentioned but infantilizing way that many clinical staff members used with patients. "Yes, dear, we all work here. Some of us work here as
staff and others work very hard to get better. Why don't I make a call and find
out on which floor you belong?" I was shocked at being mistaken for a patient. I
told her that she didn't understand, that she should call my supervisor to verify
that I really was an employee. Again, the patient smile. Realizing that she had
the power to limit my freedom, I became frightened, the experience began to feel
unreal, and I wondered if this could really be happening to me. It was. I became
a bit agitated and tried again. And again. She said I was becoming hostile (I was)
and said perhaps I needed to take something to calm down if I couldn't calm down
on my own. Life got easier after I had my own set of keys because the keys made
my identity clear; I was not one of them.

Years later I could look back at this episode and think: So, this is what it
was like to be a mental patient. You are not taken seriously, you have no credibility, your freedom to come and go is taken away. I learned a lot there. I was
told that the schizophrenic patients could not be treated with psychotherapy,
only managed with medication, and was advised not to bother listening too
carefully to what they were saying because it was meaningless. Although many
of the patients had a diagnosis of schizophrenia and spoke to some extent in
the language of primary process, I found that if I listened closely and carefully,
some of what was thought to be meaningless seemed to have meaning for them
and made sense to me when I could supply some of the linguistic links that they
omitted. I was able to do this when I could bend my unconscious to meet theirs
in the space where they veered away from reality. Schizophrenia was becoming less scary. I began to think that maybe schizophrenics could be treated with
psychotherapy. Certainly I had no training to do it other than my own experience of being listened to as an analytic patient, but it took no training for me
to listen to them and find that what initially seemed mysterious and remote
became more understandable.

Like most clinical social workers, from the beginning of my career I worked
with many patients considered to be untreatable by means of psychoanalysis or
psychoanalytic psychotherapy. At that time treatment by social workers was typically supportive, as training for more demanding work was not so readily avail-

able. Fortunately, my own treatment was with an analyst who was a social worker, one of a number who had obtained psychoanalytic training from the few "renegade" analysts who were courageous enough to train lay analysts in the way Freud wanted, at a time when the American Psychoanalytic Association's policy was to exclude nonmedical professionals from training.

From the beginning of my career I worked with patients who lived in the most impoverished and traumatic environments, and who had to adapt to human jungles in order to survive. I worked with the urban poor in the toughest neighborhoods of New York's Lower East Side, with survivors of the Holocaust, and with hospitalized mentally ill adolescent girls from Brooklyn's ghettos who, for their own safety, carried switchblades. I worked in the department of psychiatry in a municipal hospital in a rough Bronx neighborhood, a hospital that has since been razed, paved over, and turned into a parking lot. I did psychotherapy on the street, on the fly, in snatches of brief contact in hallways, in the emergency room, by phone, in formed and in unformed groups, and, more traditionally, behind closed office doors by appointment.

Later, working in both psychiatric and medical settings further stimulated my curiosity about the mind–body relationship of several patients who had decidedly mysterious relationships to their own bodies. There was a 13-year-old girl, a psychiatric inpatient at Kings County Hospital, a city hospital in Brooklyn, who kept using her left hand to try to "catch" her flailing right arm that looked as if it were running away from her or did not even belong to her body. There was a 15-year-old girl thought to have attempted suicide whom I was asked to see in the Fordham Hospital Emergency Room. She had carved "The New York Dolls," the name of her favorite rock group, into her arm with a razor blade. She expressed no wish to die; she felt only warmth, relief, and no pain. Carla, at 19, was a puzzle to the dermatology clinic, where she was repeatedly treated for skin infections on her left arm. She was given oral antibiotics and ointments, which she used as prescribed. Her skin condition did not improve. In fact it got worse. She developed open sores and pus-filled lesions. What she did not tell the clinic personnel was something I learned after a few weeks of psychotherapy, that she regularly raked her infected arm hard with her metal-bristled hair brush, promoting and maintaining the outward signs of something very wrong on the inside. Also at Fordham was the schizophrenic woman I treated. When I became pregnant and the pregnancy became apparent, she asked about it and I told her that yes, I was pregnant and would in time be leaving the hospital. There was no expression of feeling about this, but the following week and the weeks after, she arrived looking quite pregnant. Her periods had stopped, she said, her breasts were tender. I referred her to the OB-GYN clinic, but oddly they found she was not pregnant. I called and they agreed to examine her again and again, the report was negative. So was a third. When I called yet again and they said quite definitely that she was not pregnant, it finally occurred to me that this was a case of pseudocyesis ("hysterical pregnancy"), something I had read about as one of those mysterious leaps from the mind to the body. At New York University's Rusk Institute for Rehabilitation Medicine, I worked with Tommy, an 8-year-old boy who had become paralyzed from the waist down. He drove the medical staff to distraction by regularly digging into his legs with pins, scissors, pens, or any sharp object he could find, continuously infecting and reinfecting himself.

The experience with Tommy caused me to think about the drug addicts with whom I had worked in a detoxification center before entering social work school. Many seemed to be as addicted to the act of sticking a needle in their arms as they were to the heroin that they injected into their bodies, and some could even get high injecting water. I was asked to run a weekly group therapy session. I wanted to get them to think about something other than drugs. Whether it was because I had no training for what I was doing or that the power of the addiction was extraordinary, or probably both, I found that group therapy became immediately an animated exchange of favorite "recipes" for getting high. These men seemed addicted to sharing their recipes, entering altered states of consciousness as they spoke of how they would "shoot up two nickel bags of horse, take a couple or so bombitas, then a bottle of Thunderbird" or advising, "no, man, bombitas aren't worth shit; you take cibas, you are *gone*, out of *sight*."

One of the positive aspects about not being a professionally trained drug counselor in the 1960s was that nothing was expected of us in terms of effecting any significant change. We were just meant to help the addicts go through the detox program. Most of the patients had done time in prison for drug-related crimes. Most had come into the detox center for "three hots and a cot," three cooked meals a day and a bed, to escape the harshness of the addict's life in winter—sleeping in alleys or on rooftops—or to cut down on their habit to make it less expensive. We were expected to do intake drug histories, counsel patients as needed, and try to dissuade them from signing out against medical advice so that they would complete the thirty-day detoxification period. We had not yet experienced the often stultifying influence of dogmatic theories, training institutes, or teachers and analysts whom we had idealized to quench a youthful impulse that ran toward rescue fantasies. This allowed some freedom for innovation, if one was inclined, and after the group therapy experiment, I was. I decided to try a different group approach, using acting for its expressive potential. Addicts were some of the best actors I knew, their bravado and swagger covering a lifetime of hurt, violence, and trauma. Bored with waiting for their thirty days of passive detoxification to be up, they picked themselves up from their beds, their interminable games of checkers, their hoarded stashes of cigarettes and Kool-Aid, to follow me into the dayroom, muttering self-conscious jokes about their "acting careers." I was surprised to see how readily they gave themselves to improvising a scene when a situation was given to them. Even more surprising was that although initially they managed to introduce drugs into every improvisation, after some time this stopped, and they became engrossed in the acting. To my astonishment, after an hour and a half had elapsed and dinner was announced, they did not want to stop. They asked if they could continue the next day. Two men told me with tears in their eyes that this was the first time in many years that they felt normal, the way they do when they were "high." Beyond the initial rush, what they craved from the drug experience was the feeling of normality and well-being that so eluded them. They had been able to use the freedom to play, to enjoy for awhile a sense of creativity and well-being, the wonderful sense of being part of a group, like kids at school putting on the senior play.

The women addicts once put together a variety show to dispel their boredom, and one act was unforgettable. A woman pantomimed to driving jazz the sequence of getting sick, going out to turn a trick, meeting her connection, copping a few bags of heroin, inserting them into her vagina for safekeeping until she got home, tying off her arm to prepare the vein, preparing the syringe, then injecting herself, feeling a rush of pleasure, then her body relaxing into limpness. What was astounding about this was that the others watching seemed to be mesmerized, going into a trancelike state with the performer in which their muscles moved, tensed, and then relaxed in concert with her. A roomful of women got high together without taking any drug and reached some erotic crescendo and release, a most powerful interaction between mind, emotion, and body. I was peering into the mystery of dissociated states and wanted to understand more.

Several years later in the early 1970s there occurred a disturbing moment in my life that fueled a fierce interest in understanding the strange, trancelike states of mind of those involved in the various religious and mental health cults that seemed to be cropping up. Transcendental Meditation (TM) was very popular at that time and my brother not only practiced it but had become a TM instructor, going to Spain to learn whatever mysteries were involved from the Maharishi Mahesh Yogi's videotapes. The Beatles had studied with the Maharishi and their album, *Magical Mystery Tour*, reflected it. TM was in the air. It never occurred to me at the time that TM could be harmful. I learned the method myself but found it annoying, finding the yogic breathing I had learned in college better for relaxation. In one shocking moment, however, when my brother was talking with me and my husband about TM, I realized that he was talking like a robot, like a human machine. When I asked him thoughtful questions about his TM practices, he could not answer, except to recite from memory what I later came to understand were the rote teachings he had committed to memory, the TM "party line." He was talking only to my husband and me and yet he addressed us as "ladies and gentlemen," the same way he might have addressed a roomful of people who had come with their flowers, fruit, and money for their initiation into TM. There seemed to be nothing behind his eyes when I looked into them, no emotion, just a void, blankness. Ever since that moment I have been struggling to understand what happened. How could a personality change so suddenly? How could an intelligent person suddenly lose the ability to think? To feel? How could someone who had been there all of a sudden not be there?

A few years later I treated my first patient who had been profoundly damaged by her cult experiences and then a few others whose experiences in EST (Erhardt Sensitivity Training, later known as The Forum), in nominally Christian sects, and with various Eastern guru entrepreneurs had left them in what seemed to be ongoing states of confused floating and dissociation. Ultimately, I integrated what I had learned from my personal and clinical experiences and from doing consultations with people who had had a family member lost to a cult. I came to understand how the strange process of what had happened to my brother, the process that had caused him to snap, had also happened to lesser or greater degree in those who harm themselves. I also came to understand the importance of ongoing active intervention to correct the enormous cognitive distortions both in cult members and in those who harm themselves.

I learned that dissociation was essentially a phenomenon of those who do not experience the unity of mind and body. After getting my master's in social work, when I was studying with Dr. Gertrude Blanck and the late Rubin Blanck at the Institute for the Study of Psychotherapy, Gertrude Blanck made a statement—about people with borderline ego organization and those who had an inordinate narcissistic investment in their bodies—that stayed with me, providing much food for thought: "They tend to live more in the body and less in the mind." I came to think of the patients I have described above and many others as living more in the body and less in the mind. Their experience of events that one might expect to be experienced emotionally were not, but were experienced by them as physically charged experiences. I came to understand that living more in the body and less in the mind was a certain form of adaptation to their environment— a psychosomatic adaptation.

Even after going into private practice and seeing more middle-class suburban patients, I soon realized that many of the people I saw with borderline personality organization, dissociative disorders, posttraumatic stress disorders, psychosomatic disorders, and pronounced sadomasochistic pathology had suffered the effects of violence. While many came from environments that superficially looked good, from intact families, some even with high-achieving functional parents and attractive, affluent homes, they nonetheless came from environments of neglect, abuse, or other trauma. I became more aware only in the past decade that those who actively engaged in self-harm behavior seemed to be repeating the violence they had suffered or witnessed passively, inflicting it upon their bodies.

After postgraduate training in psychoanalytic psychotherapy, psychoanalysis, and child and adolescent treatment, I decided to get my doctorate in clinical social work. During this time I was fortunate to have the experience of teaching first-year medical students about psychopathology and the role played by psychosocial factors in the etiology and maintenance of illness and recovery from illness. This stimulated more thought about how the mind and body can work synergistically and unconsciously to inflict harm on the body. Soon after, I undertook training in treating patients with eating disorders, and came to understand eating disorders as a paradigm for understanding psychosomatic processes. I learned that all disease is psychosomatic and somatopsychic, in that psychological and somatic factors are always present to a greater or lesser extent, actively intertwining at many levels (Weiner and Fawzy 1989).

Having obtained specialized training in eating disorders, I began to study the strong association between binge and purge behavior and self-mutilating behavior. I learned a great deal about this association and saw these behaviors in relation to other forms of self-harm such as drug and alcohol abuse, anorexia nervosa, compulsive eating, suicide attempts, compulsive sex, shoplifting, compulsive shopping and spending, accident-proneness, and compulsive risk taking. I thought that what I was learning would be helpful to clinicians, researchers, and patients.

Many colleagues were repelled by the nature of my study, others were fascinated. Some began to look at their skin picking, nail biting, and autoerotic habits in a new way that was somewhat disturbing to them. Some wondered if they too were "self-mutilators." Applying that label to themselves seemed to be the equivalent of acknowledging a stigmatized status, one shared with hospitalized psychiatric patients and prisoners. If these acknowledged behaviors are forms of relatively mild self-mutilation, perhaps the difference between "us" and "them," self and other, the normal and the pathological, is not quite so great as we like to think. The more I came to think this way, the more I continued to find it unsettling, disturbing my sleep and my dreams as I had to wrestle more and more with what I was coming to acknowledge and understand in myself. At times I thought I had bitten off more than I could chew, and wanted to turn back. Despite these reservations, what remained constant was the passion for knowledge and the fascination of discovering and exploring a mystery.

I came to understand that nail biting and other habitual behaviors were low key versions of human impulses that were articulated far more powerfully by the severe eating disordered and self-mutilating behavior of the subjects in my study. I appreciated how very human these behaviors were, how many functions they could serve, and how many meanings they could have. As I learned how necessary and useful they had been, I could better appreciate the mysterious creativity of the unconscious in creating them. Borrowing from Joyce Mcdougall's provocatively titled book, I join her in making A *Plea for a Measure of Abnormality*. If we understand and accept our own very human impulses, we can more readily find empathic identification with our patients, which can only promote better informed treatment, and we can come to see those who severely harm themselves as being as much like ourselves as they are different.

Acknowledgments

To Hunter College High School, for treasuring and cultivating an adolescent girl's intellect and curiosity. To my classmates and friends from Hunter, my first co-travelers of the life of the mind. To teachers Charles Raphael, English teacher at Hunter, who introduced me to the wonders of stream of consciousness, which opened up worlds to me; and to Joseph Imperial, for convincing my mother that I needed to be there.

To the memory of my mother, Raye Klayman, who struggled to make this wonderful opportunity possible.

To Robert J. Berk, Ph.D., for that for which words are not enough.

To Gertrude Blanck, Ph.D., from whom I learned so much in so many different ways. For the largeness of spirit not only to tolerate my criticism of some of her ideas but to appreciate the thinking behind it. For me, that was a gift worth the world.

To Professor Martin Bergmann, who taught and stimulated so much.

To John Kerr, for directing my mind down the path of attachment theory, where I found that I was already there.

To Jason Aronson and Michael Moskowitz, for the opportunity to transform my fantasy of writing a book into a reality. And to Cindy Hyden, my editor, for a brief but wonderful time. And to Judy Cohen and David Kaplan, for their expert editorial work, and to Norma Pomerantz—a great team.

To the Rivertowns' Artists and Writers Group, who listened, laughed, recognized my creative struggle, and inspired me.

To Janet Murphy and the staff at the Hastings-on-Hudson Public Library who good naturedly honored my almost constant requests for interlibrary loans and journal articles.

To writers Catherine Taormina, and Ruta Mazelis, for their contributions to this book, and for helping me better understand the role of self-harm in their lives and in their healing.

To Joyce Kraus Aronson, Ph.D., whose friendship and support are treasured. Her scholarly editing of key psychoanalytic concepts in eating disorders, *Insights in the Dynamic Psychotherapy of Anorexia And Bulimia: An Introduction to the Literature* (1993), has been invaluable to me in formulating my ideas about self-harm.

For their encouraging words and help in ways large and small: Myrna Armstrong, Ed.D., R.N., Evan Bellin, M.D., April Benson, Ph.D., Rev. Hillary Bercovici, Ph.D., Maureen Burke, R.G.N., R. M. N., Lynda Chassler, Ph.D., Karen Conterio, Anna Christake Cornwell, Ph.D., Barbara Ehrenreich, Ph.D., Armando Favazza, M.D., Susan Gombos, M.S.W., Judith Greif, R.N., M.S.,Walter Hewitt, R.N., Dutch Holsinger, Rev. Betty Hudson, Patrick Kavanaugh, Ph.D., Edward Khantzian, M.D., Caroline Koblenzer, M.D., David Krueger, M.D., Craig Johnson, Ph.D., Roberta Markowitz, M.S.W., Janice Mclane, Ph.D., Dolly Moon, M.A., C.S.W., Vivian Pronin, M.A., Jean Sanville, Ph.D., Lynda Schare, Ph.D., Andrea Schneer, M.S., C.S.W., Marge Slavin, M.S.W., Jeffery Smith, M.D., Rabbi Noach Valley, Walter Vandereycken, M.D., Marcy Viboch, M.A., Karen Walant, Ph.D., Pat Williams, M.S.W., C. Philip Wilson, M.D., Margaret Woodruff, Ph.D., and Stephen Zimmer, C.S.W.

To Rabbi Daniel Brenner and members of the Westchester-Riverdale Reconstructionist Group for stimulating discussions that were food for mind and soul.

To my wonderful, funny son, David, whose drive and ambition continue to inspire me. And finally, to my husband, Stuart, my sun of a zillion rays—for enriching my life, sharing everything, giving so very much, and tolerating the disruption this book made to our life. For his marvelous humor, which helped me keep my feet planted on the ground and helped me maintain my own sense of humor through the hardest of times. For meals cooked, and groceries bought. Without him, this book would never have been possible.

Introduction

Suddenly self-cutting, a clinical problem that evokes considerable anxiety, seems to be almost everywhere, bursting onto the cultural scene in very much the same way eating disorders exploded into our awareness twenty or thirty years ago. Both are hot topics now. After years of researching the relationship between two specific kinds of self-harm, bulimic behavior and self-mutilating behavior, I am asked to lecture on how to get patients to stop cutting themselves, or starving themselves, or bingeing and purging, and I am asked to do this in an hour. It is all too easy to focus on stopping self-harm without understanding it. The behavior is only the tip of the iceberg.

Self harm is about people who cannot live peacefully in their own skin, whose emotions are not experienced in their mind but in and through the immediacy of their bodies. It is about individuals whose predominant mode of self experience is sadomasochistic pain and suffering, and whose most comfortable terrain in which to live is the "borderland" (Novick and Novick 1996). Although written primarily for the clinician, there is much here for any reader whose interest has been captured by the violent destructiveness to others and self that has ascended to the foreground of our cultural consciousness. This includes those people whose lives are wrapped around a self-destructive core. Any thoughtful reader who wants to understand more about why we are hearing so much about self-mutilation, tattooing, body piercing, food-related disturbances, substance abuse, sadomasochism, and other disturbing trends in the youth culture will find something of interest here.

This is a book for clinicians who may or may not have psychoanalytic training. Whether one comes from a psychoanalytic, family systems, or cognitive-behavioral orientation, a psychoanalytically informed case formulation offers a good opportunity for designing an empathic and pragmatic treatment meant to transform the nature of the sadomasochistic attachments. A psychoanalytically informed case formulation can be quite useful not only in informing a psychoanalytic treatment per se but also in designing a group therapy program, cognitive-behavioral treatment, family systems treatment, or a largely supportive treatment for self-harming patients.

In this book I attempt to make self-harm understandable as a creative unconscious solution to formidable problems of living. It may be a dark kind of creativity, but the paradox is that even the most seemingly self-destructive acts often have creation as their goal. Clinicians must understand and appreciate the creative functions of self-harm behavior and their creative etiology. Helping a patient to give up self-destructive behavior and relationships is a complex and circular process, requiring the clinician to appreciate how the libidinal and aggressive drives and a sense of self have become trapped in the body's symptoms. If the heart is the representational source of our emotionality, then telling the patient to "amputate" the self-harm symptom is equivalent to telling him to eat his heart out or to cut his heart out.

Many self-harming patients will say that they would give up their bodily symptoms if only they could, but because they know no other way to live, they simply cannot give it up. This is where we need to start, because even though clinicians can get patients to give up the self-harm behavior, getting a patient to give it up before he is capable of functioning without it can result in even more severe self-harm. Self-cutting and eating disorders are disturbing symptoms, and we hope we can help our patients who are attached to pain and suffering to find more growth-enhancing attachments. In this age of managed care, the focus is on symptom reduction through behavioral treatment, psychopharmacology, and tiny bits of psychotherapy—short shrift to patients whose difficulties require complex and necessarily longer-term treatments.

Some time ago, I got a call from a clinician who worked with psychotic patients at a prestigious teaching hospital and was interested in eating disorders. She told me that as the patients on the eating disorders unit got better (getting better was measured behaviorally in terms of weight gain and stopping bingeing and purging), many of them began manifesting psychotic symptoms just at the time that discharge plans were being arranged. The plans for discharge were halted and the patients were transferred to her unit, where their psychotic symptomatology was the focus of treatment, paid for by insurance companies using managed care criteria. I suggested that to understand the phenomenon of eating disorders, one must know something too about the kinds of severe ego and psychosomatic regressions that can occur when the patient is forced to give up symptoms before the ego is able to relinquish them. The emerging psychosis can be an iatrogenic illness, precipitated unnecessarily by the patient's treatment. Managed care, although committed to cost-efficiency, was actually promoting iatrogenic illness by insisting on short-term, symptom-focused treatment, and then having to spend even more money to pay for the treatment of the iatrogenically induced illness!

In my research, I began looking for a way to illuminate a dark mystery, that of self-inflicted harm and its mysterious companion, self-inflicted pain in those who need to cut or scratch their skin, rip up their insides with self-induced vomiting or abuse laxatives violently, or other self-destructive acts. I wanted to understand the demonic powers by which some lives are lived. I wanted to better understand the concept of the *It* in Georg Groddeck's *Book of the It* (1923). Groddeck never clearly defined the *It*, but it was virtually synonymous with the forces of the id. In fact Freud (1923) derived the word *Id* (*Es* in German) from Groddeck. Groddeck spoke of the mind and the body not as separate entities but as facets of the whole, and said in a letter to Freud that "the distinction between mind and body is only a word, not an essential distinction. . . . The body and mind are a joint thing which harbors an It, a power by which we are lived, while we think we live" (Grossman and Grossman 1965, p. 69). Once we can face our deepest and darkest urgings, our *It*, said Groddeck (1923), we will be free to live in harmony within ourselves.

Novelist E. L. Doctorow described the creative process in writing as "going down to the rag bin of your mind and pulling up whatever you can find and somehow stitching it together, making a whole something out of little bits and pieces (Lahr 1998)."[1] Healthy artists or writers have the ability to reach into their unconscious, into the whirling chaos of primary process, to create something new of aesthetic value in the transitional space between the unconscious and the conscious, and then resume functioning in the ordered thought of secondary process. The borders are not threatening to creative people with intact ego functions, because the regression to primary process is a controlled regression in the service of the ego, and so they can readily emerge from it to use the bits and pieces they have come up with to fashion something new and of enduring value to society. The self-harmer, on the other hand, does not dip, but instead plummets down precariously into the unconscious mind, retrieving bits and pieces of memory—cognitive memory, memory traces, and somatic memory—to create various self-harming acts. Like the poem or painting that is meant to communicate to others, the self that is harmed also serves as unspoken communication to others, and sometimes it serves as a presymbolic communication to the self. For the self-harmer the regression to self-harm may devastate and engender more pain and suffering, and sometimes death. Yet strange as it may sound, some have been able to transform the enactments on their bodies into a communication to the self, using their self-harm to grow into a newer sense of self, one with a greater aware-

---

1. I thank Jeanette Bertles for introducing me to this quotation and for pointing out its source.

ness of options and choices that has enabled them to relinquish their self-harm. I have been helped to understand this last point through dialogues with writer Catherine Taormina and writer and publisher Ruta Mazelis, of *The Cutting Edge*, both of whom have lived with and relinquished self-harm.

The concepts about self-harm discussed in this book have evolved from my training, clinical experience, research, and self-analysis. In conducting a study on the relationship between two very similar yet different kinds of self-harm behavior, binge-and-purge behavior and self-mutilating behavior, I found that these two severe and mysterious forms of physical self-harm were prototypes for understanding other kinds of self-harm.

CONCEPTUAL THEMES

Psychoanalysis is given to metapsychology, simultaneous multiple points of view, rather than mutually exclusive dichotomous categories. We need a broadened integrative psychoanalytic frame of reference with which to understand and treat patients attached to self-harm, one that can transcend disciplinary boundaries and intellectual disciplines. This is not the same as a random eclecticism that takes bits and pieces from potentially incompatible models of therapy (Holmes 1996). Attachment theory offers a new paradigm that can synthesize and integrate the best ideas from different disciplines within such a broadened frame. We can look through the lens of attachment theory in order to tolerate ambiguities and dualities, to appreciate the dialectics of attachment and autonomy, control and dyscontrol, spoken and unspoken, mind and body, the revealed and the hidden, the sacred and the demonic, prey and predator, the wish to know and the wish not to know.

There is, I suggest, a relationship between the culture of violence in which we live and the increasing tendency of human beings in Western societies to inflict violence not only upon others but upon themselves. Our attraction to violence may well be rooted in the trauma experienced by our prehistoric ancestors when they were preyed upon by carnivores bigger and stronger than themselves, early in our evolutionary history when lions, tigers, raptors, and dinosaurs roamed the earth hungry for flesh and blood (Ehrenreich 1997). In the process of thousands of years of evolution, prehistoric man became transformed from being prey, occasional food for bigger carnivores, to becoming a meat-eating predator, hunting and preying upon other animals. According to Ehrenreich, man's propensity for bloodshed is derived from ancient blood rites of human and animal sacrifice, which were performed by early man to reenact their terrifying experience of predation by stronger carnivores, a way of mastering the trauma and a way of appealing to the gods for mercy and healing.

We know all too well that sometimes man, like the other animals, preys upon his own species, and sometimes man, like the other animals, takes his own body as the object of prey and preys upon himself, creating his own blood rites and sacrificing his flesh to his own internalized demonic gods. While the popular "inner child" concept often helps people develop a sense of empathy for themselves and their needs, which they have denied, what is lacking but equally needed to complete the picture is the concept of the "inner predator," that destructively demonic part of the self that resides in all of us, that can come to prey upon and take over the self. We also need a sense of empathy for the dark impulses to do so and greater understanding of the spiritual dimension of our patient's lives, whether within the confines of organized religion or not. Bollas (1997) has said, "Perhaps we need a new point of view in clinical psychoanalysis, close to a form of personal anthropology" (p. 7). Whether the reader practices psychoanalysis, psychoanalytic psychotherapy, or family systems therapy, understanding the concepts of the prey-to-predator transformation and sacrifice can enrich the treatment of those who harm themselves.

Given the recent findings of biological psychiatry in understanding the psychobiology of trauma, we must consider how psychobiology and neuropsychology can help us to understand self-harm. Given the findings of evolutionary psychology about the evolutionary origins and functions of anxiety (Marks and Nesse 1994), we must consider how self-harm may have evolved in the life of an individual as a means of defending against extraordinary anxiety. We must also ask how self-harm can be understood in relation to suicide and in relation to sadomasochism, either the wish to inflict pain and harm on another or the wish to inflict pain and harm on oneself.

Self-harm can be best understood by the idea that psychological symptoms are caused by more than one factor and can serve multiple functions in the psyche (Waelder 1936). Various forms of self-harm can be understood as compromise formations (Brenner 1982), solving conflicts among and between the psychic apparatus (ego, id, superego), the repetition compulsion, and the demands of the outside world. In this era of Freud-bashing, those who have been quick to dismiss Freud's theories of the instinctual drives and the etiology of trauma will need to reconsider Freud's contributions in order to understand the origins of self-harm.

Various forms of self-harm—drug and alcohol abuse; compulsive sex, gambling, shopping, or spending; shoplifting; and the quest for danger and near-death experiences—can also be understood as attempts at self-medication. That is, they are the attempts of desperate people to interrupt or terminate an intolerable mood or emotional state, or more simply put, to feel better. As with the self-medicating use of drugs or alcohol, these attempts at self-medication can develop into an addictive cycle.

The developmental point of view requires that we explore self-harm in the context of how it developed throughout the phases of childhood, adolescence, and adulthood, considering what led up to it, what came after, what has continued, what has fallen by the wayside, and what has been transformed. Child therapists know that the task of treating the child is to remove the stumbling blocks that impede healthy development. Because the developmental point of view helps us to identify how these obstacles developed and the developmental tasks that should be achieved when they are removed, it is invaluable in pointing a direction for both the clinical treatment of self-harming children and adults and the preventive early intervention or developmentally informed later interventions with self-harming infants and children.

The universality of self-harm may be difficult to consider because its primitive nature tends to evoke considerable anxiety in civilized people. We need to look at the apparent increase in self-harm in relation to the dramatic shifts for both sexes in terms of body image and gender role expectations brought about by the sexual and cultural revolution of the 1960s. At the same time, we need to acknowledge that self-harm is not peculiar to contemporary Western culture, but has existed in diverse cultures and religions, and in mythology from the beginning of history.

While certain forms of self-harm are acknowledged and discussed in our culture, others are not. But we must consider that self-harm not only may be far more common than has been acknowledged but also may be universal in human beings. Accepting its possible universality allows us to relinquish the artificial and defensive "us" and "them" categories that marginalize our patients and keep us from understanding them in ways that can be truly healing.

The concepts of adaptation and attachment theory are key to understanding the universality of self-harm as they offer the potential for integrating into psychoanalysis concepts from other disciplines. They serve as valuable bridges to object relations theory that can be used to understand how human self-harm is related both to self-harm in other animals as well as to our need for a feeling of connectedness to others.

Heinz Hartmann brought together concepts from biology, anatomy, psychology, and sociology to inform his understanding of how human infants adapt to their environment (Blanck and Blanck 1974). Adaptation is "primarily a reciprocal relationship between the organism and its environment" (Hartmann 1939, p. 24). To adapt, the infant must discharge instinctual drive energy outward to the exterior of its body and must develop instincts for protecting and caring for the body self. Hartmann, however, was referring to an "average expectable environment," in much the same way that Freud's theory of neurotic conflict assumed that the environment of the person with the neurosis was both average and expectable. And today more and more of the people seeking treatment present with borderline personalities, dissociative disorders, and posttraumatic stress disorders. Many have had to adapt, not to average expectable environments, but to human jungles in order to survive, and they have come to prey upon others so that others cannot prey upon them. From poor families and affluent ones, these children have adapted to their environment abusively and violently. Others of their ranks are wild and savage only to themselves, preying upon their own bodies in an adaptation that is steeped in pain, violence, and sadomasochistic experience. Unfortunately, Hartmann's obtuse theory of adaptation did not include the clinical material necessary for bringing it alive for clinicians. This book should serve to fill that gap.

What is the difference between man and the other animals? Until recently we have thought that the distinguishing features are man's ability to use language, to make and use tools, to have a sense of consciousness about himself, and to have the ability to transmit culture. Each of these distinctions has crumpled and we have come to understand more and more that what may be thought to be unique about human beings is also characteristic of other animals (Candland 1993). Ethology, the scientific study of animal behavior, has produced a body of knowledge on animal self-harm and the nature of early attachments that can be applied to understanding human self-harm. For example, hair pulling, head hitting, head banging, face slapping, eye and ear digging, self-biting, and skin scratching are seen in confined monkeys and other animals, and are comparable to mutilative behaviors in humans. Animals, like humans, are known to refuse to eat after being separated from their mothers. Animals manifest their response to separations and disorders of attachment much as humans do. Understanding how animal self-harm evolved will provide further understanding of how human beings can come to prey on their own bodies like the most savage of animals, thus helping clinicians better understand how profoundly deep is the ego regression in the act of self-harm.

Like the concept of adaptation, the greatest contribution of attachment theory is that it offers a rich potential for integration of concepts from other disciplines, including evolutionary biology, ethology, psychoanalysis, cognitive psychology, chaos science, and nonlinear dynamics. Attachment theory is a systemic theory, seeing the individual not in isolation but in reciprocal relationship, initially to a primary attachment figure, then to secondary attachment figures within the family, and then to the larger society (Holmes 1996). The key premise of research-based attachment theory is that there is a biologically based attachment system characteristic of each species that attaches the offspring to its caregiver in order to protect it from predators in the environment (Bowlby 1969) and to promote the development of self-regulatory functioning (Hofer 1995). Intimate behavior, especially intimate touch, is at the heart of the attachment system and is central to the existence of all animals (Morris 1971). It is intimate touch that attaches the infant securely to his mother and the mother to her infant, making her a secure base for him. With a secure atttachment the child can come to tolerate separations and develop a basic sense of trust. The theory provides a firm psychobiological framework for appreciating the importance of the mother–child relationship in ensuring that the child survives and thrives, not only in the attachment to the mother or caregiver but also in other future attachments. Man needs to touch and to be touched, to love and be loved. Whether we use Fairbairn's concept that infants are not only instinctually driven but object seeking, Melanie Klein's theory of the interface of very early developmental events and primitive cognitive mechanisms, Winnicott's conclusion that the infant cannot be understood apart from its interaction with the mother, Mahler's observationally based theory of separation-individuation, Stern's concept of interactive attunement mechanism's in the mother–infant relationship, or Kohut's theory of self-object relations, what we really are talking about are the ways in which human beings become attached after birth to their caregivers and subsequently to others. Attachment theory can help us to understand self-harm by illuminating what goes wrong in the attachment system that predisposes human beings to forming strong attachments to repetitions of trauma, to internalized violent and pain-inflicting objects, to painful affect, and to somatic pain.

The research and clinical literature on attachment theory has provided a great deal of food for thought. Especially exciting has been the work of Jeremy Holmes (1996) and Peter Fonagy and associates (Fonagy 1997, Fonagy et al. 1995, Fonagy and Target 1995) in using attachment theory in adult psychotherapy and violence. The work of Felicity de Zulueta (1994) in using attachment theory to understand the increasing violence in our society, Barbara Ehrenreich (1997) in tracing our attraction for war and violence to prehistoric man's fear of powerful animal predators, and Reid Meloy (1992) in using attachment theory to understand the violence of the most bizarre homicidal acts have been both evocative and provocative in helping to clarify, inform, and differentiate my own ideas about the violence in self-harm. Especially important in the development of my ideas about attachment has been Hans Loewald's seminal paper, "On the Therapeutic Action of Psychoanalysis" (1960), which continues to inspire my theoretical and clinical thinking.

Hofer's (1995) synthesis of neurobiological concepts from ethology with psychoanalytic concepts has provided a unified psychobiological theory for understanding human attachments and emotional and physical responses to separations and losses. Hofer's theory also provides a valuable lens for understanding the psychosomatic processes underlying disorders of self-regulation, illness and self-harm. I am indebted to Graeme Taylor, whose integrative book, *Psychoanalytic Medicine and Contemporary Psychoanalysis* (1987), introduced me to the concept of attachment theory and its relation to physiological regulatory processes, thus enabling me, without the benefit of medical training, to understand these and countless other concepts in psychosomatic medicine. Discussions of such concepts with the psychosomatic study group of the Psychoanalytic Association of New York, guided by C. Philip Wilson, has taught me a great deal as well about psychosomatic processes. The International Federation on Psychoanalytic Education's 1998 conference was an extraordinary event that brought together individuals interested in psychoanalysis to consider the question: "How Will the Body Speak in the 21st Century?" Allan Schore's (1997) exciting integrated theory of the imprinting of early mother–child interactions on the brain not only illuminates how earliest attachment experiences shape the child's regulatory processes in the brain but also provides a conceptual model for understanding how subsequent secure attachment experiences can alter the earlier imprinting. Similarly Bessel van der Kolk's (1994, van der Kolk and Fisler 1994) research in integrating the neurobiology of trauma and self-destructive behaviors with attachment theory has been exciting and inspiring.

While we may know through our clinical work that a strong and secure attachment to a therapist can change our patients' "wiring," Schore's work has demonstrated that psychotherapy can produce changes in the brain as significant as those produced by psychotropic medication and perhaps even longer lasting. In this era of managed care and quick fix solutions, Schore's work provides the empirical support needed for psychoanalytically informed psychotherapy in general and in its treatment of self-harm. Schore (1997) has said that the regulatory processes that get disrupted in infancy can get repaired in psychotherapy. Schore's work also highlights the importance of expanding our vision and thinking across a spectrum of other disciplines.

Like other animals, we human beings are capable of violence to others and ourselves. However, we are quite different in that we are "as a species, quite alone in our capacity to murder in cold blood, to torture one another and to threaten our species' very existence" (de Zulueta 1994, p. vii), by means of killing off others of our species or ourselves. We must recognize our primitive and violent inclinations if we are to become capable of restraining them in ourselves and understanding them in others. Physical violence is the language of those who, lacking the ability to use metaphor or symbol to express emotion or unspeakable pain, use the body to speak for them. In those who tend toward self-harm, these acts serve to narrate that which their words cannot say or their minds cannot remember. In the acts of self-harm they are more like feral animals, living primitively and viscerally in the bodily experience of bared fangs, tensed muscles, and bloody talons.

The fields of ethnology and anthropology provide a cross-cultural perspective from which one could understand the adaptive aspect of self-harm in diverse cultures the world over. For example, if bloodletting could be used by indigenous people of New Guinea and was routinely prescribed during the American Revolution for yellow fever among Washington's troops, the claim of self-cutters that they feel healed by their cutting places their self-harm in a tradition of healing that spans history and cultures. The members of snake-handling churches risk getting bitten by poisonous snakes to achieve a state of religious ecstasy. Similarly, seeking out pain, starvation, and mutilation was in the medieval Christian tradition that continues today far more than is usually thought. Religious self-harm is similar to the disordered eating and self-mutilating behavior of those who use such behavior to purify and cleanse themselves of the continuing aftereffects of severe childhood physical and sexual abuse and other trauma. Today we are seeing a multitude of young people in industrialized cultures all over the world with tribal-like markings, "modern primitives" who have had their bodies pierced, branded, tattooed, and scarred by others or who scar their own bodies themselves or create their own home-made marks. Why do they mark and harm themselves in these ways? How do these practices relate to tribal practices? Are they, in fact, the new tribal practices of contemporary global tribes? The tribe of the disenfranchised and alienated? The tribe of the freak? The tribe of the traumatized and abused?

ORGANIZATION OF THE BOOK

Part I, "The Mysterious Borderland of Self-Harm," serves as a map of new territory, introducing the reader to the self-harm concept, its spectrum, paradoxes, and universality. Part II, "Neglect, Violence, and Traumatic Attachments," explains the origins of self-harm in experiences of violence, abuse, and neglect. Attachment theory explains how such experiences and the psychosomatic nature of the trauma response promote an addictive-like attachment to pain and suffering. The perspectives of evolution, religion, mythology, and contemporary culture are presented so that those who prey on themselves can be understood within a larger context as having been transformed from the status of being prey to the status of predator.

Part III, "The Body Speaks," explains the creative power of the unconscious in directing the construction of symptoms that can perform so many functions, and introduces the concept of self-harm as gestural articulations of trauma. The language of self-harm as articulated by patients and those who participated in my study is presented. It explains how various kinds of self-harm can become forms of self-medication, the specific kinds of self-harm serving as the drug of choice uniquely suited by the individual to what ails him. It explains what self-harm can do for someone, how it can regulate moods, affect states, relationships, and self-esteem, express unthought and unspoken emotion, and reenact earlier trauma. Gender differences in self-harm behavior are discussed, including the apparent tendency for self-harm behavior to be more common in women. The phenomenon of symptom substitution is addressed—when one self-harm behavior is given up or renounced, often another form of self-harm crops up to substitute for it. The body modification culture and the culture of the "freak" will be discussed in light of what is known about self-harm, attachment theory, and self-medication.

Part IV, "Clinical Implications," presents the implications for this understanding to the diagnosis, assessment, and treatment of those whose emotions bypass their mind and are expressed through bodily self-harm. The influence of my training with Gertrude and Rubin Blanck, who developed and taught a model curriculum for training in psychotherapy at the Institute for the Study of Psychotherapy (G. Blanck 1998), is profound. Their psychoanalytic developmental ego psychology is a model that does not see either conflict or deficit as an all-or-nothing proposition, but is based on the concept that building ego functions increases the structuralization of the ego, which can ultimately make a patient with ego deficits more capable of sustaining the demands on the ego made by a more intensive psychotherapy. The work of treatment will be to provide an environment in which a safe and secure attachment relationship can grow, and to hold and contain the patient while undertaking the work of decoding their bodily enactments. The aim is to transform the harmful bodily enactments by building in patients a capacity to reflect upon their experience, a symbolic leap from the body to the mind. Inspired by Loewald's (1960) "On the Therapeutic Action of Psychoanalysis," a concept of how this is accomplished by means of the therapeutic process is proposed. The relationship of enactments on the body and enactments in the transference/countertransference matrix is discussed, with special considerations for helping clinicians deal with countertransference issues and avoid becoming secondarily victimized by the treatment. Handling group contagions of self-harm is discussed as well. In addition to implications for the treatment of those who self-harm, there are implications as well for early intervention and prevention in schools, medical practice, social service agencies, and mental health programs.

The appendix, "The Study and Transitional Space," is devoted to a description of the study, with emphasis on it as a transitional space, an intermediate area of experience between the researcher and the subjects. It provides readers with an interest in research an understanding of the study to which I refer throughout the book. For those not usually interested in research but who are considering working with these patients, it provides an understanding to other clinicians of what I have learned in the study's transitional space so that they too can, as I did, come to feel less afraid of working with these challenging and often fearful individuals who require lots of transitional space.

The voices you will hear in this book are those of patients, of people who participated in my study, of theorists, clinicians, researchers, and writers. The words of patients are not always verbatim, having been altered at times for instructive purposes, and some case vignettes are composites, created also for instructive purposes.

PART I

THE BORDERLAND
OF SELF-HARM

*To seek out in a world full of joy the one thing that is
certain to give you pain, and hug that to your bosom with
all your strength— that's the greatest human happiness.*

Jean Giraudoux, *Ondine*

1

The Mystery of Self-Harm:
Concepts and Paradoxes

Symptoms belong to the realm of semiology;
they are signs that suggest a mystery.

Hamburg, "Bulimia:
The Construction of a Symptom"
in Bemporad's and Herzog's (1989)
Psychoanalysis and Eating Disorders

Many patients come into treatment complaining of an endless sense of aloneness and psychic deadness. They want to get back to the land of vibrant living where life has meaning. Those who can articulate this pain are the fortunate ones because they know what it is to feel alive and are troubled by the loss of their spirit (Bollas 1997, interviewing Michael Eigen). By entering treatment they turn to another human being in the hope that their spirit can be rekindled. It is the unfortunate ones who often do not know or remember what it is like to be alive in body and spirit. They may feel like the walking dead but may not even be able to say that they feel dead inside; instead, they may harm themselves in one way or another.

Those who harm themselves have received ongoing messages—from family, peers, and the media—about their worth or lack of it, about pain, pleasure, violence, power, death, sex, God, and beauty. Self-harm is a particular kind of masochism, the embodiment of a determination to punish, castrate, or annihilate the self, but it is more than that.

For some who are deadened by depression, feeling bodily pain is to be jolted momentarily out of a depressed state and to come alive once again. For those who are deadened by dissociation, inflicting bodily pain on themselves is like turning on the switch that makes them feel real once again. For those who live with a constant anxious hypervigilance that deadens them to pleasure and joy, inflicting pain to their bodies can provide them with a release that is as close to joy as they will get. To feel pain in the body is to experience the body as alive and vital, a very welcome relief that mitigates the severity of the physical pain.

As clinicians, we have values that we take for granted and bring implicitly to our work—that life is to be preserved, to be bettered, to be lived. These values may conflict with the ways that some of our patients live their lives. We want to help our patients find the freedom to live their lives more fully. Food is meant to sustain life and bring pleasure, not torture by self-starvation, vomiting, or laxative abuse. Blood is meant to flow through our veins, nourishing our cells and sustaining our lives, so the thought of someone deliberately shedding his or her blood may make us cringe in fear and revulsion or may make our own blood boil. People who make suicide attempts, mutilate their bodies, have eating disorders, or are dependent on alcohol or drugs disturb and frighten us, shaking up our assumptions about human nature. Although the term *self-destructive* is more familiar and is usually used for such people, it seems to presume that the destruction of the self is the person's primary intention. It is not nearly so simple. The term *self-harm* is a more neutral term to designate a continuum of behavior that results in harm to the self. It does not presume a primarily self-destructive intention, which makes it preferable to the term *self-destructive*. It may be more accurate to say that both self-destructive as well as life-affirming impulses exist in all of us, in different balances and at different times.

THE DEATH INSTINCT REVISITED

Some self-harming patients are attracted to self-destruction in a strangely erotic or romantic dance. Freud's (1920) theory of the life and death instincts explains certain fundamental attitudes in relation to life. In Freud's theory of the death instinct, the person withdraws from human connections and retreats into a narcissistic position, silently driving him- or herself toward death. Freud emphasized that it was only through the activity of the life instinct that this death-like force was projected outward as destructive impulses to objects in the outside world. He assumed that the life and death instincts—or the constructive and destructive aspects of the personality—are in constant conflict and interaction. As Menninger put it, "To create and to destroy, to build up and to tear down, these are the anabolism and catabolism of the personality, no less than of the cells and the corpuscles—the two directions in which the same energies exert themselves" (Shneidman et al. 1994, p. 18). This conflicting interaction is an unstable fusion, that is, the "erotic [life] instincts and the death instinct would be present in living beings in regular mixtures or fusions, but 'defusions' would also be likely to occur" (Freud 1920b, pp. 258–259). No one of us evolves completely free from the upsurge of self-destructive tendencies. Some of us manage to balance the conflicting tension between the constructive and destructive tendencies, acting only occasionally on the self-destructive wishes, and others establish a very different kind of equilibrium, in which the self-destructive impulses prevail.

Steiner (1996) formulated how the conflict between the life and death instincts has deepened and supplemented the mental conflict theory, the central theory of classical psychoanalysis. The early mental conflict theory stressed the conflict between unconscious impulses and drives and the demands of reality. Then with the introduction of the structural theory, the conflict between the ego and forces from the id and from the superego became more important. Ultimately, however, the conflict was formulated as one between the life and death instincts, and innate destructiveness was seen to set limits on what psychoanalysis could achieve (Freud 1937). That is, each individual must negotiate the conflict. When he cannot, he develops symptoms as a compromise and uses maladaptive mental mechanisms to defend himself and his objects. These mechanisms become embedded as permanent personality features and may give rise to illness or to serious character disorders. With Freud's discovery of transference and resistance, a theory emerged in which the conflict can be worked through in the analysis because during treatment it is relived in relation to the analyst (Freud 1914b). The goal of treatment was to help the patient understand his unconscious processes in order to resolve the conflict in healthier ways, in particular through the use of insight. Both self-knowledge and control over his impulses are part of these goals, as suggested by the adage, "Where id was, there ego shall be" (Freud 1933, p. 80).

PURGING, BLOODLETTING, AND EXORCISING THE DEMONS

Until the beginning of the nineteenth century, treatment of the physically or mentally ill in the Western world involved getting rid of something evil that was foreign to the individual—a spirit, demon, or toxic substance—that had invaded the body (Rizzuto 1985). Or it was thought that the four basic humors or temperaments—sanguine, phlegmatic, melancholic, and choleric—had become unbalanced and could be rebalanced by bloodletting, blistering, purging by vomiting or anal purgatives, or other potions that would cleanse the body. George Washington was one of the most famous victims of this kind of healing. Physicians trying to save him from a high fever hastened his death by blistering his arms and legs, purging him with laxatives, and bleeding him repeatedly, withdrawing around half of his blood. These same practices were believed to rid the body of the demons that were thought to dwell within the ill individual. Even today when we say "God bless you" or "gesundheit" to someone who has sneezed, blessings are invoked because of the belief that sneezing expels the demons. In some Eastern cultures, tattoos with religious significance are thought to banish the demons. So what we might regard as our contemporary afflictions—excessive exercise, self-starvation, self-induced vomiting and diarrhea, self-mutilation, and body modifications (tattooing, body piercing, etc.)— fit within a long and established tradition of health and healing.

Freud wrote about demons and states of possession (1923b) and told us that sometimes neuroses "emerge in demonological trappings" (p. 72). He told the story of a painter who had made a pact with the devil, promising to belong to him body and soul, and who was redeemed from the pact by the Virgin Mary. Nonetheless, the demonic and the sacred are concepts that psychology, especially psychoanalysis, tends to discount. But many of these patients do seem possessed, if not by demons, then by monsters, and at times may even verbalize this. "It's as if there's a monster inside me, telling me to do these things, and I can't resist." Today we are seeing increasingly larger numbers of people who are trying to heal their broken souls and spirits with the help of vomiting and other purging, bloodletting, tattoos, body piercings, and other contemporary exorcisms.

THE FEAR OF MADNESS

Many clinicians tend to avoid understanding those with such problems as eating disorders, substance abuse, self-mutilation, compulsive gambling, stealing, shopping, and compulsive sexual behavior. In addition, those whose physical illness has a large psychogenic component are not the kind of referrals we tend to welcome, nor do we tend to welcome patients with dissociative disorders, who can evoke a great deal of anxiety and threaten to overwhelm our emotional resources. They can intrude into our lives, fantasies, and dreams in ways that can make us want to shut them out of our lives. For the past twenty years or so, using the label "borderline" has been an easy way to create a defensive distinction between self and other. When these patients are treated it is usually primarily by medication or behavioral modalities that do not require truly understanding these patients. Sometimes such treatment is ineffectual, and often may even be destructive and traumatizing.

It is very difficult to treat patients who court death. It is challenging to connect empathically with them, so we tend to resist the complex attachments that must develop if we are to treat these patients. It is much easier to see them simply as the sum of their symptoms, and to collude unconsciously with them in maintaining their symptoms and the sense of identity that is bound up in them. Understanding the mystery of self-harm, like understanding the mystery of schizophrenia (Karon 1992), means getting in touch with the darkest, most violent, and primitive aspects of ourselves, a venture into unknown territory that evokes fear. It means bending toward the patient's unconscious to face the monsters and demons in them and in ourselves. It means facing truths about ourselves, our families, and our society that we do not want to face. Trying to understand self-harm means entering into our patients' darkest states of being, to tolerate dwelling there for a time, confident in one's ability to emerge from it. "Mysteries—if we reinvest the concept with something of its ancient prestige—designate a truth *necessarily* closed off from full understanding. They remain always partly veiled in silence . . . they introduce us to unusual states of being which, for a time, we enter into and dwell within. . . . Mysteries disturb the world we take for granted" (Morris 1991, pp. 23–24).

THE BODY

The body has become the locus of subjectivity, and is linked to language, feeling, pleasure, pain, power, and history. And so what we do to and with our bodies, what and how we eat, how we dress, how much space our bodies occupy, the daily rituals through which we attend to our bodies, are all part of our unconscious individualism. The body provides a home for the self.

What is it—this thing, this flesh, this cabin of our consciousness, this sailboat of our soul?

The body: we stuff it, starve it, expose it, cover it, excite it, drug it, destroy it. It is the source of our lust, and its object. It sates and is sated. It is the house of our appetites. In the body is our idea of pleasure.

And our idea of pain. It smells, it swells, it stretches, it sags, it decays. It will never again be what it was before. It is our personal metaphor of time—and death. [From the back cover of *Granta*, 39, Spring 1992]

We have polarized our images of the body, portraying it in art and literature as either wholesome or diseased, unified or fragmented, a sacred temple or a hungry monster. The mind-body split has existed not only in medicine but in Western culture in general. More recently, our culture, even more than psychoanalysis, has seen a dramatic return to an interest in the body, holistic health, and an effort to heal the mind–body split.

The human body stands as a symbol of society and its values. The "body politic" is divided into left and right, while the "social body" is compartmentalized into upper, middle, and lower segments which are governed by a disembodied "head" (Polhemus 1988). We describe behavior in ways that are both corporal and social: A person may be upright, uptight, straight, bent out of shape, tight-assed, twisted, loose, upfront, hard-headed, soft-hearted. At the same time, inside and outside describe both physical and social boundaries, and so a popular song of years ago referred to love as "getting under one's skin" while ending a relationship may be called "cutting her loose." Anthropologist Mary Douglas has analyzed the symbolic interface of the physical body and the social body: "The physical experience of the body, always modified by the social categories through which it is known, sustains a particular view of society. There is a continual exchange of meanings between the two kinds of bodily experience so that each reinforces the categories of the other" (Douglas, *Natural Symbols*, p. 65, quoted in Polhemus 1988, p. 12).

Despite the efforts of Freud and the early psychoanalysts in understanding how libido and aggression had become trapped in the body's symptoms, the importance of bodily experience has been largely neglected until the recent focus on the intersubjective and interrelational has made psychoanalysis begin to turn its interest to the body as the subject of experience. The ascetic view of the body has become woven into the landscape of Western culture. According to the ascetic writers (Saint John of the Cross, Saint Catherine of Siena, etc.), the "body of desire," with all its cravings excited by the phenomenal world, must be mortified or obliterated (Podvoll 1969). Self-cutting and self-starvation mortify the flesh on a major scale, while the most common and even ordinary self-harm—picking at one's skin, overeating, chewing on one's cuticles—does it on a minor scale. It is most intriguing, then, that self-harm has neither been well defined nor understood in the clinical or research literature. Clinicians and researchers have not explored the mysterious aspect of human experience that, more than any other, bridges the chasm between "us" and "them," and allows us to see people who harm themselves as less human than ourselves. This chapter introduces the concept of self-harm and discusses the spectrum of human self-harm behavior, which may encourage readers to become more acquainted with their own individual repertoire of self-harm behavior, certainly not an easy or welcome acquaintance to make. It does, however, promise to be a fascinating one that can help us to better understand our patients and engage them in a treatment that is "experience-near."

SYMPTOMS AND LANGUAGE

To navigate the terrain of self-harm, one needs to understand the mysterious language spoken by the symptoms.

> Symptoms . . . are signs that suggest a mystery. . . . The symptom is necessarily ambiguous. . . .
> We can welcome symptoms as clues to an underlying process. Naturally we are first impressed by the pain of the symptom itself, yet we are also confronted by uncertainty, mystery, and the possibility of many meanings. . . . The psychiatric symptom is at once a source of distress to the patient, a complex assortment of unconscious meaning, a form of communication, and a cause for our own discomfort as we seek to unravel its interweavings. . . .
> Symptoms can be seen as complex acts of communication. . . . A symptom, then, is a clue to multiple contexts of communicated meaning. It reveals and conceals simultaneously. [Hamburg 1989, pp. 131–134]

The language of self-harm is the language of violence spoken on the body. Learning the language means having a tolerance for seeing the essential unity in opposite ends of the pole, for tolerating contradictions, dualities, and paradox. It means developing an appreciation for the resourceful creativity of the unconscious in constructing the symptoms.

THE PROBLEMATIC CONCEPT OF SUICIDE

The term *self-harm* is now used differently from the way it had been used in the older literature, in which it was synonymous with attempted suicide and parasuicide, a suicide-like activity such as self-mutilation or suicide gestures (Hirsch et al. 1982, Kreitman 1977). These synonyms are problematic.

We know that among borderline patients, the rate of completed suicide among those who engaged in parasuicidal behavior is twice the rate of those who do not engage in this behavior, which suggests that parasuicidal behavior is the best predictor of subsequent suicide (Stone et al. 1987). In addition, borderline patients who frequently mutilated themselves have significantly higher mean scores on the Beck scale for suicidal ideation, are more likely to have attempted suicide, and are more likely to have attempted suicide more often than a group of infrequent mutilators and a group of nonmutilators (Dulit et al. 1995). Certainly, these findings compel us to understand the relationship of self-mutilation and other parasuicidal behavior to completed suicide. These acts of self-harm result in the deliberate infliction of harm upon the individual's body. The harm may cause injury to body tissue, may or may not cause pain, and may or may not be life threatening.

The word *suicide* has too many unclear and contradictory meanings to be scientifically or clinically useful (Shneidman 1993, Schneidman et al. 1994). Suicidologist Edwin Shneidman's (1973) early definition is "Suicide is the act of self-inflicted, self-intentioned cessation" (p. 383). Yet how can we know with any certainty that a person who has caused his own death had the intention of doing so? How can we know that even if the individual leaves a suicide note stating his intention, he is not imagining that at the very last moment, someone or something will come along to rescue him? How accurate can we be in assessing the degree to which a person has the intention of ending his life? Many individuals are suicidal only for a brief period, so the person who actively seeks his own death on Monday may find himself quite glad on Tuesday that he was not successful.

There is no agreed-upon definition of actual suicide, and there is no way to know with certainty any individual's intention to commit suicide (Ivanoff 1991). Realizing the problems with his earlier definition, Shneidman implored clinicians to abandon terms like *suicide attempt* or *gesture* and restrict themselves to evaluating the lethality of the act and the psychic pain of the individual contemplating death. To reduce the level of lethality, the clinician must view suicide as a multidetermined act aimed at decreasing the level of psychological pain. That is, the patient suffers from a "psychache" and wants relief from pain and resolution of conflict. Choosing death is a quick, uncomplicated resolution of the tension between living and dying, and so despairing patients who cannot tolerate ambiguity and who are impulsive are at special risk. We need to understand the individual's basic orientation toward death, that is, the role of the person in his own demise (Shneidman et al. 1994). Does he play a direct and intentional role in his own death? Does he play a more ambivalent indirect, partial, covert, or unconscious role in hastening his demise? Or does he play no significant role in his own death?

When we think about self-harm in relation to suicide, then we think of the more severe and dramatic forms of self-harm such as self-cutting. Cutting has been aptly called "a bright red scream" (Strong 1998) and is the stuff of drama. Drops of blood oozing from self-inflicted cuts excite our emotions and bring to mind acts of violence and "the sameness of all living creatures under the skin" (Ehrenreich 1997, p. 25). Self-harm can be directed at the body's external surface, the skin, as in most forms of self-mutilation, or can be directed in various ways to the deeper recesses of the body's interior, to the fat, nerves, and guts.

PAIN AND SUFFERING

The Stoic split between body and mind, like the Christian split between body and soul, indicates how ancient the desire is to assign pain wholly to the flesh.
David B. Morris, *The Culture of Pain*

To understand the pain and injury that a human being inflicts upon his body means to understand the depth of emotional pain that requires such expression. We think that pain is either physical or mental, reflecting the dichotomous thinking inherent in the traditional medical model of illness. "These two types of pain, so the myth goes, are as different as land and sea. You feel physical pain if your arm breaks, and you feel mental pain if your heart breaks. Between these two different events we seem to imagine a gulf so wide and deep that it might as well be filled by a sea that is impossible to navigate" (D. B. Morris 1991, p. 9). Yet the gulf between the two is not so wide at all. There is no limit to the means by which human beings can harm themselves. Bodily self-harm can cause pain and suffering, but sometimes this pain is welcome because it can divert one from one's emotional pain. Inflicting pain upon oneself can also give rise to pleasure, and so some come to seek and embrace pain. Sexual masochists get erotic pleasure from physical pain, and moral masochists create their own emotional suffering. When we talk about pain, we are not on solid ground. The suffering of self-harm, like the suffering of passionate love, has to do with mystery, with the pursuit of that elusive something that constantly escapes one's grasp, with illusion, with the forbidden, the secretive, and with danger (Viederman 1988).

Pain is more than the result of a biochemical process in the brain involving nerve pathways and bodily reflexes (D. B. Morris 1991). Suffering implies a type of damage that has gone beyond the body to afflict the mind and spirit as well (D. B. Morris 1991). The taste for suffering has something to do with sadomasochism, but can take human behavior far beyond the exotica of sadomasochism. Lingering emotional distress afflicts the body just as chronic bodily pain takes its toll on the emotions and spirit. "A deep sorrow or grief that does not begin with pain very quickly produces it. Loss and isolation can cut like a knife" (D. B. Morris 1991, p. 247). Grief or anger can be stored in the muscles of a tense neck or in unrelenting headaches. "Pain, no matter what its cause, is a strange and difficult phenomenon. Its hardness and horrors collapse normal life: pain . . . is the 'unmaking of the world.' . . . Our normal lifeworld dramatically does recede when pain is intense" (McLane 1996, p. 108). What most matters about pain may well be the personal and social meanings with which we and our surrounding culture endow it (D. B. Morris 1991).

SELF-HARM AND PAIN IN THE CONTEXT OF CULTURE

Although the mental health professions have considered all self-injurious behaviors in terms of pathology, most societies sanction some of these behaviors. A valuable way of understanding self-harm is by identifying which of these behaviors receive social approval and which receive social disapproval. There are at least four basic constellations of social attitudes to these behaviors (Kroll 1993). In the first, the self-injurious behaviors express positive social values, and the self-harming person, for example the person who goes on a political hunger strike, is accorded a great deal of social approval. Public self-harm is, above all, a protest of the weak against the powerful as well as a means of honoring and appeasing the weak and the powerful (Kroll 1993). The second constellation consists of those self-injurious behaviors that appear to have no social value and are publicly condemned, and the self-harming person is regarded as having a mental disturbance, such as in eating disorders, self-mutilation, and substance abuse. Paradoxically, self-starvation and bulimic behavior are devalued socially even though their apparent goals—weight loss and slimness—are socially approved. The third constellation is an ambiguous range of self-injurious actions considered to be pathways to socially valued performances, but are met with disapproval when disclosed publicly, such as professional ballerinas who starve themselves or competitive athletes who abuse exercise and steroids. The fourth constellation is "lifestyles" that are associated with a higher than usual risk of illness or accidental harm, for example cigarette smoking and use of other mood- or consciousness-altering substances, unusual exercise training, unhealthy diets, sexually related social behavior, and body modifications (piercing, tattooing, scarification). In the cases that come to the attention of the mental health professions, an important component of the self-harm behavior consists of some degree of public demonstration of one's "wounds," with an expectation of evoking a response from others.

In most cultures throughout history there have been socially acceptable forms of self-harm within the context of religious and healing rituals, cultural rites of passage, social stratification, and self-adornment and beautification. The Western healing traditions of bloodletting, vomiting, and anal purging continue to the present day, transformed and shaped by the forces of history and culture. For example, the self-starvation and abuse of laxatives that are common in what is today called eating disorders can be traced back to the last quarter of the nineteenth century, when physician John H. Kellogg and his brother invented Kellogg's Corn Flakes and established the Battle Creek sanatorium, where colonic purging, exercise machines, and low-calorie and high-fiber regimens were the rule. The message was that weight loss and keeping one's colon clean with large quantities of bran and herbal laxatives purified and cleansed one's soul, bringing one closer to God. This is not so dramatically different from what is predominant in our culture today: a sense of moral and spiritual self-righteousness and goodness achieved by strict dieting, weight training, and aerobic workouts. So it is just a bit of a leap to understand the logic of bulimics, who persist in trying to rid themselves of the badness within through vomiting and the use of laxatives. We see it in the Overeaters Anonymous groups, whose doctrine has members believing that if they place their faith in God or a power higher than themselves and stick to their food plan, the evidence of their faith will be apparent in the resulting weight loss.

As eating disorders increase in prevalence in the Western countries, they also increasingly affect immigrants who have become Westernized. Interestingly, large numbers of people with anorexia and bulimia have been reported in Japan (Hsu 1990), an affluent nation that has become Westernized. While a strong African-American cultural identity may afford black women a tolerance for a body size larger than the anorectic or tubular-shaped feminine ideal as well as some protection against a preoccupation with slimness, as more black women become upwardly mobile they tend to adopt the feminine ideal of the dominant culture, which puts them at risk for eating disorders in at least equal proportion to whites (Chandler et al. 1994, Pumariega et al. 1994). The same is true for Hispanic women (Thompson 1994). In the Southwest, Native-American subjects were found to be more prone toward disordered eating than Hispanics and Caucasians (Smith and Krejci 1991), possibly influenced by the unusually high rates of alcoholism found in Native-American culture (Holderness et al. 1994). Contributing influences may be traditional practices, specifically fasting among the Pueblo for ceremonial cleanliness (Benedict 1934) and the use of emetics, bleeding, purging, and sweating (Vogel 1970).

To What Lengths for Beauty?

Across cultures, men are attracted to women with narrow waists and full hips, busts, and lips, all of which are signs of fertility. From an evolutionary perspective the attraction ensures that sufficient pregnancies result for the survival of the species *Homo sapiens*. What is advantageous from an evolutionary perspective has become an aesthetic preference that certain cultures have exploited. Despite this, the feminine physical ideal has oscillated throughout history depending on whether woman's reproductive capacities were or were not being celebrated. In the past several decades the feminine ideal of beauty has undergone radical transformations, from an ideal that glorified a bottom round and broad enough to carry a fetus to term and full breasts for nursing, to an elongated tubular emaciated body. Historically, it has been expected that women be willing to endure far more pain and suffering for the sake of their appearance than men, whose attractiveness was not so dependent on their physical appearance. A heavy man with power and money might be called portly and considered attractive, while a heavy woman is simply called fat.

Today the expectations are converging in a unisex standard. Women tweeze their eyebrows; remove facial or body hair by shaving, waxing, or electrolysis; diet or exercise stringently to reduce the size and shape of their bodies; chemically bleach, curl, or straighten their hair; and have expensive cosmetic surgery. In 1921 the first Miss America was soft and plump; today's Miss America is quite thin, has "buns of steel," and may well have had cosmetic surgery. For women, the body ideal has shifted radically from curvy to tubular, at least in the lower body, appearing more like a prepubertal asexual lower body, which is attached to a grotesquely bosomy top. Similarly, increasingly greater numbers of men are spending hours in the gym, dieting stringently, and having cosmetic surgery, all in the quest for health and fitness. Many men style or replace their hair with permanent waves, hair coloring, or hair replacement surgery, while some shave, wax, or use electrolysis to make their bodies and their heads virtually hairless.

Marking and Mutilating the Body

Self-mutilating practices have been sanctioned for centuries in many cultures, from male ritual nose bleeding in New Guinea that is thought to be a protection against illness and a form of male menstruation, to the finger amputations common to some Polynesian, African, North American Indian, and New Guinea tribes, to the head slashing of a Moroccan cult, to the self-flagellation and other self-mutilation endemic in Christianity. The latter includes flagellant Christian cults from the eleventh century on (Favazza 1987), numerous nuns and saints of the Middle Ages who were known to starve, purge, flagellate, and scar themselves (Bell 1985), and even in the self-flagellation of today's Roman Catholic Opus Dei movement.

We regard permanent markings on the body as belonging to primitive people, not to the civilized being that is Western man.

> From Africa to Asia, the Arctic to the South Pacific, tribal peoples cut, shave, dyed or decorate their hair; paint, tattoo, scar or pierce their flesh. . . . Some bind the heads of their infants, stretch their necks or compress their waists. Most groups attach feathers, shells, bones, flowers, leaves or ornaments made of metals or some material to their bodies. No group of which I am aware does all these things but—what is more important—*no group does none of them.* [Polhemus 1988, p. 31]

No culture accepts the body in its natural state. Makeup, body paint, war paint, tattoos, body piercings, and scarifications have existed throughout time in cultures everywhere. The marks tell stories, personal history written on the body. Cultures everywhere use the body to inscribe messages about the society and about the place of the individual in the society, and to define human nature (Polhemus 1988). While the tendency is universal, the particular way each group decorates itself is the result of cultural factors. Tattoos are more prevalent among people whose skin is light enough to display a tattoo, while scarification is more prevalent among darker-skinned peoples whose skin forms darker keloid scars when cut. Tattooing has been a universal practice, reaching its height in the Pacific Islands, where they have had religious meaning, then decreasing under the influence of Christian missionaries. In Japan, however, the tattoo folk art of *irezumi*, associated with the lower social classes, geishas, and criminals, is still practiced. *Irezumi* artists cover the client's entire body with very colorful designs of fish, dragons, flowers, snakes, gods, and famous lovers, designs that have been described as "subtle, repulsive, magical, seductive, sensuous, three-dimensional, thought-provoking and macabre" (Ackerman 1990, p. 100). Japan has a particular fascination with the perverse, erotic, and sadomasochistic aspect of tattoos (Favazza 1996). For example, a Japanese wearing the work of a grand tattoo master may donate his skin to a museum or university upon his death. Tokyo University has three hundred of these bizarre framed "masterpieces." Czar Nicholas II of Russia and George V of England were tattooed by a famous Japanese artist, and a number of fashionable people in London had patriotic tattoos done at the royal coronation in 1901 (Favazza 1996).

In Western culture tattoos and other permanent markings have identified groups with unconventional or antisocial subcultures: bikers, skinheads, English punks and Teddy boys, prisoners, gang members, prostitutes, and homosexuals. A tattoo was the mark of a street tough who might start a barroom brawl and was a common initiation ritual of a sailor on leave. It was a mark of aggression, of those whose masculinity was measured by physical prowess and ability to withstand pain. Incarcerated Hispanic males developed a convention, since adopted by non-Hispanics, of having a small tear tattooed at the corner of the eye for each year spent in prison. However, nipple and genital piercings were fashionable among royalty in Victorian England. Prince Albert reportedly had his penis pierced in a way that allowed him to tether it to his leg so that he could fit into the tight pants that were customary. Today the "Prince Albert," as it is called, is one of the most popular genital piercings (Vale and Juno 1989).

From prostitutes to aristocrats, tattooed women have always been regarded as subversive (Mifflin 1997). The height of subversion was the development of a small cadre of tattooed female tattoo artists. A woman's tattoo, whether so public that all the world can see it or private so that only a spouse or lover can see it, is a way of making public what is private, an illicit compromise between the wish to exhibit one's body and the constraint to keep it private. Once again, the British aristocracy had the privilege to go beyond the social boundaries, and many upper-class ladies, including Winston Churchill's mother, were tattooed. Middle- and upper-class women flirted with tattoo in the suffragist 1920s and then again at the birth of the women's movement in the 1970s.

Tattoos were usually done by a man of working-class background (Sanders 1989). Common designs were crude pictures of nude women, predatory animals, or symbols of death. The hippies popularized body painting in the 1960s and early 1970s, and even today face painting for children is a popular feature at church sales and suburban fairs. For a growing subculture within evangelical Christianity, religious tattoos have become an expression of individuality, identity, and faith. In the 1970s the punk movement's practice of inserting safety pins into their faces was a forerunner of the tattoos and piercings of sadomasochists and disaffected young people. These signs of affiliation to a marginal subculture are becoming more socially acceptable and normative, indicating that once again the borders dividing socially acceptable self-mutilation from deviant self-mutilation are changing, as is clear in fashion trends and the practices of young people. Researchers for the First Collegiate Body Art Project at Rutgers University (Greif & Hewitt 1996) launched a study of collegiate body art through the Internet, obtaining data from 766 students in twenty universities (nineteen American and one Australian). Almost every student with a tattoo or body piercing had arrived at college without it but had acquired one or more body modification in college. They represented all racial, religious, and ethnic groups, and included those who were academically outstanding and those who were marginal. Myrna Armstrong, a nurse at Texas Tech University, advocates for health education programs to inform students about the risks inherent in obtaining a tattoo, while Clint Sanders, a tattooed sociologist at University of Connecticut and expert on the sociology of tattoo, serves informally as campus tattoo consultant.

Today, almost half of all tattoos are done on women, many of them career and professional women (Armstrong 1991). The designs are usually small and feminine, and tend to be placed on parts of the body usually covered by clothing, to be viewed and enjoyed by those with whom they are intimate. Bolder women may have a tattoo that is meant to be openly displayed, such as a floral design on the wrist, or a tribal-like bracelet on the upper arm or ankle. Many current tattooists were artists originally, have had formal art training, and regard themselves as artists working on human canvas.

What is a culturally acceptable form of self-mutilation in one era shifts with time, and we are in the midst of a transition. In the 1960s a man's pierced ear signified his homosexuality, while the particular ear pierced signified his sexual availability or commitment to a partner. In this country in the first half of the twentieth century, girls and women wearing earrings in their pierced ears were readily identified as foreigners, Mediterranean gypsies, or other "undesirables," while "real Americans" (e.g., white Anglo-Saxon Protestants) wore clip-ons. Whereas thirty years ago, middle-class parents might be horrified if their 18-year-old daughter came home with her ears pierced, her adolescent "declaration of independence," today it is not unusual for parents and children to have piercings in various parts of their faces and bodies and parents sometimes even accompany their adolescent child to the tattoo or body piercing studio.[1]

All cultures have rites of passage into adulthood. In Western culture they have traditionally had to do with male drinking, while today binge drinking is expected of male and female students in high school and college. Fraternity hazing rituals often include tolerating the pain of tattoos, beatings, and cutting rituals, and drinking toxic quantities of alcohol. Binge eating and purging parties for women are reported in many boarding-school and college dormitories. We cannot assume anything at all about what any self-harm behavior means to any individual or what role it plays. What is socially acceptable, even desirable, within a subculture, may be repugnant to the larger mainstream culture. The social acceptability of the behavior itself says not very much about the person performing the behavior, the presence or absence of psychopathology, or the nature of any existing pathology. Two different individuals may perform similar behavior for very different intrapsychic, interpersonal, social, and cultural reasons. All such contextual factors must be considered together in attempting to understand the self-harm behavior of any individual.

THE LANGUAGE OF PAIN AND
VIOLENCE SPOKEN ON THE BODY

Pain speaks of our bodily existence when spoken language cannot. Pain speaks and writes on and through the body, signifying what words cannot say. If

---

1. When I was conducting my study on the relationship between bulimic and self-mutilating behavior, I visited a few body-piercing and tattoo studios to enlist the help of the proprietors in recruiting subjects for the study. Sitting in the waiting area next to a table displaying magazines about body art, nipple and genital piercings, and sadomasochism, was a middle-aged couple. They were waiting for their 16-year-old son, who was in one of the cubicles getting his septum pierced.

the language of pain fails to communicate, if it cannot be heard or read by another, it becomes woven into the fabric of the "speaker's" existence. Pain "unweaves the self until the self is nothing but pain" (D. B. Morris 1991, p. 254).

> What does matter then is: How can I get the pain to end, and when? Why do I hurt? Will it ever go away? . . .
>
> Pain *refers* to the disintegration of the wounded person and to her need for reintegration, and *expresses the value* of the persons harmed, her wholeness, and her wished-for unwounded connection to the world. Even the cries, screams, moans, grasping of wounds, rocking back and forth of physical pain are sounds and movements which are part of the gestural basis of language. [Merleau-Ponty 1962, pp. 185–187]

> But if these expressive aspects of pain are hindered . . .—if the wounding is not communicated . . .—pain reiterates. It is not resolved, but becomes part of the lived structure of the human being suffering it. [McLane 1996, p. 108]

Those who harm themselves are speaking a language we must try to understand. They make gestures—pushing food away, picking or scratching at their skin, slicing into their flesh, sticking a finger down their throat to vomit—that signify who they are, how they have lived, and the pain about which they cannot or will not speak. Throughout this book, self-mutilation and disordered eating are considered in depth. These behaviors express and regulate pain and cause pain, injury, and death. The pain and signifying of those who harm themselves through self-mutilation and disordered eating provide a template for understanding the pain and signifying found in the broader continuum of self-harm.

THE SPECTRUM OF BODILY SELF-HARM

Self-harm is not limited to self-cutting, probably the most dramatic form of physical self-harm and the one that evokes the most anxiety in us. Identifying the spectrum of self-harm is helpful in removing some of the veil of mystery about the more extreme forms of self-harm such as disordered eating and self-mutilation, and places them in a continuum.

Self-Mutilation

Mutilation is associated in our minds with both the demonic and the divine. In 1969 the world was stunned by the gruesome murders of actress Sharon Tate and her houseguests and Leno and Rosemary LaBianca committed by the Manson Family. Ever since "Charlie's girls" Leslie Van Houten, Susan Atkins, and Patricia Krenwinkle appeared in court with crosses carved into their shaved heads, cutting has been associated in the mind of the public with the demonic. "No one with a heart and a soul could have done what these defendants did to these seven victims. . . . These defendants are human monsters, human mutations," said prosecuting attorney Vincent Bugliosi (Conway and Siegelman 1995, pp. 219–220). However, the pain of a bleeding, mutilated martyr is at the center of both the Oedipus myth and the story of Christ. In Christian countries, the story of Christ's martyrdom occupies a central position in the minds and hearts of the people, consciously, unconsciously, or both, and is reflected in themes of sacrifice and atonement that are heard in the words of many self-harmers. Were it not for the discomfort many clinicians feel with religious imagery, the story of Christ might have come to occupy the same central position the Oedipus myth has occupied within psychoanalysis (Grotstein 1997). The Oedipus story of a tragic forbidden unconscious male sexual yearning for his mother, is the Passion Play of psychoanalysis. Yet until recently there has been relatively little written about the actual act of self-mutilation, which is as intrinsic to the myth as incest and patricide.

> Near the conclusion of *Oedipus Tyrannus* the chorus and two messengers speak alone before the closed doors of the palace. Inside, hidden from view, King Oedipus has just learned the terrible truths he so stubbornly pursued: that he unknowingly killed his father and married his mother, the queen Jocasta. One of the messengers explains what happened next inside the palace. Just moments before, we are told, Jocasta hanged herself. Oedipus then tore the brooches from her dress and plunged them deep into his eyes. "No sluggish, oozing drops," the messenger reports, "But a black rain and bloody hail poured down." The flood of gore from his ruined eyes, the messenger says of Oedipus, even now runs down his face and stains his beard.
>
> Only after this terrifying verbal preparation do the doors of the palace open. We behold the once mighty king now blind, broken, soaked in his own blood, and anguished with the guilt he feels for a crime he committed unknowingly. When Oedipus finally speaks, what we hear is not words but only a single, repeated cry of agony: speech rolled back into mere sound and torment. This is the stark revelation toward which every act and speech of the entire drama have been relentlessly aiming: a frozen moment of pain that contains nothing except the mutilated human body and its wordless suffering. [D. B. Morris 1991, pp. 247–248]

For medieval Christians, pain served as a sign and means of contact with the divine, inspiring many saints to shed their blood as martyrs and inspiring numerous others to mimic them. Both Oedipus' and St. Lucy's acts of self-enucleation makes us cringe in horror, as do other major acts of self-amputation, such as cutting off the penis, hand, fingers, or toes. These acts occur with sudden violence, involve a great deal of tissue damage, and are found primarily in psychotic states or in those who are acutely intoxicated (Favazza 1987, Walsh and Rosen 1988, Winchel and Stanley 1991). Patients' explanations for this behavior often refer to biblical texts and to sexual themes (Favazza 1987, 1996).

Then there are acts of stereotypic self-mutilation—head banging, eyeball pressing, finger biting—that have fixed, often rhythmic patterns, and are thought to be without symbolic meaning. They are most commonly seen in institutionalized mentally retarded individuals and may be associated features of autistic disorder, acute psychotic states, schizophrenia, Lesch-Nyhan and Tourette syndromes, and obsessive-compulsive disorder.

Although others who have studied self-mutilation have defined it as the nonlethal infliction of injury upon one's body that results in tissue damage, (Favazza 1987, 1996, Kahan and Pattison 1984, Pattison and Kahan 1983, Russ 1992, Walsh and Rosen 1988, Winchel 1991, Winchel and Stanley 1991), it is best that it not be defined according to lethality, which is the outcome and not necessarily the intent. It is preferable to define it descriptively as the infliction of injury upon one's body that results in tissue damage or alteration, without inferring assumptions about intent. Some superficial to moderate acts of self-mutilation might strike one initially as being startlingly pathological, while others are so common and ordinary that it may seem odd to refer to them as self-mutilation. Other forms of self-mutilation include burning oneself, peeling off layers of skin, sticking oneself with needles or pins, scratching oneself, cutting oneself, picking at one's skin or blemishes, popping pimples, interfering with wound healing by attacking scar tissue or pulling off scabs, pulling out one's hair, rubbing away layers of skin with erasers, and severe nail and cuticle biting. Most people who self-mutilate do so in several different ways. A survey of 250 self-mutilators (Favazza and Conterio 1988) found that 78 percent used multiple methods, the most prevalent of which was cutting (72 percent), followed by burning (35 percent), picking at wounds or otherwise interfering with wound healing (22 percent), hair pulling (10 percent), and bone breaking (8 percent).

While cutting may strike us as violent and dangerous, this is often an emotional reaction to the drama surrounding it rather than to the actual danger to the person doing it. It is important to distinguish between wild and out-of-control slashing and the "delicate self-cutting" (Pao 1969) more commonly known to clinicians—superficial controlled cuts typically to the wrist or arm that usually require little or no medical treatment. Cutting is prevalent in patients with personality disorders, posttraumatic stress disorder, and dissociative disorders, who report experiencing little or no pain or a localized pain that is far more tolerable than their more diffuse emotional suffering. Some cutters cut their thighs, abdomen, breasts, or even lacerate the vaginal canal. The cuts may be simple lines or a word, name, or symbol engraved in the skin. The location and appearance of the scars often allude to some veiled meaning.

A chilling practice among groups of adolescents is sharing cutting instruments, with possible exposure to the risk of infection including human immunodeficiency virus (HIV) and hepatitis. For example, among seventy-six adolescents hospitalized in psychiatric facilities 46 reported cutting themselves and 50 percent of them shared their blades with others (DiClemente et al. 1990). The risk is even greater in gangs of intravenous drug users, in whom the knowledge of the risk they are taking increases the thrill. The use of drugs or alcohol may precede the self-cutting, diminishing inhibitions, judgment, and the degree of pain felt, and giving the person greater courage to cut more deeply and violently.

Body Modifications

Those who have a penchant for permanent markings may employ someone else to tattoo, pierce, cut, or otherwise mark their bodies, which is a passive form of self-mutilation. Often they bridle at the term *self-mutilation* because of the connotation of psychopathology, and prefer the term *body modifications*. They may be ignorant of the real or potential dangers or find the pain and danger to be exciting. (Most body modifications are done without anesthesia.) Physicians and dentists have seen an increase in problems associated with body modifications, which is not surprising since piercing is really a form of minor surgery involving the insertion of a needle into a body part supplied by major nerve centers and blood vessels. Studio piercings and tattoos are done by unlicensed personnel who may have minimal or no knowledge of anatomy. A Mayo Clinic study found that nearly 25 percent of people with congenital heart disease who had their bodies pierced developed endocarditis, a potentially life-threatening heart-valve infection. Tongue piercing, done with a needle with a diameter seven times greater than that used for dental anesthesia, can cause puncture infection, chronic pain, soreness, chipped teeth and broken fillings, permanent numbness, loss of taste, and interference with speech, chewing, and swallowing.

There has been little consideration of the risks involved in introducing permanent ink into the body or of transmitting blood-borne pathogens through the inks or needles. Tattoo pigments are laden with mercury or chromates, are neither standardized nor approved by the Food and Drug Administration for intradermal use (Armstrong 1991, Armstrong and McConnell 1994), and can, along with unsterilized needles, be tainted with the hepatitis C virus. An outbreak of hepatitis was traced to a tattoo parlor in New York City in 1961, leading to a ban on tattooing that remains today. Oddly enough, New York City is home to many body-piercing studios even though piercing carries many of the same risks as tattooing as well as some additional ones. While there have been no reported cases of HIV infection traced to tattooing or body piercing, studies of "body art" among students (Armstrong 1991, Armstrong and McConnell 1994, Greif and Hewitt 1996) found that some piercings did not heal and some students had become infected with hepatitis. Traditionally, girls and women from certain ethnic groups have pierced each others' ears, which is far less risky than piercing other parts of the body. Earlobes consist of mostly fatty tissue and few blood vessels or nerve endings that can be damaged. More risky are the homemade tattoos and piercings, some made by children as young as 8 who use pins, needles, or pens to insert colored India ink, carbon, charcoal, soot, or mascara into the skin.

As the shock value of tattoos and piercing wanes, branding, a mark traditionally denoting ownership of animals, is gaining popularity. Branders heat thin slivers of steel to extremely high temperatures and apply it to the skin. Blood vessels are cauterized on impact and the tissue heals to form keloids or scar tissue that is usually raised. The greatest danger is caused by branders who may not get the brand hot enough for branding but hot enough to cause serious burns and infections. While most of us are pleased when our wounds heal without causing scarring, there are those who have designs cut into their skin expressly for the purpose of leaving permanent raised dark scars, a practice called scarification. As the cuts begin to heal naturally, the healing process is deliberately thwarted by rubbing alcohol on the wound and igniting it, rubbing vinegar into the wound, rubbing ashes or ink into the wounds to color the tissue, and picking off the newly formed scabs.

Certain kinds of self-mutilation are meant to enhance sexual pleasure. Some individuals have their nipples or genitals pierced to increase their own excitement, while some have their tongues pierced and a "barbell" inserted for the purpose of providing greater sexual stimulation to the partner during oral sex. Others may frequent clubs where they are likely to find "vampires," people who enjoy bloodletting and bloodsucking (Ramsland 1998).

Mutilating Surgery

Some individuals manage to get doctors to perform intrusive medical procedures or unnecessary surgery on them. These may at times be cases of Munchausen's syndrome or sex-change surgery, but the majority are cosmetic surgeries—tummy tucks, face lifts, rhinoplasty, breast enlargement, breast reduction, penile enlargement, eyelid surgery, liposuction—that have become increasingly common in both sexes. With newspaper ads for penile enlargement surgery, it should be no surprise that the newest development on the cosmetic surgery horizon is a procedure called "aesthetic labioplasty," or surgical "beautification" of the labia. As for facial surgery, the injection of animal collagen to make lips fuller has become a popular procedure despite the fact that it can result in a disease of the connective tissue (Lappe 1996). Although most reputable hospitals require intensive training for their residents, board certification is not required to perform plastic surgery. In fact, in New York and California there are no regulations regarding who can perform tumescent liposuction, which is the most popular cosmetic surgery in the country and more risky than is commonly known. Unfortunately, too many people are more concerned about the before and after computer imaging they see during a consultation for cosmetic surgery than they are about the physician's qualifications.

For centuries male infant circumcision has been a common religious practice among Jews and in the twentieth century was the most frequently performed operation in the United States, performed primarily for nonreligious reasons despite medical controversy about whether this operation affords health advantages. Pulitzer Prize–winning author Alice Walker helped expose to the Western world the practice of female genital mutilation in Africa in her 1992 novel, *Possessing the Secret of Joy*, sparking an international debate on the issue. African midwives have been traditionally trained to perform these mutilations on young girls for the purposes of providing a "chastity belt" for women until marriage, and to contain their sexual appetites. Women with mutilated genitals experience unusual pain during intercourse and childbirth and medical complications in childbirth.

Female genital mutilation is currently practiced openly in central Africa and the Middle East. According to the United States Centers for Disease Control and Prevention, there are an estimated 168,000 women in this country, mostly from central Africa, who have undergone female genital circumcision or are at risk for having it. Although it is not openly acknowledged, some American doctors currently perform the operation on the daughters of African emigrants when they or their parents request it (Abel 1996). What is also not so well known is that the mutilation of women by means of gynecologic surgery such as genital circumcision and unnecessary hysterectomy has been practiced throughout the history of medicine, and continues today in "civilized" and Third World cultures (Shorter 1992). In fact, clitoridectomies have been practiced in England, Europe, and the United States as remedies for chronic masturbation, nymphomania, and hysterical seizures; the *American Journal of Obstetrics* published numerous papers from 1869 until World War I praising and reporting clitoridectomy (Shorter 1992). The procedure became so institutionalized as a panacea that some women requested it.

Fighting Fat: The Desperate Quest for the Magic Bullet

Although obesity is an enormous American health problem, the number of overweight adults and children continues to increase because of overeating and under-exercising. It is very easy to become fat in the Western world because human beings continue to prefer food dense in calories that was an adaptive preference when we were evolving prehistorically in an environment where food was scarce (Logue 1986), a preference that is now maladaptive. The increase in obesity parallels the increasing cultural obsession with weight, dieting, and exercise and the increase in eating disorders, providing those with anorexia and bulimia with a culturally acceptable rationalization for their illness. For the first time in recorded history individuals are dieting and exercising excessively in the name of self improvement, suffering from too much of a good thing (Yates 1991). This is less a problem in Europe where people are not so fat-phobic. They eat smaller portions but savor their food more, maintaining lower body weights and suffering less with eating disorders.

In America, miracle diets, drugs, surgeries, and other "magic bullets" prevail, leading Americans down a desperate and often dangerous path of weight loss and health regimes.

The Keys study (Keys et al. 1950) during World War II is the classical study of the mental and physical effects of semi-starvation that led to the recognition that severe and prolonged dietary restriction can lead to serious physical and psychological complications. Many of the symptoms once thought to be primary features of anorexia nervosa were found to be symptoms of starvation (Wooley and Wooley 1985). The experiment involved carefully studying young, healthy, psychologically normal men while restricting their caloric intake. For the first three months the volunteers ate normally, and in the next six months they were restricted to half their former intake and lost, on average, 25 percent of their former weight. At the same time hypochondriasis, depression, and hysteria increased.

The caloric intake in the Keys study was at a level that is greater than many weight loss programs permit. What makes the Keys study so important is that the 25 percent rapid weight loss of the subjects is paralleled by a 25 percent rapid weight loss by those who meet *DSM-IV* criteria for anorexia nervosa. Many of the experiences observed in the study volunteers are the same as those experienced by patients with anorexia nervosa: dramatic increase in preoccupation with food, decreased interest in sex and activity, increased hunger, episodes of binge eating, obsession with food, and bizarre and secret food rituals. The study showed that tormenting and obsessive thoughts about food are an inevitable result of starvation and the semi-starvation that characterizes most weight loss diets, predisposing one to develop the ravenous "ox hunger" that defines bulimia, to binge, to lose control of eating, and to purge. It explains why many who became anorexic after experiencing rapid weight loss on a restricted diet began to experience bouts of bingeing and purging. For many these bulimic episodes alternated with severe dietary restriction, sometimes called bulimarexia, or anorexia nervosa, bulimic type. For others the bulimic episodes continued. Thus, many bulimics envy the control over the impulse to eat exerted by anorexics and consider themselves to be "failed anorexics." In the rarely discussed eating disorder status hierarchy, anorexia reigns as "queen" while binge eating or compulsive overeating is of the lowest status, one of the seven deadly sins (gluttony).

Fat has gone from being a symbol of health, prosperity, and well-being to a sign of moral, psychological, and physical disorder. "Fat" has become the new "F-word" or dirty word, and "fat-free" has become a national mantra, with children as young as 5 or 6 becoming phobic about consuming any fat. The compulsion to exercise excessively and to develop perfect fat-free bodies is especially intense among those involved in careers or sports that have stringent weight requirements, such as ballet dancing, figure skating, swimming, cycling, gymnastics, running, modeling, and wrestling. Gymnasts present with the highest rates of eating disorders found in any sport; 20–25 percent become bulimic. Wrestling competition, like boxing and the martial arts, is conducted in weight classes, and many high school and college wrestlers use vomiting, diuretics, and excessive exercise to lower their weight. Recently three college wrestlers died within six weeks of each other during strenuous weight loss workouts (Litsky 1997). Male and female body builders are as obsessed with ridding their body of fat as much as anorectics and bulimics. They will go to grotesque lengths to achieve huge striated muscles and the "cut" or "shrink wrapped" look, stripping themselves of all subcutaneous fat to reveal the full definition of their muscles. "Cutting" involves strenuous dieting, often with nutritional additives or fat solvents, a process of intentional dehydration to minimize the amount of water retained in the hypodermis. The dehydrated skin cannot maintain the correct body temperature, and so despite their bulk, body builders are often cold. Someone with a well- 'cut' body will have less than 4 percent body fat, a level reached only among starvation victims (Lappe 1996). Although the body must look vital and youthful, one Mr. Universe commented on a television documentary, "By the time we are on stage, we are more dead than alive."

In the 1960s and 1970s, diet doctors dispensed dexamphetamine diet pills freely and a generation of women walked around tolerating heart palpitations, anxiety, and sleeplessness, even risking drug-induced psychosis in order to lose weight. In the 1980's the very popular liquid protein diets were associated with gall bladder disease and hair loss.

The fen-phen phenomenon has been extraordinary. On the basis of one study of 121 obese patients who had lost an average of 30 pounds on a combination of fenfluramine (an appetite suppressant related chemically to the amphetamines) and phentermine (a serotonin regulating drug), and despite the fact that it was not approved by the Federal Drug Administration, the word spread about fen-phen and doctors were inundated with requests for the drugs. A huge industry in diet "pill mills" was spawned, exploiting the 30 percent of their female clients with diagnosable or subclinical eating disorders and depressions, who suffer from magical thinking, convinced that if they simply become thinner their lives will be transformed. They have the obsessional "diet head," living lives of yo-yo weight cycling, going from weight loss from the latest diet to reinforced obsessional thinking about food and compulsive binge eating, to the newest diet, and on and on. Even after extensive media coverage of the linkage of fen-phen and Redux with serious heart-valve damage, sales of these drugs nearly tripled from 1995 to 1996, and many enraged dieters demanded that their doctors prescribe the pills despite the recall. Weight loss centers that had done a big business in fen-phen did an about face, advertising their concern for their patients' well-being by promoting the "natural" way to weight loss with dangerous herbal remedies and other diet drug substitutes.

Those desperate to lose weight may turn to street drugs like cocaine and amphetamines. Metabolife, one of numerous "fat burners" containing ephedrine, an adrenaline-like substance that speeds up metabolism and increases heart rate and blood pressure, has become extremely popular, selling as well as Prozac and Viagra. People have been demanding products made with Olestra, a fat substitute, even though Olestra may interfere with the absorption of necessary vitamins and minerals and can cause a condition euphemistically called "intestinal leakage" as well as diarrhea and gas. Many have been taking Xenical (orlistat), a prescription fat blocker that can result in the same difficulties associated with Olestra.

Overeating and Obesity

People who eat so compulsively that they become morbidly obese put their health at great risk. Morbid obesity may decrease longevity and aggravate the onset and development of cardiovascular difficulties, hypertension, high cholesterol levels, diabetes, sleep apnea, or other pulmonary problems, gallbladder and other digestive diseases, trauma to the bones and joints, and certain cancers, specifically prostate and colorectal cancer in men, and gallbladder, breast, cervix, endometrial, uterine, and ovarian cancer in women (Bray 1986). The frequency of abnormal labor and delivery is higher in obese women.

Anorectic Behavior

The image of a bleeding and mutilated Christ is also an image of an emaciated and dehydrated Christ. The anorectic operates under the assumption that she can transcend the flesh and not need what other human beings need in order to live.

The physical complications of anorexia and bulimia can be life threatening, yet it is disturbing to know that many psychiatrists, non-medical therapists, and primary care physicians overlook and fail to diagnose eating disorders (Hornbacher 1998, Sharp and Freeman 1993). Many anorectics have an intense obsessional fear of being fat and an encapsulated delusional inner representation of their body as fat and grotesque. Others are compelled to punish themselves by starving themselves, purging their bodies violently and painfully, and exercising to the point of pain and injury and beyond. They progressively and rapidly lose more and more weight, allowing their emaciated bodies to feed off themselves, thus cannibalizing their own muscle tissue, including cardiac muscle. Aptly, the earliest account of the anorexia nervosa syndrome in 1694 was called "Nervous Consumption" (Morton 1694).

Although anorexics often minimize their difficulties, nonetheless some die suddenly from heart arrhythmias, renal malfunctions, circulatory failures or suicides. According to the American Anorexia Bulimia Association, each year 150,000 American women die of anorexia. Some anorectics improve enough that their medical risk ceases to be an immediate concern, but nonetheless torture themselves with diet, weight, and body image preoccupations, remaining chronically ill throughout their lives. There are many kinds of anorectic behaviors, some that might strike one as being startlingly pathological and others that are very common in our culture as ordinary culturally acceptable weight control practices.

Anorectics are often irritable and depressed and may have difficulty concentrating, thinking clearly, and making decisions. Their moods are often labile, going from the manic exhilaration that comes with losing weight to crashing depression and self-loathing. Endocrine and metabolic abnormalities include yellowing of the skin, impaired taste, and hypoglycemia. Other common symptoms are constipation, bloating, abdominal pain, cold intolerance, lethargy, hyperactivity, low blood pressure, dizziness, dry skin, and pitting edema. Often there is the growth of a fine downy hair (lanugo) that covers the limbs and face, the body's adaptation to hypothermia in much the same way as fur is the body's adaptation for animals in cold climates. Anorectics may suffer from leukopenia, low white blood cell count, non-menstrual bleeding or the loss of menstrual function (amenorrhea), and loss of libido. Often, there is bone loss. Even the brain may undergo structural changes such as loss of brain tissue and enlargement of the ventricles, which may be reversible when weight normalizes.

In her 1998 memoir, Marya Hornbacher described compellingly the medical and mental toll taken by anorexia. She had become ugly, like a monster. Her hair had fallen out; her skin was "the color of rotten meat." Her brain would not work and she felt "like an ice cube." Where there once was flesh, there now was space, and the spaces were growing larger and larger. "I put toilet paper in my shoes so the ground wouldn't slam back at the bones of my feet when I walked, jarring me and making me dizzy . . ." (p. 267).

Those Who Purge to Binge

Marya, old and wasted beyond her 23 years, speaks: "Bulimia is linked . . . to periods of intense passion, passion of all kinds, but most specifically emotional passion. Bulimia acknowledges the body explicitly, violently. It attacks the body but does not deny. It is an act of disgust and of need . . . the bulimic impulse is more realistic than the anorexic because, for in its horrible nihilism, it understands that the body is inescapable" (Hornbacher 1998, p. 93).

The word boulimia means ox-hunger in Greek and has been defined in terms of binge eating, the consumption of what most people would regard as large amounts of food, usually over a concentrated period of time (American Psychiatric Association 1994). There are problems with this definition because it does not take into account the subjectivity factor; what one person might consider to be a large amount of food might be regarded as small by another. The binge is usually ended by a purge, which serves the purpose of allowing individuals to continue to binge without fear of weight gain, popularly expressed as "having your cake and eating it too." These are the individuals who seek the experience of satiety and fullness. For them the purging is a necessary evil, a means to an end. They may account for approximately 85 percent of those who meet criteria for a DSM-IV diagnosis of Bulimia Nervosa. Bulimia can be more dangerous than is usually thought because it can go undetected for a long time by family members and physicians, as the bulimic can maintain a normal body weight and appearance even while putting her life at continual risk.

"I Purge, Therefore I Am"

Cardiac arrest is the most common cause of death among bulimics and among anorectics who binge and/or purge. Some anorectics starve themselves and if they eat so much as a spoonful of food, feel compelled to purge several times immediately. Because so much of the literature on bulimic behavior focuses on binge eating, the severity of the physical and psychological problems of the person who starves and purges or who binges in order to purge are easily overlooked (Farber 1995a, Garner et al. 1993, Tobin et al. 1992). There are those who binge so that they have something to purge, a significant group barely even mentioned in the literature (Hall and Beresford 1989). This group, whether they binge or whether they starve themselves, seeks the experience of the purge, the violent cramping and pain, and will induce severe purging to a life-threatening degree. They use multiple means of purging and will purge very frequently. In fact, laxative abusers have an increased probability of making suicide attempts or other self-injurious behavior and have a higher rate of prior inpatient treatment for depression (Mitchell et al. 1986). Further, much of the morbidity and mortality in patients with eating disorders may be a consequence of purging behaviors (Sharp and Freeman 1993).

Those who purge very frequently and severely tend to be an extremely masochistic group who seek the violent and intense experience of pain, cramping, and injury and the resulting emptiness, dehydration, and internal bleeding (Farber 1995a). Their purging is a literal form of self-mutilation from the inside out, as it lacerates organs and causes internal injuries and bleeding. They attack their bodies internally in much the same way that self-mutilators attack their bodies externally. They might consume a large amount of food so that they can have the experience of vomiting or anally evacuating it. To make sure they get rid of every last morsel, they may consume foods of only one color, or may binge on foods organized by color and eaten in a certain order, a ritual called layering.[2] That is, they may mark the beginning of the binge with orange foods, progress to green, then white, and so on, and when they see they have vomited food in the reverse order, they can be certain they have rid themselves of all of it. This process may be marked not by one but by many purges for each binge, even resulting in several waves of dry heaving. Some patients may purge as many as 40–100 times during any discrete binge period which might last as long as two or three hours (Hall and Beresford 1989). For them, the binge might be a necessary evil, or it may be the experience they seek along with the violent purge.

The pain and serious complications of bulimic behavior are more often the result of the purging rather than the binge itself (Johnson and Connors 1987). Chronic purging may result in menstrual irregularities and other endocrine difficulties, and has been associated with peripheral nervous system changes. Vomiting

---

2. While I knew of this ritual involving food of different colors, it was Star Qualter, M.S.W., a student in my eating disorder seminar, who introduced me to the term *layering*.

also results in electrolyte abnormalities caused by the severe depletion of certain trace minerals, primarily sodium and potassium, necessary to maintain the integrity of many body systems. Such electrolyte imbalance can lead to cardiac arrhythmia and muscle weakness. Gastric acids remaining in the mouth after vomiting may cause dental cavities, erosion of the dental enamel, soreness of the throat, hypersensitivity of the teeth, reduced salivary flow, swelling of the parotid salivary gland resulting in a "chipmunk cheeks" appearance, and gum disease, and vomiting may cause cuts or calluses on the finger used to stimulate the gag reflex. Vomiting also leads to fluid loss and dehydration, which may result in retaining water, excessive thirst, decreased urinary output, and dizziness. It can severely affect the gastrointestinal system, resulting in ulceration of the esophagus, loss of the gag reflex, and subsequent reflex regurgitation.[3] Some may use syrup of Ipecac, a poison antidote, to induce vomiting, putting them at great risk for cardiac arrest and sudden death. Chronic laxative use results in loss of bowel function, laxative dependence, and serious effects on the renal and gastrointestinal systems (Willard et al. 1989), while the use of diuretics can have severe consequences on renal function and fluid and electrolyte balance. The excessive use of saunas to induce water loss and "exercise bulimia" (Yates 1991), severe exercise to "undo" the binge, are both forms of purging that can result in dehydration. When several purging methods are used in combination, the potential for pain, serious medical complications, and death are multiplied many times over.

When the body is already in a severe deficiency state due to starvation, the assaultive effects of bingeing and purging or severe purging alone can be even more life threatening, as Marya Hornbacher (1998) elaborates.

I went in search of a scale.

Seventy.

I took off my belt and shoes.

Sixty-seven.

That's when I began bingeing. . . . everything is a blur. . . .

. . . . It feels . . . as if you are possessed . . . your body . . . wants to live. You want to die . . .

---

3. People who have been purging chronically and severely often do not need to induce vomiting mechanically by sticking their fingers down their throat but find that they can vomit automatically. Some deliberately focus upon disgusting thoughts to stimulate the gag reflex. One of my patients would imagine that the food she had eaten had been in the toilet bowl, mingling with feces and urine.

Sixty-five.

. . . . You can't stay alive very long when you're not eating at all, or when everything you eat is thrown up.

Sixty-one.

. . . I bought laxatives and began eating a box of them every day. Trouble was, there wasn't any food in my system. I was shitting water and blood . . . we are running through the streets trying to find an open store where we can find more food. We are buying ipecac . . . we eat on the subway . . . and we . . . sit down on the floor and stuff the rest of the food into our mouths, choking . . . and then we stand up and drink the whole bottle of ipecac . . . and then the floor comes flying at our heads.

I lay there, praying . . . to either throw up or die, dear God . . . and then I threw up horribly and blacked out again.

. . . I wanted so badly to be dead.

Fifty-five.

I think I'm dead.

Finally.

Fifty-two.

Then everything goes white. [pp. 267–279]

Bulimic behavior can be found not only in those who meet DSM-IV criteria for Bulimia Nervosa, but also in those who meet criteria for Anorexia Nervosa, Bingeing/Purging type, as well as in those who have disordered eating that does not fall into these discrete categories, the individuals who may receive a DSM diagnosis called Eating Disorder Not Otherwise Specified. However, there is disagreement about whether anorexics who only purge are more similar to the "pure" restrictor anorexics and should be grouped with them, or whether they are more similar to the anorexics who both binge and purge and should be grouped with them (Nagata et al. 1997). DSM diagnostic categories fail to consider the influence of developmental factors on the evolution of an eating disorder and do not consider that an individual with anorexia nervosa may convert from one subtype to another in the course of the illness or come to fulfill DSM criteria for Bulimia Nervosa. It is in the border between one diagnostic subtype and another, or between one diagnostic subtype and something that has no name where the most telling psychosomatic processes occur.

Those who do not meet *DSM* criteria for Anorexia Nervosa or Bulimia Nervosa fall between the cracks, and have illnesses most likely not to be studied. These may include those patients who do not have typical bulimic symptoms but present instead with atypical gastrointestinal difficulties that have been diagnosed as ulcerative colitis, Crohn's disease, or irritable bowel syndrome. What may not be considered by physicians and therapists is the possibility of a secretive purging component to these illnesses, with patients inducing severe diarrhea by typical or atypical methods. For example, a colleague referred an 18-year-old college student to me for consultation, who complained that she at times suffered diarrhea within ten minutes of eating, and at times would awaken at night with a stomach ache and diarrhea. In two or three months she had lost at least eleven pounds from her small frame. She was able, reluctantly, to divulge a secret that she "did something" with her mind right after eating that results in diarrhea, that is, she performed some mental process that made it occur. I had also seen a woman who had been treated medically for years for ulcerative colitis and more recently for self-starvation, self-induced vomiting, and laxative abuse. Another had Crohn's disease and bulimia nervosa at the same time. Patients can make themselves sick in many different ways. One is rumination, which may be present in anorexics and bulimics more than has been thought (Tamburrino et al. 1995). Rumination is bringing up into the mouth food that has been swallowed and which may have been partially digested, to be rechewed and reswallowed. Interestingly it often has a cognitive counterpart, mental rumination, the thinking about or daydreaming about food, working the same thought over and over again. Purging can occur in bizarre and peculiar guises, including the documented case of a woman who regularly donated her blood to blood banks in order to purge her system of the "internal pollution" her bingeing had caused (Ghadirian 1997). Clinicians should know that the body can be exploited in unlimited and dangerous ways not to be found in the *Diagnostic and Statistical Manual of Mental Disorders.*

OTHER SELF-HARM IN THE SPECTRUM

In the quest for the elixir of youth, people are flocking to medical anti-aging specialists, contemporary Ponce de Leons who may be doing far more harm than good. Most are plastic surgeons by training who go far beyond plastic surgery to hormone replacement therapy with testosterone, melatonin, DHEA and the costly growth hormone hGH, vitamin supplements, dermatology, physical therapy, and other procedures. "We're not about growing old gracefully. We're about never growing old," (Kuczynski 1998, p. 9) said the president of the American Academy of Anti-Aging Medicine. Despite their claims for hGH injections, the National Institute on Aging found that the side effects can include diabetes, pooling of fluid in the skin, joint pain, and carpal tunnel syndrome.

In his offices on what might be called Plastic Surgery Mile on Manhattan's Park Avenue and in Smithtown, New York, Dr.Bruce J. Nadler performs the standard symphony of plastic surgery procedures and is popular with the youth-elixir crowd. He says he has more than 50 patients on hGH; he and his wife also take it. A competitive body-builder by hobby, Dr. Nadler likes to show visitors to the New York office a picture of him clad only in a bikini-brief bathing suit, posing next to his silver BMW Z-3 convertible. [Kuczynski 1998, p. 9]

Those with limited finances can turn to the do-it-yourself approach, dosing and megadosing themselves with these and other hormones that are readily available commercially. Ever since the men's impotence pill, Viagra, hit the market, many men are taking it without a prescription, with the result that a number with heart conditions have died of heart attacks. Some women have been taking it too even though at the time of writing, Viagra had not been tested on women. Similarly, a million American adolescent girls and women have been using Accutane for treatment of acne, even though the FDA linked it to human fetal malformation and miscarriage.

Still another kind of self-harm is that practiced by those with physical illnesses who chronically seek medical care and just as chronically refuse to comply with the treatment. These care-seeking, care-rejecting patients may spend a lifetime going from doctor to doctor, managing to defeat their doctors while becoming yet even more ill. (Chapter 15 features such a case.)

Certain sexual practices such as anal intercourse, "fist fucking," and insertion of sharp objects into the anus, urethra, or vagina can lacerate delicate mucous tissue and transmit infection, notably hepatitis B and HIV. The danger inherent in sexual sadomasochism can be far greater than either the psychiatric literature or the S & M aficionados would indicate, with an estimated 50 deaths per year resulting from erotic hanging or asphyxiation (Litman and Swearingen 1996). Many chronically suicidal patients in time reveal a pattern of sadomasochistic sexual activity, either with partners or alone, and there have been media accounts of murders that occurred within the context of a sadomasochistic relationship. The damage done to one's life through moral masochism, the unconscious seeking of self-sabotage, failure, and self-punishment, is immeasurable and quite common.

Then there is the category of behavior that may be harmful to the self in ways that may result ultimately, although less directly, in injury or in physical illness—drug and alcohol abuse, smoking, compulsive sexuality or unprotected sex, accident proneness, physical risk taking, and repeated involvement in abusive relationships.

As more and more people in the United States have been laid off from their jobs or live with that threat, drug abuse problems have been increasing. The obsession with weight loss is often a factor in many women turning to the use of crack cocaine or methamphetamine to control their appetite. Methamphetamine, "Mother's Little Helper," is a cheap source of energy and stamina for many women who work twelve hour waitress shifts or for many single mothers who juggle jobs,

children, and housework. The addiction to alcohol and drugs is a progressive journey during which chronicity and tolerance is established, transforming what may
have initially been occasional substance abuse into a life-threatening addictive
path. The addiction to the adrenaline rush of power behind the wheel of a car
("road rage") has become a national problem and danger.

Self-harm is manifested not only in physical symptoms but in shame, anguish,
isolation, and alienation, all of which inflict injury to one's self-esteem. For
example, shoplifting, compulsive gambling, compulsive shopping and spending,
and moral masochism can all result in the kind of pain and suffering that leaves
no detectable physical mark. It is thought that 3.8 million adults in the United
States and Canada suffer from pathological gambling, which is prevalent among
adolescents and those with psychiatric and substance abuse problems, and which
accounts for increases in stealing, in bankruptcies, and is a factor in lost jobs,
marital problems, domestic violence, and welfare costs. Credit card debt is a
national problem, while shopping and spending have become the preferred way
for many to spend their weekends and vacations. Compulsive shopping or buying is a significant problem for as much as 10 percent of the population, and one
out of 12 Americans is overwhelmed by debt (Benson 2000). Men in positions
of great power have been known to sabotage their success and bring humiliation
on themselves, most notably, Bill Clinton, the president of the United States,
whose sexual indiscretions and subsequent lies have been rampant. When one's
lifestyle has become organized around self-harm of any kind, the person has
become firmly attached to self-inflicted suffering.

THE SELF-HARM CONCEPT IN THE LITERATURE

Self-harm is a relatively new concept in the scientific literature, including
the literature on self-care, body alienation, self-mutilation, and eating problems.
Popular books about specific kinds of self-harm are increasingly being published,
notably eating disorders, substance abuse, and self-mutilation.

Caring for the Body, Caring for the Self

The concept of the self-care functions of the ego (Khantzian and Mack 1983)
evolved from the consideration of several theories: the self-preservative or ego
instincts (Freud 1913b), the adaptive function of the ego in helping the human
species survive (Hartmann 1939), the importance of the quality of nurturance
and care in the earliest phases of the mother–child relationship (Kohut 1971,
Mahler et al. 1975, Sandler and Sandler 1978), a developmental line from irresponsibility to responsibility in body management (A. Freud 1966), self-regulation
(Greenspan 1979), and psychosomatic disorders (Krystal 1978, Nemiah et al.

1976). Khantzian and Mack (1983) postulated that the child's ability to care for and protect himself becomes internalized and developed through the experience of being cared for and protected by a nurturing parent. If we apply this concept, then accident proneness, impulsive or violent behavior, weight disturbances, substance abuse, and other forms of self-neglect or self-destructiveness can be considered signs of failure in those functions of the ego that warn, guide, and protect individuals from dangerous involvements and behavior.

Krueger (1989) has elaborated the evolving mental representations of the body as it becomes woven into the development of the body self and psychological self (see Chapter 5). Those lacking a consistent and accurate image of their body self often use self-stimulation to regulate affect, including the use of food, drugs, alcohol, sex, cutting, exercise, and impulsive or compulsive behavior. Because the body self cannot sufficiently contain the developing psychological self, these individuals fail to develop the use of symbolic language and must rely on their bodies to speak for them.

Walsh and Rosen (1988) developed the concept of body alienation, "a pervasive pattern of disrespect, discomfort, and debasement of their physical selves" (p. 70) indicating an individual's feeling alienated from his or her own body and promoting a negative and/or distorted body image. Based on Walsh's study of adolescent self-mutilators, it was found that a sense of body alienation was the most powerful predictor of self-mutilating behavior. Of the numerous ways through which these adolescents expressed their body alienation, the relationship between eating disorders and self-mutilation yielded the highest correlation.

From Self-Mutilation to Other Self-Harm

Several other concepts were developed for understanding self-mutilation, out of which developed a scientific interest in understanding other kinds of self-harm. A deliberate self-harm (DSH) syndrome had been proposed for inclusion in the *Diagnostic and Statistical Manual* (DSM) characterized by multiple episodes of deliberately physically self-damaging acts of low lethality, often associated with alcohol abuse, including skin carving, wrist cutting, biting, burning, eye enucleation, amputation of tongue or ear, skin ulceration, and genital mutilation (Kahan and Pattison 1984, Pattison and Kahan 1983). Individuals "with apparent consciousness and willful intent perform(ed) painful, destructive, and injurious acts upon their own bodies without the apparent intent to kill themselves" (Kahan and Pattison 1984, p. 19). These acts differed on the basis of their lethality, repetition, and the directness of the harm.

Favazza (1987, 1996) and associates (Favazza and Conterio 1988, Favazza and Rosenthal 1990, Favazza et al. 1989) extended the DSH syndrome concept, regarding it as a class within a larger category of self-damaging behaviors that differ on the basis of the lethality, repetition, and the directness of the harm.

A high lethality single episode, indirect type of self-injurious behavior would be the deliberate termination of dialysis treatment by a person with severe kidney disease. A corresponding direct type of self-injurious behavior would be completed suicide from shooting oneself. Chronic alcoholism and heavy cigarette smoking are examples of low-lethality, multiple-episode, indirect self-injurious behavior; DSH is a corresponding direct behavior. . . . Single-episode acts of self-mutilation such as eye enucleation or hand amputation are direct, medium lethality behaviors. [Favazza 1987, p. 207]

Subsequently, Favazza and Simeon (1995) subdivided superficial self-mutilation into compulsive and impulsive self-injurious behavior according to the characteristics of the act. They categorized hair pulling, skin picking, and severe nail biting as compulsive, characterized by habitualness and repetitiveness, and associated with greater resistance to an ego-alien urge. Skin cutting and burning, in contrast, was categorized as impulsive, characterized by its episodic nature and extreme gratification, and was associated with ego-syntonic (acceptable to the ego) urges that were often triggered by events and involved little resistance.

These definitions enhance the body of knowledge about self-harm but are problematic, raising a number of provocative questions. How can we even be certain of the deliberateness of the act of direct self-harm is if it is committed in an altered state of consciousness such as that produced by mind-altering drugs or alcohol? How can we know that what appears to be "conscious and willful intent" really is? Things are often not as they seem, and what may seem to be a self-destructive act committed with conscious and willful intent may in fact be an act meant to ensure survival and committed in a dissociated state of consciousness.

We tend to ignore the many less dramatic forms of self-harm that may or may not take the body as its target, directly or indirectly. Robin Connors' (1996a,b, Trautmann and Connors 1994) clinical and personal experience as a self-injurer led her to writing about self-injury in trauma survivors. She has categorized self-injury as one of a possible four categories that constitute a broad continuum of self-harm. The first is body alterations, direct self-chosen changes to the body, such as tattoos, ear piercing, eyebrow plucking, cosmetic surgery, ceremonial or initiation scarring. The second is indirect self-harm, in which one's physical or psychological well-being is harmed even though the apparent intent is not to harm the self. This can include substance abuse, overeating, dieting, smoking, remaining in damaging relationships, and having unnecessary surgeries. The third is the failure to care for the self, such as is found in excessive risk-taking, accident proneness, or failure to get necessary medical care. The fourth is self-injury, direct actions that injure the body and that do not appear to fit the categories of body alteration, for example, cutting, head banging, burning, gouging, slapping, hair pulling or plucking, harmful enemas or douches, inserting dangerous objects into the vagina or rectum, picking at nails and cuticles until they bleed, hitting oneself, ingesting sharp objects, using erasers to rub and burn the skin, and biting oneself. Although there is, expectably, substantial overlap in

Connors' descriptive categorization of extremely complex human behavior, hers are, to my knowledge, the most thoughtful and thorough.

What can be most useful is a schema for assessing self-harm in a way that has direct and practical implications for treatment. Toward this end, it is proposed that self-harm be assessed according to the following criteria: the potential lethality of the behavior, the frequency or repetitiveness, the directness of the harm, chronicity, the extent to which the behaviors are compulsive or impulsive or both, the extent to which the behavior is acceptable to the ego (i.e., how ego-alien or ego-syntonic it is), the level of consciousness or dissociation that accompanies the act, the adaptive functions that are served by the self-harm, the degree to which the intent is suicidal, sadistic, or masochistic, how much pleasure is derived from the self-harm, and the multiple psychic functions served by the behavior. This assessment schema will be further elaborated in Chapter 13.

Symptom Clusters and Hunger Diseases

Clusters of self-harm behaviors are often found in the same individual so often that clusters of drug or alcohol abuse, binge eating, self-mutilation, suicide attempts, or hypersexual behavior, are commonly regarded as presumptive of a diagnosis of borderline personality organization (Goldstein 1990, Kernberg 1975, Kroll 1988, 1993, Walsh and Rosen 1988). What is less commonly known among clinicians is that both eating disordered and self-mutilating behavior are frequently found in those with dissociative disorders (Bliss 1980, Herman 1992, Putnam et al. 1986, Shapiro 1987, Torem 1986, van der Kolk 1987, 1989, 1994, van der Kolk et al. 1991, Vanderlinden and Vandereycken 1997), and in those with posttraumatic stress disorder (Herman 1992, Kroll 1988, 1993, Putnam et al. 1986, Shapiro and Dominiak 1992, van der Kolk 1987, 1989, 1994, van der Kolk et al. 1991, Vanderlinden and Vandereycken 1997). In fact, childhood trauma in which the child's body has been assaulted or violated sexually, in combination with a lack of secure attachments, may be the common denominator underlying the development of borderline personality, PTSD, dissociative disorders, eating disorders and self-mutilation.

There is a remarkably strong empirical association between eating-disordered behavior and self-mutilation that has major implications for understanding self-harm processes. Favazza (1987, 1996, Favazza and Conterio 1988, Favazza et al. 1989), having found that as many as 50 percent of female chronic self-mutilators have a history of anorexia nervosa or bulimia, proposed that self-mutilation and eating disorders are manifestations of the same pathological process. In several studies of patients who were identified as self-mutilators, 57 percent to 93.3 percent of self-mutilating subjects had concurrent eating disordered symptoms (Coid et al. 1983, Rosenthal et al. 1972, Simpson and Porter 1981, Walsh 1987, Yaryura-Tobias and Neziroglu 1978, Yaryura-Tobias et al. 1995). In studies of patients diagnosed with bulimia nervosa (which did not distinguish between those whose binge eating was followed by purging and those whose binge eating was not followed by purging), 8.9 percent to 26.6 percent of bulimic patients reported concurrent self-mutilating symptoms (Garfinkel et al. 1980, Turnbull 1989, Welbourne and Purgold 1984, Yellowlees 1985). Favazza and colleagues (1989) found that of the 50 percent of female self-mutilators who reported concurrent symptoms of disordered eating, 35 percent reported the syndrome of bingeing and purging, leading the authors to hypothesize that individuals with eating-disordered behavior, especially those who binge and purge, are at high risk for self-mutilation. Supporting these findings are those of Vanderlinden and Vandereycken (1997), who found that in the group of ninety-four female psychiatric inpatients that they studied, almost half reported at least one form of self-injury in the past year. These studies confirm what is known from the research literature, that self-injury is a greatly overlooked problem in psychiatric patients in general and in eating-disordered women in particular (Figure 1–1).

Some authors have pointed out the similarity of bulimia nervosa and both types of self-mutilating behavior—the milder, more habitual type and the more severe and impulsive type (Favazza and Simeon 1995)—to other impulse control disturbances and obsessive-compulsive disorders. All are marked by irresistible urges to commit the act, mounting tension when the individual tries to resist the behavior, and relief following the act (Simeon et al. 1992). Furthermore, all are associated with dysregulation of serotonin (5-hydroxytryptamine [5-HT]) and seem to respond positively to 5-HT reuptake inhibitors.

FIGURE 1–1. Association between eating-disordered behavior and self-mutilating behavior.

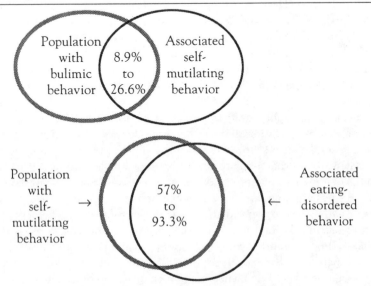

There have been startling findings of surgical bloodletting (venipuncture), a very unusual form of self-mutilation, in three female medical students in England, each of whom had a long history of anorexia followed by bulimia (Parkin and Eagles 1993). All had engaged in other acts of self-mutilation before resorting to bloodletting, which started when all three had developed expertise in venipuncture and had access to the necessary implements, and declined when the implements became less readily available. Two of the three reported having been sexually abused. Each subject seemed to derive similar psychological benefit from the bloodletting as they did from their bingeing and purging—relief of anxiety, tension, and anger. One believed that letting out a liter of blood at a time would help her lose weight. In the case of the bulimic woman who had donated her blood every three months for ten years, she reported feeling relieved and elated each time. She fantasized about watching the last drop drain from her body, wondering if she would evaporate and disappear at the same time (Ghadirian 1997).

If a patient went to a physician for relief of depression, despair, or overwhelming anxiety, it would be shocking if the doctor were to prescribe that she throw up after all her meals. If the patient were to complain that the prescribed "medicine" was too unpleasant to take, it would be even more shocking if the doctor responded, "Don't worry; you'll get used to it. It's an acquired taste." Yet for many, purging their meals or cutting or burning themselves may be initially a frightening thing to do, but many do acquire the taste for it as they find it brings relief. Many others quickly acquire a taste for many other potentially self-harming behaviors. An illuminating concept is Battegay's (1991) concept of hunger diseases, various disorders based on lack of self-esteem in which people are driven to possess and consume people and/or things in an addictive manner. Those with hunger diseases may medicate themselves through bulimic or anorexic behavior, self-mutilation, drugs, alcohol, sex, gambling, shopping, shoplifting, and power seeking in relationships. When one hunger disease is given up or renounced, often another will appear as a substitute if the insatiable hunger or yearning still remains.

Similarly, several other clinicians and researchers have noted the substitution of self-mutilating behavior for bulimic behavior and vice versa (Battegay 1991, Favazza 1987, 1996, Favazza and Rosenthal 1990, Welbourne and Purgold 1984, and Wilson 1983, 1986, 1988, 1989). A symptom substitution formulation has been proposed by Wilson (1983, 1989), expanding the idea that bulimia and self-mutilation are manifestations of the same pathological process. Wilson suggests that if symptoms are cleared before there has been adequate change in the underlying neurosis and object relations, the bulimic ego functioning may be replaced by "bulimic equivalents" such as self-destructive acting out, another addictive disorder, another psychosomatic symptom, neurotic symptom formation, or severe regressive symptom formation.

Expanding Favazza's idea that eating disorders and self-mutilation are different manifestations of the same pathological process, Heller (1990) studied a group of bulimic inpatients, a group of self-mutilating inpatients, and a third group that was both bulimic and self-mutilating, comparing their level of object relations and symptom choice, and found that the symptoms are differing manifestations of a similar illness in the borderline range. Cross (1993) compared bulimia with delicate self-cutting in relation to the dynamics of female body image and feminine development, and postulated that they were concrete bodily externalizations of similar psychological problems and emotional experiences. Miller (1994) found clinically that various kinds of self-destructive behavior, including alcoholism, drug abuse, anorexia, bulimia, and self-mutilation, are all part of a cluster of behaviors and problematic relationships common to women who were abused, violated, or neglected as children. She suggests that such clusters are indicative of a trauma reenactment syndrome. Similarly, Lacey (1993) has proposed the category of impulsive personality disorder, characterized by bulimia, substance abuse, overdosing, self-mutilation, and stealing, and often associated with a history of sexual abuse. More recently, we have learned that these symptom clusters are the frequent sequelae of Post-Traumatic Stress Disorder (PTSD), especially the kind of chronic PTSD that is associated with the most chronic and cumulative psychic trauma (Farber 1995a; van der Kolk 1988) and a diagnosis of borderline personality disorder.

To understand how and why self-mutilation and disordered eating have become so linked in the lives of so many individuals, we turn to a concept introduced by Armando Favazza to understand self-mutilation. Throughout history, contends Favazza (1987), all mutilation of the skin, including the communal self-mutilating ritualistic practices of various cultures worldwide as well as pathological self-mutilation, is deeply embedded in elemental experiences of healing, religion, and social amity. Extending Favazza's concept, we can understand disordered eating in the same way. Self-mutilation and disordered eating are both rooted in the most primitive experiences of emotional healing and fellowship (Farber 1995a) that are derived from the ritual sacrifice of humans and animals and cannibalism. Derivatives of these most primitive roots can be found in religion, mythology, rites of passage, contemporary culture, and in the child's most basic experience of learning how to eat and feed himself (Malcove 1933).

In my study I compared binge-purge and self-mutilating behaviors in order to understand and explain the strikingly strong association between the two as well as the similarities and differences between the behaviors (Farber 1995a). Bulimic and self-mutilating behaviors serve very similar multiple psychic functions in survivors of childhood and adolescent trauma, especially the trauma of physical and sexual abuse and medically related trauma. The findings suggest that a prolonged history of direct assault to their bodies combined with a lack of secure attachments underlies the development of depression and chronic and cumulative PTSD, predisposing these individuals to rely upon two peculiarly special but very harmful "talents." First, they rely upon a specially developed ability to go into dissociated states in order not to know what it is that they are experiencing. Second, they know that there is no one there to protect or soothe them so they rely upon their bodies very early in life for self-soothing purposes, developing self-injurious behavior and feeding and eating problems, which are the precursors to the development of adolescent and adult self-mutilation and bingeing and purging.

Both self-mutilation and bingeing and purging serve numerous psychic functions: to regulate mood, affect, and states of hyperarousal and dissociation; to express emotion; to serve as compensatory attempts to differentiate self from object; to better develop a fragmented sense of body image by defining and differentiating inner and outer body boundaries; and to master the aftereffects of severe childhood trauma by means of psychophysiological addictive reenactments and management of dissociative processes and hyperarousal states. The longer they binged and purged, the more likely they were to develop severe self-mutilating behavior. When they stopped or decreased their bulimic behavior, other self-harm behaviors such as drinking, self-mutilation, suicide attempts, reckless driving, drug abuse, increased sexual activity, excessive shopping, shoplifting, unnecessary surgery, and allowing others to cut, brand, pierce, or tattoo them cropped up to substitute for or alternate with the bulimic behavior. The most powerful of these substitutes was severe self-mutilation. Severe purging and severe self-mutilation are equally powerful and dangerous forms of self-medication, making it likely that one could readily substitute for or alternate with the other. The findings of the study suggest that when these two most powerful forms of self-medication fail to relieve the sufferer of her psychic pain, the only self-medication left to try is the lethal one, suicide.

The findings of my study also predated and were supported by the most recent research (Favaro and Santonastaso 1999), which found that at least one form of self-mutilating behavior was reported by 123 (70 percent) of the 175 bulimic subjects studied. In this study 139 (79.4 percent) were purging bulimics, while 39 (22.3 percent) were nonpurging. In the Italian study skin cutting and/or burning, considered by the authors to be an impulsive form of self-mutilation, was reported by 39 subjects (22.3 percent), and severe nail biting, considered compulsive, was reported by 80 (45.8 percent) of all subjects and hair pulling, also considered compulsive was reported by 62 (35.4 percent). The compulsive forms were predicted by a short duration of illness and a greater lack of interoceptive awareness, while the impulsive forms were predicted by the presence of a history of sexual abuse and greater depression. Although the cutting and burning was not associated with lethal intent, they are significantly associated with suicide attempts. Because suicide is one of the most frequently causes of death among bulimic patients, it is extremely important that attention be paid to suicidality and depression in bulimic patients.

In comparison to the findings of Favaro and Santonastaso, not only did a much greater percentage of my subjects report self-mutilating behavior, they also reported much higher percentages of severe self-mutilating behavior and presented a far more pathological clinical picture. That is, 75 of 99 (75.8 percent) bulimic subjects reported severe self-mutilating behavior such as cutting, burning, or needle-sticking (Farber 1995a). The differences betweeen the findings of my study and the Italian study can be attributed to the differences in the design of the studies. In the Italian study, the sample consisted of patients diagnosed with purging and nonpurging types of bulimia who had been referred to an outpatient unit, which suggests a certain relative stability to the clinical picture and better prognosis. The majority of subjects in my study, on the other hand, were those who binged and purged and were recruited from newsletters for abuse survivors and for people with dissociative disorders, skewing the sample much more toward a chronic and extremely unstable group with a history of numerous hospitalizations and much poorer prognosis.

SELF-REGULATION, SELF-MEDICATION, AND SELFOBJECT HYPOTHESES

The only antidote to mental suffering is physical pain.

Karl Marx

Khantzian's (1985, 1989) view of addictive suffering is that addiction to drugs or alcohol is an attempt to seek relief from emotional suffering that occurs in those who have not developed their own inner resources to defend adequately against affects and drives. Individuals try to self-medicate with various classes of drugs, choosing a drug that corresponds to the emotional state or mood that the addict wants to stimulate or sedate. For example a depressed individual might use cocaine or other stimulant because of its energizing qualities. Individuals suffering from feelings of emptiness, coldness, and isolation might use alcohol or other drugs with sedative qualities to counter these feelings. Those individuals who are frightened that their rage and aggression may erupt in a wild and out-of-control fashion may choose narcotics for their antiaggression action. Similarly, Brisman and Siegel (1984) used the self-medication hypothesis to explain the similarities between bulimia and alcohol abuse, supporting the view that it is the psychic function served by the drug of choice that is more important than the specific qualities of the drug. They have found that bulimic behavior, much like alcoholic behavior, serves ego-compensatory needs in the absence of the ability to adequately regulate and modulate emotions, moods, and tensions. Similarly, others have viewed bulimia and other eating disorders as attempts at self-regulation of mood and affect (Brenner 1983, Goodsitt 1985, Schupak-Neuberg and Nemeroff 1993). Stolorow's (1986) expanded concept of the selfobject (Kohut 1971) is instructive. "The term *selfobject* does not refer to environmental entities or caregiving agents—that is, people. Rather it designates a class of psychological *functions* pertaining to the maintenance, restoration, and transformation of self experience" (p. 389). Krueger (1997) has found clinically that food can serve as a selfobject in eating-disorder patients.

Extending the self-medication concept, it is proposed that both eating-disordered behavior and self-mutilating behavior might be the attempts of desperate people to interrupt or terminate a dysphoric mood or affect state or alleviate their psychic suffering in much the same way that others may impulsively or compulsively use drugs, alcohol, sex, gambling, shopping, and other addictive-like behaviors (Farber 1995a). That is, for those who chronically starve themselves, binge and/or purge, or self-mutilate, these acts themselves should be regarded as serving as their drug of choice or as their selfobject.

SELF-REGULATION AND ATTACHMENT THEORY ILLUMINATE SELF-HARM

Attachment theory (Bowlby 1969) is the application of the study of animal behavior to human behavior. Its fundamental premise is that there is a biologically based attachment system characteristic of each species that brings a newborn close to its caregiver in order to protect it from predators or other harm in the environment. Providing a sense of security, then, is the principal role of the attachment bond (Bowlby 1969). This theory provides a substantial psychophysiological framework for understanding the importance of the mother–child relationship in regulating the infant's metabolic, neurochemical, sleep-wake, cardiovascular, and endocrine systems, and in ensuring that the child survives and thrives not only in his childhood environment but also later in life in other significant emotional attachments. There is compelling evidence that all early-forming psychopathology constitutes disorders of attachment and manifests as failures of self and/or interactional regulation (Schore 1997).

Despite the biological and ethological dimensions of attachment theory, Bowlby's work grew out of psychoanalysis, specifically the British object relations school, and was very much influenced by Melanie Klein. According to Bowlby, the infant needs bonds with others as much as he needs food; the various ways these bonds develop and become organized in infancy and childhood are the major factors determining whether a person becomes a mentally healthy adult (Bowlby 1969, 1974, 1979). Jeremy Holmes (1996) has advanced attachment theory as a "new paradigm" for use by psychotherapists, for whom the therapeutic alliance, or attachment bond, is the basis for successful psychotherapy.

Because attachment theory helps us understand how the child comes to grow and thrive in his environment, we can also use attachment theory to help us to understand why some children do not grow and thrive but grow up with major deficits in self cohesion and ego functioning. The theory can be used to understand how a child can instead grow up with grave problems in the self-care functions of the ego, resulting in the failure of the ego to warn, guide, and protect him from dangerous involvements and behavior. The theory can help us to understand not only why the attraction to violence and bloodshed is universal in human beings, but why in some individuals it is inordinately articulated as violence aggressively directed toward the self. It can explain how the child who has suffered traumatic disruptions of attachment can readily fall prey to self-harm and to others who will abuse, neglect, or exploit him. As is elaborated in Part II, the attachment to suffering is both the cause and the result of self-harm, and represents an attachment to early experiences of neglect, abuse, and other trauma. A person who behaves characteristically in self-harming ways has a very peculiar and perverse relationship to his or her self, ranging at worst from fatally self-destructive to at best disrespectful and uncaring.

THE PARADOX OF SELF-HARM

Many people who harm themselves describe their relationship to their self-harm in much the same way that people locked into unhappy relationships describe their relationship to their partner: "I can't live with her, but I can't live without her." People who harm themselves will tell you that this is not a choice that is theirs to make, that they would give it up if only they could. They are attached to this behavior in much the same way that people remain attached to teddy bears, or other "warm fuzzies" or even to an unhappy relationship. Many say that if they did not have their eating disorder, or self-mutilation, or drug or alcohol abuse to sustain them through extraordinarily painful times, they would have killed themselves. That is, for many the self-harm may well be the lesser of two evils. Those who may be trying to give it up are comforted through their painful "abstinence" by knowing that they can always return to the self-harm to see themselves through the toughest times; it is an ace up their sleeve. For many, self-harm is a way of surviving, a way of managing to live their life, something that they may have great difficulty articulating. In fact the part of their brain that deals with cognition may not even know that they know this, but their body knows it exquisitely in the reflexive-like way the hand grabs for the food, shoveling it into the mouth, or the way the hand reaches for the razor blade to draw it across the arm. The writings and drawings of survivors of severe sexual and physical abuse express the role of self-harm in their lives. Survivors explain that while others may view self-harm negatively, they see it as their closest friend, enlivening a deadened or depressed self or terminating other intolerable mood and affect states. Those who routinely flirt with danger say that it makes them feel alive, and if the price they have to pay is that they hurt themselves in the process, it is a price they are willing to pay. Their acts of self-harm make them feel whole and complete, restoring them to a higher level of functioning and well-being. Acts of the most violent purging and self-mutilation may function immediately as instant Prozac or instant Xanax—fast, effective, and costing absolutely nothing, at least in dollar amounts. They require no prescription and can be administered as needed. So much of its appeal is that it requires just the self, no one else.

Many who harm themselves in these ways describe the sense of aliveness and well-being experienced afterward as healing, a redemption borne of pain and suffering. Others describe it as cleansing or purifying. Others speak of offering their pain up to God for the sake of healing or forgiveness. Even within the sadomasochism subculture, many maintain that it is a healing experience to be able to trust one's partner to inflict only the degree of pain or stimulation that is craved—no more and no less. For many, self-harm is a way both to revere and negate death's power.

Even some individuals who have tried suicide and failed find that for a time they feel restored and healed by the experience. Perhaps they are taking the ultimate risk, submitting to God or fate, and finding themselves healed by the process. Perhaps they are the ultimate twelve-steppers, "letting go and letting God." Perhaps all self-harm is experienced, if only for a brief delicious moment, as a resurrection from the ashes of destruction, like the phoenix rising. It is that moment that is longed for, lived for, craved and savored by those who desperately attach themselves to self-harm. "For as we have worked to mitigate suffering it has been impossible to ignore the fact that lives can be captivated by it, that self-torture is one possible construction for a life, and that the slave clings to its master with as much force as the master clings to its slave" (Montgomery 1989a, p. ix).

2

How Common Is Self-Harm?

When we remember that we are all mad,
the mysteries disappear and life stands explained.

Mark Twain, *Notebook*

When having to endure the pain of a medical or dental procedure, one may find oneself digging one's fingernails into one's hands, diverting oneself from the pain of the procedure by inflicting a different kind of pain on oneself.[1] Better to control one kind of pain than to be controlled by another kind. This illustrates the pleasure principle, which holds that the aim of all psychic activity is to seek pleasure and eliminate unpleasure (Freud 1911, 1915a). When one is in pain, a diversion from its source can be very welcome in providing a sense of control over the pain. For the woman in labor, for example, the concentration on patterned breathing may divert her from her pain sufficiently so that she does not require pain medication; it also provides a sense of control that itself is a source of pleasure. This is the basis of self-harm: the substitution of one kind of pain for another to divert oneself from the original pain.

---

1. I am grateful to Dr. Stuart Farber for providing this observation.

THE UBIQUITY OF SELF-HARM

Self-harm seems to be everywhere—in the media, popular music, MTV videos, and literature. It is about people who cannot tolerate feeling emotional pain, people hungry for higher highs, ecstasy, intense experience, and unparalleled stimulation despite the harm it causes them. Many of those who came of age in the 1960s, whose rallying cry was "sex, drugs, and rock and roll," have raised a generation of children who expect that they should be feeling good all the time. And so they have developed little tolerance for what Freud called the ordinary misery of everyday life, the anxiety, depressed feelings, shame, and guilt that are part of being human. For Freud, happiness was to be found in the experience of loving and working, but for so many today, happiness means being "blissed out" in ecstatic states or the numbness of feeling no pain. "If it feels good, do it!" Those who seize on something or someone in a frenzied quest to feel good deny themselves the opportunity to develop an ability to tolerate, think about, reflect on, and contain their unpleasant feelings.

Twelve-step meetings and other self-help groups focus on helping people give up their dependence on alcohol, drugs, food, sex, gambling, and abusive relationships. These programs offer a sense of community and a means of attachment for those in need. For those whose dependence on the Internet has become problematic, there is Internet Anonymous. For those prone to alcohol dependence, there is Alcoholics Anonymous, which has become the prototype for other twelve-step programs such as Overeaters Anonymous, Cocaine Anonymous, Co-Dependents Anonymous, Narcotics Anonymous, Debtors Anonymous, Gamblers Anonymous, Fear of Success Anonymous, Hair-Pullers Anonymous, Obsessive-Compulsives Anonymous, Self-Mutilators Anonymous, Incest Survivors Anonymous, and Sex and Love Addicts Anonymous. There is Mail Order Anonymous, for the many people whose catalogue and television shopping is out of control, and Communications Anonymous, for those who are overly dependent on cellular phones, beepers, faxes, and e-mail. One of the newest twelve-step programs is Adrenaline Addicts Anonymous, for those who are addicted to the adrenaline rush produced by extreme stress and hyperarousal. This concept of addiction, crucial in understanding self-harm, is supported by the field of brain studies and the psychobiology of trauma.

The self-help movement is not limited to group meetings and nonprofessionals. Some support groups are led by professionals. Statewide and national self-help clearinghouses put people in touch with groups. There are newsletters, recovery conferences, recovery trips, reunions, and cruises. The recovery movement, based on the disease model of recovery from alcohol addiction, is a major force in the self-help movement as well as an enormous industry. For example, the Schneider Institute, an inpatient program for "food addiction" sends newsletters to "graduates," offering "booster" meetings, reunions, and recovery cruises designed to recharge spiritual batteries.

In Contemporary Western Culture

Self-harm of all kinds is increasingly featured in the media and contemporary literature. Newspapers, popular magazines, and television news programs feature stories about substance abuse, eating disorders, adolescent suicide, gambling, compulsive shopping, and compulsive sex. We are fascinated with Hollywood stuntmen or people who hang glide or bungee jump, whose experiences with danger make them come alive. Gyms increasingly have simulated rock-climbing walls and emergency rooms treat increasing numbers of bicyclists, motorcyclists, roller bladers, and skate boarders.

S&M

Our culture is fascinated with the potential for bondage and danger that is inherent in any human bonding (Merkin 1997). Sadomasochism has gotten a glamorous make-over in the media as an "alternate lifestyle," making it easier for people with an inclination in this direction to try it out. The "art" of sadomasochism is in its theater, in its exciting simulation of harm and high-risk violence in a consensual enactment of a master–slave relationship. In *The History of Sexuality*, Foucault (1977) discusses the dialectics of power in relation to the body and the individual's right of power over his own body. Foucault has been extensively involved in the sadomasochistic subculture (Litman and Swearingen 1996). His work has given sadomasochism a dangerous cachet as the "intellectual's sexuality." He advocates the "limit experience," a particularly pleasurable kind of pain in which mind and body are pushed to the breaking point. Cultural icon Madonna, whose history of abuse and abandonment makes it easy for many teenage girls to identify with her, is seen in MTV videos and in her book *Sex* in a variety of sadomasochistic scenarios. We see S&M garb in the fashion and advertising worlds, selling black leather corsets along with Absolut vodka. The look of the dark side has become fashionable. Adolescents adopt the S&M look, wearing Fetish nail polish and Blood lipstick. The Internet is filled with images of sadomasochism and serves as a meeting place for victims and victimizers.

When S&M is promoted as simply a spicier, more interesting option, the equivalent of a mango or passionfruit alternative to what is called "vanilla" sex, when it is described as something that fills the void left by giving up drugs and alcohol, this is an attempt to transform sadomasochism from the status of a perversion to that of a superior lifestyle or to a therapy. When a dominatrix proclaims in newspapers or on cable television that S&M is "an extremely positive life force streaming through me," then sadomasochism is being plugged in much the same way enthusiastic talk show guests extol Prozac as an agent for personality change. What the S&M proponents do not address is that when there is an enactment of a master–slave relationship, there is always the enormous potential for what was initially consensual activity to become nonconsensual brutality that can result in death.

An alarming trend is the growth of S&M clubs in urban areas. Members are primarily "white, middle-class, baby boomer professionals . . . with enough discretionary income to indulge in some trendy outlaw eroticism" (Blau 1994, p. 41). Practices such as dripping hot wax on bare flesh, cutting, whipping, and administering electric shocks are common and provide opportunity for strangers to join in. In La Nouvelle Justine, a New York cafe named after the Marquis de Sade novel, the waiters simulate various S&M scenarios with each other and with customers. Vampire clubs named Fang Club and Mother have been featured in the Styles section of The New York Times. Clinical psychologist Katherine Ramsland is considered an expert on vampires and a participant observer of the culture. Her book, Piercing the Darkness: Undercover with Vampires in America Today (1998), is an underground guide, informing readers where they can get fangs custom made and where they can meet those who role-play at being vampires and those who drink the blood of others.

The New York Press, a free weekly newspaper, features a regular column by "Mistress Ruby," who makes her living by dominating and inflicting pain upon people. Recently, at a conference on women's sexual freedom at the State University of New York at New Paltz, there were how-to demonstrations of S&M practices. There are even self-help books for sadomasochists co-authored by Dossie Easton, a practicing psychotherapist in San Francisco. The Bottoming Book: How to Get Terrible Things Done to You by Wonderful People (Easton and Liszt 1996) provides information to masochists on how to get other people to dominate them while the companion book, The Topping Book: Getting Good at Being Bad (Easton and Liszt 1995), advises on how to dominate or inflict pain on others. Piercings, brandings, scarification, and other body modifications have been crossing over from the S&M subculture into the mainstream.

The Self-Help Movement

Bookstores feature endless books for helping individuals to conquer a variety of behaviors and ways of thinking that are harmful to the self. Codependent No More, a paperback, was on The New York Times best-seller list for over one hundred weeks and sold over two million copies (Kaminer 1993). A sampling of others includes Self-Defeating Behaviors: Free Yourself from the Habits, Compulsions, Feelings, and Attitudes that Hold You Back; You Can't Say That to Me! Stopping the Pain of Verbal Abuse—An 8-Step Program; Why Weight? A Guide to Ending Compulsive Eating; Facing Love Addiction; When Money Is the Drug: The Compulsion for Credit, Cash, and Chronic Debt; Overcoming Overeating; Out of the Shadows: Understanding Sexual Addiction; How to Break Your Addiction to a Person; Bulimia Nervosa and Binge Eating: A Guide to Recovery; When Society Becomes an Addict; Victim No More: Your Guide to Overcome Revictimization; Do I Have to Give Up

Me to Be Loved by You?: The Workbook; and *End the Pain: Solutions for Stopping Domestic Violence.* And finally, there are books on the self-harm inherent in depending on popular psychology: *Self-Help or Self-Destruction? Ten Pop Psychology Myths that Could Destroy Your Life* and *The Codependency Conspiracy: How to Break the Recovery Habit and Take Charge of Your Life.*

The market for many of these self-help books is overwhelmingly female. Only some of the titles are addressed explicitly to women: *Fat and Furious: Women and Food Obsession; Men Who Hate Women and the Women who Love Them; Women Who Shop Too Much: Overcoming the Urge to Splurge; Women Who Do Too Much: Stress and the Myth of the Superwoman; Fat Is a Feminist Issue; Smart Women, Foolish Choices: Finding the Right Men, Avoiding the Wrong Ones; Women Who Love Too Much: When You Keep Wishing and Hoping He'll Change; Meditations for Women Who Do Too Much; Ten Stupid Things Women Do to Mess Up Their Lives; Women Who Hurt Themselves: A Book of Hope and Understanding,* and *Quick Fixes and Small Comforts: How Every Woman Can Resist those Irresistible Urges.* A *New York Times* bestseller for several years, *Reviving Ophelia* (Pipher 1994) explores how our culture threatens the healthy development of teenage girls, promoting the development instead of eating disorders, self-mutilation, suicide attempts, substance abuse, and submission to people who are emotionally and physically abusive.

Self-Harm in the Media

The recovery culture promotes the disclosure of private anguish to strangers (Kaminer 1993) and television talk shows reward people for entertaining the audience with details about their addictions, incest, divorce, and abusive relationships. Individuals with little sense of privacy and boundaries are willing to collude in their own victimization and degradation.

Popular magazines, television series, and talk shows present eating disorders and substance-abuse problems in the lives of glamorous people as simply part of an exciting lifestyle. Women's magazines publish articles on eating disorders along with new diets to try and articles on how cosmetic surgery is the best in "make-overs." Countering the trend to glamorize these problems are a number of books depicting the very real consequences of the obsession with becoming thin. Caroline Miller, a Harvard graduate and author of *My Name is Caroline* (1988), writer Elizabeth Wurtzel, Harvard graduate and author of *Prozac Nation* (1994), psychologist and writer Lauren Slater (1998), author of *Prozac Diary*, and writer Naomi Wolf, a Yale graduate and author of *The Beauty Myth: How Images of Beauty Are Used Against Women* (1991) all state that large numbers of their female classmates in high school and college starved themselves and purged to achieve a degree of thinness that was never enough. Both Miller and Wolf found that the pressure to compete for thinness and for academic and sports achievement cost them their health. Marya Hornbacher (1998) wrote of her intense flirtation with death that began at age 5 with an obsession with thinness.

Kitty Dukakis, wife of the 1988 presidential candidate Michael Dukakis, disclosed her personal battle with alcoholism. Similarly the problems of numerous show business celebrities with drugs, food, and alcohol have been revealed on television news features. In a television interview, actress Margot Kidder revealed the physical and emotional suffering and self-neglect she endured while suffering manic-depressive illness.

Drug abuse, alcoholism, suicide, compulsive sexuality, and eating disorders have been featured endlessly in films and magazine articles. Ingmar Bergman's film *Cries and Whispers* depicted a woman cutting her vagina in a moment of despair. More and more people are "coming out of the closet" in the media about their self-mutilating behavior in much the same way that people began to come out about eating disorders in the 1970s. In 1985, Karen Conterio, a former self-mutilator, appeared on the Phil Donahue show speaking about her self-mutilation (Favazza and Conterio 1988); over a thousand daytime viewers, most of them women, called in, saying that they too mutilated themselves. They were sent the Self-Harm Behavior Survey, the first instrument devised to gather information on self-mutilation in a standardized manner. A year later Hartgrove Hospital in Chicago opened the first inpatient facility in the country for self-injurers and established a toll-free telephone number (1-800-DON'T-CUT) for self-injurers wanting information about their disorder. This program has since relocated to MacNeal Hospital in Berwyn, Illinois.

Actor Johnny Depp, one of whose major roles, oddly enough, was Edward Scissorhands, acknowledged in a popular magazine that he had cut himself many times. *The New York Times Magazine* featured an article about a black adolescent girl, girlfriend of a gang leader in Brooklyn, who at times of desperation takes a blade and gently runs it down her arm, enjoying the sight and feel of the red drops oozing from the cut (Le Blanc 1994). *The New York Times* reported that in Recife, Brazil, where there is a growing population of runaways and other street children, many girls who have taken to prostitution slash themselves in fits of despair or rage (Schemo 1996). *The New York Times Magazine* also published a comprehensive story about self-mutilation, the cover page and table of contents proclaiming "Whenever Jill McArdle felt bad, she didn't starve herself the way an anorexic might. She secretly burned her arm or sliced into her leg until she felt better. Doctors call that self-mutilation and they're seeing more and more of it. . . . In an age of tattoos and nose rings, self-mutilation is the latest expression of adolescent self-loathing" (Egan 1997). Two years later the same reporter wrote about anorexia and self-mutilation as "power suffering"—self-inflicted suffering that provides the sufferer an otherwise lacking sense of control over her life much like the voluntary self-starvation and other mortification of the flesh provided the mystic medieval saints. Probably the most well-known example is the late Princess Diana, who inspired passionate devotion and whose death was marked by a public demonstration of grief. In Princess Di, as in the medieval female saints, a personal charisma and a wish to help others was intertwined with the same self-inflicted suffering—anorexia, bulimia, self-mutilation. The increased visibility of self-mutilation in the media may explain why advertisements for ointments "effective on scars resulting from surgical incisions, burns, and traumatic events" have become quite prominent.

Drug and alcohol abuse is so widespread among high-power executives that more than a quarter of all Fortune 500 companies screen their employees for illicit drug use. Employee assistance program magazines have featured articles on self-injury as a hidden problem among women in the workplace (Golden and Walker-O'Keefe 1988, Witherspoon 1990). Even *Miss Manners*, the contemporary etiquette advice column, featured a letter inquiring about the proprieties of social interactions with several severely anorectic women who have refused treatment. "Friends who see them at these [social] events don't know how to treat the situation. Do they smile and kiss them as though everything were normal? Do they murmur a few words of concern? Or do they take more drastic action, such as calling an ambulance? Nobody wants to be rude, but letting someone die is bad manners, too, and anorexia kills" (Martin 1989, p. 117). Most recently *Dear Abby* featured a letter from a reader who participates in an Internet forum for self-mutilators, to let others prone to self-injury know of this source of help. There is also a very informative and well-researched Web Page called "Self-Help for Self-Injury" that can be of value for self-injurers and therapists working with them (http://www.mindspring. com/~thefly/ selfinjury.htm). Numerous online forums address the self-harm associated with substance abuse, eating disorders, self-mutilation, depression, abuse, and trauma.

Self-Harm in Literature and the Arts

Self-harm has long been depicted in literature. In Ovid's *Metamorphosis* there is a reference to bulimia, self-mutilation, and self-cannibalism. Having scorned the gods and having violated the sacred groves of Ceres, Erysichthon was punished by famine and a wild craving for food: "At last when . . . his grievous malady needed more food, the wretched man began to tear his limbs and rend them apart with his teeth and, by consuming his own body, fed himself" (quoted in Parry-Jones and Parry-Jones 1993, p. 394). Dr. Samuel Johnson, the famous eighteenth century English lexicographer, was described by his companion and biographer, James Boswell, as having bitten his nails and scraped his fingers until they were red, gorged on food, and hit his legs continually (Parry-Jones and Parry-Jones 1993).

Eating disorders were described in literature primarily by women writers as early as the nineteenth century. Catherine Earnshaw, the heroine of Emily Bronte's *Wuthering Heights*, was thought to be anorexic, as was Emily Bronte herself (Levine 1990). Fictional accounts of disordered eating were featured in modern literature by Margaret Atwood (*Lady Oracle, Cat's Eye, The Edible Woman*), Joyce Carol Oates (*American Appetites, Solstice, Them*), Mary Gordon

(*Final Payments*), Susan Sussman (*The Dieter*), Amy Tan (*The Joy Luck Club*), Mary Gaitskill (in her novel *Two Girls, Fat and Thin*), and Alison Lurie (*Fat People*). Kafka's *The Hunger Artist* describes the existential predicament of a man compelled to starve himself in a cage in full view of the public. For the young-adult market, there is *The Best Little Girl in the World*, a novel by Steven Levenkron about an anorexic adolescent girl, which has been made into a television movie.

Representations of mutilating and self-mutilating behavior are also featured in literature. Kafka's *In the Penal Colony* describes a machine upon which people are mutilated before being executed. Hazel Motes in Flannery O'Connor's *Wise Blood* pokes out his eyes with a stick to cleanse himself for his sins and purify himself. There is even fiction about adolescents who self-mutilate, *Crosses* by Shelley Stoehr and *The Luckiest Girl in the World* by Steven Levenkron. Erotic piercing was noted in Margaret Atwood's (1989) novel *Cat's Eye*: "Some men have carrots between their legs. They aren't really carrots but something worse. . . . Some men have their carrots pierced and rings set into them as if they are ears" (p. 98).

Tashi, a peripheral character in Alice Walker's best-selling Pulitzer-prize novel *The Color Purple*, is the focus of her later novel, *Possessing the Secret of Joy*. Tashi, the daughter of American black missionaries in Africa, wanted to demonstrate her to loyalty to the Olinka tribe, whose tribal customs were increasingly taken away by whites. She reluctantly submitted to the ritual of female genital circumcision, enduring long-lasting emotional and physical trauma, repeated infection, and medical complications as a result. Eventually she came to remember the circumstances under which her older sister died as a result of genital circumcision: "Underneath a tree, on the bare ground outside the hut, lay a dazed row of little girls, though to me they seemed not so little. They were all a few years older than me. Dura's age. Dura, however, was not among them; and I knew instinctively that it was Dura being held down and tortured inside the hut. Dura who had made those inhuman shrieks that rent the air and chilled my heart" (Walker 1992, p. 75). She became obsessed with razors and began cutting herself, thus repeating and reenacting the trauma by actively inflicting on herself that to which she passively submitted. "At first she merely spoke about the strange compulsion she sometimes experienced of wanting to mutilate herself. Then one morning I woke to find the foot of our bed red with blood. Completely unaware of what she was doing, she said, and feeling nothing, she had sliced rings, bloody bracelets, or chains, around her ankles" (Walker 1992, p. 51). Somalian model Waris Dirie, an outspoken activist against female circumcision, spoke out in a newspaper article about her own genital mutilation at age 5, telling of how the procedure killed her younger sister and two cousins (Abel 1996).

The main character in Kathryn Harrison's *Thicker Than Water*, who was involved in an incestuous relationship with her father, starved herself, binged and purged, beat herself with a paperweight, picked at scabs, and took morphine. An incestuous relationship looms again in Harrison's *Exposure*. The main character is a diabetic who starved herself, used amphetamines to induce dissociated and comatose states, and shoplifted. In her memoir *The Kiss*, Harrison wrote about the incestuous relationship with her father and the bulimia, anorexia, and self-mutilation that she struggled with even before the relationship began, but that worsened after it began. In *Holy Hunger*, an Episcopal priest (Bullitt-Jonas 1999) wrote of her life-threatening binge eating as a thwarted spiritual desire. The female protagonist in Atwood's *Cat's Eye* binged, peeled the skin off the bottom of her feet, chewed her cuticles until her fingers became infected, bit her lips until they bled, and cut herself. The association between bulimic and self-mutilating behavior was noted by the late writer and gay activist Paul Monette (1992), who wrote about his friend Edie, who plucked out her eyebrows, lashes, and pubic hair, then cooked and ate "six bags of groceries—a ten-pound roast, a turkey, two pounds of bacon, on and on, all night long. Every half hour or so she'd go into the bathroom and throw it all up" (pp. 252–253). Alfred Kinsey, the pioneer sexual investigator, revealed that he had punished himself for his homoerotic feelings by shoving a toothbrush into his urethra (Jones 1997).

Erotic vampire literature has become increasingly popular, presenting the image of ordinary people transformed by certain life events into enacting a previously latent unquenchable thirst for blood. Anne Rice's *Interview with the Vampire* is the startling erotically charged confessions of a man seduced by another vampire into piercing the flesh of rats, roosters, other human beings, and his own flesh in order to drink their blood, and who in turn seduced a young woman, transforming her into a vampire. A film and the *Vampire Chronicles* series followed, as well as compilations of underground vampire erotica by other authors. Playing upon the fascination with vampirism, recently Barnes and Noble hosted an Anne Rice book signing, in conjunction, amazingly enough, with a Bellevue Hospital blood drive. Blood donors were eligible to receive a prize of autographed copies of the *Vampire Chronicles*.

Female Perversions, a startling and controversial film, is based on psychoanalyst Louise Kaplan's book of the same title. According to filmmaker Susan Streitfeld, the goal of the film was to expose women's secret, self-destructive behaviors, and to look at them in a larger social context.

Autobiographical accounts by public figures, writers, mental health clinicians, and others feature their struggles with various kinds of self-harm behavior. In *Drinking: A Love Story* Caroline Knapp, daughter of psychoanalyst and psychosomaticist Peter Knapp, discussed her battle with drinking and self-starvation, and the struggles of acquaintances with alcohol and other forms of self-harm such as bulimia, compulsive stealing, and drug dependency. In *Note Found in a Bottle: My Life as a Drinker*, Susan Cheever (1999), a writer and alcoholic like her father John Cheever, wrote of her life of drinking, fasting, bingeing, purging, and casual sex.

In my senior year I thought I had a weight problem so I stopped eating. When I was hungry I would eat three cookies from a stash I kept in a bag in my dorm. Sometimes I fasted for days; I liked the light-headed feeling fasting gave me and I liked getting thin. Then I would break the fast. I spent hours thinking about what I might eat. Usually it was something odd but delicious, like a jar of strawberry jam or a can of salted peanuts. Then I would get sick and vomit. Food was a problem, but drinking was the answer to a series of problems. I don't even remember what I drank most of the time. I just drank the way everyone I knew drank. Sometimes I forgot what happened when I drank; so did everyone. [pp. 42–43]

Similarly writer Pete Hamill wrote of his fight with alcoholism, while actress Ali McGraw wrote of her problems with compulsive sexuality. World-famous mountain climber Jim Wickwire wrote a memoir, *Addicted to Danger*, telling how despite his repeated promises to stop climbing, the fears of his wife and young children, and the deaths of several climbing companions, he could not stop. Psychiatrist Kay Redfield Jamison, who has written numerous papers and books on mood disorders, went public in *An Unquiet Mind* on her personal history with the self-harm of both suicide attempts and noncompliance with treatment resulting from her battle with manic-depressive illness. Similarly in *Welcome to My Country* and *Prozac Diary*, Lauren Slater, a practicing psychologist, disclosed her experience with self-mutilating behavior, anorexia, and severe depression, and psychiatric hospitalization. Journalist Elizabeth Wurtzel traced her bouts with severe depression, self-cutting, and suicide attempts in her autobiographical *Prozac Nation: Young and Depressed in America—A Memoir*, while writer Susanna Kaysen, in *Girl, Interrupted*, disclosed her history of suicide attempts, self-starvation, and self-cutting while a patient in psychiatric hospitals.

Self-Harm in the General Population

Normative Behavior in Women?

> *But from the moment my mother and I first walked into My Darling Daughter and I tried on a forest green pinafore with sprigs of violets, to the day I walked into Chandler's Shoe Store and bought my first pair of heels for twenty-six dollars, . . . shopping has occupied a place next to food in my life as an activity that promises sensual pleasure, excitement, and relief from whatever is disturbing me.*
> Geneen Roth, *Appetites: On the Search for True Nourishment*

Can we know just how pervasive self-harm behavior is in the nonclinical population, and which kinds are most frequently and consistently used? Can we know when ordinary and normative behaviors that can become harmful to the self actually become harmful? Can we know the boundary that is crossed when one enters the arena of self-harm? A survey was conducted of a self-selected sample of 1,661 women on "quick fixes," or behaviors they frequently used to make themselves feel better, which had become a problem for them to control (Witkin 1988). Each woman reported at least one "fix" that had become problematic. The most frequently and consistently used "fix" was food, usually eating too much in binges or overeating at meals or "grazing" throughout the day, but also included dieting, self-starvation, and the syndrome of bingeing and purging. Shopping for food in the supermarket, women are assaulted at the checkout counters with magazines touting the latest quick weight loss miracle diet. They have ranged from various high-protein/low-carbohydrate diets like the Stillman and Scarsdale diets, the high-carbohydrate/low-protein diet, the high-fat/no-carbohydrate diet, the Hollywood all-fruit diet, the grapefruit diet, the all-you-can-eat ice cream diet, the cabbage soup diet, the Zone, and many more. The second most frequently used "fix" was shopping, with half as many women listing shopping. Between 20 and 27 percent shopped as a quick fix, except the divorced group, which shopped even more. Some shopped by mail or through the Home Shopping Channel, some bought and returned clothing, some shopped for friends and family, some just browsed but could not let themselves have anything, some shopped only for a bargain or a "steal," while others in fact did steal or shop-lift. Some specialized in shoes, housewares, or makeup, or collected antiques. There were numerous variations on the theme, but the theme was that they all shopped as a quick fix.

Other fixes listed included telephoning, redecorating, yelling, cleaning, fantasies, working too hard, TV watching, beauty makeovers, napping, masturbating, sexual flings, gambling, alcohol, prescription or nonprescription drugs, caffeine, and smoking. Some favorite fixes were short-term fun or temporary "time-outs," such as doing their nails or rearranging the furniture, but other fixes were major life changes meant to distract these women from their real problems, and were as drastic as having a baby, moving, and getting married. No other fixes, however, were shared as consistently as food and shopping. I have found this consistently as well in the women I see for treatment of eating disorders, who often reveal that their shopping is almost as much a problem as their eating.

Freud said that all women are clothes fetishists (Rose 1988). Shopping has been so associated with vanity and shallowness that until the recent interest in the culture of the body, women's concerns with their bodies, feminine beauty, shopping, and fashion were dismissed by clinicians and academics as subjects too frivolous for scientific inquiry. Because clothes are the most intimate objects we own, they are closely associated with personal identity. Women patients in treatment with a female therapist often comment easily on the therapist's clothing, shoes, hair style. Recreational shopping is normative for women, and has much to do with identity and meaning, depending on the context. Clothing and shopping for clothing can be a normal pleasure or it can be a fetish (Richards 1996).

The compulsive accumulation of, and hunting for, clothing can be pathological, and for many may result in debt, shame, and interpersonal conflict.

In the 1950s when most married middle-class women were full-time homemakers, women were exhorted to buy themselves a new hat if they were feeling blue. With the advent of plastic credit cards, shopping malls, television, and online shopping, shopping has become an easy sport, recreation, and in a large proportion of women, self-medication. Shopping is the most public, quintessentially feminine of the quick fixes. Men who enjoy shopping are suspected of homosexuality. Women affix bumper stickers to their cars—"I shop, therefore I am," "I brake for all garage sales," "When the going gets tough, the tough go shopping." Shopping has long been the subject of jokes by male comedians who describe the aggression in women as they stampede to the bargain tables. This aggression inspired the title of late writer Erma Bombeck's book, *All I Know about Animal Behavior I Learned in Loehmann's Dressing Room*. Shopping has been called "retail therapy." Loehmann's is a legendary national chain of discount designer clothing stores for women; the opening of the Manhattan Loehmann's was noteworthy enough to take up two-thirds of a page in the Styles section of *The New York Times*: "In the almost two weeks that it has been open, it has been like a cartoon caricature of chaos: women rushing from rack to rack, searching for the ultimate bargain. I enjoyed the thrill of the action. It was like playing the slots in Las Vegas" (Prager 1996, p. 53). Shopping together is a common activity for mothers and daughters. The advertising campaigns of clothing stores appeal to the "bargain lust" and compulsivity of many of their clientele, to the passionate yearning for shopping, and the thrill of "illicit" purchases.

Women meet to shop and have lunch. While social shopping and eating go hand in hand for many women, far less public and social is the secretive and shameful thinking, feeling, and behavior involving food and/or shopping that is an integral and intimate part of so many women's private lives, when a relationship with food or shopping has gotten out of control. Krueger (1988) found clinically that compulsive shopping and spending form a specific psychodynamic complex with common developmental precursors of pathological narcissism, while Mintz (1992b) found shopping to be a form of bingeing on clothing, displacing inner needs from inside to outside the body. For many woman for whom shopping is self-medication, the anticipation of shopping, like the anticipation of a food binge or sex, provokes a state of heightened arousal that is then followed by a progressive spacing out or dissociation as they roam through the aisles in search of the perfect item. The depersonalized state distances the shopper from the feelings of emptiness or anxiety that triggered the shopping expedition. Stores pipe in hypnotic music to induce spacing out, as women browse the aisles in various degrees of dissociation, like women in *The Stepford Wives*.

Traditionally it has been considered feminine for women to be involved with food shopping and cooking for their families, but openly enjoying eating with gusto has long been considered unfeminine. Women, especially in the middle and upper classes, have long been expected to eat like birds in public. For some women, eating is so shameful that they eat in their sleep by sleepwalking to the refrigerator. Strict dieting and constant obsessional thinking about food and weight, like shopping, have come to be regarded as quintessentially feminine in our culture. Many compulsive eaters are also compulsive shoppers, holding dual membership in Overeaters Anonymous and Shopaholics Anonymous. I have found that approximately 70 to 80 percent of the women in my therapy groups for women with compulsive eating problems also are compulsive shoppers. Several years ago, after I agreed to appear on a morning network television news program to talk about bulimia, the thoughts that quickly came to mind in anticipation of being viewed so publicly were what to wear, crash diets, and cosmetic surgery. It was striking how the anticipation of being viewed publicly by so many increased my body image concerns so dramatically for the moment. As is often the case, the line between the normal and the pathological is not a clear and discrete one.

"Everybody and Their Mother Has a Tattoo"

Tattooed and pierced models have been increasingly featured in the media, and so it was inevitable that the new line of Barbie dolls would have a tattoo on their abdomen, a ring through their nose, and come with temporary tattoos for children to apply to themselves. Some dermatologists have developed collaborative working arrangements with tattoo artists, to whom they refer patients who want the "permanent makeup" (tattooed eyeliner, eyebrows, lipstick) that is becoming quite popular in women of all ages. In the absence of government regulation, the Alliance of Professional Tattooists educates members about sterile procedures, offers complete infection-control guidelines, and information regarding blood-borne pathogens. Their goal is to keep tattooing safe and legal (Krakow 1994) by having tattooists comply with the same Occupational Safety and Health Administration (OSHA) regulations required of physicians and dentists. Similarly, the Association of Professional Piercers has been formed.

Tattooists historically learned the trade by apprenticeship, and currently those who provide body piercing, branding, and scarification services teach their skills to others individually or in group classes. The Gauntlet, an international chain of body-piercing studios, has existed since 1975, and is the grandfather of piercing studios. The School of Professional Body Piercing in San Francisco claims to "prepare those with the proper attitude and aptitude to deliver competent, professional body piercings in a commercial, semi-commercial, or amateur setting" (Musafar 1992, p. 31). A studio in New York State advertises ritual and ceremonial piercing and tattooing, and the proprietor enjoys lecturing at colleges about her work.

When tattooing was for "tough guys," the tattooists were tough and the tattoos were crude. The trend toward tattooing becoming mainstream has earned the disdain of old-timer "outlaw" tattooists like J. D. Crowe: "Women? Men? It's not even a statistic anymore. Straight, sensible businesswomen get tattoos. It's just not that big a deal. Instead of what your mom's going to think, now people bring their moms. . . . In the 1960s you got tattooed to be out. Now you get tattooed to be in" (Krakow 1994, pp. 96–97). Tattooing has become so upscale that many tattooists today consider themselves artists, and indeed, some of their work is quite beautiful. No longer so hot and spicy, tattoos lost their shock power to body piercing, which also is gradually becoming passé, although nipple and genital piercings still have considerable shock value.

Throughout history, burning, branding, and tattooing was the mark of ownership of prisoners and slaves. Prisoners of the French Revolution were tattooed on their faces with a fleur-de-lis and Nazi war prisoners had numbers tattooed on their arms. These markings were a natural for adoption by the sadomasochistic subculture. Today, branding seems to be crossing over from the sadomasochistic subculture to become the new shock wave in body art. Dr. Norman Goldstein, a professor of dermatology and expert on body modifications, has said: "People want to do the ultimate so they'll start off getting tattoos. But everybody and their mother has a tattoo. Then they'll go into piercing. But everyone's doing that. So the people who get branded seem to want to go to the max. Short of total body mutilation, where digits are amputated, branding is the next step" (personal communication). There have, in fact, been reports of a trend for amputation of digits in Europe. It seems that no sooner can one even think of what outrageous thing might be next, that the unthinkably outrageous is here, and what had been outrageous is instantly old news.

CONTAGION AND GROUP FACTORS IN SELF-HARM

For he today that sheds his blood with me shall be my brother.
William Shakespeare, *Henry V*, IV, iii

Although self-harm in groups is not as common as solitary self-harm, it is commonly found in closed institutions (prisons, psychiatric hospitals, residential treatment facilities) where the most basic bodily functions (eating, sleeping, elimination) are closely scrutinized and regulated. The nature of institutional life exacerbates psychopathology by taking away control and promoting feelings of despair and desperation, resulting in the use of regressive self-harm to express a sense of control and despair. An adversarial "us" versus "them" mentality readily develops between staff and patients or inmates. Self-harm promotes a sense of strength and competence in outwitting and torturing the staff. Once one person begins harming himself, the behavior tends to spread to other inmates by means of a contagious group process that is often triggered by a loss or separation. For example, contagion episodes of self-mutilation occurred in treatment centers after a favorite staff person had announced he would be leaving the center. These contagions present enormous management problems for the staff, whose anxiety about the self-harm seems to have a contagious aspect, too.

> Today the nurse reports several incidents of cutting, the word itself stabbing into our peace of mind. "Who?" "How many?" "How deep?" we wonder as another female patient is named as the latest cutter. In the last month, six of our fifty patients have begun to cut themselves on different parts of the body but mostly wrists or thighs. We always seemed to be capable of dealing wih a single cutter, but now a new anxiety emerges: the women have opened a competition, daring each other on, cutting deeper, spreading the wound to the body politic, as we all worry if one of *our* women—I now speak of course of our patients—will cut herself and mark our coupling with this act of . . . Act of what? [Bollas 1992, pp. 137–138]

When adolescents at a residential treatment center were observed for signs of a self-mutilation contagion, self-mutilation was found to have occurred in clusters throughout the year, suggesting that the adolescents were triggering the behavior in each other (Walsh and Rosen 1985). Similar findings were made in a study of "carving" done at a Canadian correctional facility for adolescent girls where "carving parties" were de rigueur, and in a prison study of contagion factors in male inmates who had inserted foreign bodies such as pins, paper clips, pens, pencils, or paint chips into their urethras (Ross and McKay 1979). In a study of adolescent psychiatric patients, these inpatients were distinguished from adolescents with no psychiatric history by self-made tattoos or other self-inflicted scars (Michelman et al. 1991). Just as obtaining a body piercing or tattoo is one of the new initiation rites in college, self-injury seems to be the rite of passage of hospitalized psychiatric patients. The boys' multiple cuts and self-inflicted cigarette burns were often done in groups in the hospital, playing "chicken" to show how tough they could be, how much pain they could tolerate without showing emotion. Boys and girls in street gangs may cut and burn themselves or acquire a piercing or tattoo. For example, young men incarcerated in a juvenile institution in Puerto Rico may have several tattoos, but two are typical: the name of the gang to which they belong inscribed on their hand and the first name of their mother on their back (Carrasquillo-Ramirez 1998). Latino gang girls belonging to Club Fuck in Los Angeles all wore small colored rings in their nasal septums. The fervor generated in contagion episodes of cutting probably makes it more likely that some will cut in groups, increasing the dangerous possibility that they may share the same blade or knife, increasing their risk for human immunodeficiency virus (HIV) transmission.

Cutting together is often the focus of a "blood brothers" ceremony (DiClemente et al. 1990), the commingling of blood symbolizing that the participants share the same blood and are family. Testifying at the trial of alleged Mafia boss Vincent Gigante, gangsters Philip Leonetti and Peter Chiodo described having their trigger fingers pricked as they swore their oaths in blood at their Mafia induction ceremony. The Bloods are a violent gang that originated in Los Angeles in the 1970s and spread to New York in the early 1990s. Their factions have names such as Gangsta Killer Bloods and Blood Stone Villains. Their motto, " Blood in and blood out," means "You have to draw blood to get in . . . and your blood has to be drawn to get out—meaning you have to be killed or they have to cut you to leave." The New York City Bloods have been linked to a number of razor attacks on subway riders, thought to have been part of an initiation rite.

"Fat talk"—programmed conversation about hating their bodies and wanting to be thin—is female conversational "rap." Little girls as young as 7 or 8 who receive "skills training" in this kind of obsessional thinking by the women who serve as their role models—their mothers, sisters, peers, actresses, fashion models—speak "fat talk." It is an identifying link with the peer group and spreads the contagious obsession with dieting and thinness. There is the element of contagion in simply hearing about eating-disordered behavior; many students have gotten the idea of purging as a means of reducing emotional tension or as a method of weight control after having heard a psychoeducational program meant to educate them about the hazards of such behavior. They selectively perceive what appeals to them about the media presentation of eating disorders, just as they selectively perceive only part of what is presented in eating-disorder prevention programs. Rather than getting the message that eating disorders are dangerous, far too many are getting the message that eating-disordered behavior is not only a very efficient way to control one's weight, but also a good way for an outsider to become an insider. In a study at the University of Toronto, when a female college freshman was assigned at random to a bulimic roommate, she was five times more likely to have tried purging by the year's end than a similar freshman who was not assigned to a bulimic roommate (Rodin 1992).

On college campuses bingeing and purging parties have become an alternative to sororities for becoming part of a social network and an equivalent initiation rite. While many girls participate initially to be social, a number of them find that the purging provides a release of tension and a sense of well-being that they have been missing. What may begin as a social ritual can readily precipitate the onset of an eating disorder in someone whose ego structure welcomes it. Girls may compete for status by demonstrating that they can starve themselves better than any of their friends, or purge themselves of the most food. In a personal account of her struggle with bulimia, Caroline Miller (1988) reported learning of purging techniques from two high school classmates who binged and purged together, enjoying such a special secret. Just as the alcoholic who drinks with his drinking buddies can convince himself that his drinking is purely social, it becomes easier for those who starve or binge and purge together to convince themselves that they do not have a problem. Certain message boards on the Internet meant to be online support systems for recovering bulimics and anorectics are serving as sources for harmful ideas, such as how many laxatives to take for a quick fix, spreading the word about how to use fen-phen, herbal stimulants, and thermogenics for quick weight loss, and how to fool eating-disorder professionals into thinking their patient is gaining weight.

Recently, a Dateline television program exposed the brutal violence in the Marines' secret gold wing initiation ceremony. The gold wing pin has several sharp posts protruding from it. Newest members of the Corps are expected to stand bare-chested in a row as around thirty older members, including commissioned officers, each in turn push, twist, and grind the posts into the potential gold wingers' chests. Despite the screaming and bleeding, the drunken Marines persist, and conclude by shoving each new member's head into the wall, then pouring beer down his throat to welcome him into their ranks. The sense of instant bonding through violence was striking, with members saying: "It makes a man out of you," "The great thing is the bond you feel with the others." The 20/20 show exposed similar secret hazing at the Citadel, the South Carolina military college. "Knobs" told of having to ask the upperclassmen to hit them, as well as being expected to stand at attention as upper classmen set their clothing on fire.

Contagion episodes of suicide attempts often follow a suicide gesture, at-tempt, or successful suicide by a peer. Suicides increased following newspaper coverage of a suicide, and increase according to the intensity of the publicity and the prestige of the publicized suicide (Phillips 1996). Editors have learned to be extremely cautious about the kind of coverage given to a suicide, and those who work with adolescents have learned to make themselves especially available after a suicide or attempt. Suggestible youngsters are all too prone to idealize or romanticize the successful suicide, and are at particular risk at the time of or around the anniversary of a suicide. There are suicide watches in some local schools in my area in March, as suicides and suicide attempts have occurred around this time for a number of years. They increase as spring arrives, the time of Christ's crucifixion and resurrection, when desperate people believe that they will be reborn after they have died.

Late in February 1997, Kathy, a high school senior whom I knew, who lived on the street where I live and practice, jumped to her watery grave from the George Washington Bridge into the Hudson River. This occurred almost two years after the suicide of a younger student in her school, whom she did not know. This 14-year-old boy had lain down on the railroad tracks that ran par-allel to the river and was killed instantaneously by a train. Grief-stricken class-mates spontaneously erected a shrine to his memory at the tracks. Kathy had been deeply disturbed by this episode, and had set up her own personal shrine to his memory in her room. At the memorial service for her, it was disturbing to see that a shrine to her memory had been similarly created. Her graduation photo was displayed along with a brutal suicide note found in her car, that ended with the words "Please burn me!" A poem was displayed, copies of which were distributed to all present, and was read aloud in unison by those present. It was filled with images of sunlight, gentle rain, birds, and morning awakenings, and ended with the words, "Do not stand at my grave and cry . . . I am not there . . . I did not die." This romanticization of her death was far from the harsh reality that Kathy's unrecovered body was whirling around somewhere in the river, and it served to transfer the mantle of sainthood onto her. The community feared yet another teen suicide, and terrified parents and teachers wondered who would be next. In the weeks immediately following, four more students in this small high school made suicide attempts. Just a week after the suicide, early in March, a 15-year-old girl from an adjacent town came into treatment with me, a day after she had an almost irresistible impulse to throw herself down a ravine into a stream that flowed into the river. Only a day or so before, a schoolmate had taken an overdose of pills on the fourth anniversary of her mother's death. The power of suggestion on the peer group is not to be underestimated.

The power of an individual's religious or spiritual beliefs can seduce him into seeking out danger or welcoming dangerous situations. Believing that God will heal them, some Christian Scientists have refused medication for themselves and their children and have died. Those who believe in astrology believe the time of the vernal equinox, March 21, when winter ends and spring begins, has mystical importance. Mass suicides in religious cults have also been found to occur at around this time, and the potential for such mass suicides is especially great at the time of the millennium, when the era of physical life may end to be replaced by "everlasting life." The potential for self-harm contagion in the various cyberspace communities is enormous as well. The Heaven's Gate cultists who committed mass suicide were computer scientists who had a Heaven's Gate Web page, conveying their belief that the body is "just so much hardware . . . just dead meat, a container for the brain."

Once an individual allows his ability to think critically to be co-opted by the power accorded to a powerful leader, the potential for self-harm is enormous. The minds of cult members can, under certain conditions, become reduced to the mentality of the horde (Freud 1921). We are accustomed to thinking of cults as religious groups with varying degrees of destructiveness inherent in their beliefs and practices, but there are also destructive political cults, martial arts cults, diet cults, and psychotherapy cults. Each cult's lifestyle is different, but many are closed systems, living together essentially cut off from the rest of the world, with members living with a minimum of sleep, food, or privacy. Cults have been promoted by numerous celebrities. For example, George Harrison's (of the Beatles) hit record, "Hare Krishna Mantra," promoted the spread of the Hare Krishna movement, while the Beatles, actors Mia Farrow and John Travolta, magician Doug Henning, and many others spoke glowingly of their involvement with Transcendental Meditation (TM), Scientology, and other cults. The Maharishi Mahesh Yogi, founder of TM, became a celebrity as did former TM promoter Deepak Chopra.

TM, often regarded as a harmless technique to induce relaxation and relieve stress, is regarded as one of the most harmful cults by those who study cult involvement. Advanced TM'ers are taught to develop "supernormal powers" such as levitation ("yogic flying"), omniscience, and invisibility, and are trained to relinquish critical thinking and to induce altered states of consciousness to the point that they occur automatically with little or no effort (Ryan 1993). There is empirical evidence that depersonalization, derealization, tic disorders, and seizures have occurred with extensive meditation, as well as reports of a high incidence of psychiatric hospital admissions, suicides, self-mutilation, child abuse, and neglect among those living in the TM community in Fairfield, Iowa (home of Maharishi International University).

Cult members may turn over all their money to the leader, rejoicing in their poverty while applauding the luxurious lifestyle of the leader. Members of certain cults may consent to allow themselves to be abused physically or sexually by the leader or his henchmen, even offering their children for such abuse, considering it a sacrament. The Garbage Eaters Brotherhood on the West Coast considers it a sacrament to rummage through dumpsters for food, to eat food that has spoiled. Violent diarrhea and vomiting are signs of their devotion. When they are ordered to marry a partner chosen by their leader, cult members obey. When they are told that they shall take up poisonous serpents or drink strychnine to demonstrate their faith in God, many do. When they are ordered to be celibate, they obey, and like some in the Heaven's Gate cult, may even have themselves castrated. When they are ordered to cut themselves in pacts of fellowship, many obey. When systematically programmed to cut themselves or take poison or lethal drug overdoses in pacts of suicide, they obey.

The world has been rocked in the past two decades by the news of mass cult suicides. At the urging of their leader Reverend Jim Jones, most of the 913 people in the Jonestown cult in Guyana died after drinking grape juice laced with cyanide. In Waco, Texas, eighty members of the Branch Davidian cult gave up their lives at the urging of their leader. In Europe and Canada, seventy-four members of the Order of the Solar Temple doomsday cult took their lives. In San Diego thirty-nine cyber-geeks, members of the Heaven's Gate cult, videotaped their good-byes to the world before they and their leader ritualistically took their lives.

PROCESS FACTORS IN CONTAGIOUS SELF-HARM

Several different interacting factors found to contribute to contagions of self-mutilation (Walsh and Rosen 1988) can inform our understanding of other contagious self-harm as well, including self-starvation, bulimic activity, binge drinking, drug use, and suicide. First, those who mutilate themselves were found to have primitive patterns of communication, a limited ability to use verbal means for expressing themselves, particularly for expressing emotions. For such individuals, self-mutilation delivers a powerful emotional message in concrete, visible, and physical fashion. It expresses a wish for acknowledgment or a wish to affiliate with others in the group, in much the same way that a special gang handshake does. Because minor slights or insensitivities are often experienced as major narcissistic injuries within the group, jealousy, rage, and panic may ensue, with self-mutilation expressing attack and accusation, retaliation and revenge. The message expressed for groups of incarcerated gang members is, "We only know how to destroy what others have constructed" (Carasquillo-Ramirez 1998).

Second, their self-mutilating behavior may be used to have an interpersonal impact on others. Some self-mutilators delight in shocking or disgusting others by exhibiting their wounds. At times a patient will self-mutilate prior to her therapist's leaving for vacation, a gesture meant to keep the therapist from leaving, or a young woman might self-mutilate after her boyfriend breaks up with her, an act meant to restore the relationship.

The third factor is the influence of the peer group itself. When individuals mutilate themselves in a group, the drama, intensity, and "realer than life" quality of the experience cements the bond so that more ordinary group experiences pale in comparison. Thus, the friendships of self-mutilators are usually experienced as more meaningful and intense than other friendships. While in an ordinary friendship, girls might exchange rings or woven bracelets to demonstrate friendship, self-mutilators might cut themselves together in a special ceremony or cut each other. Repeated exposure to a group of self-mutilating peers provides a modeling influence that makes the behavior more attractive and lowers an individual's resistance to participation. The lowered resistance plays an important role in contagion episodes; the normal tendency not to self-injure is reduced as a group momentum of disinhibition mounts. At such times, then, someone who fails to self-mutilate may appear utterly deviant to his peers. Within the group, a hierarchy may form based on the severity of self-mutilation; that is, those who cut most often and deepest are highest in the pecking order. There develops a perverse pleasure in violating taboos and reversing the status hierarchy, the destruction of old values to create a new anarchy. So when one member shifts the equilibrium by self-mutilating, others may need to reestablish their position within the hierarchy, self-mutilating even more severely to demonstrate that they will not be outdone.

A fourth factor is that of competition for staff resources. In treatment programs the time and attention of staff members is filled with meaning, as staff members may be perceived as parental figures with links to the outside world, as alternately harsh and punitive or wise and caring. Obtaining the attention of staff members becomes a way of a patient's obtaining high status for himself, and self-mutilation is a behavior bound to generate a great deal of staff attention. So for many patients self-mutilation may become their primary means of initiating contact with staff. Those patients who do not mutilate see that those who do often receive medical attention to their wounds, adjustments in their medication, additional hours of therapy, and intense staff scrutiny, and they are tempted to follow suit. At Grandview, a Canadian institution for behaviorally disordered adolescent delinquent girls, where almost every girl had cuts and scars from self-inflicted wounds, one of them explained the predictable order in chaos:

> Melinda told us that by their carving, the girls controlled what she called the "Grandview emergency machine." When the girls carved they started a chain reaction: the supervisors called in head supervisors; the head supervisors called the duty administrator; the administrator came running and summoned a retinue of professionals—the nurse, the doctor (if you cut deeply enough), the ambulance (if you really do it right), the caseworker, the male staff (if you are obstreperous about it or keep cutting instruments in view), and even the psychiatrist (if you threaten to keep doing it). Virtually guaranteed was a visit to the school's director. It was all so predictable. [Ross and McKay 1979, p. 134]

We can understand a great deal of the process and dynamics occurring in those whose self-harm is done within the context of a group. If we examine the self-harm chain reaction through the lens of chaos theory and information theory (Conway and Siegelman 1995), we discern a process by which an individual becomes caught up in the spiral of self-harm. This process can be understood as a communication disease caused by the ongoing impairments of mind that lead to snapping, the physical breakdown of a person's entire ability to make sense of his experiences. When we understand the need for people to feel attached to groups, we can understand how sometimes that need can lead to being caught up in a cataclysmic death cycle, such as happened in Jonestown and Waco. When we know that members of a group may turn over their well-being and their mortality to a powerful leader, we can understand that group members can be bound to charismatic and narcissistic leaders and to each other in destructive and perverse attachments.

SELF-HARM IS AS OLD AS TIME

Self-mutilating practices have been culturally sanctioned for centuries across cultures. Herodotus provided the oldest literary account of self-mutilating behavior, describing how Cleomenes, a Spartan leader gone mad, took a knife and starting with his shins "sliced his flesh into strips, working upwards to his thigh, hips and sides until he reached his belly, which he chopped into mincemeat" (Favazza and Rosenthal 1990, p. 77). Biblical accounts can be found in the New Testament. Mark told of Jesus's encounter in the lands of the Gadarenes with a despondent man infested with demons who "always, night and day, was in the tombs, crying and cutting himself with stones." Despite the commandment that man should multiply, Jesus is said to have favored self-castration, self-enucleation and the self-amputation of limbs:

> There be eunuchs which have made themselves eunuchs for the kingdom of heaven's sake. He that is able to receive it let them receive it. [Matthew 19:12]
> Wherefore if thy hand or thy foot offend thee, cut them off, and cast them from thee: it is better for thee to enter into life halt or maimed, rather than having two hands or two feet to be cast into everlasting fire. . . . And if thine eye offend thee, pluck it out, and cast it from thee: it is better for thee to enter into life with one eye, rather than having two eyes to be cast into hell fire. [Matthew 18:8–9]

While the Old Testament forbids the infliction of injury on the self (Leviticus 19:28), the custom of mourners ripping their clothing is a cultural transformation of the impulse to tear one's hair or flesh. Many Orthodox Jews today will tear a garment and wear it throughout the period of mourning, while Conservative and Reform mourners customarily wear a small piece of ripped black ribbon on their lapels as a symbol of their grief.

Despite the drama of self-mutilation, it has been a poorly studied phenomenon (Winchel and Stanley 1991), only recently getting much scientific attention. The epidemiology of self-mutilating behavior has never been studied, except in over-inclusive studies of direct self-harm that included not only self-mutilating behavior but drug overdoses, self-poisonings, failed suicides, self-asphyxiations (Walsh and Rosen 1988), and underinclusive studies of wrist-cutting (Clendenin and Murphy 1971, Weissman 1975). Only rough estimates of incidence can be provided. Walsh and Rosen's (1988) review of the epidemiological literature suggests that the incidence of self-mutilation during the 1970s and early 1980s ranged broadly from 14 to 600 persons per 100,000 population per year. Favazza's (Favazza and Conterio 1988) estimate of the incidence of self-mutilation, based on inferences of disorders with which self-mutilation is associated in the DSM-III (borderline personality disorder, histrionic personality disorder, antisocial personality disorder, anorexia nervosa, bulimia, schizophrenia, major depression, and multiple personality disorder) is 750 per 100,000, or 2 million people in the United States, an underestimate quite close to the upper end of the range estimated by Walsh and Rosen. While the statistics differ, it is agreed that self-mutilation is a far more common behavior than is realized (Favazza 1987, 1989, Favazza and Conterio 1988, Walsh and Rosen 1988). In a study investigating the dress and body markings of 100 adolescent psychiatric patients (both hospitalized and never hospitalized), the hospitalized patients had a significantly higher incidence of self-inflicted scars than the nonhospitalized patients (Michelman et al. 1991). Dress, haircuts, and other individualized expressions of appearance did not differentiate the hospitalized from the nonhospitalized group, and the findings suggested that psychiatric hospitalization was a predictor of self-inflicted markings (Michelman et al. 1991).

In the Roman Empire perverse orgies of sex, eating, purging, and drinking went on for days among the wealthy, with revelers throwing up into special urns strategically placed for that purpose so that the bingeing could continue. Certainly, eating-disordered behavior and alcohol abuse have a long history, going back in time long before alcohol abuse, anorexia nervosa (Gull 1874, Lasegue 1873), and bulimia (*DSM-III*) were identified as medical syndromes. The clearest early account of what might have been the condition known today as anorexia nervosa was by Richard Morton (1694), a London physician, who reported on two cases of what he regarded as "Nervous Consumption" caused by "Sadness and Anxious Cares." One was an 18-year-old woman and the other a 16-year-old boy, both of whom had become emaciated because they refused to eat. However, it was not until the late nineteenth century that the syndrome currently called anorexia nervosa emerged as a distinct syndrome with the almost simultaneous medical reports of Gull (1874) and Lasegue (1873). Self-flagellating practices as well as self-starvation and self-induced vomiting were noted as early as the thirteenth century in such Roman Catholic mystics as Saint Catherine of Siena and Saint Margaret of Cortona (Bell 1985). In many of the grand spa hotels of Europe even today, gluttony, followed by purging, is de rigueur. Guests indulge in a sumptuous dinner of many rich courses, and the following morning drink various mineral waters that induce diarrhea, in an effort to rid their bodies of food consumed the night before (Harrison 1996).

There have been inconsistent findings in studies of the incidence and prevalence of what has been called bulimia (*DSM-III*) or bulimia nervosa (*DSM-III-R*). Early findings indicated that bulimia, using *DSM-III* criteria, was a relatively common disorder affecting from 10 to 20 percent of female college students (Halmi et al. 1981, Katzman et al. 1984, Pope et al. 1984, Pyle et al. 1983, but more recent research using *DSM-III-R* criteria, perhaps sensitive to the popular exaggerations of the disorder, reported dramatically lower prevalence rates ranging from 1 to 5 percent of female college students (Coric and Murstein 1993). Coric and Murstein (1993) found that a considerable percentage (11.3 percent) of female college students in a nonclinical random sample fully met *DSM-III-R* criteria. This prevalence rate is toward the middle of the spectrum of earlier reported prevalence rates based on *DSM-III* criteria, but higher than two studies (Drewnowski et al. 1988, Schotte and Stunkard 1987) that used *DSM-III-R* criteria and reported rates of 1 and 3 percent, respectively. The number of college men reporting the termination of binge-eating by self-induced vomiting doubled from 1980 to 1983 (Pyle et al. 1986), while the reported prevalence of binge-purging behavior in a sample of college males was 6.1 percent compared to 11.9 percent in females (Halmi et al. 1981). The prevalence of eating disorders in men is reported to be higher in dancers and professional athletes, particularly wrestlers and marathon runners (Yates 1991), populations that overvalue thinness and fitness.

Other major difficulties in studying eating-disordered and self-mutilating behavior, especially in nonclinical samples, are that those who suffer from these illnesses tend to be ashamed and secretive about it, and tend toward minimization or concealment. This is especially true of men with eating disorders, who may feel a sense of shame at having a disorder regarded as a woman's illness.

GROOMING AND ATTACHMENTS GONE HAYWIRE

Through animal studies we can better understand certain pathophysiological mechanisms and social factors in the attachment system that may play a part in human self-harm. Human beings harm themselves in response to a separation or the threat of separation; does animal self-harm occur as well under similar circumstances? Human beings turn their aggression against their own bodies in the form of self-harm; what is the extent to which this hyperaggressiveness is derived through experiences in the environment and the extent to which this unusual degree of aggression is innate, derived from a constitutional predisposition? All primate infants, including humans, depend on their caregivers for help in regulating emotional states. Primates who have experienced an early lack of parental responsiveness and are left to their own devices to regulate physiological states may develop a deficit in their ability to modulate physiological arousal, making them more vulnerable to automutilation, feeding disturbances, and aggressive acting out (van der Kolk and Fisler 1994).

In his review of the literature on automutilation, Favazza (1987) has found that some mutilative behaviors appear both in animals and humans and are comparable. Hair pulling, head hitting, and skin scratching are seen in confined monkeys and in about 17 percent of normal children. Animals that are socially isolated mutilate themselves in higher rates; monkeys raised with infrequent social contact often become self-mutilating adults. Animals and humans claw, bang their heads, scratch, gouge, or bite themselves. Because human beings have evolved to become tool users, they may use razors or broken glass instead of teeth or nails. The more severe acts, such as head banging, face slapping, eye and ear digging, and self-biting, are seen in laboratory monkeys and in severely mentally retarded humans.

Heroin, caffeine, alcohol, and amphetamine all may precipitate self-mutilation in animals and humans, probably through their effects on neurotransmitters in different parts of the brain. Animals and humans may use automutilation as a means to increase or decrease arousal, for its self-regulating effect. Just as monkeys who are agitated or enraged become calm after harming themselves, human beings too find relief after harming themselves. Winchel (1991) noted that automutilation is common to animals confined to zoos, stalls, and laboratory cages, and speculates that "aloneness affect," the experience of feeling utterly alone, may be a contributing factor. Heller (1990) has noted that most self-mutilating incidents in psychiatric hospitals occur at night or on weekends, times when physicians and therapists are unavailable. Although a loss or separation is known to be the precipitant of self-mutilation in humans (Favazza 1987, Walsh 1987, Walsh and Rosen 1988), I would wonder, too, if a biological substrate, perhaps a constitutional endowment of greater than usual levels of aggression, is not a factor in animal automutilation and human self-mutilation that interacts synergistically with the separation factor to produce the self-mutilation.

Studies of animals, especially nonhuman primates, have demonstrated how self-destructive they can become when forced to endure a prolonged or permanent separation. Jane Goodall, who has worked with chimpanzees in Africa, describes grief in a chimp family.

I would strongly suspect that the kind of affection between a chimp mother and her offspring and a human mother and her children is very, very similar. The motivation to protect, to nurture, and to suckle is very close in both species. Flint's grief at his mother's [Flo's] death, for example, underscores this point. Flint had been with his mother when she died while crossing a stream. For three days after her death, Flint returned to her body and tried to extricate maggots from the corpse. Within a week following the death of his mother, Flint became so lethargic and depressed that he lost a third of his weight. He exhibited all the signs associated with severe depression; he refused to eat and would sit huddled up in a ball. On the fifth day, Flint met his sister, Fifi, and it seemed as if her presence would help him relax. When she moved away, we were sure that Flint would follow. Although Fifi waited patiently, Flint lay down under a bush. During the last two weeks of his life, he hardly moved at all. The day before he died, he returned to the place in the stream where his mother had been. He spent a long time looking at the rock on which she had been before he moved away. [Hansburg 1976, p. 229, quoting from Goodall's book, In the Shadow of Man]

In a review of studies on eating and hunger disturbances in both animals and humans, transmitter brain chemicals such as endogenous opiates, serotonin, dopamine, and norepinephrine were found to influence hunger (Battegay 1991). These substances are associated with mood and affect, which influence food intake in several ways: the frequency of eating, the quantities consumed, the rapidity of eating. In studies of animals and human beings, the somatic substrate seems to be connected quite closely with the psychological situation of eating. There is a failure-to-thrive syndrome in both animal and human infants in which growth difficulties stem from problems in regulating food intake in the context of a disturbed mother–child relationship (Battegay 1991). The monkeys studied by the Harlows were separated from their mothers and raised by mother surrogates, created from wire structures covered with terrycloth to which milk bottles were attached (Tomkins 1962). These monkeys became attached to the surrogates and grew and developed normally, while their counterparts raised by wire surrogates that were not covered with synthetic fur failed to develop normally. Similarly, the failure to thrive syndrome in human infants has been documented (Chatoor 1989, Satter 1986, 1990, Spitz 1945, 1946). Growth problems are attributed to food refusal, vomiting, and rumination, all of which have been found to develop from a disturbed mother–child relationship.

While cats are ordinarily clean animals, requiring a clean litter box in which to deposit feces and urine, when the relationship to its owner is disturbed, the cat may protest the neglect or abuse by urinating or defecating where he is not supposed to, much the same way that insecure children soil or wet themselves or bulimics make their smelly mess.

In studies of rats, food refusal not only corresponded to complex psychological behavior, but also had somatic factors found in neuronal and metabolic processes (Battegay 1991). Both human beings and pigs can develop self-starvation. Although anorexia in pigs develops after weaning as wasting pig syndrome or after farrowing as thin sow syndrome, anorexia has been noted in particular in those pigs that have been bred for extreme leanness (Treasure and Owen 1997). Similar syndromes have occurred in sheep. There is a striking similarity in the onset of anorexia in humans, which often occurs after a period of extreme dieting in order to lose weight. Both psychological and somatic factors interact in complex ways in human beings who refuse to eat; although anorectics, when they refuse to eat, are extremely hungry, they deny their physiological hunger but display their emotional hunger instead, by starving themselves. As the illness progresses, they actually lose the sensation of hunger and continue to waste away without having to exert much effort to control or deny their hunger. When a rat's access to food is restricted to 60 to 90 minutes a day and when it is given free access to a running wheel, the rat will progressively increase the amount of running it does and will also frequently decrease the amount of food it takes in, even to the point of running itself to death (Epling and Pierce 1996). The parallels with food restriction and excessive exercise in anorexia nervosa are striking.

Three forms of animal obesity have been studied extensively and are useful for a better understanding of human obesity (Keesey 1986). First, there is a genetically transmitted obesity, a form of obesity in rats inherited as a single recessive gene. At the same time those rats who had this form of obesity also were found to have a reduced rate of resting metabolism, which seems to defend the obesity and can prevent further weight loss. Thus, they are thought to defend an elevated set-point weight. Those who have studied set-point theory in humans have found that some human beings are genetically predisposed to being heavy, regardless of dietary restrictions, and may even gain more weight when they attempt to diet. Second, there is a diet-induced obesity in rats that is similar to that in humans. When offered certain highly palatable diets or a cafeteria selection of junk foods, the normal resistance of rats to weight gain can be overcome and obesity results. Third, hypothalamic obesity, associated with irregularity in the satiation center of the brain (ventromedial hypothalamus), has been found in studies of rats, other rodents, cats, monkeys, and humans. It is thought that this irregularity is a factor in overeaters eating so quickly and in their gulping their food that they do not allow themselves the opportunity of experiencing their physiological hunger. Not taking the time to savor the food or experience their increasing satiation, they feel hungry and continue to eat, remaining insatiated and insatiable.

Overeating and binge eating in humans have been found to be associated with emotional deficiencies in early childhood (Battegay1991, Fairburn 1985, Fairburn and Wilson 1993). Although excessive consumption in humans can take the same form it does in animals, that is, gorging or overeating, the insatiable hunger can be experienced as a hunger for warmth, stimulation, and fusion with others, a narcissistic hole (Ammon 1979) that must be filled with alcohol, drugs, excessive clothing, money, or sex.

When we examine the grooming behaviors that are characteristic of each species, we can understand animal and human self-harm as biologically based grooming behaviors that have gone haywire in response to attachment disturbances. Several years ago when I was in a pet shop, I noticed a large tropical bird in a cage. Ordinarily he probably would have been one of those splendid, flamboyantly colored birds, but in the pet shop, however, he looked peculiarly pathetic. He had virtually no feathers on his chest, having plucked them out in the preceding two weeks, since the time his owner had boarded him in the shop while she was on vacation. In attributing human qualities to this bird, I assumed that either the anxiety or the loss experienced in the separation was a main factor in this poor bird's mutilating himself. (Favazza [1987] refers to automutilation rather than self-mutilation in animals, stating that he does so because it is not known whether an animal has a true sense of self. When Koko, the lowland gorilla who knows sign language, takes questions from America Online subscribers, and when the linguistic communications of dolphins are recorded, it becomes less clear-cut just what it is that differentiates *Homo sapiens* from the rest of the animals.) I speculated that the bird, acutely missing his owner's gentle stroking its feathers and her soothing words, in some peculiar twist of nature, had replaced the stimulation of her touch by the sad and desperate touch substitute of plucking out its own plumage. I then discovered that some species of tropical birds in captivity, thought by their keepers to become moody or bored, will react by biting or plucking their feathers. Some even become denuded and an occasional bird will literally pluck itself to death, when a "blood feather" is wrenched loose, resulting in excessive, sometimes fatal bleeding (Smith 1980).

Some self-injurious human behaviors may be grooming behaviors that have somehow gone awry. Although cats spend a great deal of their waking hours in grooming themselves, they tend to spend even more time in grooming themselves when they have inadequate stimulation. The same may be true for many narcissistic women, who fill empty unstimulating time with experimenting with hairdos, manicures and pedicures, facials, and shopping. Grooming is an activity that cements social ties and solidifies attachments (Dunbar 1997), as is clear by the attachments so many women make to their hairdressers.

Many nail biters note that they bite their nails when bored; the nail biting may be a way of obtaining stimulation quite like the feather plucking of captive birds (Smith 1980). Nail biting may be a behavior that emerged from biologically adaptive urges that have gone astray, similar to the urge that could have been inherent in what drove early man to remove ticks, fleas, or leeches from his body and the bodies of his kin. Thus, some aspect of the urge to bite or pick at one's nails may have been engendered from a drive that otherwise serves to promote bodily health through self-grooming. For example, because early man had no artifacts with which to trim, moderate nail biting and picking was probably the main method of nail grooming for thousands of years. In fact, many people who are not habitual nail biters will resort to nail biting to trim a ragged nail when a nail file or clipper is not available.

Hair pulling (trichotillomania), like nail biting, is a remarkably widespread practice, and may also derive from early grooming behavior, when touching another's head was reserved for only the closest of intimates, among both humans and animals (Morris 1971). Because hair is a touch receptor, touching someone's hair may set off an intense and stimulating sensory experience. "Any first -time touch, or change in touch (from gentle to stinging, say), sends the brain into a flurry of activity. . . . We set in motion our complex web of touch receptors" (Ackerman 1991, p. 80). "One hair can be easily triggered: If something presses it or tugs at it, if its tip is touched, if the skin around it is pressed, the hair vibrates and sparks a nerve. . . . Hairs make wonderful organs of touch" (Ackerman 1991, p. 87). Cleaning, grooming, washing, and oiling the hair have always been important adjuncts to its cultural use as a sexual signal. If one were to observe the monkeys or apes in the monkey house of a zoo, one can see from the way one monkey works lovingly on the head of its companion that the cleansing alone cannot account for the relaxed ecstasy of the monkey being groomed (Morris 1971). Nuns, sworn to celibacy, appear asexual, covering body and hair with a habit and veil. Similarly, Muslim women cover the head and face as well as the entire body, while Orthodox Jewish women cover their hair, exposing it only to their husband's view.

Women look forward to the intimacy of the hair salon, where they can enjoy confiding aspects of their personal lives to their hairdressers as much as they enjoy having their hair and scalp massaged and shampooed. In the earlier periods of human history, however, professional hairdressers were a rarity. Touching the head became reserved for one's parent, lover, or a close friend or relative of the same sex. When a child grows up without a mother to lavish loving attention on her in the act of grooming, or when maternal grooming is harsh and without tenderness, grooming can become a harsh activity. When the mother pulls the comb through tangled tendrils of hair without regard for the pain she is inflicting upon the child, grooming can readily become associated with the pain of pulled hair. Or when the child is left alone to care for her hair herself, the abandonment may stimulate the wish to feel her head caressed. For such a neglected child, the physical pain experienced in pulling out her own hair may be a welcome diversion from the emotional loneliness.

SELF-HARM AND ASSOCIATED PSYCHOPATHOLOGY

As one might expect, the most severe kinds of self-harm seem to be more prevalent toward the most severe end of the diagnostic spectrum. We know that borderline personalities demonstrate an inability to self-regulate and form stable self and object representations (Grotstein 1990). Those with narcissistic personalities, although somewhat more advanced developmentally, also exhibit insecure attachments and manifest impairments in self-esteem regulation and disturbances in the representation of the self in relation to others. The various forms of eating-disordered and self-mutilating behavior, alcohol and drug abuse, compulsive sexuality, shopping, spending, stealing, gambling, risk taking, and involvement in a series of relationships are all manifestations of failures of self-regulation derived from disorders of attachment. They can be found in those who have diagnoses of dissociative disorders and posttraumatic stress disorder, anxiety and mood disorders, personality disorders, psychoses, and addictions. This suggests, then, that self-harm belongs to no one discrete diagnostic category but may well be an integral part of all psychopathology.

Dissociative Disorders

The psychological substrate for precipitation of a physiological regression to illness is a regressed ego state, as described by Schur (1955) but also including fluctuations in the level of consciousness and the use of more primitive defenses (Giovacchini 1993, Reiser 1966). Bach (1985) regards narcissistic patients as demonstrating a characteristic altered (regressed) state of consciousness involving disturbances of self, and body image, hypochondriasis, thermal and boundary sensitivity, and difficulties with eating and weight regulation. Living so much in this altered or dissociated state would make such people prone to the development of illness associated with these bodily experiences such as eating disorders, body dysmorphic disorder, and Raynaud's disease.

Many bulimics and self-mutilators regress to trancelike dissociated states, usually depersonalization and derealization, before and during the episodes of bingeing and purging and before and during episodes of self-mutilation (Farber 1995a,b). They are often the same individuals who, as abused and traumatized children, developed an unusual ability to dissociate, which enabled them to endure painful, often violent bodily assaults and intrusions by experiencing them as if they were being done to someone else. The more they need to use dissociation in this way, the more they develop their ability to use it, becoming unusually adept at dissociating without even trying. The use of dissociation as a defense becomes automatic, as it becomes woven into the fabric of their developing personality, predisposing them to severe bulimic and self-mutilating behaviors. People who have experienced severe cumulative trauma such as physical and sexual abuse or the trauma inflicted unknowingly on children by intrusive coercive medical and surgical procedures tend to feel as if they have little control over their bodies and lives. So to seize one's own body and actively cut, burn, starve, stuff, or purge it provides a needed sense of control. Interpersonal and intrapsychic conflicts are displaced, concretized, and enacted within the psychic space that dissociates psyche from soma (Sacksteder 1989a, b), producing self-harm behavior. The ability to numb oneself to emotional pain can develop in childhood as well with those who have suffered the trauma of object loss and separations. Although many people find that their ability to dissociate becomes a finely honed instrument over time, others may find that this ability instead diminishes. When the ability to numb oneself is desperately wanted but not readily available, alcohol or various drugs promote the numbing.

Both abuse survivors and Vietnam veterans suffer from severe drug and alcohol abuse resulting from their efforts to medicate themselves for the aftereffects of extreme trauma. Herman (1992) has found that eating disorders, self-mutilation, and substance abuse may be symptomatic of the posttraumatic stress disorder associated with physical and sexual abuse, while Miller (1994) found that eating disorders, self-mutilating behavior, substance abuse, and involvement in abusive relationships are manifestations in women of a trauma reenactment syndrome. A sense of numbness can occur during experiences that replicate the ego-state associated with the trauma. During the Persian Gulf War, many Vietnam veterans watched the television news coverage for hours in a trancelike state, picking at their faces, neck, and arms, often until they bled (Dennis Babik, personal communication).

The findings of the author's study (Farber 1995a) suggest that it is the severity of trauma experienced in childhood and adolescence, particularly the cumulative trauma of violent sexual and physical abuse maintained in a climate without secure attachments, that is the key factor in the development and maintenance of dissociation, self-injurious habits, and eating-disordered habits in childhood. The severity of trauma is also a key factor in the development in childhood of a sense of body alienation, making the individual prone to the development of eating-disordered behavior, self-mutilating behavior, and other forms of self-harm later in adolescence and or adulthood. All forms of self-harm, including substance abuse, compulsive sex, shopping, reckless driving, other risk taking, and involvement in abusive relationships, seem to be desperate efforts to medicate the self.

Obsessive-Compulsive Disorder and Obsessive-Compulsive Spectrum Disorders

There are similarities between obsessive-compulsive disorder (OCD) and the ritualistic, repetitive self-harm behaviors such as hair pulling, nail biting, skin picking, self-mutilation, and eating disorders (Hollander 1993, Hsu et al. 1993, Simeon and Hollander 1993). Those with eating disorders are obsessive and compulsive about food and body image (Hollander 1993, Johnson and Connors 1987). The obsessional thinking about food, and the rituals around eating, purging, exercising, and weighing oneself are so similar to the OCD obsessions and compulsive washing, checking, and repeating rituals that they can be considered a counterpart. Some of the ritualistic aspects of bingeing and purging include the shopping for and bingeing on only certain foods, ensuring privacy by turning off the phone, secretly consuming those foods in a certain self-imposed order so that certain colorful foods, when vomited, can serve as markers indicating the beginning of the binge. Other ritualistic behaviors include compulsive calorie counting, weighing oneself several times daily, compensatory exercising for a specific length of time, scrutinizing the contents of the purge, and cleaning and deodorizing the bathroom after purging. Some of the ritualistic aspects of self-mutilating behavior include the secretive hiding and assembling of self-mutilating instruments, ensuring privacy by turning off the phone, scrutinizing the injury, and cleaning the instruments, the injury, and the site of the self-mutilating act. Some bulimics (Hall et al. 1990) and self-mutilators (Favazza 1987) report very similar rituals in which they deliberately arrange to collect and save their vomit or blood in containers.

For some patients, hair pulling is compulsive, serves to reduce tension, and is ego dystonic (alien to the ego); for others, it is impulsive, pleasurable, and ego syntonic (acceptable to the ego). When the hair pulling is ego dystonic, there is a motivation to give up the symptom, which makes the individual more likely to respond to psychotherapy or to the same medications that are effective for OCD, namely the selective serotonin reuptake inhibitors such as Prozac, Paxil, and Zoloft (Hollander 1993). In fact, Prozac (fluoxetine) has received U.S. Food and Drug Administration approval for the treatment of both OCD and bulimia nervosa (Breggin and Breggin 1994). Luvox (fluvoxamine), used for treatment of the symptoms of OCD, has been reported to be effective for reducing the compulsion to shop, reportedly problematic for ten million Americans, 85 percent of them women. It is thought that there is a serotonergic mediating mechanism in the pathophysiology of self-mutilation (Hollander 1993, Winchel and Stanley 1991, Yaryura-Tobias and Neziroglu 1978, Yaryura-Tobias et al. 1995). It has been found that the modulation of serotonergic systems reduced compulsive cravings and impulsive behavior (Hollander 1993), and therefore may play a role in reducing addictive behaviors such as binge eating and substance abuse. Recent research suggests that bulimic behavior, self-mutilation, and compulsive shopping and spending can be manifestations of OCD and/or an impulse disorder. The clinical analysis of episodes of these behaviors can be found to have elements of both.

Sadomasochism

All self-harm has a strong masochistic element, whether it be a physical masochism, in which pleasure is combined with bodily pain, or moral masochism, in which pleasure is combined with the pain of self-inflicted emotional suffering. Some bulimics have been found to be repeatedly involved in sadomasochistic sexual relationships (Cross 1993, Hall et al. 1990, Heller 1990, Johnson and Connors 1987), that is, in relationships combining sexual pleasure and pain (Grossman 1991). Self-cutting and other forms of self-mutilation offer direct libidinal gratification of both sadistic and masochistic wishes (Asch 1971, Crabtree 1967, Graff and Mallin 1967, Kernberg 1992, Novotny 1972). A group of bulimics who purge most severely were also found to mutilate themselves severely as well (Farber 1995a). Some of them tended to become most attached to the pain and degradation of severe purging with laxatives, while those who harmed themselves the most severely with purging and self-mutilation tended also to involve themselves with extensive tattooing, body piercing, and scarification. A strong masochistic orientation was found in patients who presented with subclinical eating disorders (Lerner 1991). These were college and graduate students who did not meet strict criteria for a diagnosis of anorexia nervosa or bulimia nervosa, but nonetheless suffered from episodes of bingeing, occasional vomiting, weight fluctuations, excessive exercising, perfectionistic strivings, and overreliance on the body as a means of expressing affect. The masochistic orientation was linked to a disturbed mother–child relationship, a delusion of omnipotent control, and a core unconscious masochistic fantasy.

Some patients with borderline personality organization behave in a masochistically perverse way that seems devoid of safety features and has a quality of danger that may lead to self-mutilation and even accidental death (Kernberg 1992, Litman and Swearingen 1996). The men studied by Litman and Swearingen were all deeply depressed and preoccupied with death. They seemed to use their perversion as a defense against suicide, as an effort to overcome loneliness, depression, boredom, and isolation. The sadomasochist protagonists became the producer, director, author, and chief actor in their own dramatic scenarios, and eroticized a situation of helplessness, weakness, and a threat to life that they then overcame and triumphed over. Betty Joseph (1982) found that some individuals who lacked warm contact early in life and who had a violent parent became masochistically addicted to the experience of near-death; they take exquisite pleasure in coming as close as possible to self-annihilation. They may experiment with erotic strangulation, with the most violent and painful experiences of sadomasochism, or with the pleasure in becoming so dehydrated from purging that only the machinery of the hospital's intensive care unit maintains the connection to life. They flirt wildly with death, and sometimes die in the process. Some of those who engage in these practices are more intentionally suicidal. Patients in treatment for chronic suicidality often reveal a pattern of sadomasochistic sexual activity (Litman and Swearingen 1996).

Kernberg has found that some borderline patients, whose self-mutilating behavior has an erotic quality, represent the most severe level of masochistic sexual perversion and malignant narcissism. Using Kernberg's (1992) nosological spectrum of masochism, when self-mutilation is found in someone with a neurotic level of ego development, aggression is recruited in the service of eroticism; at borderline levels of masochism, eroticism is recruited in the service of aggression; and at the deepest level of masochism, eroticism fades out completely, leaving an almost pure culture of aggression. It is thought that integral to every perversion is an eroticized childhood trauma that the person is trying to master (Bach 1994, Stoller 1985). If we define perversion as the erotic form of hatred (Stoller 1985), these kinds of sadomasochistic self-harm behaviors represent the erotic form of hatred toward both the self as well as the object. If we define perversion as the lack of capacity for whole-object love and treating a person like a thing (Bach 1994), then in a perversion the loveless individual uses another person like a prosthesis to allow himself the semblance of feeling love. It is also suggested that those who use their own bodies in this way may be thought to suffer a perversion. In fact, self-cutting, hair pulling, self-starvation, and bingeing and purging have been characterized as forms of female perversions with pronounced sadomasochistic and exhibitionistic elements that parody the feminine stereotyped models of submission and purity (Kaplan 1991). Parry (1934) found that prostitutes and male homosexuals get tattooed to satisfy strong masochistic-exhibitionistic drives. Those eating-disordered and self-mutilating individuals whose lives center around their self-harm behavior maintain a sadomasochistically perverse relationship to themselves in which they sadistically torture and take control of their bodies and masochistically take pleasure in being tortured and controlled. In this perverse scenario they play the part of the torturer as well as the tortured, continually enacting the beating fantasy regarded as the essence of masochism (Freud 1919, Novick and Novick 1996). They remain ruthlessly and narcissistically self-sufficient, their omnipotent sadomasochism disavowing the need for another human being.

Disorders in both food intake and elimination may lead to subsequent disturbances in the capacity to work, and may develop in women who fear their ambitious aspirations (Bergmann 1988, Krueger 1984). Eating disorders or other self-harm or self-sabotage may develop as a way for women to thwart their success not only in work but in love as well.

Addictive and Impulsive Processes

Addiction is a life-threatening journey (Jellinek 1994), with the attachment to drugs, starving, bingeing, purging, self-mutilation, compulsive sex, compulsive spending, sadomasochistic activity, or risk taking having the potential to become an addiction that gains control over one's life. All these forms of self-harm can provide rapid, striking, and short-lasting relief. These mood-altering substances and activities can produce an initial state of euphoria, soon to be followed by a depressed state, a high soon followed by a low, which is remedied by taking "the hair of the dog," that is, more of the self-harm activity to relieve the pain, in an endlessly vicious cycle.

Low self-esteem is a crucial factor in all addictions, leading to the use of various mood-altering activities and substances, from cocaine to skydiving, to alter neurotransmission and thus change the way people feel about themselves and the world. These and other compulsive activities can alter the neurotransmission of the brain chemicals that control emotion, perception, and bodily functions (Milkman and Sunderwirth 1987, van der Kolk 1994, van der Kolk et al. 1991, Winchel and Stanley 1991, Wurtman et al. 1981). On a neurobiological level, addiction can be understood as the self-induced changes in neurotransmission that result in behavior problems (Milkman and Sunderwirth 1987). Serotonin deficiencies have been implicated in compulsive self-mutilating behavior (van der Kolk, 1991, 1994, Winchel and Stanley 1991) and bulimic behavior (Wurtman et al. 1981). Changes in dopamine levels were found to play a role in the psychopathology of pathological gambling (Bergh et al. 1997).

Both bulimia and self-mutilation are thought to be impulse control disorders that were associated with other disorders of impulse control including drug and alcohol abuse (Lacey 1993, Lacey and Evans 1986). Not surprisingly, both bulimics and self-mutilators demonstrated high rates of substance abuse (American Psychiatric Association 1994, Holderness et al. 1994, Walsh 1987, Walsh and Rosen 1988). It makes a certain kind of sense that in someone who grew up in a home where one or both parents abused drugs or alcohol, what readily develops is a model of identification with a substance-abusing parent or a mood-altering activity. Food, too, is a substance that children have easy access to when in need of relief from emotional pain. Many children grow up with food having become their drug of choice, and they may well develop an addictive-like relationship to food. Because drugs and alcohol are often abused for their numbing effect, individuals who cannot dissociate sufficiently to numb themselves may resort to drugs or alcohol to promote dissociation. Heller (1990) reports patients have told her that they have used drugs or alcohol to ward off the intolerable feelings that lead to self-mutilation, and then while under the influence of drugs or alcohol may self-mutilate even more severely than usual. Several patients have told me of similar experiences in which they have used alcohol or marijuana to numb dysphoric affect, and then with the resulting loss of inhibition will tend to binge more readily.

While working with heroin addicts on a detoxification unit I found that these patients were as addicted to the furtive ritualistic behavior—copping drugs, preparing to shoot up, and injecting the drug—as to the opiate effect of the drug.

Those who binge and purge often seem to have developed an addictive-like relationship to both the rituals surrounding the bulimic episode as well as to the actual acts of bingeing and purging. Self-mutilators, too, are similarly addicted to the act, the rituals, and the ambience, developing increasing tolerance and increasingly larger and more frequent "doses" of the self-harm acts. Similarly, in eating disordered behavior and self-mutilating behavior, the behaviors seem to become more severe over time in a way that suggests that the patients have become "hooked" (Farber 1995a, 1997). The anorectic's weight loss increases as her eating and food-related behavior becomes more and more bizarre, and she weighs herself and exercises more frequently as the illness progresses, in much the same way as the alcoholic develops a tolerance for alcohol, drinking larger and larger amounts more frequently. In those who binge and purge, the binges become greater and more frequent over time, as do the purges. Over time the self-mutilator self-mutilates more and more frequently in a manner that suggests his behavior is out of control (Favazza 1987, 1994, Favazza and Conterio 1988, Favazza and Rosenthal 1990, Favazza et al. 1989, Walsh and Rosen 1988). The rituals of shopping for a binge, secretly stashing food away, stealing food from a store, and sneaking food from friends and family all resemble the "copping" rituals of drug addicts. Even the terms used mimic those of the drug addict. Bulimics often talk about their food as a "fix," and describe the experience of convulsive vomiting in the way that heroin addicts describe the erotic rush as the drug enters the bloodstream. Bulimics speak of eating "junk" or "shit"; the drug addict takes junk or injects "shit." Favazza (1987) found that when self-mutilating patients were prevented from mutilating themselves for a prolonged period of time, they experience symptoms reminiscent of drug or alcohol withdrawal, such as agitation, irritability, fear, hallucinations, and paranoia.

Just as addictive alcoholism is a progressive disease in which over years there is a crucial loss of control over intake (Jellinek 1994), the behavior of chronic bulimics and self-mutilators follows a similarly progressive and addicting course (Farber 1995a), a four-component cycle: (1) preoccupation with the behavior; (2) ritual preparation for the symptomatic behavior that helps to induce a disso-ciated mental state, usually either depersonalization or derealization or both; (3) compulsivity to perform the behavior; and (4) shame and despair. Many bulimics have reported that the more they have binged and purged, the more they wanted to and the more frequently they had to. Like many drug addicts, many self-mutilators who stick pins into themselves, or seek out others to do so by means of tattooing, acupuncture, or unnecessary medical procedures, may be "needle freaks" (Levine 1974), addicted to the behaviors surrounding the act of self-in-jection as much as to the actual act of self-injection (Farber 1995a). In addition, the addiction to these self-destructive behaviors may well represent a psycho-physiological addiction to trauma, a compulsion to repeatedly and unconsciously reenact and express through bodily self-harm severe trauma suffered in childhood (Farber 1995a, van der Kolk 1988, 1989).

Interestingly, it was found in a study of those who binge and purge that the more chronic this behavior was, the more strongly it was associated with the development of severe self-mutilation (Farber 1995a). The bulimic behavior became increasingly more severe over the years of chronic and progressive use. The severity of the purging behavior increased over time; the subjects purged more and more frequently and used multiple methods of purging, and the severity of the self-mutilating behavior increases significantly. The severity of the purging was also associated with increasingly severe self-mutilation. Thus, the chronicity of bingeing and purging behavior was found to be predictive at the trend level[2] ($p < .10$) of the development of severe self-mutilating behavior, and the severity of purging was associated with the development of severe self-mutilation. This suggests that with more chronic and progressive binge and purge behavior, not only are stronger and stronger doses of bulimic behavior required to get the needed soothing effect, but also, over time, the progressively more severe purging behavior itself loses its self-medicating effect as the tolerance for it increases, and it leads to the progression to increasingly severe self-mutilation. The addictive-like bulimic behavior, over time, becomes addictively transformed into an increasingly severe syndrome that includes severe purging and severe self-mutilation. It may even become further transformed to include an addictive-like relationship to body piercing, tattooing, and branding. Or the addictive bulimic behavior may be replaced by severe self-mutilating behavior or body modifications. The body modification industry not only is aware of the addictive-like relationship to these behaviors that may develop, but also capitalizes on it. One body piercing and tattoo studio advertises: "Welcome to your new addiction . . . delicate to deadly designs."

Personality Disorders

The borderline diagnosis has provoked enormous controversy, having become an all-purpose category for difficult patients. Similarly, the term *borderline* has crept into our culture and into the discourse of psychologically informed laymen: "She's so borderline-y." To be diagnosed as having borderline personality disorder (BPD) the patient must satisfy five of the nine *DSM-IV* diagnostic criteria (American Psychiatric Association 1994), two of which are "recurrent suicidal behavior, gestures, or threats, or self-mutilating behavior" (p. 654) and "impulsivity in at least two areas that are potentially self-damaging: e.g. spending, sex, substance use, reckless driving, binge eating" (p. 654). It has been sug-

---

2. When $p > .05$ but $< .10$, it is not at a statistical level of significance but nonetheless denotes a trend finding, meaning that the difference or association is worth taking seriously. It is important that statistical significance not be confused with theoretical or practical significance (Reid and Smith 1981).

gested that clinicians incorrectly tend to use self-mutilation alone as a sufficient criterion to diagnose BPD.

Even when the DSM criteria for BPD are strictly adhered to, the diagnosis is a controversial one, an outgrowth of political struggles in American psychiatry. It is based only on observable symptoms without consideration of the underlying structure of the personality. A far more comprehensive diagnosis would be a psychoanalytic developmental diagnosis that includes an assessment of the structure of the ego in which the symptom is embedded (Eissler 1953), that is, regarding borderline pathology not as an entity, but as the vast developmental territory of severe personality disturbance in which there are chronic impairments in adaptive functioning in social, interpersonal, or occupational roles. In Kernberg's (1975) schema of borderline personality organization, very different from the DSM borderline diagnosis, those with this diagnosis differ from neurotics by employing primarily primitive defenses, such as splitting, denial, displacement, projection, magical thinking, projective identification, introjection, and turning against the self. These borderline phenomena and others, including the failure to have attained self and object constancy, the intolerable conflict between the wish to merge versus the fear of merger, and the lack of signal anxiety, are thought to have their origin in failures in development in the separation-individuation phase or rapprochement subphase (Blanck and Blanck 1974, Kernberg 1975, Masterson and Rinsley 1975). Consistent with this is the view that the etiology of borderline personality is a developmental disorder of character that leads to an arrest of object relationships at the stage of the transitional object (Modell 1963).

The most frequently noted characteristic of those in the broad borderline range is an impairment of attachment relationships, that is, an impairment in their attachment to internalized objects as well as to real objects in the external world. I would propose that those who binge and purge, self-mutilate, or otherwise characteristically harm themselves are either arrested at or regress to a pretransitional level of object relations in which either borderline or narcissistic features are prominent. Those with personality disorders are given to repetitions and reenactments of early experience. Their splitting of self and object representations makes them prone to narcissistic rage and to expressing their anger and emotional pain through the body, making them more prone to self-harm. In both borderline and severe narcissistic personalities there is a preoccupation with bodily experience that represents an attempt to establish or restore body integrity (Krueger 1989).

Walsh and Rosen (1988) have reviewed the studies regarding the association between self-mutilating behavior and BPD, and found empirical support for the association in both directions: borderlines have been found to be frequently self-mutilative, and self-mutilators have been found to be frequently diagnosed as borderlines. Heller (1990) has found that subgroups of bulimics, self-mutilators, and bulimic self-mutilators all had differing manifestations of what was a similar illness found in a similar character structure. Most of her subjects were found to be functioning in the borderline range. Similarly, the psychoanalytic literature on alcoholism was traced from its early conceptualization as a manifestation of oral narcissism, latent homosexuality, and repressed aggression to the current view of its being a manifestation of ego deficits and poor affect tolerance (Levin and Weiss 1994). In both the older and newer views is the implicit notion of alcoholism as a developmental disorder of a borderline nature. That is, most alcoholics are borderline, narcissistic, or both. They tend to have had a relationship with their mothers that discouraged the communication of the normal developmental need for help, in which their mothers could not serve to regulate their infant's physical or emotional states. Left alone to soothe themselves, they developed deficits in their self-regulatory abilities. As adolescents and adults they found alcohol to be a potent regulator.

Bulimia nervosa is considered to be a disorder characterized by numerous ego deficits, particularly alexithymia (Cochrane et al. 1993) and impulsivity (Garner 1993, Reto 1993). However, only one-quarter to one-third of the eating disorder population has been found to manifest ego deficits and symptoms characteristic of borderline disorders, while the majority have been found to present with false-self/narcissistic characteristics (Johnson 1991, Johnson and Connors 1987). In her study of bulimics' conceptualizations of their disorder, Teusch (1988) found that the sample was well above average in level of ego development, suggesting that bulimics may function at a higher level of ego development than is usually reported in the literature. Aronson (1986) found that there was no correlation between the severity of the symptoms and the level of object relations or developmental deficits in normal-weight bulimic women. That is, patients with equally severe eating-disorder symptoms were found to have diagnoses in the neurotic, character-disordered, or psychotic range. This suggests that those patients presenting with bulimic behavior, like those presenting with self-mutilating behavior, are subject to premature and inconclusive diagnostic labeling, often as borderline personalities.

Thus, there is disagreement about the alexithymia construct and whether bulimics suffer from it. Alexithymia is considered to be an arrest of ego development in which individuals have failed to develop the ability to use words as symbols to describe their emotional states. Nemiah and colleagues (1976) believe that there is a hereditary constitutional defect in psychosomatic patients that results in the ego's failure to fantasize, dream, and use words symbolically to describe and identify feeling states, a point of view supported by Krueger (1989), Lichtenberg (1983), Taylor (1987) and Taylor and colleagues (1991). On the other hand, the editors (Wilson et al. 1983) and other contributors to *Fear of Being Fat* (Gerald Freiman, Melitta Sperling, Howard Welsh, Charles Sarnoff) do not believe that what appears to be a presymbolic and nonconflictual presentation is caused by a constitutional ego defect but is instead the result of a defensive ego regression from intrapsychic conflict whose etiology derives from infancy and early childhood. These authors believe that with careful psychoanalytic work, the fantasies accompanying the impulse, action, and defense can become available. Similarly, there are some individuals who function at a relatively high level of object relations and have the capacity to use words expressively and symbolically, who may regress to a presymbolic alexithymic level at times of extraordinary stress or after suffering an acute trauma. At such times they may self-mutilate. Their self-harm may reflect a constitutional endowment with more than the usual share of aggression that becomes directed at the body and self at such difficult times. While they may at times exhibit what are thought to be borderline features, they may not be characteristically alexithymic or borderline.

Bulimic behavior was found to be used as a means of regulating affect in borderline bulimics; they reported significantly greater reductions in both anxiety and depression than did non-borderline bulimics (Steinberg et al. 1990). Alcoholics, too, were found to use alcohol as a means of regulating affect (Khantzian 1997).

Both impulsivity and severe bulimic symptomatology were associated with and predicted by a history of physical abuse (Reto et al. 1993). Lacey (1993) proposed the existence of a syndrome, impulsive personality disorder, based on finding a core group of bulimic women characterized by numerous self-damaging and addictive behaviors, specifically substance abuse, overdosing, self-mutilation, and stealing, as well as a history of sexual abuse. In a study of self-mutilation in personality disorders, the degree of self-mutilating behavior was correlated with impulsivity, chronic anger, and somatic anxiety (Simeon et al. 1992). Vanderlinden and Vandereycken (1997) describe a group of eating-disordered patients seen in their clinic in Belgium who also exhibit serious dissociative symptoms and impulse control problems. They behave in ways that are harmful to themselves, engaging in self-mutilation, excessive drinking, drug use, and impulsive sexuality. Often they have a history of severe trauma, notably sexual and physical abuse.

Both bulimic and self-mutilating behavior may be symptoms of the narcissistic disturbance that arises in patients who, as children, never received the loving care, warmth, and stimulation (tactile, visual, and acoustic) needed for becoming a healthy adult. Their self-harm reflects a hunger for these missed experiences. However, it is not only deprivation that can be a factor in the development of a hunger disease leading to self-harm. Those who were cared for excessively and indulgently and those who were stimulated excessively in early life can come later in life to hunger for what they had received excessively. Another factor in the development of self-harm is the creation of a false or ideal self, built up in childhood, in a constant effort to receive approval or love, by those who had to adapt constantly to their parents' expectations. When bingeing and purging and self-mutilating behaviors become severe and addictive in nature, such persons would meet Kohut's (1977) criteria for narcissistic behavior disorder, the "temporary breakup, enfeeblement, or serious distortion of the self, manifested predominantly by alloplastic symptoms, such as perversion, delinquency, or addiction" (p. 193).

Kernberg (1992) has found that tendencies toward chronic and potentially severe self-mutilation and nondepressive suicidal behaviors frequently accompany the syndrome of malignant narcissism, and that the self-mutilating behavior reflects an unconscious identification with a hateful and hated object.

Mood Disorders

The mood disorders have been found to be associated with bulimia, anorexia nervosa, self-mutilating behavior, and sadomasochistic sexuality. Although there is controversy about the idea that eating disorders are variants of affective disorders (Polivy and Herman 1993), a review of the literature revealed, however, that there is considerable overlap between anorexia nervosa and depression (Levy and Dixon 1985). It is necessary to determine if the depression is a manifestation of an independent diagnosis of major depression or dysthymia or if it is related to the eating disorder alone, as a product of failure of impulse control or impaired relationships. Symptoms noted in both include insomnia, depressed mood, loss of libido, and a disturbance in concentration. Also, an anaclitic depression has been found to underlie anorexia nervosa (Sugarman et al. 1981). The anorectic symptomatology was found to serve as a defense against the sense of depression, and the experience of loss and helplessness to which anorectic individuals are prone in the face of separation experiences.

A minority of patients with bulimia have been found to have a coexisting affective disorder (Fairburn 1985). Depression and substance abuse were about 4 times greater in the group of women treated for bulimia than in bulimics in the general population (Bushnell et al. 1994). In clinical practice, bulimic, anorectic, and self-mutilating behavior as well as substance abuse often serve as defenses against depression and as ways of regulating mood and affect. Borderline bulimics reported significantly greater reductions in both anxiety and depression following the binge-purge episode than nonborderline bulimics, who reported a slight increase in depression following the episode (Steinberg et al. 1990).

The severity of purging has been found to be associated with greater disturbance in a number of areas, including depression and increased and more severe self-mutilation. Patients who employed more than one purging strategy were found to be more disturbed on a number of psychiatric indices, including state and trait depression (Tobin et al. 1992). Patients who purged more severely, in terms of frequency and number of methods, had higher scores on a suicidality scale and self-mutilated more severely than patients who purged less severely (Farber 1995a). Self-mutilation, especially self-cutting, is thought to be a means to alleviate depressive affect (Bach-Y-Rita 1974, Favazza 1987), and may be used to counter the vegetative signs of depression that have been associated with self-mutilation (Kahan and Pattison 1984, Pattison and Kahan 1983) such as overeating and sleeping. Cutting and burning oneself may temporarily alleviate depressive affect by providing a welcome distraction and by providing physical punishment in addition to their self-punishing thoughts. In fact, the findings of my study suggest that patients who suffer from the depressive affect and anxiety associated with abandonment depression and posttraumatic stress use the most severe purging and self-mutilation as a means of enlivening a deadened self. Many of them do not binge at all; some use both self-starvation and severe purging. Clinicians who must evaluate and effectively triage self-harming patients would benefit from utilizing the severity of purging (number of purging strategies as well as frequency of purging) and the severity of self-mutilation as indicators of the severity of depression and other possible comorbidity.

Psychosomatic Disorders

Both eating disorders and self-mutilation can be regarded as psychosomatic disorders, real illnesses that are either produced or maintained by a disturbed mind–body relationship (Weiner and Fawzy 1989). These include not only the disordered eating and self-mutilating behavior per se but also the numerous medical and psychological problems associated with them. In fact, anorexia nervosa has been regarded as the quintessential paradigm for understanding psychosomatic disorders (Kaufman and Heiman 1964, Lowy 1983). In people who develop eating disorders as well as other psychosomatic disorders, it is thought that there was a failure in the mother's ability to handle and nurture her child, so that an integrated sense of a mind–body self, or what I like to think of as a self housed in the body, does not develop. There occurs a split between the soma and the psyche (Winnicott 1949), a dissociated space between the body and the mind; the child is not able to experience his psychological self as housed in his body, but instead experiences primarily a depersonalized bodily self. In anorexia there is a dichotomous split between the mind and body in which the patient cannot tolerate or identify unpleasant emotional states but instead uses her body via the eating disorder to solve these psychological problems. That is, the person's "solution" to the problem of unpleasant emotional states that she cannot tolerate experiencing is to master and control the body. That is, starving her body, exercising it excessively as if it were a machine, stuffing it with food and then purging it, or cutting, scratching, or burning it is a concrete, bodily solution to complex psychological problems.

Engel and Schmale (1967) found a relationship between real, threatened, or symbolic object loss and the onset or exacerbation of illness. They found there was an intervening transitional psychobiological ego state between the object loss and the onset of illness. This transitional ego state, the "giving up/given up" complex, occurs when defenses or methods for coping with the loss have not yet developed, and are associated with depressive affects of helplessness and hopelessness thought to initiate autonomic, endocrinological, and immunological processes that lower resistance and allow illness to develop. Such a transitional ego state seems to be operative among those who use disordered eating, self-mutilation, and other psychosomatic illnesses to regulate dysphoric affect, especially in association with an actual or perceived loss of an important relationship. Similarly, Masterson (1972) found that when the adolescent perceives that his struggle for separation and individuation (Mahler et al. 1975) is punished by his mother's emotional abandonment of him, he usually gives up the struggle by succumbing to illness. Much of the time the illness to which he succumbs is an eating disorder, self-mutilation, or other illness alarming enough to cause family members, the mother especially, to rally to his side. While his falling ill makes it seem that he has given up the struggle, it may be more accurate to regard his illness as an escalated unconscious attempt to capture his mother's love and attention.

Sperling (1978) has found that the dynamics in anorexia nervosa and in ulcerative colitis are similar somatic expressions of depression. The coexistence of asthma and anorexia has been noted in the literature (Mintz 1989, Silverman 1989), an involvement of two physical systems that serve as lifelines. I have treated a young woman who suffered from asthma since early childhood, and at different times from anorexia nervosa, bulimia nervosa, and compulsive eating; I am currently treating a woman who suffers from asthma, which began in early childhood, and compulsive eating.

Some theorists posit that there is a psychotic core (Grotstein 1981, McDougall 1989, Taylor 1987, Tustin 1981) or a black hole (Grotstein 1981) in the ego, a sense of "private madness" (Green 1975) that contributes to somatic illness. This can be understood in relation to bulimic and self-mutilating episodes and to sadomasochistic sexual practices. That is, these kinds of self-harm are often used defensively by individuals when they fear that they will go crazy. For them, resorting to "mad" behavior serves as a defense against the fear of going mad.

Others, echoing Winnicott's (1949) concept of the dissociated mind–body split, propose that various ego defects, such as somatization (Dunbar 1954, Schur 1955), alexithymia (Krueger 1989, Krystal 1978, Nemiah et al. 1976, McDougall 1989, Taylor 1987, Taylor et al. 1991, Terr 1973, 1990), a split-off regressed part of the ego (McDougall 1989, Wilson 1989, Wilson et al. 1983), operatory thinking (Marty and de M'Uzan 1963), and regressive dissociative states (Giovacchini 1993, Reiser 1966) contribute to somatic illness. Others conclude that it is a disturbed mother–infant relationship (Benedek 1949, 1959, Mahler and McDevitt 1982, Mahler et al. 1975, McDougall 1989, Pines 1980, Sperling 1978, Winnicott 1949) that results in the various ego defects that contribute to the development of psychosomatic difficulties. In patients inclined toward psychosomatic solutions, the body has been found to express what cannot be said verbally. Two crucial questions are: Who is speaking when the body speaks? With whom is the body speaking? (Deutsch 1959). This is particularly true for those who have suffered severe trauma. Either lacking the ability to use words for expression of affect or regressing to a dissociated state that precludes verbal expression of affect, these individuals are prone to using their bodies to serve as the arena for ego-state reenactments of the trauma (Terr 1973, 1990), such as are often found in conversion hysteria, disordered eating, and self-mutilating behavior, or for specific or diffuse sensation in the affected part of the body (Bass and Davis 1988, Farber 1995a,b, 1997).

Interestingly, the majority of patients diagnosed as having multiple personality disorder report binge-purgeing behaviors (Kluft 1993, Torem 1986) and self-mutilating behavior (Bliss 1980, Kluft 1993). In addition, these patients as a group reported an extensive array of somatic symptoms and many illnesses; they frequent physicians' offices quite often, use medications excessively, and invite unnecessary surgeries (Bliss 1980).

ADAPTATION AND DIMENSIONS
OF THE SELF-HARM SPECTRUM

The human tendency for self-harm is complex and multidetermined. To understand self-harm behavior, each act of self-harm must be considered along the dimensions introduced earlier: its lethality, degree of repetitiveness, directness, degree to which the behavior is compulsive or impulsive, extent to which the behavior is acceptable to the ego, level of consciousness or degree and quality of dissociation maintained during the episode, degree to which the intent is suicidal or sadomasochistic, expressive functions served by the behavior, and other adaptive functions that the behavior serves. (The clinical assessment of self-harm is discussed in Part IV.)

The notion that self-harm can serve adaptive functions can be best understood through understanding the concept of adaptation, which evolved from Hartmann's synthesis of concepts from animal studies, psychology, biology, and culture and anthropology in order to expand psychoanalytic conceptualization (Blanck and Blanck 1974). Finding that drive theory was not sufficient to explain the relatedness that exists between the self and the other, or the self and the object, his interest turned to understanding the functions of the ego. Hartmann (1939) defined adaptation as an ego function, "primarily a reciprocal relationship between the organism and its environment" (p. 24). He provided a way of understanding how each side of the reciprocity and interdependency, the infant (the organism) and its mother (the environment), contributes to it.

On the side of the infant, the infant develops functions that can be used for adaptation. The infant develops the ability to act upon itself (autoplastic activity) and the ability to elicit responses from the environment (alloplastic activity). The adaptive function, along with the other ego functions, develops from inborn ego apparatuses. Under normal developmental conditions, the ego functions remain in the conflict-free sphere, but under the influence of traumatic developmental circumstances, the ego functions may become involved in conflict, rendering them compromised for continued development. Hartmann formulated the idea that on the side of the environment is primarily the mother and her maternal needs, which reciprocate the infant's needs, and then behind the mother stand the husband, the family, the social structure. Hartmann assumed that the environment was the "average expectable environment," or, using Winnicott's (1965) language, that the mother was the "good enough" mother who could reciprocate the infant's needs, not perfectly but well enough to promote healthy development of the infant. For example, at the time the mother is experiencing the fullness and slight engorgement of her milk-laden breasts, the newborn's hunger cry and suckling at her breast is reciprocated by the mother's let-down reflex, and the subsequent flow of breast milk into the infant's mouth as he continues to suckle thus relieves the mother of the pain of engorged breasts. Both baby and mother bask together in the glow of well-being created by this reciprocal relationship. In this way the baby and mother fit together by means of this regulating process to maintain the interdependent equilibrium.

How well or poorly they fit together can be influenced by constitutional factors or the external environment of the partners. A problem arises if, for example, the mother has little ability to produce milk for her baby. A positive adaptation can develop if her sense of self-esteem is sufficient for her to get beyond this disappointment, obtaining maternal pleasure through holding and singing to her baby as she bottle-feeds him. An unfortunate possibility, however, is that the mother feels maternally deficient and may become angry at her baby, causing her to pull away from him and reject him in other ways, severely rupturing the bond between the two or precluding it from developing. The infant can respond to this faulty adaptation by refusing to eat when offered formula or other food, possibly developing ultimately into a failure-to-thrive syndrome. The cover drawing of Battegay's (1991) book, *Hunger Diseases*, is a disturbing picture of a mother turning away in despair, her shriveled and bony infant lying unheld and untouched in her lap. Hartmann (1939) asks, "Is the relationship of the child to his mother or the care of children not a biological process?" (p. 33), and answers, "In our opinion the psychological is not an 'antithesis' to the biological, but rather an essential part of it" (p. 34). When the environment is not an average expectable environment, when there has been the reciprocal need to adapt to trauma, the child's adaptation will reflect that trauma and in some way repeat it.

How can the self-harm behavior that is symptomatic of underlying pathological processes be understood according to the principle of overdetermination, the idea that psychological symptoms are caused by more than one factor? How can these symptoms be understood as serving multiple functions (Waelder 1936)? How can these symptoms be understood as compromise formations (Brenner 1982), solving a conflict among the psychic apparatus (ego, aggressive and libidinal drives, superego), the repetition compulsion, and the demands of the outside world? How can the patient's unconscious selection of the symptom or symptom cluster be understood? What are the expressive functions served by the symptoms?

NAVIGATING THE BORDERLAND
AND EXPLORING THE MARGINS

How do we come to know our experience? To know what it is we have experienced in our lives, we must take it in and metabolize it just as we must eat and metabolize food, so that it becomes part of our lived self, just as our food becomes absorbed.

Human experience is composed of the dialectical interplay between three different modes of generating experience: the depressive mode (Klein 1964), the paranoid-schizoid mode (Klein 1964), and the autistic-contiguous mode (Ogden 1989, 1990). The depressive position, the most mature form of psychological organization, is marked by true symbol formation, which "allows one to experience oneself as a person, thinking one's thoughts and feeling one's feelings" (Ogden 1990, p. 71). In the paranoid-schizoid mode, there is virtually no real difference between the symbol and the symbolized. When the symbol and the symbolized are equivalent, this mode of symbolization is called a symbolic equation. The autistic-contiguous mode is even more primitive, the most rudimentary sense of self formed by the rhythm of sensation, especially the sensations at the skin's surface. Because it is basic to the earliest relations with objects—the nursing experience and the experience of being held, rocked, sung and spoken to—it is a mode that is very difficult to describe in words. These three modes exist in all of us in a dialectical relationship to one another, with each "creating, preserving, and negating the others." The thought of a single mode of functioning without a relation to the other two modes is, states Ogden, "as meaningless as the concept of the conscious mind in isolation from the concept of the unconscious mind; each is an empty set filled by the other pole or poles of the dialectic" (pp. 69–70). "The autistic-contiguous mode provides a good measure of the sensory continuity and integrity of experience (the sensory 'floor'); the paranoid-schizoid mode is a principal source of the immediacy of concretely symbolized experience; the depressive mode is a principal medium through which historical subjectivity and the richness of symbolically mediated human experience are generated" (p. 92).

Psychopathology can be thought of as a collapse of the abundance of experience generated between these poles, in the direction of any one of the poles.

> Collapse toward the autistic-contiguous pole generates imprisonment in the machinelike tyranny if attempted sensory-based escape from the terror of formless dread by means of reliance on rigid autistic defenses. Collapse into the paranoid-schizoid pole is characterized by imprisonment in a nonsubjective world of thoughts and feelings experienced in terms of frightening and protective things that simply happen and cannot be thought about or interpreted. Collapse in the direction of the depressive pole involves a form of isolation of oneself from one's bodily sensations and from the immediacy of one's lived experience, leaving one devoid of spontaneity and aliveness. [Ogden 1990, p. 92]

A transitional area of experience exists between the inside of the self and what is outside the self, between that which is normal and that which is pathological. The body is the dwelling place for the self, at the surface of which is the skin, the body's largest sensory organ, of which our hair, nails, and teeth are derivatives. The transparent cornea of the eye is covered by a layer of modified skin; the skin turns inward to line our bodily orifices, our mouth, nostrils, and anal canal, creating a transition between what is outside and what is inside. Even our soft inner organs are covered by a skin-like membrane, an internal skin. Our skin marks the boundary between what is self and what is outside the self. At the same time that the skin is a boundary, it is also permeable, a sieve that allows for exchange of gas, moisture, and nutrients (Lappe 1996). The skin is the body's edge, and yet "it is a profound paradox of nature that the boundary where we leave off and our external environment begins is demarcated by an organ with so few sensory systems and nerves" (Lappe 1996, p. 15).

Because nature is no fool we have, instead, at the body's edge, the organs that allow us to perceive the world outside ourselves—our skin for touching and being touched, our eyes for taking in what we see, our ears for taking in what we hear, our nose for taking in odors and scents, our mouths for taking in food and drink, our synesthetic sense for weaving different senses together so that the stimulation of one sense stimulates another. Our senses help us to make sense of life, to detect the world through the "radar-net of our senses," to define the edge of consciousness (Ackerman 1990). Our senses can connect us to pleasurable memories, as in Proust's famous limeflower tea and madeleines or when we seek out the "comfort foods" of our childhood, or they can connect us instantly to traumatic memories from the past. "Most people think of the mind as being located in the head, but the latest findings in physiology suggest that the mind doesn't really dwell in the brain but travels the whole body on caravans of hormone and enzyme, busily making sense of the compound wonders we catalogue as touch, taste, smell, hearing, vision" (Ackerman 1990, p. xix).

We all have a psychosomatic potential. We need to take in and metabolize our experience. Metabolizing pleasurable memories is easy for most of us. Metabolizing traumatic memories, on the other hand, is not as these memories are more likely to be repressed, or what is a more serious problem for development, to be dissociated and stored in the body. We want to keep from knowing what horrific thing happened, to keep it out of our consciousness. The lengths to which we might go to keep from metabolizing what we do not want to know is astonishing. We manage to dissociate our affect from the cognitive memory of the event, speaking blandly and matter-of-factly about what we endured. The experience, while in consciousness, is not metabolized. The metabolism of experience requires that the cognitive memory and the affect connected to it become joined together in consciousness. Or we may dissociate the memory entirely, and not having a place in our consciousness, the total experience is stored in the dissociated space in the body. The body then comes to know what the mind does not remember. But unmetabolized experience has a power and energy of its own. Like a piece of food lodged in the throat, we must either swallow and metabolize it or discharge it. Violent force may be needed to dislodge it, such as in the Heimlich maneuver. In any case, unmetabolized experience pushes for discharge, for motor release. The body arranges for motoric discharge, exercising madly even when the body is beginning to break, shoving monstrous portions of food into the body, only to purge it even more violently, dancing wildly, the hand punching out the window, the blade in hand cutting the flesh. We come to live on "the primitive edge of experience" (Ogden 1990), in the borderland, the body speaking "that which is known but not yet thought" (Bollas 1987, p. 4) or speaking that which is known but not known at the same time, the dissociated doublethink.

It is a silent voice and it is bodily language that must be decoded. They take what had been stored inside and bring it outside, to be seen and heard. "There will be no sound . . . only unfelt and silent pain which makes its appearance in another pain, self-inflicted, and when that second, collateral pain emerges, it will articulate in blood or blisters the open definition you desire, although it may not be in a language you care to see. This, it says, is pain, and this is real in any language you care to speak" (McLane 1996, p. 111). And so the person must learn through her body how to speak of the unspeakable. Through her body she might learn to articulate her experience, especially if she has another to help her decode and to listen to the dark terrible voice. This is the borderland, the space between the borders that separate the DSM diagnostic categories, the crack through which many patients fall and become lost. It is a broad territory, ranging from the shocking and dangerous behavioral and relational manifestations of psychotic and borderline patients to the far milder and benign manifestations in neurotics. The borderland is the place where significant personal meaning is experienced in enactments on the body and in reenactments in relationships. Some people live most of the time on the primitive edge of experience, while others drop in from time to time to visit, but do not for the most part live there.

Although many of us are careful today not to allow our skin to tan enough to peel, we probably can remember the days when we cultivated a tan, and what it was like when the tanned skin started to peel. A dry thin translucent layer starts to slough off, the edges pulling away from the moister healthy skin beneath. There is just enough edge for fingers to grasp carefully, a gentle assist to the body in shedding this now superfluous layer. Just as Mount Everest invites climbing, peeling skin seems to invite peeling, a kind of ritualistic grooming behavior akin to the way a cat will lick and pick at its coat. I can recall this as an event in summer camp, an activity when a girl's tan would start to peel. She'd lie face down on her bed, as the rest of us stationed ourselves around her, jockeying for position to peel off the most inviting looking sheets of dead skin. A passage in Kathryn Harrison's (1991) novel *Thicker Than Water* beautifully describes this fascination.

Later that night, before she dresses for a date, she lies on the bed in her underwear, facedown. I sit on the firm cushion of her bottom, knees straddling her hips, and carefully, carefully, I pull the dead tan skin off in big strips. Where it has started to bubble between her shoulder blades, I pull gently, my fingers trying not to tear. It's very hot this evening and her sweat gathers in tiny blisters that lift the dead skin away from the fresh layers underneath. When I'm finished peeling, her back is all smooth and coppery. . . . When I hold it up to the light, I can see a pattern of tiny holes where little hairs were growing. [p. 52]

In her novel *Cat's Eye*, Margaret Atwood (1989) also has written a startlingly graphic description of deliberate skin peeling and chewing. This skin, however, is not dead skin; it is live and vital tissue.

I peeled the skin off my feet . . . at night, when I was supposed to be sleeping. . . . I would begin with the big toes. I would bend my foot up and bite a small opening in the thickest part of the skin, on the bottom, along the outside edge. Then, with my fingernails . . . I would pull the skin off in narrow strips. I would do the same to the other big toe, then to the ball of each foot, the heel of each. I would go down as far as the blood. . . . In the mornings I would pull my socks on over my peeled feet. It was painful to walk, but not impossible. The pain gave me something definite to think about, something immediate. It was something to hold onto. . . . I chewed the ends of my hair, so that there was always one lock of hair that was pointed and wet. I gnawed the cuticles off from around my fingernails, leaving welts of exposed, oozing flesh which would harden into rinds and scale off. . . . I did these things constantly, without thinking about them. But the feet were more deliberate. [p. 120]

Children bite or pick at their skin, hair, or nails (Buxbaum 1960). Young children like to taste and chew the products and secretions of their own bodies, including mucus, fecal matter, or blood, so it is no coincidence that a gooey substance called Slime is a favorite toy of preschoolers. It is also in the nature of human experience for young children to rock themselves, bang their heads, suck their thumbs, or chew their tongues (Silberstein et al. 1966). These are normal phenomena in infants that satisfy an instinctual need and facilitate motor and ego growth and development (Lourie 1949). Children tend to select these techniques opportunistically, depending on the age at which tension arises and the availability of particular sensations at that phase of their development (Silberstein et al. 1966). In the process of training our children to be polite, civilized human beings, these urges come under the influence of the ego and superego. They become dormant in later childhood, reappearing in preadolescence and adolescence, to their parents' dismay. Preadolescent boys love "gross out" foods like an aerosol foam that oozes out of their mouth or a viscous green candy called Snot. They pull "boogers" from their nose to flick at a friend or fart on demand. Even college students, girls included, are known to keep BM charts on the wall of the communal bathroom, charting the size, shape, degree of firmness, color, and smell of their bowel movements.

But when infantile motor or oral behavior patterns become prominent in the child's personality, they serve other needs, including the expression of pleasure, expression and relief of tension and anxiety, and provision of a form of compensatory satisfaction, and they then persist past the infantile period. They may serve transitional functions, substituting for the soothing rocking, crooning, and holding that an attentive and attuned mother can provide. While most observant parents have probably noted such behavior in their young children, it is also in the nature of human experience to be so disgusted by it that they fail to remember it and fail to acknowledge the remnants of these behaviors in themselves. And so when at the playful performance art show *Blue Man Group*, the actors and participating members of the audience regurgitate what seem like endless streams of goo, it acknowledges these infantile remnants and the audience roars with laughter.

What distinguishes those who peel off the dead skin of already peeling suntans and those who scratch or tear away at live tissue? Or to put it another way, if we regard the skin as the body's container, what distinguishes those who peel off a dead layer of epidermis containing no nerves or blood vessels from those who peel off an integral layer of living dermal tissue? In the former there is an integrity to the skin that allows an unnecessary layer to be shed, as a snake sheds his skin or a butterfly his chrysalis. In the latter, there is the removal of the boundary between life and death. That is, it is the skin that is the boundary between life and death, with skin continually generating a layer of dead tissue that serves as a "life-preserving outermost layer of the body" (Ogden 1996, p. 181). Peel off the life-preserving dead layer and you have begun to skin someone alive.

Perhaps somewhere in between the normal and pathological is a primitive impulse to self-grooming that has gone awry. Freud (1937) wrote, "For every normal person is in fact only normal on the average. His ego approximates to that of the psychotic to a greater or lesser extent; and the degree of its remoteness from one end of the series and the proximity to the other will furnish us with a provisional measure of what we have so indefinitely termed an alteration of the ego" (p. 235). Where is the line between ordinary grooming behavior and self-harm? Between tweezing ones eyebrows to get a more fashionable look, and compulsively plucking out all the eyebrow hairs? Where is the line between ordinary nail biting and the kind that results in infected and bleeding fingers? Similarly, should we regard the normative female obsession of girls and women with thinness and dieting as skills training for anorectics- and bulimics-to-be? This obsession with thinness and fitness, the culturally acceptable fear of being fat, is the bridge between the woman who is continually "dying to lose ten pounds" and the woman who is at risk for dying from an eating disorder.

The transitional space (Winnicott 1953), that intermediate arena of experience between that which is normal and that which is pathological, is the most interesting space to explore. It is the border lines and the marginal space, the edge and the space "between the thumb and the teddy bear" (p. 230), that invites exploration to those whose fear does not stand in the way. Novick and Novick (1996) have described the "borderland" as follows:

> Many theorists have described omnipotent fantasies as part of borderline disorders. Borderline patients were first described in 1884 in the journal *Alienist and Neurologist* by Hughes and Russell. They referred to such patients, however, as "borderland patients," which seems clinically very apt. . . . We too prefer describing a place to labeling a person. When a patient is called "borderline" there is an implication of difference from us, with an assumed scale of superiority ranging from normal down to neurotic, borderline, and then psychotic. But when a patient is operating in a borderland we can join him there if we have the bravery, skill, and desire to do so. If we are secure in our original identity, we may safely travel and explore, trying to see the other place through this person's eyes. [p. 356]

A social work graduate student gave me the following poem, written by her roommate, part of a collection entitled *Chalkboard with a Bad Eraser*, which was subsequently published in 1996. The poems are dark and disturbing, having to do with abuse, self-hatred, sadism, masochism, and self-harm.

Song of the Brufiliac

Hello. My name is Catherine Taormina

I am a brufiliac.

I am 5 months pregnant but

the doctors say there is no

child in my womb.

I started irritating when I was 13 mostly

because of physiological changes but now I feel this

irritating is soothing. It is, simply, cost free & doesn't directly harm

anyone (as far as I know of)

except me.

My first infliction began after a visit to a neighborhood dentist. I had received a large dose of his venom and unconsciously bit my cheek. After the anesthetic wore off, my cheek was left with a dangling piece of flesh which became a new playtoy for my tongue. Tongue. How many times do I have to tell you not to rip your taste buds off when you have a sore on your tongue.

My tongue-n-cheek had a problem for the next seven years. That then diminished with the stomach, thigh & ass problems. When my stomach didn't get food, my thighs & ass were happy. And when my stomach did get food, my thighs and ass were livid. Oh, it is worthy of mention that 4 years into my first infliction hand and ear frequented each other quite often & hand simply shredded ear to bits. It was awful. Ear never did anything to hand. Then every so often my playtoy would be spontaneously recovered.

As I grew, my skin received parcels with fat white presents & hand left ear for face, back & chest. In the prime of adolescence I plucked my pubes out one by one & continue to do so on boring occasions. It kinda looks gross. In time, some things grated on my brain and I'd scratch the outside covering. These past 4 years have been especially hard & I've lost a lot of hair unnecessarily. This last soother remains with me today but my nose mediates between the two. My nose is also a mediator for operation belly-button.

So I know I'm a brufiliac. I know its a problem but I don't want to stop. It's like blistiks on chapped lips or water for a shriveled stomach. I enjoy what I do. As I said, this irritating is soothing. Two negatives = a positive, and I can go on and so I'm here because this hurt will harm. [Taormina 1996]

The borderland is where Eve, a self-destructive masochistic woman in the film *Female Perversions*, lives. Screenwriter Susan Streitfeld said online: "It's a very freeing book because it ultimately talks about behavior in terms of attaching it to history, society and family. So it's not as if I'm the only person with this behavior in the world and I am fucked up around it." Actress Tilda Swinton who played Eve, said: "[Her character] is a mirror. It invites projection—the kind of projection that might be very scary for people." Kathleen Wilkinson, reviewing the film, said, "Whether it's eating a one-pound bag of M & Ms, hoping for approval from an unavailable parent, or shopping obsessively, everyone can relate to some aspect of Eve's disorder."

In the film *The Pillow Book*, the body is written on as if it were paper, and becomes a text, carved on the skin with ink and blood. Those women and men who write the stories of their inner pain on and in their bodies are really speaking to and for the rest of us. They are expressing on our behalf those biologically based primal and universal urges that most of us cannot tolerate recognizing in ourselves. Bodily self-harm is a psychosomatic manifestation, and all of us have a psychosomatic potential that can come alive when circumstances in either our inner world or in the external world overwhelm our usual ways of coping (McDougall 1989). It can be a tendency to pick at scabs or cuticles, overeat, or pop pimples. Stoller (1991), in *Pain & Passion*, asks rhetorically, "How common are the little sadomasochisms of everyday life, covert but observable: the skin pinching, cuticle tearing, gum picking, colonic treatments, deep massage, hairpulling-dreamy-self-and-other-stimulations?" (p. 23). These "little sadomasochisms" may be manifestations of a secret that we all want to keep from ourselves, that deep within us exists an encapsulated psychotic core (Freud 1937), our own bit of "private madness" (Green 1975, p. 3).

Neurologist Oliver Sacks is brilliant, talented, and admittedly quite eccentric, with a touch of the autistic in him. In his search to understand people afflicted with grotesque neurological conditions strange enough to be fascinating ("fascinomas" as they are known), Sacks makes "the alien familiar and the familiar new" (Angier 1998, p. 33). He sees aspects of himself in people so afflicted and aspects of them in himself. In looking at those individuals who inflict harm on themselves, we undoubtedly all will, if we are honest with ourselves, find aspects of ourselves in people so afflicted and aspects of them in ourselves. Wendy Lesser (1995), in reviewing Sacks' An Anthropologist on Mars, summarized as follows: "Everybody is peculiar. . . . Oliver Sacks wants us to know that we are all links in the great chain of weirdness" (p. 1).

3

Not Wanting to Know about Self-Harm: Trauma, Violence, and Chronic Mental Illness

In a world full of universal deceit,
telling the truth is a revolutionary act.

George Orwell, *1984*

It is easy to dismiss as meaningless gibberish what the mentally ill have to say and to put them in the category of "other." To hear of experiences of terrible physical and sexual abuse in families is too painful, and so we have not wanted to believe them. It is only recently and reluctantly that we have begun to understand the role of trauma, especially the trauma generated by violence and abuse, in producing the severe symptomatology that we associate with mental illness. With this understanding comes a greater readiness to understand the development of self-harm behavior within the context of trauma and violence. As will be demonstrated, self-harm occurs when the self treats itself as other.

DEINSTITUTIONALIZATION AND THE CHRONIC MENTALLY ILL

We initially modeled our treatment of the mentally ill in the United States after the private English madhouses, where patients were treated with cold baths, forced dunkings, and bloodletting. As treatment of the mentally ill became more "sophisticated," we have instead warehoused such patients in state mental hospitals, where many of them lived for many years, neglected, mistreated, or abused. Those who spoke of experiences of beatings, neglect, and sexual abuse tended not to be believed, their voices often muted or silenced by drugs.

Some patients diagnosed with chronic schizophrenia have filled state hospital beds for decades, receiving minimal clinical reevaluation and often incorrectly diagnosed for a lifetime. The introduction of antipsychotic drugs in 1954 initiated the move toward the grand-scale deinstitutionalization of the chronic mentally ill, when very ill patients were discharged into communities unprepared to care for them. New York State was among the earliest to initiate the use of the new drugs chlorpromazine and reserpine in the public hospitals, and within a year the population in these hospitals began to decline as large numbers of long-term chronic patients were discharged (Shorter 1997).

With deinstitutionalization, the population in the hospitals shifted as more and more patients who had cut their wrists or made suicide attempts were admitted. In 1966, in a paper presented to the American Psychiatric Association, Graff and Mallin stated, "In the past several years wrist slashers have become the new chronic patients in mental hospitals, replacing schizophrenics" (1967, p. 74). In their summary the authors state, "This pattern, stemming from early maternal deprivation, is embedded in their inability to give and receive verbal communications meaningfully. Therapy is directed at fostering more mature methods of giving and receiving love" (1967, p. 79). Numerous reports on self-harm had begun to appear, in which attention was directed at trying to understanding its meaning. Psychoanalysts have contributed many theoretical considerations of childhood self-injury and adolescent and adult self-mutilation (Beres 1952, Bornstein 1953, Boyer 1956, Buxbaum 1960, de Young 1982, Doctors 1981, A. Freud 1949, Gardner and Cowdry 1985, Graff and Mallin 1967, Green 1978, Greenberg and Sarner 1965, Grunebaum and Klerman 1967, Kafka 1969, Kernberg 1987, Kris 1956, Kwawer 1980, Lourie 1949, Mannino and Delgado 1969, Menninger 1935, Nakhla and Jackson 1993, Novotny 1972, Pao 1969, Podvoll 1969, Richards 1988, Rosenthal et al. 1972, Schur 1955, Shapiro 1987, Silberstein et al. 1966, Simpson 1980, Simpson and Porter 1981, Sperling 1968, Stone et al. 1987, Sylvester 1945, Wechsler 1931, Wilson 1989). Attention to the meaning of problematic eating behavior began in the early 1950s, when psychoanalyst Hilde Bruch began to see anorexic patients with some regularity and published several books about eating disorders (Bruch, 1973, 1978, 1985). Several others have focused psychoanalytic scrutiny on eating disorders (Aronson 1986, Chatoor 1989, Goodsitt 1985, Johnson 1991, Ritvo 1988, Sacksteder 1989a,b, Sours 1980, Sperling 1953, 1968, 1978, Sugarman and Kurash 1982, Wilson et al. 1983, Zakin 1989).

Unfortunately, this scientific yet compassionate interest in those who harm themselves was the exception rather than the rule. A harsh, punitive attitude toward self-destructive patients prevailed, as represented by Jack R. Ewalt, president of the American Psychiatric Association, who noted the change in the chronic psychiatric population in his 1964 presidential address: "Our long difficult cases increasingly consist of the character and personality disorders, the wrist slashers, the promiscuous, the improvident and lazy, and the aggressive reactions. We must learn to care for them" (Shorter 1997, p. 61). As one might expect, such moral judgment and abhorrence of these difficult cases would present a major obstacle in learning to care for them. History has shown that this marked antagonism became the prevailing attitude toward the increasing number of chronic patients with severe self-harm symptomatology.

With deinstitutionalization, large numbers of such patients were among those discharged en masse into communities ill-equipped to care for them in municipal hospitals or regional psychiatric units in general hospitals. Community mental health centers were created to care for them, psychiatrists administered large doses of medication and social workers and psychiatric nurses managed the care of these difficult patients, many of whom made what were considered suicide attempts or gestures by cutting themselves, or were given to bingeing, purging, drinking, and drug use. Often they were given a perfunctory diagnosis of borderline personality disorder. If they cut themselves frequently and spoke of hearing voices (Graff and Mallin 1967), they were especially likely to be diagnosed as schizophrenic. Whether considered borderline or schizophrenic, the labels followed most of them for a lifetime of revolving-door hospitalizations and careers as mental patients.

Patients' attempts to harm themselves are often treated punitively by hospital staff, who respond, understandably, with frustration, anger, and anxiety at this behavior they do not understand. Many of these patients are women who have suffered severe abuse and may be overmedicated so that, zombie-like, they no longer have sufficient energy to harm themselves. Or they may be placed in four-point restraints, legs spread-eagled, and left alone for long periods. Basic bodily functions may be supervised and monitored closely and intrusively, as when patients are restrained from using the bathroom after a meal in order to prevent them from vomiting or when a staff member accompanies them into the bathroom. All too frequently their behavior is dismissed as the manipulations of mental patients who "just want some attention."

THE RESISTANCE TO UNDERSTANDING
THE ORIGINS OF TRAUMA

The sexual abuse of children is found with uncanny frequency among school teachers and child attendants, simply because they have the best opportunity for it . . . and fantasies of being seduced are of particular interest, because so often they are not fantasies but real memories.

Sigmund Freud, *Three Essays on the Theory of Sexuality*

I therefore put forward the thesis that at the bottom of every case of hysteria there are one or more occurrences of premature sexual abuse, occurrences which belong to the earliest years of childhood but which can be reproduced through the work of psycho-analysis in spite of the intervening decades.
Sigmund Freud, *The Aetiology of Hysteria*

The development of severe self-harm arises within the context of trauma, and when not correctly diagnosed and treated, can develop into chronic mental illness. Probably a substantial component of the illness is iatrogenic, as will be explained. To understand the origins of self-harm, it is necessary to understand the etiology of psychic trauma. Such understanding has been greatly confounded because Western culture has fiercely resisted understanding the etiology of psychic trauma since a century ago, when Breuer and Freud provided a clinical explanation for it. Freud's original theory of the effect of trauma and childhood abuse, his "source of the Nile" solution to understanding hysteria and conversion hysteria, was virtually ignored until three decades ago.

The study of psychological trauma began with the startling recognition that the etiology of hysterical illnesses in many of Freud's female patients could be traced to the trauma of having been sexually abused in childhood, often by a close relative (Breuer and Freud 1893, Freud 1896). Freud proposed that repressed mental content associated with the traumatic event had become transformed into physical symptoms. Freud (1896) explained that the child is damaged by the overstimulation of his sexuality because "injuries sustained by an organ which is as yet immature, or by a function which is in process of developing, often cause more severe and lasting effects than they could do in maturer years" (p. 202). With great pride in this monumental discovery, Freud presented these findings to the Society for Psychiatry and Neurology in Vienna, ending his talk with an optimistic challenge to the psychiatric community to use this new understanding for the benefit of patients traumatized by sexual abuse and incest. "The new method of research gives wide access to a new element in the psychical field of events, namely, to processes of thought which have remained unconscious. . . . Thus, it inspires us with the hope of a new and better understanding of all functional psychical disturbances. I cannot believe that psychiatry will long hold back from making use of this new pathway to knowledge" (p. 221).

Not only could psychiatry hold back from making use of this new pathway to knowledge, it could not at all tolerate hearing Freud's explanation and was enraged by it. His professional community turned on him ferociously, humiliating and ejecting him from the professional nest. A deeply wounded and angry Freud wrote to Wilhelm Fliess: "A lecture on the aetiology of hysteria at the Psychiatric Society met with an icy reception from the asses, and from Krafft-Ebing the strange comment: It sounds like a scientific fairy tale. And this after one has demonstrated to them a solution to a more than thousand-year-old problem, a 'source of the Nile'!" (Schur 1972, p. 104). To be accepted once again by his peers, Freud did not actually renounce the seduction theory as he has been frequently accused of, but he retreated from it somewhat, allowing for the possibility that the patient's accounts of incestuous sexual abuse could also be fantasies. Freud (1905a) tried to soft-pedal his shocking discovery by saying seduction is not required in order to arouse a child's sexual life, as this can occur from the child's being innately disposed toward polymorphously perverse sexuality.

> The continual disappointment in my efforts to bring any analysis to a real conclusion; the running away of people who for a period of time had been the most gripped [by analysis]; the absence of the complete successes on which I had counted. . . . Then the surprise that in all cases the *father*, not excluding my own, had to be accused of being perverse—the realisation of the unexpected frequency of hysteria, with precisely the same conditions prevailing in each, whereas surely such widespread perversions against children are not very probable. (The perversion would have to be immeasurably more frequent than the hysteria, because the illness, after all, occurs only where there has been an accumulation of events and there is a contributory factor that weakens the defence.) Then, third, the certain insight that there are no indications of reality in the unconscious, so that one cannot distinguish between truth or fiction that has been cathected with affect. (Accordingly, there would remain the solution that the sexual fantasy invariably seizes upon the theme of the parents). [1897; quoted in Masson 1984, pp. 108–109]

At the same time, however, Freud continued to maintain that some reported seductions are undoubtedly real. Sandor Ferenczi (1949) challenged the "repudiation" of the seduction theory, declaring that it is trauma, particularly sexual trauma, that is a pathogenic agent and that sexual abuse of children is common, and received a response from the psychoanalytic community that was similar to the response Freud received (de Zulueta 1994). It was, nevertheless, the theory that it is the child's sexual fantasy rather than the trauma of an actual seduction by the parent that remained the prevailing psychoanalytic theory of perversion, a theory championed today by those who do not want to believe, as Freud did, that some reported seductions were real. The net result was that Freud's original theory of the effect of trauma and childhood abuse was virtually ignored until three decades ago, when a number of other factors converged to make the area of trauma ripe for study.

There has been a flood of reported cases of sexual abuse in the United States, from 6,000 cases in 1976 to 300,000 in 1993 (Ney 1995), evoking a split in the psychotherapeutic field between believers and nonbelievers, and intense and acrimonious debates about the credibility and accuracy of recovered memories of traumatic experiences, especially childhood sexual abuse. The passionate emotions stirred by the issue, the inflammatory media coverage, and the extension of scholarly and clinical disagreements into expert testimony in the legal arena have resulted in polarized positions and vicious debates that obstruct opportunities for dialogue. History does truly repeat itself.

WARTIME VIOLENCE

After World War I Freud addressed the role of wartime combat in the etiology of trauma (de Zulueta 1994), finding that the symptoms of shell shock in soldiers returning from the front could be explained by the repetition compulsion, the way the mind mentally repeats stressful experiences in order to integrate them (Newcombe and Lerner 1982). Once again, Freud was linking the development of psychological symptoms and the experience of psychological trauma. Since World War II, Western culture began paying increasingly more attention to the traumatic effects of violence. During and after the war, medicine struggled to find ways to treat and understand the somatic effects of overwhelming anxiety on millions of soldiers. Fairbairn (1952) and Kardiner (1941) studied the war neuroses, as they were called, Bettelheim (1943) wrote about the concentration camp survivors, and Grinker (1953) found that the symptoms of combat stress syndrome in soldiers (vomiting, diarrhea, headache, tachycardia) represented a dissolution of healthy adult psychological organization and a regression to a far more primitive visceral mode. These observations and those of the post–Vietnam War era, when American psychoanalysts began working with traumatized war veterans, stirred a widespread scientific interest in the concept of psychic trauma and its relation to illness.

HOLOCAUST SURVIVORS

Out of the interest in the traumatic effects of combat, there developed an interest in studying the effects of cataclysmic violence on concentration camp surviors, other survivors of the Holocaust, and the children of Holocaust survivors. An in-depth study was done, using psychoanalytically gathered case material, of the aftereffects of the Holocaust on the surviving victims, their offspring, and the offspring of the Nazi perpetrators (Bergmann and Jucovy 1982). Increasingly, the Nazi perpetrators and the culture of Nazism have come under historical and scientific scrutiny in attempts to understand how ordinary Germans, including physicians (Lifton 1986), not only complied with Hitler's orders but also participated directly in the murders of millions of Jews and others (Goldhagen 1997). According to psychoanalyst Alice Miller (1983), the violence of Nazi Germany can be partially attributed to its traditional child-rearing patterns, which have been aimed at producing extreme obedience. Such training often involved physical and emotional abuse. Hitler himself was reported to have been the victim of the most severe physical and emotional abuse; in a probable identification with the aggressor, he managed to unite the German nation to repeat the trauma they endured, making the Jews and other "undesirables" their victims.

RAPE, DOMESTIC VIOLENCE, AND CHILD ABUSE

As we have become aware of the destructive consequences of war-related trauma, we have become increasingly aware that romantic relationships and parent–child relationships often constitute a combat zone of a different kind, arenas for the infliction of severe physical and psychic trauma (Herman 1992). We have become increasingly more aware of the prevalence and sequelae of child abuse, domestic violence, and rape. Almost half of the 188 psychiatric inpatients interviewed by Carmen and colleagues (1984) had histories of physical and/or sexual abuse, with females far more likely than males to report a history of abuse. Abused males were more likely than abused females or other males to have abused others. In a study of 190 consecutive psychiatric outpatients, 22% were found to have been victims of physical or sexual violence, most of whom (81%) were women who continued to be victims (Herman 1986). Studies of adult rape victims and battered women have found that many were abused physically and sexually as children, and tended to be abused or raped by their spouses or others in adulthood (Browne and Finkelhor 1986). Similar findings have been found consistently in numerous studies that have come to the forefront of interest in research and in clinical communities around the world, affirming what Freud had tried to tell the world about trauma a century ago.

The diagnosis of borderline personality disorder has been associated with a history of abuse, particularly sexual and physical abuse (Herman et al. 1989). However, as they worked with many survivors of severe physical and sexual abuse, van der Kolk (1987) and Herman (1992) came to see a consistent pattern of hyperarousal alternating with numbing; numerous other symptoms such as sleep problems, dissociation, rage, suicidality, self-mutilation, and drug and alcohol addiction; and relationship difficulties similar to the combat syndromes described earlier by Freud and Kardiner. These survivors of prolonged and repeated childhood trauma were the same patients who had become the new chronic psychiatric patients, filling the mental health system's beds, often misdiagnosed and maltreated. By now it has been well documented that over half the self-injurious nonpsychotic patients in psychiatric facilities (in- and outpatient) have been sexually or physically abused in childhood or adolescence. Many clinicians working with the severely traumatized proposed that a diagnostic formulation was needed that went beyond the concept of simple posttraumatic stress disorder, one that takes into account severe, prolonged, and cumulative massive psychological trauma. The diagnoses these patients frequently received in the mental health system, borderline personality disorder, somatization disorder, and multiple personality disorder, became controversial. The borderline diagnosis, because it came to be applied readily and indiscriminately to troublesome patients, was charged with derogatory meaning. Herman (1992) proposed that all three diagnoses be considered variants of complex posttraumatic stress disorder, as each was thought to derive its characteristic features from a form of adaptation to a traumatic environment. The diagnosis of complex posttraumatic stress disorder was thought to inform a direction for treatment, to normalize and validate a trauma survivor's emotional reaction to past events, and recognize that such reactions are maladaptive in the present. It is a diagnosis meant to clarify that the clinical picture of a person reduced to basic concerns about survival is not necessarily the clinical picture of underlying character. The same clinician researchers (van der Kolk et al. 1991) found that histories of childhood sexual and physical abuse were highly significant predictors of self-cutting and suicide attempts. While childhood trauma was found to contribute to the initiation of self-destructive behavior, a lack of secure human attachments was thought to help maintain it.

THE LINK BETWEEN SELF-HARM
AND TRAUMA IS ESTABLISHED

Since Anna Freud's (1946, 1949) efforts to understand various infantile habits and behaviors, numerous child psychoanalysts have tried to understand infantile and childhood eating, feeding, and self-injurious behaviors (Boyer 1956, Buxbaum 1960, Garma 1953, Greenberg and Sarner1965, Krueger 1989, Mannino and Delgado 1969, Monroe and Abse 1963, Selvini-Palazzoli 1974, Silberstein et al. 1966, Sperling 1968, Sugarman and Kurash 1982). Unfortunately, as interest increasingly turned away from psychoanalysis to other psychotherapies and to biological psychiatry, the richness of this body of work was appreciated only by the dwindling numbers of the psychoanalytically minded.

In the early 1950s, however, psychoanalyst Hilde Bruch began to see numbers of anorexic patients and published a book about eating disorders in 1973. By the mid-1970s a handful of specialists were treating people with eating disorders, and by the early 1980s a heightened interest in eating disorders pervaded not only the clinical literature but the media, instigating much investigation of the etiology and treatment of eating disorders. As the public became aware that eating disordered behavior was a known diagnostic entity with available treatment, more individuals with these disorders began to present themselves to clinics and physicians for treatment.

The same sequence of events has begun to occur with the phenomenon of self-mutilation, about which there have been numerous written efforts to understand it from an analytic perspective (Asch 1971, Bollas 1992, Buxbaum 1960, Crabtree 1967, Cross 1993, Doctors 1981, Emerson 1914, Friedman et al. 1972,

Greenberg and Sarner 1965, Kafka 1969, Krueger 1989, Kwawer 1980, Mannino and Delgado 1969, Monroe and Abse 1963, Siomopoulas 1974, Silberstein et al. 1966, Sperling 1968), efforts that are not widely known. There is, however, a current growing awareness of and fascination with self-mutilation that seems to parallel the earlier growing interest in eating disorders (Favazza and Conterio 1988). While both were thought to be rare but fascinating disorders, there is increasing awareness that self-mutilation, like eating disorders, is far more common than had been thought. There has been an explosion of clinical and research literature citing not only eating disorders or self-mutilation separately but also the comorbidity of eating disorders and self-mutilation together as the frequent sequelae of traumatic abuse (Cross 1993, Farber 1990, 1991, 1994, 1995a, 1997, Miller 1994), evidence of a paradigmatic shift (Kuhn 1962) taking us full circle back to trauma. We are picking up today where Freud left off, trying to lead his colleagues to understand the harmful consequences of trauma.

In 1985 an episode of the Phil Donahue television show featured self-abuse, and Karen Conterio, a therapist and research associate working with Dr. Armando Favazza in studying self-mutilation, spoke about her own experiences with self-mutilation. After the show more than a thousand people contacted Ms. Conterio, identifying themselves as self-mutilators, and 250 participated in a survey. Around half of them had been hospitalized, 57 percent had also taken at least one drug overdose, and a third expected to be dead in the next five years (Favazza and Conterio 1988). Not long after this study, Shelley Goldberg, an alcoholism counselor whose skull was completely bald and covered with sores and postules as a result of his hair pulling and head gouging, appeared on the Larry King show to talk about his experience.

Self-mutilation was in the media, and was being recognized, studied, and talked about in much the same way that eating disorders had burst into the nation's consciousness. In 1986, in a collaboration between Dr. Allen Showalter and Karen Conterio, Hartgrove Hospital in Chicago opened the first inpatient facility in the country designed specifically for patients with characterologic or affective disorders who repeatedly injure themselves (Karen Conterio, personal communication). Although self-mutilation had begun to be studied by clinicians and researchers (Favazza 1987, Favazza and Conterio 1988, Favazza and Rosenthal 1990, Favazza et al. 1989, Rosen et al. 1990, Russ 1992, Simeon et al. 1992, Walsh and Rosen 1985, 1988, Winchel 1991, Winchel and Stanley 1991), it was not until it was associated with the trauma of sexual abuse that it was accorded major scientific attention. Armando Favazza's *Bodies Under Siege: Self-Mutilation in Culture and Psychiatry* (1987) was reissued as a revised second edition in 1996 as *Bodies Under Siege: Self-Mutilation and Body Modification in Culture and Psychiatry*. In the preface to the second edition Favazza described the great difficulty he had in getting the book published the first time, receiving numerous rejections from publishers. By the time he revised the book the subject of self-mutilation had gone from receiving a very chilly reception to becoming a hot topic. In nine years the association with trauma and the highly visible and disturbing wave of body modification had made a big difference.

Trauma studies began to look at not only the prevalence but also the destructive consequences of abuse, and feminist researchers especially studied the effects of physical and sexual abuse on women and children. In *Trauma and Recovery: The Aftermath of Violence, From Domestic Abuse to Political Terror*, Judith Herman (1992) bridged the experience of war veterans, prisoners of war, Holocaust survivors, battered woman and children, rape victims, and victims of child sexual abuse to integrate an understanding of the effects of a wide range of traumatic experience on people's thoughts, feelings, and behavior. In 1994 the New York State Department of Mental Hygiene sponsored a statewide telecast on self-mutilation (Favazza 1994), which was viewed simultaneously by the clinical staffs of several New York State psychiatric centers.

Although the association between eating disorders and sexual abuse had already received scientific attention, the association of both eating disorders and self-mutilation within the context of trauma did not receive serious scientific attention until the last decade (Cross 1993, Farber 1991, 1995a,b, 1996a,b,c, Heller 1990, Miller 1994).

In 1996 for the first time in the history of New York, the New York State Mental Health Association sponsored a statewide conference for clinicians, researchers, and survivors specifically to address the treatment of sexual-abuse survivors diagnosed with serious mental illnesses. This conference represented a public acknowledgment that sexual abuse is a major factor in the mental illness seen throughout the New York psychiatric system. Elaine Carmen, M.D., in her keynote address spoke about how psychiatric hospitalization in the Massachusetts system often revictimized and retraumatized patients who had already suffered severe trauma. Mary Auslander, M.S.W., the plenary speaker from the New York State Office of Mental Health, spoke powerfully from the dual viewpoint of an administrator in the mental health system and as a former hospitalized mental patient who experienced the revictimization and retraumatization firsthand. This landmark conference has since become an annual occurrence, bringing together abuse survivors and members of the helping professions, some of whom are also survivors, to build better community resources for trauma survivors. It provides an opportunity for survivors to speak directly about their experiences and an opportunity for clinicians to receive further training and support, and a chance for dialogue between the groups. I did a presentation at the first conference, *Eating Problems and Self-Mutilation in Survivors of Sexual Abuse: Self-Destructiveness or Survival Tools?* (Farber 1996a), a public acknowledgment that both self-mutilation and eating disorders are major problems in abuse survivors diagnosed with serious mental illness that evolve as attempts to cope with the emotional consequences of trauma. Soon after, I did a presentation at the Fifth International Research Conference at the University of New Hampshire, "Bulimic Behavior and Self-Mutilating Behavior as Self-Regulatory Attempts in Trauma Survivors" (Farber 1996c).

We are late in coming to know this about self-harm, in the way that paradigms spin themselves out slowly over time, stumbling over obstacles and fighting resistances as ideas evolve and undergo transformations. Our tardiness in acknowledging the prevalence of self-harm is tied to our tardiness in coming to acknowledge the prevalence of violent trauma in our culture and the tendency toward violence in ourselves. Yet this knowledge has been stored for years in the bodies of the mentally ill and the survivors of trauma. They have written and continue to write about it in *For Crying Out Loud*, in *Body Memories*, in *The Healing Woman*, and in numerous other newsletters for survivors of incest and sexual abuse. They write about it in *The Cutting Edge*, a newsletter for women who live with self-inflicted violence. They write about it in newsletters for those with eating disorders, for those with dissociative disorders, for those who pull out their hair, for those who are tortured by endless obsessional thinking and compulsions. They write about it in radical feminist newsletters and in newsletters for men who have been sexually abused. They speak of it in meetings, in therapy, in speakouts, and in cyberspace. Some of those who have lived with their own self-harm have become the clinical social workers, psychologists, and psychotherapists who speak, teach, and write about self-harm with great courage and dignity (Burstow 1992, Connors 1996a,b, Conterio and Vaughan 1989, Favazza and Conterio 1988, Favazza et al. 1989, Miller 1994, Trautmann and Connors 1994). They are our bridge to understanding self-harm. For far too long those who have lived with the self-harm born of trauma have needed clinicians to listen to them and learn from them (Farber 1998a,b).

It is hardly by chance that *The Scream*, that famous swirling image of horror and dread painted over a hundred years ago by Norwegian artist Edvard Munch, is turning up everywhere—on T-shirts, posters, and coffee mugs. There is a *Scream* pillow with a built-in shrieking voice, a Pontiac commercial that exploits the image to sell cars, Halloween masks inspired by the movie and *Scream* dolls. We hear it in heavy metal rock music and see the image of *The Scream* as the background for an Internet site on self-injury. For many abused and traumatized people who have plenty to scream and cry about, self-harm is what happens when screams are not listened to.

PART II

NEGLECT, VIOLENCE, AND TRAUMATIC ATTACHMENTS

The passion for destruction is a creative joy.
Graffito written during French
student revolt, May 1968

4

Suffering and Self-Harm:
Treating Oneself as the Other

Today violence is the rhetoric of the period.
Jose Ortega y Gasset,
The Revolt of the Masses

DEHUMANIZATION OF THE OTHER
AND VIOLENT SUFFERING

From the beginning of time human beings have preyed upon others defensively so that they cannot be preyed upon. We still tend to disavow our violent
impulses, projecting them onto the other. Those who have suffered extreme narcissistic injuries will tend far more toward dehumanization of the other, bolster-
ing themselves at the expense of the other by unconscious projection of their own
hatred and destructiveness. Sometimes they even come to turn that hatred and
destructiveness upon themselves, treating themselves as the other.

EFFECTS OF VIOLENCE

There is a link between the high levels of violence in our culture and the
effects of a traumatic childhood and adult abuse. It is the victims' compulsion to
repeat the trauma coupled with an inherent degree of aggression that is at the
heart of the traumatic origins of violence. It is through the compulsion to repeat

the trauma that violence begets more violence, either outwardly or inwardly directed. The experience of having been abused as a child is a major factor in a wide range of health problems, including major depression, posttraumatic stress disorder, substance abuse, eating disorders, self-mutilation, dissociative disorders, and somatization.

Although most violent crime is committed by males, girls now account for one-fifth of juvenile arrests, and more violent female criminals than ever await execution on Death Row. We are seeing an increase in "girl rage," as one newspaper called it. Violent crimes by adolescent girls and women and physical fights between girls are more common in schools. Unprecedented numbers of American girls and women are learning how to knock out, maim, and even kill men who assault them, a protest against the "femininity training" that has made them the targets of men's aggression. The self-defense movement for women trains them to embrace violence as a way of fighting back. All of this may reflect just the beginning of an outward response to the shadow of violence that has traditionally festered in women's lives.

The destructive consequences of having experienced the most severe child abuse are what Shengold (1989) calls "soul murder," defining it as

> the deliberate attempt to eradicate or compromise the separate identity of another person. The victims of soul murder remain in large part possessed by another, their souls in bondage to someone else. Thus Winston Smith at the end of 1984 loves the Big Brother who has taken over his mind. Torture and deprivation under conditions of complete dependency have elicited a terrible and terrifying combination of helplessness and rage—unbearable feelings that must be suppressed for the victim to survive. Brainwashing makes it possible to suppress what has happened and the terrible feelings evoked by the erased or discounted experiences. When it is necessary to retreat from feelings, good feelings as well as bad ones are compromised, and the victim's deepest feelings are primarily in the soul murderer (as Big Brother dominates the emotional universe of Winston Smith). Therefore murdering someone's soul means depriving the victim of the ability to feel joy and love as a separate person. In 1984 O'Brien says to Winston Smith: "You will be hollow. We will squeeze you empty, and then we shall fill you with ourselves.". . . Child abuse is a consequence of our need for dependence and our innate sadism and masochism, and it enhances that sadism and masochism in its child victim. [pp. 2, 4–5]

Having been raised in a world where sadistic violence is common to human relationships, the victims grow up feeling impotent rage. Where there often was no one who could listen to a child's pain and suffering, they developed no means of understanding, expressing, and integrating the effects of these experiences, which then become either repressed or split off from the ego. The result is that experiences may be remembered but without emotion, or emotions may be felt but remain disconnected from memory. Having been the passive victims of traumatic abuse in childhood, they will be compelled to repeat the trauma, sadistically inflicting violence on others or masochistically inflicting violence upon themselves. The children of Holocaust survivors "walk a fine line between being the fair hope of a destroyed generation and the despised object of parental aggression" (Bergmann and Jucovy 1982).

Abused men are more likely to direct this rage outward and women to direct it inward, for reasons that will be discussed further in Chapter 10. Abused women, especially those abused in childhood, are far more likely to become repeatedly involved with partners who abuse them, to stand by silently while their children are abused, and to abuse themselves. For example, writer Dorothy Allison (1988) wrote about how after a childhood of witnessing the most horrific violence in generations in her family and being the victim of that violence routinely, she began to pursue violence and long for death.

> We were so many we were without number and, like tadpoles, if there was one less from time to time, who counted? . . . They died and were not missed. . . . So I made a list . . . that one went insane—got her little brother with a tire iron; the three of them slit their arms, . . . that one drank lye and died laughing soundlessly. In one year I lost eight cousins. It was the year everybody ran away. Four disappeared and were never found. One fell in the river and was drowned. . . . Almost always we were raped, my cousins and I [pp. 14–15] . . . Like many others . . . before me, I began to dream longingly of my own death. I began to court it . . . in the tradition of all those others like me, through drugs and drinking and stubbornly putting myself in the way of other people's violence. Even now, I cannot believe how it was that everything I survived became one more reason to die. [p. 7]

The Self as Other

Victims of abuse can readily join their abusers in perceiving themselves as the other, which can ultimately result in the victims dehumanizing themselves. Whatever predisposition for sadism and masochism a female victim might have is reinforced by a culture that rewards women for treating themselves badly. Women have internalized the values of the culture, denying their natural appetites for food, sex, ambition, and freedom, in their limitless quest to become more feminine, more like what they think men want. Thus, the woman who represses her innate strength, spiritedness, and ambition will project these qualities onto her man, enacting a self-denying masochistic role. The female sense of self has been socialized to define itself in relation to the needs of others, especially men. This quest takes the form of weight control, hair and skin care, shopping to maintain a fashionable look, and a resistance to aging by any means possible. Women then make their own bodies into things, subduing, apprehending, dominating, and defeating them. Women treat themselves as slabs of dead meat, starving, corseting, mutilating, and liposuctioning themselves in an endless search for femininity and youth. "I'm going to lose these last ten pounds if it kills me" has been said by countless women, and embodying the feminine construct sometimes does kill them. Men to a lesser extent are getting an approving nod from the culture as they too dehumanize themselves as they run, starve, and dominate their bodies and their appetites.

Throughout history, self-starvation, psychogenic vomiting (Shorter 1994), and self-mutilation were psychosomatic symptoms that the unconscious mind could call forth as an expression of psychic distress. The enactment of these self-harm behaviors is a way of dehumanizing the self, turning it into other. Although the fear of being fat has been thought to be at the basis of self-starvation and purging, the work of medical historian Edward Shorter and my research suggest that the fear of being fat is rather a culturally induced artifact. Shorter (1994) notes that what was called anorexia nervosa and designated as a disease category in 1873, and became the culturally selected template for female psychosomatic expression in the middle of the twentieth century was, in reality, just an extreme form of the food refusal that had manifested itself throughout the nineteenth century in the form of stomach pain, vomiting and lack of appetite in young women. He further notes that vomiting without an organic cause is probably as old as time, and was used by patients anxious to justify their lack of appetite in terms of a legitimate nervous disease.

> Lasegue's 1873 paper , and the publicity surrounding the discussion at the Medical Society of London later that year, now forged a kind of template for self-starvation, disseminating a model of how the patient was to behave and the doctor to respond. The way had been cleared for turning a poorly circumscribed collection of symptoms revolving around food refusal into a clear-cut "disease." In this form it was launched into the twentieth century, to guide generations of young women through psychosomatic illness behavior. . . . In attempting to write its history or in constructing special eating disorder units, both groups of researchers (clinicians and historians of anorexia) lose sight of the evanescent nature of symptom choice. Granting official disease status to the phenomenon of self-starvation has in effect legitimated it, making it a desirable object of choice for many young women seeking somatic expressions of their psychic dysphoria. . . . The task of the unconscious is merely to produce behavior that will entitle the individual to a respectful medical hearing. [pp. 168–169, 192]

Even before the nineteenth century severe self-starvation and vomiting were known in female saints of the medieval era and the women who emulated them (Bell 1985). That is, their starvation and vomiting was meant to be a holy offering of suffering to God; their emaciation had little to do with a fear of being fat but much to do with the wish to become especially beloved by God, a holy Christian martyr. They made their bodies into the other, dehumanizing it in order to become other than human, saintly.

The findings of my study, exploring self-harm in women with bulimic symptomatology, suggest that an overt fear of being fat may be a cover for underlying masochistic wishes to punish oneself (Farber 1995a). The particular sample, a group of women who had experienced the most severe childhood abuse and trauma, purged, starved themselves, exercised excessively, and mutilated themselves as a means of punishing themselves for their sense of evil, or as a way of purifying what they experienced as their dirty and degraded selves, which had been beaten, molested, and raped since childhood. Or they starved themselves and exercised to the point of pain in order to become sufficiently deserving of the right to consume even the tiniest morsel of food. Their tortured body image had less to do with how fat or thin they were than with the neglect or abuse they had experienced early in life at the hands of others. Having been treated as the other and dehumanized, they too, driven by the repetition compulsion, continued to repeat the experience. They became the sadists who treated themselves as the other at the same time that they became the masochists, continually attached to the experience of pain.

When victims of violent abuse can easily convince themselves that their self-starvation and purging is simply because they want to be thin, or that their repeated cosmetic surgeries or puncturing their bodies with piercings is simply because they want a chic look, the culture readily provides a trendy template for the psychosomatic expression of the powerful attachment to abuse and violence. It can easily disguise the repetition compulsion, the repetition of the pain and punishment they were forced to endure, the endless attachment to pain, to punishment, and to those who hurt them.

The following story by a male victim of the most violent abuse was published in a newsletter called *Body Memories: Radical Perspectives on Childhood Sexual Abuse*. He tells about how he learned that violence begets violence and self-harm.

Tear Down That Wall

I.

my earliest memory: norwalk, connecticut. I was not quite three years old. father found me. blood streaming down my legs. trying to jam a pair of toenail clippers up my ass. . . . I didn't cry. until he started to hit me.

in the basement of that house. enormous monsters lived behind the water heater. he decided as a punishment. to tie me in front of it. and let the monsters come eat me. I cried a lot.

by the time I was seven. he had learned to strap me stretched naked on an ironing board. and would paddle me until I stopped crying. . . .

I'm not sure. I only remember which house and room it was in. so I would have been about eight. I was tied face down to that board. he took eleven ice cubes from the tray. (saving three for his martini). and one by one shoved them up my ass. forcing me to hold them for about an hour. give or take an eternity. while he paddled me. until I stopped crying. it hurt like hell. the cubes melted.

father drank a lot. mother drank even more. so she could forget what father did to her. regularly.

and i'd scream and shout. WHAT ARE YOU DOING?. but no one noticed anything wrong.

in that same second story room. at some point I decided. that I was too small to kill parents. and so could only kill self. . . . I jumped out the window headfirst. and broke an ankle. it was disappointing but. I didn't cry much at all.

mother came after me. when she was drunk. which was generally after 9 a.m. . . . it took me decades to understand why . . . I could not be shoved back into her vagina no matter how hard she tried. . . . the last time I ever cried. father was holding my balls in one hand. and a pair of scissors in the other. . . .

it's been more than twenty years. . . . i'd really like to weep. . . . i've tried so hard. I can't. . . .

you tell me. you . . . tell . . . me. you- TELL- ME what sort of terror. makes a three year old want to bleed? makes a seven year old want to die?

II.

chip was my pimp but. he was a nice guy. . . . I liked chip a lot. when he wasn't drunk. . . . chip had dangerous knowledge. a lot of dates. would pay good money to fuck a pretty YOUNG thing like me. . . . I had soft long hair parted in the middle. and smooth YOUNG skin. and could pass for a girl real easy . . . and over the years . . . I had an amazing variety of things shoved up my ass. and in my YOUNG mouth. I never cried. . . .

III.

. . . I didn't know it. but the first independent political thing I ever did. was walk into a domestic violence and rape crisis program. in 1976 in eugene, oregon. . . . I was sixteen . . . and said I knew a lot about domestic violence. and I wanted to help. . . . I was still pretty fucked up. . . . but even then. I knew violence was wrong. violence was evil. violence was everywhere. violence was father. violence was not crying. violence was buying things. violence was war. violence was television. violence was government. violence was men.

when I was nineteen. I tried to die again. because I knew I could never be. my ideal. because I knew i'd never even seen—my ideal. because I knew my ideal. was not even possible in this culture. this sick despicable violent disposable culture. . . . I survived that too. . . . I learned that what I had experienced was also called rape. . . . I thought rape only happened to women. . . .

now i'm thirty-three. . . . for two years i've had what I was told then was an incurable fatal disease. I was scheduled to die last year. . . . and i'm still alive. . . . ain't nobody but me going to run my death. . . . I live on stolen land. . . . I live with stolen time. . . . i'm proud of it. . . . some nights the pain is so bad. the pain is so much. my body is so weak and troubled. . . . I think a lot about dying. . . . but I keep surviving. [parrish 1993, pp. 18–20]

5

How Attachments Go Haywire

Nothing is more dear to them than their own suffering—
they are afraid that they will lose it—They feel it, like a whip
cracking over their heads, striking them and yet befriending
them; it wounds them, but it also reassures them.

Ugo Betti, *Landslide*

Attachments can be so passionate that they tie two lovers together and bind a lioness to her cub. Yet passionate attachments can become prisons, attaching one to pain and suffering the way shackles bind a prisoner. This bondage to pain and suffering derives from our primary relationships, our earliest basic attachments. The attachment the baby has to a mother or caregiver will influence the kind of attachments the child will form to others later in life. It is in an early attachment to neglect, traumatic separations, or abuse that the seeds of a deep attachment to neglectful or abusive object relations and to neglect or abuse of the self are born. The earliest attachments mold the development of the child's ability to care for himself physically and emotionally, and to feel either deserving or unworthy of good care and treatment. If he feels unworthy, he may grow up neglecting his body or being passionately attached to self-harm.

The attachment to neglect, trauma, and self-harm may even become imprinted in the child's regulatory processes in the brain and change his brain chemistry. As dire as this sounds, the good news from attachment research is that the attachment to self-harm imprinted on the brain can be biochemically altered through the development of a secure attachment relationship to a parent, friend, spouse, significant other, teacher, pet, or psychotherapist.

Despite differences in terminology, attachment theory and research, like Mahler's separation-individuation theory, is based on the poles of attachment and separation. Both develop the concept of proximity-seeking as contrasted with exploratory behavior with an awareness of the accessibility of an attachment figure. What is similar in both theories, based on observations of infants and toddlers, is that self-reliance and autonomy develop gradually as trust and confidence develop in the attachment figure. While Bowlby prefers the concept of self-reliance and the ability to find needed attachment figures in the environment when dependency needs require it, Mahler prefers the concepts of the introjection of love objects and object constancy. While Bowlby avoids the term *symbiosis*, which is considered phase-specific, Mahler and others regard the symbiotic quality as attaining internalized psychological significance. The term *symbiotic* is used here to represent greater degrees of attachment need, even when the symbiotic object no longer derives conscious or unconscious gratification from the relationship.

Attachment theory defines the inclination of human beings to form strong secure bonds with others, and explains how ruptures of these bonds, such as traumatic separations and loss, give rise to anxiety, depression, anger, and emotional detachment. Attachment behavior, seen more clearly when a person is frightened or exhausted or ill, is any form of behavior that results in that person bringing himself nearer to some other person whom he perceives as being a source of comfort and strength. The main thrust of Bowlby's attachment concept is the degree to which a child's parents provide him or her with a secure base that not only allows but also encourages him to explore further and further away from it. If the attachment figure remains available and responsive, providing protection, help, and comfort when needed, the child then can develop the psychological, emotional, and cognitive skills necessary for mastery and a firm sense of security in the world. At the same time that we understand the importance of attachment bonds, it must be recognized that solitude, the capacity to be alone and to enjoy spending time alone, and attachment are complementary, and both are essential developmental and biological needs for children and adults (Buchholz 1997).

As will be demonstrated, the child who has formed attachments in infancy that are marked by affection and security will become capable of enjoying his own company and capable of forming affectionate attachments with others. Anxious attachment originates in the individual's repeated experience of inconsistent caregiving that prevented the sense of security from forming. A pseudo-independent stance or compulsive self-reliance may appear to be the opposite of anxious attachment, but is an indicator of attachment difficulties. The pseudo-independent individual is unable to seek the love and care of others, insisting on doing everything for and by himself. He, too, has had the experience of not having his needs met and not having developed a sense of security, and has managed to convince himself and often others that he has no need of anyone else. Lacking the flexibility to bear up well under the stresses of life, he is prone to falling ill with psychosomatic symptoms. Emotionally detached individuals are not able to maintain a steady affectional bond with anyone.

Both attachment and separation-individuation theories can help us to understand how a person can become so attached to pain, suffering, and harm, including the self-inflicted kind, that he cannot imagine living without them. Attachment theory provides a relational context for identifying, locating, and understanding such disturbing feelings as separation anxiety; sadness about loss; protest and anger at separation; rage, guilt, and terror in reaction to trauma; envy of those who seem to form easier attachments; and disturbingly conflicting feelings toward attachment figures perceived as withholding (Holmes 1996). In addition, attachment theory explains how people might clutch so tenaciously at an attachment to pain and suffering that they would rather lose their life than relinquish that attachment, and how some individuals' sense of their own existence is enlivened by masochistic suffering and flirtations with death. It helps us to understand how our best clinical efforts to help such individuals fills them with such anxiety that they are determined to thwart and defeat us. Even those who consciously want to give up their self-harm may end up defeating our best efforts to help them. They emerge triumphant with their cherished spoils—their bloodied or wasted selves.

Attachment theory and research does not supersede but rather enriches many existing theoretical perspectives. It provides a new hope for working more successfully with these patients in enabling them to form an attachment to their therapist that promotes intimacy and autonomy (Holmes 1996) and further develops their ability to regulate their moods, emotions, and physiological states. Jeremy Holmes's (1996) understanding of human attachments gives clinicians a framework for thinking about relationships to human objects (persons) in one's life that can also be enormously helpful in understanding the relationship to the self and the body, especially when those relationships are harmful or self-destructive. He emphasizes that it is intimacy within the attachment relationship in psychotherapy that is the key to the development of more autonomous functioning and intimate relationships.

Attachment, however, does not necessarily mean intimacy. There are strong attachment relationships in which there is no true intimacy and no autonomy. These are the relationships based on power, in which a dependent individual is attached strongly to the other through fear and insecurity. This is commonly seen in cases of child abuse when the abused child clings ferociously to his abuser, bound to him as if magnetically. It is also seen in battered women, who, despite the availability of shelters, social services, and legal assistance, cling desperately to their abusive partners and lie to law enforcement investigators, becoming their abusers' protectors.

The work of several authors has provided an invaluable foundation for understanding the attachment to the perpetration of violence on others and on the self. Felicity de Zulueta (1994) traces how the increasing violence in modern society, including the angry self-destructiveness of young people with personality disorders, is born of the disrupted attachments associated with violent trauma, or is, as she says, "attachment gone wrong." Barbara Ehrenreich (1997) explores the mystery of the human attraction to violence and its origins in our evolutionary history. The influence of passionate attachments in love, sex, religion, and human history (Gaylin and Person 1988) has implications for understanding the attachment to violence and self-harm. Reid Meloy (1992) uses the tools of attachment theory and object relations theory to provide a lens through which we can understand bizarre kinds of violence, such as predatory stalkings and serial killings. To understand self-harm as an attachment disorder, we need to look at the contribution of the classical psychoanalytic theories of disease as well as the newer psychosomatic contributions from ego and self psychology, object relations theory, and neurobiology.

We can study attachment and separation in animals in relation to their grooming behavior to help us conceptualize primitive self-harm behaviors in humans as grooming behaviors that have run amuck in response to disordered attachments.

ATTACHMENT THEORY AND RESEARCH

Each species in the animal kingdom has its own unique biologically based attachment system that attaches its offspring to its caregiver and caregiver to its offspring in order to protect the infant from predators in the environment (Bowlby 1969). The infant clings to its mother instinctively, as the Moro response demonstrates when the infant tries to grab onto or cling to his mother when she is moving too rapidly (Brazelton 1972). The survival of the species demands that the adult female take good care of the newborn for a period that is especially long in humans because the human infant, compared to offspring of other species, is born with an exaggerated head size that requires support, and so is peculiarly helpless for a longer period of time than are other animals (Stone 1988). The mother must have a deep, indeed a passionate, attachment to the child to ensure his biological survival, and to provide the sense of security that is necessary for both the development of self-regulatory functioning (Hofer 1995) and a climate of intimacy (Holmes 1996). When closeness with the mother or caregiver is not established or the sense of security is disrupted, the child does not have sufficient protection from others who might harm him, and thus is in danger of falling prey to harm, either from predators in the environment or from himself as he turns his aggression on his body with self-harm behavior.

Hartmann (1939) believed that in the first weeks of life the newborn's means of discharging drive energy took the form of a silent physiological discharge to his body's interior. To adapt to his environment, the infant must develop the ability to discharge drive energy outward to the exterior and must develop instincts for protecting and caring for himself. If the child is to adapt to his environment and thrive within it, he needs the intimate contact with the mother that is the basis for the development of both self-regulatory functioning and the self-care function of the ego.

The primary focus of attachment theory is on how the child's inner world is influenced by the environment, or how, to use Freud's famous phrase (Bollas 1987), "the shadow of the object" falls upon the subject. While Freud's early work emphasized the instinctual basis of the mother–infant relationship, in his later work Freud (1938) spoke of the attachment to the mother: "A child's first erotic object is the mother's breast that nourishes it; love has its origin in attachment to the satisfied need for nourishment" (p. 188). The infant's powerful tie to the mother is "unique, without parallel, laid down unalterably for a whole lifetime, as the first and strongest love-object and as the prototype of all later love relationships—for both sexes" (p. 188). Attachment research has shown that a child's sense of security is greatly influenced by his parents' responsiveness, consistency, and attunement to him. Responsive mothers with securely attached children pick up their babies more quickly and frequently than do mothers of insecure children; these children experience their mothers and develop object representations of her as being a secure home base. That is, the child can tolerate her leaving because he knows she will return, and the child can leave her, to make forays into the world, knowing that she will be there when he comes back. When the handling of the child was inconsistent, unattuned, or rejecting, it led to anxious patterns of attachment (Ainsworth et al. 1978, Holmes 1996). A central assumption of psychoanalytic models is that parents respond to their children's behavior and characteristics with expectations based on their own experiences with their primary caregivers (Fonagy et al. 1995). Each mother's or father's own childhood experience will therefore influence the way he attaches himself to his child and the way that the child becomes attached to him.

Mary Ainsworth, co-developer of attachment theory, studied attachment patterns in 1-year-olds, using the "strange situation" as a measure of attachment status. Observation of behavior in the strange situation involved two 3-minute separations and reunions between caregiver and infant in a clinic waiting room. The babies considered to be secure were those who protested upon separation, and when reunited with their caregivers could be sufficiently calmed that they could return to exploratory play (Ainsworth et al. 1978). Two-thirds of normal children behave this way. Children who do not show this pattern are considered insecure and are inhibited in exploring their environment. There are three recognized patterns of insecure attachment: insecure-avoident, insecure-ambivalent, and insecure-disorganized. Insecure-avoidant children do not protest much when separated from their caregivers, and when reunited with them they anxiously hover nearby. The insecure-ambivalent children protest upon separation, but cannot be pacified when reunited. They either buried themselves in their caregivers' lap or clung furiously to them, seeming very passive or very angry. The insecure-disorganized children showed no coherent pattern of response. Some froze when reunited, and others collapsed on the floor or leaned vacantly against a wall, seeming disoriented.

These insecure attachment patterns are used defensively as strategies for maintaining contact with the rejecting or inconsistent parent. The 1-year-olds' attachment pattern has been found in long-term follow-up studies to have predictive power for subsequent behavior (Holmes 1996). The 1-year-olds classified as secure in general still show signs of security when they enter school, interacting well with classmates and teachers. On the other hand, the insecure-avoidant children were more likely to be loners, prone to unprovoked aggression, while the insecure-ambivalent children tended to be potential victims, clinging to their teachers for protection but unable to ask for help appropriately. The good news, however, is that an insecure child may become secure if his mother's situation improves or if the mother can resolve her own attachment difficulties (Holmes 1996). For example, the treatment of anxious preschool children often is not a direct treatment at all, but an indirect treatment through the treatment of the mother. If the mother can develop a secure attachment to the therapist, then an improvement in the child's attachment status often results. At times the tripartite treatment of the insecurely attached dyad, in which the therapist works with mother and child together, promotes a change in the attachment of mother to child that allows the child's attachment to the mother to become more secure.

The later attachment research moved well beyond Ainsworth's behavioral descriptions of infant attachment status to exploring the inner worlds of mother and child. In his infant observation studies Daniel Stern (1985) found that if the infant's nascent sense of self is to develop into a coherent and stable sense of self, the parent's attunement to the child's inner experience is necessary. Mary Main and colleagues researched attachment patterns in adults, paralleling the strange-situation classification. They developed and used the Adult Attachment Interview (AAI), an audiotaped semistructured psychodynamic assessment session, designed to "surprise the unconscious" into making itself known by asking questions about relationships with parents and significant others, and about experiences of loss and separations and how the subject coped with them (Holmes 1996). The AAI's scoring system is based more on the form and structure of the subject's narrative style than on the content. The adult narratives were classified as secure-autonomous, insecure-dismissive, insecure-enmeshed or preoccupied, and disorganized or unresolved. In the secure-autonomous narratives subjects speak coherently, logically, and succinctly about their past and their trials and tribulations. In the insecure-dismissive narratives subjects reveal and elaborate little. In the insecure-enmeshed narratives, on the other hand, subjects seem stuck emotionally in their history, rambling on without conclusions as if the pain from the past were alive today. The disorganized or unresolved category is rated separately and coexists with the others, referring to points in the narrative in which the logical flow is broken or disjointed. Main believes that these ruptures in the narrative may represent the emergence of previously repressed traumatic memories.

The AAI developed from a theoretical framework that predicted that there would be connections between attachment status in childhood and narrative style in later life. This hypothesis has been supported by data from other studies, showing that 1-year-olds' attachment patterns are remarkably predictive of adolescents' AAI status measured at age 16 and that the outcome of the AAI administered to prospective parents was a good predictor of attachment status of the subsequent 1-year old children twenty months later. The mothers with secure autonomous narratives had children who tended to be secure in the strange situation, while the dismissive parents tended to have insecure-avoidant infants.

Even more significantly Peter Fonagy and his associates (1995) found that the capacity to think about oneself in relation to others, what the authors term the reflective self or what in the clinical situation is usually called the capacity for insight, determines whether mothers whose own childhoods were traumatic will have infants who turn out to be insecure in the strange situation. The capacity to think about oneself in relation to others, even when one has experienced horrible trauma, is a critical protection against psychological vulnerability in the face of external difficulties.

The studies of Ainsworth, Main, Fonagy, and others demonstrate that there is a continuity of attachment over time. The attachment patterns of the parents influence the security or lack of security in their infants. The early infant attachment patterns influence school behavior, the capacity for reflection about the self in relation to others, and the capacity for intimate relationships with others. There are links between the preverbal psychobiological attachment of infancy and the verbal attachment narrative, suffused with meaning, in adult life. The strange situation measures the enactment of the child's attachment status; the AAI, in contrast, defines individuals' descriptions of their relationship to their own life. It is a movement from enactment to meaning (Holmes 1996).

Henry Hansburg (1980, 1986) studied attachment disorders in early adolescents and discovered certain self-destructive patterns.[1] He developed the Separation Anxiety Test (SAT), a projective test for adolescents for which Bowlby's analysis of protest, despair, and detachment provided a basic orientation. The SAT, consisting of twelve drawings, elicits the patterns of response with which young adolescents handle separation. Six of the drawings depict a child separating from an attachment figure in a situation designated as mildly stressful (e.g., "The child is leaving her mother to go to school"; "The mother has just put the child to bed"); the other six are considered very stressful (e.g., "The judge is placing

---

1. Hansburg dedicated the first volume to his father, George B. Hansburg, "whose inventive genius in developing the pogo stick, the baby toddler, and the baby-den set an example in fortitude and creativity."

this child in an institution"; "The girl and her father are standing at the mother's coffin"). There were several assumptions in developing the SAT. First, pictures of separation experiences can stimulate children sufficiently to be able to project their reactions. Second, children can select and report reactions to separation that genuinely reflect how they feel. Third, these reported reactions will show patterns that can be useful in diagnosis and treatment of separation problems, such as problems of attachment need (object relations), individuation (autonomy), hostility (regulation of aggressive drive), painful tension (anxiety tolerance), reality avoidance and reality testing affects, and identity stress. The superego problems center around patterns of self-love and self-esteem. Fourth, the response will help to reveal what mechanisms of defense against separation anxiety are mobilized. Fifth, the nature of object relations, whether symbiotic on one end or isolated on the other end, will be revealed. Sixth, the responses will show aspects of the capacity for autonomy that can be useful in treatment.

Using the SAT, Hansburg (1976) found that certain self-destructive tendencies emerged in early adolescents in response to separations. While psychoanalytic theory traditionally employed the concept of an attack on the introjected love object and of aggression turned inward to understand depression, suicide, and self-destructiveness, Hansburg instead gives more attention to attachment frustration with its accompanying emotional turmoil that intrudes on the capacity to cope with environmental demands. Abandonment, whether actual, perceived, or threatened, is seen as an experience that disrupts functioning capacity. "There is extensive support for the view that anxious attachment is a common consequence of a child having experienced actual separation, threats of abandonment or combinations of the two" (Bowlby 1974, cited by Hansburg 1976, p. 226). Although anger is regarded as a normal healthy component of attachment deprivation and as an effort toward regaining the association with the love object, anger can also become pathological, a serious consequence of continued frustration of the attachment need. Failure to achieve dependability from an attachment figure may lead to attacks against the self under certain conditions. Hansburg found that youngsters who experience the conflict of strong attachment need and equally strong frustration in the gratification of this need suffer from a severe separation ambivalence. This ambivalence is coupled with severe emotional turmoil, which, even if temporarily assuaged, continues as a subsurface phenomenon that will reappear, sometimes without warning, if abandonment or threats of abandonment develop or are anticipated. This turmoil will be accompanied by a great sense of helplessness, pain, hostility, intense denial, difficulties in maintaining self-esteem, and inability to face the normal identity stresses of adolescence. It is a pattern that is likely to lead to self-destructive reactivity or a psychotic break during the increasing demands of adolescence.

The dynamics of depression in adults suggest that when hostility cannot be acknowledged or expressed outwardly, it is turned against the introjected objects, which, because they are part of the self, results in the attempted or actual destruction of the self. The same is true of children, but because children are dependent on their parents, whenever children feel the threat of the loss of a love object or the loss of the object's love, they develop not only feelings of rage toward the object, but also feelings of helplessness and worthlessness, resulting in a depressive equivalent. When tension is extremely high and the defense mechanisms break down or become ineffective, suicide or suicidal equivalents may appear in the form of an attenuated attack on the introjected object, which manifests as a depression, accidental injury, antisocial acts, or other self-harm. It is a desperate effort at regaining contact with the lost gratifying object (Farberow and Shneidman 1957). Hansburg elicited patterns of response to the SAT that was easily diagnosable as a suicidal equivalent or self-destructive reactivity in children who were not diagnostically similar, who ranged from psychotic propensities to neurotic problems and character difficulties. In the presence of a strong attachment need, some children cannot accept even mild separation experiences, indicating disturbances in the separation-individuation process. This results in tremendous emotional turmoil and an effort to retrieve the lost object, but, at the same time, a lowering of self-love, corroborating Bowlby's concept of protest and despair. What ensues are strong feelings of abandonment and the inability to handle the normal identity stress and regressive pulls of early adolescence, producing an unusual combination of depression and impulsiveness, which endangers the welfare of the child. When combined with a pull toward denial, a temporary delusional reaction is possible.

The SAT was found to be appropriate as a gauge of adult separation issues, and was used to study attachment disorders in adult patients with eating disorders, with the finding that women with eating disorders in an inpatient facility manifested significantly more severe separation and attachment difficulties than is normal in adolescence and in adults undergoing developmentally based relationship crises (Armstrong and Roth 1989). Anxious attachment was demonstrated by 96 percent of the sample, and the more extreme separation depression was manifested by 85 percent. The patients made no cognitive distinction between brief, everyday leave-takings and more permanent breaks, reacting similarly to both. The clinical implications are that separations in therapy such as the end of the session, the weekend, or vacation break may reinforce patients' beliefs that long-term intimate relationships are not feasible. What is also implied is that attachment disturbances are functionally associated with specific eating-disorder behaviors. For example, restrictive dieting or self-starvation may be a means of sustaining a nurturing attachment at a safe distance, without acknowledging this need, while bingeing may fill a void for nurturance and can be a mechanism for self-soothing in those who cannot trust that an intimate relationship with significant others can meet these needs (Armstrong and Roth 1989).

Another study of attachment difficulties in adult eating-disordered patients in inpatient treatment used Pottharst's Attachment History Questionnaire (Chassler 1997). Chassler's study found that the mothers of individuals with eating disorders failed to provide a secure home base from which to separate, fostering either dependency or failing to foster autonomy. Not having had a strong attachment base in childhood, these patients enter adolescence and then adulthood without having acquired the necessary skills and resilience to deal effectively with the world. As a result, eating-disordered persons develop unconscious strategies to ensure the proximity of their attachment figures (Chassler 1997); an eating disorder diagnosis is often an effective way to get otherwise distant or self-absorbed parents to rally around the ill child. The study also linked aversive forms of discipline as a factor in the development of eating disorders, supporting Bowlby's premise that children's difficulties arise more frequently from the ill effects of premature and excessive punishment, which places a heavy burden on the developing attachment system. A history of parental threats of separation was a significant predictor of the development of anorexia nervosa and bulimia nervosa. Peer relationships were significantly and negatively affected by the attachment difficulties, supporting Bowlby's (1969) claim that an early secure base facilitates the child's ability to explore the world and to develop rewarding relationships with peers. The study has linked anorexia nervosa and bulimia nervosa to feeling unwanted. In terms of attachment theory, children feel unwanted when one or both parents persist in not responding to the child's care-eliciting behavior. Because of their attachment difficulties, these patients are usually resistant to psychotherapy, confounding the therapist's best efforts to become a secure attachment figure.

It was hypothesized that the frequency of self-mutilation would increase in seriously disturbed adolescents in residential treatment at a time of interpersonal loss (Rosen et al. 1990). Thirty-two adolescents were studied over a four-year period for the frequency of self-mutilation. It was found that each time a staff member announced he would be leaving his job, the frequency of self-mutilation increased significantly during the two-week period following the announcement and before the date of departure. Interestingly, there was no significant increase in the frequency of self-mutilation immediately following staff firings, suggesting that the time of anticipated loss was the period of highest risk for these adolescents in terms of self-mutilation. This suggests to me that the ego function of anticipation had not developed properly in these adolescents, which implies that treatment efforts should include focused efforts to develop this ego function in relation to loss. This also suggests that these adolescents were inflicting violence upon themselves to communicate what they could not say in words to the staff members to whom they had become attached, and that the behavior had an unconscious intent to coerce the staff member to change his mind and stay. That is, as long as the staff member was physically present, there was hope that he could be induced to stay, but once he had gone, the adolescents' harming themselves would be to no avail. It should be noted that the everyday separations from the therapist that eating-disorder patients must endure as well as the longer vacation separations often result in an increase in disordered eating after the separation. I would suggest that in these cases, the self-mutilation and disordered eating served transitional functions of soothing and calming the anguished self and expressive functions by bodily expressing angry feelings toward the therapist or departing staff member that they could not otherwise express in words. I suggest that the increase in these self-harming behaviors in the absence of the therapist is an indicator of severe attachment anxiety, just as other regressive behavior in patients who do not harm themselves is an indicator of lesser attachment anxiety.

Karen Walant (1995) has found that individuals prone to alcohol and drug abuse or promiscuous sex have disordered attachments, having been deprived in infancy of ongoing merger or symbiotic experiences. The standard child-rearing practices in our highly individualistic society, says Walant, often amount to normative abuse of children, forcing them to develop a premature self-reliance. As such children grow and develop, they despair of establishing meaningful human attachments and attempt to compensate for them by inducing merger states chemically through the use of drugs and alcohol. Immersive moments in psychotherapy, those memorable moments that feel like complete understanding between patient and therapist, can enable the patient to emerge from behind the alienated and detached self to build a firmer attachment to the therapist, and ultimately to others (Walant 1995).

SELF AND MUTUAL REGULATION

The mother–infant dyadic attachment as well as its separations serves as the prototype for other attachments and separations that follow, including father–infant and adoptive parent–infant attachments, friendships, couple relationships, other object relations, and the attachment of the parent to his own child. The infant's psychobiological experiences of attunement, misattunement, and reattunement construct the brain in terms of neurological connections and neural circuitry. In fact, the interaction between the mother's brain and the infant's brain is required for the baby's brain to grow (Schore 1997). In the earliest phase of the symbiotic mother–child attachment, the libidinal and aggressive drives are the point where mind and body join to bear both drive energy and affect, and to create self-regulatory processes. "All psychopathology," says Grotstein (1986), "constitutes primary or secondary disorders of bonding or attachment and manifests itself as disorders of the self and/or interactional regulation" (p. 108).

As early as the classical era of psychoanalysis, drive discharge, or the reduction of drive tension, was thought to be the governing principle during the neonatal period, following the pleasure principle (Freud 1911, 1915a). The first weeks of life are generally regarded as a stage of pre-mentation, when the infant's behavior is determined by drives in response to stimuli and the primitive ego is "first and foremost a body-ego" (Freud 1923, p. 27). Freud (1915a) defined instinct as "a concept on the frontier between the mental and the somatic, as the psychical representative of the stimuli originating from within the organism and reaching the mind" (pp. 121–122). He thought that the instincts and external stimuli both produce excitation within the mental apparatus; as the amount of excitation increases, it is experienced as unpleasurable internal tension that must be discharged.

Freud's drive theory was a model of psychosomatic process that combined two models of psychosomatic illness, the model of homeostatic disruption and the model of faulty developmental regulation. Freud believed that even at the beginning of mental life the mental apparatus constantly strives to reduce or keep constant the degree of excitation experienced within it in order to maintain a pleasurable peaceful state. The homeostatic model suggests that when excitation is blocked or inhibited from psychophysiological expression, this damming up of emotion is accompanied by visceral changes that, over time, account for pathophysiology (Freud 1920).The model of faulty developmental regulation suggests that the normal development and control over autonomic and affective processes becomes derailed, resulting in an arrest at or regression to somatic processes, manifested by massive autonomic or endocrine responses.

René Spitz (1945, 1946) found that hospitalized infants who were separated from their mothers at 6 months of age, even though they were provided the necessary physical care, suffered marasmus and even death. Marasmus, or anaclitic depression, consisted of sadness, indicators of apprehension, weeping, withdrawal, and refusal to eat. Its appearance was dependent on a good mother–infant relationship for the first six months of life, followed by the absence of the mother or caregiver for at least three months. If the mother or caregiver returned within three months, the symptoms disappeared, but if the separation continued longer, the symptoms became more severe, progressing to insomnia, weight loss, retarded development, apathy, stupor, and even death. Influenced by ethology, Spitz combined findings from animal studies with his observations to propose a new concept— that it is essential to life that the newborn's innate equipment be "quickened" through the relationship with the mother.

Bowlby's and Spitz's early studies were on a small scale, but more recently the Romanian and Russian children adopted from orphanages by American parents have become the largest group of deprived babies available for study (Talbot 1998). There are more than 18,000 of these adoptees in the United States now, and 20 to 30 percent, the most traumatized among them, are being studied. Although their adoptive parents were prepared to lavish on the children the affection and sensory stimulation they had severely lacked, this was insufficient for some of these children who manifested complex affective and behavioral neuropsychological difficulties. They spent their earliest years curled up with feeding bottles in their cribs for 18 to 20 hours a day, cared for by rotating staff who might spend 10 minutes a day talking to them or holding them.

Using ideas from ethology to bridge the gap between psychoanalysis and neurobiology, Myron Hofer (1995) has measured the nature of attachment processes and separation in rat pups, with important implications for understanding the nature of human attachments. Hofer has proposed a unified theory in which the early attachment processes can be broken down into distinct mother–infant interactions that regulate various physiological and behavioral systems in the infant. The research of Hofer and others suggests that the prototypical separation distress experienced by all mammals is the separation of the infant from the mother. More recent research has found that simulated maternal touch can restore physical regulation. For example, rat pups who were separated from their mothers for 45 minutes underwent major internal changes, including a dramatic drop in growth hormones that did not respond to injections of growth hormones. They did, however, respond markedly to touch. When a graduate student stroked the rat pups with a moist paintbrush, mimicking their mothers' tongues, their hormone levels increased (Colt 1997). Hofer has found that the separation of the infant from its mother has both an acute phase and a chronic, slow-developing, despair phase. The behavior in the acute or protest phase included agitation, vocalization, and searching for the mother, while the corresponding physiological responses included increased heart rates, cortisol levels, and catecholamines. The behavior in the chronic or despair phase included decreased social interaction, mouthing and rocking, hypo- or hyperresponsiveness, variable food intake, and sadness, while the corresponding physiological responses included weight loss, sleep disturbance, decreased rapid eye movement (REM) sleep, decreased core temperature, decreased oxygen consumption, decreased heart rate, increased ectopic beats, decreased growth hormone, and decreased T-cell activity. In short, the sudden loss of a specific maternal regulator led to a rebound response in the opposite direction, to altered patterns of function, or both.

These hidden regulators operate to some extent in separations and losses through life, but nowhere are they more apparent than in bereavement responses, which in the acute phase often resemble trauma responses. Hofer's (1995) work suggests that some of the symptoms of grief may be due to the loss of numerous real physical and temporal interactions with the deceased, as well as to the inner psychological loss of any remaining conscious or unconscious expectations of the deceased in relation to the self. The death of a parent, however, is the final separation. Anticipating the death of his father, James Atlas (1997) wrote in *The New Yorker*:

"When my father died I was for a long time *sunk*," Saul Bellow wrote to his first biographer, Mark Harris, consoling Harris on the death of his father. I think of that simple, eloquent confession whenever I come home from work and see my father, dozing on the sofa. I'm seized with a sensation of emptiness, a prefiguring of abandonment that's primal in its intensity; I felt this way, it occurs to me, when my parents left me alone at Camp Shewahmegon forty years ago and drove off down the dusty road in their old Oldsmobile, leaving me by the door of my bunk with a knapsack and a sleeping bag. How would I ever get through the night without them? How will I get through a quarter century of nights? [p. 55]

The death of both parents can leave competent mature adults feeling adrift and lonelier in this world than they ever could imagine, like orphans in the rain. *Gates of Repentance*, the Reform Jewish prayerbook for the memorial service, states, "A final separation awaits every relationship, no matter how tender. Someday we shall have to drop every object to which our hands now cling" (Stern 1978). The loss may explain why, when we are bereaved, our heart beats slower, we may fall ill or suffer physical pain, or we may sleep or eat too little or too much. Sometimes we may curl up like a fetus and cry like a baby. And sometimes the longing to be with the dead can exert its seductive pull (Freud 1913a) toward melancholia, toward suicide attempts, and toward self-harm. Blake Morrison recounted in his memoir the prolonged stages of his father's dying, and his inconsolable grief: "I feel as if an iron plate had come down through the middle of me, as if I were locked inside the blackness of myself," he wrote. "I thought that to see my father dying might remove my fear of death, and so it did. I hadn't reckoned on its making death seem preferable to life" (Atlas 1997, pp. 57–58).

The concepts of self and mutual regulation allow us a more microscopic view of the mother–infant interaction and the development of the attachment process (Lachmann and Beebe 1997). In mutual regulation, both partners actively contribute to the regulation of the exchange, but not necessarily in equal measure or like manner. The self-regulation model refers to self-comfort and the ability to regulate one's states of arousal and organize one's behavior in regular and predictable ways. In mutual regulation, experience takes on characteristic patterns— predictable coordinated rhythms, tempos, sequences, affective intensities, greetings, and separations, while at the same time self-regulatory styles form based on adaptive and nonadaptive patterns of mutual and self-regulation (Lachmann and Beebe 1997).

Human beings fit together like the pieces of a puzzle, and so examining how they fit together tells us about their mutual regulatory processes and bonds of attachment. The mother serves the biological regulation between herself and the infant in an overarching organization that we recognize as symbiosis. Oxytocin, a hormone found in human breast milk, is known as the hormone of love and attachment because it is associated with "affiliative impulses" that help form a bond between mother and infant (Angier 1994). However, there is also a biochemical process that enables adoptive parents, fathers, and others to fall in love with a baby. Cuddling and stroking a newborn, holding it against one's naked breast, and smelling its fontanel, the soft spot on its head, seem to release similar brain chemicals.

Both before and after birth, both parts of the dyad adapt to each other in the context of a developing and reciprocal psychobiologic human attachment (Benedek 1949). Breast-feeding is not only symbolic of the reciprocal attachment but also seems to be a key factor in protecting infant and mother from certain illnesses and decreasing the incidence of infant ear infections, diarrhea, allergies, and bacterial meningitis, and may also protect against childhood lymphoma, sudden infant death syndrome, and diabetes. It also provides numerous other hormones that help in tissue growth and natural opioids that may help form the baby's brain (Angier 1994). For the nursing mother, the risk of early breast cancer, ovarian cancer, and postmenopausal hip fractures is reduced. The health benefits are so great that in 1997 the American Academy of Pediatrics took its strongest stand, urging mothers to breast-feed for at least a year, six months longer than had been previously recommended, or for as long as is mutually desired. (Currently about 60 percent of new mothers breast-feed, with about 20 percent continuing beyond six months.)

Communication can regulate the ordinary operations of the brain and nervous system (Conway and Siegelman 1995), with an unconscious preverbal communication between mother and infant that begins after conception in the normal pregnancy. With conception and after the first trimester, the increased hormonal and general metabolic processes necessary to maintain a normal pregnancy produce an increase in vital energies and a calm experience of well-being in the mother (Benedek 1949). These same feelings that enhance the mother's well-being also increase her pleasure in carrying her child despite the discomforts of pregnancy. As she feels a growing ability to love and take care of her in-utero child, she feels an improved emotional balance, enhanced body image and self-esteem that enable her to master previously disturbing emotional conflicts. Studies suggest that the unborn child can see, hear, experience, taste, and even learn very primitively and experience precursors of true emotion before birth, and that a mother's chronic anxiety or wrenching ambivalence about motherhood or other persistent patterns of disturbing feeling can leave a physically based impression on the fetus that begin to shape his sense of himself (Verny 1981). There is evidence that suggests that the father, too, to a lesser degree, transmits emotional messages to the fetus.

Our first real experiences of life occurred in utero as we floated in the bath of amniotic fluid, curled up in the womb's total embrace. We swayed to the undulations of our mothers' body and we heard the steady rhythmic beat of her heart. We shared her body's rhythm and chemistry. Apparently in utero the fetus can also hear the voices of those around him, and so it registered with us that those voices were mostly calm or mostly loud and strident (Verny 1981). When the fetus is not unduly disturbed by its immediate environment or by the emotional upset of the mother, it would seem to be a blissful experience. But paradise is lost in the trauma of being born, as the infant is exposed to the shockingly sudden loss of intimate body contact. No wonder he cries as he emerges into the bright lights of the delivery room. Who would not want to go back to the womb and its lost comforts?

To compensate the infant for what was lost, the infant needs a great deal of maternal care, contact, and intimacy. At the same time, the birth experience can be considered a trauma for the mother as well, bringing with it the possibility of postpartum depression or anxiety. To compensate the mother for the loss and separation that is inherent in birth, she needs the skin contact and intimacy with her baby that comes with being attuned to his needs. So the mother has to adapt to the needs of the infant (Benedek 1949), who nature has made certain to endow with the ability to capture his mother's attention and direct it to his physiological state. Although at three weeks the infant can recognize the mother's face, he is nearsighted for about the first two months of life and prefers to look at faces and objects just ten to twelve inches away, thus keeping an attuned caregiver physically close by (Brazelton and Cramer 1990). The cries of her baby draw her close again, reassuring them both about the continuity of oneness that had been ruptured by the separation in the birth process. The mother grows in her responsiveness to her baby's cries, distinguishing her baby's cry from that of other newborns by the third day after birth, and distinguishing pain, hunger, and boredom cries by the end of the second week.

The mother's intimate embraces re-create for both mother and infant the prebirth experience; the maternal chest, arms, and hands do their best to re-create the total engulfment of the womb, as well as other womb-like elements—the mother's rhythmic rocking, rhythmic breathing, and the steady rhythm of her beating heart. Both are rocked peacefully, the infant in his mother's arms and the mother in her identification with the baby who is so cherished. The infant also has early bodily experiences of the father that influence how he feels carried and contained. In addition to being the embodiment of the outer world, the one who helps the child break the symbiotic bond to the mother, and the embodiment of phallic entry into the mother's body, the father also is the embodiment of the masculine for the child: the "textural" difference or the different "feel" of the father, the different smell, the different way of holding and carrying the child, the different way of breathing and walking, and the different voice. The father's masculinity attaches the child to him in a way that is quite different from the attachment to the mother, and so the infant is not carried or contained by the mother alone but by mother and father in very different ways (Bollas 1997).

Touch is the first important area of communication between mother and infant (Brazelton and Cramer 1990), and intimate touch is central to our existence (Morris 1971). The earliest yearnings of human infants and their overwhelming need for comfort may well set the tone for the rest of their lives. Promiscuous grapplings and the popularity of massage and other hands-on body therapies may be testimony to the "skin hunger" experienced by so many in what the anthropologists call our non-tactile Western society. Many who have been deprived of loving and intimate touch may crave the intense skin stimulation that comes from being slapped, bitten, stung, scratched, or burned. Despite what we know about the risk for skin cancer, we like to bake ourselves in the sun's rays, as if to replicate the warmth of the mother's embrace. At the beach we absorb the smell of the sea as we gaze at the water in oneness with the amniotic depths. Later we greedily savor the taste of the creatures of the sea and their liquids, as if absorbing again the contented embrace in our mother's womb. And burial at sea has become a more popular burial rite. As President Kennedy said, "I really don't know why it is that all of us are so committed to the sea. . . . I think it's because we all came from the sea. And it is an interesting biological fact that all of us have in our veins the exact same percentage of salt in our blood that exists in the ocean. And therefore we have salt in our blood, in our sweat, in our tears. We are tied to the ocean and when we go back to the sea . . . we are going back from whence we came."[2]

Skin is of fundamental importance as a means of communication between parent and child, transmitting smell, touch, taste, and body warmth (Pines 1980). Consider that premature babies who are massaged regularly gain weight as much as 50 percent faster than preemies who are not massaged. They tend to be more alert, active, responsive, and aware of their surroundings. They cry less, sleep better, have easier temperaments, are more able to calm themselves, and thus are more appealing to their parents. Enough babies born prematurely become the victims of child abuse to suggest that the difficulties in raising these children create attachment problems that may account for their becoming abused more often. Those children born with heightened sensitivities to sound or touch, for example, present more difficulties to which the mother must make the lion's share of adaptation. She must work harder to adapt to the infant because his stimulus barrier makes it harder for him to adapt. The intimate touch with which she yearns to comfort her baby may only further irritate her sensitive-to-touch child. Nothing she does is right. Even "good-enough" mothers (Winnicott 1965), who ordinarily might make a good fit between themselves and a more average baby, may not be up to this difficult task of adapting so much and so well to this unusually sensitive child. It is presumed that the attachment status of the infant depends on the "goodness of fit" between a particular parent with her own personal attachment history and the unique inborn temperament of her child. In the psychosomatic dyad, the scenario that is enacted over and over again is "Mommy I need you and you need me, too." When the mother feels useless to calm her child, she tends to feel that her child does not need her and cannot regard herself as a good-enough mother, and the attachment that is needed to protect the infant does not grow but is instead thwarted. Under such circumstances, the mother may not go the extra distance to discover what other ways might help to calm this difficult-to-calm child but may well become more likely to abuse her child, increasing the disorder of attachment.

According to Mahler and colleagues (1975), from birth on there begins a complex and circular developmental process that optimally results in the infant's awakening from a symbiotic stage and navigating through the process of psychological separation from the mother and individuation, resulting in "the psycho-

---

2. Said by President John F. Kennedy, September 14, 1962, on the eve of the America's Cup Yacht Race, to an audience in Newport, Rhode Island.

logical birth of the human infant." From the very beginning, the infant observers Stern, Trevarthen, and Brazelton agreed that the infant is alert, and Mahler too ultimately abandoned her concept of a normal autistic phase, replacing it with the concept of the infant awakening from symbiosis (Stern 1985). The newborn's tolerance for stimulation, however, is limited and he spends most of his time sleeping. But the newborn does have optimal levels of stimulation, below which stimulation will be sought and above which stimulation will be avoided, with some help from an attuned mother who serves to help the infant regulate the stimulus barrier (Stern 1985). The infant's earliest sense of himself exists prior to the development of language and self-awareness. From age 2 to 6 months the infant's sense of a core self, a separate, cohesive, bounded, and physical unit, is consolidated (Stern 1985). The first inklings of a body self come from within his own body from the very beginning through sensations, especially by proprioception (Mahler and McDevitt 1982). The subjective experience of union with another can occur only after a sense of a core self and core other exists. The mother–child relationship then is symbiotic, the essential feature of which is a hallucinatory, somatopsychic omnipotent fusion with the representation of the mother and, in particular, the delusion of a common boundary shared by the two physically separate individuals (Mahler 1968). The autistic child's awareness of his body as separate from the mother's is traumatic because he has experienced her as a limb or other part of his body (Tustin 1981, 1990).

The mother's expressive face stimulates the child's interest in it, especially her eyes, leading him to track her gaze and engage in periods of intense mutual gazing (Schore 1997), which mediates "the dialogue between mother and child" (Spitz 1958, p. 395). The infant is held by the mother's gaze and she, too, feels held and affirmed in his. In addition to gazing, vocalizations and tactile and body gestures serve as channels of communication that not only affect the infant's brain, specifically the right hemisphere, but also are required for its growth (Schore 1997).

There is a lag of around six months before the infant's experiences expand from solely body based to include the mind (Stern 1985). Thus, the mother functions as a hidden regulator of different physiological and behavioral systems in the infant, providing a physiological basis for both the development of the affective state that we call security and the beginnings of the capacity for intimacy. At the same time, the infant's sucking serves to quicken the mother's psychophysiological responses by stimulating the secretion of oxytocin, which elicits the let-down response in nursing and elicits loving and attuned emotional responses of the mother, to help her navigate that adult phase of development that we call parenthood (Benedek 1959). The goodness of fit between both parts of the psychosomatic unit serve as regulators for each part. As Hofer (1995) said, it is the mutual regulation that takes place that gives meaning to the use of the word *symbiosis*. What is essential for healthy development is optimal symbiotic gratification. It is in the gross failure of symbiosis that lies the etiology of childhood psychosis (Mahler et al. 1975), whereas insufficient gratification during symbio-sis may result in a borderline structure.

A hungry infant's cry is piercing and unrelenting, expressing a primitive psychophysiological oral libidinal tension (Jacobson 1964) that demands relief. When and how the mother gratifies the infant's hunger leads to unique experiences of pleasure and "unpleasure," which constitute the first and most important con-nection to the mother (Jacobson 1964). The cries are so painful for parents to hear that they may spend many sleepless nights doing whatever they can to quell their baby's cries—holding and rocking the baby for hours until exhausted, even driving around aimlessly so the rhythms of the car can lull the baby to sleep. For some the cries are so painful that they may provoke the parent to smother or beat the infant in order to stop him from crying.

The earliest feeding experiences regulate the psychophysiological responses of mother and infant. Optimally when the infant cries from hunger, the mother soon appears, as if by magic. It is not magic, however, but the mother's patience in determining what is wrong, that leads her to satisfy her baby's hunger. She determines that no, he is not too chilly, not too warm, not in need of changing his diaper, and yes, he is hungry. The nursing mother is glad because her breasts have become painfully engorged, and now they can be relieved by her baby. She is pleased that she could determine how to make her infant more comfortable. The moment she touches his mouth with her nipple, the infant's rooting reflex causes him to turn in the direction of the stimulus, surround the nipple with his mouth and suck. He knows the smell and taste of her milk and can distinguish it from the smell and taste of others. As he sucks she experiences the pain-pleasure of the let-down reflex and then the milk flows, mercifully relieving her engorge-ment. The infant sucks differently at the breast than at the bottle, sucking in a burst-pause pattern that suggests that babies are programmed for more social inter-action when being fed at the breast. She feels the glow of maternal love and yearn-ing as she caresses and embraces the baby and talks and sings to him. His skin is stimulated by her touch, and he further relaxes into her embracing arms, con-tinuing to suck until he is sated and asleep, and she is relieved and calm.

Sometimes though, the feeding is disrupted because the baby is crying, an indication that something is wrong, that there is a disturbance in homeostasis. In the first weeks of life the infant's physiology is not mature enough to permit sufficient discharge of drive energy to the exterior. In many infants considerable gas is discharged to the interior because the pathways to the exterior are not developed enough to allow discharge through burping or flatulence, accounting in part for the infant colic that can so unnerve mothers. Worried parents are frequently told by the pediatrician that by the time the infant is 3 months old, his systems will have matured and become more self-regulating and the colic will be gone. Until then the parents may need to learn various burping techniques to help the gas bubble rise in the infant's alimentary canal and be discharged. A relatively calm and secure mother, after determining that he has a gas bubble, holds him firmly in one of the several positions that each mother must find through trial and error to suit her baby best. As she pats or rubs him to help release the bubble, her voice, touch, and facial expression all tell the baby that he is loved and cared for. She serves as a mirror, reflecting back to him a sense of goodness and wholeness, introducing him to his body, which can produce, among other things, burps. She introduces him to his psyche when she laughs as he burps, saying approvingly "Good, good. You pushed that burp out." She introduces his mind and body one to the other, a process Winnicott (1949) called personalization, facilitating the baby's sense of his body as being the dwelling place, the home, for his developing psyche. The baby's sense of himself is forged as a good and competent mind–body self. Having been helped to expel some gas, he can now continue to nurse. As he becomes sated, he may even want to stop a while to play. Maybe he wiggles his toes, and maybe she, in turn, leans over to kiss his toes, or even engage in a game of "This Little Piggy Went to Market" until he turns again to the bottle or breast for a few moments longer. The infant, "through its cries, bodily gestures and somato-psychic reactions to stress, gives nonverbal communications that only an attuned mother or caretaker can interpret. She functions, in this respect, as her baby's thinking system, and finds an adequate response to her infant's distress" (McDougall 1989, p. 169). As his hunger is satisfied, he falls asleep in blissful comfort, while his mother rests, enjoying the interlude of separation and her increased sense of competence in her maternal role. This is the nature of symbiosis in its most literal sense. Infants arrive in the world equipped to establish an attachment relationship, equipped to keep the mother close by, and can, through their responsiveness in sucking patterns and other indicators of pleasure and pain, motivate adults to attune themselves to the infant and his needs (Ellman and Monk 1997).

The mother's capacity to be attuned to her infant, to engage in reverie, and to be free enough of anxiety to be able to be "ordinarily devoted," a good-enough mother derives from her ego strength. Winnicott (1963) called this attachment of the mother for her child "primary maternal preoccupation" (p. 85). It is an attachment that is powerful and passionate. An attuned mother stimulates her baby when he communicates to her that that is what he needs, and calms him when he lets her know that that is what he needs. As he falls asleep after draining the breast, her milk supply already is replenishing itself in anticipation of the next nursing episode, when the infant's hunger returns. Her hunger for a satisfying encounter with her infant has been fed for the time being. They continue the process of attachment by means of countless daily interactions that offer the possibilities for intimacy. Attuned mothers sleep with a level of wakefulness, listening while they sleep, attached even through sleep. Even years later mother and father may not be able to sleep peacefully until they hear their adolescent return home, secure once again. These earliest yearnings of the infant and his overwhelming need for comfort reverberate throughout the human life cycle in the need for physical contact and intimate connection (Bowlby 1969, Morris 1971).

"And for however long it is fed at its mother's breast, it will always be left with a conviction after it has been weaned that its feeding was too short and too little" (Freud 1938, p. 189).

The mother's or caregiver's availability as a secure base is the basis for the infant's emergence from symbiosis (Mahler et al. 1975). The observations of Margaret Mahler and associates of normal infants in the first three years of life demonstrated that the journey from symbiosis to separation-individuation consists of several subphases—differentiation, practicing, and rapprochement. In the symbiotic phase the infant smiles in response to experiencing the mothering half of his symbiotic self, an unspecific, social smile. The differentiation subphase occurs at around 5 months of age, and is marked by the specific smiling response to the mother, the indicator that a specific bond between the infant and mother has been established. There is a "hatching process," a gradual evolution of the perceptual-conscious system that allows the infant to remain more permanently alert when he is awake, no longer drifting in and out of alertness. At around 6 months, infants begin tentative forays into separation-individuation, with the quickening of the infant's sensory perception as the sense of touch, smell, taste, vision, and hearing are stimulated by the outside world. In time these stimuli facilitate the infant's ability to discern the self from the surroundings, thus forming the eventual boundaries of the body image. In the differentiation subphase normal infants take their first steps in breaking away physically from their status as lap babies. No longer content to mold their bodies into their mother's body when held, they strain away from her in order to get a better look at her, experimenting with touching the mother's face, pulling at her hair, knocking her eyeglasses off, putting a bit of food in her mouth. It is in these ways that the infant differentiates between his bodily self and that of the mother.

The infant also has repeated experiences of his mother's absence. With her repeated return to him when he needs her, the infant develops the idea that her existence is permanent, regardless of his state of need, that she does not cease to exist when he no longer perceives her physical presence (Piaget and Inhelder 1969). From this representation of the mother's existence as permanent, this object representation is retained in the infant's mind regardless of whether or not he needs her. That is, the mother becomes transformed from being an object who is called into existence by power of the infant's omnipotent need, to an object who exists on her own, who is not created by the infant's need. The mother may delight her baby with peekaboo games, demonstrating "now you see me; now you don't, but I am still here" (object permanence). A hallmark of increasing sense of separateness is a greater curiosity about strangers. In the more securely attached infants, the interest in strangers is more open, less affected by stranger anxiety.

Overlapping the differentiation subphase is the practicing subphase. In the early part, from approximately 7 to 10 months of age, the infant begins to delight in moving away from the mother by crawling, climbing, and standing while holding on. Even while standing up in her lap and holding onto her for support, he is looking over her shoulder at enticing vistas to be explored. He takes exquisite pleasure in his exercise of autonomous functions. In the later part of the practicing subphase, or the practicing period proper (about 10 or 12 months to 16 or 18 months), he reaches those vistas by his free and upright locomotion, often exhausting his mother as she struggles to run after and keep up with him, as he can easily disappear over a rise in the park or around a corner. His mother must be able to tolerate the anxiety of her infant's distancing himself from her, and still remain available to protect him. He does not know he needs a protector because he is "His Majesty the Baby," the king of the universe, on the move, running quickly, omnipotently exploring, oblivious of danger, drunk with elation. His is "a love affair with the world" (Greenacre 1957, p. 57). Mother is his dutiful servant, following and hovering discreetly behind with juice and diapers; he will not deign to acknowledge her presence until he needs her. Throughout the practicing subphase, she is still a safe and secure base, to which the infant returns momentarily to touch base and refuel physically and emotionally. The infant takes a more active role in determining his closeness to and distance from the mother. She is still the center of his universe. He cannot be distant from her for too long; he is, after all, only practicing; she "still is the center of the child's universe from which he only gradually moves out into ever widening circles" (Mahler et al. 1975, p. 66).

Just as this practicing period is devoted to the developmental tasks of autonomy and individuation, it is equally devoted to the seeking and creation of intersubjective union with the mother, learning that the contents of one's mind and the qualities of one's feelings can be shared with another (Stern 1985). The hallmark of this period is the child's great narcissistic investment in his own functions, his own body, and in asserting his own individuality as indicated by the "no" response (Spitz 1957) to the mother. This semantic "no," accompanied by the head-shaking gesture, is often the first abstraction the infant forms, following on the heels of tantrums. It is the "no" of a baby secure enough of his attachment to his mother that he can dare to be a separate person who can defy her. Saying no to the mother means saying yes to himself. The baby who says no requires a mother who has the ego strength to tolerate this without undue anxiety or anger.

By the middle of the second year of life, the distancing of the practicing subphase is replaced by a rapprochement, a need for closeness with the mother. The rapprochement subphase is marked by what seems like a constant concern with the mother's whereabouts and by separation anxiety, making it of utmost importance that the mother be emotionally available. This is a difficult challenge for a mother, because just as she is beginning to enjoy the freedom provided by child's apparent independence from her, his need for greater closeness can be readily regarded by the mother as regressive, and can be resented. Whereas in the practicing subphase the mother must be able to tolerate more the feeling that her baby no longer needs her in the same way, in the rapprochement subphase she must be able to tolerate the feeling that she must be almost constantly available, to be clung to or rejected. The mother's reliability as a secure base and her emotional attunement and flexibility are paramount. Simply put, mothers must be there to be left. Mother and toddler communicate more through symbolic language and play. The rapprochement subphase is the root of humankind's eternal struggle against both fusion and merger. It is during rapprochement that the elated mood of the practicing subphase and the depressive mood of the rapprochement subphase crystallize as the basic moods of the developmental expansion of the affect array (Pine 1980). If development continues unimpeded, eventually the child will have developed a fuller range of affect that may include guilt, shame, longing, dread, awe, excitement, loneliness, glee, anxiety, euphoria, and satisfaction.

If the mother is not a secure base, there to be left and to be returned to, the child's aggression, manifested as self-injurious habits or disturbances of feeding, is evoked. When this anger is experienced during the practicing subphase, the distress is often manifested as anger directed toward the self (McDevitt 1985). It has been found that destructive aggression in childhood has a hostile intent aimed at destroying a structure that has proved highly thwarting (Parens 1979). For the expression of aggression to develop in a way that promotes the development of a separate self, it needs to be expressed and contained within the context of an object relationship that will contain the child's anger. In the absence of adequate object relations, children will use any available method to substitute for a containing mother–infant relationship and to reduce tension, including thumb sucking, tongue chewing, enuresis, rocking, and head banging (Silberstein et al. 1966). Children tend to select these techniques opportunistically, depending on the age at which tension arises and the availability of particular sensations at that phase of their development (Silberstein et al. 1966). The rhythmic motor patterns of some of these activities are normal phenomena in infants that satisfy an instinctual need and facilitate motor and ego growth and development (Lourie 1949). The rate of the rhythmic movements appears to have a definite relationship to one of the time beats in the body, with usually the heart or breathing rate acting as the pacemaker (Lourie 1949). This is the most elemental form of human experience, what Ogden (1989, 1990) terms the autistic-contiguous mode, a primitive, presymbolic sensory dominated mode of experience.

It is a sensory-dominated mode in which the most inchoate sense of self is built upon the rhythm of sensation, particularly the sensations at the skin surface. The autistic-contiguous mode of experiencing is a presymbolic, sensory mode and is therefore extremely difficult to capture in words. . . . Contiguity of surfaces (e.g., "molded" skin surfaces, harmonic sounds, rhythmic rocking or sucking, symmetrical shapes) generate the experience of a sensory surface rather than the feeling of two surfaces coming together either in mutually differentiating opposition or in merger. There is practically no sense of inside and outside or self and other; rather, what is important is the pattern, boundedness, shape, rhythm, texture, hardness, softness, warmth, coldness, and the like. [Ogden 1990, pp. 83–84]

However, when such primitive modes become prominent in the child's motor patterns, they serve other needs, including the expression of pleasure, expression and relief of tension and anxiety, and provision of a form of compensatory satisfaction, and may well persist past the infantile period. They follow the pleasure principle, which regulates the need to re-create any situation—by action or fantasy—that, in the past, has provided gratification through the elimination of drive tension (Moore and Fine 1990). The rhythm of these infantile activities as well as the rhythmic stereotyped activity of hair pulling, scratching, and nail biting, and the rhythmic repetitive hand-to-food-to-mouth-and-chew-and-swallow activity of binge eating may replicate the mother's breathing or heartbeat, and therefore serve transitional functions.

Research has found that the early mother–child experiences are imprinted on the child's developing brain (Schore 1997). When the self-injurious "habits" and feeding disturbances of early childhood grow out of these experiences, these means of expressing aggression and soothing the self become imprinted on the brain, serving as the developmental forerunners of the eating-disordered and self-mutilating behaviors that we typically see later in preadolescents and adolescents. When mother–child interactions are secure and rewarding, this attachment pattern becomes structured in the brain, thus serving very well for continued healthy development. When mother–child interactions are disturbed, however, they too become encoded in the right orbitofrontal area, the executive regulator of the entire right brain, and later manifest themselves in failures of affect regulation. In fact, recent research, mostly brain-imaging studies, shows evidence of impaired right orbitofrontal activity in various psychopathologies, including autism, schizophrenia, mania, unipolar depression, phobic states, posttraumatic stress disorder, drug addiction, alcoholism, and borderline and psychopathic personality disorders (Schore 1997).

If we look at this neurobiological theory in the context of understanding what happens when a mother fails to be a good-enough mother, failing to protect the child from overstimulation by overly frustrating him by ignoring his needs, or by intruding into his quiescent states, the child does not feel held and contained, but rather experiences the very ordinary and common trauma of impingement. The feeling of containment, what Winnicott called the experience of "going on being," so crucial for psychological growth, fails to be sustained, causing cumulative psychic trauma (Khan 1963) or "strain trauma" (Kris 1956). That is, the child is not traumatized by what we ordinarily think of as "shock trauma" such as physical or sexual abuse, or physical abandonment, but is instead traumatized repeatedly over time by the nature of the mother–child interaction. So we can understand that each such impingement is encoded as an interactive representation in the right orbitofrontal area, with each ordinary little trauma adding to what came before in a snowball effect, to be encoded as cumulative psychic trauma.

While this may sound very ominous, the good news is that the right orbitofrontal area is the most plastic part of the brain. It can be modified through the establishment of a subsequent secure attachment relationship. Attachment is very good medicine that can change the structure of the brain to repair what trauma has damaged.

ATTACHMENT PROBLEMS WOVEN INTO THE DEVELOPMENT OF CRITICAL EGO FUNCTIONS

He who returns has never left.

Pablo Neruda, *Adioses*

The separation-individuation phase usually ends during the third year of life, followed by what Mahler and colleagues (1975) call "the psychological birth of the human infant," heralding the beginnings of object constancy and the consolidation of individuality. There is the evolution of a higher level of object relations, a more constant mental representation of the object regardless of the infant's need. The infant has progressed from the objectless stage of primary narcissism, through the stage of experiencing the object as only a need-satisfying object, to on the way to object constancy. There is the loss of the infant's sense of omnipotence. The infant has begun the journey of on the way to object constancy, a lifelong developmental process. Optimally the infant has reconciled and integrated the image of the good mother of symbiosis with the mental representation of the ambivalently loved mother after separation, dangerous because she is potentially reengulfing. There is no longer the need to maintain the split image of the good mother and the bad or dangerous mother. With psychological birth, gender identity is normally established. The subphase of on the way to object constancy is marked by the development of certain ego functions, among them signal anxiety, transitional object development, and a cohesive and benign body image, which fuel the development of bodily self-care.

The Failure to Develop Signal Anxiety

In the early weeks of life, if there is an abrupt rupture of the symbiotic bond, the child may feel an overwhelming and disorganizing anxiety threatening to annihilate or shatter his sense of himself. This can occur if the mother does not heed his cries, allowing him to continue to cry alone without soothing. The child who has developed signal anxiety, however, is the child who has been soothed by the mother after such a rupture or when other events have caused the infant distress, and who has developed the ego function of anticipating that the mother will come forth to comfort him. Over time, there is a transition from reliance on the mother for relief from anxiety to soothing and comforting that become internalized. These transmuting internalizations build the ego so that somewhere in the second year of life the annihilating or traumatic anxiety and reliance on the external object for emotional regulation are replaced by signal anxiety, a signal for invoking defense (Tolpin 1972). The child who is not traumatized by his anxiety, but develops the ability to heed the internal signal to defend against it, is capable of inventing a transitional object for himself, an act of supreme creativity that leads to promoting the separation-individuation process and to object constancy.

Problems in Transitional Object Development

Winnicott's (1953) concept of transitional objects, transitional phenomena, and the transitional space that the mother establishes for the child between her and the world can easily be understood in terms of attachment. Key to furthering the separation-individuation process is the development of transitional object relationships and transitional phenomena. Winnicott wrote: "I have introduced the terms 'transitional objects' and 'transitional phenomena' for the designation of the intermediate area of experience, between the thumb and the teddy bear, between the oral erotism and the true object relationship, between primary creativity and the projection of what has already been introjected, between primary unawareness of indebtedness and the acknowledgment of indebtedness" (p. 510). Winnicott calls the transitional object the first possession. As an example of transitional phenomena Winnicott refers to "the infant's babbling and the way in which an older child goes over a repertory of songs and tunes while preparing for sleep" (p. 511). Transitional phenomena thus is a term to describe activities or the mental products of these activities, for example, singing or the tunes themselves. When my son was being toilet trained, he would awaken at night and would wordlessly hurry alone in the darkened hallway to the bathroom with only the night light illuminating the darkness where unknown predators might lurk. Sometimes his courage would falter and his voice would ring out in the dark: "Talk to me while I'm making my pee-pee." Speaking coherently is difficult when one is awakened out of sleep, but "I'm talking to you while you're making your pee-pee" was sufficient. Talking to him seemed to illuminate the darkness, making it grow lighter.[3] The clumsy words were a transitional substitute for the feel of loving arms around him, holding him as securely as if he were enfolded in a warm embrace.

Contact with the mother's or another's hair or skin can play a transitional function. Anzieu (1980) presents the observation of baby Helene, as reported by Monique Douriez-Pinol, as examples of transitional phenomena that all have as a common denominator Helene's seeking contact with parts of the body or objects that either are characterized by very soft hair or are made of material that provides

---

3. This experience resonated with the title of Lynda Schare's book on dream analysis, *If Someone Speaks It Gets Light.*

a similar tactile experience of contact with skin: "Helene blinks her eyes and wrinkles her nose with an air of complete contentment when, about to fall asleep, she explores her eyelashes with a finger; she then extends this behavior to exploring her mother's eyelashes and her doll's, to rubbing her teddy bear's ear on her nose, and finally, when calling her mother back after an absence or at the approach of other babies, to touching a cat, fleece slippers, or fuzzy pajamas" (pp. 20–21).

A transitional object (Winnicott 1953) is an object the child seizes upon and holds close to himself when he is alone; he creates the illusion that he is being held and comforted by his mother. It is used when the child is in need of comfort and experiences a sense of the mother's loss, albeit a temporary one. It is a *not-me* object, not part of his body, and is usually something like a teddy bear or favorite old blanket, which may evoke the feel and smell of the mother when held close. Although it is a not-me object, the child may experience it as being part of himself and feel enveloped in safety and comfort, especially when falling asleep or experiencing other anxiety about separation from mother, and that is its function. There is a gradual transition from reliance on the mother, the infant's first object, for relief from anxiety that becomes internalized, in this way building the ego so that signal anxiety replaces both traumatic anxiety and reliance on the mother, and leads to separation-individuation and object constancy (Tolpin 1972). Winnicott related the concept of transitional objects and phenomena to developmental stages, as quoted by Barkin (1978):

> As soon as they are born [infants] tend to use fist, finger, and thumbs in stimulation of the oral erotogenic zone, in satisfaction of the instincts of that zone and also in quiet union. . . . Then after a few months infants of either sex become fond of playing with dolls, and most mothers allow their infants some special object and expect them to become . . . addicted to such objects, the first not-me possession, an attachment to a teddy, a doll or soft toy, or to a hard toy. . . . Something is important here other than oral excitement and satisfaction though this may be the basis of everything else. [p. 513]

Barkin (1978) delineates those important other aspects of the transitional object: (1) the nature of the object as either animate or inanimate, soothing rather than stimulating; (2) the infant's capacity to recognize the object as *not-me*; (3) the place of the object in relation to the child's inner reality, outer reality, and the intermediate area at the border of his experience; (4) the infant's creative capacity to create, think up, or devise an object linked to undoing the separation between mother and child; and (5) an affectionate kind of an object relationship.

To understand childhood self-harm, it is important to distinguish between transitional objects and phenomena and those objects that serve pretransitional functions. Before the development of a transitional object, the infant has objects that serve the pretransitional functions of consoling and comforting the infant in the absence of the mother (Gaddini 1975, 1978, Krueger 1989, Sugarman and Jaffee 1989, Tustin 1981). The use of these objects is thought to be a precondition for the later development of true transitional objects and transitional phenomena. Unlike true transitional objects, these precursor objects are not created out of his need for illusion (Gaddini 1975, 1978). Instead, the precursor object may be either an object provided by the mother, such as a bottle or pacifier, or it may be a part of the infant's body, such as his thumb or hair, or it may be part of the mother's body. It may be a knob of the crib, a button on his clothing, or a piece of the blanket or mother's clothing. These precursor objects are of two types—the earliest into-the-mouth type and the later skin contact/tactile sensation type (Gaddini 1975, 1978). Because these objects are experienced as "me" objects, as an extension of the infant's body, Tustin (1981) also refers to them as normal autistic objects. These autistic or precursor objects, like transitional objects, may also function as external biological and behavioral regulators until a more complex mental organization evolves (Tustin 1981). The into-the-mouth objects serve to re-create for the infant a fleeting experience of being with the mother in the act of feeding, of having the nipple in his mouth (Sugarman and Jaffee 1989). Anzieu (1990) states that skin serves transitional functions, serving as a psychic envelope, a plane of demarcation between the internal and external worlds, between the internal psychic world and the psychic world of other people. Precursor objects often involve the use of both into-the-mouth objects and skin contact/tactile objects at the same time, as when the infant sucks on his thumb while twirling his hair or rubbing a soft blanket on his face while sucking on it.

Transitional phenomena all serve the same purpose, fostering the internalization of key self-regulatory functions, thus helping the individual make increasingly complex adaptations to internal and external demands (Sugarman and Jaffee 1989). There may be a series of objects and phenomena serving transitional functions, often in a developmental line of increasing organization and complexity that parallels other developmental lines. For example, the infant may use his body as a precursor object for self-soothing, promoting self-regulation at a sensorimotor level by defining what is inside from what is outside. The toddler may create a transitional object proper, as defined above, to neutralize and internalize drive energy, to modulate the wider and more differentiated range of affects that are characteristic of rapprochement, and to promote the development of mental structure. The contents and activity of fantasy (imaginary companions, twin fantasies, the family romance, comic book heroes) play a role as transitional phenomena in the lives of oedipal- and latency-age children, promoting secondary process thinking and helping the child move further into peer relations. In adolescence, ideas serve transitional functions as symbolic representations of the youth culture promote internalization of key regulatory functions. The symbolic representations include career aspirations, music, art, literature, and adolescent mores, and usually are infused with sexual and aggressive drive derivatives in earlier adolescence. Esoteric philosophies, religious and political views, and social causes replace the more drive-infused transitional phenomena of early adolescence. Abstractness is used to render drive derivatives less real, and thus, less anxiety provoking. The adolescent can view his world in a hypothetical sense: feelings of rage do not have to lead to murder, oedipal feelings do not have to lead to incest, and yearnings do not have to lead to fusion.

Problems in Body Self, Body Image, and Self-Care

The body is the soul's house. Shouldn't we therefore take care of our house so that it will not fall into ruin?

Philo

The image we have in our minds of our own bodies is central to our concept of who we are. Freud (1923) recognized that the ego of the infant is first and foremost a body ego, and that bodily experiences are the basis for the developing ego and sense of self. Before there can be a mind, there is the body. Before there can be a representational world, there is eating and defecating. Winnicott (1949) emphasized that these bodily experiences occur within the maternal caregiving environment and are the earliest experience of the psyche-soma, the unity of mind and body. "I suppose the word psyche here means the imaginative elaboration of somatic parts, feelings, and functions, that is, of physical aliveness" (p. 244). That is, the body is experienced as the dwelling place, the home, the container for the self. The infant feels alive and vital, a sense of confidence that he can continue "going on being." The notion of the body as the dwelling place for the self is derived from Freud, who said, "The dwelling-house was a substitute for the mother's womb, the first lodging, . . . in which he was safe and felt at ease" (Freud 1930, p. 90). This psychosomatic unity is one of those things we have no reason to think about or trouble ourselves about (Sacksteder 1988), until perhaps we fall ill or are injured, or we are reminded that our bodies do not measure up to the cultural ideal of physical attractiveness. Then illness or culture can cause us, unhappily, to focus on our bodies in a way that had not been necessary before.

Anzieu's (1980) concept of the skin ego complements Bowlby's concept of attachment and Winnicott's concept of dependence. "The ego is based on a body ego, but it is only when all goes well that the person of the baby starts to be linked with the body and the body-functions, with the skin as the limiting membrane" (Winnicott 1965, p. 59). Anzieu postulates that the skin, the surface of the infant's entire body and his mother's body, is the focus of experiences that are as important in terms of their emotional value, in stimulating confidence, pleasure, and thought, as are the experiences associated with sucking and excretion. The mother's touch in caring for her baby involuntarily stimulates his skin, while intentionally caressing and touching his skin to provide pleasure. The infant receives these gestures first as excitation, then as communication. "The massage becomes a message" (Anzieu 1980, p. 29). Through these loving messages, the infant develops a skin ego, an image that the child's primitive ego uses during the early stages of development to represent itself on the basis of his experience with the surface of the body. It is a sense of security and pleasure in living in his own skin. The skin has three psychic functions:

> In its first function, the skin is the sack that holds in the goodness and fullness that accumulates from being suckled, cared for, and bathed with words. In its second function, the skin is the surface that marks the boundary with the outside and keeps it on the outside; it is the barrier that protects against the greed and aggression of others, persons, or things. Lastly, in its third function, the skin—along with the mouth and at least as much as it—is a place and principal means of exchange with others. [Anzieu 1980, pp. 29–30]

For Ogden (1996), too, it is as the boundary between inside and outside and life and death that skin has its overriding importance. "Physiologically, it is essential that one's skin be continually generating a layer of dead tissue that serves as a life-preserving outermost layer of the body. In this way (as in Freud's concept of the stimulus barrier), human life is physiologically encapsulated by death" (p. 181). Marc Lappe (1996) states, "We have tended to think of the skin as our boundary, a watertight covering that enfolds ourselves and our organs and keeps them separate from the world out there. We visualize the skin in purely Euclidean terms, as a two-dimensional sheet that envelops us in a kind of perpetual Saran Wrap" (p. 71). However, we know that the skin is both a barrier and a sieve, "denying access to the body of some things and actively encouraging the passage of others. . . . Under some conditions it lets water out, permits toxic chemicals in, and allows bacteria to reside within its own confines" (p. 70). Diane Ackerman (1990), too, writes about the functions of the skin:

> What is a sense of one's self? To a large extent, it has to do with touch, how we feel. . . . Our skin is what stands between us and the world. It imprisons us, but also gives us individual shape, protects us from invaders, cools us down or heats us up as need be, produces vitamin D, holds in our body fluids. Most amazing is that it can mend itself when necessary and is constantly renewing itself. It can take a startling variety of shapes: claws (nails), spines, hooves, feathers, scales, hair. For most cultures, it's the ideal canvas to decorate with paints, tattooes, and jewelry. But most of all it harbors the sense of touch. [pp. 95–100]

The skin is constantly mending and renewing itself, forming two new layers of cells every four hours or so and shedding cells at the rate of over a million every hour (Montagu 1971). Skin is our first medium of communication and quite literally our protector, insulating the soft tissues within the body. It can be the locus of pain or of pleasure. Skin is regarded as a window on the soul; clear skin is viewed as a sign of physical and emotional health, while blemishes and scars mark a life out of balance (Brumberg 1997). The skin is expressive, carrying its own memory of experiences as the array of life's experiences is projected onto it. What happens to the skin ego of the child whose body does not mold together with the mother's when she holds him, whose mother's body tenses when she holds him? What happens to the skin ego of the child whose mother holds him to feed him but does not hold his gaze with her own, and looks away instead? The child does not experience his skin as soft and sweet, holding in his goodness. He experiences himself as something bad that causes the mother's body to tense, or something ugly that she does not want to look at. Because the skin is such a profound organ of contact, it plays a major role in fantasies.

But of all the body substances, blood is the most symbolic. "Blood, pumped through the body by a beating heart, is the essence of the life force" (Strong 1998, p. 34). The center of the skin's vitality lies deep within the dermis, where miles of blood vessels nourish the body with oxygen and nutrients and take away metabolic by-products (Lappe 1996). Blood is spilled when we are born, as we emerge into the world drenched in our mothers' blood. We die when too much blood is spilled. When blood circulates well, it warms the body. When we die and our blood stops circulating, it may be removed from the body and replaced by embalming fluid. Blood can be healing and transformative, as in blood transfusions, but a transfusion of contaminated blood can kill. Bleeding has traditionally symbolized healing, from the bloodletting medical traditions to the religious healing that is often expressed as being washed in the blood of Christ. "Bad blood" between people poisons relationships, while getting rid of bad blood is healing and restorative. Cutting and mingling blood cements social ties and is the stuff of initiation rites. It is no wonder that its symbolic powers of healing and transformation beckon so powerfully to self-mutilators (Favazza 1987, 1996).

Scars are mysterious marks, evoking fear, revulsion, and a fascination with hearing the story of how the scars were acquired. Scars are also symbolic, providing a permanent concrete record of pain, injury, suffering, and healing (Strong 1998). "The scars of the process are more than the artless artifacts of a twisted mind. They signify an ongoing battle and that all is not lost. As befits one of nature's great triumphs, scar tissue is a magical substance, a physiological and psychological mortar that holds flesh and spirit together when a difficult world threatens to tear both apart" (Favazza 1996, pp. 322–323). In Mexican artist Frida Kahlo's self-portraits, she portrayed herself wearing a Christ-like crown of thorns, gore dripping from her many wounds. The scars represent the pain of her life: polio at age 6, her back and legs badly scarred in an accident, her struggles in her family and with her sexuality. Scars can be something to be proud of, signs that one has endured and survived. They can even be signs of a healing process that has begun. "Thus, with a few strokes of the razor the self-cutter may unleash a symbolic process in which the sickness within is removed and the stage is set for healing. . . . The cutter, in effect, performs a primitive sort of self-surgery, complete with tangible evidence of healing" (Favazza 1996, p. 280).

Krueger (1989) elaborates that the foundation for our sense of self is found in our body and its evolving representations as they form in the maternal caregiving relationship. "The mother's hands outline and define the original boundary of the body's surface: they describe a shape of which there was no previous sense" (p. 5). The body self combines the psychic experience of body sensation, body functioning, and body image (Krueger 1989). Body image refers to the mental representations of the body self and is not limited to visual images (i.e., pictures in one's head of one's body) but include the schema of all sensory input, internally and externally derived—lived experiences processed and represented within a maturing psychic apparatus (Krueger 1989). Body image is how we perceive ourselves and is the way we think others perceive us (Fallon 1990). Body image is plastic, subject to modification by biological growth, trauma, or decline. Life circumstances significantly influence body image, as do culturally bound definitions of what is desirable and attractive. Because fat is considered ugly in Western culture, "feeling fat" is a code for a discordant mind–body experience, a mood or affect experienced in the body. For example, Krueger (1989) wrote of the psychic and body image changes in a 16-year-old bulimic girl, whose experience of "fatness" was confirmed by numerous other patients of different ages who also felt fat:

> When asked to draw her body, the patient divided the page in half with a vertical line. On the left side, she drew a proportionate, distinct, cohesive body image. On the right side was a grotesquely overweight, disproportionate body that had protrusions in the stomach and leg areas. She explained that the normal-appearing image was how she looked when she felt good and things were going well for her. The image on the right represented her feelings and her image of herself when she felt bad, was depressed, rebuffed by others, or out of tune with things around her.
>
> We examined in detail her experience of these body images. When she felt good, the drawing with the accurate boundaries corresponded to the image she saw when she looked in the mirror. However, when she felt bad, she saw herself as obese and said that the image corresponded exactly to what she saw in the mirror. When I asked her what she looked at specifically in the mirror, she indicated that when she felt good, she looked at her entire body, and when she felt bad and felt fat, she looked at the inner part of her thighs and occasionally at her stomach. She saw her inner thighs and hips as rounded, concluding that they were fat and that she was fat all over. [p. 69]

The body self is a function of the mother. According to Jacobson (1964), the newborn has a primal psychophysiological self that exists within the psychosomatic matrix of the relationship to the mother. The development of an intact body image and physical boundaries, and the subsequent evolution of ego boundaries fall along a continuum, in which there is a parallel developmental line of body self and psychological self. In self psychological terms, the infant's body, affects, and movements are initially experienced through the mirroring selfobject (the mother). And in ego psychological terms: "Even if viewed from a purely biological point of view, the newborn infant is only a partial system: between the distress signal and the relief of need, there must be a mother" (Mahler and McDevitt 1982, p. 828). Soon after, in the early awareness of the body, it is immediate, felt experience, the emerging experience of unsatisfied need (e.g., hunger). Next, the body self is form, distinct patterns of behavior. By means of observation of normal infants' behavior and inferences from observations of pathlogy, Mahler and McDevitt (1982) have traced the emergence of the sense of self, particularly the body self, in the first 15 months of life. A new level of organized self-awareness begins at about 15 months, when infants come to discover themselves in the mirror and acquire the semantic "no," which encapsulates developmental statements, "I am not an extension of you and your body or your desire; this is where you end and I begin—my body is mine and mine alone. You are not the boss of me." By 18 months the infant has usually developed a cognitive sense of separate existence and body self. In normal development the experiences and images of the inner body become, and the body surface becomes organized and integrated into an experiential and conceptual whole. Finally, the body-self is a concept, a relatively stable internal frame of reference that includes bodily and emotional images, concepts, and experiences. The consolidation of a stable, integrated cohesive mental representation of one's body is a key developmental task during this period, entailing delineation of what is inside from what is outside, with clear distinct boundaries. Those involved in the marketing of children's toys and books know that children become fascinated with the insides of their bodies and their bodies' products. Taking advantage of what is called the "yuck factor," toy chemistry sets are promoted as producing something simulating mucus, and the Gus Gutz doll invites kids to reach in through the mouth and "Pull out my guts, one gross handful at a time." *Grossology*, a children's book describing body functions, proved so popular that three sequels were written.

As he develops, the normal child pays little attention to the inside of his body, although the orifices that lead to the inside are a source of exploration and pleasure. Children pay more attention to the body's surface and length, delighting in growing, seeing their height marked on measuring charts, and in getting clothing in larger sizes. In a study exploring the notions of children, they were asked what was under their skins and what was inside their bodies (Schilder and Wechsler 1935). They replied, "I [am] myself." If we regard the skin as the psychic envelope, the body's container for the self (Anzieu 1980, 1990), then having intact skin represents having an intact self (Grotstein 1990, 1993, Ogden 1990, Rosenfeld 1990). For example, after getting a cut, a normal toddler may desperately insist that a Band-Aid be put on his finger immediately to ensure that his insides will not drip out. (In the magical ways that children think, a Power Ranger or Batman Band-Aid is thought to have enhanced healing powers.) A toddler may scream in fear when his mother breaks or cuts a piece of food in two for him, for fear that if the food can be broken in two, so can he himself be broken in two. (Later, in puberty the longer and broader body surface captures far more of the child's attention, as do the hormonally induced processes occurring inside.)

The fear of fragmentation represents the fear of regressing to the infant's initial experience of his body, a fragmented one in which the borders of the various parts of the body are clearly marked (Lacan 1977). Lacan refers to these borders as cuts, like the boundary definition of cut glass or cut crystal, just as the grotesque muscle definition of body builders is referred to as the "cut" look: "The very delimitation of the 'erogenous zone' that the drive isolates from the metabolism of the function . . . is the result of a cut (coupure) expressed in the anatomical mark (trait) of a margin or border—lips, 'the enclosure of the teeth,' the rim of the anus, the tip of the penis, the vagina, the slit formed by the eyelids, even the horn-shaped aperture of the ear" (Lacan 1977, p. 315). Like the horrifying paintings of Hieronymus Bosch, the fragmented body may manifest itself in dreams as disjointed limbs or internal organs that grow wings to conduct their "intestinal persecutions" (Lacan 1977).

How the child experiences his body as he grows and develops influences the development of language and symbolic thought. The child's experiences of touch, feeding, urination, defecation, and bowel and bladder training are all experienced subjectively, endowing the involved organs with a subjective experience of victories and defeats. These organs can readily become eroticized, and so anal or urethral purging or vomiting can become a disguised form of masturbatory activity. Enuresis and soiling in the sexually abused child can serve as a form of erotic discharge (Daldin 1988b). The skin, too, can become eroticized (Anzieu 1980) and self-cutting can serve as a disguised form of masturbation (Bollas 1992, Daldin 1988a).

While we usually think of eating as an expression of orality, it can quite readily serve as an expression of anality. True orality aims at assimilating the food and leaving behind what is bad or excessive (Oliner 1988). Once incorporated, the nourishing part no longer exists as a separate entity, becoming part of the body, while the bad is eliminated as waste. "Stuffing the face" provides a visual image of how plugging oneself up with food can stuff emotions down and silence their verbal expression. Filling the stomach may provide an internal object to manipulate, to fill the emptiness, and calm forbidden genital excitement (Oliner 1988). The food-object is filling but considered bad, not nourishing. Virtually always the food that is eaten is described as bad—as junk, garbage, or even feces ("shit food"). Binge food is frequently chocolate, the color of feces. Often it is shoved in so rapidly that it is barely tasted. And so the overeater becomes the mechanized receptacle for and producer of something bad, a container for garbage, a toilet, a shit-producing factory. Filling their stomachs and intestines with "shit," they can control and manipulate it within their bodies, or they can expel it forcefully, vomiting it up or purging it anally. No wonder those who stuff themselves with food often describe themselves as feeling "like shit."

When the capacity to develop mental representations of the body and its contents, including feelings, has been interfered with, it forces the individual to rely upon the immediate experience of his own body to elicit some representation of the self (Fonagy 1997, Fonagy et al. 1995, Krueger 1997). When the parent cannot mirror a consistent sense of self for the child, the child must turn to something that is consistent to obtain some sense of self. And his body is consistently there, to be turned to in the way that other human beings cannot always be turned to. The contents of the body assume a special importance because of their permanence and because they provide an illusory sense of omnipotence. "I don't need you or anyone else. I just need my body and food." There is always blood, feces, partially digested food, urine. For the most part, food, too, is consistently there. Children can get their hands on some food, quickly consume it, and make it part of the self. So representations of the self become bound up with food, before it enters the body and after. The self becomes bound up with representations of whole food, before it is consumed, when it holds out the potential to nourish the body and become part of it, sustaining life. ("You are what you eat.") It becomes bound up with representations of food consumed by the body that cannot be tolerate or digested; it becomes bound up with the natural body wastes—feces and urine—and with the contents of the stomach and intestines that must be wasted or purged. And so it happens that an individual's sense of himself becomes bound up in images and words pertaining to waste and degradation. Their words thus become bound in bodily images. "To put it briefly, the instinctual stages, when they are being lived, are already organized in subjectivity. And to put it clearly, the subjectivity of the child who registers as victories and defeats the heroic chronicle of the training of his sphincters, enjoying (*jouissant*) the imaginary sexualization of his cloacal orifices, turning his excremental expulsions into aggressions, his retentions into seductions, and his movements of release into symbols" (Lacan 1977, pp. 52–53).

When a body image has not been sufficiently formed to sustain the stresses of developmental maturation, body image regresses along with one's functioning in response to emotional events. Self-image and body image will shift rapidly in narcissistically vulnerable individuals. In regressed states such as narcissistic rage or depression, the body image oscillates rapidly. Such individuals cannot use objective data, such as being attractive or of normal weight, to alter their notion of being ugly or fat. Instead they compulsively pursue physical attractiveness and social affirmation to serve as narcissistic supplies, compensating for an inner emptiness and attempting to insure against abandonment. Indeed, the ability of anorexics to insist not simply that they feel fat but that they *are* fat even after seeing the marker on the scale go down to eighty or seventy pounds, is delusional.

The concept of self-care is valuable in helping us understand the structures and functions of the ego that serve the survival of the self and keep the self from harm (Khantzian and Mack 1983). Self-care includes (1) an emotional investment in caring about or valuing the self, requiring that the individual have sufficient self-esteem to feel himself to be worth caring for and protecting; (2) the capacity to anticipate dangerous situations and to respond to signal anxiety by protecting oneself; (3) an ability to control impulses and forgo pleasures that may have harmful consequences; (4) a sense of gratification in mastering risky situations; (5) sufficient knowledge of the world and of oneself to allow one to survive in a threatening world; (6) an ability to assert oneself or be aggressive enough to protect oneself; and (7) an ability to choose others who will not threaten one's existence for object relationships. The capacity to care for one's own self develops out of the mother–child attachment. From infancy on, there is a subtle balance between the parents' permission for the child to take the initiative and risk and explore, and the parents' protective function, which keeps the risks within moderate bounds.

Anna Freud (1966) described how a developmental line from irresponsibility to responsibility in body management grows out of the experiences the child has in the mother–infant dyad, reminding us that it is only gradually that the child takes on the satisfaction of essential physical needs such as feeding or elimination. It is only over time that the child's ability to care for and protect himself becomes internalized and developed through the experience of being cared for and protected by parents and caregivers (Khantzian and Mack 1983). When the child is well cared for by an attuned caregiver, he internalizes the sense that he deserves to be protected and well cared for, and so comes to take good care of himself. In individuals who are prone to harming themselves or to allowing others to harm them, it is clear that the capacity for self-care has been severely impaired. They have not been well cared for and sufficiently protected from danger early on, or they have been so overprotected that they never had the autonomy and opportunity to develop the self-care functions. Not only do they fail to care for and protect themselves from others, they fail to protect themselves from themselves.

Problems in Self and Object Representations

The regulatory interactions in infancy become the building blocks from which mental representations and their related inner affective experiences are built. They induce the searching and proximity-seeking behavior toward an increasingly specific and differentiated object throughout the life span, which is the hallmark of attachment behavior. Mental representations of self and other, however, operate on a different level of organization from the hidden regulators, involving cognitive and emotional ego and self structures that over time come to be gradually and increasingly differentiated from the undifferentiated matrix of inborn ego apparatuses. These mental representations become established through the experiences of learning and through memory of past interactions. Stern (1985) has conceptualized the units of these representations into moments and scenarios that become organized in early development into internal working and narrative models.

The mother, too, develops mental representations of herself as a good mother, capable of soothing and caring for her child. The child's psychological self, that part of the self representation where the self is seen not as the physical entity but as an intentional being motivated by thoughts and feelings, develops through the perception of this self in the mother's mind (Fonagy 1997, Fonagy and Target 1995, Fonagy et al. 1995). For the infant, repeated internalization of the mother's processed image of his thoughts and feelings provides containment (Bion 1962).

In the potential borderline child, however, there remain split representations of a good and bad mother, manifested by the longing for fusion with the (good) mother at the same time there is the fear of engulfment by the (bad) mother. The potential borderline child also has an unclear gender identity derived from failures to develop a sound body image. Remaining fixated at this primitive level of object relations, as they develop into adulthood they develop the primitive defense of projective identification, projecting the bad parts of themselves into external objects (persons) in such a way that the object becomes identified with their projected parts. They then can feel threatened and persecuted by the object.

Failures in the Capacity for Reflection

For a child to move along developmentally from enactment to meaning, he must become able to be "alone . . . in the presence of the mother" (Winnicott 1958c, p. 30). When the mother can exist in the background as a quiet, nonintrusive, calm presence, her ability to let her child exist separately from her allows him to turn his consciousness away from her and back toward his absorption in solitary play. He speaks to himself in an audible inner speech, a sweet babbling singsong flow of associations. It is through this ability that a secure sense of self develops. If the mother is not there as a quiet presence, or is inconsistent or unattuned, she keeps the child's consciousness focused on her, thus preventing him from losing himself in the creativity of play. The ability to play influences the development of the infant's ability to think symbolically and to experience emotion. It is when we are lost in play that we are so much our authentic and true selves, whether that is the solitary play of the infant in the presence of the mother, the playful mind of the adult absorbed in creative work, or the free verbal and symbolic play in the presence of the therapist.

Spitz (1965) says, "Only a reciprocal relation can provide the experiential factor in the infant's development, consisting as it does of an ongoing circular exchange, in which affects play the major role. From the beginning of life, it is the mother, the human partner of the child, who mediates every perception, every action, every insight, every knowledge" (p. 95). Soon after the child can perceive objects as being separate and apart from the self, he acquires the semiotic function, the ability to represent something outside the self by means of a signifier such as a gesture or a verbal sound. The mother's attuned response to his signifying quickens the development of operational thinking and symbolization. For example, the child sees the ice cream truck coming down the street and, not yet having words, points in excitement and squeals in anticipated pleasure. His mother responds animatedly, "Look how excited you are. Shall we buy an ice cream?" Joyce McDougall (1989) describes how, in the complex mother–infant psychosomatic scenario, the mother of the infant serves as her baby's "thinking system," finding an adequate response to her infant's distress, until the time that his mental processes are sufficiently developed and organized so that he outgrows the need for her to "lend him her mind." It is then that he begins to find words himself, "small shapes in the gorgeous chaos of the world. . . . They bring the world into focus, they corral ideas, they hone thoughts, they paint watercolors of perception" (Ackerman 1990, p. 7). The mother's ability to sooth the child serves as the child's "feeling system," and by means of transmuting internalization (Tolpin 1972), what the mother had done for the child becomes something that he then can do for himself.

Fonagy (1997) and colleagues (Fonagy and Target 1995, Fonagy et al. 1995) have presented a dialectical theory of self development in which the psychological self develops through the perception of this self in another's mind. When this mirroring function is absent or distorted early in life, transmuting internalization fails to develop, promoting a desperate quest for alternative ways of containing psychological experience. Lawrence Hedges (1994) has identified a pathological organizing experience in some infants as a failed contact with an unattuned mother that becomes internalized as the lost or dead mother of infancy. This internalization of the lost mother of infancy is manifested in the infant's failure to use fantasy, symbolism, or abstraction. The capacity to develop mental representations of the body and its contents, including feelings, is interfered with, forcing the individual to rely upon the immediate experience of his own body to elicit some representation of the self (Fonagy 1997, Fonagy et al. 1995, Krueger 1997). The self representation is achieved not symbolically but through the experience of the body self.

Maurice Merleau-Ponty, a French philosopher, developed a theory of language that posits that language is an extension of our gestures (McLane 1996).[4] We interact bodily with the world, and as we do, the world comes to have meaning for us. "Speech is in fact a gift of language, and language is not immaterial. It is a subtle body, but body it is. Words are trapped in all the corporeal images that captivate the subject" (Lacan 1977, p. 87). We extend that meaning into linguistic gestures that acquire layer upon layer of cultural meaning, but these gestures are made anew in the individual gestures of each person. When an individual's interaction with the world is traumatic, and the impulse to give spoken voice to the inner pain has been thwarted, self-harm can develop as a gestural articulation of

---

4. I am grateful to Janice McLane for explaining to me the philosophical background of her paper, "The Voice on the Skin: Self-Mutilation and Merleau-Ponty's Theory of Language."

trauma (McLane 1996) as well as a perverse attack on language itself (Woodruff 1998).[5] Self-harm is, after all, an attempt to blot out intolerable thoughts or images in one's mind (Fonagy and Target 1995), an attack on the process of creating meaning (Woodruff 1998). "We come alive as human beings through our capacity to symbolize experience, but the cost of this capacity is to lose the immediacy of (bodily) experience" (Woodruff 1998, p. 3). Those who regress to self-harm cannot tolerate giving up the immediacy of experience in favor of tolerating grief and depression. To do so is to live more in the mind and less in the body. Because they live so much in their bodily experience and so little in the mind, they are addictively driven to seek and attain an impossible fusion with the body of the mother. To accept that one cannot have what is so desperately wanted is to mourn, to use language to give meaning to the loss. To use words to stand in place of that thing signified, is to destroy the immediacy and presence of the object it represents (Woodruff 1998). When confronted with their own impotence in resolving this quest and the realization that the fusion cannot occur, self-harmers cannot mourn this loss. It is too shattering to their sense of themselves. Instead, they regress to a primitive aggression, a destructive narcissism, that erupts violently against the dedifferentiated mother-body-self, once again reclaiming the immediacy of the mother, the body, and the self, in a gesture that assaults language.

---

5. I am grateful to Margaret Woodruff, Ph.D., for sharing with me her paper, "Flesh Made Word: Cutting in Search of the Mother," and her clinical experience with severe self-harming patients.

6

The Psyche-Soma and Traumatic Attachments to Pain and Suffering

Once you taste the stick, you don't want to give it up.
Reportedly said by Hedda Nussbaum, in Daphne Merkin,
"A Taste of the Stick: Joel and Hedda"

Those who have not developed a reflective self must find other ways of containing and articulating their experience. When attachments are insecure and there has been a failure to use fantasy, symbolism, or imagination to contain and express experience, there is nothing to do but call upon one's own body. Hypochondriasis, somatic illness, and self-harm are such manifestations. When experiences in life have been marked by neglect or trauma, then self-harm can develop as personal gestures that speak of these experiences. Despite the fact that those who starve themselves, abuse drugs and alcohol, and binge and purge share something in common in harming themselves, the gestural articulation is unique and individual. Each story is different.

Carla, the Hispanic patient mentioned in the Introduction, puzzled the doctors in the municipal hospital's dermatology clinic, where she was being treated unsuccessfully for a persistent skin infection on her arm. Carla could not know what unhappiness she harbored. In fact, when she arrived at the walk-in intake clinic, she could not even present herself to me as someone in need of help. She said she was there because she was doing research for a college psychology class on how mental health services could be helpful, and wanted to know if I would answer some hypothetical questions. I agreed and it was immediately apparent that the hypothetical questions pertained to a "hypothetical" potential patient—Carla. She soon acknowledged that she was there for herself. She was an overweight young woman given to overeating and dressing seductively, and feeling bad much of the time. She was also prone to rashes and told me that although she went to the dermatology clinic and used the oral antibiotics and ointments as prescribed, they did not help. In fact, despite the treatment, her rash was getting worse. She showed me her left arm, which was covered with what looked like bits of scabs, raw red tissue, and oozing sores. Her current boyfriend could not stand the way it looked, and she was afraid he would leave her.

I asked if there might be anything else she could tell me about why her rash was getting worse, and she reluctantly revealed that she regularly raked her infected arm hard with her metal-bristled hair brush. "Don't ask me why. I couldn't tell you. Sometimes, though, I just feel like I have to do it." She had had numerous one-night stands and currently was having an affair with a married man, although the intimate moments stolen with him were becoming less enjoyable.

In the second session she told me that she had told her mother about me and wanted me to meet her mother. She could not say why, only that she had told her mother and her mother had agreed to come in and see me. She told me proudly that her mother was very beautiful, which I would see. Thinking that there was something she wanted me to know about her mother that she could not tell me in words, I agreed to meet her mother, a strikingly well-groomed and elaborately dressed woman, quite vain about her appearance. Her fingernails were long and impeccably manicured, and this was before the current fashion for such long nails. Although I did not inquire about her nails, she wanted to tell me about them. They were her pride and joy. Although she could not afford salon manicures, she told me in obsessive detail how she maintained the condition of her hands and nails by avoiding washing dishes, by daily applications of hand cream, and by attending immediately to chips in her nail polish. In addition she gave herself a full manicure twice a week, spending hours on it. I commented that that must have been a difficult regimen to follow when her children were young, and soon learned that the demands of motherhood had made barely a dent in this ritual. If her baby cried from hunger or needed a diaper changed while she was repairing her manicure, the baby just had to wait until she was finished. If the baby continued to cry, she would jab the baby in the chest with a fingernail that was not wet with polish. She reassured me that she did not jab hard enough to hurt her baby, just a tiny scratch on occasion, enough to stop the crying.

As Carla's treatment continued, I came to understand how her skin, deprived of warm touch in infancy, had erupted in wordless protest. She used her hair brush to stimulate her skin in what seemed to be compensation for this deprivation and a reenactment of the jabs and scratches she had received. She had also turned to food to comfort herself and created the illusion of love from liaisons with unavailable men.

THE PSYCHOSOMATIC DYAD AND ALEXITHYMIA

The classical psychoanalysts assumed that once an ego has formed, intrapsychic conflicts can be directly translated into pathophysiological changes in the body in the form of conversion hysteria (Freud 1916). In Victorian times, Anna O. developed an hysterical pregnancy, Elizabeth von R. developed a limp, and Dora developed an uncontrollable cough, all of which were understood by Freud to mean that their bodies were speaking about repressed sexual desire and about unspoken loss. These symptoms demonstrated what Felix Deutsch (1959) called the "mysterious leap from the mind to the body." According to Deutsch, the body is in a continual speechless dialogue with the environment, with the individual, and with the various parts of the personality, a dialogue that can be decoded through psychoanalysis. The classical formulation did not consider that in the primitive mind of the infant, another mysterious leap can occur, but in the opposite direction. That is, the infant begins to experience his bodily sensations and some of his biological processes as actual mental events (Taylor 1987). When this primitive mentation continues into adult life and becomes embedded in the personality, the body then becomes the stage where emotional expression occurs in what is often a dramatic presentation. Emotion then is not experienced mentally but instead is expressed bodily, through a particular body organ or system that is predisposed to comply somatically (Freud 1905a). Thus, a disorder of emotional expression is created in which the predisposed individual develops a psychosomatic illness or inflicts harm upon his body. An incest survivor who has had incestuous intercourse may develop numerous gynecological problems and/or may be prone to mutilating her genitals. Or if the hand was used to fondle the genitals of a parent, the hand may become arthritic or may become an even more direct target for aggression, as the individual punches her hand through windows or into brick walls.

As the infant grows and develops, at those times when her ego cannot defend against painful affect she might regress to an undifferentiated somatic phase of development, thus retracing and strengthening the infantile pathways to the interior, laying down psychophysiological mechanisms for the discharge of affect (Schur 1955). Anxiety or depression become regressively resomatized, and primary process thinking prevails as thought processes regress to less abstract and more primitive levels in what Schur suggested be called "borderline states." For example, when a child suffers from psychogenic vomiting, "automatically" vomiting to express anger or disgust that she cannot know she feels and cannot express in words, the alimentary canal in general and the muscles of peristalsis in particular become endowed with an emotional valence. Each such use of the body reinforces that emotional valence, engraving it more firmly in the brain and attaching it even more strongly to that organ or organ system.

As the child grows and develops, she will tend to discharge aggressive affect to the interior of her body, experiencing it somatically as nausea, requiring discharge to the exterior by vomiting. Those whose personalities are primitively organized around expression of affect may grow up as psychogenic vomiters. One patient of mine, from latency age into her late thirties when she began treatment, had to throw up after dinner and did so "automatically," without trying. Because many adolescents or adults may have lost some of the ability to vomit automatically that they may have had earlier in life, they may induce vomiting by sticking their fingers down their throats or using syrup of ipecac. Another patient who had vomited in her latency years as an expression of affect, simply stopped in adolescence in response to an improvement in her emotional environment. But in adulthood when she could find no way to solve psychic conflicts, she regressed to vomiting once again. Initially she needed to stick her finger down her throat, but soon she found she needed no such help. Yet another patient was proud that she did not even need to use her fingers. She simply imagined that the food she had just eaten was lying in the toilet bowl along with her feces and urine and vomited quite easily.

Skin rashes can result from discharging drive and affect inward (Bick 1968, Pines 1980, Schur 1955). While the mother is handling her child, the mother's skin may convey a full range of emotions from warmth and tenderness to hatred and disgust, triggering the child to express his experience through his skin, which may itch, weep, or rage (Pines 1980). This in turn will be dealt with by the mother according to her capacity to accept and soothe her troubled child, a response that may be internalized by the infant (Bick 1968, Pines 1980). The mother, the object that contains the child, is experienced concretely as skin, and her capacity to contain the infant's anxiety is introjected by the infant (Bick 1968). Similarly, McDougall (1989) points out that the patient's experience of feeling contained by the analyst is an experience of "shared skin." In her clinical observations of women with skin diseases and the analysis of a woman with a history of infantile eczema, Pines found that babies who had eczema in the first year of life had a basic disturbance in their relationships with their mothers. Their eczema seemed to produce a profound disappointment and narcissistic hurt in the mothers and a restlessness and fretfulness in the children. The mothers, despite extended periods of trying to soothe their children, experienced great difficulty and frustration, and consequently were unable to experience themselves as good mothers.

The mother's narcissistic disappointment in the child will have a fundamental effect on the child's narcissistic structure and self representation. The pervasive fear of disintegration or loss of the self, and the need to be contained and held, affect subsequent personality formation. Otherwise emotionally deprived infants who experience extended periods of bodily soothing when ill, learn to translate psychic pain into visible bodily suffering that arouses care and concern. As this becomes embedded in their character as they grow and develop, they characteristically find psychosomatic solutions to psychic pain, reenacting the early mother–child relationship in which their mothers cared for their ill bodies but not for their feelings. In this way we can understand how children whose most satisfying experiences with their mothers were in the application of ointments to their skin eruptions might deliberately but unconsciously interfere with the healing of their skin by scratching it, pulling off scabs, or infecting it. Because harming their skin staves off feelings of inner deadness by serving to make them feel connected to the mother, cutting, burning, or scratching the skin can make them feel more alive. As McDougall (1989) puts it, "A body that suffers is alive" (p. 152). At the same time, the self-harm serves the communicative function of trying to bring the mother close, to create the sense of object constancy that has not been attained.

In the analysis of borderline adults prone to physical self-harm, Fonagy (1997) found that in their early childhood, the development of their psychological selves had been impaired by experiences of abuse and neglect. McDougall (1989) states, "A nursling, through its cries, gestures and somato-psychic reactions to stress, gives nonverbal communications that only a mother is able to interpret. She functions, in this respect, as her baby's thinking system, and finds an adequate response to her infant's distress" (p. 169). For the infant, repeated internalization of the mother's processed image of his thoughts and feelings provides "containment" (Bion 1962). "We cannot fall out of this world. That is to say, [the 'oceanic feeling'] is a feeling of an indissoluble bond, of being one with the external world as a whole" (Freud 1930, p. 65). When the world is too much to bear, when there is not that feeling of containment derived from oceanic experiences with the mother, the child may find self-injury to be a way of separating from her, cutting or scratching herself away from the mother.

In Carla's case, we can understand her rashes and promiscuity as expressions of her hunger to be touched lovingly by her mother. The physical pain she inflicted upon herself can be understood as the wish to destroy the maternal object that she has unconsciously introjected. By turning the aggression on herself masochistically, she expressed her aggressive wish to harm her mother while at the same time maintaining the libidinal tie to her. She also satisfied the superego injunction not to harm her mother, while repeating actively upon herself that trauma to which she submitted passively as a child. By exacerbating and maintaining her skin infections, she managed to get the medical staff to give her the touch and attention she craved.

The parent's inability to contain the child or think about the child's mental experience, and thus mirror it for him, may later, in adolescence, promote a desperate quest for alternative ways of containing psychological experience, which may involve various forms of destructive and physical expression toward the self and/or others (Fonagy 1997). When the parent overgratifies the child by serving as his "thinking system" relentlessly, not providing the sufficient frustration that is necessary for the development of ego functions, she conveys to the child that he has no thoughts other than those that are in her mind, that he has no mind of his own, only the "one mind for two" (McDougall 1989) that they share. When a mother cannot think about her child's somatic experience, but tells him, either through words or behavior, when he is hungry, when he needs to sleep, and when he needs to use the toilet, she is telling him that his somatic responses are not his, that what he feels in or on his body is what she says he feels. In this way she claims ownership of his body, conveying that the child's body is not his own but is an extension of hers. They share "one body for two" (McDougall 1989), which profoundly stunts the development of sexual identity and thought processes. The mother's perpetuation of the fantasy that they have one body for two, one sex for two , and one mind for two leads to feelings of inner deadness in the child, who cannot sufficiently recognize the inner stirrings of his own body, including his genitals, and of his own mind (McDougall 1989). An enormous estrangement or dissociated split between the psyche and the soma develops (Sacksteder 1988), and it is in this space that the infant begins to erect a false self (Sacksteder 1989a,b), a persona to satisfy the mother's needs, severely derailing the journey to individuation.

The individual with a false-self persona, serving the needs of a narcissistic mother, often develops into a self-denying person, eager to please others, becoming frequently a devoted caregiver of others or a superachiever in academics or athletics, like the anorexic who Levenkron (1981) called "The Best Little Girl in the World." Because the child does not value herself, she cannot really value these qualities or achievements. Her inner deadness or despair may be masked by an addictive-like dependence on significant others, who are experienced as part of herself.

Based on her personal experience, Dorothy Allison's (1988, 1992) remarkable fictional accounts of horrific physical and sexual abuse, neglect, hunger, and maternal abandonment tell us how a child was trained by her mother not to want or need, and to develop a false self. While she developed a false-self persona, a secret part of her never could stop wanting, needing, and dreaming of better things. This was what saved Allison herself and kept hope alive, to be quickened later by her ability to write about and make sense of the chaos in award-winning books.

> "Never want what you cannot have," she'd always told me. It was her rule for survival, and she grabbed hold of it again. . . . Push it down. Don't show it. Don't tell anybody what is really going on. My mama makes do when the whole world cries out for things to stop, to fall apart, just once for all of us to let our anger show. My mama clamps her teeth, laughs her bitter laugh, and does whatever she thinks she has to do with no help, thank you, from people who only want to see her wanting something she can't have anyway. . . . *Do not want what you cannot have*, she told

me. But I was not as good as she was. I wanted that dream. I've never stopped wanting it. [Allison 1988, pp. 40–42]

Because of the separation difficulties inherent in experiencing the mother's body and mind as one's own, the child has difficulty knowing what he is experiencing within himself. These children tend not to know what it is to eat when they are hungry, to be put to bed when they are tired, or to cry or express sadness in words, because the parent does not know and may not care to know that the child has physical and emotional needs of his own. The child may be raised unthinkingly according to whatever is the culturally sanctioned child-rearing practice of the day (e.g., let the child cry, don't spoil him by holding or rocking him when he's upset, feed him on schedule regardless of whether he's hungry or not, send him to his room to be alone when he misbehaves), which may further alienate him from himself. Such rigid advice was handed down from generation to generation, through Luther Emmett Holt's (1929) *The Care and Feeding of Children*, urging strict feeding habits and rapid toilet training, and John Watson's (1928) *Psychological Care of Infant and Child*, also stressing regimentation in feeding and elimination and warning parents not to hug or kiss their children. These practices were echoed in popular women's magazines, in Spock's *The Common Sense Book of Baby and Child Care* (1946), and through U.S. government pamphlets on prenatal and infant care. Parents often felt conflicted between their empathy for the child and the prescribed child-care practices. Many mothers believed that bedtime should be an unhurried time of lullabies or stories, knowing intuitively that the transition to sleep, the separation of the infant from the parent and from his own consciousness, should be gentle. Yet many of these parents allowed their own empathy for the child to be overpowered either by their idealization of medical experts or by their identification with their own parents. Bowlby (1979) commented on these practices:

> An immense amount of friction and anger in small children and loss of temper on the part of their parents can be avoided by such simple procedures as presenting a legitimate plaything before we intervene to remove his mother's best china, or coaxing him to bed by tactful humoring instead of demanding prompt obedience, or permitting him to select his own diet and to eat it in his own way, including, if he likes it, having a bottle until he is two years of age or over. The amount of fuss and irritation which comes from expecting small children to conform to our own ideas of what, how, and when they should eat is ridiculous and tragic—the more so now that we have careful studies demonstrating the efficiency with which babies and young children can regulate their own diets and the convenience to ourselves when we adopt these methods. [p. 13]

Dr. Benjamin Spock (1946), whose guide to rearing children was deemed to be as essential for new parents as a layette and a supply of diapers, later spoke of his indebtedness to Winnicott for helping him to change his early thinking about parents and children. His own experience as a child, raised by a stern, guilt-inducing mother, gave him the idea that he should have some kind of psychological training in order to practice pediatrics in a way that would satisfy mothers and could soundly inform his own thinking. The influence of psychoanalysis in general and Winnicott in particular is seen in Spock's several revisions of his book, which has changed considerably since the first edition.

T. Berry Brazelton (1972, 1974, 1981), a pediatrician influenced greatly by psychoanalysis and by attachment theory, was one of a few others who advocated an approach to child rearing that was based on empathy and respect for children's individual differences and the growing processes of mothers', fathers', and siblings' attachments to the newborn.

Eating and feeding disturbances are the earliest and most frequent disorders in children (Sperling 1978). Far too often battles for control in childhood may center around food, eating, and elimination, and for good reason; the only sense of power infants and toddlers have in a world in which they are entirely dependent on powerful adults is in the arena of eating and elimination. When mother and infant engage in battles for control around eating, with the mother insisting, begging, or pleading, the mother may win the battle of getting the child to eat what she thinks is a healthy diet and getting the child to eat what he does not like or want, but she loses the overall war, for in the process the child may internalize the experience of his body being his mother's possession, for her to control. Or the child may eat but suffer from psychogenic vomiting or diarrhea, besting the mother in the battle for control: "Maybe you can stuff things into me, but it's up to me whether I keep them in me or expel them, and in what form." Similarly, battles can be waged around toileting, with the mother insisting the child make in the potty and the child fighting back, continuing to make in his pants or becoming constipated, thus retaining some sense of autonomy by refusing to submit to the mother's insistence that he give up his feces to the mother. All these disturbances, when they are more than transient but take hold in a developing psyche-soma, are precursors to what is known today as a full-blown eating disorder or can later be manifested in other psychosomatic disorders related to feeding, such as ulcerative colitis and celiac disease, which sometimes coexist with anorexia nervosa (Sperling 1978), Crohn's disease, and irritable bowel syndrome. The early mother–child relationship acts as an early acquired constitution, predisposing the child to psychosomatic difficulties (Sperling 1978).

With the advent of puberty, when issues of autonomy, separation, and control over one's body loom large, the adolescent may resume the battle for control over her body in the form of an eating disorder, a disguised "declaration of independence," proclaiming "This is my body. I'll put as much or as little food as I want into it. I'll starve it if I want to. I'll stuff it with as much food as I want and I'll purge it with laxatives."

For some adolescents getting a tattoo or body piercing, virtually guaranteed to disturb their parents, is another kind of "declaration of independence," proclaiming not only that it is his body to do with what he wants but also an affiliation with a peer group whose values and body modifications he shares. The 13-year-old who begs, as a patient of mine did, "Mommy, Mommy, can I get a nose piercing?" is less involved in the assertion of autonomy than the child who comes home with a nose-piercing, a fait accompli. Some adolescents' self-mutilation moves beyond what is acceptable in the youth culture to the more disturbing form of cutting or burning themselves, which can also evoke battles for control with parents, medical personnel, and psychotherapists, reenacting earlier battles for control.

In those infants and toddlers who may be constitutionally strong-willed enough to provide their mothers with a formidable adversary early in life, these battles for control around food can result in infantile anorexia nervosa, a form of failure-to-thrive syndrome. Infantile anorexia nervosa is an eating disorder characterized by refusing to eat and failure to thrive that manifests during the early phase of separation and individuation, usually between 6 months and 3 years (Chatoor 1989). The mothers of these infants tend to be controlling, and are often unable to recognize, and thus they thwart, the infants' attempts at self-feeding. Subsequently, the infants refuse to eat, in a remarkably strong-willed and persistent attempt to attain a degree of autonomy and control in relation to the mother. Because of the altered caloric intake the babies' weight gain decelerates markedly. At the same time the emotional deprivation contributes to the slowing or disruption of the acquisition of emotional and social developmental milestones. It is the persistence and strong will of these babies that distinguishes them from babies who thrive in infancy but who may either submit to the mother's demands or develop the disordered eating precursor behaviors that turn in adolescence into anorexia nervosa, which becomes the adolescent form of failure to thrive; the refusal to eat results in the girl not having enough fat on her body to stimulate the secretion of the sex hormone estrogen, thus inhibiting the development of secondary sexual characteristics (e.g., breast development, amenorrhea) and causing loss of bone density. This physiological growth inhibition, combined with the disordered attachment, slows emotional and social development.

When a child is raised to meet the needs of the parent, and is neglected or abused, physically or emotionally, the child may turn to his body as the battleground for enacting a battle for control of himself and his life. A parent may "discipline" the child sadistically, attaching the child to him through pain and suffering. A parent who cannot tolerate the child's distress may punish him for communicating his distress. "What are you crying for? I'll give you something to cry about." These children do not experience themselves as a psychosomatic unity, but rather experience psyche and soma as distinct, dissociated entities. This failure of personalization, or depersonalization, the agonizing sense of not feeling real to oneself, promotes the development of a false self, developed to meet the narcissistic needs of the parent, producing what appear to be individuals with successful, even perfect functioning (Winnicott 1949), what McDougall (1989) refers to as "normopaths," persons with pseudo-normal functioning.

Infantile anorexia, later onset of anorexia, and self-mutilation represent *failures of personalization*, the term Winnicott (1949) uses to describe the child's sense of feeling real to himself and of localizing himself in his body. Depersonalization results from the mother's failure to care for and handle the infant in a way that constantly introduces the baby's body and psyche to each other and produces a sense of integration of psyche and soma. It is this persistence of a split in the patient's ego organization, or of multiple dissociations, that constitutes the true illness. Winnicott, an Englishman, wrote the word *psychosomatic* in the British style, *psycho-somatic*, using a hyphen to separate psyche from soma. That has the value of visual appeal if we think of the hyphen as representing the dissociated space where illness and self-harm can form. Similar to Winnicott's concept of a dissociated space is Ammon's (1979) concept of the experience of a hole in the ego, a structural defect in the psyche produced by disturbances in the early mother–child relationship, which the individual tries to plug with a somatic symptom or dependency on a drug or person who functions as a psychic stabilizer.

At puberty, many children who had been "perfect" can no longer stifle the feelings of resentment and anger that are necessary for the maintenance of the false self. Or they may become anxious by the psychosexual changes they are undergoing or anticipate undergoing, and develop what Freud (1918) called "melancholia of the sexually immature": "It is well known that there is a neurosis in girls which occurs . . . at the time of puberty or soon afterwards, and which expresses aversion to sexuality by means of anorexia. This neurosis will have to be brought into relation with the oral phase of sexual life" (p. 106). At puberty, the image of the body becomes infused with representations of a body that is growing larger and fleshier and producing new fluids, and with experiences of inner sensations that can be both stimulating and anxiety-producing, all of which may make adolescents feel not in control of their bodies and physical and emotional feelings. They become extremely sensitive to criticism by parents and teasing by peers, and they may imagine insults. The world seems hostile, and no place feels safe. At this time the body can be employed in relation to psychic conflict in a way that it never was used before (Ritvo 1988). It is at the point at which the false-self defensive organization of childhood crumbles and is abandoned in adolescence that the space created by the psyche-soma split is discovered and exploited by the unconscious in a drastic, malignant, aggressive bodily solution (Sacksteder 1989a,b). It is in this space, the depersonalized split between psyche and soma, that interpersonal and intrapsychic conflicts are subsequently displaced and enacted, providing a unique opportunity to pursue a sense of personal autonomy and effectiveness through a driven and perverse determination to have total control over the body.

To break free of the symbiosis, and feel separate and alive, the adolescent may need to rupture the membrane of "shared skin" by attacking, tormenting, and subduing the body by cutting or burning it, or starving it back to prepubertal hormone levels, preventing menstruation and turning back the clock on sexuality. Paradoxically this grab for freedom and separation occurs in the context of an extreme ego regression to a state in which affect and self- and object representations become less differentiated and separate. The powerful sway of this regression allows self-starvation, bulimic behavior, self-mutilation and other self-harm to take hold, in a driven and sadomasochistic determination for total control over the body and a sense of personal autonomy and effectiveness. The transitional space in which self-harm occurs becomes the adolescent's "safe space," an autistic refuge in a threatening and hostile world.

More specifically, the act of self-harm serves to displace and enact interpersonal and intrapersonal (intrapsychic) conflicts in the dissociated space in an affective regression. Differentiated affects become dedifferentiated and recondensed with one another; they become reinstinctualized and resomatized and thus cannot be verbalized. An individual who otherwise might be capable of verbalizing expressively about other emotional states is rendered incapable of identifying and talking about the primitive emotional states he experiences. Thus, mechanistically cutting or burning one's body, picking or scratching at one's skin, and other forms of self-harm arise as simplistic, concrete bodily solutions to complex psychological problems. Again, the paradox: at the moment of self-harm and self-destructiveness, the suffering body feels most alive; at the moment of symbiotic merger with the internalized object, it also feels separate, cohesive, and powerful.

Primitive defenses and regressions to altered and dissociated states of consciousness are key factors in the psychophysiological regressions to somatic illness (Bach 1985, Giovacchini 1993, Reiser 1966) and to self-harm enactments. There is a characteristic altered (regressed) state of consciousness involving disturbances of self and body, such as body image disturbances, hypochondriasis, thermal and boundary sensitivity, and difficulties with eating and weight regulation (Bach 1985). Trancelike states of depersonalization and derealization are often experienced before and during bulimic and self-mutilating episodes.

The child does not enjoy or care for her body, developing instead a persecutory, sadistic relationship with it, hating, neglecting, and cruelly attacking it. Paradoxically, the self increasingly identifies itself only with the body, as it masochistically continues to pursue ever greater heights of suffering and pain. At the same time, in the object world a similar relationship occurs as the self develops a persecutory sadomasochistic relationship with others. The self is experienced not as an intentional being motivated by thoughts and feelings, but as a painful body (Sacksteder 1988, 1989a).

Sacksteder (1988) cites Ferenczi as noting that children who are brought into the world as "unwelcomed guests" of their family are in trouble. These children know that they do not have a place in their parents' heart, that often their parents wish that they had not been born at all. This wish can be either unconscious or conscious and spoken. Wishing only to please the parents, the child's will to live may be broken. She may die readily and willingly to please the parents or may remain disposed to illness for the rest of her life (Sacksteder 1988).

She may inflict injury upon herself, as self and object representations lose whatever differentiation they had, substituting the partial sacrifice to the parents of
her injured body parts in lieu of her life, as Jill Montgomery (1989c) wrote about
her patient:

> Another woman struggling to maintain herself during my absence had a long his-
> tory of repeated psychiatric hospitalizations with anorexia, multiple suicide attempts,
> self-mutilation with cutting and burning, prolonged periods of psychotic disorgani-
> zation, and periods of mutism. The patient's mother had tried to murder her when
> she was a child and had behaved in a sadistically psychotic manner to her victim
> daughter with little intervention from family members. During my absence, the
> patient poured a pot of hot coffee on her foot and kept the wound open by cutting
> through the forming blisters with scissors. She explained, "I want to kill myself but
> I can't," and "I have to do something." Her realization, many months later, was that
> *she* was not the one who wanted her death. [p. 35]

It is no wonder, then, that those who develop perverse psychosomatic disorders suffer as well from alexithymia, difficulty in the cognitive processing of
emotions (Deutsch 1959, McDougall 1989, Taylor 1987, Taylor et al. 1991). They
have difficulty identifying emotion and distinguishing it from thought or somatic
experience. They frequently do not know what it is that they feel internally,
whether that feeling is a somatic experience such as hunger, thirst, or fatigue, or
an emotion such as anger, shame, or joy. When they can identify emotion, it
remains undifferentiated. If we think of a broad emotional range as being equivalent to a musical range of several octaves, then alexithymics play in only one
octave, a very constricted affect area. They may say that they feel good or bad,
but may not be able to distinguish further within those categories, to say more
specifically what kind of good (e.g., happy, content, elated, excited) or bad (e.g.,
sad, angry, guilty, ashamed) feeling they have. They may be able to say only that
it feels "bad." People with body-image problems may be able to say only that they
feel fat or ugly. Compare this with what David Morris (1991) has to say about
pain: "Gertrude Stein could not say truthfully about pain what she said about roses
['A rose is a rose is a rose']. It is not true that a pain is a pain is a pain: everywhere and eternally the same" (p. 28). To the alexithymic, a pain *is* a pain is a
pain. The alexithymic speaks in a way that is boring, lacking the richness that
comes from an expanded emotional range. The thinking of the alexithymic has
been characterized as operatory thinking (Marty and Debray 1989, Marty and de
M'Uzan 1963), a pragmatic and affectless way of relating to oneself and others.
The alexithymic ego style is an invaluable defensive measure against inexpress-
ible pain and fears of losing a sense of identity, of dissolving, or of going mad.
My alexithymic patients tend to speak of their lives as their personal version of
the news of the week in review, reporting on where they went, what they did,
and who said what, but with little or no affect.

Felix Deutsch (1959), anticipating the object relations focus in treating alexithymic patients with psychosomatic difficulties, posed two questions that are crucial in the treatment of psychosomatic processes: Who is speaking when the body speaks? With whom is the body speaking? For McDougall (1989) psychosomatic processes derive from complex psychic scenarios, inner "scripts" that were written in early childhood and enacted on "the theater of the body." In discussing somatizers, McDougall calls their endless lists of physical symptoms and complaints the "organ recital," a particular form of psychosomatic communication to which internists spend a good portion of their time listening.

McDougall (1989) has heard in many psychosomatic patients a terror of losing their sense of their body and individual self along with a muted search for merger with the mother. Their fantasy seems to be that they are so merged that they have one body for two, one sex for two, one mind for two, and, ultimately, one life for two (McDougall 1989). Other writers see becoming ill as representing a failure to resolve separation and individuation issues and a failure to develop critical ego functions. Both Melitta Sperling (1978) and Therese Benedek (1949) held that an unresolved mother–child symbiosis is a major causative factor in numerous psychosomatic disorders. Masterson (1972) found that when the adolescent perceives that his struggle for separation and individuation is punished by his mother's emotionally abandoning him, he usually gives up the struggle by succumbing to illness. Deutsch (1959) has suggested that if the body image cannot evolve well past the primitive stages where the subject and object are one, ego development is not possible, only a symbiotic existence, psychosis, severe illness, or death. Levitan (1989) found that the dreams of psychosomatic patients, including those of a group of bulimics, reveal a failure of the defensive functions of the ego, while Silverman (1970) found that failures in the defensive function of the ego in both waking and dream states were predictors of imminent somatic distress.

Psychoanalytic and family systems theorists have written about the role of family psychopathology in the etiology of psychosomatic illness. Wilson and Mintz (1989) trace the origins of psychosomatic symptoms back to the preoedipal years within the context of the parent-child dyad and disturbances in early object relations, and hold that underlying personality disorders and numerous failures in ego functioning are often masked by the symptoms. Through the study of over 400 psychosomatic patients, Wilson (1989) has developed a profile of the psychosomatic family, using the acronym PRISES: Perfectionism, Repression of emotions, Infantilizing decision making for the psychosomatic-prone child, the organ System chosen because of unconscious parental conflicts for the development of psychosomatic symptoms, sexual and toilet Exhibitionism whose significance is denied, and the Selection of one child for the development of psychosomatic symptoms because of unconscious parental conflicts. Wilson (1983, 1989) developed a similar profile for the families of anorexic patients, described by the acronym PRIDES: overconscientious Perfectionism,

Repression of emotions, Infantilizing decision making for the anorexia-prone child, parental overconcern with Dieting and fear of being fat, sexual and toilet Exhibitionism, and the unconscious Selection of a child to develop anorexia because of parental conflicts. The first four factors correlate with the findings of Bruch (1978) and Minuchin and colleagues (1978). Sours (1980) confims these features in his object relations family research. The anorectic patient is likely to present herself and her life as being perfect, and her parents are likely to present everything in their lives as being perfect, and under control if it were not for the one flaw, the anorexia (Bruch 1978).

These parents tend to be enmeshed, overprotective, and rigid, and there is covert marital conflict. The mothers are superficially self-sacrificing and endlessly giving, but also intrusive, overly concerned with appearances, lacking in self-esteem, and needy (Beresin et al. 1989), and have established a disturbance in the mother–child symbiosis (Sperling 1978). The fathers typically are strong, distant, successful, overinvolved with work to the exclusion of family, and often heavy drinkers. Underneath they are very needy, and they tend to dominate and control their wives. Feelings are disavowed, especially anger, to present the appearance of a loving, perfect family.

Kernberg (1975) describes how, in the formation of borderline structures, failures in the early mother–child relationship lead the child to turn to the father to meet her emotional needs. The anorectic child is required to be the symptom bearer for the family, or the peacemaker when tensions begin to show, or the confidante of an unhappy parent (Beresin et al. 1989). As the father's confidante and "Daddy's little girl," her relationship with him becomes sexualized as she is propelled into an oedipal or triangular constellation that is occasionally frankly incestuous. On the one hand this helps extricate her from the mother's frightening intrusiveness, but on the other hand, her anxiety is increased enormously for fear she will lose her mother.

Salvador Minuchin might try to help the family of the anorectic to understand the symptomatic person's illness, the nonverbal communication and main relationship-defining mode, as a precious gift or wonderful sacrifice she is making for the sake of the family because she loves them so much (Minuchin et al. 1978). Her anorexia is crucial in maintaining the family's homeostasis. Thus the ill child serves as a critical regulator for the family in the same way that the mother serves as the infant's regulatory system, and so the treatment goal is to disengage the child from her essential position between the parents and to help the parents deal with their marital problems more directly to create a new homeostasis.

Melanie was sacrificing herself for her family but she did not know this and neither did they. She came to see me while home from college between semesters. Her skin was stretched so tautly across her bones that crying made her face hurt. She seemed to feel so much that was difficult to identify. Since freshman year she had lost a great deal of weight from her small frame. Fat was her enemy and she ate nothing with fat in it and exercised for at least four hours a day. It was worse at college, as it often is when a child is physically separated from her family before she is emotionally ready to be a separate person. At home she seemed to be able to eat a bit less rigidly and was a little more relaxed. She described herself as the only child of perfectionistic parents. Her father was perfectionistic about his work and sports, spending much time away from home, not really involved in her or her mother's life. Her mother was perfectionistic about her body and the house, and was critical and controlling of Melanie. She often told Melanie what her (Melanie's) thoughts were. Yet they "told each other everything" and attended aerobics class together. Melanie was often lonely at college, and she told her father what she needed from him very explicitly. "Call me every few days. Ask how my day was. Ask me what I ate that day." Yet he would not do it. She seemed to feel that her father did not care enough about her or her mother, and that her mother cared too much for her in a way that made her angry and would not let her grow up. At the same time she felt responsible for making her mother happy. She had angry feelings but did not know what to do with them, so they became directed at her body. She loved both her parents fiercely, even though she often did not like them. She would even die for them, she said.

While the perfect and overprotective families of anorectics are characterized by the rigidity of their rules, bulimic families, in contrast, may be of the perfect or overprotective type but frequently have no rules or are inconsistent (Root et al. 1986), and may be openly chaotic, resembling substance-abusing families. In fact, it is quite common to find serious alcohol abuse in one or both parents in the families of many bulimics, fueling the violent expression of anger and releasing sexual and aggressive inhibitions that lead to abuse.

In treating eating-disordered patients, I found that their families had either an overt or covert fear of being fat. A parent often had peculiar food hoarding habits, such as the father who had his private stash of Hydrox cookies that no one else was allowed to touch, or the mother who hid candy in a certain teakettle, replenishing it when her son had depleted the supply, in an unspoken, mutually involving secret ritual. Also, a child was at times emotionally abused by name-calling, such as "fatso" or "fat pig," without there necessarily being other food-related issues in the family. Prior to adolescence the girl may have been "Daddy's little girl," having a secret eroticized relationship with the father, or the girl who had enjoyed being the father's favorite discovered at puberty that the father became more remote and unavailable, seemingly retreating from her developing sexuality, and leaving her with a tremendous sense of loss or "father hunger" (Maine 1991).

When we ask what the body is, attachment theory can help us understand how internalized attachments can find a voice in the body. Attachment theory can help us to understand how unspoken narratives can take the form of psychosomatic processes or illnesses, especially in "somatizers," those people who tend characteristically to react to psychological distress through somatic manifestations, but also in nonsomatizers, who may somatize only at those times of crisis or trauma that overwhelm our usual ways of coping. When the child has become attached to a mother who does not take good care of him, who neglects or even abuses him, he internalizes a sense of himself as someone who does not deserve good care and becomes a person who neglects or abuses himself. Failing to develop the self-care functions of the ego, he may develop various kinds of somatic disturbances, hypochondriasis, accident proneness, impulsive or violent behavior to others or himself, weight disturbances, substance abuse, and other forms of self-neglect or self-destructiveness. Through his body the child cries out in loud and compelling tones on the psychosomatic stage in a dramatic bid that the mother come forth to rescue and care for him. "Mommy I'm sick, I need you" is the script the child is trying to enact, and sometimes he is successful in getting his mother, father, and everyone involved with him to enact the scenario by rallying around him to make him better. He may evoke in his family an unheralded demonstration of caring and attentiveness, as the family pays far more attention to him in illness and self-destructiveness than ever was paid to him before he fell ill. All too frequently, once the crisis of illness is over and the child begins to get better, he is once again abandoned to neglect and indifference. To recapture the illusion that he is cared for and cared for well, he needs to fall ill again. And so he does, again and again and again, creating a personal identity and peculiar sense of security that is bound up in suffering and illness. As his body continues to speak for him through chronic somatic symptoms, he can readily develop a "career" as a medical patient, attaching himself to pain and suffering and attaching significant others to him through his illness. As his body continues to speak for him in self-harm, he can readily develop a "career" and identity as a mental patient.

From the time of the loss of the mother, whether real or perceived, or the separation from the mother and the onset of illness, there occurs an intervening transitional psychobiological ego state, the "giving up/given up" complex (Engel and Schmale 1967), or what Hofer (1995) has identified as the acute and then the chronic slow-developing despair phase. Because the infant has not yet developed the signal anxiety that can defend against overwhelming anxiety or depressive affect, the separation from the mother is experienced by the infant as traumatic, a breach in the stimulus barrier that evokes a sense of utter helplessness (Freud 1920a). This depressive affect, the helplessness and hopelessness, is thought to initiate autonomic, endocrinological, and immunological processes that lower resistance and allow illness to develop in the body part or organ most likely to comply as the locus for a psychosomatic process (Freud 1905a).When people harm themselves physically, they are most likely to direct aggression toward the body part or organ system that has become the site for somatic compliance. The hand of an incest survivor who fondled the genitals of a parent may become a direct target for aggression, as the individual punches her hand through windows or into brick walls.

When we see human beings habitually turning their aggression either against others or against themselves, we want to know the extent to which this hyper-aggressiveness is a function of their experiences in the environment or a function of an inherent or constitutional endowment of aggression. It has been suggested that specific biological factors may be operating in those who self-injure and in bulimics, which could be a factor in explaining the relative uniformity phenomenologically, the compelling quality, and the persistence of these self-harm behaviors (Russ 1992). Painful stimulation has been demonstrated to result in increased release of endorphins, which may explain why self-injurious behaviors and severe purging are repeated. Decreased serotonin levels in humans have been repeatedly correlated with impulsivity and aggression at the same time that impulsivity and aggression are associated at least as strongly with histories of child-hood trauma, including severe separation, neglect, and physical and sexual abuse (van der Kolk 1994).

Winchel (1991) offers a convincing biological theory of "aloneness affect" that is not only compatible with but also interdependent on psychodynamic formulations. When an individual is experiencing aloneness affect, its strength may be inhibited by association with others. That is, the social contact maintains a homeostasis in which there is enough aloneness affect to drive the individual to associate with others but not so much as to cause significant dysphoria or to drive undesirable behavior. When usual levels of association or social contact were not sufficient to inhibit aloneness affect, an increase in serotonin levels could reset the aloneness affect/association mechanism so that the previous level of association now became sufficient to inhibit aloneness affect. While Winchel found aloneness affect to be specific to all species who self-mutilate, perhaps aloneness affect is the response of all species who harm themselves, whether it be by self-mutilation, disordered eating, accident proneness, or other somatizations.

Clinicians treating those who harm themselves often find that the symptoms decrease with the use of the selective serotonin reuptake inhibitors (SSRIs), which increase serotonin levels. However, clinicians treating patients with the same kinds of problems also find that even without the use of such medication, there is a decrease in symptomatology that occurs when there is an increase in positive attachment to the therapist. Peter Kramer, in Listening to Prozac (1993), writes, "For the most part, in my role as psychotherapist, I acted like a medication—like Prozac—helping to mitigate my patient's sensitivity to loss" (p. 286). Winchel (1991), however, goes further: "The psychoanalytic psychotherapist actually is a neurotransmitter—a generator of signals, transduced by the receiver into neuro-chemical activity—initially just inhibiting aloneness affect but eventually helping to reset the homeostatic controls so that the system adjusts to a new level or frequency of input" (p. 12).

Who has not at least once experienced the worst aloneness and despair from which there seems to be no relief, a Sartre's *No Exit?* Who among us has never felt so despairingly alone or so impotently enraged as to want to strike out violently at ourself, tear at our hair, scratch at our skin, or throw up? We are not so different from animals who bite their tails and pluck out their feathers. Like them, our psychobiological responses to losses of our attachment objects, our aloneness affect, or the "giving up/given up" complex (Engel and Schmale 1967) can lead to self-harm, illness, or even death. These formulations imply that it is intimate attachments that can regulate the experience of aloneness affect, reducing it to tolerable levels. They also suggest that when there are no mediating intimate attachments, a person may need to turn to the painful stimulation provided by various self-harm activities to increase serotonin levels sufficient for the reduction and regulation of aloneness affect. Suggesting that aloneness is humankind's biologic destiny, Winchel (1991) states:

> But for our ability to undo our aloneness, we might all rip ourselves to bits. . . . Witness the tearing of the skin that accompanies the keening of mourning women in some Middle-Eastern cultures. The Babylonian Talmud found the behavior so prevalent (yet culturally unacceptable) that it provided a specific injunction against injuring oneself in mourning. And is the primal urge to accost the self so alien even in our own culture? In moments of stress from which no release seems immediately available, which one of us has not transiently understood the concrete meaning of the desire to pull out one's hair? [pp. 10–11]

Writer Barbara Grizzuti Harrison (1996), a compulsive eater for most of her life, wrote about a time when her fear and sense of aloneness was so intolerable that she mutilated herself. It was a time when her parents failed her terribly and even her teddy bear failed her. Her parents had left her alone while they went to play cards with neighbors across the street. She was not even 5 and was listening to the radio in bed. Listening to "The Inner Sanctum" frightened her, hearing doors creak open and the announcer inviting listeners into the mysteries of the dark. He told a terrifying story of the dead rising up out of their graves.

> I yelled out the window, . . . *Mommy Daddy Mommy Daddy Mommy Daddy come home come home!* I waited, scrunched in starchy sheets, for Mommy Daddy; and then—I heard faint sounds of laughter from the house across the alley—I waited with terror for the dancing bones . . . and then I vomited, projectile vomit gushing forth like the bones who flew like linked arrows from the ground. Then Mommy Daddy came home. . . . My mother, viewing the scene, smelling of cigarette smoke and Heaven Scent, gave vent to mutters and yelps of rage: *My clean sheets damn you work work work all I do is work.* . . . Mommy directs me . . . to scrape off the vomit; then she makes the bed (hospital corners), *All I do is work,* her voice rising in crescendo.
> I am clean (my breath stinks) between new sheets. I take my teddy bear, make inquiries of it to which there are no responses, and to punish myself and teddy

and the dark and the voices and the unforgiving night, I tear one of his sweet blind brown eyes out of its socket. I am appalled at what I have done. And then—having established who the criminal is—I gouge my wrists with the prongs of my teddy bear's eye, so as to wear the stigmata of my unnameable unknowable crime. [pp. 373–375]

When humans harm themselves, it is a sign that something has gone very wrong in the development of self-regulatory functioning and separation-individuation processes. The more severe the harm, the more severe the illness.

The more serious the symptoms of the illness, the more intense or primitive is the symbiotic level of functioning; although mild symptoms do not necessarily mean the opposite. Stating this in reverse, the greater the impairment of the sense of separation of self from object, the more severe are the symptoms likely to be. The more defective the ego is in terms of separation of self from object, the more pronounced are primitive elements in the instinctual life and strivings and the less developed is control over transformation and sublimation of the instincts. [Mushatt 1992, p. 302]

The development of self-harm during the transitional "giving up/given up" state can serve as a gestural articulation of trauma (McLane 1996), when the impetus to give spoken voice to the inner pain has been thwarted. In this ego state all has not yet been given up. There is still hope. So blood dripping from self-inflicted wounds can be the gesture that articulates grief and suffering in a way that normal tears have not been able to, offering hope that a more desperate gesture will succeed in engaging another to listen and hear what words will not say. That is, when the reality of past trauma and suffering has been ignored so "that not only language, but even normal tears no longer have meaning" (McLane 1996, p. 113), the stigmata teardrops of blood may have the power to communicate to others the depth of the sufferer's pain. The most severe bleeding and purging is the body's way of weeping. While in all psychosomatic illnesses the more serious the symptoms, the more primitive is the symbiotic level of functioning (Mushatt 1992), this can be seen very clearly and in extreme form in those who purge severely, starve themselves, and/or self-mutilate. Sometimes, when the body weeps blood and other fluids, it is heard as a wake-up call by previously inattentive or neglectful parents to focus attention on their sick child, who then improves. Sometimes the parents are able to tolerate the personal pain and anxiety of involving themselves in their child's treatment. Sperling (1978) found that simultaneous psychoanalysis of mother and child or occasionally analysis of the mother alone may be sufficient to resolve a preoedipal or preoedipally fixated child's somatic symptom picture. When the ill or self-harming adult patient has not given up and seeks help, and the parents or other pertinent family members can involve themselves in the treatment, then the need to speak the language of self-harm diminishes and words come to take its place.

FROM PASSION TO PERVERSE OMNIPOTENCE

When the body cries but the cries go unheeded, the pain needs to restate itself, repeating and repeating, even louder. What was infrequent, controlled, delicate self-cutting may become over time frequent and more violent out-of-control cutting, deep to the bone. Occasional purging may take over the person's life as she becomes determined to extract every last drop of fluid from her body, crying enormous volumes of vomit, feces, and urine, and threatening her life more ominously. Even several near-death experiences may not stop her, as the pain repeats and repeats. As McLane (1996) says, "If the wounding is not communicated or intended normality not achieved—pain reiterates. It is not resolved but becomes part of the lived structure of the human being suffering it" (p. 108). Writer Barbara Grizzuti Harrison (1996) wrote in great detail of her relationship with food from adolescence to the present, and the sense of omnipotent control inherent in it. Since childhood she had lived with pain that had become part of her "lived structure." She used eating as many people with eating disorders do in order to create a mother–child relationship in which she was both the hungry child yearning to be fed and the nurturing, constant mother whom she never had. "I love food. . . . When my lover and I separated I bought a bread-making machine. It was such a comfort to me, having something I could feed and control so that it would feed me, knowing that if I pushed all the right buttons I would get all the right results" (p. 16). For Harrison, food was her lover, her mother, her friend, her everything and everyone. This behavior paradoxically denied her needs while serving to gratify them. No lover, no mother, nobody was needed. Food was far more constant and reliable than any person could ever be.

When the body's cries are not heard, they continue to repeat themselves through increasingly severe self-harm, weaving the weft of self-harm into the warp of the personality, and increasingly taking on the nature of perverse omnipotence. When the self-harm that may have been used early on to serve transitional self-soothing functions comes increasingly over time to serve as a fetish, a devitalized object onto which mostly negative, aggressive, destructive fantasies are directed and acted out impulsively, then there is no room in the personality for object relationships. "I don't need you anymore to feel alive. I don't need you anymore to comfort me. I don't need you. I need only myself," she proclaims, in the bright loud silent voice of the body. Over time, however, the relationship of the psyche to the soma becomes increasingly persecutory and sadistic, with the psyche attacking, punishing, and starving the body (Sacksteder 1988, 1989a). At these moments there is the regression to a primitive state of rage that may be dissociated, and a regressive dedifferentiation of representations of self and other, as whatever boundaries that had existed between self and object representations disintegrate. The self-harm fails to serve transitional functions, and as it becomes more chronic and severe, it loses its ability to soothe even briefly. The symptoms become increasingly more severe and life threatening.

TRANSITIONAL USE OF THE BODY AS A FETISH

It is necessary to understand how a shift in the nature of transitional phenomena develops and changes over time, in the direction of increasingly perverse omnipotence and pseudo-independence. Those individuals who self-mutilate or binge and purge attempt unconsciously to use their bodies to serve the transitional functions of self-soothing and calming. We know that bingeing and purging indeed does serve a mood-regulating function. For example, the prebinge state in bulimics was found to be an agitated one that included feelings of boredom, frustration, and loneliness (Johnson and Connors 1987), while the binge-purge episode itself was experienced as a means of reducing tension and alleviating feelings of anxiety, anger, depersonalization, and loneliness (Abraham and Beaumont 1982, Carroll and Leon 1981, Mitchell et al. 1985). While most bulimics experienced relief from anxiety and depressive feelings during the binge (Abraham and Beaumont 1982), for many the dysphoric affect was replaced by an experience of depersonalization (Johnson and Connors 1987). Johnson and Larson (1982) found that the bingeing at some point stopped being relieving and was associated with feeling worse. The postbinge state was marked by predominantly negative feelings (Abraham and Beaumont 1982, Mitchell et al. 1985), as the bulimic came out of her depersonalized state to realize how much she had eaten and to feel shame and self-loathing. There often ensued an inner punitive dialogue between parts of the self, "You're such a pig. You are disgusting," leading her to become desperate to purge herself of the food and these feelings. Purging resulted primarily in feelings of calm and relief (Abraham and Beaumont 1982, Johnson and Connors 1987, Johnson and Larson 1982), as well as a restored sense of control, adequacy alertness, and a decline in anger (Johnson and Larson 1982). The literature on self-mutilation reveals an affect state of the self-mutilator before, during, and after the self-mutilating episode that bears a remarkable similarity to the vicissitudes of the bulimic's affect state as presented above (de Young 1982, Doctors 1981, Favazza 1987, Favazza and Conterio 1988, Gardner and Gardner 1975, Graff and Mallin 1967, Grunebaum and Klerman 1967, Novotny 1972, Pao 1969, Simpson and Porter 1981, Walsh 1987). My study (1995a), in explaining the very strong empirical association and relationship between bulimic and self-mutilating behavior, found that when a spectrum of various self-harming behaviors were assessed as to their effectiveness in helping the subjects feel better, it was the most severe purging and the most violent and physically penetrating forms of self-mutilation that ranked at the top as potent forms of self-medication.

Others have proposed that the body in fact serves as a transitional object in both bulimia (Sugarman and Kurash 1982) and in self-mutilation (Kafka 1969). Implicit in these theories is the emphasis on loss—actual, perceived, or anticipated—as a triggering factor in eating disorders (Armstrong and Roth 1989) and in self-mutilation (Hansburg 1986, Rosen et al. 1990). The bulimic, the alcoholic, the drug addict, and the self-mutilator all seize upon the symptomatic behavior, immersing themselves in the comfort it provides, much as the baby seizes upon his teddy bear or worn blanket to soothe himself in the absence of the mother. That is, the person turns to the behavior as toward a transitional object. Although the self-harm behavior serves momentarily to soothe and comfort, it fails as a true transitional object but instead serves pretransitional functions. Those who turn to a relationship with food, whether gorging, purging, or depriving themselves of it, and those who turn to alcohol or drugs taken orally are arrested at and/or chronically regress to presymbolic "into the mouth" precursor types of self-soothing, while self-mutilators, those who inject drugs, or repeatedly have themselves tattooed or pierced, are arrested at and/or regress to a pre-symbolic skin contact/tactile sensation (Gaddini 1975, 1978) type of self-soothing. Those who harm themselves in a variety of ways, turning to both pre-symbolic "into the mouth" and skin contact/tactile sensation types of self-soothing, seek out some ultimate experience of self-harm to permanently help them feel better.

The self-harm behavior fails to further the individuation of the self that the transitional object is meant to do, instead binding the individual to the abusive, neglectful, or overly gratifying internalized object. Self-harm fails to further the capacity for symbolic and abstract thinking and for tolerating ambiguities, promoting instead the use of concrete bodily activity as simplistic solutions for complex psychological problems. The person whose ego regresses into episodes of self-harm bears a resemblance to the psychotic child. The psychotic child does not have a transitional object, states Mahler (cited in Kupfermann 1996). His own body is the devitalized object onto which mostly negative aggressive, destructive fantasies are directed and acted out impulsively (Kupfermann 1996, 1998). He uses his body to soothe himself, but these devitalized objects do not aim, as transitional objects do, at maintaining the connection with the absent mother. For example, a photo included with an article on self-mutilation in the workplace (Witherspoon 1990) illustrates this point very well: A middle-aged woman wearing a bathrobe is seated comfortably in an easy chair, a pretty black and white cat curled in her lap and a look of repose on her face. She appears to be settling in for the evening, perhaps to listen to some soothing music, enjoy a cup of tea, or chat on the phone with a friend. Instead she is holding a knife to her wrist. The photo illustrates that for her, cutting is a cup of tea—soothing, calming, and bracing. The anticipation of it soothes her. Like many who cut themselves, the anticipation and preparation for cutting themselves is enough to induce a sense of calmness, and sometimes just knowing they have a razor blade readily available is sufficient. For others who feel the numbed deadness of depression, cutting, burning, or punching the wall provides the stimulation of the skin or high impact that evokes virtually immediately a sense of aliveness, representing an aggressive fusion with and attack on the mother.

It must be understood that sometimes the bulimic and self-mutilating behaviors serve as a fetish to obtain sexual arousal (Greenacre 1969). The anticipation of the act fuels the building crescendo of undifferentiated inner tension, culminating in the frenzied rhythms of convulsive purging or self-mutilation. The completed act soothes and shores up a defective sense of self for the brief time that the shoring up lasts, until it is time to do it again, and again, more severely and more frequently in the escalating spiral of addiction. When even the escalated form of the behavior fails to do what it is supposed to do, another behavior, even more severe and thus stronger, may be added to the repertoire. For the binge-purger, it may be alcohol, drugs, or self-mutilation that is added. If this is not strong enough medicine, the "aphrodisiac" may become more severe, more dangerous, and more potentially lethal. Thus, in some individuals, the self-harm serves so much as a sexual fetish that the sadomasochism can cross the line into suicide.

In common vernacular, a fetish can be an object thought to have magical power, like a lucky charm or rabbit's foot. We think of those who are overly sensitive or quick to take offense as thin-skinned, absorbing too much from the outside, while those who are tougher are thought to have a thicker protective skin. The body builders who pump iron or take steroids to build a hard muscular shell around themselves, the compulsive eaters with their insulating layers of fat, and those with a second skin of tattoos or scar tissue all may be using their bodies as fetish objects to soothe themselves and protect themself from harm from the external world. That shell is invaluable to the narcissist who has been intruded and impinged upon, building up an impenetrable boundary between himself and the outside world, fending off human relationships and potential predators. The destructive narcissists need no one, only themselves and their second skin.

THE PSYCHOTIC CORE: UP CLOSE AND PERSONAL

The alexithymic fears a confrontation with the psychotic core, that sense of private madness (Green 1975) that is split off and encapsulated in a psychotic, or the primitive destructive part of the self that is not readily accessible even in psychoanalysis. The psychotic core is thought to underlie neurosis, sexual perversion, and physical disease (Green 1975, Grotstein 1993, McDougall 1989, Taylor 1987, Tustin 1981), although it is thought to exist even in normal individuals (Freud 1937, Steiner 1981). Freud (1937) wrote: "For every normal person is in fact only normal on the average. His ego approximates to that of the psychotic to a greater or lesser extent" (p. 235).

When this psychotic core goes unrecognized and untreated (Sperling 1978, Taylor 1987), it is often experienced by the patient as a threatening black hole in the ego that must be kept at bay (Ammon 1979, Grotstein 1993). The black-hole phenomenon in autistic children was first described by Tustin (1981) as the experience of a sudden rupture in their bonds with their mothers, experienced as part of their skin surface being ripped away, leaving a black hole on the skin's surface. They tend to choose "hard" autistic objects to soothe themselves, using them to plug up their "black holes." Perhaps the dark marks left on the skin of self-mutilators is their concrete representation of the black hole, plugged up by the knife, blade, or hammer. Ellyn Shander, M.D., director of the eating-disorder unit at Silver Hill Hospital in New Canaan, Connecticut, found that many eating-disorder patients, when asked to describe themselves or draw how they feel inside, reported or drew a big black hole. That is, they experienced the black hole not on the skin's surface but in the deepest recesses of their bodies.[1] Many bulimics and self-mutilators fear they will go mad if they cannot purge when they feel compelled to do so; they may even feel that ending their life is preferable to this madness (Farber 1995a). Because they fear they will descend into a madness from which they cannot return, the regression to self-harm serves paradoxically as the lesser of the two evils, defending against an even more severe ego regression to the psychotic core. For some patients, however, an uncontrolled regression into psychosis may be one from which they cannot return.

Often the regression occurs while the individual is in a dissociated state, most often a severe state of depersonalization in which she feels unreal and emotionally numb, often accompanied by feelings that the rest of the world is not real either. At those moments of madness, the rage that she physically directs at her body feels unreal. There is little or no pain at the moment, "practically no sense of inside and outside or self and other; rather, what is important is the pattern, boundedness, shape, rhythm, texture, hardness, softness, warmth, coldness, and the like" (Ogden 1990, p. 84). But moments later, the blood she sees flowing from her cuts or the painful pounding of the hammer on her bones bring her up abruptly from her descent. There is the real and immediate need to tend to her injuries. She scurries to clean up the mess, activity that is welcome because it distances her from the fear of madness and returns her to the real world, feeling and appearing calm and competent.

The discrepancy between the self that descends to the psychotic core and the competent false self persona presented to friends, family, co-workers, and the public can be startling. Because some ego functions can be well developed and others that are primitive can be regressed to rapidly in sudden severe ego regressions, the person's life has a discontinuous Jekyll-and-Hyde quality and may be experienced as a series of unconnected episodes in which they play various unrelated parts. Under the more competent and benign appearance there is, nonetheless, a secret psychotic core. While we all may have a secret encapsulated sense of madness we fear in ourselves, in the person given to self-harm it has grown bigger and more ominous and has taken over more of the person-

---

1. Reported at a clinical staff meeting at the Wilkins Center for Eating Disorders, Greenwich, Connecticut, 1990.

ality. Issues of boundaries and ownership of the body live here in the psychotic core (Grotstein 1993). Does the body belong to oneself or to the mother or father? While children who have not been physically or sexually molested or abused struggle with this question, the question is especially pertinent for the victims of child abuse.

Grotstein (1993) states that the innocent child does not have this concern. Childhood innocence is a concept associated with Scripture and poetry, notably eighteenth-century poet William Blake, who described a state of infant and childhood bliss that imparted a sense of virtually complete protection in a trustworthy world ruled by a benign and omnipotent God. Blake's *Songs of Innocence* tell us that the innocent child believes in fairness and has an optimistic view of the world that he continues to maintain as he grows up (Grotstein 1993). *Songs of Innocence* is usually printed together with *Songs of Experience*, to show "the two contrary states of the human soul" (Bredvold et al. 1973, p. 1450). In *Songs of Experience* the sense of innocence is inevitably challenged by encounters with sexuality and the need for self-assertion; these experiences can be encountered successfully if they have a foundation in the early sense of innocence. Those who have lost innocence, among them the abused and those with borderline and other primitive mental disorders, however, experience themselves as cursed, as victims: "Patients with primitive mental disorders, in particular those who have been victims of child abuse, seem to believe that they have been robbed of their once entitled possession of a state of innocence and are now derelicts without a passport. The state of innocence conveys the state of being blessed, while its absence conveys the sense of being 'cursed' or 'fey' (in the sense of being a hapless victim of fate)" (Grotstein 1993, p. 111). While the psychotic patient seems to have already fallen metaphorically into the abyss of the black hole, the borderline patient, says Grotstein, "seems to exist on its borders, continuously experiencing a pull to fall over its edge into its awesome interior, from which there is no return" (p. 129). Self-harm is a way of living "on the edge," the borderline defense against the threat of being swallowed up by the black hole.

An act of self-harm can defend against the fear of going mad, as the acts of self-harm are experienced with an intensity and feeling of omnipotence that distances the individual from her fear. Because self-harm has a paradoxical effect frequently of restoring a sense of self-cohesiveness at a time when the person fears her self will dissolve to pieces, it serves yet another defensive function. When the self-harm is not sufficient to the task of defending against the annihilating anxiety, the despairing individual may "up the ante" and inflict even more intense, more severe harm upon herself.

A binge may then become the only way of blotting out the whole hideous muddle—because at least for the actual moments when the sufferer is shoveling food into herself, she is oblivious of everything except the food in her hands and in her mouth. When the binge is over and awareness of the rest of her life returns the wretchedness of the impact of these thoughts and feelings cannot be overestimated. . . . It is not only overdoses of whatever pills may be to hand which are tried. Desperate young women may bang their heads against the door, rub their hands or arms against rough brick walls until their skin is raw and bleeding, cut patterns into the skin on their arms or legs with razor blades or seriously slash their wrists so that bleeding endangers their life. [Welbourne and Purgold 1984, pp. 70–71]

In the self-harmer the psychotic core features the most primitive body image, what Rosenfeld (1990) calls a delusional, psychotic body image that is not limited to those who are psychotic. (It may be present in those neurotically adjusted to reality and in some psychosomatic cases, and may make its presence known in times of intense personal disorganization, such as following major surgery.) This is in contrast to the neurotic body image, which approaches normal—the notion of skin containing the body, skin representing the parents who warmly hold and contain the child's body (Bick 1968, Rosenfeld 1990, Tustin 1981).

By psychotic body image I mean the most primitive notion of the body image to be observed in certain patients whose work begins while they are already regressed or who regress during their treatment. In my view, the extreme notion of what can be conceived as psychotic body image is the thought that the body contains only liquid, one or another derivative of blood, and that it is coated by an arterial or venous wall or walls. These vascular sheaths take over the functions that normally are fulfilled psychologically by the actual skin, the muscles, and the skeleton. There is only a vague notion of a wall that contains blood and vital liquids.

In turn, as can be seen mainly in crises associated with acute psychosis, this membrane containing the blood may be perceived to have broken or to have been damaged otherwise and to result in a loss of bodily contents, leaving the body empty, without either internal or external containment or support. [Rosenfeld 1990, p. 167]

There may be a particular form of anxiety in such individuals, a terror that the boundaries of the skin's surface will dissolve, a fear that one's inner contents will drip, ooze, or leak out into endless boundless space (Ogden 1989, 1990). For them the skin is far more a terrifying sieve than a reassuring and protecting barrier (Lappe 1996). Those who are compelled to rid their bodies of virtually all fluids probably have the most primitive body image. The most severe purging behavior, in which the body is purged of virtually all vomitus, feces, urine, and sweat, and the self-mutilation by cutting and branding, in which blood and serous fluid are shed, may all be counterphobic attempts to master the fear of the encounter with the psychotic core. Instead, the person must bleed and dehydrate herself, dry herself out, lose her juice. She becomes a dried-out shell, cracked scratchy skin, drained of life. She is dry as dust, as dry as ashes.

THE PASSIONATE DANCE WITH DEATH, OR THE LAST TANGO?

Most self-harmers may not die of their self-harm. But of those who do, how do they die, those who live their lives drawn to the vortex of the black hole? To understand how self-harm can reach a level of delusion and lethality that can result in death, we need to understand that after the self-harm behavior has become chronic over many years, it takes on the characteristics of an addictive cycle that is marked at those intense moments of gravest self-harm with a delusional sense of omnipotence and immortality. When the driven nature and severity of these behaviors increase progressively, when the individual becomes increasingly preoccupied with them and attached to the ritualistic behavior surrounding them, when a tolerance to them is developed, along with an increasing sense of shame and despair, they have spiraled up into an increasingly out-of-control addictive cycle that can end in death.

The longer and more severely self-harmers purge, the more they seem to develop a tolerance to it, requiring even larger doses of laxatives, diuretics, and vomiting, and resorting in desperation to potentially lethal agents such as syrup of ipecac (Farber 1995a). When even the most severe purging using multiple methods as well as the escalation from delicate self-cutting to deeper-to-the-bone and more violent self-mutilation fails to provide sufficient relief from psychic pain, these efforts may end in death or may propel the individual to make a deliberate and calculated effort to end his life (Farber 1995a). Here the difference between behavior that is suicidal and behavior that is self-medicating is semantic and academic. Whatever the intent, which may never be really known, death may be the outcome of this perverse addictive omnipotence. No longer able to straddle the borders of the black hole, the self-harmer is seduced over the edge in a burst of passion. Like the sadomasochist who has her most intense orgasm when her partner's hands or a rope around her throat cut off her air supply, she is dancing passionately with death. Because she has so far eluded death, she is certain that she will continue to. It does not occur to her that one day death may triumph.

The starving anorectic, the anorectic or bulimic who purges violently, and the self-mutilator all unconsciously identify with the omnipotent aggressor. In that severe ego regression in which affect and self- and object representations become dedifferentiated and recondensed, the person directs her aggression against her bodily self, starving and cannibalizing her own flesh, internally mutilating and ridding her body of vital fluids and electrolytes, and/or violently shedding her own blood. She preys upon her own body like a blood-thirsty hungry beast. She cannot keep anything good or life-sustaining in her; as soon as it goes in it must go out, an endless incorporation and violent expulsion of food, vital fluids, all symbolic equations of taking in and expelling malignant introjects.[2] So as the illness feeds upon itself, growing larger and more demonic, even the smallest mouthful of food or sip of water must be expelled from the body. While it may not be her intention to take her own life, as the violent discharge of aggression oscillates crazily from self to object representation to dedifferentiated self and object representations, she nonetheless is very much in danger of doing so.

PASSIONATE ATTACHMENTS AND
THE CHILD'S SURVIVAL

While a passionate attachment to pain and suffering can lead to self-harm and even death, it is the passionate loving attachment for a mother to her child that enables the child to live and survive in the world. And that is the prototype of all other attachments. Passion and attachment are integrally related to each other in their origins. Most passionate emotions such as love and hate are adaptive in that they are based on their ability to energize attachments (Michels 1988). Rage, aggression, dependence, nurturance, and fear are all intense feelings that tie human beings to each other. The passionate attachment of two adolescents or adults can be lustful or loving or both. It is difficult to distinguish between falling in love, a phase of violent and irrational psychological passion that does not last very long, and lust. Passion, Viederman (1988) tells us, is defined initially in the *Oxford English Dictionary* in terms of pain, in particular the Passion of Christ on the Cross, the suffering of martyrdom and affliction. "One of the problems in understanding passionate love is that it is an entirely personal and subjective experience. In this, appropriately, it resembles pain" (Viederman 1988, p. 13). Lustful attachment is a passion for sexual access to the body of the desired person. It is focused on a specific person as the object of desire. A loving adult attachment may or may not be accompanied by excited sexual contact, and may or may not have begun with falling in love. It is a tie between two people who trust and have confidence in each other's loyalty or affection. In healthy adult love relation-

---

2. Discussion with Andrea Schneer, M.S.W., of her conceptualization of eating disorders as a "disorder of in and out" was valuable to me in envisioning the endless incorporation and expulsion of food, vital fluids, and malignant introjects. It also helped me to conceptualize rumination, the chewing, swallowing, and regurgitation of food, to be rechewed and reswallowed, as a muted variant of bulimia, in which the body has difficulty keeping in what it has taken in. In addition, the mental counterpart of physical rumination is cognitive mental rumination, the thinking about and daydreaming about food, which can be used as a source of pleasure or to defend against the wish for receptive pleasure (Yates 1991). For example, "The hungry anorexic woman may anticipate a meal with pleasure. The food looks delicious and she intends to devour it. Yet even before she feels uncomfortably full or uncomfortable about having eaten, she begins to ruminate about

ships there is interdependency, a tender caring for and taking care of each other that hearkens back to the early mother–child dyad.

The human infant requires concentrated attention and protection for the first few years of life and requires the mother's primary maternal preoccupation. Her passionate attachment to the child is both a biological necessity for his survival and an emotional reality. Mothers who seem not to love their children or who abuse them seem to us less than human. Yet this was not always the case. The concept of a mother's instinctive love for the child is a recent development in Western history. The history of human behavior indicates that cultural traditions and economic necessity have often prevented this passionate attachment from forming. From at least classical antiquity to the eighteenth century, it was common in northern Europe to swaddle babies at birth, tying them head to foot in bandages that were taken off only to remove urine and feces. This had the effect of reducing intimate skin-to-skin body contact with the mother, thus reducing the attachment bond. It was also commonly believed that sexual excitement spoils the milk, and because few husbands were willing to do without the sexual services of their wives for long, it was necessary for those who could afford it to send their infants out to wet nurse at some distance from home, from birth to around age 2. Women, considered the property of their husbands, could not readily insist upon the sanctity of the mother–infant bond even if they felt it. The husband's passionate attachment to his wife, and not the mother's passionate attachment to her child, was considered to be of primary importance.

Even today, with divorce occurring so frequently among couples who have been parents for only a few years, it seems that the mutual attachment of a husband and wife is seriously threatened by the mother's attachment to the infant "interloper." Societies ignorant of contraception practiced infanticide widely. There is an enormous literature on infanticide, infant abandonment, and early death by deliberate neglect in Western Europe up to and into the nineteenth century (Stone 1988). Children, even of the rich, were often treated with calculated brutality, a punishment for having been born in original sin. French and English children lived a marginal existence during the seventeenth and eighteenth centuries. Although deliberate infanticide was relatively rare among the poor, infanticide disguised in socially acceptable forms was common. For example, infants were abandoned to workhouses or foundling hospitals, and others died due to deliberate neglect. Although it was widely known that infants could die when their mothers rolled over on them in bed, this was commonly the cause of

---

things which have nothing to do with the meal. Or she may begin to read the paper, watch television, or study as she eats. In any event, she directs her concern elsewhere and she no longer pays attention to the food. She is able to sidestep gratification by disconnecting herself from the pleasurable process of eating" (Yates 1991, pp. 194-195). So cognitive rumination is akin to the difficulty in taking and keeping in malignant object representations.

many infant deaths. The mortality rate of children being wet-nursed seems to have been much higher than that of their children being breast-fed by their mothers; their deaths were regarded as routine and the child was considered to be replaceable at a later more convenient date.

Our contemporary American culture, with its thrust toward promoting self-sufficiency and independence, may well thwart the development of the strong and intimate attachments that children need. Mothers go to work early on in the life of their babies, sometimes by choice and sometimes because of economic necessity, often to the detriment of the attachment bond. Fathers, too, often are more attached to their jobs than to their wives and children. Increasingly, work is felt to be a haven from the tensions of family life. Babies are pushed to separate from the mother early on, to be weaned from breast or bottle early and to sleep alone in their cribs. More and more frequently the care of dependent children is entrusted quite blindly to day-care personnel, baby-sitters, or nannies,[3] and we have been shocked to discover that infanticide by paid mother-substitutes occurs more frequently than we would like to think. In a climate of accusations and criminal trials for child abuse, warm and caring mother substitutes may be frightened of hugging and cuddling the children in their care. Preadolescents and adolescents more often than not come home from school to empty houses at a phase of their development when their need for parental attention and supervision is greater than most parents realize. Even with the best intentions, we may be producing and raising generations of touch-deprived and security-deprived children who are more vulnerable to abuse by others.

ATTACHMENT AND DARWIN'S THEORY OF NATURAL SELECTION

INFANTICIDE: A NATIONAL TRAGEDY
The U.S. Justice Department says that five infants under the age of one, many of them newborns, are killed or left to die every week in the U.S. They account for one out of eight people murdered annually in the U.S. The majority are killed by their mothers, who either strangle or beat them to death.
The New York Post, June 23, 1997

Cases of infanticide shock us, especially those in which young single women give birth secretly and, shortly after, kill their infants or leave them to die. Often they are poor and socially isolated, but two recent cases that were especially shock-

---

3. In my clinical practice I have treated three young children who suffered the effects of multiple and abrupt separations from baby-sitters and nannies to whom they had formed deep attachments.

ing were those of well-functioning middle-class girls, whose babies would most likely have been kept from starvation by the girls' parents or by one of the many couples eager to adopt a white, healthy newborn.

According to Darwin's theory of natural selection, only the fittest creatures are selected by nature to survive, while others less fit become sacrificed. A newborn, because of the care it requires, is less fit than its older siblings. In many animal species, a mother will kill a newborn if it is not healthy or if its birth occurs at a time when there is a shortage of available food. Or under similar circumstances, a mother will stand by and not protect her child, allowing its older siblings to kill it. For example, within the nest, egret chicks are natural born killers, killing the newborn in a fight for food, dominance, and safety, while the parent egrets are co-conspirators (Kaesuk-Yoon 1996). Sharks, ants, bees, and wasps eat the siblings with whom they compete for resources. Our culturally acceptable ways for conserving resources is to practice birth control or abort a child when money is scarce or when the fetus is known to be medically compromised.

Yet when a human mother kills her newborn infant, especially if he is healthy, we assume she is depraved. In a classic 1970 study of statistics of child killing, a psychiatrist Phillip Resnick found that mothers who kill their older children are frequently psychotic, depressed, or suicidal, but mothers who kill their newborns are usually not (Pinker 1997a). From an evolutionary point of view, psychologists Martin Daly and Margo Wilson argue that a capacity for neonaticide is built into the biological design of our parental emotions (Pinker 1997a). Among all the animals, mammals are extreme in the amount of time, energy, and food they invest in their young, and mammalian mothers must decide whether to allot it to their newborn or to their current and future offspring. When a newborn is sickly or if its survival is compromised, they may "cut their losses" in favor of the healthiest in the litter (Pinker 1997a).

Daly and Wilson argue that neonaticide is a form of this triage in most cultures, including ours. In most societies, the mother may let her newborn die when prospects for its survival to adulthood are poor, either because the newborn was born ill or deformed, or because the mother is overburdened with other children, or without a husband or social support. The young women who sacrifice their newborns in our culture are similar in that they tend for the most part to be young, poor, unmarried, and socially isolated (Pinker 1997a). Resnick (1999), regarded as the nation's leading child-murder expert, said the primary reason for killing a newborn is not mental illness but rather an unwanted child.

No preparations are made either for birth or for killing. When reality is thrust upon the woman when the baby first cries, the mother wants to permanently silence the intruder. The woman is saying, in effect, "You're not supposed to be alive." . . . It's been that way for centuries in numerous cultures, whether you're talking about servant girls in 19th century England, or unwanted female children in China. . . . In a lot of these cases the choice of abortion came too late.

The decision to kill the child is made impulsively shortly after birth, before she has the opportunity and time to develop a maternal attachment (Pinker 1997a). Resnick has found that the most dangerous time of life for a child is in the first six months of life. The motives in filicide vary widely. In nearly half of the murders studied by Resnick, the killers believed they were acting in the child's best interests, with a number of them leaving suicide messages saying they could not abandon their infant when they killed themselves. "This is the time of postpartum psychoses and depression. And the younger the child, the more likely the suicidal mother will think of him as a personal possession and feel inseparable from him" (Resnick 1999). In other cases the parents believed they were relieving the infant's suffering, imagined or real. Some were driven to kill by command hallucinations, killing what they thought was the devil in the child. Some were driven to kill by delirium. Others acted out of a wish for revenge on a spouse.

The cultural expectations for mothers to love their infants passionately and protectively from the moment they see them are enormous. Many cases of child abuse are driven by the parent's wish that the child be dead, when the parent inhibits himself from fully carrying out the murderous wish. Unloving parents more often than not keep their unwanted child, but may neglect him, treating him as if he did not exist. The child who harms or kills himself may be unconsciously enacting the parents' wish that he be dead.

7

Survival and Sacrifice: When the Prey Becomes the Predator

Behold, the people shall rise up as a great lion,
and lift up himself as a young lion; he shall not lie down
until he eat of the prey, and drink the blood of the slain.

Numbers 23: 24

Darwin's theory of evolution explains not only how man's body evolved but how his mind evolved (Pinker 1997b). Combining psychoanalytic understanding with the knowledge of evolutionary biology, we can better understand the evolution of self-harm in man as a very complex form of adaptation meant to ensure physical and psychic survival. Self-harm embodies the story of transformation from prey to predator, of the weak rising up in rebellion against the strong. It is the central story in the early human narrative and the essence of religion and myth, according to anthropologist Maurice Bloch (Ehrenreich 1997).

Themes of cannibalism and predation have been prominent in contemporary theatrical productions (*The Little Shop of Horrors, Sweeney Todd*), and run through past and present culture and history, resonating with our deepest fears of predators. Mintz (1992a) points out that in *The Threepenny Opera*, Brecht compares Mack the Knife to a shark, a terrifying predator. A short story by Joyce Carol Oates (1992) depicts a middle-aged woman, hiking alone in a beautiful suburban wildlife preserve on the first warm, sunny day of spring, when suddenly she is brutally attacked by a pack of predators who are children:

The children were so young, the youngest no more than eight or nine, and very small, and there were two or three girls among them. "Yes? What is it? What do you want?" she asked with a mother's slightly restrained calm. They're only children, she told herself even as, instinctively, she took a step backward. And in the next instant they were upon her. . . . Even as it was happening, as the children swarmed over her, pummeling her with their fists, pounding, kicking, tearing, the eldest leaping up on her to bring her heavily down, savage and deft as a predatory animal, even as she struggled with them, flailing her arms, trying too to strike, punch, kick . . . she was thinking, *This can't be happening! . . . They're only children.* . . . The thought came to her too that if she surrendered, if she submitted, put up no further struggle, they would take what they wanted and leave her alone. . . . And so it was. When she stopped fighting they stopped hitting her, but in the fierce hilarity of their excitement they stripped her clothes from her, turning her, rolling her, tugging at her jeans, whooping with laughter as they tore away her brassiere and underpants, yanked off . . . her running shoes, pulled off her socks. She was too overcome with shock to beg them to stop, and the mad fear struck her that they meant to devour her alive: set upon her like ravenous animals, tear the flesh from her bones with their teeth, and eat. For what was there to stop them? [pp. 124–125]

From the suppression of Freud's seduction theory (Breuer and Freud 1893, Freud 1896) until around thirty years ago, we have been relatively oblivious to knowing the extent to which human predators took other human beings as their prey—to be beaten, molested, raped, tortured, and killed. And so much of the time it is the protector who becomes the predator: the father or the mother preying upon the child or the father preying upon the mother. Often the mother is not the actual predator but is instead the one who fails to protect the child from predators.

Those who have been preyed upon by those who are supposed to protect them are likely to become predators themselves, either preying upon others as many male victims of abuse do, or preying upon themselves, as female victims are more likely to. Sometimes those who have been preyed upon aggressively and sexually by their parents or parental figures will repeat what was done to them by inflicting a similar kind of harm upon themselves, thus transforming themselves in the process from being the passive victim of predation to the predator herself.

Paradoxically, preying upon oneself in such circumstances can safeguard the victim's life, transforming her from victim to survivor. The struggle to survive can impel people to do frightful things to others and themselves. When a child's survival is threatened because the mother fails to protect him from predators, the defenseless child becomes terrified and traumatized. He may struggle for a while to survive but if he cannot find some means of defense, may simply submit to his predator. At the same time he may turn to himself, quite literally to his own body as a means of defense and survival and take it as his prey. It is a stunning paradox that out of a need for defense against predators, those who inflict bodily harm on themselves prey upon their own bodies in the same way they have been preyed upon. Yes, despite the self-inflicted pain, suffering and bloodshed, bodily self-harm is a disguised way of putting up a fight against a predator, and of achieving, at least for one shining moment, a sense of power against him. When there are predators around, one can lie down and submit or roll over and play dead in the hope that the predator will find other prey elsewhere, or one can put up a fight. In an oddly disguised way, harming oneself can be a way of putting up a fight and defending oneself from the extraordinary despair and anxiety that comes of feeling utterly alone, helpless, and small in the face of enormous dread.

To be the predator is to be powerful, to be the prey is to be annihilated. Despite the shift from passive to active, by means of internalizing the predator-to-prey attachment and the attachment to pain and suffering, the predator-to-prey object relationship is repeated and the attachment to pain and suffering is repeated by means of traumatic reenactments in behavior, in relationships to others and to one's own body. Self-harm can keep a victim from committing suicide and can provide a means for enduring without becoming psychotic, thus safeguarding physical and psychic survival. It serves as a compromise substitute for suicide, in which the wish to inflict serious harm on oneself is satisfied but not at the cost of ending one's life (Menninger 1935). In suicide a lethal attack is directed at the whole body and relief occurs prior to the act, that is, in anticipation of death, while in bodily self-harm, the attack is on a part of the body and relief occurs following the act (Friedman et al. 1972). Thus paradoxically, self-harm can prevent or forestall suicide or homicide and is therefore an adaptive act that serves survival functions. Yes, it is harmful to the self at the same time that it functions as an invaluable survival tool (Farber 1995a,b, 1996a,b,c). Countless survivors of severe abuse have written in numerous newsletters of the use of self-starvation, bingeing, purging, and self-mutilation as survival tools.

Kim, a young woman who had been sexually abused in childhood by her father, was no longer the victim of his actual attacks but nonetheless relived the attacks mentally. Cutting herself was a way of preempting his attack as well as triumphing over it, a form of psychic survival. "Tonight I've done everything to distract myself from thoughts of cutting. . . . I feel angry and I'm not very good at that feeling. They say that behind anger is always fear. So I ask myself: 'What are you afraid of?' Well, what do you think?!! I'm afraid my father will jump right through my skin and scare the silence right out of me. When I put down this pen, who'll get me first? My daddy or me? I'd rather get there first. This belongs to me! cut, cut, cut" (Kim 1993, pp. 3–4).

THE REPETITION COMPULSION

The prey-to-predator transformation demonstrates the compulsion of human beings to repeat distressing, even painful situations in the course of their lives without recognizing their unconscious participation in bringing such incidents about or the relationship of current situations to past experiences (Freud 1920). The repetition compulsion is part of the tendency in nature to reinstate a former state of affairs, whether it be pleasurable or painful. It occurs in normal activities and relationships as well as in the transference relationship, children's play, and other behavior and attitudes characteristic of earlier experiences. That which is repeated can provide a link to the memory that has been forgotten. We see the repetition compulsion at work in the transformation of a person who had been the victim of abuse into the perpetrator of abuse, and in the transformation of a person who had been the object of her parent's sadomasochism into a sadomasochist herself. That is, the individual has been transformed from being the object of prey to being the predator in an attempt to master the traumatic experience, by turning the passive experience of being the object of predation into the active experience of preying upon other or self. There may well be a combined biological-environmental predisposition to this repetition compulsion in our ancient history, in the prehistoric period of humankind when carnivorous animals stronger and larger than humans roamed the earth, hungry for meat and thirsty for blood. Civilization, we must remember, is only a recent and so far relatively short stage of human history, compared to prehistory.

THE DIALECTICS OF SAFETY AND DANGER, PREDATOR AND PREY

The borderline and other primitive disorders, says Grotstein (1993), are an imbalance of the safety/danger dialectic in which the individual does not feel safe either from the demons in his unconscious or from the real predators in his environment. The safety/danger dialectic, employing perspectives of entitlement, innocence, self-sacrifice, disregulation, and shame, composes the borderline worldview. It is a most functional way of understanding the dilemma of the individual with a borderline personality organization: the deep longing for merger and oneness with another human being, alternating with the terrifying fear of having one's essential self swallowed up and engulfed by the other.

The person who harms himself has no internalized sense of having been cared for and protected as an innocent does. Grotstein (1993) conceptualizes innocence as the continuation of the infantile fantasy of being blessed and entitled to love and protection in a world that is basically good, from parents who are basically good. "The infant's and child's sense of innocence depends on the holding and containing capacities of the parents to bestow both meaning to inchoately chaotic feelings and reasonable guarantees of safety against predators (even including the parents themselves). It is the failure to negotiate the whirling vortex of chaos that predisposes the child to psychosis and borderline illness" (p. 111). Thus, it is the prey–predator scenarios that are prominent in individuals with borderline psychopathology because they reflect their worldview

(Grotstein 1993). Never having felt a sense of innocence or having lost the feeling of blessedness or even feeling cursed by fate right from the beginning, they instead feel a sense of shame. They feel ostracized from love and unprotected against internal and external predators. With this growing sense of anxiety and malaise, the mental representations of the parent who fails to protect them from predators become transformed into representations of the parent *as* the predator, which are internalized regardless of whether the parent has been predatory and abusive or failed to protect the child from predation by others. Even in cases of emotional deprivation, the child who feels intensely that something good was not given by the parents may retain a sense of being his parents' victim that is affectively so powerful and central as to be considered a primary unit of mental life (Pine 1994).

A similar process can occur as well when, following a serious loss, an individual fails to restore his psychic equilibrium and suffers from melancholia (Freud 1917). The processes of mourning and melancholia are similarly modeled on the infant's first experience of reality, the taking in and incorporation of food. Initially the mourner turns away from the reality of the loss of the loved one and clings to the mental representations of the lost object, turning it into an ego loss. He unconsciously manifests some of the characteristics of the lost one that preserve the sense of the person as alive. In normal mourning, the sequential stages are, first, the gradual acceptance of the loss as a reality and the world becoming cold and empty, and then the gradual withdrawal of attachments to and identifications with the lost object sufficiently so that libido is freed up so that the individual can resume life among the living. Old attachments once again provide pleasure, and there is also the possibility of establishing new attachments. Sadness, loneliness, and a capacity for mourning become tolerable dimensions of human experience in what Melanie Klein (1964) has defined as the depressive mode of experience.

It is, however, quite a different story in melancholia when the mourner maintains a very ambivalent attachment to the lost object. Because he cannot maintain the relationship, he magically restores the lost object to continue the relationship internally, a means of denying the loss. But simultaneously feelings of hatred demand the destruction of the object, so he restores the object by incorporating it as a cannibal would, unconsciously biting, mutilating, and devouring it, taking revenge on the lost object for denying him the love he craved. In melancholia he becomes a cold predator of the self, turning anger for the object against the self through agonizing self-reproach, hypochondriasis, somatization, and bodily self-harm. And there is always the danger of suicide when the internalized lost object becomes so overly cathected with aggression.

The traumatized or depressed child identifies with the parent-predator, an internalized view of the parent-as-predator that resonates with Melanie Klein's (1964) paranoid-schizoid position, in which anxieties about fear of fragmentation and disintegration lead to the mobilization of primitive defenses.

We get to look upon the child's fear of being devoured, or cut up, or torn to pieces, or its terror of being surrounded and pursued by menacing figures as a regular component of its mental life. . . . I have no doubt from my own analytic observations that the identities behind these imaginary, terrifying figures are the child's own parents, and that those dreadful shapes in some way or other reflect the features of its father and mother, however distorted and fantastic the resemblance may be. [Bloch 1994, p. 2, citing Klein]

In the paranoid-schizoid mode, there is virtually no difference between the symbol and what is symbolized. This concrete pre-symbolic mode, called symbolic equation, is quite different from the level of symbolization in the more intact depressive mode (Klein 1964), in which the symbol represents the symbolized and is experienced as different from it. In the paranoid-schizoid mode, the magical restoration of the lost object short-circuits the experiences of the depressive mode. The parent does not merely stand as a symbol of the predator but in the child's inner world actually *becomes* the predator.

BECOMING A WILD ANIMAL

It is unbearably painful to live in fear of being preyed upon, and while it is also painful to have to live with a readiness to attack as a predator, it is also the lesser of the two evils because it puts one in a position of raw power. In the face of intolerable suffering, there is a very severe ego regression from the paranoid-schizoid position to the sensory-dominated autistic-contiguous mode of self-harm, which is even more elemental (Ogden 1990). In the autistic-contiguous mode the most rudimentary sense of self is built upon the rhythm of sensation, especially sensations at the skin surface. In normal early experience there are soft impressions and hard impressions on the skin, as Tustin (1981) conveyed: "Forget your chair. Instead, feel your seat pressing against the seat of the chair. It will make a 'shape.' If you wriggle, the shape will change. Those 'shapes' will be entirely personal to you" (pp. 281–282). There is neither chair nor buttocks, but simply and literally a sensory impression. The soft impressions later come to be associated with security, relaxation, warmth, and affection. The hard angular impressions on the skin are experienced as if they were the skin itself, hard and shell-like, and come to be associated with the most diffuse sense of danger, and fantasies of a hard protective armor formed by the skin surface. "The relationship to the object in this mode . . . is a relationship of shape to the feeling of enclosure, of beat to the feeling of rhythm, of hardness to the feeling of edgedness" (Ogden 1990, p. 83).

The three modes of generating experience—the depressive, paranoid-schizoid, and autistic-contiguous—are each characterized by its own form of symbolization, method of defense, level of object relatedness, and degree of subjectivity (Ogden 1989). They exist in a dialectical relationship to each other, each creating, preserving, and negating the other. Often the regression to the autistic-contiguous mode occurs while the individual is in either a dissociated state, most often a severe state of depersonalization in which she feels unreal and emotionally numb, often accompanied by feelings that the rest of the world is not real either (derealization), an acute state of hyperarousal, or a state of angry, agitated depression. It is a visceral, atavistic attack on the self, like a wild animal attacking the self, and there is little or no pain. "There is practically no sense of inside and outside or self and other; rather, what is important is the pattern, boundedness, shape, rhythm, texture, hardness, softness, warmth, coldness, and the like" (Ogden 1990, p. 84). The regression to the immediacy of bodily experience is so startling it is like a magical transformation of a human being into a wild beast of the jungle.

FEAR OF THE BEAST

The image of the infant nursing at the mother's breast is a symbol of security, making milk and cookies at bedtime a favorite ritual for children to ease the separation from consciousness into sleep. Yet sometimes children feel abandoned to the dark shadows and shapes that lurk in the hall, and surrender to sleep means surrender to an abyss where monsters and beasts can rip them apart with razor-sharp teeth. Perhaps these fears represent retribution for aggressive thoughts and oedipal wishes, but at the same time, perhaps the fears are deeper, even primordial. Sleep is related metaphorically to death, the final separation when "like children falling asleep over their toys, we relinquish our grip on earthly possessions only when death overtakes us" (C. Stern 1978). Children's bedtime prayers reflect a fear of being killed in the night: "Now I lay me down to sleep, I pray the Lord my soul to keep; If I should die before I wake, I pray the Lord my soul to take."

Fears of predation and cannibalism abound in children's play, fantasies, nursery rhymes, favorite stories, and fairy tales (e.g., Hansel and Gretel, Little Red Riding Hood and the Wolf, The Gingerbread Boy and the Fox, Where the Wild Things Are). Often the predators are disguised as human beings, perhaps because children are predisposed to fear that their parents will actually kill them. In my clinical work with young children I have frequently found they fear human predators and seek protection against them. This fear is especially strong when the child has witnessed violence or been the target of violence. I have had to fall to the floor repeatedly and play dead when a little patient has shot me, then smiled at him from the floor to reassure him that it really was just play, then allowed myself to be resurrected and killed again, to my patient's delight. Child analyst Dorothy Bloch (1994), too, has had similar clinical experiences, leading her to conclude that the child's fear of being killed by his parents is a universal fear that is readily expressed in fantasy.

Although frequently it was deeply buried in the unconscious of my adult patients, I discovered that in children it was usually right on the surface. . . .

[The treatment] abounded in beasts, . . . in cruel witches and monsters who pursued their victims with unrelenting savagery. . . . The air continually vibrated to the rat-a-tat-tat of machine guns, corpses hung from trees, and streams ran red with blood. . . . I was instructed by a five-year-old in the slaughter of multitudes by a carefully worked out routine that inevitably ended with our dumping the imaginary corpses over the roof and then brushing "the blood and dirt off our hands." . . .

"How does it come about that the child creates such a fantastic image of its parents, an image so far removed from reality?" I concluded that children are universally predisposed to the fear of infanticide by both their physical and their psychological stage of development, and that the intensity of that fear depends on the incidence of traumatic events and on the degree of violence and of love they have experienced. . . . Why hadn't it occurred to me sooner? When I suggested it to other adults, they also expressed surprise but immediate acceptance. Why shouldn't children be afraid of being killed? To begin with, consider their size. Is there anyone more "killable"? To be born tiny and defenseless in a world where even a mouse has the advantage of mobility is surely to find oneself at the mercy of every living being. . . . Children are soon aware of their vulnerability and their dependence on the good will of their parents for their very lives. [pp. 1–4]

EAT OR BE EATEN, KILL OR BE KILLED

"The fear of being dismembered, cut to pieces, or mutilated, has a prototype in the universal experience of learning to eat," said Lillian Malcove (1933, p. 557) in an early paper. While being taught how to eat, the child sees food being cut up and broken into small pieces, and identifies with the mutilated food. He thus develops a cannibalistic notion of eating, believing emotionally in the possibility of eating people and being eaten by them. After all, teeth and fingers are used in much the same way, to tear, rip, or shred the food. These infantile cannibalistic beliefs are supported not only in childhood but in adulthood as well by the common everyday linguistic associations between love and eating. For example, children are often told "I love you so much that I'm going to eat you up," or lovers engaging in oral sex might say "I want to eat you." A father, writing about his child's first three years of life, said "That we find our own children utterly endearing is nature's way of assuring that we don't kill, cook, and eat them." And so eating comes to be equated with being eaten and being mutilated.

I can recall how my son, when a toddler, bit his finger while eating and began to cry. How had it happened? "I bit my finger because I thought it was a piece of chicken." In fact, breaded rectangles of chicken are called "chicken fingers" on menus and the term *finger food* can be understood dialectically to mean that not only can fingers be used as eating utensils but that fingers are to be eaten. Indeed, biting one's nails, cuticles, or other fleshier parts of the body constitute both eating and mutilating oneself. If one ferociously consumes large amounts of food, the binge may defend against the fear of being devoured; that is, it is better to eat than be eaten. To starve oneself and become very thin may serve as protection against predators hungry for a plumper, juicier morsel.

GHOSTS OF PREDATORS PAST AND PRIMEVAL

If we take Klein's concept of the paranoid-schizoid position and look back to prehistoric times, stranger anxiety can be seen to be a transformation of an inherent atavistic fear of being prey to the primeval predator (Grotstein 1990):

> Stranger anxiety, which is discontinuous from separation anxiety but coeval with it, seems to furnish the frightening scenarios that fill the gap of separation. It is my belief that the inherent fear of the stranger is a transformation of our inherent, atavistic fear of being prey to the immemorial predator (Bowlby, personal communication). The nature of these prey-predator scenarios is phylogenitically honed and first emerges, I believe, as inherent preperceptions as well as preconceptions, which are *released* by experiences of abandonment, neglect, and impingement to produce apocalyptic phantasmagoria . . . and which are relentlessly repeated in separations that these patients experience from their treatment in what has been termed the "gap." Stranger anxiety, which has neurodevelopmental roots . . . is probably the format of the persecutory fantasies that Klein . . . postulates comprise the paranoid-schizoid position. From another point of view, one can see how infants and primitive personalities may unwittingly superimpose prey or predator ("stranger") imagery onto the images of their parents or loved ones, as in a montage, and thereby commingle the strange with the familiar. . . .
>
> I propose that the archetypal preconceptions and preperceptions released by traumatic circumstances would be of the prey-to-predator variety and would include a lexicon of all the possible horrors of our primeval past. [pp. 141, 150]

Darwinian theory explains not only the complexity of an animal's body but the complexity of its mind as well. Even though the problem of man's enormous vulnerability to predators eluded him, an incident occurred that caused Darwin to wonder if perhaps human beings were haunted by the "ghosts of predators past." When his 2-year-old son developed a fear of large caged animals at the zoo, Darwin said: "Might we not suspect that the . . . fears of children, which are quite independent of experience, are the inherited effects of real dangers . . . during savage times" (Marks 1987, p. 112). To understand how the mind works to produce self-harm in any human being, we need to understand that our minds have been designed by natural selection to produce behavior that would have been adaptive in our ancestral environment. Evolutionary understandings can enrich our diagnostic understanding by helping us to consider psychological traits on the basis of past survival functions (Pinker 1997a). We need to consider how the crucial transformation in self-harm, the transformation from prey to predator, might have given early man an adaptive advantage.

FROM DEFENSELESS PREY TO FEROCIOUS PREDATOR

Representations of monstrous predators are ubiquitous in popular culture, reflecting the fear of predators among young and old. The U.S. Postal Service has what I call "attachment stamps," two kissing swans whose touching beaks form a valentine-shaped heart, and "predation stamps," colorful and threatening-looking dinosaurs, mouths opened to display long razor-like teeth. These are the real things, not the snuggly Barney, the-purple dinosaur that has joined the ranks of teddy bears, Big Bird, and Cookie Monster as cultural icons of childhood. Infants' sleeper suits are imprinted with teddy bears, the lovable cuddly version of another predator, the brown grizzly bear; dinosaur designs are popular for children's clothing. Children in nursery school learn the distinctions, history, and habits of *Tyrannosaurus rex*, *Brachiosaurus*, *Stegosaurus*, and *Triceratops*; New York's Museum of Natural History dinosaur room has become very popular; children and adults wait on long lines to see *Jurassic Park*. We watch ferocious beasts stalk and eat human beings. "It doesn't matter much if the beast is a fast-living 'Killer Shrew' or a sullen 'Cat People' or an abstract 'Wolfen' or a nameless, acid-drooling 'Alien.' The pattern is always the same. They dominate the genre. We are greedy for their brand of terror" (Ackerman 1990, p. 170).

Children can master their fear of predators by turning them into lovable animals like Barney, or they can defend against anxiety by playing the part of the predator. The "rapprochement games" that mothers play with their babies, the "I'm going to gobble you up" or "I'm going to get you" games may be adaptive in that, "from a mother's point of view, it is far safer for the child to fear too much than fear too little" (Ehrenreich 1997, p. 92). Many childhood games resonate with tribal initiation rites that reenact a man's primal encounter with a predatory beast: in games of knucks, the child who has lost must subject himself to being rapped hard on the knuckles with a deck of playing cards by each player; in some other games, the loser must crawl through a gauntlet, through the legs of his friends who punch and smack him as he scrambles through. Even that old favorite, musical chairs, evokes anxiety because he who does not scramble aggressively for a chair is left out in the cold, an isolate without a chair, without a community to protect him from predators. Just as the ancient Romans were entertained by blood sports that mime predation, pitting gladiators against lions and throwing Christians to the lions, we have our own genre of predation entertainment. "When Animals Attack" has become a prime-time television hit, offering taped reenactments of humans being attacked by bears or mountain lions, while audiences watch "The Crocodile Hunter" subdue and capture crocodiles and poisonous reptiles.

Human or part-human predators preoccupy us as well. Spain has traditionally adored its bullfighters, even the female bullfighters who have become popular recently, confirming that predation is not the exclusive province of men, while hunting has been taken up by women in growing numbers. Mary Zeiss Stange, an associate professor of religion at Skidmore College who wrote a book about women and hunting, "pulled the trigger of the Browning semiautomatic rifle and watched the mule buck stagger forward to collapse. Tears filled her eyes in a mix of sadness and exhilaration. It was the first time in her thirty five years that she'd killed anything more than a spider. But the remorse faded as she and her husband gutted the deer in the dusk of that cold Montana day. Stange was convinced that she was meant to hunt" (Henk 1997, p. 11). Even paintball is all about coming face to face with the fear of being hunted and shot at (Kriss 1998). "The thrill of the hunt is what it's all about, and that's something that's instinctual. It's the necessity to survive" (p. 19).

Today we avoid eating red meat for health reasons but our desire for it reflects our pleasure in having become the predator, something that the anorectic disavows. The tablecloth and candlelight in a restaurant may disguise the fact that it is far better to be eating a rare, juicy steak than to be eaten alive by a blood-thirsty carnivore. But we dare not pick up that steak with our hands and gnaw at it; that is too close to the primordial experience. Better to do that with meat that is not red and bloody, chicken for example. When we speak of "something eating me up" or complain that "they're sucking the life out of me," our language signifies the fear of being cannibalized by monsters, mutilated by vampires.

There is a fascination with vampires, blood-sucking part-human creatures with long canine teeth that drain the life out of their subjects. "Buffy the Vampire Slayer" is a television series popular with children and adults. Some people remind us of vampires as they puncture and cut human flesh, for example, surgeons, who may sublimate this wish. But for Raellyn Gallina, body piercer and scarification professional, the wish is enacted. Gallina so loves watching the blood flow as she cuts into human flesh that she is known as the "queen of blood sports" (Myers 1995). A television series called "Prey" featured a new species of man with a genetic anomaly in its blood that makes killing others not only essential to his existence but also a thrilling, pleasurable experience.

All such spectacles, says Ehrenreich (1997), offer a "safe" version of the trauma of predation, one in which we approach the nightmare—and survive. In her book *Blood Rites: Origins and History of the Passions of War*, Ehrenreich proposed that everything from war to religion to men and women's relations to violence is rooted in our struggle to combat the original trauma of prehistoric man's having being hunted by more powerful animal predators—and to remake ourselves as the hunter. Resonating with this idea, Ackerman (1990) states, "We may be comfortable at the top of the food chain as we walk around Manhattan, but suppose—oh, ultimate horror!—that on other planets *we're* at the bottom of *their* food chain?" (p. 170). We still have not gotten used to being at the top of our food chain, or we would not continue to sit in movie theaters and watch the same scary movies that turn the tables on us and make us food for the animals. On our way home from the movies, we keep listening for the sound of claws on the pavement, a supernatural panting, a vampiric flutter. We spent our formative years as a technology-less species scared for good reason about lions and bears and snakes and sharks and wolves that could, and frequently did, pursue us. You'd think we'd have gotten over that by now. . . . But civilization is a more recent phenomenon than we like to think. Are horror films our version of the magic drawings on cave walls that our ancestors confronted? Are we still confronting them? [Ackerman 1990, pp. 170–171]

PRIMEVAL FEAR OF THE PREDATOR
IN A PAST-LIFE REGRESSION

I was around four or five. I was with these people, at least two of them, a man and a woman. Maybe there were others around, I don't know. The people were strange looking, not quite human. I was with them but it was like I wasn't. They really didn't pay attention to me. They were very short and muscular but hunched over; they didn't really walk upright. And they were very hairy. Their faces were strange, too, kind of primitive and scary looking. Their jaws jutted out, their teeth were big and long. . . . I don't know where we were but the land was flat and dry. There were scrubby plants and shrubs. Not really a desert, more like a dry plain, like out west or even like in *Jurassic Park*. Then there was a roar and we all were screaming. It was a huge animal thundering toward us, it looked like an enormous lizard or dinosaur. It was many times bigger than the people. It was terrible. It was coming directly at me and no one helped. I was all alone. I don't know what happened to the man and woman but I was running away and the next thing I knew, I was lying face down on the ground and the animal was trampling me. My back was broken, I think. . . . Somehow, there I was, being carried on the animal's back as the people followed. I don't know how I got there, maybe the people picked me up and put me there after the animal stopped its rampage and calmed down. I looked so small and still, so skinny. As I looked closer, and it took awhile to realize it, I realized I was dead.

Jessie, age 42, told the above story to me after returning from a weekend away at one of the health and healing spas that are now considered vacation resorts. It was not a dream, although it sounds like one, but was what Jessie had remembered in two sessions of past-lives regression therapy. The spa owner practiced Reiki healing and past-lives regression therapy, and Jessie had always been fascinated by accounts of people who remembered past lives.

Jessie believed in reincarnation and it made sense to her that if she could anticipate a future life after her body died, she could with some help remember a past life or even several past lives. She had had lower back problems for a long time. Her former lover had given her wonderful back massages that helped for a while, but that ended when the relationship did and her back once again was bothering her. She had gone to the spa, she said, because many people who underwent past lives regressions discovered that their somatic problems, for which their doctors found no organic cause, were actually a result of terrible experiences in a past life, and if they could get in touch with these experiences, they often improved greatly.

Jessie came into treatment suffering from depression after having left her husband. They had dated in college and when she became pregnant at 19, her parents threw her out of the house and severed contact with her. With nowhere to go and no source of support, she quit college and moved in temporarily with her boyfriend's family. Lonely and essentially homeless, she was desperate for him to marry her. She took jobs where she could sleep on the premises and did this well into her third trimester when finally her boyfriend agreed to marry her. After the birth of the baby, a second followed, and Jessie initiated contact with her family. Jessie completed her college degree, went on to get a graduate degree, and developed a career in which she was esteemed and well paid.

When Jessie came into treatment she had no notion of how her child-hood experiences had skewed the direction of her life and relationships. Things with her parents were much better than years ago, she said. They resumed contact after the children were born. Although she could acknowl-edge that her environment had been a harsh one, as her father had at times beaten her and her brother, she believed she had a perspective on it that enabled her to maintain a good relationship with them: they were a product of their time, when discipline meant beatings, she rationalized. Over time, however, Jessie began to disclose just how terrifying those beatings had been. They happened when she tried to get her father to stop beating her brother, who was thin and frail like her. Her mother never tried to stop the beatings, so she had to. Her father would turn on her in a rage and she ran from him as he chased her with the belt buckle. She would hide under her bed trem-bling, until he found her and dragged her out. The marks on her lower back were still there.

Many years later, when she was married, she and her husband had gotten into an argument. He flew into a rage and began to beat her, punching her over and over again in the small of her back. He was overcome with remorse at realizing what he had done and took her to the Emergency Room. Jessie's kidneys had been badly bruised and she could not walk or stand. She did not press charges. In treatment, it took quite a while before Jessie could talk about this at all, but she did at the same time that she began to talk about the beatings by her father. Although her husband had never repeated his beating of her, Jessie came to realize that she has always harbored a fear that if she dared say the wrong thing, her husband would beat her.

Jessie's feelings about the beatings had been dissociated from the memories. When she came back from her spa weekend, she very tentatively spoke of her "discovery" that her back pain originated in another lifetime when she was trampled and killed by an enormous ferocious animal. It was

much easier for her to accept that the people she was with in another lifetime had not protected her from being trampled and killed than to acknowledge her feelings toward her father for beating her, her mother for not intervening, and both for abandoning her.

THE ADAPTATIONAL ADVANTAGE OF ANXIETY

Urban dwellers may grow up "street smart," wary of human predators.
Those who live near the jungles, mountains, deserts, or forests that harbor bears,
cougars, mountain lions, and poisonous insects or snakes take special precau-
tions not to disturb these animals, which are thought not to attack unless provoked. Yet we tend not to spend much time at all contemplating the idea that
whether we provoke their attack or not, we can be prey to the animals, a very
tasty nibble. Our prehistoric ancestors knew this better than we and evolved
to become predators themselves, hunting and preying on animals (Anderson
1986).

Although we do not often encounter ferocious predatory animals, we nonetheless have been equipped by evolution to respond to such threats instantaneously. Today's anxiety disorders may represent an exaggerated reaction of a life-
preserving neural mechanism to normal everyday social stimuli (Hall 1999). One
of the emerging theories of anxiety disorders, offered by Jack Gorman, who has
studied them for twenty years, is that each variation (panic disorders, posttraumatic stress disorder, specific phobias and social phobia, obsessive-compulsive
disorder, generalized anxiety disorder, even the stranger anxiety of infants) represents a glitch at some point in the fear circuitry in the frontal cortex of the brain
due to either an inherited biochemical predisposition (nature) or remembered
experiences (nurture). "You tweak different parts of the system and you're going
to get a different disorder. . . . You know, bang on the amygdala and you're going
to get panic attacks. Bang on the hippocampus and you're going to get posttraumatic stress disorder. You mess up the medial prefrontal cortex and you're
going to get too much worrying. They're all within the same system" (Hall 1999,
p. 70). The glitch can be exacerbated by the effects of stress, which alters body
chemistry in ways that accentuate irrational fears (Hall 1999).

The human brain contains, says Ehrenreich (1997), "at least some innate
residue of the experience of predation" (p. 89). The fight-or-flight response,
also known as the trauma response, is the most obvious example, but other
anxiety states have also been traced, at least speculatively, to the evolutionary
experience of predation (Marks 1987, Marks and Nesse 1994). Psychologist
William James, a phobic terrified of being alone (Hall 1999), said that even
though "a certain amount of timidity obviously adapts us to the world we live
in, the fear paroxysm is surely altogether harmful to him who is its prey" (Phillips
1994, p. 13).

After considering the virtues of immobility—the insane and the terrified "feel safer and more comfortable" in their "statue-like, crouching immobility"—James refers at the very end of his chapter on fear to "the strange symptom which has been described of late years by the rather absurd name of agoraphobia." After describing the symptoms, which "have no utility in a civilized man," he manages to make sense of this puzzling new phenomenon only by comparing it to the way in which both domestic cats and many small wild animals approach large open spaces. "When we see this, " he writes, we are strongly tempted to ask whether such an odd kind of fear in us be not due to the accidental resurrection, through disease, of a sort of instinct which may on some of our more remote ancestors have had a permanent and on the whole a useful part to play. . . . There is nothing really irrational about phobic terror; it is an accurate recognition of something, something that Darwinian evolution can supply a picture for. [Phillips 1994, p. 13]

"In neurobiological terms, anxiety is a close relative of panic, and akin to the constant vigilance displayed in the wild by animals which are at risk of predation" (Ehrenreich 1997, pp. 89–90). Evolutionary psychiatrists Isaac Marks and Randolph Nesse (1994) state that anxiety disorders represent evolutionary adaptations to a dangerous environment, with subtypes of anxiety that probably evolved to give a selective advantage of better protection against a particular kind of danger. Extrapolating from this theory, we can see that when it is the parent who has become the stranger, this may lead to a persistent and pronounced fear of the predator.

Consistent with this idea is that of the late Rubin Blanck (1998), who wrote that remnants of stranger anxiety that persist beyond the first year of life can become a factor in the development of hatred of the other, of racism and ethnic cleansing. That is, prolonged stranger anxiety may predispose the developing child to regard the other as predatory. In an interview in *Psychology Today* (November/December 1997), Jaron Lanier, computer scientist and researcher on the future of war, spoke of the "face of the enemy research" in which people in different cultures were asked to draw pictures of their enemies. The pictures all looked remarkably the same, with the same exaggerated canine teeth and a certain fixed and frightening expression, causing the researchers to speculate about whether at an earlier stage in the human experience we were hunted by some sort of carnivore. According to Ehrenreich (1997), we sanctify the violence committed out of anxiety about the predator and we make war sacred in the name of the new religion of nationalism. "Individually we are weak, but with God, or through 'the fatherland' or 'the working class,' we become something larger than ourselves—something indomitable and strong" (p. 16).

An evolutionary view suggests that different types of fear should be similar because reactions (e.g., rise in heart rate) that are useful in one kind of danger are likely also to be helpul in others. Furthermore, the presence of one threat makes it likely that others are present, too. General anxiety probably evolved to deal with threats whose nature could not be defined very clearly. General threats arouse general anxiety- inducing vigilance, physiological arousal, and planning for defense, while specific threats elicit specific patterns of behavioral defense. For example, high places evoke a freezing response to defend against falling; social threats arouse submission to others; predators provoke flight.

The usefulness of different kinds of behavioral responses to anxiety depends partly on the different ways in which anxiety can give protection (Marks and Nesse 1994). As shall be elaborated, these various forms of anxiety are often vital defenses used by human beings who have suffered severe trauma and abuse and are given to acts of self-harm. Escape (flight) or avoidance (preflight) parallel the body's ways of dealing with foreign material in that they can distance an individual from certain threats in the way that vomiting, disgust, diarrhea, coughing, and sneezing put physical space between the organism and a pathogen. Aggressive defense, such as clawing, biting, or spraying with noxious substances, can harm the predator just as the immune system attacks bacteria. Freezing or becoming immobile may allow one to survey, locate, and assess the danger, while at the same time deflecting attention from oneself, thus inhibiting the predator's attack reflex. Finally, to submit to and appease the predator can be useful when the threat comes from one's own group. We think, then, of submitting to a parent's beatings or sexual abuse. Multiple strategies can be used together. For example, squid escape by jet propulsion in a cloud of concealing ink. Puffer fish look ferocious and their spines harm the predator's mouth. Agoraphobics freeze in panic and then dash for home. Social phobics avoid or escape from authority figures if they can, and submit if they cannot. Obsessive-compulsives avoid "contamination" if possible; if they can't, they try to escape from it by washing or otherwise purifying themselves.

Any of these categories can involve deception (Marks and Nesse 1994), as when a cat is threatened, its fur stands on end, making it seem larger, and a frightened possum plays dead. Stranger anxiety seems to arise worldwide in infants at about 6 to 8 months of age, which suggests that a fear that is so transcultural is likely to be adaptive. At 6 to 8 months babies start to crawl away from mother and encounter strangers more often. In prehistoric times strangers were especially dangerous to infants; infanticide by strangers was so common that it was a strong selective force in primates as well as other species. Today human infants are far more likely to be killed or abused by strangers or by those to whom they are not related by blood. Thus, from an evolutionary view, predation may help explain the separation anxiety that babies begin to express at the age of about 6 to 8 months.

Mothers know not to leave their infants sitting in a stroller while they dash into the store, just as "in the archaic situation even momentary separation of the baby from its mother could mean exposure to predators and the chance of being snatched or eaten" (Ehrenreich 1997, p. 54). As the 2-year-old child explores further afield, animal fears emerge. Stimuli that come to be feared are not the imaginary "things that go bump in the night" but the ancient threats: snakes, spiders, wolves, sharks, heights, storms, thunder, lightning, darkness, blood, strangers, social scrutiny, and leaving the home range. This does not imply that these common fears per se are handed down in our DNA from generation to generation, but that the ability to feel anxiety has been transmitted inter-generationally by children's identification with adult responses to these threats. "In other words, learning, hearsay, rumor, word of mouth, subliminal suggestion, even the empathic horror we sometimes feel listening to details of a plane crash might create a hand-me-down sense of fear" (Hall 1999, p. 70). As Ehrenreich puts it, we do not inherit a fear of specific predators, but a capacity to acquire that fear through observation of and identification with adults reacting to various potential threats. That is, we inherit certain patterned responses to threats, and the threat that was originally selected for these responses was probably that of predation. This does not mean that we remember in any Jungian sense what our distant ancestors felt when seeing a peer attacked and ripped apart by a leopard, but it does mean, however, that "there was an evolutionary advantage to the ability to feel this alarm, and that this ability has been passed along to us" (Ehrenreich 1997, p. 91). It is an ability that has served as a survival tool for those who experience intrusive thoughts or feelings connected to past experiences of abuse, alerting them to beware. However, the problem with predation anxiety is that it creates a state of hyperarousal that itself becomes painful, and so many survivors will cut, burn or purge themselves to terminate it.

WE ARE THE GODS AND THE DEMONS, THE LIONS AND THE SACRIFICIAL LAMBS

Self-harmers sacrifice their blood, flesh, and sometimes even their lives to their families to preserve a certain equilibrium in the family. Even among the nonreligious, their sacrifice may have more to do with religion than we might think. Central to all religion is the concept of the sacrifice to the gods of human flesh and blood, a powerful dialectic uniting the worst in man (his destructive impulse) with the best in man (the wish to transcend those impulses). As man developed a moral sense, he experienced the sacrifice of the weak (children and the ill or deformed) to appease carnivorous deities to be a necessary but terrible transgression, and so religion evolved out of the need to transform human sacrifice from a necessary evolutionary evil into a sacred act (Ehrenreich 1997). Paramount is the image of the sacrificial lamb in Judaism and Christianity (Bergmann 1992). God demanded that Abraham sacrifice his son Isaac; at the critical moment when Abraham was getting ready to stab him and then throw him into the fire, a ram appeared, which Abraham offered and God accepted instead. God the Father sacrificed his son Jesus on the cross to redeem mankind. Human sacrifices took the form of raw human flesh or a burnt offering, what anthropologist Claude Levi-Strauss (1964) referred to as "the Raw and the Cooked." "Violence," said Girard (1977), "is at the heart and secret soul of the sacred" (p. 24). It is no wonder we so often are anxious around patients who cut, burn, or cannibalize their bodies; their behavior speaks of the most forbidden transgression.

The Jewish and Christian texts that develop the image of a loving God are Western man's greatest moral efforts to transcend the legacy of human sacrifice, which has at its root an earlier image of a ferocious deity who hungered for human flesh (Bergmann 1992). The common religious sacrifices many grow up with—refraining from eating pork, giving up meat on Friday or candy for Lent, the Islamic Halaal laws, and religious fasting—had their basis in the ancient tradition of human sacrifice, and reflect an unspoken anxiety about cannibalism (Bergmann 1992, Grotstein 1979). The sacrifice of animals, fruit, and wine became substitutes for human sacrifice. Even in the Jewish ritual of circumcision of male infants, it is believed that the infant's foreskin is sacrificed in lieu of the infant as a sign of the covenant.

There is an underlying anxiety about the Christian communion ritual, the Eucharist, which resonates with cannibalism and hints that there is a sinister side to the deity: "Who so eateth my flesh, and drinketh my blood, hath eternal life; and I will raise him up at the last day. For my flesh is meat indeed, and my blood is drink indeed. He that eateth my flesh, and drinketh my blood, dwelleth in me, and I in him (John 6:54–56). In fact, Catholic children are cautioned that they must not bite the wafer, a point made by Bergmann (1992) and writer Pete Hamill (1997) in his novel, Snow in August:

> Mumbling Latin, his left hand holding the gold chalice . . . Father Heaney deposited a host upon each outstretched tongue, while Michael held the paten under their chins. This was so that no fragment of the host, which had been transformed into the body of Jesus Christ during the Consecration, would fall upon the polished floor.
> The first woman's eyes were wide and glassy . . . The other closed her eyes tight, as if fearful of gazing too brazenly at the divine white wafer. . . . They each took the host the same way: the lips closing over it, but the mouth stretched high and taut to form a closed fleshy little cave. To chew the host, after all, was to chew Jesus. Bowing in piety and gratitude, they rose and went back to the dark pews to pray until the host softened and they could swallow. [pp. 24–25]

The paradox is that to drink the blood and eat the flesh of another is the most forbidden of transgressions while, according to Catholic doctrine, there is a transubstantiation of the wafer and the wine into "the living, risen and glorious body and blood of Christ, really, truly, and substantially present and offered in sacrifice." So Jesus is both the sacrificial lamb and, through the mystery of the Trinity, is also the demonic deity to whom the lamb is offered. The concept of the demon-god suggests that "To behave like a beast of prey . . . betokens that one has ceased to be a man . . . that one has in some sort become a god . . . On the level of elemental religious experience, the beast of prey represents a higher mode of existence" (Eliade 1958, p. 72). So to transform oneself from prey to predatory beast is to become godlike. This dialectic is most often an unconscious driving force in the psyches of those who live their lives organized around self-harm, who cannibalize their flesh or offer it burnt or bleeding to the predatory gods or goddesses they have become.

The Passion of Christ has provided Western culture with its most enduring images of sacrifice and suffering that have been absorbed, as if by osmosis, by the culture at large, with, I propose, a profound influence on the conscious and unconscious mind of children. Generations of Catholic children are raised reading and hearing *The Lives of the Saints*, absorbing blood and gore in much the same way they breathe air and drink water, while fundamentalist Protestants maintain a central image of the bloody cross. It is easy to forget that in these racially, ethnically, and religiously heterogeneous United States, European Christian origins and images are nonetheless paramount, and that anyone growing up in this culture can have such images stored away in his unconscious. Grotstein (1979) noted that in the wards of mental hospitals, quite frequently even orthodox Jewish patients had "New Testament" delusions. Writer Kathryn Harrison was born of a Jewish mother but was raised as a Christian. What stuck with her was the glamour of martyrdom. "My mother never went to temple, and I think that the faith of her forebears must have struck her as dowdy and workaday, lacking the overt glamour of crucifixion. The blood of Judaism was old and dull as a scab, whereas Christ's flowed brightly each Sunday" (Harrison 1997, pp. 102–103). Harrison's blood flowed, too, from her self-inflicted cutting, and she starved herself as well.

In adolescence, when many struggle with strivings toward asceticism, martyrdom has become an ego-ideal for far too many. Although the Catholic Church warns believers against scrupulosity (religious excess), that message is received as cognition (secondary process), while the emotional conviction that martyrlike self-harm is redeeming has no doubt been stored in early primary process thinking, in what Grotstein (1997) described as a "dual track," a dialectical interaction between primary and secondary process thinking. At times of extreme anguish, many offer their suffering up to God or to a demon-god, through starving, mutilating, and purging themselves. They prey upon their own bodies like hungry, thirsty beasts, clamoring for ever greater sacrifices of flesh and blood, transgressing ancient taboos.

"We are what we all abhor, Anthropophagi and Cannibals, devourers not only of men, but of our selves; and that not in an allegory, but a positive truth, for all this mass of flesh which we behold, came in at our mouths; this frame we look upon, hath been upon our trenchers; in brief, we have devour'd our selves (Favazza 1996, p. 62, quoting Thomas Browne in *Religio Medici*).

Bergmann (1992) holds that all religions are projective systems in which the gods are created in the image of the worshipers. This means that regardless of our patients' religious affiliation or lack thereof, we must be concerned about their internalized "deity representations." When a child projects his harsh self and object representations onto God, that child is more likely to believe that he must harm himself in order to satisfy his God.

8

Trauma, Duality, and the Transformation from Prey to Predator

The child's mind is split into contradictory fragments to separate the bad from the good. . . . This compartmentalized "vertical splitting" transcends diagnostic categories. . . . Orwell describes this in 1984. . . . Orwell's "doublethink" is a system of vertical mind-splits that makes it possible to believe that two plus two equals five.

Leonard Shengold, Soul Murder: The Effects of Childhood Abuse and Deprivation

Self-harm communicates something about personal trauma. Those who have been traumatized are likely to return to the traumatic scene in some way to repeat the trauma, perhaps talking about it with others or dreaming about it in an attempt at mastery. They might experience something physically that connects them to the trauma or they may be drawn to revisit the site physically, or in dreams, or in reenacting. Traumatized children often repeat the trauma in their play (Terr 1973).

Just as our prehistoric ancestors were transformed from potential prey to predators, we know that those who have been abused and traumatized in childhood are most likely to become predators themselves, or they will be driven to become attached to other predators who will abuse them. Traumatized children often manifest syndromes of aggressive, pain-seeking self-destructive behavior resembling the sadomasochism seen in adults (Grossman 1991). Whether they become the prey or predators, they often become self-predators at the same time, taking their own bodies as their prey. In addition there are those who, while not having been preyed upon by abusing adults, grew up being physically or emotionally neglected, and developed a false self persona (narcissistic personality) to maintain the attachment to the neglectful parent. These individuals, too, are prone to feeling extraordinarily unprotected and at the mercy of predators in the environment or predators in their imagination. These individuals, too, may grow up taking their own bodies as their prey, although not as frequently or as severely as those who suffered abuse in childhood.

These concepts help in understanding the etiology, development, and maintenance of self-harm, and in understanding those moments when a person suddenly snaps, descending into a primitive and destructive ego regression. The psychobiology of the trauma response is comparable to the animal response to the fear of predation. This chapter discusses how the self-harmer becomes psycho-physiologically addicted to the experience of trauma and self-harm by means of repetition, reenactment, and sadomasochistic experience.

CHAOS, CATASTROPHE, AND SNAPPING

Lo! I tell you a mystery.
We shall not all sleep, but we shall all be changed,
In a moment, in the twinkling of an eye.

1 Corinthians 15:51

Communication is the basic organic process that governs everything we experience and regulates the everyday operations of the brain and nervous system. Acts of speech, from sermons to hypnosis to casual chatter, as well as nonverbal communication may affect biological functions at their most basic levels and human awareness at its highest states of consciousness (Conway and Siegelman 1995). When a person is pushed to the breaking point, his nervous system may snap like a piece of brittle plastic or a rubber band. Snapping can happen

> when an individual, for whatever reason, stops thinking and feeling for himself, when he breaks the bonds of awareness and social relationship that tie his personality to the world and literally loses his mind to some form of external or automatic control. . . . It takes place as some invisible switch is thrown in the infinitely flexible human brain, whether voluntarily and in good faith or unwittingly and in a state of confusion, as personality is surrendered to some religion, psychology, ideology, technology or other recipe for living that requires no real conscience and no consciousness, no effort or attention on the individual's part [Conway and Siegelman 1995, p. 325]

Patients may report, "Something snapped inside me," or "I cannot describe it. I just snapped." To try to make sense of the experience, they might become convinced that they had gone crazy or had quite literally blown their minds. In fact, there is evidence that many kinds of experiences can cause fuses to be blown in the brain, a sudden snapping of synaptic connections and lasting neurochemical changes in the regions of the brain where thinking, feeling, awareness, imagination, and long-term memory are concentrated.

Chaos theory takes us back to the notion of chaos as a mythological concept and describes the dynamics inherent in energy transformation (Chamberlain and Butz 1998). Both Freud and Jung were deeply concerned with how energy is transformed. "It is the spirit of the chaotic waters of the beginning, before the second day of Creation, before the separation of opposites and hence before the advent of consciousness. That is why it leads those whom it overcomes neither upwards nor beyond, but back into chaos" (Jung 1957, p. 252). Catastrophe theory, its cousin, is concerned with events that happen abruptly, with discontinuous, catastrophic change of the kind described by Conway and Siegelman 1995). It provides a lens for understanding different forms of snapping—the kind triggered by a single overwhelming trauma, a more gradual buildup of stresses, or a masterfully packaged mix of communication techniques that delivers "a systematically engineered snapping moment" (Conway and Siegelman 1996, p. 210). Catastrophe theory can help explain the snapping that occurs when an otherwise loving mother beats her child, and may account for the disorientation and delusions found in many cult members and the ongoing ecstasies of many born-again Christians. It can account for those moments when a man abandons his family to take a month-long course in levitation, when a woman executive retreats to the bathroom to make herself vomit, and when a 14-year-old locks herself in her room and cuts herself. Catastrophe theory can account for the critical moment of the anorexic "knockout," as many anorexics call it, when they become exhausted and disgusted with the herculean effort needed to deny their ravenous hunger, and they suddenly crash, either having no appetite at all or giving in to uncontrollable cravings and compulsive gorging.

Long before an eating disorder begins, little girls absorb the culture's communications about weight and fat. By the time they are 11 or 12, they may repeat to their friend a variation of the female "mantra": "I'm so fat. You have such a great figure. I'd die to look like you." Simple dieting may start with fasting or very restrictive dieting. As it continues, this common dieting strategy may become like a runaway train with a catastrophic life of its own, causing a total decline of appetite, leading to profound emotional disturbance, starvation, or its extreme counterreaction, bulimic episodes (Zeeman 1976), and possibly death. Catastrophe theory depicted the abrupted change from dieting to fasting, the contradictory jump from fasting to gorging, and the journey back in therapy when the patient seems to awaken from a trance to a state of "rebirth."

The correspondence was startling between the catastrophic jumps that occur in anorexia and the sudden personality changes that may happen in cults of various kinds (Conway and Siegelman 1995). In the moment of snapping, long-term personality patterns may give way to a new personality formed from the mass of new information the person has absorbed. The signs of this information disease include physical illness, exhaustion, depression, withdrawal, overwhelming feelings of fear, guilt, hostility, violent outbreaks, suicidal tendencies, and self-destructiveness. The most alarming effects fall into the category of complex cumulative posttraumatic stress disorder and include lasting disturbances of awareness, perception, memory, imagination and other ordinary human information-processing capacities, ongoing confusion, disorientation and dissociation, recurring nightmares, flashbacks, hallucinations and delusions, uncontrollable "floating" in and out of altered states, strange psychic phenomena, and a persistence of mental rhythms, images, voices, and other repetitive thought patterns (Conway and Siegelman 1995).

TRAUMA, "ALONENESS AFFECT," AND SELF-HARM

Information disease can be produced by trauma, the most far-reaching effect of which is loss of the ability to regulate the intensity of feelings and impulses. Trauma results in affect dedifferentiation, the inability to identify specific emotions that serve as a guide to appropriate actions, and it disrupts the ability for self-reflectiveness by severing the links between the self-as-subject and the self-as-object. Without the ability to reflect upon traumatic experiences, only the body is left "to keep the score" of what has happened (van der Kolk 1994)—through psychosomatic reactions, destructive aggression against the self and/or others (Krystal 1978, van der Kolk 1994), and a perverse relationship between parts of the self (Steiner 1981).

THE TRAUMA RESPONSE

Traumatic events may involve threats to life or bodily integrity, and inspire terror, helplessness, and the fear of annihilation (Herman 1992). The victim is made utterly helpless and powerless by overwhelming force, losing any sense of control, connection, and meaning. The trauma response was first described by Kardiner (1941) as a mental disorder that affects both psyche and soma, the syndrome of shell shock or combat fatigue seen in soldiers at the battlefront during World War II. This syndrome included a pattern of intrusive hyperarousal alternating with numbing, or dissociative, responses that later came to be known as posttraumatic stress disorder (PTSD). PTSD has been observed in very different kinds of trauma: combat, rape, kidnapping, spouse abuse, natural disasters, accidents, incest, concentration camp experiences, and child abuse, suggesting a biological substrate (Herman 1992, van der Kolk 1988). Freud (1920a) postulated, "The traumatic neurosis [is] a consequence of an extensive breach being made in the protective shield against stimuli," (p. 31) fixating the individual at the traumatic scene, to which he returns over and over again under the power of the repetition compulsion.

Trauma has been defined as the experience of the sudden cessation of human interaction (Lindemann 1944), or the experience of feeling ourselves to be utterly and completely alone. It is what Winchel (1991) might call "aloneness affect," what we feel when we suffer object loss. It was, says Winchel, what Oedipus felt when he put out his eyes: "Aloneness is man' s biologic destiny—and but for our ability to undo our aloneness, we might all rip ourselves to bits" (Winchel 1991, pp. 10–11). "Acute loneliness," wrote psychoanalyst Rollo May, "seems to be the most painful kind of anxiety which a human being can suffer. Patients often tell us that the pain is a physical gnawing in their chests, or feels like the cutting of a razor in their heart region" (May 1969, p. 151). Experiences of abandonment, neglect, and impingement release "our inherent atavistic fear of falling prey to the immemorial predator" (Bowlby, personal communication cited by Grotstein 1990, p. 141).

Time and time again in the moments following the traumatic event, human beings have cried out for their mother and even confirmed atheists have been known to call out for God, reaching for attachment. The basis of crisis intervention theory (Lindemann 1944) is that after a traumatic event, an individual is unusually vulnerable and receptive, in need of establishing human connectedness. When the environment allows for comforting and soothing, the victim can speak of the traumatic event, over and over again the way trauma survivors need to; the aloneness affect gradually subsides and the person is more likely to recover. Such is the case more often for the trauma of natural disasters than for the trauma of abuse.

Experiences of abuse and neglect involve a sense of shame that isolates the victim and hinders recovery. Verbal expression may become impossible or may be expressly prohibited, and the victim may come to ignore, minimize, or trivialize his suffering. The trauma is not articulated to others or even to the self. Like the tree that falls in the forest with no one there to hear it, the trauma victim whose suffering is not heard or listened to by another experiences the trauma as if it did not happen or as trivial.

A WARM BODY IS BETTER THAN NO-BODY;
VIOLENT TOUCH IS BETTER THAN NO TOUCH

The meaning the victim gives to the traumatic experience of abuse or neglect is critical in determining its long-term effects. It is the lack of secure attachments that may produce the most devastating effects because a secure attachment is needed for the individual to be able to regulate internal affective states and to modulate behavioral responses to external stressors (van der Kolk et al. 1991). When one has suffered a trauma and is feeling unbearably alone, one seeks attachment, clinging to whoever is available.

A benign attachment makes for a good prognosis for recovery from the trauma. The child who has been beaten or otherwise abused can recover from the trauma when he has the love and comfort of family members, to whom he can articulate his experience. But when it is the parent, the one meant to protect the child from predators, who is the one who has preyed upon the child, the abuse will have its most devastating effect, for the child will reach out to the abusive parent even more desperately. Very often child protective workers investigating abuse charges find that the abused child will cling to the abusive parent and deny that any abuse has occurred. If the abusive parent is, as often happens, at times cruel and at times loving, it is the memory of the kindness that draws the child to her abuser, fueling the attachment. If there is warmth mixed with cruelty, then the possibility of obtaining that warmth once again is always there, and if it means having to tolerate beatings or curses in order to once again receive that elusive warmth, then that is the price that will be paid.

In cases of even the most extreme torture, the attachment to a malevolent object may be necessary for survival. That is, attachment to a malevolent object may be better than no attachment at all. Curling up with a warm body, even though it is the body of the one who has raped or beaten you, may be better than curling up in a ball and feeling totally alone. That is why runaway kids are readily retraumatized and revictimized by those to whom they become attached on the streets, as once again they find attachment at the hands of abusers.

Patricia Hearst, held hostage by the terrorist Symbionese Liberation Army (SLA), was starved, raped, bound, and confined in a dark closet for days on end. She shocked the nation and the world by pledging her solidarity with the SLA and joining them in robbing a bank. A nation was mesmerized by the case of the murder of Nicole Brown Simpson. How could handsome, charming football star–turned-actor O. J. Simpson have done this? Why did Nicole remain with him so long while he was beating her?

In another case of stunning abuse, a brutally beaten Hedda Nussbaum watched her adopted daughter Lisa Steinberg receive equally brutal beatings from Joel Steinberg. She stood by, wanting to call for an ambulance to help her dying daughter, but was unable to defy Joel's order not to. She watched as her daughter died. What was the nature of the diabolical bond between Hedda and Joel? Hedda is reported to have said, "Once you taste the stick, you don't want to give it up" (Merkin 1997, p. 38). In her essay "A Taste of the Stick," Daphne Merkin writes:

> Perhaps it is best—it is certainly easiest—to regard this couple as popular senti-
> ment would have it: a fiendish man, a victimized woman, a degeneration abetted by
> massive drug use, and the tragedy of a dead child. [p. 40]
> Our interpretations of what we call love vary so much as to be mutually exclusive
> a good deal of the time. Undoubtedly, Joel and Hedda's idea of love had much to do
> with their cravings and frustrations. Almost certainly the hostile symbiotic connection

that their involvement hinged on provided an emotional trade-off: Whether he was making love to her or beating her, Hedda remained at the center of Joel's attention. [p. 39]

When the trauma is not articulated to others or to the self, when the impetus to give voice to the inner pain has been thwarted, the development of self-harm can arise instead, serving to articulate the trauma through gestures (McLane 1996) such as taking a blade to one's flesh, heaving up vomit into the toilet, refusing to eat, getting one's body pierced or tattooed. When one becomes attached to one's predator, one also becomes attached to the psychophysiological experience of pain and suffering and to the response to trauma, becoming more likely to seek pain and suffering and to inflict it on oneself, over and over again.

THE TRAUMA CONTINUUM AND DEFENSIVE ALTERED STATES

Shock trauma or inescapable trauma is of two kinds. When the force of the trauma comes from nature (earthquakes, fires, floods), we speak of disasters; when it comes from other human beings (physical or sexual abuse, family violence, mugging, rape, terrorist attack, kidnapping), we speak of atrocities (Herman 1992). In children, object loss and prolonged separations should, at times, be considered as shock trauma as well, when the reality of loss powerfully and often suddenly impinges on the child's life, overwhelming the immature ego. Sometimes in adults, grief becomes traumatic.

Just as it is not recognized how often adults suffer traumatic postsurgical reactions, it is not recognized how often children may be traumatized as the result of intrusive, coercive, and painful medical or dental procedures. While in some hospitals parents are allowed to remain with children until they are anesthetized, all too often children are unnecessarily wrenched from their parents in the hospital, especially in emergency rooms. The experience of children going into surgery is often that they are strapped to a gurney, then taken from their parents to a strange room where masked strangers take away their consciousness. Even the most compassionate doctor or nurse may be experienced as a terrifying predator to a helpless, dependent child. *Ethical Issues in Medicine*, published by the UCLA Medical Center (1988), cites a letter published in *Pediatrics*, based on professional medical experience, communication with colleagues, and published surveys, claiming that the majority of hospitalized children with severe pain do not receive optimal analgesia. Surgical procedures are often performed in infants and neonates without anesthesia and postoperative analgesia. And finally, in 1999, the American Academy of Pediatrics recommended that if parents choose to have their male infants circumcised, that it be done using anesthesia.

The mother of Ted Kaczynski, the Unabomber, believed that his emotional problems and intense rage stemmed from early medical trauma. She appeared on "60 Minutes" and told how her son had been hospitalized at 9 months for a severe case of hives. Not permitted to be held by a family member, he was strapped to a table, naked and screaming, for a week. When he was reunited with his mother, she said he was unresponsive and completely limp.

When an adult survivor of trauma is traumatized iatrogenically in the course of medical or psychiatric treatment, it may well be experienced as a repetition of past trauma. In 1996 the Massachusetts Department of Mental Health Task Force headed by Dr. Elaine Carmen issued a report on the restraint and seclusion of persons who have been physically or sexually abused (Carmen et al. 1996). Because many trauma survivors have been forcibly restrained by their abusers, locked in closets or rooms, and watched while they showered or used the toilet, something so routine to hospital staff as turning off the lights in a patient's room or looking in for a 15-minute room check can be experienced by a trauma survivor as a repetition of the trauma. Adults who had been traumatized in childhood by physical or sexual abuse often are inadvertently retraumatized in hospitals. When they are restrained in four-point restraints in a spread-eagle position, it may evoke flashbacks, intrusive images, body memories, or an uncontrolled trauma response. Someone with a sexual abuse history could also be retraumatized by having staff members lie on top of her for purposes of restraint. Not understanding the response, staff will most likely respond to this behavior as a control issue, which further escalates the patient's panic.

The Massachusetts task force report confirmed what psychiatric partients have been reporting for years, that they are victimized by other patients and by predatory staff members. Many trauma survivors who were treated in hospital emergency rooms for either medical or mental health problems reported that they were treated more humanely when presenting for medical, rather than psychiatric problems. As the task force report stated, there is an enormous potential for retraumatization when a patient with a history of sexual abuse is asked by an unfamiliar clinician to remove clothing in a chaotic emergency room. The potential for retraumatization is enormous when the patient is not allowed to have a friend present during the examination, leaving the patient exposed, vulnerable, and alone. Several abuse survivors brought to an emergency room for treatment of self-inflicted injuries have told me that they were treated angrily and in some cases sadistically by the staff, who used no anesthesia when suturing their cuts, saying, "You're such a tough guy that you can stand the pain of cutting yourself, so you can be a tough guy while I sew you up." A group of mental health nurses in England founded an interdisciplinary group to improve the quality of care to people who self-injure (Maureen Burke, R.G.N., R. M. N., personal communication). The Ashworth Hospital Authority has published "Self Injury: A Resource Pack" (Baker et al. 1996).

Not all trauma is shock trauma. Strain trauma (Kris 1956) is produced by the accumulated ongoing experience of neglect, parental indifference, and insecure attachments that results in devastating effects (Khan 1963). Being neglected physically or emotionally or ignored by the parents can result in an accumulation of frustrating tensions that may cause traumatic effects that can be equal to the effects of shock trauma. Strain trauma can result from cumulative experiences of being rejected, avoided, degraded, criticized, humiliated, threatened, isolated, or exploited overtly or covertly. It can result from the child's being denied necessary stimulation and responsiveness and from inconsistent parenting. The child who experiences strain trauma and develops a false self grows up feeling that neither his life nor his body is his own. He may feel intensely that something good was not given by the parents or that something bad was wrongly given, and experiences his "ongoing painful subjective states of self" as raw wounds (Pine 1994, p. 224). He may become particularly adept at depersonalizing and inducing autohypnotic states, an ability that both defends him from psychic pain and predisposes him to become victimized and traumatized all the more readily. Like abuse, childhood neglect enhances long-term hyperarousal and decreased modulation of strong affect states. Like abuse, childhood neglect, too, can produce soul murder (Shengold 1989). "What happens to the child subjected to soul murder is so terrible, so overwhelming, and usually so recurrent that the child must not feel it and cannot register it, and resorts to a massive isolation of feeling. . . . A hypnotic living deadness, a state of existing 'as if' one were there, is often the result of chronic early overstimulation or deprivation" (Shengold 1989, p. 25).

The severity and duration of trauma and the age at which it occurs are important in determining the severity of the trauma response. Victims of severe, repetitive psychological trauma usually have a more complex symptom picture than victims of a single traumatic event. The child who has experienced numerous trauma is likely to experience the cumulative effect as more severe than the sum effect of each individual trauma. Freud (1919) postulated that the child's memory of having been beaten becomes interwoven with his fantasies about the event, and subsequently internalized, making it difficult to know just where fact leaves off and fantasy starts. Whether the child has experienced physical or sexual abuse, coercive medical or surgical procedures, or witnessed violent assault, he can readily eroticize the experience and internalize it, with perverse effect upon his subsequent development (Farber 1991). Additionally, the state of hyperarousal itself is an excitement that can easily become sexualized. It is no coincidence that a common sadomasochistic scenario is the medical one, with the masochist submitting to various intrusive probings and injections inflicted by the sternly sadistic "doctor" or "nurse." This perverse repetition is especially true when the trauma has occurred repeatedly.

While a person may integrate a traumatic experience into his life, it is beyond the scope of human experience to integrate cumulative violent intrusions and bodily assaults. Such experiences set the stage for reenactments in which the victim turns passive victimization into active self and object victimization. When the childhood traumatic experiences continue into adolescence or beyond, within

a family in which there are no secure attachments and no one to turn to for soothing or protection, the lack of secure attachments is thought to help to maintain
the self-destructive behavior (van der Kolk et al. 1991).

Those who have been exposed to interpersonal trauma at an early age have
been consistently found to have certain trauma-related psychological problems
(Herman 1992). First, they suffer from alterations in regulating affective arousal,
modulating anger, regulating self-destructive impulses and suicidal preoccupation,
and modulating sexual involvement and risk taking. Second, there are alterations
in attention or consciousness that can manifest as attention deficit disorder,
attention deficit hyperactivity disorder, amnesia, depersonalization, and transient
dissociative episodes. Third, they suffer from somaticization, typically manifesting
as digestive difficulties, chronic pain, cardiopulmonary symptoms, conversion
symptoms, gynecological problems, and sexual symptoms. Fourth, there are
chronic characterological changes in the area of self-perception, perception of
others, and relationship with the perpetrator. The victims feel ineffective, permanently damaged, guilty, responsible, and shameful, and they feel that no one
can possibly understand them. Typically, they minimize the responsibility of the
perpetrator, idealizing and adopting distorted beliefs about him or her. They
develop an inability to trust others, may become victimizers themselves, and may
become repeatedly victimized. Fifth, there are alterations in systems of meaning,
resulting in despair and hopelessness and a loss of previously sustaining beliefs
(van der Kolk and Fisler 1994).

Thus, cumulative trauma that has occurred early in life becomes woven into
the fabric of the personality, forming part of the developing self and ego structure.
While it is childhood trauma that contributes to the initiation of self-destructive
behavior, studies have found that it is the lack of secure attachments that helps
to maintain it (Farber 1995a, van der Kolk et al. 1991). There is a very strong
association between severe childhood trauma, especially physical and sexual
abuse, and the development of various self-destructive behaviors, including self-
injury, eating disorders, substance abuse, suicide attempts, and other impulsive
behaviors (Farber 1995a, Heller 1990, Herman 1992, Lacey 1993, Lacey and
Evans 1986, van der Kolk et al. 1991).

It is within a climate of severe trauma that the ability to induce dissociative states occurs and that rocking, head banging, hair pulling, nail biting, thumb
sucking, enuresis, encopresis, refusal to eat, or eating too much occurs as a substitute for a containing mother–child relationship. These early habits and symptoms
are the developmental forerunners of more full-blown eating-disordered symptoms and self-mutilating behavior (Wilson 1989) that are usually not identified
until preadolescence or adolescence. Wilson's theory is supported by the findings of my study (Farber 1995a), which found that in adult women with a history
of chronic and severe bulimic and self-mutilating behavior, the greater the number
of childhood self-injurious and eating-disordered behaviors is predictive of more
numerous eating-disordered and self-mutilating behaviors in adolescence, and

these behaviors in adolescence are predictive of their occurring also in adulthood. The subjects who had the most severe eating-disordered and self-mutilating behavior reported suffering significantly greater numbers of trauma in childhood, particularly physical abuse, family violence, and medically related trauma, as well as greater numbers of adolescent trauma, particularly physical abuse, family violence, surgical procedures, and chronic or severe illness. So, for example, the child suffering from prolonged sexual abuse who vomits and picks at her food and skin, in adolescence may well tend to pick more intensely at her skin, or gouge or cut herself, and the disordered eating will tend to escalate into self-starvation and/or purging.

Severe childhood trauma can have a profound impact on the separation-individuation process in every subphase, damaging the child's ability to distinguish the boundaries of the internal body self from the external body self and the boundaries separating self from other. Even if a child experiences beatings, and the physical abuse is aimed at the surface of his body, he can experience it at the inner core of his being (Farber 1991). Developmental theory and clinical observation inform us that both very young normal children and older more emotionally damaged children and adults have great difficulty in differentiating not only self from object but also their internal self from their external (body) self (Galenson and Roiphe 1971, Jacobson 1964, Kestenberg 1975, Krueger 1989, Mahler and McDevitt 1982, Mahler et al. 1975, McDougall 1989). An assault to the body surface may well be experienced as internal, predisposing the child toward experiencing internal somatic symptoms. Similarly, if a young child who has not yet achieved psychological birth or separateness observes his mother being violently beaten, he may well experience the beating as if it happened to him.

"DOUBLETHINK" AND THE
PSYCHOBIOLOGY OF TRAUMA

When unspeakable atrocities happen, we tend to become mute. It is as if, in a nightmare, we want to scream for help but cannot because no voice will emerge. The silence about the unspeakable is an ordinary response to the most extraordinary of events that overwhelm our ordinary adaptive abilities, such as earthquakes and child abuse. But in child abuse the child is coerced into silence by force, or by adults ignoring or mocking the child's pain. The child may ignore, minimize, or not speak of the pain. The central dialectic of psychological trauma is the conflict between the will to deny horrible events and the will to proclaim them aloud (Herman 1992). The dissociative response corresponds with the will to deny the events, while the hyperarousal response corresponds with the will to recognize and proclaim them, the conflict between the two leading to what Shengold (1989), referring to George Orwell's *1984*, has called "doublethink." In dissociation there is a split in the ego between the affect surrounding the traumatic event and the cognition of the event. That is, the affect and the thought, or memory, are dissociated from each other. One can know what occurred but can at the same time disavow the knowledge of the event, while the affect connected to the event is either displaced or repressed (Freud 1927).

"Doublethink," a political term referring to brainwashing, aptly conveys the oscillating nature of disavowal, the ability to split one's awareness of reality and one's responsibility for that awareness while not entirely denying reality. It is a peculiar means of breaking with reality without being psychotic, a form of autohypnosis to aid in the denial of reality. To engage in doublethink is to hold two contradictory beliefs in one's mind simultaneously and accept both of them as true. It is a way of playing tricks with reality and at the same time convincing oneself that reality is not being violated. "The process has to be conscious, or it would not be carried out with sufficient precision, but it also has to be unconscious, or it would bring with it a feeling of falsity. . . . Even in using the word *doublethink* it is necessary to exercise *doublethink*" (George Orwell, quoted by Shengold 1989, p. 87). Orwell (1949) understood autohypnosis:

> To know and not to know, to be conscious of complete truthfulness while telling carefully constructed lies, to hold simultaneously two opinions which cancelled out, knowing them to be contradictory and believing both . . . to forget whatever it is necessary to forget, then to draw it back into the memory again at the moment it was needed, and then promptly to forget it again, and above all to apply the same process to the process itself . . . consciously to induce unconsciousness, and then once again to become unconscious of the act of hypnosis you had just performed. [p. 36]

In the individual with PTSD, these two opposing psychological states of hyperarousal and dissociation, and their corresponding knowing and not knowing, form an oscillating but unpredictable rhythm, engraving the bimodal trauma response on the central nervous system, which creates a psychophysiological template on which further attachments will become patterned. Over time, therefore, the trauma response becomes even more firmly embedded in the central nervous system, creating an addictive response to trauma on behavioral, emotional, physiologic, and neuroendocrinologic levels (van der Kolk 1989). Hypermnesia, hyperreactivity to stimuli, and traumatic reexperiencing coexist with psychic numbing, avoidance, amnesia, and anhedonia. Attempting to defend against the pain of chronic hyperarousal, traumatized people seem to shut down and become robotic, avoiding stimuli reminiscent of the trauma and numbing themselves to both trauma-related and everyday experience (van der Kolk 1994). Because the loss of the ability to modulate affect is so profound, traumatized individuals lose the ability to use affect states as signals, so feelings are not used as cues to attend to incoming information and to reflect on feelings associated with it, but instead a state of hyperarousal is evoked that precipitates motoric discharge, a version of the fight-or-flight reaction. They go immediately from stimulus to motoric response without thinking at all about the meaning of the event. Thus, they are prone to freezing or, alternatively, to extraordinary forceful actions, overreacting and intimidating others in response to minor provocations, or to motor discharge through binge eating or shopping, purging, cutting themselves, or running.

While such defense against intolerable pain is invaluable to the child, it comes at an enormous price, the splitting of cognition and affects. That is, the price paid for not knowing is that the building blocks for memory, identity, and interpersonal functioning are profoundly impacted. They do not know what has happened, who they are, and how to have rewarding relationships. Dissociation exists on a continuum, from the normal biological dissociation when one can forget getting up in the middle of the night to go to the bathroom, to the normal psychosocial dissociation of daydreaming during a boring lecture, to the abnormal biological dissociation such as amnesia after a concussion, to the abnormal psychosocial dissociation in which there is no memory of incest (Ross 1989). The most severe dissociation occurs as a pathological response to severe trauma. When a child has been physically or sexually abused by a parent over a prolonged period, the dissociative symptoms are likely to be extreme, including, most commonly, severe and frequent depersonalization, as well as amnesia, fugue, and possibly the creation of alter personalities. When severe trauma occurs at earlier stages of development, the best that a child can do is alter his perception of reality or his state of consciousness through dissociation (Kroll 1993), resulting in the unstable split identifications (i.e., wonderful Mommy vs. Mommy the witch) that occur in borderline personalities. When severe trauma occurs at later stages of development and is imposed on a relatively cohesive personality, it contributes to dissociative identifications that are more stable because they have not become interwoven into the personality. When severe trauma occurs at later stages of development and is imposed on a borderline personality, the diagnostic picture is more likely to be what Kroll (1993) calls PTSD/borderline.

Shock trauma results in numerous biochemical changes, including alterations in norepinephrine and dopamine, serotonin, and endogenous opioid utilization. Serotonin is the neurotransmitter most involved in modulating the actions of other neurotransmitters and is responsible for the fine-tuning of emotional reactions (van der Kolk 1988, 1989, 1994). Under severe stress there is a massive secretion of neurotransmitters that accounts for the typical PTSD symptoms: hyperarousal, followed soon after by visual and motoric reliving of experiences, nightmares, flashbacks, and somatic experiences. This massive secretion of neurotransmitters accounts for the subsequent depletion of neurotransmitters that is associated with the psychic numbing of dissociative responses.

The human response to danger is very much like the animal response in terms of both physical changes and defense. Our heart rate may rise briefly, then drop, or we might faint or become nauseated, in much the same way that many clinicians respond to a patient who is dangerously self-destructive. William James pondered the nature of fear and posed a most prescient question in an 1884 article in the philosophy journal Mind. In the case of a person encountering a bear, he asked, "Does he run because he feels afraid, or does he feel afraid *after* he has already started running? Put another way, does a person have time to think something is frightening, or does the reaction to fear precede the thought?" (Hall 1999, p. 45). He concluded, "The bodily changes follow directly the *perception* of the exciting fact, and . . . our feeling of the same changes as they occur *is* the emotion" (p. 45). More than a hundred years later, researchers have put the amygdala, two bits of neural tissue on either side of the brain, at the center of the fear response. Thus, the neural circuitry of fear does not go to the thinking part of the brain but to the archaic limbic system associated with emotion. Fear is processed first from the sensory organs and liners in the cortex where conscious memories are formed before threading down to the amygdala. We experience, learn, and unconsciously commit to emotional memory numerous fearful situations without being aware of what has triggered the racing heart, the shallow breathing, and the quickened pulse (Hall 1999).

General threats of danger arouse general anxiety-inducing vigilance, physiological arousal, and planning for defense, while more specific threats elicit specific patterns of behavioral defense in individuals and groups. Just as an ancient hunter-gatherer who was excluded from the group became more vulnerable to carnivorous predators, the child who is alone is more vulnerable to predators. Our squeamishness at the sight of blood, injury, or gross deformity is a natural propensity similar to the alarm of many species when fellow members are hurt (Marks 1987). Just as the animal who senses the danger of predation may respond with aggression, a human being being preyed upon may stand up and fight, bite, scratch, or spray the predator with mace. He or she may take flight from the source of danger, or arrange to avoid an encounter with it. Just as an animal might freeze, play dead, or conceal itself by blending into the foliage, so might a human being hide, gaining the time to locate the source of danger and inhibiting the predator's attack reflex, or he may avoid making eye contact with the predator so as not to provoke a confrontation.

When the threat comes from within one's own species or group, it is probably most useful for wild animals and human beings to appease or submit to the predator. When confronted with a potential mugger or rapist, it is advised that one not actively fight unless one is skilled in self-defense. It is better to submit than risk being killed. It may also be better to be too stunned to react rather than giving in to an aggressive impulse that might be far more dangerous. Just as when a cat is threatened, its fur stands on end, making it seem larger, so too can human beings feel their body hair tingling electrically as if standing on end. When approaching the boss for a raise, one might stand up straight, take a deep breath, and puff out one's chest to disarm him. Just as puffer fish look ferocious and their shooting spines hurt the predator's mouth, the sadomasochist may dress threateningly in black leather and studded boots. A possum plays dead, just as the child who associates her father's footsteps ascending the stairs to her room with a coercive sexual encounter may feign sleep. With feigned sleep usually comes disso-ciation, a form of submission. With some, the ability to dissociate may become so well developed that the experience of abuse is *as if* it were happening to some-one else, and in those who present as having multiple personalities may be expe-rienced *as actually* happening to someone else. There is a range of altered states that can be used defensively, depending on ego structure and the level of char-acter pathology (Brenner 1994).

A dissociated state can serve to terminate an intolerable state of hyper-arousal, and a state of hyperarousal can serve to terminate an intolerable state of dissociation. Self-harm plays an invaluable adaptive role in the life of a trauma survivor by heightening and fostering dissociation and hyperarousal. In fact, binge eating, purging, excessive exercise, drug and alcohol abuse, self-mutilation, and even compulsive body piercing, tattooing, and branding can serve as "survivors' tools" for those suffering from PTSD (Farber 1995a, 1996a, b). Each of these self-harm behaviors serves a self-regulating function, terminating a prolonged period of hyperarousal and replacing it with a dissociative response, or terminating a prolonged period of dissociation and replacing it with hyperarousal. Those who binge usually find that at least part of the time they do so in a dissociated state. For some it is the dissociated state that allows them to gorge themselves in this way, while for others it is the gorging that allows them to dissociate in this way. Some whose facility for dissociation is not so finely developed may drink in order to facilitate the psychic numbing, then binge in an altered state. Soon, however, reality intrudes in the form of abdominal pains and awareness of the mess of dirty dishes and wrappers, turning the dissociation that was initially so welcome into a source of terrible pain that must be stopped. Along with pain comes the inevi-table self-loathing and masochistic need for punishment. Making oneself vomit violently or inducing the wrenching cramps of violent diarrhea can quite effec-tively terminate the dissociative episode, shock one into feeling alive and real, and punish one brutally. Similarly, self-mutilation, especially cutting, can end an intolerable period of dissociation, making one feel alive faster and cheaper than any antidepressant or antianxiety medication can, and can also provide powerful punishment.

STATE-DEPENDENT MEMORY AND
THE RETURN OF THE REPRESSED

After repeated or prolonged stress when norepinephrine, opioid, and sero-tonin depletion become conditioned responses, brain changes occur leading to excessive responsiveness at subsequent times of stress, even mild stress. Changes in the brain can cause the person to react to the usual stresses of life as if they were an inescapable trauma, and to react to anyone who even mildly resembles the original predator as if he *were* the original predator. Thus, early memories or memory traces can become activated by later events that cause a partial reliving of the earlier traumas (Freud 1896). Freud's theory about memory has been scientifically confirmed with the discovery of state-dependent learning, which tells us that the more similar contextual stimuli are to conditions that prevailed at the time of the trauma, when memories were originally stored in the brain, the more likely is the probability of retrieving those memories. Both current affects or external events reminiscent of earlier trauma can trigger an immediate visceral return to feeling as if the person were back in the midst of the original trauma. An otherwise competent woman in a verbally abusive relationship may experience herself as the terrified child she once was in a violent or alcoholic home, and may cower on the floor in terror. When disinhibition resulting from drugs or alcohol is added to this complex mix, it strongly promotes such episodes of reliving, which then take the form of violent reenactments, often directly on the body (van der Kolk 1989).

While most individuals who had been traumatized by rape, battering, or child abuse may appear to adjust socially and psychologically under ordinary conditions, they may still at times manifest the trauma response, returning to earlier behavior patterns just as animals throughout the animal kingdom do (van der Kolk 1989). When in a state of low arousal, animals tend to be curious and seek novelty, while during high arousal they are frightened, avoid novelty, and perseverate in familiar behavior regardless of the outcome. Shocked animals thus returned to the box in which they were originally shocked, and even increased their exposure to shock as the trials continued, just as abused spouses and children cling to their abusers and continue to receive even greater abuse. Novel stimuli, on the other hand, cause arousal, leading an animal in a high state of arousal to avoid even mildly novel stimuli even if it would reduce the exposure to pain.

TRAUMATIC ATTACHMENTS
AND ADDICTION TO TRAUMA

Because all disruptions of the attachment system are also disruptions of the regulatory system, they predispose the child to harm himself as compensatory attempts at self-regulation. The strain trauma of ongoing emotional neglect may predispose a child to the development of a false self, with consequential failure to express himself through words and symbols, and ego regressions to the use of the body for emotional expression (Fonagy 1997, Fonagy and Target 1995). Other childhood trauma, such as intolerable separations from significant others due to death, divorce, abandonment, or placement in foster care may lead to significant depression and depressive equivalents such as hypochondriasis and other somatization, including bodily self-harm. The opportunity to develop a secure and stable attachment can restore regulatory functioning and mediate against self-harm. If the child does not have such a vital opportunity and if he experiences prolonged trauma in adolescence, especially physical or sexual abuse or medical trauma, his develop-ment becomes organized around alternating states of hyperarousal and dissociation that become regulated by self-harm behavior. The prolonged trauma then further interferes with the child's ability to develop a self that can reflect by means of symbols and words, and therefore engraves the experience of speechless terror and the prey-and-predator attachment upon the mind-body-brain.

The child may come to understand an incestuous nonviolent relationship with the abuser as the model of love and attachment, and she may become sexuality hyperaroused precociously. When the abuser is gentle and speaks lovingly and tells her how very special she is, she is likely to feel special and loved, resulting in a particularly complex cognitive confusion. When the abuser proceeds slowly with the child, with the abuse escalating in severity slowly and over a period of time, as is often the case, the child has the unfortunate opportunity for sexual excitement to build slowly and gradually, as in adult foreplay, and to be experi-enced as loving and pleasurable.

When the abuse, whether it is sexual or physical, is violent and the child is frightened, she experiences the abuser's rage as well as any pain inflicted as an assault upon or within her body and upon the integrity and wholeness of her self. The abuser's size and strength overwhelm and terrify the child, whose only escape may lie in her ability to dissociate during the experience, who can observe her body being abused as if it were someone else's body, at the same time that she does not feel the pain. With each episode of abuse, the ability to dissociate becomes further developed, cultivated like a precious flower and treasured as a survivor's tool. As the ability to dissociate increases, so does the attachment to the abuser.

Kathryn Harrison (1997) was twenty when she was seduced by her father, and lived in dissociated servitude to him for years. She did not experience the traumatic amnesia experienced by many trauma victims but rather the particular kind of disavowal, the "doublethink" confusion and split registration in thinking in which the victim is not able to think about what has happened and must not be able to truly know what happened (Shengold 1989). Harrison could remember many details of her incestuous trysts, but could not really remember the experience.

> In years to come, I'll think of the kiss as a kind of transforming sting, like that of a scorpion: a narcotic that spreads from my mouth to my brain. . . . It's the drug my father administers in order that he might consume me. That I might desire to be consumed. [p. 70]

> . . . What he does feels neither good nor bad. It effects so complete a separation between mind and body that I don't know what I feel. Across this divide, deep and unbridgeable, my body responds independently from my mind. My heart, somewhere between them, plunges.

Neither of us speaks, not even one word. The scene is as silent, as dark and dream-like as if it proceeded from a fever or a drug. [p. 128]

. . . In years to come, I won't be able to remember even one instance of our lying together. I'll have a composite genetic memory. I'll know that he was always on top and that I always lay still. . . . I'll remember such details as the color of the carpet in a particular motel room, or the kind of tree outside the window. That he always wore his socks. . . . I'll remember every tiny thing about him . . . the pattern of hair that grew on the backs of his hands, the mole on his cheek. . . . But I won't be able to remember what it felt like.

. . . Asleep. There's the cottony somnolence of my days. There's the little trick of selective self-anesthesia that leaves me awake to certain things and dead to others. [pp. 136–137]

In the face of danger it is natural for people to seek increased attachment and when there is no one available to provide comfort and soothing, they may turn to their victimizers. The bond between the battering husband and the abused wife is like the bond between captor and hostage. She organizes her life around pleasing him. Tension builds as he expresses rage. There is the terror of the abuse, and because it is experienced in a dissociated state, it promotes the sense of un-reality. They are engaged wholly and completely with each other through violence and degradation. The explosive battering incident is followed by the tenderness of forgiveness, reconciliation, and the nonviolent physical contact that restore the fantasy of fusion and symbiosis (van der Kolk 1989). Thus, the violence-produced excitement and subsequent bliss of reconciliation are two powerful sources of reinforcement. Each of these responses, when they are placed at appropriate intervals, strengthens the traumatic bond between victim and abuser. To one degree or another, the memory of the battering incidents is state dependent or dissociated, and returns in full force during renewed situations of terror. Whatever good judgment the victim may have about the relationship becomes confused and confounded, and she allows her longing for love and attachment to overcome her better judgment (van der Kolk 1989).

Early exposure to violence or neglect produces the expectation that violence and neglect is simply the way of the world and of relationships, and serves as a template for state-dependent repetition of the childhood trauma and the return of the repressed (van der Kolk 1989). Violence and neglect thus become normal. In the most common scenario, children witness and internalize the chronic help-lessness of their parents' alternating outbursts of affection and violence. As they grow up they hope to repair the past by showering their partner with the love and service known commonly as "people pleasing," and when this fails to repair the past, they blame themselves. They alternate between expecting that their perfect behavior will lead to perfect harmony, and a state of total helplessness and futility. They regress to earlier coping mechanisms, blaming and numbing themselves.

The repetition of the trauma response and the trauma experience does not lead to mastery and resolution but rather reinforces the fixation on the trauma. The victim can become addicted both to her victimizer and to abuse, powerless to resist (van der Kolk 1989). Van der Kolk cites Solomon's opponent process theory of acquired motivation to explain addictive behavior that originates in frightening or painful events. The frequent exposure to any stimuli, regardless of whether it is pleasant or unpleasant, can lead to habituation, and withdrawal or abstinence can take on a powerful life of its own, becoming an effective source of motivation. In drug addiction, the motivation changes from getting high to controlling the painful state of withdrawal, and the abused woman's motivation changes from getting her husband to become the loving parent she never had to preventing her husband from being angry with her. The initially aversive stimulus may be perceived eventually as highly rewarding by people who have repeatedly exposed themselves to these frightening or painful situations. As Solomon says, "Fear thus has its positive consequences" (van der Kolk 1989, p. 398).

Body intimacy can have a powerful emotional impact on the attachment bond, even when the body intimacy is violent. Ethologist Desmond Morris (1971) wrote about what has become a well-known film cliché, in which two strong tough men resort to a fistfight to settle their differences.

> As the two bruised hulks sprawl weakly on the ground, sure enough, one pair of cracked and bleeding lips spits out a loose tooth, and grins admiringly at his equally beaten opponent. In no time at all, our heroes are helping one another up and crawling to the bar . . . to share a reviving drink. After this we can be sure that nothing will ever separate them again, and that they will become indomitable partners in righting all wrongs, until, at the end of the film, one of them will die bravely saving the life of the other, breathing his last gasp cradled in the loving arms of the man whose face he once succeeded in beating to a pulp. [p. 162]

The moral of this story, as Morris puts it, is that sometimes "a warm enemy is better than a cold friend" (p. 162). Mixing the bonds of love with the bonds of violence can produce a strong but confusing attachment, such as when a child is greeted every afternoon after school by her grandmother, who lovingly prepares her favorite macaroni and cheese for her and wants to know what happened at school that day, then later brushes her hair, and lays her down on the bed and inserts spoons and a hairbrush handle into her vagina. Or as one patient told me, those times when her father bought her ice cream even when her mother forbade it made her feel such love for him that at the moment it seemed not to matter that he had raised welts and sliced into her back with his belt buckle.

These early disturbances of attachment not only cause brain changes that reduce the individual's ability to cope with lesser social disruptions, but also impede the individual's ability to allow his own child to become securely attached,

230 / When the Body Is the Target

thus creating a very similar vulnerability in the next generation. Thus, the addiction to trauma and to traumatic attachments becomes handed down from one generation to the next.

SELF-HARM: SELF-DESTRUCTIVENESS OR SURVIVAL TOOL?

Shengold (1989), who found much of what he had written about the effects of abuse on the child had been foreshadowed by Ferenczi, states that the abused child changes into a mechanical robot, his mind split into contradictory fragments to separate the good from the bad. But the automaton-child has murder within and can direct the wish to kill at others or at the self. When one does not allow oneself to know what one knows, either wish, to kill the other or to kill the self, may be expressed directly at one's body in self-harm. "Doublethink" says Shengold, "is a system of vertical mind-splits that makes it possible to believe that two plus two equals five" (p. 21). Doublethink can convince the abused person that her abuser is good, and that she, the child who was abused, is bad, and that destructive wishes come from demons rather than from the self. Whether the wish is to commit murder or suicide, self-harm is the result of a conflict among aggressive, destructive impulses, the superego, and the will to live. It serves as a compromise formation to avert complete annihilation, and despite the extent of the harm inflicted upon the self, various forms of self-harm serve as survival tools and need to be so understood by clinicians.

Because of brain changes caused by cumulative trauma, those who were neglected or abused as children may crave a much greater external stimulation of the endogenous opioid system for soothing than those whose opioids can be more easily activated by responses based on more secure attachments. They are thus primed early on to neutralize their hyperarousal by a variety of addictive behaviors. The increases in endogenous stress hormones affect the strength of memory consolidation, facilitating the releasing of traumatic memories by heightened arousal. The increased release of these endogenous stress hormones also produces both dependence and withdrawal phenomena much like those of exogenous opioids, leading to various self-destructive behaviors (van der Kolk 1989, Winchel 1991), making those who were neglected or abused repeatedly especially compelled to reexpose themselves to situations reminiscent of the trauma. The "choice" of self-destructive symptoms depends on which stimuli have conditioned an opioid response. Those who suffered abandonment may be prone to self-mutilation (Farber 1995a, van der Kolk et al. 1991) and to eating disorders (Chassler 1997, Farber 1995a), with those who suffered the most severe trauma and traumatic attachments prone to both self-mutilation and eating disorders (Farber 1995a). Painful stimulation has been found to result in increased release of endorphins, which may explain why self-harm behaviors are repeated (Winchel 1991). Although neurochemical explanations of self-injurious behavior have focused on dopamine, opiate, and serotonin neurotransmitter systems, there is evidence that suggests that suicidal behavior and impulsive violence to self or others, among other variant behaviors, are associated with serotonin dysfunction (Winchel and Stanley 1991). The fact that fluoxetine has been found to be the most effective medication for the entire spectrum of PTSD symptoms suggests that the serotonergic system plays a major role in PTSD (van der Kolk 1994).

Binge eating may often serve a dissociative function for painful feelings. The binge may start in a state of eager anticipation in which the first mouthfuls are delicious, but quickly turns into an experience in which emotions, thoughts, and awareness are dissociated from the physical act; the food might as well be sawdust. Not only does inducing a violent purge terminate the dissociative state and help the individual to feel alive once again, it may well also stimulate the release of endorphins and function much as self-cutting does biochemically as a form of self-medication. In fact, in the author's study (Farber 1995a) violent purging was ranked slightly higher than cutting, burning, or hitting oneself in terms of its self-medicating strength.

The pain of cutting and burning oneself, of violent vomiting or diarrhea, may divert the self momentarily from the psychic pain of intruding memories. Blood that is deliberately shed may express tears that could not be cried and sorrows that could not be spoken. The insatiable binge may have the erotic feel of an orgy, with purging and self-mutilation representing the mounting frenzied excitement and then the explosive orgiastic release. Just as lovers rest in spent contentment, the self-harming individual, too, feels relieved and repaired, because, paradoxically, the most violent self-harm produces a temporary sense of calm and well-being. For the survivor of severe trauma, self-harm is like thumbing one's nose at one's abusers, like snatching victory from the hands of the predators to emerge triumphant. Just as soldiers marching off to war may be ready to lose their lives for victory over the enemy, the self-harmer is ready to lose flesh and blood, indeed his life, for victory over the predator. The self-harmer proclaims with his body, "No, try as you might, you cannot murder my soul."

SELF-HARM FOR HEALING AND REDEMPTION

Not only can self-harm serve as survival tools, but also the stimulation of certain nerve endings and accompanying dissociative states can promote a kind of healing and even a sense of redemption as well. This idea seems less strange when we consider the popular attraction to alternative medical practices formerly regarded as quackery: acupuncture; massage and body work therapies; chiropractic, homeopathy, nutritional, and herbal treatments; and yoga, t'ai chi, and meditation. As a culture, we are embracing the deliberate induction of healing trance (dissociative) states, in yoga, meditation, Ayurvedic medicine, holistic medicine, hypnosis and autohypnosis, deep breathing relaxation exercises, biofeedback, and eye movement desensitization and reprocessing (EMDR).

Western healers specializing in pain management (neurologists, physiatrists, physical therapists, anesthesiologists, behavioral psychologists) are increasingly using acupuncture in conjunction with traditional pain killers and other more conventional methods. It seems to have a regulatory effect on several gastrointestinal functions, including motility, electrical activity, and secretion. Acupuncture is used for the treatment of asthma, drug abuse, premenstrual cramping, smoking, nausea, and gastrointestinal disorders. Chinese physicians have used acupuncture for 5,000 years to promote healing, believing that stimulating the appropriate acupressure points with needles restores the flow of chi, the same life force that practitioners of t'ai chi hope to distribute from the center of the body to flow throughout the body. When examined under the microscope, acupuncture points reveal a greater number of nerve endings than do other skin locations. For around 5,000 years the Japanese have been using shiatsu massage, pressure with their fingers and hands on the same meridians of the body stimulated by Chinese acupuncture. Western scientists believe that stimulating an acupuncture or acupressure point causes the release of endorphins in the brain that reduce the perception of pain as effectively as a narcotic.

Cold water and heat produce a stimulation that has a salutory effect. People take bracing cold showers for this reason, or to dampen down sexual arousal. Agitated patients may be wrapped in cold wet sheets in psychiatric hospitals, and some people choose to swim outdoors in near-freezing temperatures. Members of the Coney Island Polar Bear Club in Brooklyn have been gathering on the beach for years on wintry days to swim in the Atlantic, claiming that they enjoy an unusual sense of well-being for several days after. One man interviewed on a television news show reported a history of chronic depression with difficulty getting out of bed, but since he had his first few swims with the Polar Bears, he became a regular. Similarly, eating hot chili peppers can cause a painful burning sensation in the mouth, yet many people become aficionados, "going for the burn" that creates an increased sense of well-being. Capsaicin, the active ingredient in chilis, stimulates the inside of the mouth and causes sweating and subsequent cooling, providing relief in hot climates, while capsaicin ointments have been found to relieve various neuralgias and the pain of osteo- and rheumatoid arthritis and diabetic neuropathy.

Those who cut, stick, or burn themselves seem to know something that Asian healers have known for thousands of years. Even those "needle freaks" addicted to the stick of the needle or the sensual buzz of the tattooist's needle may be practicing a kind of acupuncture in disguise, producing a new feeling of wholeness and well-being that is like a redemption or rebirth.

Although in Western culture dissociation is usually linked with psychopathology, it is also associated with healing even within the Judeo-Christian tradition. Pentecostalists may be "seized by the spirit," Christians are "born-again," and Hasidim dance and sing themselves into a trance. These ecstatic experiences are deliberately induced because of their therapeutic value (Kakar 1982). Even for those whose religious practice is not so vigorous, meditative prayer, for which there is evidence of healing power (Dossey 1993), may lead to dissociated states. Even biofeedback and natural childbirth depend on managing pain by producing a trance-like state through rhythmic breathing and concentrated focus. The dissociation that often accompanies cutting, burning, sticking, or purging, as well as these practices, is, interestingly enough, following in the tradition of healing through trance induction.

ADDICTIVE TRAUMATIC REENACTMENTS

Anger that is physically directed at the self is central to the life of the individual who has been abused and violated, leading to repetitive reenactments upon the body that have the potential to become dangerously out of control. The reenactment serves as concrete bodily repetition of past trauma, complete with alternating hyperarousal and dissociative responses. Marya Hornbacher (1998), whose battle with eating disorders has taken her to the brink of death, described the addiction to the most basic effects of anorexia and bulimia, the adrenaline rush that kicked in when she was starving, making her feel high as a kite, sleepless, and full of frenzied energy, and the heightened intense experience that eating disorders initially induce. "Your sense of power is very, very intense" (p. 105).

The secretion of neurotransmitters that occurs repeatedly in repetitions of the trauma response can make the body susceptible to a heightened somatic stimulation in general or in the part of the body that was abused or injured. This is what those in the sexual abuse survivor movement aptly speak of as "body memory." For example, the abuse victim may have sudden somatic experiences, feeling perhaps a heavy weight on her torso, thus reenacting the experience of her abuser's heavy body lying on her, or she may feel vaginal pain, reenacting the experience of forceful penetration, or she may smell the odor of the abuser's perspiration and genitalia, state-dependent memories activated by a trigger stimulus. "Smells detonate softly in our memory like poignant land mines, hidden under the weedy mass of many years and experiences. Hit a tripwire of smell and memories explode all at once" (Ackerman 1990, p. 7). Hitting a tripwire of smell can trigger other sensory memories, visual, taste, and touch, a domino effect that can open the doors to a Pandora's box of memory horrors. Soon she can go into a dissociated state that blocks all the intrusive stimuli, but this too may last long enough for it to become most unwelcome, as the experience of feeling herself unreal (depersonalization) and often the world as unreal (derealization) becomes an "aloneness affect" (Winchel 1991) too painful to tolerate.

Traumatized children often do not completely remember what was done to them but are driven by the unconscious to repeat the trauma in play or actions, and often reenact with their bodies in a psychophysiological posttraumatic reenactment (Terr 1973, 1990, 1994). The body is all about enactment, living the experience in the heart and gut, purging it into the toilet, inscribing it on the skin. Because our senses span time, the violent touch of self-inflicted pain, whether it is used to terminate the hyperarousal and flood of traumatic memory or to terminate the dissociation, immediately connects the person to the pain of trauma suffered years before. So does the taste, sight, and smell of the self-harmer's blood connect her to the trauma of her own bloodshed years ago, just as the total sensory experience of violent vomiting connects her to a childhood trauma so disgusting that it caused her to vomit then, too.

The body speaks "that which is known but not yet thought," the unthought known (Bollas 1987, p. 4). Or the body speaks that which is known but not known, the dissociated doublethink. The addiction to self-destructive behaviors represents an addiction to trauma, a compulsion to repeatedly reenact severe childhood trauma (Farber 1995a,b, van der Kolk 1988, 1989).

For example, the self-harming behavior in a survivor of sexual abuse may well be a presymbolic wordless physical reenactment of the trauma she suffered. It is different, however, in that in the reenactment she is in control and is active, in a vain attempt to master the trauma. In a depersonalized frenzy in which she identifies with the abuser, she shoves food into her mouth as others shoved a penis, fingers, or other objects into her body. Then as the identification quickly shifts to an identification with the abused, she vomits the food to rid her body of those things that were inserted by force. Or she may penetrate her flesh with a razor blade, lit cigarette, or fingernails, as her abuser penetrated her. As she watches liquid oozing from the wound, she feels pleased that the vile stuff that had been inside her (semen, the hateful parts of herself) is being expelled, leaving her clean and pure. She also has the pleasure of discharging rage and violence onto the abuser. She is both the abuser and the one being abused. She is the sadist and the masochist. She is a cool observer of her own self-abuse, like the parent who was present but failed to protect her. In the self-harming act she is all these, oscillating crazily from self to object and back again, traumatically attached to both the affects and her abuser. In another scenario, the individual who was traumatized by the terror of intrusive and painful medical or surgical procedures may repeat the trauma by sticking himself or getting others to stick him with needles or sticking others with needles. It was striking in my study (Farber 1995a) that quite a few of the subjects who reported a history of childhood medical trauma and severe self-mutilation were intensive care or emergency room nurses. It was the women who had suffered medical trauma in childhood who also reported having acquired professional tattoos and piercings significantly more than those without this history. In fact, two of them earned their livelihood as professional tattoo artists and body piercers.

While the intention of self-harm is to cheat the abuser of victory, the reality is that its severity is likely to increase over time, becoming increasingly more dangerous and more likely to result in death. Not only does the victim become addicted to the trauma response and to the attachment to the abuser, he also becomes addicted to the acts of self-harm, requiring progressively stronger and more frequent doses. Ultimately, his final act of self-harm may be a fatal overdose.

BECOMING ONE'S OWN PREDATOR

Identification is the process by which the victim becomes attached to the victimizer, or the prey becomes attached to the predator. It is a necessary step in the process by which the individual who had been prey to adult predators becomes transformed into a predator himself, preying upon his own body in reenactments of the trauma he suffered. A person can also prey upon his own body in response to an object loss that is not mourned but is instead responded to with melancholia.

Melancholia

Freud (1917) distinguished between states of mourning and melancholia in response to object loss. Mourning is the process by which one restores one's psychic equilibrium following a serious loss that may be, but is not necessarily, caused by the death of the human object. Mourning can be thought of as a derivative of the cannibalistic totem feast, in that the processes of mourning and melancholia are similarly modeled on the infant's first experience of reality, the taking in and incorporation of food. Initially the mourner turns away from the reality of the loss of the loved one and clings to the mental representations of the lost object, turning it into an ego loss. He unconsciously manifests some of the characteristics of the lost one, thus preserving the sense of the deceased as alive, a way of declaring, as Favazza (1996) put it, "He lives again in me!"

Through gradual stages the ego loss is gradually healed and psychic equilibrium is restored. The process of mourning, therefore, requires accepting the loss as a reality, experiencing the world becoming cold and empty, the gradual withdrawing of attachments to and identifications with the lost object, and finally, the freeing up of libido so that one can resume life among the living, and with that, the possibility of establishing new attachments. The person suffering melancholic depression maintains a very ambivalent attachment to the lost object who has denied him love, but because he cannot maintain the relationship he incorporates the object into his ego to continue the relationship internally. "Thus the shadow of the object fell upon the ego" (Freud 1917, p. 249). But at the same time feelings of hatred demand the destruction of the object, feelings that become directed toward the internalized object within. The person incorporates the object as a cannibal would—biting, mutilating, and devouring it, thus taking revenge upon the lost object for denying him the love he craved. The revenge can take various forms of punishment enacted on the self, including self-reproach, depression, hypochondriasis, starving, purging, and self-mutilation, as the ego becomes identified with the lost object and becomes a cold and empty predator of the self. When the internalized lost object is the target of such great aggression, the risk for suicide increases.

It is no coincidence that mourning rituals are derivatives of cannibalism. In fact most cannibalistic acts occur during mortuary rites and are considered "affectionate cannibalism, the eating of body parts of kin who have died a natural death" (Favazza 1996, p. 65). The emotions associated with "affectionate cannibalism" may be much the same as our own feelings toward dead relatives—a certain affection, but also aggression and ambivalence (Favazza 1996). In the Wari tribe of western Brazil, which practiced cannibalism until the 1960s, the eating of human flesh at funerals was thought of as helping the mourners gradually detach from the preoccupation with the dead person, because prolonged sadness was thought to endanger their health (Favazza 1996). It was thought that by devouring the corpse instead of burying it, the dead person's spirit was free to become a water spirit and then return as a piglike, hoofed animal that could be hunted and eaten in a communal feast, signifying "sadness has ended; now happiness begins" (Favazza 1996, p. 66). During the Jewish ritual of sitting *shiva* mourners gather during the seven days of observance, sharing meals together as if incorporating the spirit of the deceased with the food, a totem feast (Freud 1913b). Those paying condolence calls often arrive with cake and pastries "to sweeten the loss." Wakes involve considerable eating and drinking in the presence of the deceased. Whether the body is buried or cremated, it is consumed by the earth or sea with which it becomes one. "Ashes to ashes, dust to dust."

When mourning is impeded by great ambivalence toward the deceased and the mourner remains depressed, suffering from the loss of the object's love, he experiences an insatiable emotional hunger (Battegay 1991), which he may go to life-threatening lengths to assuage, preying upon himself in harmful ways. His desire for recognition and love from the deceased may become drowned by a hunger for food or alcohol or sex. When the hunger for touch early in life has not been met, there remains a hunger for the stimulation of the skin, even if that touch is the touch of broken glass or a razor blade upon the skin. There will remain a hunger for the touch of the abuser, even if that touch is brutal, for a brutal touch is better than none. In melancholia the individual remains fiercely attached to the predator by means of identification, preying upon himself actively much as the predatory object preyed upon him while he passively submitted.

Although the Brazilian Wari practiced affectionate cannibalism, they also practiced aggressive cannibalism, in which they ate the enemy's flesh and abused his body parts. Aggressive cannibalism, said Favazza (1996):

> serves as the prototype not only for religious self-mortification and some cases of anorexia nervosa in which one's body is treated as an enemy, but also for habitual self-mutilation among the mentally ill.

The conquering cannibal literally tastes the fruits of his victory, but victory can also be achieved by exactly the opposite action, namely self-starvation. . . .

In like manner, anorexia nervosa is an object lesson . . . a form of indirect self-mutilation in which the patient achieves victory over real and fantastic enemies through fasting. To eat is to accept the status quo. To eat is to participate in a regenerative cannibalistic ritual. To eat is to open one's self to the possibility of being devoured and to participate in the cycle of life. The episodic gorging often accompanying anorexia is a sign of weakness, a dent in the anorectic's armor, and must be undone by self-induced vomiting. Anorexia is tragic because it overshoots the mark. Once a certain point is reached, the catabolic process relentlessly feeds upon itself until the anorectic's body and will to live are shrunken. [p. 67]

Malcove (1933) stated that the fear of being dismembered, cut to pieces, or mutilated has a prototype in the universal experience of learning to eat. Murderous cannibalistic behavior and fantasy are prominent in patients with eating disorders and in those with a trauma history who often identify with toothy, hungry animals such as lizards, rats, vampires, dinosaurs, and sharks (Mintz 1992a, Shengold 1989). Probably the most famous is Freud's (1909) Rat Man, who came into analysis after a conversation with a cruel captain who told of a bound prisoner whose buttocks were exposed to rats that bored their way into his anus. Upon hearing this story the patient became obsessed with the idea that the same thing was happening to the woman he loved and might happen to his father. Shengold (1989) found that rat imagery is used repetitively by patients who have been overstimulated and who long for a means of discharge to escape from this state, and therefore emphasized the importance of teeth in the mental life of his "rat people."

Mintz (1992a) found that many anorexic and bulimic patients who identified with animals with sharp long teeth had projected onto others a phobic representation of their conflict over their own cannibalistic wishes. In their behavior the cannibalistic impulse was gratified by an almost constant chewing and swallowing. These animals and their teeth, often represented as knives, emerged in play, dreams, fantasies, and behavior, representing impulses to attack, kill, and eat up the object or part of it. Cannibalistic fantasies and impulses may be far more common than has been reported, indicating an underlying cannibalistic preoccupation in eating-disordered patients. Mintz also found that energetic sucking is a less recognized but important component in aggressive conflict in anorexia and asthma as well. I would suggest that cannibalistic fantasies and impulses may be more of a preoccupation than has been thought with those who self-mutilate. The fact that such a high percentage of self-mutilating patients also have eating-disordered behavior would suggest this, too. Whether they use their fingernails, teeth, razor blades, or knives to attack their skin, they are using these instruments in much the same way that teeth are used—to rip, tear, or shred living flesh. To eat one's prey, after all, requires that it be torn apart with claws and teeth. For example, Nakhla (Nakhla and Jackson 1993) wrote of his psychoanalytic treatment of a patient who cut herself in his office: "Grace [a self-cutter] was curious about the anatomy of her wrists and the surgical repair of them. Once when she was examining with fascination a cut on her wrist, with its beads of subcutaneous tissue, she said to me, 'It looks like a mouth of teeth. Do you see them?'" (p. 94).

Identification with the Predator

Although self-harming patients repeat and relive their earlier trauma through an identification with a predatory aggressor, often taking on the aggressor's attributes, anorectics commonly are disgusted by the idea of eating red (or any other kind of) meat. For many this is a reaction formation that defends against the cannibalistic wish. An emaciated anorectic woman in my practice would fill a large three-gallon stockpot each morning with fresh vegetables cut into large chunks, steam them, and then sit down to chew and chew and swallow and swallow for well over two hours. Often that was all she would eat all day but the rest of the time she chewed gum continuously, as many as a dozen packs a day. Gum plays a unique role in an anorexic's life because it is the only food substance that can be chewed endlessly and not be totally destroyed, because it permits patients to "chew out," attack, and destroy the ambivalently tinged introject and at the same time preserve it (Mintz 1992b). Rumination, the regurgitation, and subsequent rechewing and swallowing of food, may also serve the same purpose—to chew up, spit up, and yet preserve an ambivalently tinged introject.

Laxative use is common in anorexia, bulimia, and subclinical eating disorders, but what is less understood is that unconsciously, many use the retention and expulsion of stool as a bodily expression of their ambivalent relationship to an internalized object in much the same way they might use the consumption and retention of food. Individuals who have been neglected or abused by their parents may come to use laxatives or other purgatives to prey upon their own bodies. These tend to be the patients who binge so that they can have the experience of the intense purge. When the introject is hated, the individual may need to expel it quickly and violently from the body, using laxatives or very fibrous foods to do so. When there is a wish to destroy the object, very large quantities of laxatives or frequent enemas may be used to shred and destroy the stool-object (Mintz 1992b). They induce extraordinary pain, cramping, and at times bleeding, which may require bed rest and immediate access to a bathroom. Not only does extreme laxative abuse shred the stool, it also begins to shred and mutilate the inner recesses of the body, especially when it is combined with other methods of purging.

Just as the anorectic often is disgusted by the thought of eating red meat, the "delicate" self-cutter may be appalled by those who cut deeply and dangerously. She makes certain to use fresh razor blades and to cleanse her superficial cuts with antiseptic and prides herself on her control, and yet when she is under the disinhibiting influence of alcohol or drugs, she may find herself cutting wildly and shredding herself with any blade or bit of glass she can find, hungrier for blood than she could let herself know.

Those who tend to prey upon their bodies with the most extreme purging will also tend to prey upon themselves with severe self-mutilation (Farber 1995a). This makes a lot of sense when you stop to consider that severe purging *is* self-mutilation but from the inside out rather than from the body surface inward. Bulimics who vomit severely are more likely to abuse laxatives severely and to have abused enemas and diuretics than bulimics who do not abuse laxatives (Hall et al. 1989) and also to mutilate themselves severely (Hall et al. 1989, Mitchell et al. 1986). Severe laxative, enema, and diuretic abuse defined a population that was likely to be self-injurious, depressed, and to have abused drugs and alcohol (Hall et al. 1989). Those who purged themselves severely primarily or exclusively with laxatives seemed to have a body image far more associated with feces than with fat, their mental representations of themselves virtually entirely bound up with the equation "I *am* shit" (Farber 1995a). Just as the Nazis had mental representations of the Jews that reduced them to feces, these individuals have an anal object relationship (Grunberger 1979) with themselves, relating to themselves as if they were excrement. They prey upon themselves with severe purging and self-mutilation, with punishment, torture, self-recrimination, and self-loathing.

The Most Perverse Self-Predation

The world of perversion is an anal universe in which all differences and people are reduced to excrement. It is a world of sacrilege. The pervert sets out to make a mockery of religion and society and customary practices, according to Chasseguet-Smirgel (1984), the equivalent of devil religion. The devil is God's rival, wanting to discredit God and put himself in his place.

Several significant discrete bulimic subtypes are identified in the literature and can further help us understand the nature of the most perverse kind of self-harm in the most disturbed and difficult patients, many of whom seem to be frankly psychotic. Over 500 bulimic patients treated on an eating-disorder unit in a Florida hospital were studied (Hall and Beresford 1989, Hall et al. 1990). The subgroup identified as masochistic bulimics were extraordinarily perverse self-predators. They deliberately consumed foods or other substances that they knew would cause them agonizing pain and internal injury when they purged, and they also cut, scratched, or burned themselves. They consumed laxatives in quantities large enough to produce extreme pain and the humiliation of soiling themselves; one patient took 80 to 250 Dulcolax at a time. They consumed raw broccoli and other fibrous vegetables, barely chewed nuts and nutshells, and deliberately drank a minimum of liquid to ensure that the purge would be very rough and injurious. Some even deliberately left food in the sun to spoil before eating it, or rummaged through garbage cans to find already spoiled food to eat. (There is a religious nomadic cult that wanders from place to place, seeking out food from garbage cans and dumpsters to consume in their "sacraments.") This masochistic bulimic group was highly perfectionistic, emotionally isolated, and fearful of adult responsibility, composed mostly of young women who had become the excellent students or athletes their parents expected. Their parents were usually oblivious to any problem until a major cataclysmic event occurred, such as the onset of overwhelming depression, a suicide attempt, or loss of consciousness from a laxative overdose or upper gastrointestinal bleeding.

While those who binge and purge and those who self-mutilate often perform these acts within some ritualized set of behaviors, a bulimic subgroup that practiced unusually bizarre rituals was identified. These obsessive ritualistic bulimics also abused laxatives severely and their bulimic behavior was performed in bizarrely elaborate and compulsive rituals that often had religious overtones (Hall and Beresford 1989, Hall et al. 1990). They purged severely and obsessed about cutting off parts of their body, which suggested that this subtype is extremely close to the psychotic end of the spectrum, if not frankly psychotic. For example, a college student constructed an elaborate bulimic ritual to dissipate her anger at her mother. She built a wooden platform that she attached to the side of her bed so that she could hang over her bed and vomit into specific containers. Each container first contained a specific food that had to be ingested in a specific way prior to purging into the emptied container. While vomiting, she played specific music while looking at photographs of her mother and father which she had placed around the room. Without this bizarre ritual, her purging would not successfully discharge her anger or reduce her anxiety. Once, when the ritual was interrupted by her roommate, the roommate was physically attacked and warned that anyone who interrupted her would be beaten. Another college student enacted a grotesque ritual that mimicked the Stations of the Cross. She prepared elaborate food lists and would spend two weeks driving to various gourmet stores to buy or shoplift specific items for the upcoming planned ritual binge. The items had to be packed into a knapsack in a specific order so that they could be consumed in that order during her ritual. She would complete a three-mile course around her university campus, which had garden hoses at specific points. At each hose, she would unpack her knapsack, eat a specific food, drink a large quantity of water from the hose, vomit a predetermined number of times and then go on to the next "station." She thought of herself as a religious pilgrim purifying herself at the Stations of the Cross and had many intrusive religious thoughts. One can only imagine that each station marked her becoming closer to the ultimate sacrifice—the crucifixion and the resurrection.

The two other bulimic subgroups in the Florida study, the "Fatal Attraction" bulimics and the evocative bulimics, were self-predators and also preyed upon others. The "Fatal Attraction" bulimics, almost 3 percent of the sample, represented a bulimic syndrome in which patients reported a history of sexual abuse, usually by a family member or authority figure (teacher, minister, doctor, dentist) and subsequently used their sexuality to entrap married and unmarried males in authority.

While people with eating disorders are usually secretive about their behavior, there are those who are frankly defiant and flaunt it provocatively, like 10 percent of the bulimics in the Florida study designated as overt or evocative bulimics (Hall and Beresford 1989, Hall et al. 1990). They prey upon significant others by emotionally torturing them. This subgroup was composed of adolescent girls whose previously stable behavior changed suddenly and drastically until it was necessary for them to be hospitalized. They had difficulty in school and with authority figures, and flaunted their bulimia by leaving containers of vomit around the house. They reported that their parents were too busy and did not care about them. Their behavior was erratic, impulsive, and willfully defiant, refusing to follow household or school rules. Many shoplifted, and were truant and promiscuous. While a mother of a bulimic might feel rejected (and ejected) to see the food she had prepared continually vomited by her child, when the child almost literally rubs her mother's face in the vomit, the unneutralized rage is not defended against by the symptoms but is enacted in a process that seems very close to primary process thinking, or psychosis.

In the following examples, it is astounding how long each family tolerated the torture their daughter inflicted on them.

A 14-year-old girl brought home five-gallon containers from a donut shop, placed them in her closet where she would vomit into them and ultimately fill them, then seal them with their plastic lids. As a container became filled, she would stack it on top of another, building a tower that she called her shrine. The distraught parents finally went to a local physician for advice and were told to ignore the behavior, that it would pass. Later a psychologist too advised them to ignore this "attention-seeking" behavior. The girl continued to vomit into buckets that she then placed throughout the house until the family could no longer tolerate the smell. When her mother tried to remove them, the patient hit her. Finally, the family arranged for psychiatric hospitalization.

An 18-year-old college student vomited into Big Gulp cups (oversized soda cups), leaving them in every room of the house. When her parents confronted her, she became so enraged that they backed off. When they stopped removing the offending cups, she became enraged and began vomiting in her mother's fine china cups, leaving cups full of vomit in every room. She and her mother had a violent argument when her mother told her to get out of the house. She struck her mother and later attempted suicide.

The mother of a 16-year-old girl was certain that her daughter was deliberately vomiting food. She confronted her, telling her that she knew what was going on because the daughter didn't clean up the mess very well and there was the odor in the bathroom. Despite this confrontation, the daughter denied vomiting, sarcastically asking her mother, "Mother, what is your *problem?*" The mother was hurt, angry, frightened, and confused. Any further attempt to speak to her daughter provoked an onslaught of verbal abuse. When she stopped trying to talk to her, she found the next morning that her precious Limoges china teacups, collected lovingly over the years and grouped together on a piece of handmade lace to form the dining table center-piece, were all filled with vomit.

Bizarre blood rituals were reported by Jay Kwawer (1980), who treated a young woman in intensive psychotherapy in an open psychiatric hospital. During her eighteen months of treatment, whenever she felt abandoned by her therapist or others she mutilated herself with knives, pins, razor blades, and broken glass, saving her blood in containers and on tissues. She treasured the blood relics, and looking at the vials of blood, while knowing she could cut if she wanted to, helped her refrain from cutting. As she cut less, she continued to save the blood in containers so that she could drink some every night. Even talking of these vampiristic rituals with her therapist gave her great pleasure and comfort.

REGRESSION TO THE IMMEDIACY
OF BODILY EXPERIENCE

At the moment of self-harm, the person seems to regress from the preda-tory paranoid-schizoid position to the far more primitive autistic-contiguous mode, a regression to the immediacy of bodily experience. Although our skin is the body's edge, both a barrier and a permeable boundary (Lappe 1996), a collapse into the autistic-contiguous mode may reflect the overwhelming anxiety of fearing that one's insides will not be contained by the body but will drip out, falling into an endless void (Rosenfeld 1990), thus evoking the defense of self-mutilation or severe purging.

Mutilation of one's skin causing fluid to drip out may serve as a counter-phobic response to the overwhelming fear that one's insides will drip out; so may the massive loss of fluid caused by vomiting, anal and urinary purgatives, and ex-cessive sweating. Tattoos, extreme muscularity, and layers of scar tissue from self-inflicted wounds all may form a "second skin" psychic armor. In bodily self-harm, the individual may shift from the paranoid-schizoid to the autistic-contiguous mode, "a form of self-soothing that is 'perfect' in a way that no human being can possibly be" (Ogden 1990, p. 90), like masturbation compared to a lover's less adequate touch. Whether it be drumming one's fingers, cracking one's knuckles, twirling a lock of hair or rhythmically pulling out strands, biting one's lip, raking one's fingernails over one's skin or scraping a piece of glass or a razor blade over it, playing with one's genitals with one's fingers, sucking one's thumb or drag-ging on a cigarette, or picking at a sore, these activities are predictable and reliable, always having the same sensory rhythms and qualities, always there when needed. For very fearful, untrusting people, relying on what is machine-like for soothing is far better than relying upon another human being.

These experiences in the autistic-contiguous mode represent experiences of self-predation that are especially valued by those who have suffered extreme neglect and abuse. Having little symbolic means of expression, the body becomes his voice, and he becomes a predator of himself in an attempt to master overwhelming fears of being preyed upon. For those who have been doing this for quite awhile, it feels impossible to resist the impulse to collapse into the autistic-contiguous mode, experiencing the rhythmic repetitive pulling of one's hair, cold hard steel piercing warm soft flesh, the sizzling smell of lit cigarette on flesh, or violent cramping and heaving. In speaking of the body as the silenced voice, McLane (1996) reminds us that so much of the darkest side of ourselves has its basis in the ancient rituals of blood sacrifice, mutilation, and cannibalism:

> This voice is so appalling that even the self speaking in wounds cannot stand to hear it. For who can really bear to be their own torturer? Who can look into their own eyes and see the three-headed-baby nature of themselves? Some people can look into a mirror and call their self-wounding tattoo-art, body-piercing, religious ecstasy, a drug trip, psychoanalysis. But these terms themselves are an artful arranging of cooked bits on a plate to disguise the fact that one is eating pieces of bloody dead animal. Who can take off their skin and dance around in their bones . . . without wanting to throw up? No one I know of. . . . This voice is too terrible to contemplate. [p. 111]

Feeding the Hungry Beast (Primitive Sadomasochism)

Beasts (Satan is often referred to as the Beast), monsters, and demons are convenient to have around when one has a need to project the bad parts of oneself elsewere, while angels, currently very popular, proclaim our goodness and protect us from harm. Comedian Flip Wilson proclaimed his innocence from wrongdoing by simply saying, "The devil made me do it." The internal predator is often experienced as a beast or a monster inside, telling the person to cut herself, telling her that she does not deserve to eat or to have anything good inside her. Mary's father raped her when she was 14. A year later she had put on thirty pounds. She wrote:

> There is someone who can be very happy and someone who no longer wants to eat and puke, but as many voices scream that I am a hypocrite, a tart. If I hurt myself I come to feel more quiet. But the beast inside me directly breaks free: give me food, I have to get food. You are a SWINE, Mary, a BEAST. Sell your BODY, put yourself NAKED in the street and have yourself FILLED UP. Let them all MAKE LOVE with you. [Vanderlinden and Vandereycken 1997, p. ix]

244 / When the Body Is the Target

The internal predator is experienced as something foreign, evil, and demonic, not part of her suffering, good self. Despite the conscious wish to get better and stop harming herself, she battles minute to minute or hour to hour to resist the power of the beast. Each time she yields to the beast's power and harms herself is proof to her of her inherent badness, and all the more reason to sacrifice herself to the beast in an effort to appease it. Or, conversely, the wish to expel the beast might compel her to bleed, burn, or purge it out, ridding herself of evil so that she can experience herself as good. The power of the beast increases over time, the self-destructive core growing bigger and fatter as it takes over more and more of the patient's psyche in the same way an invading army occupies and controls another country.

When the patient's illusion of omnipotence is challenged, the immediate sense of defeat and humiliation unleashes the destructive "monster" that restores the sense of omnipotence. Anthony Bateman (1998), using the distinction proposed by Rosenfeld (1987) in which thick-skinned narcissists are inaccessible and defensively aggressive, while thin-skinned narcissists are fragile and vulnerable, has found that narcissistic and borderline patients mostly move between thick-skinned and thin-skinned narcissistic positions. Depending on whether thick- or thin-skinned elements are at the fore, such movement gives an unstable clinical picture that increases the likelihood of enactment in the form of violence either to others or to the self.

The monsters that are unleashed contain mental representations of the object that have been split off from the sense of the self in a psychic maneuver meant to avoid introjection or the internal presence of the "bad" object (Rizzuto 1985). Because the individual cannot save the "good" object from contamination by the bad, an action is required to rid the self of the bad object. In the bulimic the good food-object is experienced as turning sour, poisonous, and must be purged. The anorectic experiences eating as a massive forced incorporation of the toxic maternal object or as an incestuous penetration requiring that she keep the maternal object or incestuous paternal object out by refusing to eat or by purging. The self-mutilator experiences the internal presence of a bad object that she must rid herself of so that she can feel good. A subject in my study wrote the following when asked to describe the experience of mutilating herself: "I feel too much. I hurt. He hurts me over and over in my mind and it all comes back and I can't get it out and I am scared. I feel bad, evil, trapped. I cut 'me' out of her body." For another subject, vomiting and exercise were not enough of a sacrifice for the beast, who demanded more. "Emotions, usually anger or pain, build to intolerable levels. Rather than feel them, I begin to feel fat and to hate my body. Exercise and vomiting was not enough. I also had to punish my body. I wanted to see blood come out. I wanted scars all over. I'd dissociate and start cutting and burning." No matter how hard a person tries to expel the monster within, it is always there, an unacknowledged part of herself unappeased and hungry for more sacrifice.

Destructive Narcissism

This relationship with the internal predator can be understood in terms of the concept of destructive narcissism (Rosenfeld 1971, 1987, Steiner 1981). This is quite different from the narcissistic rage (Kohut 1972) that occurs when a patient reacts to a narcissistic injury by feeling humiliated or denigrated, but may remit readily when the patient once again feels understood by the therapist. In comparison, the destructively narcissistic patient feels only contempt for the therapist who seems kind, loving, and understanding. All his energy goes into remaining sadistically "strong" (Rosenfeld 1987), and he regards warm feelings in himself and others as a weakness. These patients are prone to developing a negative therapeutic reaction, fighting with all their might to hold onto the sadism. Because they cannot allow themselves to acknowledge the libidinally needy part of the self, they disavow it. This allows them to collude with the destructive narcissistic organization in their personality without knowing that they are doing so, and thus they collude with the destructive part of the self in encouraging violent attacks against the self. The destructive part of the self is highly organized "and may appear in the patient's material as a Mafia-like gang dominated by a leader who controls the members by promising benefits and threatening punishment" (Steiner 1981, p. 241). The destructive part of the self presents itself to the suffering good self in several ways: first, as a protector from pain; second, as a servant to its sensuality and vanity; and third, covertly—when the individual tries to resist the destructive regressive force—as the brute, the torturer. In her book *Prozac Nation*, Elizabeth Wurtzel (1994) describes the growth of her destructive narcissism as an enormous roach, growing and overtaking her: "I had metamorphosed into this nihilistic, unhappy girl. Just like [Kafka's] Gregor Samsa waking up to find he'd become a six-foot-long roach, only in my case, I had invented the monster and now it was overtaking me" (p. 40).

Claude-Pierre (1997) describes this state of mind as a mental civil war, in which a healthy part is pitted against another encapsulated part, conjured up in the victim's mind as a physical being, perhaps a monster or beast that is unrelentingly critical and hateful, urging the person to hurt or kill herself. "It tells its victim: Everyone HATES you. You only cause trouble. There's nothing you can do right. You are demanding, selfish, greedy, and mean. Things will never work out for you. You make the world miserable. A person like you doesn't deserve any pleasure. . . . You're fat and gross and ugly. Your father will die in a plane crash if you eat. You should burn in hell. You don't deserve to live. . . . You should die" (p. 38).

A woman wrote to Claude-Pierre, describing the monster's voice as flat and lifeless, having no features, no feelings; it doesn't matter how fast one runs to escape it, one can never run fast enough. The monster is hateful, a creature that thrives on ruin and destruction. Claude-Pierre compares it to a parasite preying on the host (the good self), trying to consume it. As the beast grows larger, the individual will try to bargain with it for small favors, promising not to eat supper tonight if the beast allows her to have one grape now, promising to run for three hours if it lets her eat a bowl of strawberries.

This is not, however, a good innocent self caught in the grip of a beast, or a dear sweet angel besieged by an evil tormentor, as Claude-Pierre seems to think. It is far more complex than that, a perverse relationship within parts of the self, with the healthy part colluding and allowing itself to be taken over by the destructive part (Steiner 1981). This is done, however, so that the individual both knows what she is doing at the same time that she does not allow herself to know that it is she and not some evil monster doing it. (Commonly, we hear people refer to excessive self-indulgence in something they know is bad for them as "going to hell with myself.") Once again, there is a comparable perverse duality operating. It is disavowal that allows her to have this perverse relationship with parts of herself and allows her to be seduced by madness. It is disavowal that is externalized in the transference and gives rise to the perverse flavor of the interacting transference–countertransference processes.

The Suffering Martyr Is Fed to the Hungry Beast

The beast within is hungry for food and thirsty for blood. Nothing else will satisfy. When his voice is resisted, it grows louder until it is an insistent deafening roar. The self-harming person sacrifices her body and her blood to the beast. Seduced by the psychotic core of her own mind to regress to the deepest most destructive part of the self, the beast in the mind preys upon the healthier part of the self and cannibalizes it. The person who is preyed upon by the beast and the beast itself are one and the same. That is, the one who is cannibalized is one and the same as the cannibal, greedily licking her lips as she watches her flesh disappear from the bone. Her ravenous thirst requires more blood, yet the more of her own blood she drinks, the more she wants. She devours more and more of herself, feeding on her dying, singing love songs to death. The sacrifice is delicious, a process she extends and elaborates on so that she can savor it a long time, as if it were the best of Perugina dark chocolate.

Despite the pain of their self-sacrifice, the sacrifice is delicious. Those who have religious symbols carved or tattooed on their skin may also be signifying that they have been sacrificed to satisfy the appetites of hungry beasts.

"Sometimes I feel like my purpose in life was to be abused. . . . Two men, possibly three, sexually assaulted me at different times in my life," said Marcia, a 32-year-old mother of three who participated in my study. She has carved several crosses into her left arm. She reported a childhood history of family violence, and physical and sexual abuse. As a child she vomited and had diarrhea, had a poor appetite, refused at times to eat, ate non-edibles, bit her nails until they were bloody and sore, chewed and swallowed her hair, and had frequent accidents and several surgeries. Early in adulthood she began cutting and sticking herself quite frequently. She said that she had affairs, after which she cut herself with razors, and once threw herself down the stairs. She wrote that the last time she cut herself was after having sex that she did not really want. She has carved the word *hate* on her left leg, along with *hate*, *bad*, and *slut* on her left arm. The word *hate* is so well cut into her arm, she says, that it will never go away.

Becoming the Omnipotent Demonic God(dess)

The devil can cite Scripture for his purpose.
Shakespeare, *The Merchant of Venice*

Monsters can be predatory gods and goddesses who eat and regurgitate human beings in order to renew them. To transform oneself from potential prey to predatory beast is to become godlike, and various cultures have provided prototypes: Zeus, who was rumored to demand the annual murder, dismemberment, and devouring of a child at Mount Lykaion; Titan Cronus, who required human victims to feed his voracious appetite; Kali, the hungry, bloodthirsty goddess; Artemis, a "lion among women" who killed at her pleasure. The predator goddess in Anatolia was Cybele, in Egypt was Sekmet, in India is Durga, also known as Kali, in Sumer was Inanna, in Canaan was Astarte, and in Bali was Rangda, the bloodthirsty, child-eating demon queen. But none surpasses Kali for bloodthirstiness. According to Hindu belief, today's era (*yuga*) is called the Kali Yuga and the destroyer goddess Kali reigns (Montgomery 1995). The Kali Yuga is thought to be the final era before the world dissolves, the era in which we repudiate our gods, extinguish rather than revere life, the era in which our goodness is overwhelmed by our destructiveness. While the Kali Yuga may be the Hindu version of "millennium madness," there is much about the goddess Kali that resonates in Western culture with the destructive narcissism of those who harm themselves. The demon god(dess) can slay others and the monstrous demon god(dess) can also be slain by humans in secret rites, his violent death becoming the central mystery. Above all other monsters, it is the serpent that is the fundamental symbol of evil. The paintings of Hieronymus Bosch, which depict aggressive images tormenting humankind, contain images of the mouth and cloaca becoming transformed into demons (Lacan 1977). It was the serpent in the Garden of Eden that, through Eve, induced Adam to eat of the tree of knowledge, thus forfeiting his innocence and creating the original sin. To eat of and be eaten by evil is to become a monster.

The person who has been preyed upon by internal or external predators and then becomes a predator himself is in his own way an omnipotent and demonic god or goddess, unleashing the beast upon the self in a passionate orgy of destructive narcissism that can profoundly harm or even kill him. To understand how this perverse omnipotence and pseudo-independence develops, one must understand how the discharge of aggression increasingly shifts in the direction of deadly encounters that can end in death, and for this we must understand grandiosity and omnipotence. "Human aggression is most dangerous when it is attached to the two great absolutarian psychological constellations: the grandiose self and the archaic omnipotent object" (Kohut 1972, p. 378).

Like the sexual sadomasochist, the self-harmer experiences a sense of destructive omnipotence and sadistic pleasure at inflicting pain and humiliation upon herself, playing the part of the torturer as well as the tortured while she either enacts the beating fantasy or reenacts the traumatic experience of having been abused physically or sexually or both. She is hardly aware that her life is hanging in the balance because the destructive omnipotent parts of the self are defensively split-off from the healthier part, remaining all-powerful in isolation. All that is taboo, forbidden, or sacred is turned upside down and reduced to excrement (Chasseguet-Smirgel 1984). Meaning is reduced to excrement.

What Mara Selvini Palazzoli (1974) has said of the anorectic is true for the bulimic and the self-mutilator:

> Her mind is made up that the body can and must be subdued in the long run. But *this type of acarnality is not a death wish*—quite the contrary. It is, essentially, an unrealistic tension and a rejection of existence *qua* living and dying in one's body. More precisely it is a rejection of death as a biological fact, and with it a rejection of aging, corpulence, and existential decay. In short, the anorexic turns her back on the existentially inevitable, on everything that is imposed by, and inherent in, her corporeality. . . . In fact, anorexics look upon their possible deaths as so many accidents, but never as something that they themselves may be courting. . . . These patients play with death like children who think they can disappear by shamming dead. Incapable as they are of facing reality or even, as we shall see, of comprehending their own physical needs, they delude themselves into thinking that they can tamper with their bodies as they please. This I have observed with utter astonishment even in one of my patients who was a doctor, who in theory at least, was fully familiar with her biological processes and nevertheless treated her own body in the most absurd and anti-scientific, and sometimes even magical, way, thus ignoring the most elementary tenets of medical science. [pp. 81–82]

It is difficult, if not impossible, to imagine one's own death, and certainly impossible to experience it. "Our own death is indeed unimaginable, and whenever we make the attempt to imagine it we can conceive that we really survive as spectators. . . . At bottom no one believes in his own death, or to put the thing in another way, in the unconscious every one of us is convinced of his immortality" (Freud 1915b, p. 289). Yet it is probably a universal wish to know what it feels like to be dead. Out of fear, one can deny that death is right there and imminent, as the anorectics Selvini Palazzoli described do, or one can rush to the arms of death, longing to know it intimately. Marya Hornbacher (1998) wrote about how, even when dying of her eating disorder and having been given by doctors no more than a week to live, she experienced an erotic pull toward death, an excited longing to know death intimately, like a lover. She found dying very exciting. Death can reach out with the seductive call of a siren. The French call orgasm *la petite mort* ("the little death") because it is closest to death, the ultimate surrender. First, in the throes of ecstasy we experience full aliveness, then there is the peak of orgasm, experienced as the obliteration or death of the self, and then finally there is regeneration, or rebirth, as seventeenth-century poet John Donne wrote in "A Valediction: Forbidding Mourning." Freud (1913a) wrote about the seductiveness of death in "Theme of the Three Caskets," and when expressing supreme pleasure, some express it by saying, "I thought I'd died and gone to heaven."

It is no wonder, then, that despite how drastically her behavior threatens her life, the self-harmer may act as if she has everlasting life. Each glimpse of death can feel like the beginning of life. She acts as if she has no need to take the steps the rest of us mortals must take to maintain and preserve our lives. "To risk death can mean having the strength to have no needs, to have an identity at last" (Sprince 1988, p. 81). Going even further, Lacan (1977), reformulating Freud's concept of the death drive, conceptualizes the taking of one's own life as the ultimate freedom:

> Man's freedom is entirely inscribed within the constituting triangle of the renunciation that he imposes on the desire of the other by the menace of death for the enjoyment of the fruits of his serfdom—of the consented-to sacrifice of his life for the reasons that to give to human life its measure—and of the suicidal renunciation of the vanquished partner, depriving of this victory the master whom he abandons to his inhuman solitude. . . .
> It is in effect as a desire for death that he affirms himself for others. [pp. 104–105]

The right to decide life and death has been historically the privilege of a sovereign power. Like a god, just as he had given his subjects life, so he could take it away (Foucault 1977). Today, death has become the most secret and most private aspect of existence. Suicide, still a crime in many states, was considered so because it usurped the power of death which the sovereign alone had the right to exercise. The popular contemporary feminist heroines Thelma and Louise (from the film *Thelma and Louise*) chose to drive their car over a cliff to their death rather than lose their freedom. They were even more than heroines; they became twentieth-century goddesses. The right to do whatever one wants with one's body and one's life (Foucault 1977) has been taken up as a cause célèbre by many of those who practice sexual sadomasochism and vampirism.

In those involved in self-harm behavior, the sadomasochistic psychopathology joins in the personality with the perverse relationship between parts of the self, in which destructive narcissism gains a hold on the healthier aspects of the personality. Destructive and aggressive narcissism reigns omnipotent and supreme with the help of "doublethink," that deadly ability to know and at the same time not let oneself know what one knows. There may even be in some a "dual track" oscillation between primary and secondary process thinking about Christlike images (Grotstein 1997), not letting oneself know that one is the actual sacrificial offering and at the same time the fierce deity to whom the sacrifice is offered.

What it means matters not to her, the self-harmer; it is all a crazy game of Russian roulette. While flirting passionately with death, her self-harm transforms her; she feels all powerful and immortal, like a goddess. Her ravaged and emaciated body evokes the Passion of Christ. Like Christ, in suffering and (near) death she will be reborn and live forever. And so the whirling and twirling and dips and turns of the death dance become faster and faster in an exhilarating blur. "Ecstasy means being flung out of your usual self, but that is still to feel a commotion inside. Mysticism transcends the here and now for loftier truths unexplainable in the straitjacket of language; but such transcendence registers on the senses, too, as a rush of fire in the veins, a quivering in the chest, a quiet, fossillike surrender in the bones" (Ackerman 1990, p. 302).

She is the masochist, coming alive with pain and suffering at the same time that she is the sadist, all-powerful in inflicting suffering. She is the prey and she is the predator, the sacrificial offering and the demonic deity to whom it is offered (Eliade 1958), dancing an ecstatic macabre dance. In describing the pain of self-mutilation McLane (1996) uses language that sounds very much like the pain suffered in the living body of Christ: "The primary pain of abuse is experienced as the structure of the world itself, something that has been taken in like the nerves absorb lead or hemoglobin inhales carbon monoxide. But these metaphors are incorrect, because . . . a primary pain is absorbed into itself and becomes the living body. What happens is substitution, but of one life for another" (p. 110). It was Christ's suffering that is believed to have redeemed humankind and it is the pain absorbed by the self-harmer that is believed on some level to redeem the sufferer and give her everlasting life.

The starved and bleeding body of Christ is the symbol of rebirth and renewal, the season of resurrection, the season of spring. The skin, too, constantly mends and renews itself, and so it should be no surprise that many who mutilate their outer or inner skin, even coming close to death in the process, feel renewed and reborn. Many who self-mutilate may carve a cross or other religious symbol into their flesh, signifying their self-sacrifice, while some who claim they were victims of satanic abuse may carve satanic symbols, such as 666, an upside-down cross, or a pentagram. An elderly patient whose self-starvation began at age 3 with an identification with Christ suffering on the cross, would offer her suffering up to God until old age. Another patient had to be transferred from an open psychiatric hospital to a closed unit when her purging and cutting had become quite dangerous and she could not stop. The unit was, in her words, a snakepit, and as she looked at her body swollen with edema and she had the realization of how very close to death she had come, she had what she described as a religious experience in which God visited her, and she felt that she had been resurrected. Several days later she was readmitted to the open unit determined to live for a long, long time. We should beware of such professed determination. Feeling renewed by a close brush with death is no reassurance that the person will not do it again. Feelings of renewal are fleeting, and may need the "booster shot" of yet another close call with death to regain the feeling of renewal.

Tina, a 37-year-old subject in my study, was a victim of childhood physical and sexual abuse, witnessed family violence, and suffered traumatic separations and placement in care in her adolescence. At the same time she suffered from diabetes and skin rashes, and she displayed head-banging behavior. She began at this time picking at her skin, cutting and sticking herself with pointed objects, and burning herself. She also alternated between starving herself and bulimic behavior, beginning her bingeing and purging at 14. For her, the purge is the more intense part of the experience. She consumed poisonous cleaning agents and food that had spoiled. "I am trying to kill myself, but in a nonconspicuous way—I cannot slit my wrists, because I just can't bring myself to do it that way but I have a great desire to harm myself in other ways that will end my life. . . . I get a new 'renewal' in positive spirit when I live through each suicide attempt, although I would like each to be the last." She has taken syrup of ipecac, diuretics, laxative pills and suppositories, enemas, even opium and heroin to induce purging. She also acknowledges that she has gotten physicians to perform surgery that was not medically necessary, including a double mastectomy, a facelift, and a hysterectomy. She has purposely overdosed on drugs and alcohol in attempts to kill herself. She said that before she cuts or sticks herself, "I feel my heart racing and a very big build-up of stress and panic." She feels unreal, as in a trance. "I feel as though I am losing touch with reality—and that the only thing that matters is to harm myself. . . . I hate myself and the hate actually builds up to a point that I want to kill myself and end the mental pain. . . . Physical pain is renewing 'life' (pain is the start of a relief)." She has acquired many "professional" body piercings (eleven earlobe piercings, three piercings on other parts of her ear, three nostril piercings, two nipple piercings, and a genital piercing). She read about my study in a notice in the *Piercing Fans International Quarterly*, an expensive magazine catering to those with a special interest in body piercing and sadomasochism. Not surprisingly, she also has a tattoo of a skeleton on her abdomen.

Hornbacher (1998) wrote about her experience with self-harm in terms of religious, masochistic suffering. She described her pain as ascetic and holy, the dark place of her mind blending in her memory with the dark womb of the church, associating the chants and prayer fugues with the erotic energy she received by carving a small cross into her thigh with a nail. She describes herself as being both a "top" (dominant) and a "bottom" (submissive), and as having a twisted sado-masochistic holy life. Hornbacher's account exemplifies Stoller's (1985) concept of perversion as the erotic form of hatred, the common feature of which is the desire to inflict harm, either physically or by means of humiliation. When there is physical pain, humiliation may be implied, and not a part of the overt scenario. In any case, the dehumanization of the bottom (masochist) and the gross dramatized expression of powerlessness for the bottom and of power for the designated top (sadist) is grossly emphasized in the overt scenarios. It is important to note that it is not only overtly sexual sadomasochistic enactments that can be intensely exciting; sadomasochistic enactments that are not overtly sexual can also be intensely exciting.

Overt sadomasochism is all about theater, with its dramatic props (black leather, whips, masks, dungeons, etc.) exaggerating the titillating simulation of harm and high risk. When sadomasochists play, they not only spend much time and effort setting a scene, but once they start, they spend hours at their games, catering to each other's desires and the need not to exceed the other's bounds, before arriving at an emotional catharsis. For some this is foreplay before orgasm, for others it is the end of the scene. By virtue of the top's exaggerated dominant position, the fantasy of omnipotence is maintained. It is also maintained for the bottom as well, for in consensual sadomasochism, the bottom can halt what is happening by uttering a previously agreed upon "safety" word and then the game is over. However, the potential for danger is enormous in these scenarios, because the presumed safety of the bottom may be only a presumption, especially when new unfamiliar partners are frequently sought. When sadomasochistic activity is solitary, bondage deaths may occur when partial asphyxiation involving nooses, gags, plastic bags, or gas inhalation "accidentally" becomes total asphyxiation (Litman and Swearingen 1996). Skin eroticism (Krueger 1989), the erotic focus on skin stimulation and warming, can come from being beaten, from rubbing or picking at infected areas, from having one's skin pierced or tattooed. For some who purge or self-mutilate severely, this sadomasochistic activity can be quite erotic. For anyone involved in sexual sadomasochism, it is not easy to distinguish those who play at harm, in an effort to undo or master the effects of harm inflicted on them early in life, from those whose intent is real harm, also an attempt to master early trauma. And as with any compulsive activity, playing at harm can escalate over time to real and potentially dangerous harm.

In a sex column with a question and answer format in The Village Voice, the columnist (Savage 1996) posts a question from a Chicago woman in her twenties who likes being treated roughly sexually. He refers to Dossie Easton, co-author of two books on S&M, The Bottoming Book: How to Get Terrible Things Done to

You by Wonderful People (1996) and The Topping Book: Getting Good at Being Bad (1995).

Easton, a licensed marriage, family and child counselor with a private practice in . . . San Francisco, has been into S&M for almost 25 years. Before she "came out" about her desires, she found herself in a similar situation to the one you describe. "I spent my idle youth hunting down rough trade in the streets of New York, and I finally wound up with a first-class batterer. So I'm not surprised she found somebody who was really exciting who turned out to be a 'headcase.'" Savage says, "It's like this . . . if you bop through life hoping to meet men who by chance happen to share your desires, or if you encourage the men you're involved with to be 'slightly physically abusive,' you may well find yourself with a man who will use your desires as a pretext to abuse you. A man who is openly into SM, who has thought about it and read about it and is involved to some extent in the SM community is a much safer bet. He's likely to know what boundaries and limits are; to possess a vocabulary that allows him to articulate his desires and help you articulate yours; and to understand where fantasy ends and reality begins. . . . As for your abusive parents, Easton says, "There are many people into SM who experienced abuse, and many who have not. I am an abuse survivor myself, and SM has not made me sicker than my parents did. If anything, it's made me healthier. I've been bottoming since 1974, and I just get stronger all the time, and more assertive." If the abuse and neglect you suffered as a child trouble you, Easton strongly suggests you find a therapist, one who is "trained in working with child abuse but is not prejudiced against SM. Your local SM group will know who those people are. Too many therapists will say your desires are sick and you should just get rid of them. Not only is that not possible, but what I found in my 25 years of SM is that the experience is very empowering for me. I'm in control of it, making conscious decisions. My friend who plays the dominant has my safety as her chief concern. I can ride this rollercoaster knowing it has been safety-tested. SM has made a major contribution to my healing from child abuse, and I have seen it in other clients I've worked with" [Savage 1996, p. 121]

In the world of people in search of others to inflict pain on them, the dominant, or top, may be regarded as a healer of sorts, and the personal attachment to that healer can become quite strong. Among the many role-playing scenarios enacted by sadomasochists, that of sadistic nurse and submissive patient is quite popular. Personal advertisements for an S&M experience promise one with a nurse/mistress in an "authentic medical exam room," which may closely resemble a physician's examination room except for the presence of whips and handcuffs. "Nurse Wolf . . . described one of her favorite roles as that of a nurse in a medical scenario. I could see the white shoes, the nurse's white outfit, the brisk gestures, the busy hands. She was in her early thirties, attractive, the picture of health, still looking like the Texas cheerleader she once was. . . . In her studio she had a medical room and a lot of implements: forceps and scalpels and electrical devices" (Theroux 1998, p. 50).

254 / When the Body Is the Target

In the case of Marya Hornbacher, who plays the part of the sadist as well as the masochist, this is no theatrical scenario; this is not play. It is the real thing, destructiveness at its most demonic. When Freud (1923) spoke of a "daemonic force at work" (p. 35) in the traumatic neurosis, he was speaking of the rage, hatred, and terror that continue in the dialectic of trauma. We can trace that hatred and traumatic terror in the following story, written for Robert Stoller (1985) by one "erotic vomiter" about another:

> She says she began to actively masturbate at about age 11 years. She was caught by her step-father, who placed her across his lap and spanked her very hard. She said she could feel his penis against her stomach (erect?). She began to vomit and came to orgasm, the best and most intense sensation she has ever had.
> She began to have sick spells, especially in the presence of dominant males—teachers, principal, stepfather, uncle—. . . She says that she doesn't get any pleasure from regular sex, but does enjoy giving head, yet says she rarely has an orgasm—with the exception of manual masturbation or a vomiting episode. During masturbation her fantasy primarily consists of being an executioner in a men's prison and vomits when the prisoner is twitching in death. They are usually prisoners who are being hung [sic] for the rape and death of a small child. She occasionally fantasizes the crime, and it seems to make little difference whether the child is male or female. She has also vomited with an accompanying orgasm, during the actual crime [rape] fantasy, at the moment of penetration [of the child] by the criminal. [pp. 159–160]

The rage, hatred, and terror engendered by trauma live on in sexual perversions, eating disorders and other addictions, narcissistic character disorders, and borderline personality disorders, which all have in common a lack of capacity for whole object love, and a tendency to treat another person as a thing rather than a person (Bach 1994). Much character pathology can be understood as derailment from the path toward whole object love to perverted object relationships. The fundamental developmental issue for such patients is the failure to resolve separation from the maternal figure, with the perverted object relationship functioning for the loveless like a prosthesis, providing the illusory sense of feeling loved (Bach 1994). Such patients have prominent sadomasochistic fantasies because sadism is rooted in the denial of separation and masochism in the fear of it. The sadist refuses to accept that the object is lost, desperately attempting to recapture it and obtaining excitement from punishing the object. The masochist, by contrast, identifies with the lost object and denies the loss by finding substitutes to whom he desperately clings, preferring pain to object loss. Excitement comes from the pain that tells the patient the object is still there. Because they have not had the transitional space necessary to form an autonomous sense of self, they cannot use symbols or tolerate ambiguity, paradox, or multiple viewpoints (Bach 1994), and so regress in the act of self-harm to a dedifferentiated bodily means of enacting the relationship of predator to prey. At some moments the individual is the predator, sadistically mutilating and devouring her prey. This can switch within seconds and the individual can then become the terrified creature, frozen masochistically still as she receives the burns, blows, or slashes on her body. The bodily acts are presymbolic, a symbolic equation, in which the part of the body being attacked does not symbolize the object being attacked, but is experienced concretely as the object. They attack their bodies as animals attack their prey, a primitive, visceral experience that precludes the possibility of using language to create meaning. It functions, therefore, as an attack on language and the creation of meaning (Woodruff 1998).

For some there may be a startlingly dangerous regression to a primitive dissociated state of dedifferentiation in which one is the actual sacrificial offering and at the same time a horrific satanic deity to whom the sacrifice is offered. Kathleen, a young woman who participated in my study, wrote that her religious background was Roman Catholic, "officially, by day" but also wrote that her upbringing was involved with something that sounds cultic and ominous, called "darkoneness HCTUHC." Note the frightening nature of Kathleen's ego regression, the progressive nature of the dissociative responses that occurred in the process of filling out the questionnaire, and the remarkable dedifferentiation of self and object representations.

Kathleen, a 27-year-old white single woman who is unemployed and lives with her aunt, stated that she dropped out of her second year of graduate school after she was gang-raped. She hates everything about her body except her eyes. Through her childhood and adolescence she experienced family violence, sexual and physical abuse—hundreds of episodes of sexual abuse. She recalls "spacing out" as a child. Anorectic in childhood, she developed bulimic episodes in adolescence. "I don't plan it anymore. It happens when I'm either tense and emotionally upset, with no release or anyone to talk to . . . or it happens at night when I am bored . . . or if I eat too little for a few days I am likely to binge. Truly *binge* eating was when I was 19 years old—after a long bout of anorexia but I kinda binged when I was 11, 12, 13 . . . but maybe it was normal teen snacking—after school would eat *lots* of ice cream and cookies."

She has vomited as frequently as eight times a day and has used at times ninety Ex-Lax and twenty diuretic pills. She has consumed large quantities of the usual foods people tend to binge on, but points out emphatically, using several exclamation points, that she never eats meat. Using her vegetarianism to deny her predatory instincts, they are revealed nonetheless in her consumption of nutshells, Clorox bleach, and syrup of ipecac. The purge is by far the more intense part of the experience. She uses Clorox because it "cleans out my system" and also causes the most intense purge. She wrote that purging "feels great but then my mind still counts the calories. They're not all out. I will weigh more tomorrow." She has been bingeing and purging for eleven years and is not sure if she intends to harm her body. She did, however, write that she has not consumed these items in order to kill herself. She developed arthritis in adolescence. She has mutilated herself in several ways since childhood and throughout her life. She reports banging her head, biting her nails and cuticles severely, picking at her skin, cutting herself, sticking herself with pins, burning herself, and snapping a rubber band against her wrist until it is swollen and bruised. She has been accident-prone since childhood and has crashed her car and overdosed on drugs many times. The word HATE was carved on her arm when she was 9, also some symbols of a religious sort, but she is not sure who did these things: "I don't know if I did it or he did. I just woke up with them." She wrote that she had been pierced, tattooed, branded, or scarred more than ten times by her abusers. In the past year she had deliberately injured herself more than fifty times, at times needing medical attention. Most of the time before she self-mutilates (often after a bulimic episode), she reports that she does not feel real. In answer to the question, "In your own words, can you tell me about this?" she wrote the following, using the lower case *i*, a graphic representation of her self-esteem, which changes to the upper case *I* toward the very end of the questionnaire when she states her determination "to *fly* away":

> Usually i go away in my mind. i feel like a child again and she is saying over and over, "You're bad, you're evil. I am going to punish you, hurt you." The blood brings the evil out . . . i float away. . . . i go away after cut cut cut and blood drips all over her arms and it is good. Keep cutting. Nothing hurts me. i am made of iron. . . . i feel too much . . . i hurt . . . i am scared. He hurts me over and over in my mind and it all comes back and i can't get it out and i feel bad, evil, trapped. i cut "me" out of her body. . . . i feel justly punished and it feels better. i am evil but i paid the price. i feel relieved to a certain degree. Now I must hide my arms again though. . . . There is so much to tell about all this—but i can't sort out the words. The behaviors bring relief but i'd give them up if i only could. I really don't care anymore . . . too many hospitals, doctors, medicines, ECT [electroconvulsive therapy], sodium amytal, restraints, questions. I just want to *fly* away. . . . I will.

Kathleen's shift from referring to herself in the lower case *i* to the upper case *I* seems to mark her fusion with the demonic beast to become the demonic omnipotent goddess, perhaps even Lucifer him/herself. More than any other subject's, Kathleen's response to the questionnaire chilled me to the bone. This is the universe of sacrilege, in which the self-harmer puts herself in the position of God, becoming through a terrible process of destruction the creator of a new kind of sacrilegious reality in which the world is reduced to excrement (Chasseguet-Smirgel 1984). "All that is taboo, forbidden, or sacred is devoured . . . disintegrating the molecules of the mass . . . in order to reduce it to excrement" (p. 4). Unleashing uncontrollable narcissistic rage upon her body, she feeds the illusion that she is an omnipotent goddess flying through eternity. "Led on by hubris, 'the artful universe' of perversion dethrones God-the-Father and rewrites the Bible. It aims to transmute reality, to revert to confusion and chaos" (p. 10).

Blood, Vomit, and Feces: Totems or Transitional Phenomena?

We tend to respond fearfully and anxiously to an individual's shedding his own blood or deliberately vomiting because these acts represent taboos and transgressions. We are commanded "Thou shalt not murder," and commanded to preserve life above all else. There is a taboo against spilling one's own blood or otherwise harming oneself. According to Freud's (1913b) theory of taboo, the most primitive source of the taboo lies in the fear of demonic powers hidden in the object. If the object is touched or used wrongly, it is believed that the demonic power takes its vengeance by casting a spell over the wrongdoer (Freud 1913b).

"A totem," wrote Frazer in his first essay on the subject, "is a class of material objects which a savage regards with superstitious respect, believing that there exists between him and every member of the class an intimate and altogether special relation. . . . The connection between a man and his totem is mutually beneficent; the totem protects the man, and the man shows his respect for the totem in various ways" [Freud 1913b, p. 103, quoting James G. Frazer, *Totem and Exogamy*, 1910]

Totemism is directly connected with a belief in the spirits, in animism. Originally all totems were animals regarded as the ancestors of the different clans and inherited only through the female line (Freud 1913b). Freud wrote that Frazer's first psychological theory of totemism was based on the belief in an eternal soul, and the totem provided a safe place of refuge where the soul could reside and thus escape the dangers threatening it.

If we examine the bizarre ritualistic behavior around cutting and saving the blood and vomiting and saving the vomit in containers, Freud's theory makes eminent sense. The blood that is deliberately shed or the vomitus deliberately vomited is believed to have extraordinary demonic powers, much like religious relics. The bones and body parts of the saints became objects of reverence and are at times used in healing practices (Favazza 1996). No wonder clinical staff members respond with terrible fear and anxiety when patients assault them with the sight of their blood. When understood in this way, it is no wonder that anyone who tries to interfere with these rituals involving collecting and keeping blood or vomit will have to contend with the rage of the ritualist. To confiscate containers of a person's precious bodily fluids, which are believed to be the source of omnipotent power, is the equivalent of cutting off Samson's hair, leaving the person bereft and impotent. Kwawer's (1980) patient, described earlier, cut herself, collecting the drips in a small container that was hidden, like treasure, in her closet. Just knowing it was there had the power to calm her at difficult times. At times she opened the container and sipped the blood, delighting in telling her analyst the details of the vampire-like rituals. Blood is life, and vampires drink deeply of the blood of the living to give themselves eternal life. Sometimes vampires drink deeply of their own blood to provide themselves with everlasting life.

I was told of a bulimic patient who became very frightened of vomiting into the toilet for fear that her vomit would clog up not only the sewage system of her apartment building but the New York City sewage system. She would instead vomit into plastic bags, which she would tie closed, and then would distribute the next day on her way to work in various public garbage cans. She was so convinced of her omnipotent power that she had to protect the city from the demonic power of her vomit, making certain to place the bags of vomit into different cans each day so that city officials could not detect a pattern that could be traced to her (Ellen Steingart, M.S.W., personal communication). The word *demonic* can aptly describe Bollas's (1992) imaginative effort to put into words the self experience of a female cutter in the hospital.

> I hear A cut across her stomach. All the way across it. A deep cut. She bled through her analytical hour, but Dr. Z knew nothing as she sheltered beneath her lovely Scottish sweater, its heavy braid soaking up the sacrament. Moments before the session's end she lifted the sweater to reveal the cut and Dr. Z's face became horror. He closed his eyes. . . .
> I have not done that yet, but A did it to Dr. Z with that wonderful great cut across her belly. "Have a look at this, you coal miner of the unconscious, open your eyes to this fearsome cunt, with no pubic fleece to protect your gaze from its object: a hole that bleeds and bleeds and bleeds. Look at this, you coward!" [pp. 138–140]

For many, even a tattoo or body piercing is believed to have a totemic power to heal or grant wishes. It provides a sense of protection in much the same way as a cross or religious medal does, and a sense of wholeness or completion as well. "In New Guinea the Roro people, who tattoo themselves extensively, describe the un-tattooed person as 'raw,' comparing him to uncooked meat . . . the Roro see the tattooed man as 'cooked meat,' transformed by a human process and thus given a social identity" (Vale and Juno 1989, quoting Victoria Ebin, *The Body Decorated* 1984, p. 121). A significantly large number of the women who participated in my study, abuse survivors who reported the most severe purging and self-mutilation, had also acquired studio tattoos and piercings, suggesting that all were unconscious attempts at self-healing. Raellyn Gallina, a body modification professional said, "Sometimes women have had a traumatic experience and they'll want to reclaim their sexuality in a way by having a nipple or labia piercing; this becomes a *reclaiming ritual* that helps undo a lot of shit from their past. And from that moment forward they can go on. Sometimes that happens" (Vale and Juno 1989, p. 105).

Another who believes tattoos and piercings can transform people arranges ceremonies to enhance their power. Friends are invited, and there may be chanting and burning herbs or incense.

"We are all connected as we gather together to support and help nurture the growth and transformation of the celebrant. I usually break the silence by speaking about the symbolism of the chosen design and the auspiciousness of the time chosen for this transformation. I then ask the celebrant to tell in his own words what the tattoo will accomplish. Each remaining participant then offers a word, idea, blessing . . . whatever . . . to help charge this tattoo talisman. The energy is raised, grounded, and the clasped hands are released. We begin the tattoo" [Mifflin 1997, p. 108, quoting Pat Sinatra, owner of a tattoo and piercing studio]

Sitting around a dinner table, we lift our glass and drink to life ("L'chaim!"), health, ("Salud!"), and good appetite ("Bon appetit!"). We may utter a blessing over the food that sustains our life. So of course we tend to respond passionately to self-harm as an assault on life and health. But to those who purge, cut, or mark their flesh with tattoos and piercings, their vomit, feces, blood and "magical marks" contain magical power over their life.

PART III

THE BODY SPEAKS

This is a world of bodies
each body pushing with a terrible power
Each body alone racked with its own unrest.

Peter Weiss, *The Persecution and Assassination of Jean-Paul Marat,*
as Performed by the Inmates of the Asylum of Charenton
under the Direction of the Marquis de Sade

9

The Body Speaks That
Which Cannot Be Spoken

Some people experience their painful subjective self states as raw wounds (Pine 1994). These are wounds that do not really heal and that demonstrate a readiness to bleed like stigmata. "An unacknowledged trauma is like a wound that never heals over and may start to bleed again at any time," wrote Alice Miller (1983, p. 81). The scars tell stories, personal history written on or in the body. Sometimes they are visible, but sometimes the scars, like those of many abuse survivors who carve on their breast or inner thigh or lacerate their vagina, are not readily visible. Sometimes the scars are invisible, like those of the bulimic who bleeds internally, whose scarred and damaged interior tells a story. Just as Tolstoy said in Anna Karenina that "every unhappy family is unhappy in its own way," each unhappy story told by the body is uniquely unhappy in its own way.

We cannot assume that one person's bulimic episode is like another's, or that one person's experience of cutting or skin picking is the same as another's. Understanding compromise formation to be that which solves an intrapsychic conflict among the ego, the id, the superego, the repetition compulsion, and the demands of the outside world, creating a psychic equilibrium (Brenner 1982), then we understand that what may appear to be quite the same behavior in two different people is the symptomatic manifestation of two unique and different compromise formations. That is, the symptomatic behavior itself needs to be understood within the context of the individual's ego structure (Eissler 1953) and in terms of the multiple functions that that symptom serves for that person at that time (Waelder 1936).

If the individual's psychic equilibrium can shift, then so can his subjective experience of the type of self-harm behavior(s) used; for example, self-cutting may be experienced one way one day and somewhat differently the next day by the same person. In answer to my questions asking subjects to write what their experience usually was of both the binge–purge episode and the self-mutilating episode, one subject wrote, indicating that there is no bulimic episode or self-mutilating episode, only uniquely different experiences. Another wrote: "I wish I could describe each and every time I binge and purge or hurt myself because it's always so different."

SELF-HARM AS ATTEMPTS AT SELF-REGULATION

All sorts of behavior commonly regarded as self-destructive can be understood as attempts at self-medication, the attempts of desperate people to interrupt or terminate an intolerable mood or emotional state and to feel better. We rely on three distinct types of experiences to achieve feelings of well-being: soothing or relaxing experiences, excitement, and fantasy (Milkman and Sunderwirth 1987). Those who rely excessively on soothing will gorge themselves with food, television watching, alcohol and depressant drugs. Their craving for relaxation may stem from the wish to reduce either externally or internally generated discomfort. The search for tranquillity may be an effort, conscious or unconscious, to keep a lid on their own hostility, which threatens to erupt. In contrast, those who crave excitement may take a counterphobic stance, actively confronting a world seen as hostile, persecutory, or threatening, or their yen for excitement may serve the defensive function of masking and enlivening a depressed and deadened sense of self. They may be given to the excitement of flirting with death, through repeated drug overdoses, reckless driving, starvation, sadomasochistic practices, or other courting of near-death experiences. The third group, made up of those who are compelled by fantasy, enjoy the activation of the right hemisphere of the brain, pursuing mystical experiences of oneness through the use of marijuana and hallucinogens, making deliberate attempts to induce trances by means of meditation, chanting, and sleep and food deprivation. Some creative people may even become so addicted to the creative "high" that promotes the feeling of oneness that they crave more and more of it, losing their ability to regulate cycles of work and rest, consciousness and sleep. They then resort to drugs and alcohol to help them sleep and to caffeine, amphetamines, or cocaine to get them going again, ending up with multiple addictions.

The child who has suffered a traumatic disruption of attachment experiences difficulties in his self-regulatory abilities. He may suffer in the extreme with his affects and states of consciousness, seeming not to feel emotions at all, or feeling them so deeply and intensely as to be overwhelmed by them. He may not feel anger at all or may experience it as an overwhelmingly explosive and dangerous force. He may feel intensely anxious and angry or numb or deadened, and may turn to self-harm as a means of trying to regulate himself and make himself feel better. The questions to be kept in mind are: What does this self-harm do for you? Was it different today compared to yesterday?

I examined the behavioral sequence and the affect state before, during, and after the self-harm episodes in numerous subjects and found that they all bore a striking resemblance in that they served to regulate states of mood, affect, and consciousness. How this occurs was expressed by several subjects in my study (Farber 1995a).

> I feel stress and panic inside. I eat to vomit. My decision to vomit is made before I eat. The vomiting helps the panic and constant running feeling inside. I feel not in balance.

> I starve myself and then eat a regular meal and throw up. i take lots of laxatives, diuretics, and enemas all the time, so nothing stays in me. Sometimes I freak out and think I didn't throw everything up and then I take ipecac and get deathly sick. Then sometimes I start all over again and eat more but usually it's just once—then I get a tranquil feeling and relax.

> [Cutting] is someplace you go when you're about to get too angry or too sad— Nowhere land.

> I eat to numb when feelings are overwhelming. Sometimes bingeing is a lesser alternative to self-mutilation.

> I pick at scabs on my head. I've done this since adolescence. I find the activity soothing—and am trance-like while doing it.

One subject, who identified herself as having multiple personality disorder (MPD), wrote;* "I do not eat a lot at one sitting—but rather eat a little all day— then at night I wake up and vomit. Sometimes I feel very sick and need to vomit but just can't, this is when I will make myself. We eat when memories are coming—when we feel scared of sexual feelings—anger, strong feelings."

---

*Because someone presents herself as having MPD does not necessarily mean that she does, only that she thinks she does.

TRANSITIONAL FUNCTIONS
OF THE BODY IN SELF-HARM

Self-harm behavior serves pretransitional functions, the into-the-mouth and skin contact/tactile sensation (Gaddini 1975, 1978) types of self-soothing that do not promote autonomy but instead promote dependence on and addiction to the self-harm behavior. Both the into-the-mouth and the skin contact/tactile sensation type can be found in many nail and cuticle biters and hair pullers. The experience is quite similar for both. There is an increased sense of tension present immediately before pulling out the hair. For some, tension does not necessarily precede the act but is associated with attempts to resist the urge. There is gratification, pleasure, or a sense of relief when pulling out the hair. Some individuals experience an itchy sensation in the scalp that is relieved by pulling hair out, and others describe it more specifically as an erotic itch. According to the Trichotillomania Learning Center, almost half of hair pullers acknowledge some degree of oral activity involving hair—they may examine the hair root, twirl it off, rub the hair along the mouth, chew the end of the hair, pull the strand between the teeth, or eat it. Nail and cuticle biters describe a similar experience, and so it is not surprising that many hair pullers are also nail biters. Many binge eaters and overeaters do not purge but use their nail biting or hair pulling to serve the same psychic functions as purging.

Pulling out the hair represents an attempt to separate the self from the maternal body, while saving or eating the hair represents an incorporation of and identification with mother and reassurance against her loss. As long as there is hair to pull out and to incorporate, no one else need be depended on to help soothe the suffering self, and no one then will disappoint. The body is there and is reliable, a fetish from which separation becomes impossible. The following was posted on an Internet trichotillomania bulletin board:

> When I am in a bad bad low, I pull (among other acts harmful to my person), but when I pull, I feel worse. I was shocked at the amount of hair I found in the carpet of my car today. When I got out to put gas in my car, my shoe trailed a bunch of hair the likes of which you've never seen and I was horrified. All that used to be on my head! How can I do this to myself! The sad thing is, I'm typically aware of when I'm pulling. I get the urge, I chastise myself for wanting to pull again, but then I say "screw it" and I go ahead and pull anyway. This makes me feel horrible. It seems like a downward spiral.

Eleanor, a 42-year-old divorced mother with a history of childhood sexual and physical abuse, enclosed a letter along with her completed questionnaire. Most of her self-harm was of the tactile kind (hair pulling, cuticle and nail biting, picking at scabs), but she also reported swallowing her hair from the time she was a child. Her hair pulling was so severe that at times she was almost completely bald. She thinks that her hair pulling is in some way connected to her experiences of sexual abuse.

> Before I begin pulling out my hair I may feel bored, anxious, or needing something I can't quite find. . . . I know this is going to make me ugly, but the short-term relief is greater than the knowledge of the long-term results. . . . I'm usually in the car or talking on the phone at home. Sometimes when I read. It's an act of comfort, or the stroking part [of my hair] is. The pulling out part is to me like I want me, and the swallowing part is like I'm getting me back. . . . It doesn't feel like harm. It doesn't hurt. It feels good and I realize when I pull out my hair that I like to do it. I just don't like the way I look afterward.

HOW THE BODY SPEAKS

Speaking of one's experience makes it real. To know what is inside oneself, one's thoughts, sensations, and feelings, one must be able to speak about one's experience and about one's inner world. But because some people may not be sufficiently articulate, they supplement their verbal communication with gestures or body language.

Self-harmers have a broad range of ego development. Some can speak articulately and think symbolically, manifesting a high level of ego functioning in some areas. But when it comes to talking about their inner experience, they regress to the use of operatory functioning and concrete unexpressive language, becoming alexithymic. Their regression from the symbolic mode serves as an attack on the process of creating meaning (Woodruff 1998). Those who are arrested at a lower level of development, who have never developed the ability to use words symbolically, are also prone to using their bodies to speak expressively about their experience, and they too regress to a more primitive and dedifferentiated level.

Experiences of neglect and trauma cause pain, but that pain has frequently been silenced. Instead, it tunnels underground in the body and repeats itself in different form, such as linguistic gestures or uttered sounds. Scratching, cutting, or starving oneself; vomiting; drug or alcohol abuse; getting involved in abusive relationships; and scarring, tattooing, or repeatedly piercing one's skin—all these are gestural articulations of trauma that need to be decoded as such. Pain is written on and in the body through emaciation, scars, violent cramps, tattoos, piercings, brandings, and whippings. These gestures say what cannot be said in words. They acquire layer upon layer of cultural meaning. In order to navigate the terrain of self-harm, one needs to become familiar with the language spoken by the symptoms. Language is based in gesture and utterances, that is, the basis of language is gestural (Merleau-Ponty 1962). First there was gesture and uttered sound and then there was the word. Between the most primitive gestures and symbolic language is a large spectrum.

In response to the question about how the bingeing and purging usually happens, one subject in my study wrote this primitive, concrete reply: "Yellow the color . . . Yellow good cheese danishes, chicken eggs, scrambled & fried, corn muffins, rolls, f.fries, potatoes, bread, breaded fish, corn flakes, cake, cheese, cheeseburgers, grapefruit juice, peaches." To most people, a list of foods that are yellow is meaningless. Presumably the subject was writing about "layering" her food by color, a ritual written about elsewhere in this book. I can presume this because I have supplied the missing linguistic links and because I know about this practice. That is, I have created meaning out of a written description of primitive gestures. Translating this into implications for treatment, this is what the therapist would need to do if the patient spoke this way. That is, the subject's response suggests a psychotic regression, an inability to use secondary process thinking to respond, and the therapist will need to lend her ego functions to the patient with the aim of promoting in the patient an identification with the therapist's ego functions.

Here are the words of several who seem to have virtually no awareness that their self-harm does something for them, very concrete responses but less primitive than the one above. When asked the same question one subject wrote very concretely: "I'll go for hours, days without eating, then buy a whole bunch of candy that's easy to throw up. Eat all the candy I can fit in my stomach, drink some water, and throw up in the toilet, shower or sink." "I haven't binged for several years. I restrict my food, and after every meal I stick my finger down my throat and throw up." "I pick up a razor and cut. No thought and no feeling. I am drawn to it." The awareness of having no thought and no feeling indicates some thought. Another wrote: "I find all the sweet and fattening stuff around the house and eat as much of it as I can, but not so much that others will notice that it is gone. I chew quickly and drink a lot of liquids. I wait about 1/2 hour, then go to the toilet and put my fingers down my throat. . . . I have six scars on my wrist about ½ inch in length. They kind of look like the rungs on a ladder."

For many self-harmers, the words I feel *fat*, *disgusting*, and *grotesque* have become easy, culturally acceptable utterances that serve as a cover for dysphoric affect. Fat is not a feeling, but for many American girls and women, it has become a short-circuited way of transmitting what they have difficulty in using symbolic language to convey—that they are feeling sad, depressed, angry, guilty, anxious, or ashamed. When asked to say something about how the act of bingeing and purging usually happens, many spoke of feeling fat or disgusting prior to, during, or after the binge, or feeling fat when they ate very little, or having thoughts about how fattening the food was. One subject wrote, "I eat and eat and eat for about 2 hours, then I feel disgusting and fat and throw it all up." Another wrote, "Starts by picking at things, then speeds up. Eating fast triggers me. It gets rapid till my pulse is going fast and I have a buzz. Then intense guilt overwhelms me and I really have to fight the urge to undo my terrible act (by vomiting) for fear of weight gain and other terrible things." We would have to wonder what terrible act (sexual? cannibalistic? murderous?) she needs to "undo" by vomiting, and we would have to wonder what are the other terrible things that she cannot name.

Weight gain is only the least, and perhaps the most easily mentionable, of the "evils." An 18-year-old girl about to leave home for an Ivy League college embellished the words *fat* and *disgusting* with a few minimally emotionally expressive words—*nervous, edgy, tense*: "I come home, feel nervous, edgy, disgusting. Mom and everyone else is busy so I can't talk to anyone. I go and eat to shut my nervousness up. Then regardless of how little I ate, I feel bloated, tense, disgusting, fat, nauseous, and force myself into the bathroom to vomit. Sometimes I don't even binge, just vomit after breakfast or lunch because I feel too fat or nauseous or generally too disgusting for words."

Others wrote about their self-harm also using somewhat expressive language. Some spoke of how their self-harm served to avert suicide, and several of those who identified themselves as having MPD explained that the different personalities created an equilibrium, a system of checks and balances in which punishment was meted out to the self at the same time that suicide was averted. Some of the most bizarre, severe, and potentially lethal kinds of self-harm were reported by those who claimed to have MPD, the behavior only a hint of the bizarre and "soul-murder" experiences they have had. The MPD is the ultimate in dissociated "doublethink."

Susan, a 41-year-old divorced woman who identifies herself as having MPD, lives on disability payments. She reported a history of child sexual and physical abuse and family violence, daily incidents too many to remember. She wrote that she cuts and burns herself; sticks herself with pins; bites her nails and cuticles until they are infected and bloody; starves herself and binges; purges with vomiting, laxatives, and enemas; and has deliberately overdosed on alcohol and pills:

> Extreme stress builds up. Tranquilizers don't help. I get suicidal. To stop the suicidal feelings I smoke marijuana, which puts me in a better mood but causes me to eat too much, as guilt and punishment. . . . I thought O.D.-ing was an easy way to kill myself but I have been on life supports a number of times and still survived. Now I think a gun would be most efficient. . . . [Regarding her self-mutilation] I'm in a trance or hypnotized. Or I feel I'm not a real human being, but unworthy of life and subhuman. The trance usually starts after I have the strong negative feelings. I have strong feelings of suicide—usually triggered by memories of abuse from my childhood. Because I am a multiple, voices suggest ways to hurt myself without killing myself. (1) Sometimes it is to prevent a suicide attempt. (2) Sometimes it is a punishment. (3) Sometimes it is anger at my body for being attractive—I try to destroy its beauty so men won't be attracted. . . . I have cut every part of my body. Some are patterns or designs— especially on wrists, ankles. Up and down legs. Most patterns involve numerology—cuts look the same but must have unequal numbers that add up to a prime.

Carola, a 21-year-old high school senior who also identified herself as having MPD and a childhood history of ongoing sexual and physical abuse and family violence, wrote that she began vomiting at age 5 or 6, and at around that time began having skin rashes, banging her head, refusing to eat, and severely biting her nails and cuticles. Between ages 6 and 9 she began to ingest cleaning fluids, crushed glass, and food that she knew had spoiled, and injected bleach into her arm, although she is not certain if she had the intention of killing herself. She also began cutting herself, sticking herself with pins, and having frequent accidents. At 10 she began purging with ipecac, laxatives, diuretics, and enemas; burning and hitting herself; and cutting in her vagina and throat. In the year in which she participated in my study she deliberately injured herself more than fifty times, requiring a great deal of medical attention. She reports that the self-injury makes her feel somewhat better than before and that the purging makes her feel much better. Shopping used to make her feel much better but not any more. Her self-harm seems to be telling us that she felt alone, orphaned, damaged, and dirty:

> I "stock up" on food for several days or weeks, usually hiding it under my bed (though I live alone). I feel very guilty when even buying food. Then something will make me "have to" eat it all (usually I barely taste it). Then I use a stomach feeding tube (for orphaned puppies) down my throat to make myself vomit. I vomit for at least an hour. . . . I have also attempted to inject bleach into my arm. I feel dirty inside, especially after eating. I need to be cleaned out. I also feel the need to punish myself. . . . I have MPD and I usually just become numb before I switch. Katy, the alter that does this [self-injury], states that she does it to prove to herself that she is real, has blood, feels pain (physically), etc. . . . I am usually "half there" for a short period of time before I am completely gone and another alter takes over. I don't remember any of the injuring. . . . I am not actually present when it happens, but after, I "wake up" confused and bleeding or whatever. I feel tremendously guilty and I am the one who has to clean up the mess, go to the hospital for stitches, etc. However, I do feel a sense of relief after the cutting has occurred, and I have cut myself a small amount to prevent anything worse from happening. . . . I do not feel any physical pain when the injury has been self-inflicted.

In contrast, Vicky wrote about how her psychotherapy helped her to become more aware of how her self-harm expressed and regulated feelings and helped her to soothe herself, if only briefly:

> When I binge and purge, it is always to relieve feelings that seem intolerable, whether it be anxiety, fear, loneliness, and sometimes feeling really good. When I first started I had no idea why I was engaging in this behavior, but as I progressed in therapy I came to connect my behaviors with other experiences. By bingeing and purging many things happen. (1) Focus is on something other than feelings (distraction). (2) Feelings repressed seem to be "let out." (3) I become numb and disso-

ciated in the process. (4) I felt calmer afterwards, at least for a short period of time. (5) I felt "clean" afterwards. . . . I felt like I couldn't feel, like maybe I wasn't really alive—by burning myself, I felt something! A validation I was alive. . . . I feel like I am in a trance, like it's not really me who is harming myself. I know I wasn't the person that I usually am. I feel very dissociated and distant from myself. . . . I had repetitive thoughts about burning myself, and I wanted to know if I would see it when I was burned (I did, but I could make myself dissociate and then not feel). Afterwards, I was proud of myself and and felt I had done something that was special. It felt good to feel bad. It's strange but I felt strong for being able to burn myself—also I had a secret that no one else knew about. . . . I felt like I deserved to feel pain. The laxative abuse was the most harmful because of the severity of my abuse. I couldn't see the laxatives as being self-abusive until I was in therapy a long time, but the physical pain of laxatives was worse than anything else, including burning, that I did to myself. It felt better to be in pain than to feel good.

APPROACHING SYMBOLIC USE OF LANGUAGE

Self-harm can develop as a gestural articulation of trauma (McLane 1996) as well as a perverse attack on the creation of meaning (Woodruff 1998). "We come alive as human beings through our capacity to symbolize experience, but the cost of this capacity is to lose the immediacy of experience" (Woodruff 1998, p. 3), to lose that which is desired, the illusory experience of fusion with the object. When the immediacy of the bodily experience is given up, the illusory but thrilling experience of fusion with the object is given up too. This is a tremendous loss, as nothing else can be as intense as the immediacy of bodily experience. To accept that one cannot have what is so desperately wanted is to mourn the loss of sadomasochistic excitement and to use language to give meaning to the loss. Some individuals have found that their self-harm behavior has helped them articulate to themselves and to others what it is they have lost. That is, the self-harm has been an invaluable tool for helping them bridge the gap from bodily articulation of pain to verbal symbolic articulation of pain. When self-harm can function in this way, it can be considered to serve transitional functions (see Chapter 16).

In the following account, the experience of purging is somewhat less expressive and more concrete than the experience of self-injury.

Judy, an 18-year-old, is about to go off to a competitive college in another state. The only potentially traumatic experience she reported was the separation of her parents when she was a young child; however, she is unsure if she had had coercive sexual contact as a child or adolescent. She recalled being a poor eater in early childhood. She began restricting her food intake during the latency-age period, and began inducing vomiting at age 13 or 14. The purging began at the same time she began mutilating herself in various ways—hitting herself, squeezing pimples, biting her hands and the inside of her cheek, and scratching her arms, legs, and stomach with her fingernails, scissors, glass, and knives. She mutilated herself several times in the year in which she participated in the study, and has never required medical attention for her injuries. She mutilated herself a few times shortly after purging. Although she reports that "spacing out or going numb" was something she used to do as a child, only occasionally does she currently space out, and not before or during mutilating herself. While mutilating herself she feels as if everything is too much. Over two years after the onset of her purging and self-mutilation, she began bingeing. She does not often binge, drink, use drugs, shop or exercise when feeling bad. She will occasionally eat when feeling bad but not large amounts. The purge is usually the most intense part of the bulimic experience. Occasionally she will steal loose candies from the supermarket. At times sex makes her feel better. She was the subject quoted above, who reported that she felt "nervous, edgy, and disgusting" about how much she ate and then forced herself to vomit.

In answer to the questions about her experience of mutilating herself, she wrote that she never has a sense of not feeling real, just feeling too much, everything is too much.

> An overwhelming guilt, self-hatred, blame, or anger at outside things (other people, uncontrollable events) rises up in me. I feel helpless in some bizarre sense underneath this wave, and feel trapped, as if this is the only way to let it out, the only sensible way to let the wave pass on is to punish myself, see my own blood well up out of the scratches, feeling nothing else to be done. [I feel] tense, as if I don't belong in my own body, hate—hate—hated myself—I feel frantically horrible . . . hatred, confusion, frenzy. [With the physical pain comes] release of hatred of self/release of anger at others, i.e., release of emotional pain when actualized as physical pain.

She is more emotionally expressive when writing about her self-mutilation than when writing about the bulimic behavior. The fact that she occasionally mutilates herself shortly after an episode of purging alone or eating and purging suggests that the purging, even though a more intense experience than the eating, is at times not sufficient to calm her, and so she must up the ante by going on to mutilate herself. Her emotional expressiveness is associated more with self-mutilation than with the purging, suggesting that she *needs* to self-mutilate in order to get more in touch with her emotions. It would seem that for her, the act of mutilating herself serves to help her body to speak to her mind and helps her to feel and express the emotions verbally. It would seem that verbalizing these emotions and exploring their origins in treatment might help her develop greater ability to express herself symbolically, lessening the need for the self-harm.

BODILY REENACTMENTS SPEAK TO THE SELF

In addition to serving self-regulatory and expressive functions, some experiences of self-harm can serve as a means of reenacting split-off dissociated experiences. For example, here is one subject's answer to the question, If you like, please tell me in your own words how the act of bingeing and purging usually happens.

It starts with an image that flashes into the mind. The fear immediately follows, the internal chanting, "That didn't happen to me. It didn't happen." Panic starts to rise in my throat like poison. I have to eat. But you're not supposed to do that. I don't care. I jump into my car and fly to the supermarket. I hurry through the aisles, grabbing things off the shelves, throwing them into my cart. All I can think about is getting home again so I can eat. My body trembles in anticipation.

Once home, I begin the routine. I know it well. I start the rice pilaf on the stove and put one frozen pizza in the microwave, one in the oven. On the table I have all the makings for cheese subs, along with a bag of Doritos, jar of picante sauce, and jalapeno cheese dip. There is a box of chocolates for dessert, which I start into now, while waiting for my rice to cook. I can put the subs together while munching on Doritos and dip. Today I tell myself I'll have only two sandwiches, although in my heart I know I'll eat all six, as I always do. Oh, there goes the timer on the stove. At last, the rice and pizza are ready. I've already eaten two subs, ¼ bag of Doritos, and half a box of chocolates. I spread my feast on the table before me. Oh God, I am so happy. There is nothing in this entire world that can make me more content than the food I love. I am a queen and these are my riches spread before me. I have all that I have ever needed or wanted in my life. I am so very thankful that I am entitled to such joy, such pure satisfaction. I can't get enough. I begin to stuff the food in great gulps in my mouth: six subs, two pizzas, an entire box of rice pilaf, the bag of Doritos, picante sauce, cheese dip, the chocolates, and the two-liter bottle of Diet Coke. I can't get enough. I don't even know what it is that I'm eating anymore. Was that a chocolate? Or pizza? It doesn't matter. I just know that I can't stop. I gorge myself as though I'll never eat again. I cannot get enough. I continue to eat in a frenzy until every last bit of food is gone. It is then that I look in horror at the mess left on the table and realize what I've done.

You've done it again, you fat cow. You're so weak, such a loser. The self-hatred sets in. Worse than that is the panic—all those calories. I can feel them padding themselves onto my body. My hips are fatter than when I sat down to eat ten minutes ago. Or was it a half hour ago? An hour ago? How long has it been? I don't know. I lost track of time. All I know is that I have to get rid of the food. I move my body, groaning in protest, from the kitchen to the bathroom. How many times am I going to do this? Why can't I just stop? I will, but not now. I'll just get rid of it today, and I'll never do it again.

I am an expert at this. No finger in the throat for me. No ipecac syrup. I just tighten my stomach muscles and on cue, it all starts to come. There is so much relief when I see the food coming out looking somewhat similar to the way it did when it went in. This means it hasn't begun digesting yet; the calories are not yet packing themselves onto my body. I kneel there, my head hanging in the toilet bowl, heaving. The vomit splashes me in the face. I am so disgusted. I have vomit on my face and that is still not enough to make me stop. I keep tightening my stomach muscles. The food keeps coming. My face and hair are speckled with tiny bits of vomit. I hate myself. I am so very tired of living my life in the toilet bowl. This is what you deserve, you fat cow. I flush the toilet so it won't overflow and begin the process again. I will flush six or seven times more before I'm through. I briefly wonder what my upstairs neighbors think of a single person flushing so many times. I'm embarrassed but not enough to stop.

Anything with cheese is always hard to get up. It packs in so tightly. Sometimes it lodges in my throat, cutting off my air supply. I can't force it up. I can't push it back down. For a split second, I know I am going to die. This is how they will find me, my head immersed in vomit. This is my disgrace. A life of struggling to survive, flushed down the toilet. *It's what you deserve.* The hateful voice that I know as my own continues to batter and abuse me. I finally force the cheese out. Relief. This time I did not die. I should stop now but there is still more food left. I'll just get that out, and then I'll stop. I'll never do it again.

Finally I rise to my feet, weak and covered in a cold sweat. I make my way to the bedroom and collapse onto the bed.

While it cannot be known with certainty if the episode truly is a reenactment because we do not have the actual clinical material that would tell us, the sequence of events and thought process strongly suggest that it is.

The flashback image of sexual abuse intrudes into consciousness, evoking fearful hyperarousal. She shifts from the image to an obsession with eating, thus shifting the locus of anxiety from the disturbing abuse image to food, the lesser of the two evils. She must eat in order to distance herself from this terrible image. The anxiety shifts to getting the food for the binge, which in turn shifts into an erotic experience. "My body trembles in anticipation." On the surface it would seem that her body trembles in anticipation of the food she will consume. What seems sufficiently disguised is that the anticipation of the binge allows her to reexperience the probable excitement of anticipating the sexual act in a way that is acceptable to her conscience. Driving to the store, shopping for food, cooking the rice and preparing the sandwiches are disguised ritualized forms of foreplay, a way of anticipating what she will put into her body that masks the forbidden and dissociated pleasure in what others had put into her body. The initial joy at the beginning of the binge represents the exhilaration of an oedipal triumph and illusory sense of omnipotence and satisfaction of all her needs. "I have all that I have ever needed or wanted in my life."

This joy quickly turns sour as what had seemed to be the satisfaction of her incestuous desires soon became fraught with dysphoria, causing her to stuff ever greater quantities of food in herself. The triumph has become instead an indiscriminate desperate craving that can never be satisfied. Such precocious sexual hyperarousal cannot be satisfied and only leaves her feeling extremely aroused with no hope of release. Reality intrudes, confronting her with the actuality of the binge and then the punitive self-hatred mantra starts: "fat cow," "loser." She immediately tries to undo what she has done in a frenzy to "get rid of it," to undo the sexual act and cleanse herself of the shame she feels. She resolves that she will never do this again, but she is drawn back to it, attached to the pain of physical and emotional suffering, attached to the degradation of engaging in forbidden acts, attached to the shame of the forbidden pleasure she experienced, attached to the need for punishment. The repeated vomiting, the convulsive heaving do not really cleanse her but only serve to immerse her more in her own degradation. She degrades herself with vomit the way others may have degraded her with semen. She wallows in it while at the same time desperately trying to cleanse herself. What seems to have been an exciting reenactment of her childhood incestuous experiences created only an increased self-loathing.

It should not be surprising to discover that this same woman also turned to self-cutting to relieve her pain, and wrote equally articulately about the function the cutting served for her and how she ultimately was able to give it up. She said that she is going to write a book on self-mutilation.

I would like to share some of my thoughts and feelings—words from a former cutter. I've not self-injured in almost four years now—four years of intense personal growth and healing. In this time I've come to several realizations.

I believed that cutting relieved the excruciating pain. It didn't. It only acted as a deferral. I now know that there was/is *no way* to avoid it. Not only did I eventually have to go through the pain which I sought so desperately to obliterate it from my consciousness *anyway*, but I also had to deal with the pain of knowing that I will live with the scars for the rest of my life, scars that make me think twice about swimming in a swimming pool or wearing shorts on a brutally hot day when around people whom I don't know well. Scars that will sometimes bring me up short in the middle of some happy, contented moment to slap me in the face with the old pain. Scars that label me abuser—for I did, in fact, physically abuse an innocent who never deserved it—I abused myself.

I believed that cutting was a healthy alternative to suicide. These days, I imagine a dear friend, struggling with horrific memories of sexual abuse and the daily fight not to end her life. I don't offer her a razor blade to help her make it through another day. I offer her my love, compassion, hugs. I offer my help in managing the practical aspects of safety: calling a therapist, arranging hospitalization. Did I deserve anything less? I believe that isolation was the smoke screen that made self-injury appear to be an attractive, healthy choice.

I believed that I had no choice back then. Believe me, I have not forgotten the horrible, overwhelming urges. I *did* feel as though I had no choice—and perhaps then I truly didn't. Cutting seemed to fulfill so many needs and substitute for so many skills that I simply did not possess. I still have the same past today that I had back then. (Unfortunately, I was never able to come up with a way to change that—though not for lack of trying.) I still experience and deal with the pain. I made a choice nearly four years ago. That choice was to not only keep my physical body alive, but to let my spirit and my heart also live. I didn't wake up one day and "choose" to never cut again. It was a terribly long process in which I chose to learn new coping skills, to take the frightening risk of letting others into my life, risking abandonment. I made some mistakes, trusted the wrong people, but chose to keep trying. I chose to learn new ways of communicating and expressing my pain, to say "I'm hurting. I'm frightened," rather than choosing to write my pain on my body in blood. I've chosen to cry out loud when that's what I need to do.

Flo, a 27-year-old woman with a master's degree wrote about what seemed to be reenactments of ritual abuse. She wrote that she lives on disability payments and was raised with a combination of Protestant and satanic beliefs and practices by a mother who had MPD and was involved in a satanic cult. As an adolescent she "almost became a Roman Catholic nun." She wrote that ethnically she is Jewish and currently identifies herself that way. During or after bingeing she has ingested cleaning fluids and other poisonous cleaning agents, vinegar, decaffeinated coffee to which she is allergic, and food that has spoiled. She wrote that others had carved a Star of David on her right thigh along with many other burns and cuts, and that she used to cut satanic and Latin phrases into her legs. She also has burned and stuck herself. She describes what it is like when she cuts herself: "I can get so dissociated I'm completely out of my body and into the past (abuse)—memories of chanting, being hurt, and numbing my body to cope become real to the present situation and I'm in the same dissociated 'trancelike' state."

REPETITIVE THEMES

From my study, my clinical work, and from the media, I have heard repeated thematic undercurrents that made clearer the paradoxes that can be embodied in an act of self-harm. Some of the most prominent threads have to do with the dialectics of inner and outer: the inner "true" self and the outer "superficial" self, boundaries between inside and outside, and outer scars as expression of inner feelings. Others have to do with doing and undoing, good and evil, purity and filth, fear of sexuality and expression of sexuality, pain and pleasure, physical pain and emotional pain, having control and losing control, self-protection and self-harm, sadism and masochism, wish for success and the fear of success, wanting to be invisible and wanting to be seen, shame and purification, deadness and aliveness, and self-destruction and self-healing. The theme of punishment to achieve a sense of justice was pervasive, as was the theme of balancing the scales between good and evil, justice and injustice, right and wrong. Often several such themes were woven together in one narrative.

Inner and Outer, Show and Tell

For many the physical pain and disfigurement represented by their scars and emaciation was infinitely preferable to feeling the inner emotional pain. One woman who stated she has MPD wrote that the blood she deliberately sheds is a visible substitute for "tears we couldn't cry." A number of subjects wrote that the scars and injuries visible on their bodies made their inner pain visible, made the inside and the outside congruent, while others wrote that they injured parts of their body that would not be readily visible.

Georgia wrote that she picks vigorously at her face shortly before she has to make an important appearance, such as for a job interview, yet she had plastic surgery to remove the facial scar someone else inflicted on her. An attractive model/actress, she sent professional photos of herself in seductive garb and poses, in contrast with the self-hatred she struggles with, about which she wrote at length. She wrote of her distrust of men. She starves herself and smokes pot to control the compulsion to eat but nonetheless binges and purges with vomiting, laxatives, and enemas. She had tried to kill herself and used to cut and pick at herself in her teens and hurt herself in other ways:

> Eating habits coincided with onset of severe depression. . . . My depression has been successfully treated but the eating habits continue. . . . I just want to concentrate on my career, the gym, and kicking this habit. I take vitamins, fat burners, and ephedrine hydrochloride to get me moving. I take high doses of vitamin C and Glutofac—a high-potency metabolic supplement with anti-oxidants . . . with a lot of minerals.
>
> I used to cry hysterically and punch and hit myself, throw my entire body into a wall repeatedly, slap and hit (clenched fists) my head and face, bite myself extremely hard, punch myself in the stomach repeatedly, scream at myself in a mirror as though it was another person. . . . I included pictures because one of my biggest problems was getting people to realize how easy it is to hide as long as you look okay. People should never judge by looks because if someone is intelligent and can paint a pretty picture, people don't suspect anything! Then, when tragedy strikes everyone is shocked. "Such a beautiful, happy girl. Why would she do such a thing? She had no problems." Sure!

The external evidence of self-harm serves as a concrete physical representation of emotional pain. The outer gestures articulate the inner pain. One woman wrote:

> I feel hurt, like I'm in trouble, or like I'm exposed (e.g., publically criticized, made to feel stupid or worthless) and want to be invisible. Yet at the same time since I'm sort of half "better." I can no longer completely repress or deny or split off when I feel ignored, awkward, chastised, or "wrong," etc. So I hurt myself to show I'm stupid,

worthless and also to *show* I'm hurt—something that never "showed" in my past even though the abuse was severe. . . . I think enough not to do things that "show" if I have any public appearances where I'd have to explain it. . . . I was never noticed or believed enduring tremendous pain from abuse and I still believe that unless you can "show" a sort of wound no one will believe how bad the pain is.

Some self-harmers find their self-harm to be more ego-alien, less acceptable to the ego. Many of those who do practice the less dangerous, more repetitive hair pulling, skin picking, and nail/cuticle biting. Sherri wrote the following on a hair-pulling (trichotillomania), bulletin board on the Internet:

> I think the saddest thing about trich is that it makes us fear looking anyone directly in the eyes. And this is extremely hard on high school kids because, at that age, outside appearance is so important to everyone that it could make or break a young person's self-esteem. I know how it feels to constantly keep your eyes roaming so that no one is permitted to look into them. I know what it's like to check the bathroom mirror over and over to make sure my "eyebrows" haven't rubbed off. I know the fear you have to hide as you try to slink behind your hand, resting your face on it with your elbows on a desk just a few feet away from a friend who you just KNOW is wondering "What the HELL is wrong with her?!? Why doesn't she have any eyelashes and eyebrows?" I know the sick feeling in your stomach you can get from walking in on a conversation your friends are having about mascara or eyebrow waxing. In high school, it seems like you need approval from everyone—and whether or not they even pretend to like you is based on superficial and silly things.
> It's true—the eyes ARE the windows to the soul! I used to believe that because of trich I was a freak and that having no eyelashes meant my "soul" seemed ugly and shabby to anyone who tried to glance at it. I would positively CRINGE everytime I thought someone was looking near my eyes. But now I see that a little thing like having sparse eyebrows or bald eyelids could never tarnish the beauty of my soul. No matter how plain and bare the frame is, what's behind the window is just as beautiful. And (just maybe?) with a less ornate frame, it's easier for others to see the vulnerable and beautifully human soul each one of us posesses.

Several women who have had mastectomies have refused reconstructive surgery, choosing instead to have designs tattooed on their chests. For some these tattoos symbolize that their sense of themselves as women goes deeper than what one sees on the surface. Some human immunodeficiency virus (HIV) patients announce their status in a very personal and permanent way, through an HIV tattoo. These markings speak of attempts to banish the shame and secrecy that often accompanies an HIV or cancer diagnosis, and challenge the public's notions of health and illness in a provocative way at a time when newer treatments have made living with these illnesses a reality, not necessarily a death sentence. Such tattoos can also make a preemptive strike against social or sexual rejection by disclosing the wearer's status and thus screening out those who might be frightened away by it.

My Body, Myself: Control and Loss of Control

For many, harming their own bodies represents an active means of being in control of one's own body, a way of taking control of it just as others controlled it in the past. Jean, a 34-year-old married woman with a long history of severe childhood physical and sexual abuse, wrote about her disordered eating and self-mutilation:

> I cut my wrist while in sexual abuse treatment (inpatient). Just had to do it once. Wanted to experience this pain. Some kind of fascination, something special. Before going into treatment, my husband had to hide our knives. I hadn't had memories, yet had an overwhelming desire to cut my wrists. . . . I just want a release or I feel so angry. Often it's either I want to binge or cut. I'd probably cut more if my husband weren't around. . . . I wish I could get away with it more—you lose your freedom, people lock you up. You lose your credibility. It feels like I'm empowered, like I'm making a statement, "This is MY BODY. I can do with it as I choose and you can't stop me!"

Joan, a 41-year-old married woman with a similar history, identified herself as having MPD. Starving herself, purging, burning and cutting herself all give her a needed sense of control. Her bingeing represents a loss of control:

> After days of forcing myself not to eat or eating as little as I can to keep from being dizzy, I lose control. I think to myself, eat just a little, then stop. I'll be OK. But after one bite I lose track of time and it feels horrible. The sick "full feeling" is horrible! It feels like I'll explode I have to get it out! It feels like I'm suffocating and dying! . . .
> I have taken water pills and Ex-Lax to the point of passing out. Yes at times I have wanted to die. To me, it would be the only freedom and peace I have ever known. Until that time comes, this is my way of control. . . .
> [About her burning and cutting], it's a feeling of not being real. I have a need to prove to myself that I am by bleeding. It's my way of being in control. This time I control the stop start, not the abusers. . . .
> I pull away to the hiding place with the others. The body is our unit. We don't wish to die, we only want to be real and control how we feel. . . .
> Rejection—we feel unloved, unneeded and therefore [why be]. If some of our others were not watchful, many of the cutters would have destroyed the body by now, we have compromised—(1) We cut but not to harm, only to release pressure. (2) The watchers will make sure the cutters stay in control. (3) We have rules for the extent and amount of damage. . . . To us, controlling the body shows the abusers they didn't win.

Acquiring a tattoo or body piercing is for many adolescents and marginalized people a way of proclaiming ownership of their bodies. Long before tattooing and piercing became popular, it was part of initiation rites in some black fraternities to tattoo or cut identifying marks in initiates, a volitional sign of connection with similarly marked Africans who had been taken from their tribes by slave traders. The Nazis tattooed the Jews, but today we see Jews wearing their Jewish identity on their tattooed bodies. For example, a young photographer, Marina Vainschtein, has made her body a living witness to the Holocaust. Tattooed over much of her body is a Star of David, an angel of death wearing a gas mask, naked corpses hanging from gallows, and images of some of the medical experiments performed on children. The event that triggered using her body to speak so dramatically about her Jewish identity was hearing a Holocaust survivor speak at her high school about having survived seven death camps (Strong 1998). It can also be a sign of another significant life transition in adulthood, of separating the self from others who have been exercising control over the individual's personal choices.

> [My friend and I] both talked semi-seriously about getting a tattoo. I mentioned it to my husband and he was adamantly opposed—only certain seedy types get tattoos. He didn't want someone else touching my body intimately, which is what a tattoo would involve . . . even if it were just my arm. He was against it, which made me even more for it. . . . I finally really decided sometime last year when my marriage was coming apart. It started to be a symbol of taking my body back. I was thinking that about the time I got divorced would be a good time to do it. [Sanders 1989, p. 43]

Big and Small, Fat and Thin

The dichotomous issues of wanting to be important and noticed, on the one hand, and wanting to fade into the woodwork and become invisible, on the other, are often expressed in terms of size and weight. The issue of being too large and taking up too much space is often expressed as being too fat. And yet for many who claim to hate being fat, on an unconscious level being fat is what they want. Being fat may mean being a person of substance and taking up space, while being thin means shrinking down to nothing, not noticeable. Yet for many, becoming as thin as possible has become the ultimate in perfection. Those who are unusually fat or thin capture our attention.

In Günter Grass's novel The Tin Drum, Oskar, the protagonist, gets smaller and smaller and smaller inside himself because he has no sense of self. Alice in Wonderland experiments with becoming unusually large and unusually small. Peggy Claude-Pierre noted of the many anorectic patients writing to her at the Montreaux Clinic in Canada, that as their eating disorder progresses, their words become tinier and tinier, as if they were trying to disappear altogether. Sometimes they include an apology, asking to be forgiven for the size of their handwriting: "I didn't want it to take up space." This is a phenomenon I noted too in the handwriting on the questionnaires and letters sent to me by the subjects in my study (Farber 1995a). Many of the most chronic patients, who had the most severe bulimic and self-mutilating behavior had very small, constricted handwriting, and many tended to use lower-case letters for their name and the pronoun *I*, an expression of their feeling small and insignificant. Claude-Pierre (1997) reported that as the patients at her clinic start to get better, their writing changes noticeably to a more usual size.

The other side of the coin is that one of the many functions that excess fat serves for compulsive eaters is to make them large, so that they take up space and are "substantial." Being fat may have unconscious meanings of being somebody, getting noticed. Not surprisingly, as children, they were not acknowledged in their families; what *was* acknowledged was their increasing obesity. Although being taken by their mothers to diet doctors and Weight Watchers was exceedingly painful to them, it was better to be noticed for being fat than not noticed at all. Many found that as they lost weight, there was an anxiety about being thin. Losing weight was associated with loss of a sense of themselves and a loss of maternal attention. For some, not having a barrier of fat around them made them sexually and emotionally vulnerable, just a body, a thing to be used for the gratification of others. Some used their fat as a barrier to intimacy, putting a distance between themselves and others who might hurt them. Jackie, an obese bulimic who cut and picked at herself and has walked in front of cars and driven recklessly, wrote about how her fat protects her: "I am medically considered to be morbidly obese. At 5'8" I weigh 300 pounds. . . . I eat to protect myself from men and sexual come-ons. I gained weight and snuck food at about nine years of age and became fat quickly after being raped by my father at age 8. . . . I've been in the hospital for dissociative disorders. . . . I've been living in hell most of my life it seems, and I'm now involved in a very exhausting uphill struggle for survival and healing."

A woman in her late thirties in treatment with me recalled that her fat served as a means of getting the holding and affection she did not know she craved in adolescence. Her mother, emotionally and at times physically abusive, did not notice her unhappiness but did notice her corpulence, taking her to diet doctors for shots of amphetamines and strict diets. Some boys teased her for being fat but also knew that if they spoke affectionately to her, they could use her sexually. Because she so wanted to be touched and held, their caresses were far preferable to her mother's slaps. During these incidents she felt cared for and special and could "forget" temporarily that she was a fat girl.

For some, becoming exceedingly thin serves a protective function sexually by keeping men at a distance. Losing enough weight to become amenorrheic was an aim for Kate, a 27-year-old who became anorectic at age 12 and bulimic at age 18, during a period when she witnessed family violence and suffered loss of a parent.

Food has controlled my life 14 years. At 5'5" my weight has fluctuated from a brief low of 92 to a high of 135 pounds. Above 125 pounds feels hopeless and suicidal. My period completely stopped for three years as my body fat was evaluated at 5 percent. This past year, I have been heavy. My period returned in April. The flow is *much* heavier than before and lasts longer. . . . I am struggling, but determined to lose weight and drop my body fat to a level where my period will stop. I was raped at age 21 or 22 and have not been sexually active since.

Masochism and Sadism

Sadomasochistic practices can serve to punish, but even though they flirt with death and can lead to death, they can also serve the will to live. Eating disorders have been found to serve as punishment for and sabotage of creative, financial, or professional success (Bergmann 1988, Krueger 1988). Georgia (introduced above), wrote how she must masochistically punish herself for her success in her acting and modeling career.

> It always stems from a feeling of anxiety, frustration, or lack of self-worth. I love that empty feeling. Also, it keeps me from being successful. When I feel as though I'm accomplishing something or have a potential success, I feel out of control, and must check myself. I eat things I'd enjoy, except they are forbidden, even in small quantities. Hopefully soon I can conquer these impulses. It's very methodical, hard, and uncomfortable. I use objects (spoons, toothbrushes, tongue depressors) in order to make my body release the food . . . immediately after a binge.

The theme of the self-harm serving extreme sadomasochistic aims is clear in some responses. Celia, a mother of three with a long history of childhood sexual and physical abuse and family violence, wrote of having frequent accidents, biting her nails, and cutting, sticking, and burning herself. She wrote that she "had affairs then emotionally abused self and cut with razors, threw self down the stairs." She has carved the words *hate, bad,* and *slut* on her left arm, and *hate* on her left leg. "The last time I cut was after sex that I didn't really want. . . . When I cut I feel like (1) I deserve to be hurt. (2) Takes me away from my emotional pain. It bothers me to see the scars on my body. The word *HATE* is so well cut into my arm that it will never go away. Sometimes I feel like my purpose in life was to be abused. . . . Two men, possibly three, sexually assaulted me at different times in my life."

Becky, a woman with a similar history, wrote of her masochistic assaults on her body, including picking at her skin, picking the skin off her lips, chewing the inside of her mouth, and shoving bottles up her vagina. "I usually start feeling self-hatred and want to destroy myself and whatever I choose, be it sexual mutilation, bingeing and purging, chewing at the inside of mouth, etc.—these feelings become so strong and overwhelming that I feel the only way out is to give into the self-destructive act."

Julie, another woman with a similarly horrific history, also wrote of her assaults on her body including her genitals, as if punishing them for having been sexually abused. She has binged and purged severely, starved herself, picked at her skin and cuticles, cut and burned herself, and poured hot wax on her eyes and face.

Regarding the bingeing and purging. Sometimes I get up in the A.M. and it will last all day long until about 4:00 P.M., when I work. Then when I get off work I feel shaky. I know I need sugar. So it will start again with mostly candy. I will purge 10–20× during one binge. . . .

I feel nothing. It's just like a machine getting up and sticking a knife or something up inside its vagina. . . . I don't have a set pattern of how it happens. The vaginal abuse is more like a machine. The cutting happens usually when I have to get something out of my body, either emotional feelings like anger or physical things that was put in me that I can still feel inside now. . . . Sometimes it not about feelings at all. It's more about that this is what I am *supposed* to do to my body/ to myself.

In *Bob Flanagan: Super-Masochist* (Juno and Vale 1993) and in Sundance award-winning documentary film, *Sick: The Life and Death of Bob Flanagan, Super-Masochist*, Bob Flanagan physically demonstrated and told how discovering in childhood various painful and bizarre masturbatory practices enabled him to adapt to and survive a fatal illness. He used these practices to battle against death until ultimately cystic fibrosis killed him at age 43. He was expected to die much earlier but credits his S&M practices—tests of pain and endurance—with giving him the strength to cling to life as long as he did.

Born with cystic fibrosis, a hereditary disease that causes the lungs, pancreas, and intestines to become plugged up with thick mucus, Bob was not expected to live to adulthood. He lived with his impending death a constant presence and no sense of control over his body. He witnessed one sister die in infancy of the disease and another die at age 21. When he was a baby, his hands and feet were strapped down while doctors inserted needles into his lungs and physical therapists pounded on his chest to release the mucus that was choking him. He also had to endure the severe stomachaches and painful bowel movements that were part of the illness, and soon discovered that when he rubbed against the sheets and pillows to soothe his stomach, it became quite erotic and he started to masturbate that way. "One way of taking control of the stomachache was to turn it into an orgasm" (Flanagan quoted in Juno and Vale 1993, p. 12). Being tied up flat to a bed became one of his favorite positions. He linked his fascination with bondage to his life of illness and constant thoughts of his death: "In order not to be terrified of it, I sexualized it" (p. 36). Aware that he had no real control over his life, he craved surrender, but a controlled surrender—"I determine the surrender and who I surrender to" (p. 56). His masochism was his adaptation to a life of pain. "I was born with a genetic illness that I was supposed to succumb to at two, then ten, then twenty, and so on, but I didn't. And, in a never-ending battle not just to survive but to subdue my stubborn disease, I've learned to fight sickness with sickness" (p. 73).

Flanagan tortured himself in private, tying himself into crucifix-like positions and whipping himself—conducting his own personal Stations of the Cross—before meeting the woman who became his life partner and personal dominatrix. She spanked and whipped him, ordered him to cut and brand her initials into his skin, to submerge himself in ice water, to hang ten-pound weights from his penis, to sew his lips closed, to put needles through his penis—to which he gladly submitted. He sewed up his scrotum and nailed it to a board. They began performing these private rituals publicly, first at sex clubs and then at prestigious art galleries and museums. Museum installations included videos of medical procedures he was forced to endure that he then incorporated into a "masochistic cystic fibrosis lifestyle."

Wanting Sex and Disavowing Sex

A number of subjects wrote of their fear of men or their own sexuality. One wrote that her emaciated and scarred body, so repulsive to men, gave her a feeling of power and protection against the enemy. Having stopped menstruating only added to her sense of power; no man could impregnate her. Some used the word *orgy* to describe the binge, and a few wrote that purging was like having an orgasm. A number of subjects described the rituals attending their bulimic and self-mutilating episodes with words usually used to describe sexual excitement and orgasm.

Delia was uncertain if she had been sexually abused as a child but knew she had been physically abused. She describes how the act of bingeing and purging feels quite sexual: "I'll feel real nervous and tense and then it'll build until I can't take it and in a sense, it's sort of like a sex [build-up]. I start to settle down when I eat and the throwing up is kind of like an orgasm. I usually feel extremely relaxed after I vomit." It is to be noted that she uses the words *build up* again, here to describe the self-hatred she feels when cutting, burning, and sticking herself. Perhaps the self-mutilation serves as punishment for sexual pleasure and gratification of sexual wishes at the same time: "I just build up such an incredible amount of self-hatred that I can't keep it in anymore. I'll just cut myself real hard and deep and watch it bleed. I almost always feel better the next morning."

Jody's extreme and bizarre self-harm may well be connected with sexual abuse in childhood and unconscious forbidden sexual feelings. She jams a spoon down her throat in order to purge, and has been bingeing and purging since she was 8. At that time she began pulling out her hair, biting her nails and cuticles badly, and picking, cutting, and sticking herself with pins. In adolescence she began using laxative pills, suppositories, and diuretics, and began burning, scratching, and punching herself. During binges she has consumed nutshells, coffee grinds, large amounts of syrup of ipecac, dirt, hair, and paper. She is uncertain if she was sexually or physically abused as a child

or whether she dissociated as a child, but seems to wonder if it has something to do with being a virgin at 27. Feeling "freakish," she has made several suicide attempts.

> Most times I feel like if I don't binge, I'll die. . . . I binge until I can't even
> sit up straight then purge and start over. . . . [It is] maybe subconsciously as
> some kind of punishment . . . to turn me off from ever bingeing again. . . .
> [About my self-mutilation], it has usually happened following a buildup of
> intense feelings I don't understand. They weren't sad or angry or anything,
> just INTENSE. . . . Then I'd feel confused, then I'd anticipate that rage or
> uncontrollable sadness might come. . . . Usually it feels like a combination of
> justice (punishment I deserved) and a relief from intense feelings. . . .
> I have no conscious recollection of ever being sexually molested, yet I am
> 27 years old and have never been intimate with anyone. I am repulsed by
> physical contact and have only kissed when extremely drunk. Since I stopped
> drinking 2½ years ago I've not even dated for fear of what is expected of a 27-
> year-old woman. I have known many, many women, even others with eating
> disorders, but I do not know of even *one* other 27-year-old virgin. I often
> wonder how this all relates. I feel like such a freak and the constant "Why
> don't you date?" questions make me think about it and feel ashamed about it
> to the point of feeling suicidal.

Quite a few made a connection between their bleeding or purging as a means
to cleanse or purify themselves, or to release the evil inside them, like an exorcism.
Rita, a 20-year-old, wrote that she had taken as many as sixty to seventy-five
laxative pills and thirty diuretics at a time to purge. She binges in order to purge:
"When I'm alone, hurt, depressed, lonely, stressed, pissed off, or just plain hungry then I eat. Whatever it is I feel guilty. I feel dirty, out of control, and that I
will throw up. . . . The guilt is what makes me purge. Then I feel clean, uncon-
taminated, in control."

To Feel Bodily Pain Is to Come Alive

To walk through life deadened by depression or numbed by dissociation is
to feel dead inside. Bodily pain can jolt one momentarily out of a depression or
dissociated state and make one come alive again. To feel pain in the body is to
experience it as alive and vital, a welcome relief that mitigates the severity of
the physical pain.

To know what is in the body, to see the bone and ligaments, to feel one's
heart beating or abdomen cramping, is to know that the body is real. To see and
feel the layers of skin that separate inside from outside is to differentiate the
boundaries of the body and its separate parts. Mutilation of the body surface may
be a way to find out what is inside. Because such individuals think in terms of
symbolic equations, they may not know that what they are also looking for, besides

blood, bone, and ligaments, is a sense of what is there emotionally. To know that there is something there emotionally is to know that they exist. To feel pain is to feel oneself real and alive again, like a resurrection from the dead.

"From My Suffering Will Be Born New and Everlasting Life"

Themes of suffering and mortification of the flesh had to do with religious healing and redemption, with clear identifications with Christian martyrs, saints, and Christ himself. For some, the blood they shed was the blood of the lamb that washed and cleansed their souls and delivered them into a new and everlasting life.

For Christine, her suffering was meant to save her father's soul and was insurance that he would be admitted to heaven.

Christine, a 43-year-old married woman, heard about my study while touring a college campus with her 17-year-old daughter. She spotted a stack of my questionnaires in the health office and was intrigued to find that it was relevant to her.

She wrote about her religious scrupulosity as an influencing factor in inflicting pain and mutilation on herself. She indicated that she was sexually abused by "a family member" but was not certain whether this occurred before age 10 or not. Interestingly, her binge-purging behavior began at age 30, which suggests that memories of the abuse may have begun to occur at this time.

Her father died when she was 12, another critical trauma in her life. Believing that no one is admitted directly to heaven, she was convinced he was in purgatory for an indeterminate period of time until his soul could be purified sufficiently to justify his admission to heaven. She was also frightened that he may have died in a state of mortal sin, which meant he would never be admitted to heaven. She believed that if she prayed a great deal and suffered pain, she could offer the suffering up to God and in that way could obtain "days of indulgence" or days of pardon from her father's sentence in purgatory. She was convinced that the more praying and suffering she did, the sooner he would be granted admission to heaven. She began to hurt herself, careful that no one see her injuries because allowing them to be seen by others was to commit the sin of pride and self-righteousness. She began chewing the inside of her mouth and cheek, causing large ulcerations, something that she still does at times when feeling anxious. She would deliberately bend her legs in a manner that would cause pain while praying. Although she appeared to be kneeling in prayer in church, she was actually supporting herself on her elbows on the pew in front of her, causing herself more pain. Each time she prayed she tried to do this for an even longer period of time to build up endurance. For her, the suffering seemed to serve as an "act of contrition" for her father's sins, a sacrifice that she believed was necessary to save her father's soul.

10

Self-Harm, Gender, and Perversion

Masochism is a short cut to true intimacy . . . full of denials, evasions, fractured meanings, and lost hopes for love and meaningful communication. Masochism becomes the alternative to genuine loving when anger and disappointments are suppressed but not forgotten, when an attachment is betrayed, and when the pain is disowned and displaced.

Ann Greif, *Masochism: The Treatment of Self-Inflicted Suffering*

Is self-harm a problem primarily for women? Both the research data and clinical observations on eating disorders and self-mutilation suggest that these specific problems are far more prevalent among females but are increasing in males (Beresin et al. 1989, Brumberg 1988, Simpson 1980, and Walsh and Rosen 1988). The continuum of self-harm behavior goes beyond eating disorders and self-mutilation and has not been studied systematically. Yet the more severe forms of self-mutilation (Pao 1969) and successful suicides are more common among men, and men with eating disorders are even more preoccupied about food and weight than women with eating disorders (Kearney-Cooke and Steichen-Asch 1990, Mickalide 1990).

"Drinking someone under the table," once the mark of a "man's man," has become acceptable for women in high school and college. Both substance abuse and gambling, previously thought to be male problems, are proving to be equal-opportunity problems. How men and women harm themselves is a function of culturally derived gender expectations as well as gender-different lines of body image development. That is, bodily self-harm develops out of an individual's developing relationship to his or her body through the phases of early childhood, adolescence, and adulthood, and out of culturally influenced expectations of how one's body should look and be used.

Just as conversion hysteria in Victorian times was understood by Freud to speak of the strangulation of women's drives, today self-harm is the way the body speaks of sexual desire, destructive narcissism, and the continual struggle between the ego and the libidinal and aggressive drives.

GENDERED EMBODIMENTS OF SELF-HARM

There has always been an oscillation between the construct of woman as body—carnal and fleshy—and woman as spirit—ethereal, even sickly and close to death. Only in the past twenty years or so has the subjective experience of the body emerged as a topic of interdisciplinary inquiry and research, and feminist theories have focused on the female body as the site where representations of difference and identity are inscribed. Simone de Beauvoir's pivotal question "What is a woman?" has evoked the idea popular in some feminist circles that the whole idea of woman is a social construct—that woman is not born but constructed by a system that regards man as self/subject and woman as other/object, defined and evaluated by her biological processes: menstruation, pregnancy, childbirth, nursing, and menopause (Conboy et al. 1997).

Making the body docile and controllable (Foucault 1977) has become a hallmark of contemporary culture (Bordo 1997) and a dominant theme in adolescent development. The interaction of culture and development creates a powerful tendency for adolescents of both sexes to devote themselves to having dominion over the body. Traditionally, women have been expected to deny their potentially dangerous appetites for food, sex, and ambition, to shape a nonthreatening docile body, to internalize and embody all the values of domesticity. Girls are socialized to become women through very complex regulatory practices that increase their ornamental value: weight control, skin and hair care, makeup, shopping, accessorizing, and resistance to aging. When women hunger for a sense of danger that they cannot directly acknowledge, shoplifting is a covert feminine way of expressing aggression, an external feminine expression of unfeminine feelings.

Both sexes are "biologically born" and "culturally made." They develop in very different ways that can explain the differences in how they harm themselves, but for both sexes, self-harm is associated with masochism, trauma, and depression.

MASOCHISM AND GENDER

Masochism embodies a determination to punish or annihilate the self. When the developing self is thwarted, the resulting devaluation is central to the shame and masochistic surrender to others that is so seen more frequently in women. Both sexual masochism, in which erotic pleasure is combined with bodily pain, and moral masochism, in which pleasure is combined with the pain of self-inflicted emotional suffering, are rooted in feminine identifications, predominantly with a preoedipal maternal figure (Greif 1989).

> The clinical reality of masochism is that it is almost invariably tied to disillusionment with parental figures on whom the self has been passively dependent. Masochism is by definition the consequence of thwarted passivity rather than the cause or the inversion of passivity, feminine or otherwise. Masochism contains often, if not always, a mocking transformation of passivity into something deadly, grasping, and noxious, something hardly passive at all. What has come to replace the need of the child is the assertion of paralysis by an enfeebled self, a self both dynamically clinging and dependent for reasons of displaced aggression and also, for some individuals, authentically underdeveloped to the tasks of love and work. [p. 5]

It has been found clinically that in children who become masochistic, there is a sadomasochistic quality to the parents' marriage, usually with the wife assuming the role of victim to the husband's more powerful stance (Greif 1989). Maureen Howard's (1996) memoir makes the point:

> At home, to irritate us all, my father sat down to dinner in his undershirt. . . . My mother might say, "Put a shirt on, Bill," but could not pursue the matter. He was perverse and crude, a man who must have his way. I was humiliated by the scene between them: his childishness—demanding ketchup and ice water, finding fault with the butter fresh from the dairy, . . . thrusting his freckled hairy chest out defiantly. Her painful submission to him brought a short uneasy peace. Then he was angrier than ever and provoked a fight with me or George for not helping our mother. Couldn't we see how dragged out she was, all afternoon cooking the pot roast, baking apple pie? How many families did we think were waited on hand and foot by a blessed martyr? How many of our friends, . . . were eating her homemade chocolate cake? You bet your life they're eating crap off Louie's shelf your mother wouldn't feed to the dog. And weren't we chauffeured to our lessons—clarinet, elocution, and dance? For what? For us to sit at the table and be distressed . . . by his undershirt? . . . George and I were miserable choking down the chocolate cake or custard, whatever gift had been given us that day by our sainted mother. [p. 73]

These inequalities of power make love confusing for the child who thus equates it with the giving over of control and autonomy. To be good is to submit one's will to the parent or husband, to be seen and not heard, to become invisible, selfless. The cultural stereotypes reinforce this distortion, making little girls who feel unlovable especially vulnerable. And so the notion grows that submitting one's will to others is the embodiment of femininity and is simply how girls and women should be.

It is a factor in the perverse relationship many females have with their ambition, creativity, and competitiveness that either does not allow them to produce what they are capable of, or if they can produce the work, they may end up destroying it or preventing it from gaining recognition. For some women each professional or love relationship progression is met with a regressive food binge, shopping spree, or other self-sabotage whose aim is the maintenance of old attachments. Women who distinguish themselves from their female peers often fear being rejected by them, a punishment for the equivalent of an oedipal triumph. Eating disorders frequently develop in women who fear their ambitious aspirations, who are afraid to achieve what they most desire (Bergmann 1988, Krueger 1984).

TRAUMA AND GENDER

Both male and female trauma survivors harm themselves in ways that are similar psychodynamically but present quite differently. They are compelled to repeat the trauma but in different ways. Male trauma survivors who mutilate themselves tend to do it more violently and to express their violence outward, compared to females, who tend toward more superficial self-mutilation. Andrew is a 22-year-old college student in Scotland who was raised by a mentally ill mother. He blames himself for both his grandmother and grandfather dying in his presence:

It's that feeling again. You wake up and see blood stains on your sheets and on your carpet. Books and bits of paper strewn all over your room. Broken furniture. That familiar sting on your arms, on your torso. Your face is smeared red. . . . You can hardly get yourself up; you haven't eaten for three days and you've lost a lot of blood. . . . You try to piece together exactly what happened last night. . . .

You'd been working all day, wanted to go out and . . . enjoy yourself. . . . Went to the liquor store, bought something to drink, sat in your room, listening to your favorite violent and depressive music. Something is welling up inside you . . . any minute you're going to explode. Your eyes become watery, you start crying. The crying becomes shouts, yells, screams. You try and hold yourself down. Start kicking the door. Throw stuff across the room, out the window. You can't calm down. . . . You dig your nails into the skin on your wrist. Can't feel anything. . . . You take your shirt off, look in the mirror. Hate, disgust, frustration, anger, regret. Almost like a ritual, without even thinking what you're doing, you pick up the razor blade . . . blood dripping down. Rub in some antiseptic, do it again, do it until you're calm, you're satisfied. [Strong 1998, pp. 1–2]

Men tend to be the perpetrators of violence on others, while women tend to be the perpetrators of self-inflicted violence and the victims of others' violence. For example, a male trauma survivor may provoke fights and get himself beaten up, while a female trauma survivor may enact violence more directly upon her body with a knife or razor blade and may involve herself repetitively with abusive partners. This male pattern of self-harm has been found in the adolescent boys charged in an epidemic of multiple-victim school shootings across the country in 1997 to 1999 that culminated in the massacre at Columbine High School in Colorado. The first of the shootings was in many ways a blueprint of what was to follow. A 14-year-old honors student walked into his algebra class and shot his teacher and two students. He had thought it would be "pretty cool" to go on a shooting spree just like the lead characters in the film *Natural Born Killers*. In all of these teen killers, a pattern emerged in which the boy felt inferior, was picked on and bullied, and harbored anger toward some student or teacher. The boys complained of being fat, near-sighted, short, or unloved. Most of them were suicidal and of above-average intelligence. All left clues or warnings. One left a last will and testament, saying, "I do this to show society, 'Push us and we will push back.' I suffered all my life. No one ever truly cared about me." All suffered from serious depression, and seemed to want to end their lives in a blaze of terror. When cornered after the killings, they said, "Kill me," expressing a wish for "suicide by cop."

It is not yet known what trauma Buford O. Furrow, Jr. suffered that played a part in a most recent high-profile hate crime, a planned attack on a Jewish community center in California. What is known, however, is that Furrow, a member of the Aryan Nations, opened fire in August 1999 with an Uzi assault-style machine gun on preschool children, injuring five people, and in a later attack killing a Filipino postal worker. Furrow's hatred knew no bounds and could be turned on himself as well as others. He had a long psychiatric history of evaluations and brief hospitalizations, and a history of violence. He was known to slash his arms deeply, to drink until he blacked out, and to espouse a deep hatred for Jews and nonwhites.

Men are socialized to behave more actively and aggressively and so are more likely to inflict upon others that which had been inflicted upon them. It is too feminine to allow others to harm them, but provoking someone else to harm them is thought of as the ultimate in masculine behavior. Women, on the other hand, are socialized to be nice, and may allow themselves to be hurt rather than object, for fear of hurting the other. Many women have had the experience of men rubbing against them sexually in a crowded bus and have responded nonverbally by trying to move away, but have not spoken or shouted out loud to protect themselves for fear of embarrassment or behaving in a way that is not "nice." Many men do not seek help for their eating-disordered or self-mutilating behavior, convinced that these are women's illnesses. In fact, males with an eating disorder are more likely to be confused about their gender identity (Hunter 1990, Woodside et al. 1990). But put a gaunt-looking man in running gear and hardly anyone would guess that he might be anorectic. Or if the bulimic young man just happens to be on the wrestling team, his teammates are not likely to think anything is wrong when he vomits before weighing in, as many of them are doing the same thing.

DEPRESSION AND GENDER

When women are depressed they either eat or go shopping. Men invade another country.

Comedian Elayne Boosler[1]

Depressed women are more likely to swallow their anger or bite their tongue, metaphors that legitimize burying their anger under a lot of food or injuring themselves. Men are more likely to express it outwardly in actions or words. As with trauma survivors, depressed women are more likely to express their feelings concretely and directly against their bodies, while men are more likely to express their anger outwardly toward others. Can we know to what extent the gender difference is a function of culture or of biology?

Women suffer from depression in much greater numbers than men, for reasons that may be attributed both to biology and culture. Dysthymia, major depression, cyclothymia, and bipolar disorder have been found to be more common in women than men (Reus 1984). There may be gender differences in brain function, as depressed men respond best to drugs affecting the neurotransmitter systems involving both norepinephrine and serotonin, while women respond better to drugs that affect only the serotonin system. In cross-national epidemiologic studies of major depression, the rates of major depression were higher for women in all ten countries studied, with women universally at two to three times the risk of depression compared to their male counterparts (Weissman et al. 1996). The differences for rates across countries suggest that cultural differences may affect the expression of the disorder. While not conclusive, studies have shown that men and women differ in their capacity to generate and metabolize serotonin, the neurochemical most strongly implicated in depressive disorders, with men synthesizing 52 percent more serotonin than women. It is unclear whether women's lives and experiences cause them to synthesize less, whether they are inherently less capable of generating and synthesizing serotonin, or whether some interaction of factors is involved. But if generating and synthesizing seratonin is a crucial issue for more women than men, then perhaps the many women who inflict pain and injury to their bodies have found a short-term "solution" to the serotonin problem without the help of psychopharmacology. Self-cutting profoundly and immediately is associated with increased levels of serotonin and the resultant experience of well-being. I am not aware of research that has found an association with severe purging and the neurotransmitter system involving serotonin, but I would wonder if severe purging, which also promotes a sense of well-being, might also work in much the same way.

---

1. Thanks to Todd Essig, Ph.D., for posting this joke online in the Psychoanalytic Connection. It was also heard on the Home Box Office cable TV program, "Comedy Central."

Like all stereotypes, the gender stereotype has a kernel of truth: men vent their rage outward while women vent it on themselves. Masculinity has long been associated with physical strength and the willingness to tolerate physical pain and bloodshed, expressed in an automobile bumper sticker that reads: "Give blood— play rugby." As Adrienne Rich said: "Most women have not even been able to touch this anger except to drive it inward like a rusted nail" (1977, p. xvii).

Terrence Real, psychotherapist and co-director of the Harvard University Gender Research Project, said that it is now more acceptable to admit to depression when it is "severe and biological, an acute disease-like condition," but emphasized that speaking about the less severe but more prevalent forms of depression was still considered "wimpy," more like a personal weakness. Rather than showing the classic signs of acute depression, the most depressed men expressed their distress in an unholy triad of masked ways: (1) self-medication to enliven dead feelings by drinking, drugging, womanizing, compulsive working, eating, or spending; (2) pulling away from relationships, intimacy, and from life itself; and (3) lashing out, which runs the gamut from increased irritability to domestic abuse and violence (Real 1997).

Whether the expression of aggression is inward or outward, both kinds of violence assault thinking, meaning, and language. They represent attempts to be rid of intolerable thoughts or fantasies that were originally the thoughts of the parent (Fonagy and Target 1995), thoughts about wishing the child were dead or never born. Self-directed violence may reflect a wish to attack the thinking of the same-sex parent, with whom identification is more painful and inescapable. It may be more common in women than men because the intolerable mental presence of the same-sex parent would be experienced inside the female's mind but outside the male's (Fonagy and Target 1995). In cases where the child's sense of identity is diffuse and poorly separated from that of the mother, the relationship with the mother cannot be reflected on or thought about. The son or daughter who feels trapped by or engulfed by the mother may seek a solution in an attack upon the "mother inside the self."

WOMEN TAKE THEIR MEDICINE; REAL MEN DRINK YOU UNDER THE TABLE

Holding one's liquor has long been associated with masculinity, whether it be construction workers ending the day with a six-pack, or executives sealing a deal over a two-martini lunch; using street drugs is associated with a sense of violence and danger that is stereotypically masculine. Prescription medication is considered far more feminine than alcohol or street drugs. For years women who feel trapped by the circumstances of their lives have been seduced by the promise of energy, stamina, and a sense of well-being to be found in the antidepressants and tranquilizers that are heavily advertised in women's magazines. They have been prone to abusing these medications and other drugs that suppress appetite, such as crack cocaine and methamphetamine. Women demand and easily receive prescription drugs from their doctors, who receive free gifts including luxury vacations from pharmaceutical companies and financial incentives from managed care to prescribe these medications.

Nonetheless, middle-class "recreational" heroin use has become more common among both men and women. As former heroin user Linda Yablonsky (1997) says in *The Story of Junk*, "Heroin plays with the soul—or whatever it is that makes a person uniquely appealing and distinguishable. Like an enveloping shadow dissolving day into night, it sneaks across your vision and tries to put it out, whatever that joy is by which you live, it creeps inside and pushes you down, making you smaller and smaller, a tiny flame burning down" (p. 4).

Marty's mother would comfort him after he had been beaten and verbally abused by his father, but she could not protect him. He was supposed to become a professional man, to make something of himself to please his father. He regarded himself as a "fuck up" because he worked at skilled manual labor. Marty grew up to beat up others before he could get beaten up. He was sent away to private military schools where he was no match for packs of boys who beat him regularly. He was forced once to perform oral sex on another boy. He became a cocaine user and an alcoholic, always "sucking on a bottle." After giving up drinking and drugs in AA, he became a compulsive eater. Always projecting his wish to victimize others, he constantly found predatory intent in everyone. To him, the whole world is out to get him. He'd shout at me, "What makes you so much fucking better than me? Your fucking credentials, living in a nice house?" He drove at high speeds on the highway, chasing anyone who had cut him off, determined to crash into the offending car, shouting, "Don't fuck with me!" It seemed a miracle that he had not killed someone or himself.

He once had a coughing jag during his session; he had no cough drops and a drink of water did not help. I had some throat lozenges and offered him one, which he eagerly took, immediately biting and crunching it to bits. Bone crusher, I thought to myself. What I said out loud was that it couldn't be very soothing to his throat if he didn't allow it to dissolve. He laughed sheepishly and said he always does that, he can't allow anything to dissolve in his mouth, he has to chew it up right away. It was much like his tendency to chew me up.

Jill, age 20, had just gotten a medical leave from college because she was depressed. She could not return until she was significantly better. She was emaciated, her clothing hanging from her frame. She had lost twenty pounds after the boy she had lost her virginity to dumped her. He was sleeping with lots of girls and no longer had time for her. Although she wanted to be the only one he slept with, she would have settled for being one of many, but did not even have that option. She could eat very little and the little she ate she could not keep down. Her hair was dull and lifeless, probably from malnutrition but also because she constantly attacked her wavy hair with hot irons and chemical straighteners, spending up to two hours on her hair before school. In the week before she came to see me, she managed to get herself to school, albeit hours late, but immediately compared herself to other girls she saw and was convinced that she was ugly. Her fair skin was too fair, when all her friends had olive skin. She hated her hair and skin, insisted her eyes were too small, that she was very ugly. (She wasn't.) Her eyes were ringed by bizarre-looking black makeup, "raccoon eyes," to make them look larger. Although her former boyfriend treated her terribly, she kept pursuing him, convinced that he wanted nothing more to do with her because she was not good enough for him and was too ugly. Her mother was too depressed to notice what was happening, and had in fact been so depressed for most of Jill's life that she was unable to care for her daughter. Had her father not taken charge of the situation and brought her to the attention of the college counseling department, she would have continued on this dangerous downward spiral.

GENDER DIFFERENCES IN SELF-HARM IN INSTITUTIONS

The nature of institutional life and the power structure in closed institutions, such as hospitals and jails, foster the spread of self-mutilating and eating-disordered behavior. Psychiatric patients often pick up tips from other patients on how to purge more efficiently or weigh in at a more respectable weight or how to hide cutting instruments. Having dominion over their bodies means having power over their "jailers," and so self-harm often has a manipulative quality, with an aim to outwit the staff or obtain a transfer to another hospital ward or to the prison infirmary. Rape and other violent assault is a problem in male prisons, and so at times male prisoners may threaten others by cutting themselves. The nonverbal message is "Don't fuck with me. As easily as I'll hack my arm to shreds I'll slice you up, too. Don't try me." When violent male prisoners are kept in solitary for the protection of other inmates, they may cut or bite themselves or even swallow razor blades. "They evoke the men in Dante's lowest rung of hell, frozen up to their necks in ice, gnawing on one another's heads" (Real 1997, p. 147).

As many as 50 percent of prisoners exhibit self-injurious behavior (Haines et al. 1995). Self-injury is common enough in male and female inmates to be considered a normal coping mechanism in prison, and incidents may not even be recorded except when severe medical problems or bizarre patterns of self-mutilation arise. The more bizarre patterns are more common in male prisons, where inmates have inserted objects into their urethra, banged their heads against the walls, and swallowed razor blades (Rada and James 1982). A male inmate who learned of my study wrote to me about his practices of erotic strangulation and infibulation, in which the foreskin of the penis is sewed closed to make erection or masturbation very painful (Farber 1995a).

GENDER DIFFERENCES IN EATING DISORDERS

It appears that while the clinical features and outcome of eating disorders in males and females are similar (Crisp et al. 1986, Schneider and Agras 1987), there are also several differences. First, the man who develops anorexia nervosa or bulimia tends to lack a sense of autonomy, identity, and control over his life, and seems to exist as an extension of others and to serve the needs of others in order to survive emotionally, quite like the girl who develops an eating disorder (Kearney-Cooke and Steichen-Asch 1990). He may well have come from an environment that could not validate his strivings for independence, leaving him at risk for symptom formation later in life. He may have been teased about his body shape, increasing his vulnerability about his body image. Like the girl, he tends to identify with his mother rather than with his father, which leaves his masculine identity in question (Kearney-Cooke and Steichen-Asch 1990). Like the girl, he may have an incomplete and distorted sense of his body, experiencing his own and his mother's body as one indivisible unit, as one body for two, expressing emotion somatically (McDougall 1989). Like the woman with an eating disorder, he is deeply affected by a culture that emphasizes thinness and fitness. Although their preoccupation with food and weight seems feminine, the manifestation of their eating-disordered behavior is in the traditionally male arena of athletics, typically wrestling and marathon running (Mickalide 1990, Yates 1991). Like most male marathon runners they may have begun dieting in order to become fit rather than to lose weight (Yates 1991). Both male and female athletes begin dieting to become fit, and become as compulsive about dieting as they are about exercise. In an upwardly escalating spiral, they often exercise to compensate for food consumption, a pattern often called "exercise bulimia," and may also binge and/or purge. Many male bulimics induce vomiting and starve themselves to "make weight," and jockeys "waste" themselves through restricting food intake, excessive sauna use, purgatives, abuse of appetite suppressants, and self-induced vomiting (Mickalide 1990). Men with eating disorders are usually even more preoccupied about food and weight than women, showing more hyperactivity, sexual anxiety, and a more intense achievement orientation (Fichter et al. 1985).

The second difference is that there is a higher prevalence of homosexual or bisexual preference and more problems with drugs and alcohol among the males than the females (Schneider and Agras 1987, Woodside et al. 1990). Their early history was characterized by trauma, including physical and sexual abuse, abandonment, and death of an important relative, which was not characteristic of heterosexual eating disordered men (Herzog et al. 1984, 1990). These experiences were, however, quite similar to the early experiences reported by self-mutilating adolescents, and were also found to be predictive of self-mutilation and associated with severe body alienation in adolescence (Walsh 1987, Walsh and Rosen 1988). Therefore, homosexual eating disordered men tend to have had the childhood experiences that are predictive of self-mutilation and associated with severe body alienation in adolescence. Homosexual and bisexual eating-disordered men tend more toward body alienation and self-mutilating practices, including tattooing and body piercing, than heterosexual eating-disordered men. Like female self-mutilators, men who cut or pierce their flesh or have others do these things to them may be expressing very concretely a feminine wish to be penetrated sexually while enacting the masculine wish to penetrate.

BODY ALIENATION

Alienation from the body (Walsh and Rosen 1988), especially from the sexual body in adolescence, is crucial to the development of bodily self-harm. Girls are more prone than boys to body alienation in adolescence because their attitudes toward their bodies are more readily influenced by powerful, complex, and confusing bodily experiences. Specifically, partially internal genitalia, menstruation, abrupt changes in body contours in puberty, and pregnancy all contribute to a confusing experience (Cross 1993), that evokes fantasies of the female body as a source of danger, power, and transcendence, in much the same way that men have always found women to be mysterious and dangerous. It is no wonder that the female genitals are often cryptically referred to as "down there," even by adult women. "The sex organ of a man is simple and neat as a finger; it is readily visible and often exhibited to comrades with proud rivalry; but the feminine sex organ is mysterious even to the woman herself, concealed, mucous, and humid, as it is; it bleeds each month, it is often sullied with body fluids, it has a secret and perilous life of its own" (de Beauvoir 1949, p. 386).

To be alienated from one's own body speaks of depersonalization, the dissociation of psyche from soma, in which the body is regarded as separate from and different from self, or is regarded as Other. "Women watch themselves being looked at . . . thus turn [themselves] into an object. . . . [the woman] comes to consider the surveyor and the surveyed within her as the two constituent yet always distinct elements of her identity as a woman (Berger 1972, p. 47). Confounding the difficulty in differentiating her self from the other is the fact that the anatomical similarities between the female child and her mother create a greater difficulty for the girl in distinguishing her physical separateness (Ritvo 1988, Zakin 1989). The mother's tendency toward overly identifying with the child of the same sex is yet another factor that can serve as an impediment to self and object differentiation for both mother and daughter, maintaining a preverbal merger described as "one life for two, one body for two, one mind for two" (McDougall 1989). When the girl becomes accustomed to regarding her body as other and treating it accordingly, asserting control over the body readily takes on the dynamics of a master-and-slave scenario.

CHILDHOOD BODY EXPERIENCE

Boys know their sexual parts better than girls because they can see their genitals and feel them with their hands. As toddlers they masturbate more frequently and more directly than girls. Touching the penis is a direct source of lifelong pleasure and comfort for males. The boy uses his body to comfort himself in a way that furthers his sense of mastery and autonomy, while girls' anatomy puts them at a disadvantage that may predispose them to using their bodies in more pathological ways to comfort and soothe themselves. Girls' genitalia are mostly hidden from their view, so they cannot show off and compare their genitals or touch them to comfort themselves as readily as boys can. The little girl feels freer to explore her body only when the mother is accepting of her female child and delights in her (Lax 1994). Because frequently she is not allowed to explore her vaginal opening freely so that she can know better how she is constructed, she does not really know how this opening connects her surface to her interior, and she may imagine being closed up or sealed over internally.

Boys know that urine comes from their penis because they can see it as they hold the penis while urinating. Girls have difficulty knowing where their urine or where stimulating genital sensations come from. Because of physical proximity the little girl tends to associate the bladder and urethra with the inner genital, experiencing sexual stimulation from the bladder and urethral sensations of urinary retention and enuresis (Bass 1994, Kestenberg 1975; Richards 1992). Urination, suggests Richards (1992) is the original model of internal sexual sensation for women. Just as little boys play at controlling their stream, little girls play with controlling the sphincter muscles, practicing control over excreting urine, which can serve to express sadistic and sexual aggression (Bass 1994). It is easy for the little girl to imagine that she discharges urine from her clitoris, viewing it as a little penis (Bass 1994, Shengold 1989).

The girl's genitals become a source of confusion and anxiety, as they are experienced only when aroused and even then are difficult to localize (Kestenberg 1975). Genital excitation may be associated with messing and with explosive loss of control, which make it frightening (Gilmore 1998). In early childhood, Kestenberg suggests, a tendency toward externalization begins for girls, an attempt to transform these diffuse, ambiguous, and passively experienced sensations into more focused forms of discharge involving external organs, objects, or people. This lays the foundation very early for the tendency toward taking what is experienced inside the body and externalizing it through purging, excessive exercise, and self-mutilation, even though these externalizations may not manifest until preadolescence or later. For girls who have been sexually abused, their genitals are even more a source of confusion, and urination and soiling can become a form of erotic discharge (Daldin 1988b), paving the way for purging to become a disguised sexual perversion later in development.

The little girl has difficulty knowing not only what is inside her but also has greater difficulty than the boy in differentiating her body from that of her mother. In this situation, the little girl has greater difficulty in saying no to the mother and may fail to develop the no response, a major psychic organizer. She cannot say no because she cannot know that "I am not you and I do not have to say yes to what you want. I am different from you, a separate person."

Little girls go from playing with Beanie Babies to Barbies to sexy Spice Girls dolls in décolletage and hot pants. Against their better judgment some mothers give in to their daughters' demands for similar clothing, while others enjoy dressing their little girls this way. Those mothers who are overly concerned with thinness readily transmit this message to their little girls by putting them on diets and underfeeding them. In fact, some of the children of mothers with eating disorders have been underfed and are physically underdeveloped and frail. I treated a 5-year-old boy who was naturally quite thin, but recently had begun refusing food, telling me, "Nobody likes a fatso." His beloved nanny was trying to become a model and was on a very restrictive diet. Her obsession with thinness had begun to take hold of the little boy. In a therapeutic nursery for young children of mothers with eating disorders, these children were obsessed with food and, when no restrictions were put on their eating, were inclined to stuff themselves. Some little girls as young as 5 or 6 are asking their mothers to put them on diets. "No fat, Mommy!" If the mother agrees, she is transmitting to her daughter that her little body with its baby fat is somehow bad or wrong as it is.

ADOLESCENT DEVELOPMENT

My face is a fucking mess
I wish I lived in Iraq
　　　　Catherine Taormina, *Chalkboard with a Bad Eraser*

Today's girls have options as never before and the feminist message has been that they could have it all. They expect that they can be all things: powerful in business or the professions, super-moms, gourmet cooks, and alluring sexpots, all at the same time. Upon adolescence girls are confronted with a "crisis of connection" in which they feel compelled to adapt to psychologically debilitating sex-role stereotypes, expecting that they should live up to an idealized and superficial version of care and nurturance in womanhood while at the same time being strong and autonomous like boys (Gilligan 1982, Steiner-Adair 1991). The same girls who at age 9 know what they think and believe and can hold their own with boys, at 13 and 14 are devastated by this crisis of connection. They have trouble saying no to sex they're not ready for, to promiscuity, drugs, and alcohol. Coming of age in this culture is frightening and confusing, a no-win situation for many that can drive girls to self-negation and self-harm.

> Just as planes and ships disappear mysteriously into the Bermuda Triangle . . . the selves of girls go down in droves. . . . In early adolescence . . . girls' IQ scores drop and their math and science scores plummet. They lose their resiliency and optimism and become less curious and inclined to take risks. They lose their assertive, energetic and "tomboyish" personalities and become more deferential, self-critical and depressed. They report great unhappiness with their bodies. . . .
>
> Many of the pressures girls have always faced are intensified in the 1990s. Many things contribute to this intensification: more divorced families, chemical addictions, casual sex and violence against women. Because of the media . . . girls live in one big town—a sleazy, dangerous tinsel town with lots of liquor stores and few protected spaces. . . . This combination of old stresses and new is poison for our young women. . . . Adolescence has always been hard, but it's harder now because of cultural changes in the last decade. The protected place in space and time that we once called childhood has grown shorter. There is an African saying, "It takes a village to raise a child." Most girls no longer have a village. [Pipher 1994, pp. 11–28]

The adolescent both inhabits and is inhabited by the body (Phillips 1994). The subdued self erupts in puberty, forcing adolescents to grapple with the intensity of their feelings. When adolescents spend much time alone, they are alone in the presence of their body and so their own body becomes an intense preoccupation. The adolescent further differentiates himself and discovers his capacity for solitude by taking risks with his body, endangering it and experimenting with it. The body is tested to see if it can be relied upon as a holding environment, a self container (Phillips 1993). Because of the girl's confusing experience of puberty, endangering herself through attacking the body becomes more of an issue for girls.

The Mysterious Uncontrollable Feminine Body

The adolescent body is often described and experienced as fragmented body parts rather than as a whole integrated body, adding to the girl's experiencing her body as an object alienated from the self (Cross 1993). Girls have historically attained puberty earlier and more abruptly than boys, but today it occurs earlier than ever, especially for black girls, and girls as young as 7 or 8 find that their bodies have become even more mysterious and alien almost overnight (Gilbert 1997). With puberty comes a natural and necessary increase in body fat. Breasts, thighs, and hips develop faster than the girl's psyche, having a deep, often disturbing effect on her feelings and fantasies about her body (Cross 1993). Body image is disrupted by these changes, influencing teenage girls' very changeable views of their own attractiveness. Girls tend to think of their bodies primarily in terms of their physical appearance, while boys tend to think of their bodies in terms of how effectively it functions (Rosenbaum 1979).

Nonetheless, boys entering puberty whose mothers are obsessed with weight may become overly concerned themselves with their size and weight. At a presentation I did at a middle school, two 11-year-old boys who looked fine and healthy expressed a concern about being too fat. In the past year, each had gained a few pounds, which alarmed their mothers and which, in turn, had begun to alarm them. They were very relieved to hear that if they have grown in height, as they had, it was natural and normal for their weight to increase to accommodate the increase in height. It made sense to them but they were puzzled about why their mothers seemed not to know this.

Menarche is a central organizing experience for girls (Kestenberg 1975) that can be progressive or regressive. Optimally, seeing and feeling the menstrual flow and feeling menstrual cramps can help to create a clearer sense of the vagina and uterus, facilitating a visceral sense of ownership of her reproductive organs and increased pride in her reproductive capacity. For many girls, however, the onset of menstruation has a regressive effect on their sense of control over their bodies, experienced as a failure to control the body (Kestenberg 1975). Before a predictable cycle is established, her period may arrive at a time when the girl is least prepared for it, interfering with her life, staining her clothing, and creating embarrassment. Sanitary napkins, like diapers, cover both anus and vagina, further evoking anal themes (Cross 1993). Many girls have the same anal preoccupations as the toddler who is being toilet-trained—fear of being messy, smelling bad, and soiling—which Madison Avenue affirms with ads for unnecessary douches and genital deodorant sprays.

Adolescent girls masturbate less frequently and less directly than adolescent boys (Blos 1962, Rosenbaum 1979). Many discover orgasm and aspects of their own anatomy through their relationships with boys, or as Cross (1993) puts it, a boy may discover a girl's vagina and clitoris before she does. Because she does not psychologically "own" her vagina and is unfamiliar with its contours, during intercourse the penis may be experienced as a disturbing "other within" (Cross 1993). The first time she had sexual intercourse, a patient of mine was afraid that her husband's penis would not be able to penetrate her, maintaining a fantasy that a metal plate was embedded in her vagina and would block entry. Because a girl may fear her vagina being closed up or sealed over, self-inflicted cuts may represent attempts to master this anxiety by creating "little vaginas" that bleed (Bollas 1992).

All the pubertal changes that mark the girl's transition to womanhood may stir up memories of repressed or dissociated experiences of sexual abuse, of a time when, despite her wishes, her childish body was not within her control. Her adolescent sexual arousal may bring her back in time to when she came to be overly aroused as a child, an exciting and frightening time. Being flooded with dissociated memories of forbidden experience may only exacerbate the feeling of wanting to control her body, making her more likely to harm or punish it.

When Saying No to the Other Is Saying Yes to the Self

The ability to say no in early childhood is a developmental milestone, an indicator of a certain degree of psychological separation and autonomy. Many girls can say no until early adolescence, when they seem to regress and lose their sense of being a separate self. They have great difficulty saying no to boys and actually forfeit the right to say no, forming a false self presentation designed to please boys. Many frequently end up having unwanted sex. They think that virginity is an embarrassment, even an aberration. I was told of a disturbing conversation a middle-aged woman had with her daughter, a new college graduate. The daughter's boyfriend wanted her to get her tongue pierced in order to enhance his pleasure when she fellated him. She did not know if she was "supposed to." Just as girls were "pinned" in the 1950s and 1960s with their boyfriends' fraternity pins, increasingly more of today's high school and college girls are wearing a "secret pin," a stainless steel ring piercing their labia, a token of the intimate secret that they share with their boyfriend (Brumberg 1997).

A father can provide a much-needed counterpoint to the girl's pressure to submit if he can admire her admirable traits and love her as she is. If he can admire her intelligence, creativity, or athletic talents, or takes pleasure in his daughter's company, he can thus help her find value in qualities not tied to notions of her sexual desirability, providing a sense that she can have a relationship with a male that does not require her submission. But fathers too frequently disappoint their daughters by failing to meet this developmental need.

Some of those girls who cannot say no to sex may stop eating or may eat huge amounts, allowing their emaciated or obese bodies to say no for them by warding off unwanted sexual attention. The anorectic's periods may stop, thus effectively saying no to pregnancy. Or some may have unwanted sex but then undo or say no to the experience by purging themselves with vomiting, laxatives, or cutting themselves.

Another false self presentation is the seductive female "stud," sexually casual and indiscriminate. Her behavior ensures that she will always have some male companion while at the same time defending against the tremendous vulnerability she feels around boys. She may tease and frustrate boys in mildly or not-so-mildly sadistic ways, at the same time that she enters into relationships with boys who are unavailable, domineering, or abusive. She can attain a vicarious mastery over her sexuality by becoming adept at manipulating a boy's passions or by establishing sexual power over a boy who abuses but desires her (Cross 1993).

And She Shall Have Dominion Over Her Body

And God said, Let us make man in our image, after our likeness: and let them have dominion over the fish of the sea, and over the fowl of the air,

and over the cattle, and over all the earth, and over every creeping thing that
creepeth upon the earth.

Genesis 1:26

When there is little in an adolescent's universe over which he or she can have dominion, then dominion can be enacted upon one's own changing and out-of-control body. Adolescents of both sexes may feel prey to this changing body, uncertain if their brains are in their head or their genitals. Erections can occur publicly to embarrass a boy. A 14-year-old girl complained to me, "It's like my boobs have mind of their own. I wake up and there they are, bigger than yesterday. I wish I could get a halt and desist order."

Despite the hardness of their dress and manner, adolescent girls feel vulnerable to intrusion and invasion from male inspection, sexual penetration and impregnation, and maternal demands and criticisms (Sours 1980). Mothers may become anxious over their daughters' weight gain and take them to diet doctors. Taking control over their own bodies provides adolescents with the sense that they are in control of their life. The involvement in sports that so often gives adolescent boys a means of mastery over their bodies and a constructive means for socializing can do the same for girls (Zimmerman and Reavill 1998), serving as a powerful antidote to destructive body preoccupations.

Controlling the body is an all-consuming project for girls (Brumberg 1997), many of whom request and are getting cosmetic surgery as birthday presents: collagen-enhanced lips, rhinoplasty to shorten their noses, and breast implants. It is no surprise to discover that girls often are following in their mothers' footsteps or living out their mothers' unrealized self-improvement campaign. They may respond to parents who seem not to really see their daughters but see only the superficial, the way writer Kathryn Harrison did. Raised by a neglectful, abusive mother who literally did not see her, who slept the days away with her eyes covered by a slumber mask, little Kathryn stood by the foot of her bed, praying silently for her mother to wake up and notice her. The only time her mother seemed to notice her was when Kathryn was injured in an automobile accident and when they sat next to each other in church. When she was 15, however, her mother did notice her weight gain, and nagged her endlessly about it. Almost predictably, Kathryn's starving escalated. "Do I want to make myself smaller and smaller until I disappear, truly becoming my mother's daughter: the one she doesn't want to see? . . . Or am I so angry at her endlessly nagging me about my weight that I decide I'll never again give her the opportunity to say a word to me about my size. You want thin? . . . I'll give you thin. I'll define thin, not you. Not the suggested . . size six but size two. . . . Anorexia can be satisfied; my mother cannot" (Harrison 1997, p. 39).

Boys and girls may get themselves tattooed and pierced to assert their ownership of their bodies and marking them as unique from others while at the same time as a member of the peer group. These markings often produce disturbing reactions in others, effectively keeping them at a desirable distance, a new version of the proverbial demand for privacy posted on a teenager's door: "Keep out. This means you" (Martin 1997). They may play with their bodies by shaving their heads, piercing their eyebrow, or wearing outrageous clothing for the sheer fun of seeing Mom and Dad "freak."

They may play with their bodies sexually, through masturbation. Some girls feel so vulnerable to invasion by boys that their sexual play may be with another girl, a way of separating from the mother while merging with her. Anxieties about pregnancy echo other preoccupations about fullness and emptiness, self and non-self, inside and outside, and may be enacted through vomiting, diarrhea, rapid weight gain or loss, purging, and self-cutting. Both ascetism and intellectualization are the significant defenses of adolescence (A. Freud 1966), with asceticism being the more ego restrictive, repudiating sexual and aggressive feelings by means of stark vegetarian macrobiotic diets or kneeling in prayer. Some adolescents, especially those whose bodies have been abused by others, may feel especially desperate to wrest control over their bodies, and starving or stuffing themselves with food, purging, cutting, burning, or tattooing themselves may provide them with the temporary sense of autonomy and control that they crave. Elizabeth Wurtzel (1994) wrote how she began cutting herself at age 12 while listening to the music of the Velvet Underground:

> I guess the cutting began when I started to spend my lunch period hiding in the girls' locker room. I would bring my . . . black and silver Panasonic.. and I would listen intently to the scratchy sound of the tapes I'd accumulate. . . .
> And so, sitting in the locker room, petrified that I was doomed to spend my life hiding from people this way, I took my keys out of my knapsack. On the chain was a sharp nail clipper, which had a nail file attached to it. . . . So I took the nail file, found its sharp edge, and ran it across my lower leg, watching a red line of blood appear on my skin. I was surprised at how . . . easy it was for me to hurt myself this way. . . .
> I did not, you see, want to kill myself. Not at that time, anyway. But I wanted to know that if need be, if the desperation got so terribly bad, I could inflict harm on my body. . . . Knowing this gave me a sense of peace and power, so I started cutting up my legs all the time. . . . I collected razor blades, I bought a Swiss army knife, I became fascinated with the different kinds of sharp edges and the different cutting sensations they produced. I tried out different shapes—squares, triangles, pentagons, even an awkwardly carved heart, with a stab wound at its center, wanting to see if it hurt the way a real broken heart could hurt. I was amazed and pleased to find that it didn't. [pp. 38–41]

Early Adolescent Versus Late Adolescent Onset of Self-Harm

The onset of self-harm is an unconscious means of warding off the transition from childhood to adulthood. Those teens whose self-harm symptoms appear in early adolescence are more fragile than those whose symptoms emerge later (Levy-

Warren 1996). The earlier in development that the self-harm becomes intertwined in their personality, the more deeply embedded it will be. For example, bulimia that had its onset later in adolescence is generally more accessible to treatment than earlier-onset bulimia because these girls' personalities are not as dominated by the symptom complex (Levy-Warren 1996). Levy-Warren (1996) found that the fathers of these girls have a profound influence on the development and psychic meaning of their bulimia. The early adolescent bulimic often turns to her father for the nurturing that she has felt deprived of by her mother, but then flees the disturbing sexuality of the oedipal situation, regressing back to the safer, more easily regulated oral/anal stages. The late adolescent bulimic, however, seems more often riveted to the phallic/oedipal stage, feeling a conflicted triumph over her mother that may contribute to her contemptuousness of women. While she treasures her special relationship with her father, its persistence makes relationships with other men extremely difficult. When a father reacts with anxiety at the sexual change in his adolescent daughter and distances himself from her or when a mother reacts with a sense of envy or competition, this joins with the girl's own fear of growing up, affecting her sexuality, body image, self-esteem, and identity all the more.

When a girl with a lesbian orientation develops an eating problem, it will tend to be compulsive eating and she may become overweight. Her body image problems may be manifested by self-mutilation more than by starving and purging. She might value her body for its strength and its functioning more than adolescent girls typically do, and so she may take control over her body by developing her muscularity and athletic ability. She may be more inclined to get herself tattooed or pierced. If she experiments sexually with other girls, the loving, touching, and caring by another female may provide the acceptance of her body that she could not find from her mother and can serve to enhance her body image. She may be prone, however, to tolerate an abusive relationship with a woman as other girls might tolerate an abusive relationship with a boy.

Infirmity and Body Self

The development of an illness or disability as result of an accident in adolescence can have a profound effect on the sense of bodily integrity for boys and girls alike. In the midst of making greater moves toward independence, becoming immobilized, even temporarily, and having to be cared for by adults will probably be experienced as a narcissistic injury. When illness is chronic, the effect is far worse. Even an illness of the adolescent's own making, kept a secret for years, can become worse over time and threaten independence. This was the case with Allie, whose secret eating problem came to frighten her enough to seek help.

Allie, an 18-year-old college student, complained that for the past 2½ years she would at times suffer diarrhea within ten minutes after eating, and would awaken at night with a stomachache and diarrhea. This had been going on for some time, usually in response to events in her life that were stressful, but in the past year had become more constant and was interfering more with her life. Although she had dieted strictly and made herself vomit to control her weight in fifth grade and then later to relieve feelings of anxiety and depression, she had stopped doing this in eighth grade. No one had known about it; it had been her special secret. In the past few months, however, she had lost at least eleven pounds. The gastroenterologist who examined her was disturbed by the weight loss and nocturnal symptoms, which were atypical for an irritable bowel syndrome. It seems that even though the diarrhea consciously disturbed her, she felt guilty for eating, not believing herself worthy to have anything good in her. She was able to acknowledge that "I do something with my mind" right after eating that produces diarrhea. It had started to frighten her when it got out of control.

Adolescents may fight having to be cared for or having to care for themselves. Those with juvenile diabetes must test their blood, manage and take their insulin, and be vigilant about their sugar intake. Their daily life with friends who consume quantities of sweets and beer is a chronic reminder that something is wrong with their bodies. Without the motivation to care for themselves, they may deny their condition and neglect their care, resulting possibly in a life-threatening diabetic coma or developing over the long term blindness, kidney damage, or loss of limbs. Some diabetic patients who also are bulimic omit or reduce their insulin to control their weight, while others may overeat in response to a hypoglycemic reaction.

Gerri, age 18, was a diabetic. "No big deal. I don't sweat it." That was an understatement. According to the pediatric endocrinologist who had been following her since she was diagnosed at 13, she had been sent to camps for diabetics and had been in groups for adolescent diabetics, to no avail. She was a compulsive eater, too, and used food to calm her anxiety and relieve her depressed feelings when she could not smoke pot or drink. As her pot smoking had increased, so had her eating, a result of the "munchies." She frequently forgot to take her insulin. Once when she was high and forgot that she had already taken her insulin, she injected herself a second time and ended up in the emergency room.

Gerri met me for the first time wearing a T-shirt emblazoned with the logo, DRUNKEN UNIVERSITY. Under that it read, "Alcoholicus consumptis maximus." When I commented on it, she quickly replied that she had not selected the shirt; her mother got it from a thrift shop and gave it to her. Actually, she said, her father should be the one wearing it—he no longer worked and sat home all day drinking. She explained that she should have graduated from high school the spring before but instead was referred to a special academic program for "bad kids." She had been arrested a year before for disorderly conduct. "This dumb-ass bitch started up with me. I was minding my own business." All the cops in her small town knew her. She was biding her time in this program, bored with the level of the work, which was for "dummies." Her real problems began the year before when her best friend, who had been her only close friend, had sex with Gerri's boyfriend. Now her friend and former boyfriend were going together. She was trying to be "cool" about it and still hung out with them. She had no choice, really; if she did not, she would have no one in her life.

Someone new she was becoming friendly with was a feminist; she loved the idea that "women can do things guys can do and don't have to take shit from guys." She wanted to be like that. She was no dummy, she explained, she was smart enough to become a veterinarian, which is what she wanted to do. And she could become one. Only, she just goofed off too much. Before she was sent to the special program, she had been truant almost all the time, sleeping late, watching television during the day, then going out to hang out with her friends, with whom she smoked "blunts" (cigar wrappers filled with marijuana) and drank "forties" (40-ounce bottles of beer). Pot was her favorite. She was a little concerned that her dealer bought his supply in an area where lots of people had gotten very sick and one even died after smoking pot laced with hairspray or rat poison. It hardly concerned her that her pot smoking promoted her binge eating. In fact, she invoked her doctor's authority, insisting that "the doctor said" that depending on the time of day she smoked, pot could actually have a healthful effect on her blood sugar levels. Going blind from diabetes was not a real worry, not yet, because it takes years and years for that to happen. Her vision, which was 20-20, was just a little blurred, she was young, and had a long way to go before going blind.

Eugene, age 15, was from an immigrant family. Both parents worked hard and had high social and educational aspirations for their children. His father was a tyrant in the family and could tolerate no opposition from his wife or three children. Eugene was referred to me after having been suspended from school. His entire life was out of control. Both his diabetes and his behavior had been out of control ever since he was diagnosed with insulin-dependent diabetes at age 13. He had attended three different schools in three years. His parents took him out of the local high school, where he presented behavior problems, and enrolled him in a private Catholic prep school that subsequently suspended him. He enrolled in another Catholic high school and had already been suspended, but his mother was working on trying to convince the nun who was the principal to give him another chance. The final straw for the principal was when Eugene, who was not even supposed to be in school, walked into the cafeteria, stood up on the table where his friends were sitting, and dropped his pants and "mooned" everyone.

Eugene wanted to be a physician but had trouble concentrating in school. He hated his home and felt depressed there, mostly because his father was always yelling at him and cursing him. All he could think of was being with his friends and what he would do after school. He spent most of his time at his friends' homes or at his girlfriend's home.

It had not always been like that. At one time his father paid attention to him and they "hung out" together. Everything started to change after he was diagnosed. At first, he took better care of himself, managing his insulin and his diet. But he couldn't stand how badly his father treated his mother, and he tried to protect her by demanding that his father treat her with respect. His father hit him across the face. Things only continued to deteriorate from that time on. Eugene became the bad one in the family and felt more and more that he did not belong at home, only with his friends. But his friends changed with each change of schools, and being the new kid in school was hard. But he did make friends. When they drank beer and soda and ate sweets, so did he. They knew of his diabetes and tried to help him but he had already developed an "I don't give a damn" attitude. His eyes had the telltale pearlescent look of a diabetic whose blood sugar was very high. He had lost around fifteen pounds from his already slim body.

Adolescent Suicide

The adolescent girl's particular difficulties in separating from the mother put her at risk for self-harm, including suicide. It is thought that adolescent suicide attempts involve an attack on the internalized object, invariably the mother, by a child unable to give up the libidinal tie to the mother (Friedman et al. 1972). *Vivienne: The Life and Suicide of an Adolescent Girl* (Mack and Hickler 1981) is a portrait of a troubled girl and an examination of adolescent suicide and the culture that fosters it.

Vivienne was little more than 14 when she walked into her mother's silversmithing studio in their suburban Massachusetts home and hanged herself. It was just four days before Christmas, and Vivienne's home was in turmoil as the family was preparing to move to another community where Vivienne's father, a Unitarian-Universalist minister, would assume the ministry of a church. Vivienne was an intelligent and sensitive girl with a gift for writing, leaving behind a long diary and personal journal, a collection of her poems, compositions, and letters to a former teacher whom she had adored. The diary chronicles her inner experience in the three years before she killed herself, after several aborted attempts. The writing was collected by Holly Hickler, a writing teacher at Vivienne's school, who co-authored the book with psychiatrist John Mack, in collaboration with Vivienne's parents, brother, and sister.

Vivienne never was comfortable with her body. She was teased about her overbite as a child and she was always somewhat overweight. She would gorge on sweets and then try to starve herself. At 10 she had a pelvic examination that was so traumatic that she never again "wanted to go near a doctor who was going to explore those regions" (Mack and Hickler 1981, p. 153). Entering a new school where she was cruelly teased by schoolmates, Vivienne became deeply attached to John May, her sixth grade teacher. She called him at home, and sent him letters, journal writings, and poems that were dedicated to him, and received letters from him in return. Vivienne tended to take on the burdens of other family members, but with May she could unburden herself. May knew he had become important to her, but had no idea just how important until after her death.

The news that May was planning to leave the area to return to his native California hit Vivienne very hard. The anticipation of losing him triggered a downward spiral, and then he left. Vivienne became even more depressed and withdrawn, a depression that resulted ultimately in suicide. She read Sylvia Plath's *The Bell Jar*, the story of Esther Greenwood, a virginal young woman living in New England in the 1950s. Esther, a thinly disguised Plath, was tormented by whether to maintain her purity or lose her virginity. She also could not decide whether she wanted marriage or a career as a writer. Tortured by impossible choices, suicide increasingly emerged as a solution to her dilemma, foreclosing the need to make a decision and releasing her from her conflicts. Esther planned several different ways to end her life, forming various mental images of how she would look dead, and then made several suicidal "experiments."

The first hint of suicide is in Vivienne's journal. She identified with and idealized Sylvia Plath, and came to think of death as beautiful like a cloud. "Vivienne had transformed death from something dreaded and bleak to an idealized realm. Rather than a feared or awesome prospect, death became a solution for Vivienne by virtue of being itself distorted into the perfect and self-completing object she had always been seeking" (Mack and Hickler 1981, p. 163). Just as Plath played at being dead and made "practice" suicide rehearsals, Vivienne's playing at being dead escalated into her first attempt to strangle herself. Less than six months later the rehearsal became the final act.

This is the night of July 9; a Monday. I have spent the past half hour in the back bathroom trying to strangle myself, and sending a prayer. The prayer was not strong enough. I never could pray. You can tell when a prayer doesn't get through. I believe it is a sign to check with the validity and sincerity of it. But I have been able to practice how to strangle (myself) all the same. I know that I will need the knowledge some day soon. There are two effects to clutching your throat. I have not had enough time to study the reasons for this. However, one is life and one is death. . . . Life comes in the form of a whitened face and a sensation of tingling through your whole body while you sway back and forth. When you let go, you make jerking motions with increasing speed. This is the more horrifying of the two effects. Death comes as an increasingly darkening face and unrestrained thin breathing, which I am sure would soon die away altogether. Your head pounds painfully and in the mirror I had the privilege to see for myself what my dead face will look like immediately after the killing. Somehow this effect is much less upsetting than the first. Perhaps this is a sign that my prayers are being considered. [Mack and Hickler 1981, pp. 71–72]

Later she wrote across the wall of the bathroom: DEATH IS GOING TO BE A BEAUTIFUL THING. The next day she wrote again to John May, flippantly masking the desperation she felt about not hearing from him in a while: "Dear Mr. May, Would you please write? You know it's very hard to write to a person when you don't even know where he's at! How about a letter? Do I hear a postcard? Anything?" She went on to report the suicide attempt in matter-of-fact tone, and perhaps enlivened by her brush with death the night before, she spoke of her determination to live for another year. Feeling good, she wrote that she had begun writing again and included four poems for him to read and critique, all of which referred to death. Then two days later she wrote to him again in a matter-of-fact tone in which she described activities with friends. But she wrote at the end, "I wish so much I had some friends to be with but I don't, so I'm writing this one" (Mack and Hickler 1981, p. 77).

Then a week before her fourteenth birthday, Vivienne again wrote to May: "One guy tried to rape me five days ago, and I haven't seen him since." Two weeks later she wrote, "Three times, three people in the last 2½ weeks, have tried to fuck me. Twice I was good and stoned and once I was bored stiff. But each time, I just thought to myself—God! Is this all there is? Not only is there no true love, no giving—but this is all as routine as taking your vitamins in the morning. I don't see how you get Saturday night 'fun' out of it" (Mack and Hickler 1981, p. 157). When boys made aggressive sexual moves on Vivienne, she was curious to try it and go along with it as her sister did, but she became frightened and ended up frightening the boys away by pretending to drop dead. She would pretend to faint, and would go limp as her eyes rolled back, and her breathing became shallow. She and her sister would laugh about her "dead" act. Mack and Hickler noted how very unprotected Vivienne felt sexually. Indeed, she seemed to think that only death could protect her from sexual intrusion. "The American culture in which Vivienne was growing up was particularly destructive to a child of her sensitivities and vulnerabilities, and contributed ultimately to her death" (p. 157).

PREGNANCY AND BREAST-FEEDING

For many women, the experience of carrying a pregnancy to term or breast-feeding their infants can become a newfound source of body image enhancement. But for those women whose body image faltered badly in infancy, childhood, and adolescence, it is likely to falter with pregnancy and breast-feeding, which revive earlier feelings of loss of bodily control (Cross 1993). Women who had eating disorders earlier but thought they had recovered may be at risk for relapse during or after pregnancy. For many women infertility or the inability to breast-feed can confirm an already negative body image.

A large-breasted patient had to search for bras with H cups at the end of her first trimester, fearing her breasts would get even bigger when she breast-fed. She said, half laughing and half crying, "They're like the damned monsters that devoured Cleveland." In pregnancy the fetus, the "other within," is focused on, and the woman may feel, as one patient said, as if she had been invaded by aliens. Anal themes of losing bodily control through her water breaking or loss of bowel control during delivery may emerge. The mother-to-be must get used to another change: the vagina has a new function as the birth canal, and thoughts of pushing an infant through it may further evoke fears of being invaded or ripped apart by force. Writer Barbara Grizzuti Harrison described it as "like shitting a watermelon." The new mother's breasts, formerly focused on as objects of sexual desire, come to be the objects of her infant's hungry desire. The patient above who had to get very large bras came to despair when nursing, spending so much time at it that it felt like her breasts were no longer her own. "I might as well just hack them off and throw them in his crib. They're not mine anymore." Nursing breasts secrete milk and leak at embarrassing times. These changes can make her feel less attractive and evoke feelings of anal messiness. Weight gain and the dramatically changing body shape suggest to the woman that she has become fat and that her body is no longer in her control. Those who have suffered from eating disorders in the past may once again become symptomatic, trying to take control of a body that feels out of control by starving it or by bingeing and purging. Some compulsive eaters continue to overeat when pregnant, running the risk of developing diabetes during the pregnancy.

THE AGING PROCESS

Middle age is when your age starts to show around your middle.

Bob Hope

Self-harm can begin at any time of emotional crisis in the life cycle. While both sexes are equally prone to the effects of aging, the aging process tends to exacerbate an already existing sense of body alienation among women that can precipitate the development of an eating disorder later in life. Women tend to gain weight from age 30 on. The physical changes of menopause further assault the body ego: body shape changes, becoming thicker through the middle and flabbier overall; facial muscles slacken; wrinkles and gray hair become more prominent; hot flashes intrude; insomnia and memory loss exacerbate feelings of the other-ness and uncontrollability of the body.

The transitions from adulthood to middle age, to menopause and to old age are all vulnerable times for women when anxieties about their bodies may increase along with harmful practices meant to undo the effects of aging. Baby-boomer women can become as competitive about their looks and fitness as younger women, and can become more inclined to resort to disordered eating practices and cosmetic surgery to maintain a youthful appearance.

While there has been little written or known about eating disorders in old age (Hsu and Zimmer 1988), the bodily changes, loss of function, and shifting body images in elderly women would seem to create a climate in which eating disorders might develop more frequently than has been thought. The body may decline to the extent that it requires care from others, reviving dependency issues, and incontinence evokes once again regressive anal preoccupations. For some, only starving or suicide offers any hope of feeling in control. Probably a lot more elderly women have undiagnosed eating problems than has been thought.

In the older woman with an eating disorder, her illness may have had its onset many years earlier. Self-harm that began in adolescence can become woven into the fabric of the personality, becoming a chronic illness that continues well into adulthood, middle age, and even old age. A study (Rosenzweig and Spruill 1987) investigated the incidence and severity of bulimic-like behaviors in middle-aged women retrospectively—the post-World War II baby-boomer women who had been in college when stick-thin model Twiggy appeared on the fashion scene (1965–1966). Their use of fasting, diet pills, laxatives, diuretics, and vomiting to reduce and control their weight increased significantly from their high school to their college years, and continued to increase from their college days until the time of the study.

It has been my privilege to treat a 67-year-old woman who had been suffering from infantile anorexia nervosa, and I have had the unique opportunity of tracing the development and vicissitudes of the eating disorder from an infantile failure-to-thrive syndrome (Chatoor 1989) to anorexia with bulimic features and its chronic continuation into adulthood and old age (Farber 1992). To my knowledge, there is no other similar case in the literature.

When we began our work together Claudia was 67, 5'3½" tall, and her weight had been stabilized at 82 pounds for the past three years. She had always been severely underweight and sickly except during adolescence, the happiest time of her life, when she weighed 122 pounds. Her lowest weight was 61 pounds at age 30. She was repelled by her emaciated body, but had come to regard her eating problems as part of who she was, something she had to live with.

Claudia was told that although she was of normal weight at birth and nursed well at her mother's breast, she soon seemed to lose interest and appetite, becoming a frail, severely underweight baby who developed as a sickly and emaciated-looking child. She was born when her older sister was 4. Her mother, preoccupied with marital problems, her husband's rages and his alcoholism, was probably depressed. While she may have been a "good enough" mother of symbiosis to Claudia until she was 5 or 6 months old, when she became pregnant with a third child at this time, the pregnancy undoubtedly depleted her of sufficient libidinal investment in Claudia. When Claudia was 14 months old the third child was born prematurely and was very ill. Claudia's mother undoubtedly was overwhelmed by the needs of such a sick infant, the normal neediness of baby Claudia, and her oldest daughter, still a dependent young child of 5. It seems fair to assume that essentially Claudia was emotionally neglected and abandoned, which created a profound emotional hunger for her unavailable mother that could not be satisfied.

Superimposed upon this trauma was an infantile neurotic conflict that Claudia developed at around age 3 when she began deliberately starving herself after a crucial incident. She had overheard her father crying that he had lost all his money in the 1929 stock market crash and now the family would starve to death. There would be no food, the family would go hungry, and there was nothing to do. Fearing the end was near, she remembered thinking that if she made the sacrifice of rationing food to herself in tiny portions, she could extend the food for the family and thus "buy" them days of life. A devout Catholic, she also believed that just as Jesus sacrificed his life for the salvation of mankind, she could offer her pain and suffering up to God and obtain mercy for her family. So to prepare for the famine to come, she began eating even less than before, never telling anyone why. She had heard about the poor hungry children in the world, and knew it was a sin to eat when they were so deprived. She knew that to suffer and offer her suffering up to God would make her special in his eyes and ensure her a place in heaven next to him. And so when Claudia's mother, who knew that steak was one of the few foods that she enjoyed, would cut a piece of her own portion to add to Claudia's plate, coaxing her to eat it, Claudia always refused, feeling an exquisite virtue in denying herself, even though she wanted the meat very much. And so the anorectic battle for control was launched.

She was enrolled in first grade at age 4 in a parochial school run by the same order that her anorectic aunt took her vows in. Not wanting to burden her mother, she never told her that she hated the school and most of the nuns, whom she described as harsh, cruel, and frightening. She wanted only to stay home but did not say so for fear of burdening her mother. Denying her own needs and hungers had become woven into the fabric of her being. The nuns held her aunt up to her as a model of virtue and threatened to tell her aunt if Claudia was "bad." Claudia would get so anxious in school that her stomach would churn. At around age 7 she began vomiting in class and chewing her nails and cuticles so badly that her fingers bled.

At around the same time she began making confession and taking communion, priding herself that she could fast more easily than the others before receiving the sacrament. Then she felt guilty of the sin of pride. At times she had no sin to confess but was afraid to say so, for fear the priest would say, "What do you think you are, perfect?", and then she would be guilty of the sin of arrogance. So she would plan to lie to the confessor and say she had lied three times. Then regarding the lie she was telling the priest as a fourth, she would confess that she had lied four times. She would be given absolution, and would do her penance, which she found meaningless. At other times she might feel so guilty for angry thoughts about the nuns that she did not feel at all absolved by the priest and so saying even a hundred Hail Marys would not have been sufficient.

When she did the Stations of the Cross she would weep for Jesus, who gave up his life so that she and the rest of humankind might live. That she should suffer too seemed the least that she could do for him. She was often ill, and prone to chronic headaches. She was frequently tested for tuberculosis, because it was thought that TB was consuming her body tissue and causing her emaciation. She was taken from physician to physician to find out what was wrong with her. While her mother prayed that Claudia did not have tuberculosis, Claudia prayed for the diagnosis, thinking that if at least she were very sick her mother would have to take her out of school and care for her at home.

Life improved in high school when she was enrolled in a coed Catholic high school taught by nuns and priests. She loved this school, finding the coed faculty more normal and natural than nuns alone. With great trepidation she dared to question church doctrine, something she had never done before, and found that a Jesuit priest encouraged her to continue to question, an experience she found exhilarating. He was so different from her angry, melancholic father. She began to feel strong and finally began to thrive, gaining enough weight so that menstruation began at 13. At fifteen she weighed 122 pounds. Her headaches and nailbiting stopped. For the first time she had friends. She met the boy who later became her husband, attracted to his lively, upbeat manner which was so different from her father's. She enjoyed chaste kisses and cuddling with him.

Adolescence presented a second chance (Blos 1962), and she was able to enter the relationship with her boyfriend with a sense of trust in a man. That hope died when one day he forced himself on her and raped her, though she did not even know then that it was rape and only realized it many years later in treatment. She told no one about it, believing him when he said that she now belonged to him and they would marry. She felt she had to marry him because no decent man would want her, and so she married him at 18 and relocated far from her family where he was stationed in the service. His drinking quickly became problematic and he was verbally and physically abusive, while she felt powerless to do anything about her life. Her anorexia reappeared and she discovered that when she made herself vomit she felt better. Despite losing a great deal of weight, she conceived and delivered her first child at 19, then another two years later. Thoughts about ending the marriage surfaced but were quickly repressed as unthinkable to a good Catholic. At 24, upon her husband's discharge, they came back east and temporarily moved in with her family until he found work. After a third child was born and they were still being supported by her family, she suggested to her husband, who spent his days drinking, that perhaps *she* should find a job to support them. When he agreed, she kicked him in the behind and threw him out. (Later in treatment, she said that one of the big regrets of her life was that she had not kicked him in the testicles when she had the chance.) Finally she obtained a legal divorce, but continued to feel guilt and shame about it. Weight loss continued.

When she was 30 her mother died of breast cancer. Claudia nursed her until the end, watching her grow more and more skeletal. During this time her father, too, lost a great deal of weight and became even more depressed. Claudia's weight dropped to 61 pounds and she could barely walk. She recalled that after her mother's death she wanted to die and join her, "to fade away like a flower, like her, with her." What stopped her was her determination to care for her three boys and her father. Her father's depression deepened, he stopped eating completely, and died in a nursing home of starvation. Becoming disillusioned with Catholicism, Claudia defiantly began eating meat on Friday, long before it was permitted. She went to work as a school secretary to provide for her family.

Charles and Julie, a wealthy childless couple who had been family friends, became like parents to her and her children, taking them to dinner and on vacations, even housing them on their estate. Coincidentally, Dr. Hilde Bruch, known for her pioneering work in eating disorders, was a personal friend of the couple and they had consulted her about Claudia. They convinced her to undergo evaluation at a university medical center, where she was diagnosed at 35 as having atypical anorexia nervosa. She forced herself to eat in front of Charles and Julie, but avoided eating with anyone else to protect her odd eating behavior from the scrutiny of others. She became an artist of deceit, playing with bits of food to appear as if she were eating and throwing food away when no one was looking. Her illness disturbed and puzzled her. She once met Dr. Bruch at Charles and Julie's home.

She could not bring herself to talk to her about her eating problem, even though she wanted to very much. If Dr. Bruch had broached the topic Claudia would have gratefully spoken about it. She really was waiting for someone who might understand. But Dr. Bruch did not ask and so Claudia, a "good little girl" who did not speak unless spoken to, said not a word about it.

She had a brief courtship with a kind and gentle man, then abruptly refused to see him any more or answer his calls. They had never shared more than chaste kisses, yet she convinced herself that his only interest in her was as a sexual conquest. She had begun taking college courses with the encouragement of her adolescent son Rudy, who was eager to see his mother get out and mix with people. Rudy suddenly became very ill with nephritis but ultimately refused the dialysis that could have saved his life, insisting that he would not live married to a machine. Claudia wanted him to have dialysis but finally stopped trying to deter him from his decision. She remained stoic, and her self-induced vomiting increased, as she expressed her emotions through her body. During Rudy's final hospitalization, she would vomit into the hospital toilet before going into his room with a cheerful face. Later we were to understand together that she was vomiting away her anger at him for not choosing to live, for abandoning her. He died at 18. She had no memory of the funeral or the period shortly after his death. She quit her courses, could not sleep, began smoking heavily and drinking herself into a stupor in her bedroom. She went into an alcohol rehabilitation center and then began attending Alcoholics Anonymous.

She continued eating very little and making herself vomit, but managed to work as a secretary. At 58, with the urging of Charles and Julie she was reevaluated at the same medical center that had diagnosed her earlier. Weighing 74 pounds, she was hospitalized immediately for treatment, comprised of frequent feedings and a demand that she gain weight. Battling for control, she lied to her physician, gained just enough to warrant her discharge, and then defiantly lost the weight once again.

She had no friends except Charles and Julie, with whom a triangular relationship developed. She adored Charles. He never told her what to do but respected her autonomy and was gentle. She dared to be feisty with him. When he died, he left her a small trust fund, which enraged Julie, who turned away from her and soon died. Claudia felt bereft and frightened, once again an orphan. The diminishing stamina produced by her eating disorder and her age forced her to retire from her job, creating an emotional crisis. Without the structure and the social aspect of the workplace she had trouble coping with feelings of sadness, loneliness, and anxiety. She kept up with AA meetings, enjoying being around people, but did not participate actively. She enrolled once again in courses, hoping new activities might distract her from her feelings, and was delighted and surprised to discover in her sixties that she had real talent in art. A newspaper article about the opening of a private eating disorders clinic intrigued her and offered hope. She made an appointment and presented herself there, and so our work began.

SADOMASOCHISM AND OTHER PERVERSIONS

Freud (1905a) considered a perversion to be a fixed and urgent sexual behavior that deviated in object choice and/or aim from the accepted adult norm of heterosexual adult intercourse. For Freud, perversion was the obverse of neurosis; that is, those with perversions did what neurotics only fantasied about—beating or being beaten by a sexual partner—or some other form of "kinky" sex. He recognized that all perverse behaviors are normal to the child at some time in childhood, making a disposition to perversions a fundamental human characteristic. Current thinking about sadomasochism and the other perversions expands the concept of perversion to include not only sexual perversions but also perverse elements in personality and object relations. When we consider that the individual who is prone to self-harm makes himself into an object to be tortured and humiliated, we must consider the object relationship he has with himself as a sadomasochistic object relationship.

The Widening Scope of Sadomasochism

The term *sadomasochism* is used to indicate a spectrum of fantasies and behaviors that are characterized by pleasure obtained through hostile aggression and destructiveness (Grossman 1991). The spectrum includes infantile self-injury, sexual perversions and perverse fantasies, and unconsciously motivated behavior that leads to apparently accidental suffering and "bad luck" (Grossman 1991). The essential elements of sadomasochism are thought to be the beating fantasy (Freud 1919), a core delusion of omnipotence and externalization (Novick and Novick 1996). As Stoller (1991) says, "There is no sadomasochistic perversion: there are many sadomasochistic perversions" (p. 8).

Perversion, for Bach (1994), is the opposite of mature love—it is treating another person as a thing rather than a person. That is, the loveless individual uses another person like a prostheses to allow himself the semblance of feeling love. It can be manifested in its overtly sexual form in sadomasochism and other sexual perversions, but also in narcissistic character disorders, anorexia, bulimia, and borderline personality disorders. Such patients have sadomasochistic fantasies because sadism is rooted in the denial of separation and masochism in the fear of it. Whereas in the classical perversions the split ego is patched by a fetish, in sadomasochistic relationships it is patched by the mode of relating. The sadist, refusing to accept that the object is lost, tries desperately to recapture it, getting sexual excitement from punishing the object. The masochist, on the other hand, identifies with the lost object and denies the loss by finding substitutes to whom he desperately clings, preferring the pain to object loss.

Integral to every perversion may be an eroticized childhood trauma that the person is trying to master (Bach 1994, Stoller 1985). There is the wish to harm the object, an act of revenge that converts the childhood trauma into adult triumph (Stoller 1985). The common features are suffering, eroticized pain or flagrant or implied humiliation, and the expression of powerlessness for the recipient of pain and power for the sadist. Perversion is the erotic form of hatred (Stoller 1985); the person with a perversion does not make love but makes hate (Kaplan 1991). Hate can be made in overt sexual activity, in object relationships, and in the relationship to the self. Hate can be made when the object or self is regarded or treated as feces. The person with a perversion can "make hate" secretly by starving or mutilating or otherwise punishing himself.

Looking at perversions as both sexual perversions and perverse object relations provides us with a new and functional way of examining both the erotic relationship and the object relationship that the self-harming person has to himself and others. Kernberg's (1992) classification of sadomasochistic phenomena is valuable for assessing the quality and potential lethality of self-harm. In high level or neurotic character pathology, masochistic personality traits reflect a harsh superego, an overdependence on acceptance from others, and difficulties in expressing aggression that tend to produce depression (Kernberg 1992). At this higher level sexual masochism usually takes the form of a scenario enacted in a context of an object relation that is experienced as safe; that is, hostile aggression such as spanking or light bondage enhances their eroticism. Those with a sadomasochistic personality disorder, however, behave toward their partners with alternating sadistic and masochistic behavior, both within and outside of overtly sexual situations, justifying their sadism on the grounds that they feel victimized and treated poorly. In these patients, an erotic relationship becomes the playing field for their aggression (Kernberg 1992). Individuals with a far more primitive self-destructiveness lash out aggressively toward the outside or onto their own bodies. In those with borderline features, the self-destructiveness emerges at times of intense rage or times of agitated depression. In those individuals with malignant narcissism, their self-destructive behavior occurs when their sense of grandiosity is challenged. In those with certain atypical psychotic conditions that mimic borderline pathology, a psychotic process may underlie their very idiosyncratic and cruel self-destructiveness, creating a tendency toward the most bizarre rituals around purging, cutting, and other self-mutilation.

The more hostility and destructiveness prevail in perverse behavior, the more dangerous and life-threatening the sadomasochism becomes. Toward the more severe pole of masochistic character pathology, there is an increase in primitive and severe aggression along with a very primitive level of object relationships and defenses. At the deepest level of masochism, eroticism fades out completely, leaving the field to what seems to be an almost pure culture of aggression (Kernberg 1992). Those whose self-harm is embedded in such primitive pathology are in extreme danger of killing themselves or allowing themselves to be killed. This most malignant kind of self-destructiveness functions as addiction to near-death that dominates their lives (Joseph 1982).

Female Perversions

Female perversions are different from the gender stereotype of the male pervert. The aim for men is an outside object while women focus their perversity at their own bodies or at objects they regard as their creation, such as their children (de Zulueta 1994). Whether the woman has an active or an impoverished sexual life, the perversion is meant to deceive her about the taboo and shameful elements in her sexual life, including masturbatory equivalents and enactments of taboo sexual activity. Girls and women tend to be involved in a sadomasochistically perverse relationship to their own bodies, in which they simultaneously sadistically torture and take control of their bodies and masochistically take pleasure in being tortured and controlled.

Self-cutting, hair pulling, self-starvation, and bulimic behavior can be considered forms of female perversions with pronounced sadomasochistic and exhibitionistic elements that parody the feminine stereotyped models of submission and purity (Kaplan 1991). Some of the normative female beautification behaviors—dieting, eyebrow tweezing, and the like—can actually serve as a template for the development of self-cutting, hair pulling, self-starvation, and binge-purging behaviors in women, grooming behaviors gone awry. Kaplan considers these behaviors as well as the exaggeratedly "feminine woman," dressed to titillate in stiletto heels and revealing clothing, to be exaggerations or caricatures of female virtues. Many women get a perverse erotic pleasure in the act of spending money for clothing or from shoplifting items. Spending recklessly or shoplifting both have a seductive power for women who feel they have retreated from life as an adventure, the trademarks of a silent and cunning "secret society" of women dominated by consumerism (Merkin 1997). "Shoplifting . . . is sort of sly, like poisoning. . . . Poisoning being a kind of women's murder, don't you think?" (Merkin 1997, p. 245).

In the clinical vignette that follows, Val's eating disorder has reached the most primitive levels of sadomasochism, forcing her husband to realize his masochistic collusion in his own humiliation.

Several years ago a man called to arrange a consultation for himself and his wife. Jim and Val had been married for a year. Jim said that both of them were very disturbed about a problem in their marriage and were ready to do whatever it took to make things better. Both were in their early thirties and held responsible administrative positions. He had known before marrying her that she starved herself and purged and had several medical and psychiatric hospitalizations. She had been honest about this—her honesty was one of the things he loved most about her. He had been able to handle it, but recently it was getting to him more and more. She had been sent to the emergency room several times in the past few months when she had passed out at work or had a seizure. His anxiety about her health was affecting their marriage, but he was sure that with some help they would be all right. A day after the appointment was made, Jim called again, asking me to see them sooner; something had occurred in the interim that felt urgent. I moved up the appointment.

Both were attractive people, or more correctly, I could see that Val had at one time been attractive. Her skin was a grayish-green, her emaciation was startling, her hair was dry and lifeless. I wondered how her company tolerated her illness.

The problem was his fault, Jim said. He was willing to shoulder the blame for not living up to their agreement that they would accept each other as they were and not try to change the other. He was finding that he could not do this. He was tormented with anxiety and nightmares. It was starting to interfere with his functioning at work. When he tried to talk with her about it, she spoke reasonably and was calm and collected. He was the one at fault, she said, because he kept "losing it" when trying to talk with her. I noted the cool and poised pleasure she took as her husband's anxiety escalated. He was starting to perspire while she maintained a pasted-on smile. She did not understand what the big deal was, she said calmly; she had told him all about her eating disorder and had hidden nothing from him, so how come he was getting so unglued? He said that her eating problem had gotten so bad recently that he was frightened she would die. It had never been this bad but since they had gotten married it had gotten so much worse. "One of these days," he said, "you're going to be taken to the E.R. and you're not going to come back. I'll have to bury you." He was not trying to get her to give up her eating disorder per se, but this was getting too scary. He started to cry.

I asked Val to tell me something about her eating problem. No one had been able to help her, she said, and the best in the field had tried. Triumphantly, she rattled off the names of some of the most prominent clinicians whose efforts she had thwarted. When I asked about how her illness was interfering with her functioning at work, she calmly said that she does her work so well that they would never let her go, that they know that they simply have to put up with her episodes. Jim was simply getting himself in an uproar for nothing. She'd had to have emergency treatment more times than she could remember and she had not died yet. Then she smiled a slow strange smile and said that Jim had not even told me the worst of it, that there was more. "Why don't you tell her all about it, honey?"

He began to tell me about the incident that prompted him to ask me to move up the appointment. He said he was used to her having to get up at night; she took diuretics and laxatives before going to bed and got up to use the bathroom several times each night. But that night the smell awakened him; he woke up to find the bed completely soiled with liquid feces and some had even gotten on him. Val was just lying there in a pool of it, awake but with a "funny look" on her face. He did not think he could live like this; it was too much. She calmly said that she had done nothing wrong; it was he who was at fault for not being able to accept this, for not keeping to their understanding. This is who she was; it was no secret, and he had to accept her as she was, "warts and all." It was clear that she enjoyed the humiliation of soiling herself and got great pleasure in traumatizing and humiliating her husband. She had established an anal object relationship (Grunberger 1979) with herself and with him, treating him like shit and turning the marital bed literally into a toilet. Jim said he had a lot to think about; he did not think he could remain in the marriage any longer. He knew he could not tell anyone why. It was bad enough that I, a stranger, knew about this. As the extent of his masochistic collusion in this relationship became clearer to him, this was the ultimate humiliation. They left and I never heard from them again.

11

The Addiction to Wanting

It can be said that all vile acts are done to satisfy hunger.

Maxim Gorky, *Enemies*

Hunger is a terrible pain and suffering deep in the self. When it is not satisfied, it can fill a person with a longing so deep and powerful that it can impel
one to scratch ones flesh, devour whatever can be devoured, or punch out windows. Writer Dorothy Allison (1992) knows this all too well:

> Hunger makes you restless. You dream about food—not just any food, but perfect
> food, the best food, magical meals, famous and awe-inspiring, the one piece of meat,
> the exact taste of buttery corn, tomatoes so ripe they split and sweeten the air, beans
> so crisp they snap between the teeth, gravy like mother's milk singing to your blood-
> stream. When I got hungry my hands would not stay still. I would pick at the edges
> of scabs, scratch at chigger bites and old scars, and tug at loose strands of my black
> hair. . . I'd chew my fingernails or suck on toothpicks and read everything I hadn't
> read more than twice already.[p. 71]

Not all hunger comes from a stomach that has been empty too long. Sometimes it comes from a self that has felt empty and lonely too long, that craves
the feeling of living full, warm, and juicy in one's own skin. When the hunger to
live fully alive is thwarted, it may manifest itself as a hunger disease.

"DO NOT WANT WHAT YOU CANNOT HAVE"

Hunger can be expressed through means other than wanting food (Fenichel 1954). Battegay's (1991) evocative term *hunger disease* refers to the emotional problems based on lack of self-esteem, in which people are driven to possess and consume people and/or things in an addictive manner. They may hunger for food, drugs, alcohol, money, clothing, power, or sex; they may crave physical pain or suffering. Yet no matter how much they get, it is not enough. The hunger is insatiable. These problems are thought to derive from childhood when the child's hunger for closeness, warmth, and stimuli were either inadequately met or overly gratified, resulting in a continual experience of insatiable hunger, a narcissistic hole (Ammon 1979) that must be filled with a constant supply of human objects or substances.

As the expression "food is love" implies, many who feel empty inside express it through oral incorporative behavior, incorporating food, drugs, and alcohol in a way that serves as the prototype for other non-oral behavior. Unlike the anorexic who denies the extent of her hunger, the compulsive eater or the bulimic turns expectantly to food as at one time she had turned to the maternal object for gratification. But food, like the maternal object, fails to satisfy, and in desperation she consumes more and more. Even the nature of her relationships has an oral incorporative quality, as if wanting to devour the other person. When the relationship to the early maternal object has been bound up with much destructive aggression, the eating may have a particularly oral sadistic quality, as if wanting to shred the object to bits with the teeth, and crunchy or chewy foods may be preferred. The bulimic's inner experience is as if the food had gone bad and must be expelled, representing the inability to contain representations of an object so tinged with anger. When the rage is so great that it evokes wishes to punish the object severely, the purge may be especially painful and violent, expressing sadistic and expulsive elements.

When narcissistic needs are not gratified, this failure results in different kinds of psychopathology that involve destructive greed and insatiability, envy and devaluation, regressive fusion, and the dismantling or expulsion of what is incorporated (Battegay 1991). Using disordered eating as the prototype, we can see that in disorders as diverse as hair pulling, nail biting, skin picking, cutting, and compulsive shopping there is the dialectic of the wish to incorporate and merge with the object and the wish to expel and become separate from the object. In hair pulling, the individual plucks out her own hair, a part of her self, thus making it separate from herself, an attempt to separate the self from the maternal body. In the angry zeal to get the offending hair-object out, she may gouge out pieces of scalp beneath the surface. In a kind of reversal of the bulimic binge–purge syndrome, those who save or eat the hair after pulling it out are first "purging" and then "bingeing," expelling the object and then reincorporating it/her. Similarly, the nail biter chews and bites off pieces of nail, cuticle, and sometimes even the surrounding outer skin layer, all parts of herself. If she further chews and swallows the piece of nail or cuticle or skin, she thus reincorporates the object after sadistically punishing it. Even in cutting, pimple popping, interference with wound healing, and other skin mutilation, the individual may take an inner substance from the body (blood, mucus, pus) and may taste it and eat it. Chasseguet-Smirgel (1995) said that these "cases . . . involve . . . some unappetizing forms of autoerotic behavior in which the secretions and/or excretions of the patients' own bodies take pride of place and give rise to secret practices which cannot be confessed to. . . . Admittedly, all of us to some degree or other indulge in hidden autoerotic activities, but those of my female patients are characterized by great *violence* against themselves" (p. 456).

When narcissistic needs go unmet in a child, it is easy for her to convince herself that she does not need closeness, warmth, and self-affirmation from anyone. She splits off the libidinally needy part of herself, presenting a pseudo-independent caricature as if to say, "I don't need anything from you or anyone else." Or as Kathryn Harrison (1997) said: "The dizzy rapture of starving. The power of needing nothing. By force of will I make myself the impossible sprite who lives on air, on water, on purity" (p. 41). The problem with the false self persona is that she comes to believe it is true, that she does not want what she cannot have.

DESTRUCTIVE NARCISSISM AND HUNGER DISEASES

To deny one's neediness is to suffer "a disorder of the recognition of desire" (Ogden 1989, p. 214). Those with hunger diseases often become anxious because they know they want something but cannot allow themselves to know what it is. Not only does the narcissistic self organization prevent access to the needy part of the self, it may actually encourage violent attacks upon it if any move toward a dependent relationship is made (Rosenfeld 1971). The knowledge of what is desired becomes defensively split off from consciousness only to become attached to other things, all of which can become obsessional objects of desire. As Elizabeth Wurtzel (1994) said, "There was never any pleasure . . . in any of the drug use. . . . I was loading myself with whatever available medication I could find . . . to get my head to shut off for awhile. . . . It was all desperation. . . . I would find myself, whenever I was in anyone's home, going through the medicine cabinets, stealing whatever Xanax or Ativan I could find, hoping to score the prescription narcotics like Percodan and codeine. . . . I was consumed by depression and by the drugs I took to combat it" (pp. 107–109).

The desire for the object comes before its acquisition (Lawrence 1990), something known quite well by those in the field of advertising. Adjacent to a display of boots in the window of a women's shoe store on Madison Avenue was the slogan "OBJECTS TO DESIRE." A beautiful piece of glass elicited the desire to steal it in Daphne Merkin.

I am browsing with a friend in one of those . . . shops dedicated to the selling of beautiful, largely unnecessary objects. It is the kind of store whose enticingly arrayed goods seem expressly put in the world to elicit desire in its most abstract form, rather than to satisfy any conceivable human need. So my friend and I . . . are cruising by a sparkling display when I say to her, *sotto voce*: "If you weren't here, I'd take one of those." Take without paying, I meant. We are standing in front of a bowl filled with fake hard candies, ingeniously designed to look like the real thing, only prettier. Imported from Italy, these small glass bonbons are luxuriously tagged at ten dollars apiece. I think how good they would look in my living room, and how no one in the store would be any wiser if I were to pocket one or two. Indeed, I reason to myself with an impassioned lack of logic, I would be righting the scales of mercantile justice on behalf of all my fellow consumers, since the candies are so prohibitively overpriced to begin with. [Merkin 1997, p. 239]

Shoplifting is what the criminologists call a "dark number." Those who overspend or shoplift often have the sense of enraged entitlement common to many who have been deprived in childhood—the sense that the world owes them something, and that if it is not forthcoming, they have a right to take it. Objects become transfigured into magical objects of desire, and a credit card becomes a piece of magic plastic that provides them with easy access. One patient, who had already declared bankruptcy, wrote checks in amounts she knew her account could not cover, simply putting that knowledge "away" in some dissociated place. "In the depth of my worst depressions . . . [shoplifting] gives me a strange sense of accomplishment. I walk out and feel so good for a little while. It creates the illusion that the world is available for the taking. . . . When I was depressed, the physicalness, the rush of it, cheered me up" (Merkin 1997, pp. 242–243).

Buying may be a small part of most people's daily routine, but for others it is a central part of their existence. Uncontrollable urges to shop or buy can only be relieved by buying (Faber 1992).[1] That which is acquired provides only a transient satisfaction, fueling the compulsion to buy more and more. It is the wanting and anticipation of obtaining the object that is the most exquisite pleasure, which is repeated over and over again (Lawrence 1990), with the shopper sometimes buying the same item she had already bought. The "bulimic shopper" shops with abandon, but returns much of what she buys. The "anorexic shopper" does not buy, but wanders through stores, looking hungrily at the displays, allowing herself to have nothing. The shopper who allows herself to buy only picked over shopworn items or clearance sale bargains is like the purging anorexic, who eats just a little but cannot let herself have anything really good. "Revenge shopping" entails running up a large credit card debt to punish a parent or spouse.

Whereas everyday shopping for one's family may be chore or a routine, for the compulsive shopper anticipating a purchase is exciting, transcending thoughts

---

1. I am grateful to April Benson, Ph.D. for her insights into compulsive shopping and her extensive bibliography on the subject.

of mortality and destructibility. "The function of buying or shopping is to transcend the death fear and impose the feeling of immortality and permanence on the ephemeral individual" (Lawrence 1990, p. 68). Making the purchase, the shopper may feel powerful and immortal, in contrast to some elderly people who buy only fruit that is ripe enough to eat in the next day or two, rather than buying unripened fruit that may outlast them (Lynn Tepper, Ph.D., personal communication).

The attention from sales personnel is often an important element, and so the actual purchase may be postponed in order to extend the period of attention from the sales person (Faber 1992). Relationships with sales personnel may develop so that the salesperson may phone the shopper to let her know that items she might like have arrived in the store, thus feeding the shopper's illusion that she is specially cared for. Compulsive shoppers feel good and powerful when shopping but deflated, guilty, or embarrassed when it is over. Once the new acquisition has been worn or displayed, it is no longer new and it loses its ability to provide pleasure, and something else is then wanted. Purchases accumulate, devitalized power trophies that sit unused in the closet, often never even removed from the original packaging, to be returned or ultimately discarded.

Men's compulsive buying is often disguised as "collecting," the selecting, gathering, and keeping of objects of desire (Muensterberger 1994), while most outright compulsive shopping is done by women, who tend to buy objects to enhance their beauty: clothing, makeup, shoes, and jewelry. In our consumer culture, wearing an expensive designer dress may provide the shopper with a sense of personal worth; the beautiful dress is viewed as an extension of the body, the elegant shoe as an extension of the foot, the glistening jewel as an extension of personal beauty (Lawrence 1990). Shoes are particularly desirable for women because even when a woman feels she has become too fat or old to be attractive, the foot in a beautiful shoe can still look very sexy. Acquiring beautiful clothing or jewelry to adorn the outside of the body may shore up a defective sense of self in the same way that stuffing the body with food does, so it is no surprise that compulsive eating and shopping tend to go together (Farber 1995a, Krueger 1988, Mintz 1988, 1992b).

The act of acquisition provides such a heady experience that it is repeated over and over again. This is true also for those who hunger for the next sexual conquest and indulge in binges of frantic sexuality. Anorexia nervosa patients display their emotional hunger by starving themselves physically, while bulimics and overeaters display their voracious cannibalistic hunger through futile repetitive attempts to incorporate a sense of love and fullness in themselves. The hunger for drugs and alcohol, too, often reflects the unspoken need to overcome narcissistic emptiness by producing a temporary sense of well-being. The craving for the violent purge or the blade slicing into their flesh is a hunger for a balance between intense stimulation and the calm that comes after the storm. The hunger for power and control can be an aphrodisiac, resulting in an insatiable desire to hurt and control others. It leads them to try to control increasingly larger numbers of people, puppets whose strings they manipulate. They reward their puppets and seek vengeance against those they cannot control. Their narcissistic hunger drives them to perversely degrading anal object relationships (Grunberger 1979) in which they treat people like shit. In their hunger for power, they become consumed by their own desires, devouring so much and so many that they cannot digest what they have consumed (Battegay 1991), and may sow the seeds for their later fall from power.

Some people hunger for the painful, even abusive relationships that they need as the focus of their inner lives, maintaining an attachment to partners or spouses who will deprive, hurt, or abuse them. In its most extreme form the masochist's intense appetite for physical or moral suffering (Nacht 1995) can function as an addiction to near-death (Joseph 1982). In her essay "Spanking: A Romance," Daphne Merkin (1997) described her concerns about having begun to enact her masochistic fantasies, how indulging it awakened a hunger for more dangerous S & M, and her fear about where this might lead. Hunger, we see, is at the core of the most dangerous and destructive narcissism. Dorothy Allison (1988) described the hunger for violence and death that accompanied her life of abuse and victimization: "Like many others who had gone before me, I began to dream longingly of my own death. I began to court it . . . through drugs and drinking and stubbornly putting myself in the way of other people's violence" (p. 7).

THE ADDICTION TO MORE

Hunger diseases become more severe over time in a way that suggests an underlying addictive process. The anorectic's weight loss increases as her eating and food-related behavior become more and more bizarre, and she weighs herself and exercises more frequently as the illness progresses, in much the same way as the alcoholic develops a tolerance for alcohol, using larger and larger doses more frequently. In those who binge and purge, the binges become greater and more frequent over time, as do the purges. Patients talk about their passion for self-destructive behavior as addictions; they speak of being hooked and needing a fix: a food fix, a gambling fix, a sex fix, a shopping fix, an Internet fix.

Just as eating quantities of sweet or salty food develops a greater yen for it, as patients begin indulging their self-destructive impulses, they want more and more. For example, initially the binge-purge sequence or self-mutilation can occur infrequently, but over time can become a several times weekly occurrence, then escalate to several times a day, becoming more severely out of control. Just as drug addicts can be as addicted to the behaviors associated with drug use as to the drug itself, bulimic behavior, with all its attendant rituals, has the potential to become addictive, as can self-mutilation. It is the loss of control over the addictive substance or behavior that determines addiction. The same components that compose the alcohol addiction cycle also compose the addictive cycle of those with hunger diseases: the preoccupation with the behavior; a ritualistic preparation that helps induce a dissociated state; a sense of being compelled to perform the behavior; and the sense of shame and despair when the act is completed, compelling the individual to search once again for another fix, thus perpetuating the vicious cycle. When the addictive cycle is fully established, it becomes an autonomous closed system that feeds on itself and develops a destructive life of its own, a Frankenstein's monster.

SYMPTOM SUBSTITUTION

Because those suffering from hunger diseases constantly need people or things to compensate for their hunger, when they renounce the substance, relationship, or activity, they suffer great emotional pain. At this critical time, alcoholics or drug addicts may relapse to using their drug of choice or substituting another addictive substance, especially an oral substitution such as smoking or overeating.

For example, in the film *Clean and Sober*, an older man, an abstinent alcoholic who has become a twelve-step sponsor, is waiting in a coffee shop to meet the younger cocaine addict he is sponsoring. He is wolfing down a large piece of chocolate layer cake and washing it down with a chocolate ice cream soda. Having given up alcohol, he has turned increasingly to food to medicate himself for whatever ails him. In *Drinking: A Love Story*, Caroline Knapp (1996) described her battles with alcohol and anorexia, chronicling how her and her friends' use of starving, vomiting, stealing, drugs, and drinking all served to divert and distance them from their painful emotions and feelings.

Symptom substitution in the bulimic has been well explained by Wilson (1983, 1989), who proposes that if symptoms are cleared before there has been sufficient change in the underlying neurosis and object relations, the bulimic ego functioning may be replaced by "bulimic equivalents," such as self-destructive acting out, another addictive disorder, another psychosomatic symptom, neurotic symptom formation, or severe regressive symptom formation. The theory is supported empirically by the findings of my study (Farber 1995a), in which a group of bulimic women reported that after stopping or decreasing their binge–purge behavior, a significantly high number of behavioral equivalents appeared. Specifically, after giving up or decreasing their bulimic behavior, the largest number of women increased their shopping or overspending (Table 11–1), a finding consistent with other studies in which the comorbidity of compulsive buying and binge eating was determined (Faber et al. 1995, Witkin 1988). ("When the going gets tough, the tough go shopping.") After shopping, the behavioral equivalents, in the order in which they were used by the largest numbers of women, were drink-

Table 11–1. Symptom Substitution after Stopping or Reducing
Binge–Purge Behavior

Symptom	X
Shopping	.64
Drinking	.51
Self-mutilation	.44
Suicide attempts	.44
Reckless driving	.34
Drug use	.33
Sex	.30
Shoplifting	.23
Allowing others to cut, brand, pierce, or tattoo them	.17
Unnecessary surgery	.07

From Farber 1995a. X = mean frequency of number of times the behavioral symptom was reported as either having replaced binge–purge behavior when it had stopped, or having appeared when it had diminished (measures the degree to which a self-medicating behavior appears to substitute for binge–purge behavior either by replacing it when it has stopped or appearing when it has diminished).

ing; self-mutilation and suicide attempts (equally); reckless driving; drug use; increased casual sexual encounters; stealing; allowing others to cut, brand, pierce, or tattoo them; and medically unnecessary surgery.

ADJUSTING THE MEDICATION

When one object of desire is substituted for another, a relatively satisfactory equilibrium can occur if the substitute symptom has a self-medicating strength equivalent to that of the original symptom (Farber 1995a). Although shopping was a very popular replacement for bulimic behavior, a finding supported by other clinical observation and research (Krueger 1988, Mintz 1992b, Witkin 1988), apparently it was not a sufficiently strong dose of self-medication to be an adequate substitute for the bulimic behavior. This suggests that when compulsive shopping and spending also failed to medicate the self, then drinking was resorted to, which may provide some explanation for the significant association between bulimia nervosa and alcohol abuse (Garfinkel et al. 1980, Holderness et al. 1994, Lacey 1993). When the drinking subsequently failed, too, then self-mutilation and suicide attempts were resorted to in equal measure.

When subjects in the study were asked if they had ever deliberately harmed their body shortly after a binge–purge episode, sixty-one out of a total of ninety-nine subjects said they had. Two subjects reported that this occurred once, thirty-one reported that this occurred a few times, twenty-four reported that this occurred numerous times, and four reported that this occurred every time, all of which suggests that the bulimic behavior had not provided sufficient relief and had to be bolstered by an additional dose of self-medication of similar self-medicating strength.

When the behavioral equivalents or substitutes were ranked in terms of their self-medicating strength, purging was ranked the strongest, followed in order by cutting, burning, or hitting oneself; hair pulling; severe nail/cuticle biting or piercing; exercise; bingeing; shopping; taking drugs; drinking; casual sex; and shoplifting (Table 11–2). Purging and self-mutilation proved to be similarly potent forms of self-medication for the bulimic women in the study, which suggests that if an individual stops or diminishes either her purging or self-mutilating behavior, it is likely that it will be replaced by self-mutilating behavior or purging respectively.

Whether an individual gives up the addictive-like behavior "cold turkey," out of a determination to live without it, out of a wish to please a therapist, or because the cravings have been diminished as a result of medication, doing so can upset a defensive structure in which the addiction was an integral part and leave the person prone to regressing (relapse) to the use of another destructive addictive-like behavior.

Dina, age 23, was one of numerous children from a large, chaotic family. Her mother was overwhelmed and neglectful; two sisters remember being

Table 11–2. Self-Medicating Strength of the Self-Medicating Behavior (Theoretical Range 0–5 Using Mean

Symptom	X
Purging	3.74
Cutting, burning, or hitting oneself	3.60
Hair pulling, severe nail/cuticle biting, piercing	3.51
Exercise	3.22
Bingeing	2.95
Shopping	2.79
Drug Use	1.99
Drinking	1.96
Sex	1.68
Shoplifting	1.16

From Farber 1995a. X = mean frequency of number of times the symptom was reported as being the strongest self-medication in alleviating dysphoric effect (measures the relative self-medicating strength of each behavior as they cumulatively serve as "strong medicine" in alleviating dysphoric effect).

beaten by their father, although Dina has no memory of this. As a child she hungered for her mother's attention, discovering she could get it when she was sick. Dina managed to get sick frequently, and she reported that she even managed to convince her doctor and a surgeon that her appendix should be removed, although it was not infected. She enjoyed recuperating at home. For years Dina suffered from depression, out-of-control binge drinking, casual sexual liaisons that at times seemed compulsive and other times impulsive, binge-eating and purging, compulsive bargain-hunting, and shoplifting. Her destructive symptomatology was at an all-time high when she began treatment.

She had a promising position in a male-dominated profession and made decisions that could make the difference between life and death for others. She was living with a married sister and could not say no to her frequent and unreasonable demands, giving in to them because they always seemed more important than her own. Then her anger would slowly build until it was discharged in a foul explosion; then she would binge and purge or drink, or both, to calm herself. At the beginning stage of treatment she often came to her sessions hung over. She enjoyed presenting herself as zany, madcap, unpredictable, enjoying hearing her co-workers say, "Oh, Dina is a *trip!*" She bragged of wild exploits: climbing out of the window in the middle of high school English class as a whole classroom laughed and applauded, oiling her bikinied body and lying down on a beach chaise with radio blaring right in the middle of the driveway of her workplace, having intercourse in the Jacuzzi with a man she had just met at the health club as the janitor walked in on them. Yet it appalled her that people might think of her as cheap or "easy." She had had a few affairs with married men. She was forced to leave a job after having been accused of running up a large long-distance phone bill through the illegal use of someone else's phone card.

She regarded her slightly overweight body as gross and repellent, and her rather pretty face as ugly, too, magnifying minor skin blemishes into huge blights. She was remarkably out of touch with the internal sensations that signal the basic human needs to sleep, to excrete, to eat and drink. Frequently she will eat when she is very tired. She has gone for as long as seven hours without urinating because she was unaware of the need to urinate until she found herself dashing to the bathroom as urine poured down her legs uncontrollably. She would stay awake for over twenty-four hours, enjoying the feeling that she was above the need to sleep. She abstained from food in the same way, enjoying saying no to food in public for hours on end, then finding herself in an out-of-control binge in private.

She called one afternoon to cancel her appointment, having just been picked up for shoplifting. After years of shoplifting, she was finally caught, and she was stunned. She was forced to recognize that her life was out of control and she was afraid that she would end up killing herself deliberately or being killed by her way of life. She arranged to be hospitalized voluntarily, something I had tried to convince her to do long before. While in the hospital she was put on Prozac and began attending daily meetings of Alcoholics Anonymous. When she was discharged and resumed her treatment, she no longer drank and the urges to binge and purge were almost completely gone. She could even recognize that she missed it. She was attending meetings of Alcoholics Anonymous six days a week and stayed clean and sober until one afternoon she arrived for her session stinking drunk, having driven over thirty miles in that condition. I had her call friends to come take her home and drive her car back.

She stopped drinking again but she began to have impulses to drive off bridges and to cut herself. When I asked what the cutting would do for her, she said she felt like a balloon about to burst; popping it open would release the tension. Frightened of these impulses, she finally agreed to add a second weekly session of therapy and began to call me between sessions on occasion.

Allowing herself to feel more securely attached to me allowed her to explore the self-destructive impulses that were frightening to her. Dina recalled that when she was around 10, her sister teased her about a large brown mole on the back of her thigh, taunting her that it looked like a piece of shit stuck there. Dina responded to the taunting by taking a paring knife and cutting the mole away. Ten years later she became transfixed by the crease in her eyelid while looked in the mirror as she applied her makeup. As she put it, she wanted to know about the place where her eye and eyelid met, the place that separated inside from outside. So she picked up a razor blade in a trance and slid it slowly across her eyelid crease, watching in excited fascination as drops of blood appeared and slowly dripped down her cheek. If Dina had not been in psychotherapy, which helped her explore the meaning and psychic functions served by the self-harm behavior, and if she did not have a safe attachment to her therapist, undoubtedly self-mutilation and suicide attempts would have emerged to replace the drinking and bulimic behavior.

THE STRONGEST MEDICINE FOR THE DEEPEST PAIN

We want immediate relief from pain—not insight, understanding, or the development of the capacity to bear the pain. Dina's pain required a combination of "medicines" which she took as needed. Getting picked up for shoplifting was a wake-up call that helped convince her of two things: that her once-a-week treatment was not sufficient and that she could not continue acting like this. The individual may start with a relatively mild medicine and if the desired relief is not obtained, may increase the dose of the same medicine. Then if that is not enough, a new kind of medicine, stronger than the first may be added. And then perhaps another. The strongest and most unrelenting pain requires the strongest medicine to alleviate it. When Dina gave up two crucial self-medications, the binge-purge behavior and the drinking, her pain worsened despite the fact that she was on antidepressant medication. The impulses to kill herself or cut herself became the stronger medicines that beckoned to her.

The findings of the study discussed above has implications for understanding how self-harm develops as self-medication for hunger diseases, and how severe purging and severe self-mutilation become unusually potent and potentially addictive. The sample was one of chronically self-harming women with a median age of 28.5, whose bingeing and purging endured, on average, almost 13 years, and their childhood and adult self-injury endured for around 21.5 years. This suggests that in those with hunger diseases there are infantile and childhood developmental precursors to the more full-blown eating disorder and self-mutilation syndromes that developed later. Over time, when these perverse soothers failed to provide sufficient self-medication, other soothers of a stronger and more severe kind emerged to provide the strong self-medicating effect that was needed. Clusters of such behaviors were formed, unconsciously self-prescribed by the individual according to the unique pain of the hunger disease.

As has been discussed, severe purging, suicide attempts, and certain kinds of self-mutilation, specifically self-cutting, burning, and hitting oneself, seemed to function as the strongest kind of self-medication for a group of bulimic women survivors of the most severe childhood and adolescent trauma (Farber 1995a). While we cannot know whether these findings are based on memories of real events, on fantasies, or on fantasied elaborations of real events, what we do know clinically and empirically is that fantasied elaborations of traumatic memories most often evolve from real events (Berliner and Williams 1994, Davies and Frawley 1994, Williams 1995). Memory may disort some of the details that speak of an essential truth. In the context of the most unspeakable cumulative trauma—physical and sexual abuse, medically related trauma, neglect and repeated experiences of loss, abandonment, or separation—these individuals developed a terrible sense of body alienation and sense of their bodies as damaged, dirty, and worthless. The body alienation allowed them to develop an unusual defensive ability to induce dissociation and hyperarousal, to somatize in general, and specifically to regulate their overwhelming anxiety and depression by means of bodily self-harm. They live primarily in the paranoid-schizoid mode (Klein 1964) and regress to the autistic-contiguous mode (Ogden 1989, 1990), governed by the pattern, boundedness, shape, rhythm, texture, hardness, softness, warmth, coldness of an object—by cutting, purging, and burning themselves, living "on the primitive edge of experience."

THOSE WHO NEED THE STRONGEST MEDICINE

My study also compared several different subgroups of women with bulimic symptomatology, shedding light on the relationship between different kinds of self-harm and different varieties of hunger disease resulting from childhood and adolescent trauma. To understand how these subgroups were identified, it is necessary to discuss briefly the basic design and hypotheses of the study. (See the Appendix for more information on the study.)

It was an exploratory cross-sectional survey, originally meant to compare those who binge and purge but who do not self-mutilate with those who binge and purge and also self-mutilate. Adult subjects were purposely recruited from several sources: a campus of the State University of New York; newsletters for people with eating disorders, obsessive-compulsive disorder, trichotillomania, dissociative disorders, and survivors of sexual abuse; self-help groups and clinicians known to serve these special populations; tattoo and body piercing shops; and a magazine for those with special interests in body piercing. Of all the 110 people who responded, 11, including the three men who responded, did not meet selection criteria and so were not included. Of the 99 subjects only 10 reported no current or recent self-mutilating behavior, making it necessary to divide the sample into two comparison groups different from those originally planned. The first was women with bulimic symptoms who did not mutilate themselves at all or mutilated mildly (nail or cuticle biting, hair pulling, skin picking), called the Mild group ($N = 24$). The second, the Severe group ($N = 75$), was women with bulimic symptoms who reported current self-mutilating behaviors that either carried the potential for severe tissue damage and infection (cutting, sticking, or burning themselves, trying to break their bones), or who indicated that they performed any of the behaviors in the mild category severely enough to cause severe infection or injury.

It was hypothesized that compared with the bulimics who mutilate mildly or not at all, those who self-mutilate severely will tend to have had more severely traumatic childhood and adolescent experiences. In other words, the more severe self-harm was expected to correlate with the more severe trauma, and it did. Specifically, the Severe group reported having experienced greater numbers of traumatic experiences in childhood and adolescence than the Mild group: more family violence, physical abuse, and severe or chronic illnesses in childhood as well as more family violence, physical abuse, sexual abuse, surgical procedures, and chronic or severe physical illnesses in adolescence. Thus, severe self-mutilation and purging turned out to be probable indicators of severe childhood and adolescent abuse and other trauma.

It was expected that the Severe group would have had more severe childhood self-injurious and disturbed eating or feeding habits when compared with the Mild group, and this hypothesis too was supported. The Severe group reported more numerous childhood self-injurious and disordered feeding habits and adolescent self-mutilating and disordered eating behaviors. Thus, the greater the number of childhood eating and self-injurious habits is likely to be predictive of greater numbers of adolescent eating- disordered behaviors and self-mutilating behaviors, both of which are predictive of severe adult eating-disordered behavior and self-mutilating behavior. The chronicity of the bulimic behavior was found to be meaningful at the trend level of significance ($p < .10$) in terms of predicting the development of severe self-mutilation. The findings suggest that as binge-purge behavior increases in severity over time in an escalating and addictive pattern, the nature of the bulimic behavior shifts to creating a more intense and violent purge, while the milder self-mutilating behavior over time shifts to more intense and violent self-mutilating behavior, with increased risk for suicide.

It was expected that the Severe group would have other emotional and physical symptoms that are more severe than the Mild group, and this hypothesis also was supported. Although there were no significant differences in scores between the Mild and Severe groups, both groups had unusually high scores in somatization and childhood onset dissociation. The Severe group reported significantly higher scores on dissociation, number of somatic illnesses, and suicidality than the Mild group. This means that self-mutilation and suicide gestures should be regarded as indicators of a hunger disease so severe that they might ultimately require death as the strongest self-medication.

It was expected that the Severe group would engage in the more severe binge-purge behavior and this was supported in part: the Severe group used significantly more numerous purging methods, and purged more severely (a meaningful trend finding of $p \leq .10$), but no significant difference was found in the severity of their bingeing. Both Mild and Severe groups consumed nonedible substances as part of the binge, including nutshells, cleaning fluids, Drano, food or drink that had spoiled, worms, dirt, bones, shampoo, crushed glass, hair, paper, plant food, coffee grinds, large amounts of vinegar, nail polish remover, rubbing alcohol, mercury, money, scouring powder, and aluminum foil. The comments they added suggest that some of these items were ingested to cleanse their bodies of all foulness, to punish or mutilate themselves internally, or to kill themselves.

It was expected that the binge-purgers who self-mutilate severely would experience the purge as the experiential apex or most intense part of the binge-purge episode. The Severe group did tend to experience the purge as the apex of the binge–purge episode (a meaningful trend finding of $p \leq .10$) in comparison to the Mild group; the subjects deliberately sought to induce the severest purging to experience the intense stimulation and pain.

It was expected that the binge-purgers who self-mutilate severely would have a more negative body image. While both groups reported quite negative total body image scores, the Severe group reported a significantly more negative total body image than the Mild group. The Severe group reported significantly less satisfaction with their appearance, specific parts of their body, and total body image. Both groups reported that their self-esteem was bound up with fluctuations in weight and that they "felt fat" at their present weight. It would seem that the women who binge and purge believe they can improve the internal psychic representations of their bodies through the "medicine" of weight loss. Those who binge and purge and self-mutilate are perhaps demonstrating that they already know unconsciously that weight loss itself is not a strong enough medicine to effect a change in their body image, and that adorning their bodies with the scars of self-mutilation is an outward message to the world of the low esteem with which they regard their bodies.

SPECIAL SUBGROUPS WITH MOST SEVERE HUNGER DISEASES

Within the Severe group, several overlapping subgroups were identified as manifesting some unusual differences in the ways they binged, purged, and self-mutilated. Several of these groups had the most extreme scores, indicating that they were to be located toward the most severe end of the self-harming spectrum and most likely suffered the most severe personality and dissociative disorders, with some probably frankly psychotic. These were women with the worst hunger diseases, and included those who thought that they had multiple personality disorder (MPD) (N = 10), those who indicated that they experienced ritual abuse (N = 10), and a very large body modification subgroup (N = 19) who reported having themselves tattooed or pierced by others. Two groups were distinguished by the prominence of their laxative abuse: those who preferred laxatives for purging (N = 9) and those whose purging behavior began with laxative abuse (N = 14). This group's self-harm was not as extreme as the Severe group in general. Although sexual orientation was not inquired about, a small subgroup of women voluntarily indicated that they were lesbians (N = 4). This group was too small to form a subgroup profile, and each of the four had experiences of trauma and self-harm that were more diverse than similar. However, what distinguished this subgroup from the larger sample was a difference in body image.

Multiple Personality Disorder Subgroup

The write-in answers to various open-ended questions indicated that some subjects believed they were suffering from MPD. For example, some specifically stated "I am MPD"; some said they had been diagnosed with MPD; others referred to themselves in the plural as "we" or "us," in a context that indicated that they believed they had more than one discrete personality; others referred to conflicts between alter personalities. Although whether these subjects actually suffer from MPD or not cannot be known, the severity of their past experiences and current symptomatology distinguishes them from others with extremely severe experiences and symptomatology. In fact the mean scores of the MPD subgroup (N = 10) were higher than the mean scores of the Severe group in most critical measures. They reported more childhood feeding problems and self-injury, more childhood and adolescent trauma of all kinds—repeated physical and sexual abuse, medical and surgical procedures, family violence, childhood illnesses, and traumatic separations. Their defensive use of dissociation began earlier in childhood. Their bulimic and self-mutilating behavior was even more chronic, more severe, and occurred more frequently, and they reported more self-harm behaviors of all kinds. Their dissociation was more severe and they reported more physical illnesses as adults. They reported even greater negativity about their body image in general, and their self-esteem was especially affected by fluctuations in their weight.

Their bingeing and purging and their self-mutilation were different from the rest of Severe group's. Both their bulimic and self-mutilating behaviors were more chronic; they used fewer purging methods but purged more severely, consuming more nonedible items, especially those that were caustic or poison. The sequence of behavior and the affect state before, during, and after the bulimic episode differed from those of the Severe group on average, and the experience of self-mutilation was qualitatively quite different; rather than reporting a sense of relief from depersonalized or hyperarousal states, often they would have no memory of the self-harm episodes or not remember it until later. When they did remember it, they usually said that the behavior was not meant to make them feel better but was the attempt of an apparently violent and sadistic alter personality to punish them. Sometimes they spoke of other personalities making sure that the punitive alter did not do too much damage.

The total self-medicating strength of not only their bulimic and self-mutilating behavior but of all their self-harm behaviors was less than that for the Severe group, and they scored higher in suicidality than the Severe group. This suggests that this group was experiencing minimal relief from pain while using the most severe of all self-harm behaviors, and was therefore the subgroup most likely to succeed ultimately at suicide.

Marietta is a 30-year-old single white woman who lives alone and is employed. She heard about the study through a newsletter for survivors of incest or sexual abuse. She stated that she was raised in both Catholicism and satanism. She exists in a severe depersonalized state most of the time. She stated that she had been physically and sexually abused since early childhood and continues to be so abused.

As a child she had ulcerative colitis and asthma, and developed arthritis in adolescence. She binges and starves herself, purging exclusively with laxatives and diuretics. She often feels nauseated, has diarrhea or constipation, stomach trouble, cold limbs, breaks into cold sweats, is short of breath, has heart palpitations. She picks at herself, burns herself, bangs her head, has frequent accidents, has had several surgeries, and cuts herself, frequently needing medical attention. She has carved upside-down crosses (satanic symbols) on her arm and leg. She reports negative feelings about her stomach, hips, thighs, genitals, and buttocks, and that she has negative feelings about her male alter's chest. Since shortly after stopping or diminishing her binge-purge behavior she has begun mutilating herself, abusing drugs and alcohol, and shopping compulsively, and has made suicide attempts. She wrote: "When I hurt myself I usually don't remember it happens until after it is done. I have a trance memory. Then another personality comes out to harm the body. I have multiple personality disorder. My personality was told never to tell anybody about the abuse."

Ritual Abuse Subgroup

Experiences of ritual abuse have been reported in numerous newsletters for abuse and ritual abuse survivors, in the *Cultic Studies Journal*, in *Recovery from Cults* (Langone and Eisenberg 1993), and in investigative reporting of vampire cults (Ramsland 1998). The ritual abuse subgroup ($N = 10$) overlapped greatly with the MPD subgroup and presented an even more alarming picture. The findings (Farber 1995a) suggest that the experience of being victimized by the most egregious assaults to their bodies in the most malevolent families has produced individuals with the most severe psychopathology. They are even more at risk for suicide for two reasons: first, they have been indoctrinated to believe that to sacrifice their life for the cult is not only a duty but an honor, and second, they may well have internalized the cult's injunction that if questioned by outsiders about the cult, they must kill themselves to protect the cult from detection. They may go to their deaths willingly as some of those at Jonestown or Waco did, believing that their parents, or cult leaders, or God or Satan is pleased by their sacrifice. All but one subgroup had carved or burned words or symbols on their bodies: "HELP," "HATE," "KILL," "PAIN," "Die Fat Whore," "Bitch," "Slut," crosses, and satanic symbols (pentagrams, upside-down crosses, and "666"). One had cut her own satanic and Latin phrases on her body and also had a Star of David cut on her body by someone else. Another was Kathleen, whom you read about in Chapter 8 (see page 255).

Lesbian Subgroup

The four women who indicated that they were lesbians constituted 4 percent of the total sample, an incidence in the study population that was consistent with the findings in other studies of bulimic women (Johnson and Connors 1987). Lesbian women in treatment for an eating disorder typically are bingers and overeaters who do not purge or diet; in fact, obesity is a major health problem for this group. Research suggests that lesbian women may overvalue thinness less than heterosexual women, and may value muscularity, physical strength, and larger size to a greater degree (Striegel-Moore et al. 1990). This subgroup was, in fact, different from the Mild and Severe group in terms of body image; although the internal representations of their bodies were poor, they were not as poor as in the Mild or Severe groups. They were less dissatisfied with the size and shape of their bodies and were more satisfied with specific parts of the body about which eating-disordered women tend to be very critical. They rated their calves, arms, breasts, and buttocks in the fairly positive range, while the total sample rated calves, arms, and breasts in the neutral range, and buttocks in the negative range. Three of the four lesbian women binged and purged and had periods of starving themselves, making them atypical of lesbians with eating disorders, and the same three had carved or burned words or symbols on their bodies: "HELP," "HATE," "HELL," a heart covered with barbed wire, other hearts, crosses, flowers, and initials.

Body Modification Subgroup

Those in the body modification subgroup (N = 19) reported that they had had their bodies modified by tattoos or piercings (other than ear piercings). The subgroup greatly overlapped with the 21 percent of the total sample who reported that they had cut, scratched, or burned words, designs, or symbols on their bodies. Seventeen subjects of this subgroup reported current severe self-mutilation in addition to allowing others to mutilate them. Some of the designs were decorative, but others reflected a preoccupation with death, rage, pain, suffering, sorrow, satanism, and self-hatred.

Although the body modification subgroup reported even more severe child and adolescent trauma in general than the Severe group, the specific trauma of childhood and adolescent sexual abuse was less. What was distinctive about these subjects' history is that they were beaten more and suffered more medical and surgical trauma. This subgroup dissociated less severely than the Severe group and had even less childhood-onset dissociation than the Mild group. While the intrusive procedures may have been experienced as much as a physical violation as sexual abuse, the key difference was that these violations were not performed by their parents and were without sadistic intent. Having had to endure injections, needle sticking, and surgery probably created an unusual adult tendency to try to master the trauma by engaging others to inject and pierce them or even by becoming professional body piercers and tattoo artists themselves. During their adolescence they suffered the additional traumas of family violence, placement in foster or group care, and loss of a parent through death or separation even more than the Severe group. This subgroup also began bingeing and purging and self-mutilation earlier and had more severe eating problems and self-injury in adolescence than the Severe group. They no doubt came to rely far more on the group in institutions for a sense of belonging and family; other needy teenagers abused and alienated from their parents became like family. It was probably while in these institutions that scarring themselves became their self-styled initiation rite.

This group somatized even more than the Severe group, which might be expected from their having their earliest years involved so much with physical illness and surgery. Although most of these subjects both mutilated themselves and had body modifications done by others, two of them reported that they had engaged in severe self-mutilating behavior several years ago but had stopped. Bree, a young woman who was not a subject in my study, elaborates on this behavior (Strong 1998).

> Bree, age 26, had a long history of cutting, starving herself, bulimic vomiting, purging, punching walls, biting and scratching her body, smashing her legs with a baseball bat, smoking marijuana, and using amphetamines and other drugs. She had a childhood history of sexual abuse and was brutally raped at 13. Not surprisingly, she has prostituted herself. She has given up her self-mutilation as well as the drug and alcohol abuse that went with it, and even her smoking, greatly improving the quality of her life. What has replaced these forms of self-harm is getting herself tattooed and pierced, which she considers an improvement. "I know if I go back to drugs they will kill me. . . . So sometimes I feel like cutting is the only thing I have left, the only really satisfying release in these situations where the pain is too great. Fortunately, because I'm not doing drugs, I'm not coming across situations that are too painful too often anymore" (p. 186). She has displaced some of her impulses to injure herself into getting herself tattooed and pierced, and laughs that "I can at least pretend that's healthy. . . . I think it's art. . . . But the fact of the matter is when you get pierced or tattooed, you do have a big needle going through your skin. I definitely have a fascination with the sadistic, masochistic, darker kind of stuff. I guess this is the most positive expression I've found so far for that side of me" (p. 186). For her the tattooing and piercing are both self-medication, with an opiate-like high and a rush, but the effect of the tattooing lasts longer than that of the piercing. "About an hour into it, you feel like you've got the heroin nods. . . . I remember looking forward to that feeling the last time I got a tattoo. It feels like you're on drugs without the negative effects" (p. 186).

Almost all the subjects in the body modification subgroup reported that it was shortly after stopping or diminishing their bingeing and purging that they either began or increased their body modification and other self-harm behavior, substituting more self-harm behaviors for the bulimic behavior than the Severe group. Even though they used fewer and less severe self-mutilating behaviors than the Severe group, the total self-medicating strength of all their current self-harm behaviors combined was greater. This suggests that the tattooing and body piercing not only substituted for the severe self-mutilation but also added to the self-medicating strength of all their self-harm behavior to provide an unusually powerful dose of self-medication. This group had even more negative body images than the Severe group, but they "felt fat" less than did the Mild and Severe groups.

Despite the self-medicating power and extreme stimulation provided by tattooing, piercing, and erotic piercing particularly, it was not powerful enough to awaken their dissociated and deadened body-selves, and the body modification subgroup scored even higher than the Severe group on suicidality. Only individuals with great difficulty in experiencing pleasure could tolerate such extremes of pain and stimulation or could inflict it on others. Only individuals with the most damaged body image could regard the mutilation of such sensitive and intimate parts of the body as adornment for the sake of beauty. As in other addictive behaviors, a tolerance for the "drug of choice" seems to develop over time, going from piercing and tattooing nonerogenous parts of the body to erotic piercings and tattoos. When the tattooing and piercing that once may have enlivened a deadened self comes to lose its self-medicating strength, the risk for suicide is greatest.

Neela, a professional body piercer and tattooist, had to be excluded from the study because she did not meet the criterion of bingeing and purging in the past year. Nonetheless, her responses provide a very instructive profile. She is over 31, a former bulimic who began inducing vomiting at 19, developed a penchant for laxatives which induced the most intense purge, stopped purging at 21, substituting self-starvation and binge eating alternately. She reports a history of family violence and childhood physical abuse. From early childhood on she picked at herself, and from age 19 to 30 she continued to cut herself and stick herself with pins. Soon after stopping the binge-purge behavior, she began having her body pierced and tattooed, and a career of piercing and tattooing others. She now owns a tattoo and body piercing shop. She reported that her body is almost fully covered with tattoos and she has had her earlobes, nostril, septum, and nipple pierced. She states that the tattooing does not make her feel better, in fact it makes her feel worse. She just cannot stop.

Subgroup of Those Who Reported Laxatives Produced the Most Intense Purge

From the subgroup of those reporting the purge as the apex of the binge–purge episode, another smaller subgroup was created of those who reported that laxatives usually produce the most intense purging experience ($N = 9$). This group was atypical of both the Mild and Severe groups in several ways. First, they experienced even greater numbers of trauma than the Severe group. In childhood this subgroup experienced more physical and sexual abuse and medically related trauma than the Severe group. The physical and sexual abuse continued in adolescence, during which the subjects also experienced family violence, placement in foster or group care, and loss of a parent. With that history, one might expect that they began dissociating in childhood even more than the Severe group, became ill a lot more, and had a greater number of disturbed feeding and self-injurious behavior, but, interestingly, they did not. They reported dissociating less, and having fewer illnesses, feeding problems, and self-injurious behaviors in childhood than did the Severe group. As adults they dissociated about as much as the Mild group but less than the Severe group and their suicidality was less than that of the Severe group.

Second, although the severity of their self-mutilation was less than that of the Severe group (they mostly picked at themselves or bit their cuticles severely), the frequency and the chronicity of their self-mutilating behavior was greater than both the Mild and Severe groups (they had been mutilating themselves on average 23 years). They also somatized even more and had an even larger array of symptom-substituting behavior. However, they had fewer eating problems in adolescence and began their bulimic behavior later in life, at about 23 years of age, compared to both the Mild and Severe groups. Their bulimic behavior, on average, had been chronic for twelve years. Despite the fact that the purge was the apex of their bulimic experience, it was less so than for both the Severe and Mild group. They used fewer purging methods and so both the severity of their purging and the self-medicating effect was less. This suggests that their primarily laxative purge, though stronger than other kinds of purging, nonetheless was not as powerful as they wanted it to be and did not produce the desired effect. In fact, the number and total strength of all the self-medicating behaviors they used lacked power, making it likely that they would escalate the severity of their already most chronic self-mutilating behavior.

They reported even greater body image negativity, but it was expressed much less in terms of dissatisfaction with their weight, which when combined with the paramount importance of laxatives in their lives, suggests that this is a group of women whose raison d'être has become focused not on ridding themselves of as much fat as possible but on ridding their bodies of as much fecal matter as possible. They relate to their bodies and selves as if they were excrement. Their extraordinary obsessive and compulsive involvement with their feces is a somatic means of enacting what they cannot express verbally, which may provide some explanation of their high somatization score.

The unusually late onset of bulimic behavior in this group, at 23, might suggest that it was at this time in their lives when these women began to remember and reexperience the violence of the abuse they suffered, accounting for the worsening of symptomatology commonly noted clinically when abuse survivors begin to recover traumatic memories (Davies and Frawley 1994, Herman 1992, Miller 1994).

Subgroup of Those Whose Purging Began with Laxatives

Overlapping considerably with the group that purged primarily with laxatives and presenting quite a similar profile was another small subgroup of subjects ($N = 14$) who reported that their purging began with laxative abuse rather than vomiting, a feature that was atypical for both the Severe and Mild subgroups and for bulimics in general. In fact, nine of this group used only laxatives to purge. For this group their bingeing and purging were at times equally intense. This group differed from the group that purged primarily with laxatives in that some of them did not limit their self-mutilation to the milder skin picking and cuticle biting.

One subject from this group is a 29-year-old white single woman living with her "long-term partner" (a phrase that suggests she may be living with another woman in a lesbian relationship) and working as a school psychologist, pursuing a Ph.D. in clinical psychology. Some responses regarding past trauma suggest considerable confusion about what actually occurred. For example, she indicated that between the ages of 6 and 9 she suffered "verbal sexual abuse," but then indicated that she had had sexual contact that she had not consented to but was uncertain if this occurred before age 10 or if it involved a family member. She reported having had a poor appetite and pulling her hair from early childhood through adolescence, picking at her skin from early childhood to the present, and severe nail and cuticle biting from latency through adolescence. She began bingeing and laxative use at 18, self-starvation soon after, and began self-induced vomiting at 26, at times using syrup of ipecac. She has taken as many as seventy laxative tablets at a time. She has also used enemas, fasted, and exercised excessively. She finds the binge and the purge are equally intense experiences. She began self-mutilation shortly after stopping or diminishing the binge–purge behavior. She has hurt herself deliberately more than fifty times in the past year, requiring medical attention two to five times. She currently picks at herself, cuts herself, sticks herself with pins, burns herself, has frequent accidents, deliberately deprives herself of sleep and water, trying to dehydrate herself. She carved a cross on her arm and cut teardrops onto her face. She is quite articulate in describing her self-mutilation.

> Emotions, usually anger or pain, build to intolerable levels. Rather than feel them, I begin to feel fat and to HATE my body. Exercise and vomiting wasn't enough. I also had to punish my body. I wanted to see blood come out. I wanted scars all over. I'd dissociate and start cutting and burning. It was a release, an absolution for my sin of being alive, a way to make my pain visible. I also would rub on cuts when I was hungry to associate pain with hunger, and therefore not to eat. I also liked the attention my therapist gave my cuts.

The Subgroups and the Meaning of the Obsession with Thinness

While most of the subjects had an overt fear of being fat and an extremely negative body image, many of those who suffered the most egregious abuse had little to say about weight concerns and wanting to be thin. This group included four subgroups: those who reported that laxatives produced the most intense purge; those who reported that their laxative use preceded or precluded vomiting; those who had themselves tattooed, pierced, or branded; and the lesbian subgroup. They wrote in a way that indicated that at the moments of self-harm their thinking was at or approaching primary process and that they regressed to a psychotic level. They wrote in a very driven manner about wanting to hurt and punish themselves, about needing to evacuate their bodies of all filth. Although all but the lesbian group reported that their self-esteem fluctuated with changes in their weight, they used the word *fat* not to describe their bodies but to flagellate themselves verbally, suggesting nonetheless that they may not be so concerned with weight as with self-punishment, self-hatred, and anality.

ATTACHMENT AND HUNGER DISEASE

We all have our own personal idiosyncratic repertoire of self-medicating behaviors, our "quick fixes and small comforts" (Witkin 1988) that come in handy in difficult times to soothe and calm ourselves. Some may not be harmful—we may clean out our closets, balance our checkbooks, play soothing music, rearrange the furniture, go for a drive or walk or run— but others have the potential to be—we pour ourselves a drink, or devour what is in the refrigerator. If our early attachments have been secure, we will know better what it is that we want or need and we will not lack recognition of what it is that we want. We will not want what we cannot have or never had, but will tend to want what we have had that was good, to re-create earlier warm and comforting experiences. When we are hungry we will eat; when we are tired, we will rest. And when we have had a tough day and are in need of comfort, we might settle in with what was comforting in childhood: a warm bath; a "comfort food" meal; changing into cozy pajamas; reaching out to touch and be touched, physically and with words. When our early attachments have been insecure, we will tend to want what we cannot have or never did have. It is not the wanting or the hunger that is problematic, but the lack of recognition of it. It is the blind looking for what one hungers for in objects, substances, and relationships that cannot provide it that is ultimately harmful.

PART IV

CLINICAL IMPLICATIONS

Orthodoxy of any kind forces us to live on the capital accumulated by previous generations, and this is the enemy of creativity.

Martin Bergmann, "Asking for Freud's Blessing"

12

The Attachment Paradigm

Recent attachment research supports the view that the development of a healing narrative—the Shakespearean injunction to "give sorrow words"—is the key task of psychotherapy. This work can be usefully informed by attachment ideas and research findings.

Jeremy Holmes, Attachment, Intimacy, Autonomy

The treatment of self-harming patients can be challenging and difficult. We cannot predict which patients in the borderline range will do well in treatment, and therapists are reluctant to invest themselves in a treatment that feels like a gamble. A few long-term follow-up projects at Chestnut Lodge (McGlashan 1986) and from New York State Psychiatric Institute (Stone 1990) have shown that some borderline patients do well, whether they have received intensive explor-atory therapy, supportive therapy, or hardly any therapy in the years following discharge from the index hospitalization, while others do poorly, regardless of the kind or amount of therapy received (Kroll 1993). Despite our best efforts and expert training, self-harming patients may continue to suffer and may even die as a result of their own actions. On the other hand, this knowledge should pro-vide us some sense of perspective and humility, serving to temper our rescue fan-tasies, and providing a certain freedom for clinicians to take on the challenge. For many of these patients, treatment with a therapist who is ready to stay the course may work out very well.

Psychotherapy process and outcome research have found that therapy suc-cess is correlated not with a specific technique or orientation but with two fac-tors related to attachment (Kroll 1993). The first is the "fit" between patient and therapist, something that may be apparent within the first few sessions. A good fit augers well for the formation of a secure attachment. The second is some degree of supervision, peer group supervision, or consultation for the therapist (Kroll 1993), which provides the therapist with the supportive attachment to trusted colleagues or supervisors he or she will need to maintain a sense of safety and security in conducting a potentially tumultuous treatment. No therapist can provide constancy and reliability if he or she is constantly caught up in the whirlpool of anxiety evoked by the patient's self-destructive threats and actions. This chapter and those that follow address clinicians with or without psychoanalytic training, and present the conceptual, organizational, and clinical principles of an empathic and pragmatic psychoanalytically informed treatment.

The principles come from a developmental psychoanalytic framework for conducting a psychotherapy that is contained in the patient–therapist attachment relationship. This does not necessarily mean that the technique itself is psychoanalytic, but rather that concepts of psychological defenses, a dynamic unconscious, resistance to treatment, and transference, countertransference, and enactments are operant, and that interactional processes between patient and therapist are emphasized. As Loewald (1960) said, it is the significant interactions between the patient and the therapist that ultimately lead to structural changes in the patient's personality. That is, ego development is resumed in the therapeutic process whether it be from a point of relative arrest or from a higher level. These concepts are necessary for making sense of patients' wildly oscillating wishes for intimacy and fear of intimacy, their boundary issues, their impulsivity and despair, their cognitive confusions, their sense of damage and inadequacy, and their difficulty in tolerating disturbing inner monologues and the intrusive images, thoughts, and memories created by trauma (Kroll 1993). The understanding of patients' boundary issues will help the therapist exercise concern about the patient's safety without being overly protective, set limits around which the treatment will be conducted, and determine how elastic those limits can be.

The therapist will need flexibility to combine supportive and exploratory techniques and to provide the patient with strategies for tolerating the impulse to harm herself and the dysphoric affect associated with the impulse. When the patient has developed the ability to curb and contain her self-harm impulses so that they pose little danger, she may be ready to allow herself to live more in the depressive mode of experiencing emotion and may be ready for the treatment to deepen by addressing the intrapsychic.

Getting to this point in treatment is a three step process involving controlling the self-harm behavior sufficiently so that the underlying problems can be addressed, thus making the self-harm and related symptoms unnecessary for self-regulation. First, patients must be helped to take responsibility for using the strategies or tools that can bring about a shift in their view of their self-harm from being out of their volitional control to within their control. Second, patients must be helped to begin to view and use the therapist as a transitional object in the service of developing the means to withstand the destructive impulses and to begin to identify and regulate affect. In this process, as attachment is strengthened, the self-harm behavior may diminish greatly or be relinquished. Third, self-harm can also be modulated by the effects of cognition, which seems to be as effective as the selective serotonin reuptake inhibitors (SSRIs) in diminishing the trauma response and other anxiety disorders, and seems to provide even more enduring success. The drugs may do this by dampening the activity of the amygdala biochemically, while cognitive-behavioral therapy does it, researchers believe, by strengthening memory circuits in the cognitive parts of the brain through the repetitive exercises that are the hallmark of this kind of therapy, thus allowing the reasoning brain to override the amygdala (Hall 1999).

It is not relinquishing the self-harm behavior that heals the patient. Rather, as she comes to be healed, she is more able to give it up, although at times it may beckon and call seductively. What is crucial is not so much the siren call but whether and how the patient tolerates and contains the beckoning and calling. We all have to wrestle with the call of old destructive solutions. None of us can expect to extinguish our demons forever, but we can find ways to keep them from enslaving us.

Therapists are faced with the limitations of the settings in which they practice, and the limitations of insurance and managed care. Thus, many difficult patients are deemed untreatable and are denied adequate coverage for their care. For many such patients, twenty outpatient visits a year or a one-week hospital or day hospital stay is grossly inadequate. Medical and psychological care meted out in the briefest symptomatic treatment, as is the current trend, results over time in increased expenditures in emergency room treatment, increased medical care, and revolving door hospitalizations. A wise investment of clinical, emotional, and financial resources may cost more initially but is likely to result in positive clinical changes that help patients live in the real world rather than in the expensive world of illness—hospitals, emergency rooms, and physicians' waiting rooms. Because of the tenacity of the symptoms and because treatment requires the exploration of how the symptoms became embedded in the personality, the optimal treatment is likely to be long-term and more frequent than once a week.

Managed care is not interested in optimal treatment, only the minimum and most "cost-effective" treatment. However, if case managers can be convinced that the dollar cost of providing more intensive outpatient treatment is likely to prevent the greater cost of a higher level of care, they may be inclined to authorize it. As so often happens, patients feel forced to change therapists as their insurance coverage changes. Therapists may want to consider approaching the managed care company with the idea that a wiser investment of financial resources would allow patients to continue in treatment with the therapist of their choice rather than disrupting attachment bonds by forcing patients to change therapists as their insurance plans change. Insurance companies need to know that by adhering inflexibly to these rules, they will be inadvertently fostering the maintenance of self-harm.

Because both patient and therapist need to have a more expanded "holding environment" than is usually found in psychotherapy, the psychotherapist may not be the sole source of treatment for the patient, and the therapist may need to consult collaboratively with supervisors, peers, physicians, nutritionists, nurses, and others. It is hoped that the following chapters will inspire new and creative ways of using and altering the existing resources more efficiently and productively to help these patients.

THE THERAPEUTIC ALLIANCE AND SADOMASOCHISM

The therapeutic alliance, sometimes called the working alliance, is the means by which therapist and patient work together toward the same end. In less disturbed patients, it is thought that treatment proper starts once a therapeutic alliance has been established. Some individuals are thought to need a period of preparation for becoming a patient, a period of ego-building treatment, by which already existing ego functioning is strengthened and other ego functions are built, so that the ego can be drawn into the treatment process (Blanck and Blanck 1974). This has been described by Rubin Blanck (1998) as a process of building "psychological connective tissue." We need to begin where the patient is, and many self-harming patients are at a level where their ego deficits make the capacity for a therapeutic alliance extremely difficult. In fact, the most pronounced features *are* the difficulties that characteristically arise in their treatment to obstruct the development of a therapeutic alliance (Kroll 1988). Because features in their personalities get in the way, developing a therapeutic alliance with patients with significant sadomasochistic pathology can become the major focus of treatment. That is, the therapeutic alliance may represent the end point of successful therapy, not the mechanism by which therapy works (Kroll 1993). For other patients, the development of a therapeutic alliance may represent the beginning of the development of a reflective self that can tolerate a therapy that is more intrapsychic in focus.

Again, the outcome research shows that when therapy is successful, it has to do with the "fit" between patient and therapist. This illusive concept of fit may have more to do with the therapeutic alliance than has been thought. In outcome studies done in the fields of psychiatry, counseling, and psychotherapy, the quality of the working alliance was a critical factor in predicting outcome (Kroll 1988). Definitions of the therapeutic alliance have been problematic because of attempts to describe it as "out there" in the patient rather than characterizing it as an "in-between" clinical, relational concept requiring input from both patient and therapist. A useful formulation has been proposed by Novick and Novick

(1998): "The therapeutic alliance is a way of looking at the entire clinical field, a lens, that allows for heightened attention to the capacities and motivations, conscious and unconscious, from all levels of the personality and all stages of development, that enter, for both patient and analyst, into the specific collaborative tasks of each phase of treatment, to the resistances and conflicts that arise around these tasks, and to the therapeutic change in motivation during the course of analysis" (pp. 827–828).

The formation of a therapeutic alliance is a collaborative effort that is necessary for therapeutic change. The alliance lens highlights the motives and capacities of both patient and therapist for collaborative work on certain tasks (Novick and Novick 1998b). The working alliance is based on the conscious and rational wish to be rid of suffering (Greenson 1978). That is, patient and therapist work collaboratively together toward the goal of discovering and finding alternatives to sadomasochism (Novick and Novick 1998b). Elements of the therapeutic alliance may be spoken of in various terms, such as Bion's (1962) "the container," projective identification (Klein 1964), and the analyst as new and real object (Loewald 1960) or as a transformative object (Bollas 1987). When the patient is desperately attached to his omnipotent functioning and sadomasochistic object relationships with himself and others, this poses the most formidable resistance to the development of a therapeutic alliance.

"THERE IS NO ONE THERE FOR ME"

What is often diagnosed as depression is the sadomasochistic need to live in a world of psychic and physical pain in order to feel safe, connected, and powerful (Novick and Novick 1998). A central theme of many patients, but especially those whose lives are organized around self-harm, is that "there is no one there" for them, a theme that speaks of a lack of secure attachments; earlier in life there was no one home emotionally in a consistent and reliable way. To have nobody (no body) makes one turn aggressively to one's own body in order to feel that there is somebody (some body) there. "I feel alone and I am afraid that nobody is there anymore. . . . I cannot trust anyone and nobody puts his trust in me. Nobody, no body! I only have my own body . . ." (Vanderlinden and Vandereycken 1997, p. x).

At the heart of psychotherapy is a safe and secure human attachment that has the potential to alter and even repair the attachments to pain and suffering encoded in the brain in those who harm themselves. The intimacy in the attachment relationship provides a corrective emotional experience for individuals who fear that intimacy will engulf and swallow them whole, whose solution is an endless oscillating quest for and flight from attachment. It furthers the development of the patient's ability to regulate moods, emotions, and physiological states, a maturation that is related to the capacity for reflective thinking. It is intimacy within the attachment relationship in psychotherapy that is the key to the development of more autonomous functioning and intimate relationships (Holmes 1996).

SUPPORTIVE ATTACHMENTS

Support is the basis of all psychotherapies, whether it is essentially a supportive psychotherapy, expressive psychotherapy, or something in between (Holmes 1996). Ego psychology is based on the structural model of the mind, the ego being the mediator between id (instinctual) impulses, the demands of reality, and the strictures of the superego (conscience and ego ideal). Freud (1923) defined neurosis as a turning away from reality, and so the aim of all psychotherapy is to make a better adjustment to reality. In expressive psychotherapy, this is done primarily by strengthening the ego in a process involving interpretation, regression, and insight by which primitive and maladaptive defenses are replaced by more mature, flexible, and better-adapted ones (Holmes 1996). In traditional supportive psychotherapy the ego is accepted more or less as is, while the therapist attempts to modify the demands made upon it.

Combining elements of both, Blanck and Blanck (1974) proposed an ego psychological model of psychotherapy, sometimes called psychoanalytic developmental object relations treatment, in which faulty ego defenses are not accepted as is but are built and strengthened along with other ego functions. The Blancks taught this model curriculum for training in psychotherapy at the Institute for the Study of Psychotherapy before the deficit-conflict controversy emerged and, anticipating more recent psychoanalytic developments, long before attempts were made at integration. It is a model that does not see either conflict or deficit as an all-or-nothing proposition, but is based on the concept that building ego functions increases the structuralization of the ego and is essentially supportive, and that a patient with well-developed ego functioning is more capable of sustaining the demands on the ego made by a more intensive psychotherapy. The aims of treatment are determined by the therapist's assessment of the patient's ego deficits and the separation-individuation inadequacies. The therapist using this approach functions at times as a new real object (Loewald 1960), providing the consistency, reliability, and caring that foster a secure attachment, and using the attachment relationship to promote ego development. That is, the ongoing ordinary reliability of the therapist, the face-to-face interactions that promote safe and secure attachments, can change the way the patient's brain is wired so that the work of ego building can be tolerated in the present, and more exploratory work can be tolerated in the future. Whether the therapist is operating in a supportive or exploratory mode may be less important than the level and shifts in process as they occur in therapy (Kroll 1988). Druck (1999), one of the contemporary analysts attempting to integrate the conflict-deficit polarities, urges that the therapist must consider whether a particular intervention at the specific moment in treatment will tend to be stabilizing or destabilizing, as patients with deficits may shift between levels of structural capacity and function.

Jeremy Holmes (1996), referring to Harry Stack Sullivan's Cinderella metaphor, suggests that although "supportive psychotherapy has long been the poor relation of the psychotherapies, a Cinderella stuck at home doing the routine psychiatric chores while her more glamorous psychotherapeutic sisters are away at the ball, . . . attachment theory may be the much-needed fairy godmother for supportive psychotherapy" (p. 117). Supportive psychotherapy, metaphorically a base mineral like copper, has generally been held in considerably lower esteem than the "pure gold" of psychoanalysis. "The very word *support* has music hall overtones, evoking the image of a truss, a cumbersome and noncurative holding operation, much inferior to a definitive hernia repair" (p. 117). We tend not to appreciate sufficiently how inherently supportive the nature of the attachment relationship is in psychotherapy (Holmes 1996). Support is what makes the patient feel that finally someone really *is* there for him and "may be compared with invisible foundations upon which all buildings rest, and the external buttresses that some, especially those in poor condition, require" (p. 119). "Support often makes its presence known by its subsequent absence. Only when our lower limbs or the foundations of our dwellings develop problems do we become grateful for the support they normally provide" (p. 121). This is true of virtually all health care and psychotherapy, and even the cognitive-behavioral therapists and psychopharmacologists are beginning to acknowledge that if patients are to ingest and digest their prescribed treatments, a supportive attachment is essential. Without a supportive base, treatment will fail.

Support is composed of the therapist's punctuality, reliability, attentiveness, and nonjudgmental acceptance of the patient, and of the working alliance between them. These features occupy the foreground in supportive psychotherapy and the background in the expressive or directive psychotherapies. All psychotherapies contain the components of support, directiveness, and expressiveness in varying proportions at different times in the treatment (Holmes 1996). For example, in psychoanalysis the element of support may shift from background to foreground at times of emotional crisis in the patient's life. If excessive problems with mood or anxiety make an expressive treatment inadvisable, the clinical picture may shift once psychotropic medication is prescribed, with many patients then more able to tolerate and benefit from a more expressive psychotherapy. So at the beginning the treatment may need to be primarily supportive and then shift at the appropriate time. An important difference between the supportive and exploratory modes is the use of the transference. In supportive psychotherapy, a positive transference is fostered and maintained but usually not acknowledged or discussed, while in exploratory treatment, working with the transference, especially the negative transference, is a central feature. The negative transference can ruin the treatment while the positive transference, and not insight, is

"what turns the scale" (Freud 1916, p. 445). Just as the supportive and exploratory components intertwine, so do process and content, making for a dynamic
interplay between process and content, support and exploration (Kroll 1988).

TYPICAL PROBLEMS IN TREATMENT

The therapist's attitude and demeanor must present his conviction to the
patient: "You can get through this and I can help you to do that." If there is
anything that makes a patient even more anxious and dashes any sense of hope,
it is a chronically anxious therapist with whom a meaningful attachment is problematic. And if treatment can help the patient give up his attachments to pain
and suffering, to repair what got disrupted in infancy, the therapist will need
to create an environment that promotes the development of a secure and safe
attachment for both patient and therapist.

Therapists' Training

Complicating the picture further is that the majority of patients in therapy
are treated by clinicians who are not well trained in conducting a psychodynamically informed psychotherapy and who have not themselves experienced a long-
term psychoanalytic psychotherapy or psychoanalysis as a patient. Basic licen-
sure or certification requirements are no guarantee that the therapist is qualified
to conduct a treatment that is more than a basically supportive one. Using their
own intuition, common sense, and humanity, therapists piece together bits of
technique and theory acquired along the way, and essentially fly by the seat of
their pants, doing the best they can, often with considerable discomfort about
whether they are proceeding in the right direction. Sometimes the patient responds well to the treatment and sometimes treatment is a disaster for patient
and therapist. All therapists bring their own personal history to the treatment,
and when their own issues intrude, which is inevitable, those who have not had
a personal or training analysis will be especially handicapped at dealing with their
own countertransference responses.

Reducing the World to Trauma and Survival

Errors are made in all treatments but when they are made with severely self-
harming patients, the consequences are likely to be greater. Serious errors are more
likely to be made when the therapist works without adequate training and in isolation. Patients with a history of abuse may attract therapists who also have an
abuse history, who are unusually susceptible to projecting their own victimization history onto a patient, or whose unresolved history will be stirred up by the
patient's reports of similar trauma (Vanderlinden and Vandereycken 1997).

"Trauma is contagious" said Judith Herman (1992, p. 140), meaning that all therapists working with trauma patients run the risk of developing symptoms of vicarious traumatization. Listening to and accepting our patients' stories of the worst kind of victimization and sorrow can be overwhelming, filling us with disgust, fury, and helplessness. We often feel incompetent to respond and may feel angry at the patient for provoking such feelings in us. Repeated exposure to such stories of human cruelty may cause us to lose faith in the power of the therapeutic relationship and to feel far more vulnerable than ever (Herman 1992). As Vanderlinden and Vandereycken (1997) point out, under such circumstances it is easy for therapists to narrow the psychological world of patients to one of trauma and survival. When that occurs, therapists may become overly detached to defend against the emotional impact, which may result in an identification with the offender and a tendency to blame the victim for what happened. Or the therapist may become so overidentified that he starts to mourn or experiences the patient's pain so much that he may try to rescue the patient or assume too much responsibility for his life.

Self-Care for the Therapist

Working with patients with such difficult histories can test our psychological strength, making it especially necessary that therapists exercise certain preventive measures. Therapists must have realistic treatment goals in mind, taking into account the patient's problems and the therapist's expertise. Therapists with a flair for the dramatic may be especially at risk and put their patients at risk. Even in the most obvious cases of traumatization, the drama of confrontation and recovering memories may result in further trauma (Vanderlinden and Vandereycken 1997).

Consultation with supervisors and colleagues experienced in working with traumatized patients is more likely to keep the therapist from becoming vicariously traumatized by the work (McCann and Pearlman 1990) and from committing serious errors. Some interesting alternatives to traditional consultation have been proposed. A collaborative model of supervision acknowledges that although the supervisor brings more clinical experience and, in some areas, more wisdom than the supervisee, it can be shared in a way that recognizes the knowledge and experience of the supervisee (Etheart and Perkins 1998). This collaborative model creates a safe environment that recognizes common ground, rather than emphasizing the supervisor's power. When transference–countertransference issues lead to an impasse in working with self-destructive patients in an inpatient setting, requesting a consultation intervention often results in removing the obstacles to progress (Sansone et al. 1994). Similarly, difficulties in the treatment of eating-disordered patients could be resolved through psychotherapeutic partnering, a challenging multidimensional collaborative approach (Benson and Futterman 1985).

Therapists treating such challenging patients must have a good balance in their professional and personal lives, which may mean reducing the number of patients seen and creating clear boundaries between their professional and personal lives. Allowing a 24-hour availability for contact may be a temporary necessity in the beginning of treatment or in specific times of crisis, but should resolve in due time. Both patients and therapists need a social support system to prevent the therapist from becoming the patient's only significant other (Vanderlinden and Vandereycken 1997). "The therapist's personal life should be emotionally rich and psychologically strong enough to nourish his or her professional life, and not the reverse" (Vanderlinden and Vandereycken 1997, p. 169).

Therapeutic Ambivalence: Fearing and Supporting Self-Harm Symptomatology

Symptom management must be a focus of treatment, for which a psychoanalytic model lacks some practical value, and so many who have been analytically trained may decline to treat very self-destructive patients. Clinicians in hospitals, mental health clinics and social service agencies, however, may not have the option to decline to treat self-harming patients and may be required to treat patients they are not prepared to treat.

In addition, clinicians may feel ambivalent about patients who harm themselves. If patients continue their self-harm behavior in the hospital, they may be placed on one-to-one observation; they may have their razor blades, shoelaces, cigarette lighters, and matches taken from them; they may be searched for drugs or prohibited from using the toilet unsupervised shortly after eating, to prevent purging. All eating, toileting, and self-care activity may be controlled and monitored. They may be rewarded with extended privileges for stopping their self-harm behavior while at the same time the institution unwittingly encourages and reinforces the problematic behavior. Expected to stop harming themselves, they may receive simplistic explanations about how and why they cannot stop harming themselves, "as if self-injury under altered states of consciousness, such as trance or dissociated states, is the logical, understandable, and inevitable response to present-day distress and emotional overarousal over past events, especially childhood sexual abuse" (Kroll 1993, p. 95). Expected to become autonomous adults who are able to care for themselves, they may be treated like completely dependent children whose every move must be monitored and controlled.

If inpatient or day-hospital treatment is to be successful, clinicians and administrators must heed the fears and suspicions of formerly hospitalized patients. The hospital milieu has the potential to provide a safe place and a "holding environment" for the patient only if thoughtful consideration is given to exercising control and providing containment in a way that minimizes the experience of retraumatization and maximizes the opportunities for the patient to act autonomously (Shapiro and Dominiak 1992). For example, when the locked adolescent unit in a private psychiatric hospital was changed to an open-door unit, there was a marked diminution in disruptive and self-destructive behavior. The success of this transition was attributed to the unambivalent commitment to the open-door policy by staff leaders, development of empathic containment approaches, and staff responsibility for the design of these approaches (Crabtree and Grossman 1974).

Therapists often fear that the patient is or could become suicidal and that they will be held liable for their patient's self-destructive behavior. The climate in mental health and medicine has become increasingly more litigious in this country, making the legal issues of greater concern here than in Canada or abroad. There have been increasingly more lawsuits against psychotherapists for unethical or substandard practice. While self-harming patients may require hospitalization at points in their treatment, sometimes the inclination to hospitalize the patient is made out of the need to assuage the therapist's anxiety.

So for a number of reasons, clinicians may feel impelled to reduce symptomatology as quickly as possible and by any means possible. Symptom management must always be an integral part of the treatment focus, but focusing primarily on symptom reduction may have the opposite effect of inducing patients to cling to their symptoms even more defiantly. For many, losing their symptoms is tantamount to losing their best friend. For others, losing the symptoms means losing their best defense against a descent into psychosis or suicide. All defenses must be respected and treated with care, even when those defenses are potentially life-threatening symptoms. Untrained therapists have little understanding of how symptoms function and tend to view them, as managed care does, as something to be eliminated as soon as possible and by any means. When patients are viewed and treated as a bundle of symptoms, we unconsciously collude with them in maintaining a sense of identity that is bound up with their symptoms. Fighting to hold onto the symptoms can feel to them as if they are fighting for their life.

Chronic Patienthood as an Identity

As much as patients complain of their symptoms, we must never lose sight of how important their symptoms are and the functions they serve. We know that individuals with bipolar disorder are often loath to take psychotropic medications because they will lose the manic episodes that let them feel omnipotent and alive. Those with schizophrenia may also become very attached to their illness, refusing to take their medication, like the 29-year-old schizophrenic man who pushed a woman off a subway platform to her death, or the Yale Law School graduate who stabbed his pregnant fiancée to death. A fine balance must be reached between respecting the patient's autonomy and intervening when his behavior threatens the life of another or himself.

The fear of giving up the symptoms was described by Ken Steele, a man who finally decided to relinquish the voices that spoke to and about him from the radio

360 / When the Body Is the Target

and television, making him feel special and powerful (Goode 1999). "You are the star. Everybody on TV is talking about you. They're talking about you on the Johnny Carson Show" (p. 1). The symptoms had defined who he was during his "32 year cross-country schizophrenic odyssey" and made him a star in his own horror show. Making the decision to take and stay on antipsychotic medication required a willingness to let go of this feeling of specialness. It happened when he met and came to trust a new therapist who could tolerate the whirlwind his treatment had become. But on the day when he realized his hallucinations had actually stopped, he curled up in his bathtub in a fetal position for four days, debating whether to tell his doctor the voices were gone and wondering what he would ever do without them. He comforted himself that if the ordinariness of being without his symptoms became too painful, he could always stop taking his medication. He had to grieve the loss of his symptoms, a profound loss that therapists are inclined to overlook.

Psychologist Lauren Slater's grief when Prozac released her from her symptoms was stunning and disorienting. She had been diagnosed with obsessive-compulsive disorder, considered a secondary rather than primary diagnosis (Slater 1998) when she began taking Prozac, and apparently was not in psychotherapy at the time. Her long history of psychopathology included attempted suicide, self-mutilation, and anorexia, and resulted in five hospitalizations. She has carried a diagnosis of borderline personality disorder since she was 19, and a diagnosis of severe and recurrent major depression. She has loved being ill since childhood, and so when Prozac released her from her disabling symptoms, she was grief-stricken.

When I was a girl I loved fevers and flus and the muzzy feeling of a head cold, all these states carrying with them the special accouterments of illness. . . . I loved my illnesses. I loved my regal mother bending to the mandates of biology, allowing me to rest and watch TV. She even read me stories, sitting at my bedside.

Illness was a temporary respite, a release from the demands of an alienating world. . . . Getting better was a grief. . . . You wanted to weep. Prozac, too, made me want to weep. Prozac, too, was a grief, because it returned me to the regular world with consequences I never expected. . . .

Doctors assure the public that psychotropic drugs don't get a patient high; rather, supposedly, they return the patient to a normal state of functioning. But what happens if such a patient, as I was, has rarely if ever experienced a normal state of functioning? What happens if such a patient has spent much of her life in mental hospitals, both pursuing and being pursued by one illness after another? What happens if "regular life" to such a person has always meant cutting one's arms, or gagging? If this is the case, then the normal state that Prozac ushers in is an experience in the surreal, . . . a disorientation. . . . Thus Prozac . . . blissed me out and freaked me out and later on . . . sometimes stunned me with grief. [pp. 21–25]

Clinicians must carefully consider what it means to a patient to give up an identity organized around chronic patienthood. To be certain, it can ultimately feel like a rebirth, but it is one that requires the slow and gradual death of the false-self identity as a chronic patient. When the patient does not experience himself as giving up the symptoms but as having them taken away from him, this is likely to evoke a regressive clinging to them as a means of retaining autonomy. We need to remember that the identity of chronic patients is to some extent a false self that has been created by patient and caregiving professionals (Montgomery 1989b); that is, it is an interweaving of the primary psychopathology and iatrogenic pathology. Giving up that identity means loss, sadness, and guilt that needs to be worked through in treatment.

TREATMENT OBJECTIVES

The overall task of treatment is twofold: first, to help the patient move from living primarily in the immediacy of bodily experience to living primarily within a reflective self in a representational world; and second, for the attachment relationship in the treatment to serve as a bridge to new and different relationships in the real world. The primitive, regressive, and sometimes psychotic personality must be prepared for what Grotstein (1993) called the weaning-into-reality process by having the patient's needs addressed by empathic attunement and attachment.

Before the patient can come to care for himself and develop a reflective mind, he must feel cared for and protected and know that his well-being is foremost in the therapist's mind. To create the capacity for reflective thought, a working relationship must be established in which the patient feels a sense of security and safety that over time can come to change the encoded traumatic attachments in the brain. Because the expression of emotions is so concrete, impulsive, body focused, and destructive, treatment should aim at helping these patients develop a capacity for taming their aggression and impulsiveness, altering a negative body image, and developing a greater capacity for self-care, affect tolerance, and containment, and a greater ability to use words symbolically.

To structure the therapy the therapist must consider the psychological makeup of the patient and the relationship of his ego structure to the attachment system. Treatment must address three central issues: the pathological split between mind and body, the perceptual and conceptual disturbances, and the severe ego regressions suffered (Sacksteder 1989a). The treatment must grow organically out of a diagnostic assessment that considers ego structure, self experience, and the self-harm behavior. The cornerstone of treatment should be an individual psychoanalytic psychotherapy based on ego-psychological principles, that is, a treatment that considers the ego structure of the patient's personality and how attachment difficulties are reflected in impairments of the ego. The therapist will need to consider how the self-harm behavior serves defensive needs, and will need to examine the patient's ego defenses in terms of their adaptive and destructive aims and goals. Treatment should be tailored to the specific needs of the patient as defined by diagnosis, and so some may be better suited to a primarily exploratory approach while others may require a primarily supportive treatment.

FOCUS ON INTERACTIVE PROCESSES

The cornerstone of therapy is the attachment relationship formed in the therapist–patient dyad, essentially an interactive system. Because the treatment of personality-disordered patients is characteristically marked by transference–countertransference (i.e., attachment) problems, the therapist must concentrate primarily on the process of the interaction between himself and the patient (Kroll 1988), identifying problematic interactions as they occur and providing support toward mutually changing the process. When possible, exploration of the problem between the patient and therapist is related to other similar patterns in the patient's life. All processes that interfere with the development of a safe and secure attachment must be identified, with the aim of developing in the patient of a sense of active responsibility in becoming a partner in the process of change. Within this structure, key themes such as victimization, loneliness/emptiness, incompetency, and entitlement will arise and provide the subject matter. Because of the nature of the self-harm, often the treatment requires the use of cognitive-behavioral techniques for symptom management. Other treatment modalities may be needed as well, such as group and family treatment, the expressive therapies, medical monitoring, and nutritional counseling.

The therapist–patient relationship plays a great role in how other treatment modalities and other professionals are introduced into the patient's life, and in the patient's ability to begin to extend the trust she has found with the therapist to these other professionals. A successful referral to a physician, nutritionist, and family therapist goes way beyond giving the patient a name and phone number.[1] The first such referral the therapist makes serves as a bridge connecting the patient to others in the object world. The therapist– patient relationship thus can help the patient extend her sense of trust to others, and start to build a needed social support system.

ENGAGING THE PATIENT

Why do we wish to be remembered, even when none remain who looked upon our face? Surely, though it must retain an element of self-consideration, it is a last acknowledgment that we need to be loved; and, having gone

---

1. I am grateful to Richard Steinberg, M.S.W., who was a model of how a successful referral should be made.

from all touch, we trust that memory may, as it were, keep our unseen presence within the borders of day.
> William Soutar's diary, 1943, quoted by Thomas Mallon,
> *A Book of One's Own: People and Their Diaries* (1986)

Why does anyone go into treatment? The conscious wish is to be rid of suffering (Novick and Novick 1998b) and the unconscious wish is to be known and remembered by another. The therapeutic alliance (Greenson 1978) is based on both these objectives, which must be kept in mind in treating people who cling to suffering and present great difficulties in participating in a therapeutic alliance.

Engaging self-harming patients is the most crucial task as they frequently arrive for the initial consultation with certain expectations on the basis of past experience or hearsay. It is always a good idea to initiate a conversation about how they feel about being there. I use the word *conversation* deliberately because treatment should be an extended conversation in plain English, not ponderous pronouncements by the therapist or extended inquiries. Conversations are mutual, having to do with the easy way words ping-pong back and forth, creating invisible arcs of attachment. At times the therapist will be quiet while the patient develops his thoughts or clarifies feelings, while at other times, the patient is quiet while the therapist tells him something he thinks will be helpful for him to think about. Patients want what we all want—to speak, to be listened to and heard and held in the memory of another. They want to "live out loud," and be heard.

To engage patients in a treatment relationship, certain obstacles need to be removed, such as focusing on the pathological aspects of their self-harm behavior. This is old news that they have heard many times before and may well be the way that they think of themselves: mad, out of control, and simply crazy to be doing these things that they must do in order to live. They may believe that they are beyond hope and understanding. So if their therapist joins them in focusing on the pathological aspects of their behavior, as undoubtedly many before have done, they are likely to experience that therapist as punitive and sadistic. To join with them in their own assessment of themselves as worthless, contemptible, and out of control is to re-create an abusive or sadomasochistic relationship from the past.

It can be an unexpected, even disarming, surprise for the patient to meet a therapist with a genuine interest in wanting to understand the self-harm behavior. To disarm a patient is to remove his hostility or suspicion, at least temporarily, substituting a sense of intrigue with the therapist instead which creates a wonderful window of opportunity. The therapist's interest in the adaptive value of the self-harm gives the patient the idea that perhaps there is a method and reason to her madness, which is a new and welcome way of thinking about herself, one that emphasizes something good and healthy in her. The collaborative nature of the work becomes clearer as the therapist expresses interest in working together with the patient to help her to understand and articulate the functions of the self-harm behavior. If in the first session the patient can walk away intrigued with the idea that she does what she does in order to feel better, she can moderate her harsh judgments about herself. To tell the patient that you understand her self harm to be saying something that she cannot say in words immediately takes her behavior out of the realm of craziness into the realm of communication. Establishing the adaptive context of the behavior as a frame of reference serves as an anchor for the therapist, too, as this perspective can be easily overwhelmed by the patient's resistance and provocative behavior.

The therapist's attitude of curiosity and willingness to serve as a navigational guide to uncharted psychological territory provides hope, helps engage the patient's curiosity about herself, which is a healthy narcissism, and provides motivation for the patient's observing ego to develop. Then the patient starts to feel that she has more control over herself than she had thought. Because control is a major issue with these patients, this is a crucial turning point. Such an approach enhances the patient's self-esteem while engaging her in wanting to understand more and talk more with the therapist who has seen some value in her illness, and therefore in her.

THE TREATMENT FRAME

No rule is so general, which admits not some exception.
Robert Burton, *The Anatomy of Melancholy* (1621)

The therapist should establish certain boundaries from the beginning that spell out the responsibilities of patient and therapist for maintaining the treatment, framing the basic arrangements. When treatment times are arranged, the patient should understand that the therapist is holding this specific period of time for him, in return for which he will expect the patient to be there. The therapist's own policies regarding cancellations, fees, make-up sessions, and availability for receiving telephone calls should be discussed. The issue of confidentiality must be discussed, including those breaches of confidentiality and privacy if managed care is to be involved in the treatment.

How treatment is to be paid for must be discussed at the outset. Most patients plan to use their health insurance and yet are strikingly unaware of its limitations, especially managed care plans. If a good rapport is established and the patient is eager to return, she will dismiss the issue of payment, saying that the treatment is important and that she will find a way to pay for it. It is a very poor idea to begin a treatment that may have to be disrupted; undertaking and sustaining treatment requires that both therapist and patient assume certain responsibilities. Patients must consider realistically that when their insurance is exhausted, they will need to take personal responsibility for payment, and so must consider thoughtfully what they can afford and whether there are any alternate resources available. The therapist may need to consider whether he will adjust his fee. Not to confront these realities is to collude with patients in denying their importance and can result in the ultimate destruction of the treatment.

The issue of boundaries, as Grotstein (1993) elaborates, goes to the very heart of treatment. Ordinarily, commonly held boundaries benefit both the patient and the therapist by reducing potential anxiety and conflict over the procedures of psychotherapy. Many self-harming patients (and others in the borderline range) live by the unspoken credo that the rules do not apply to them, and so despite the boundaries the therapist has created, will try to alter these rules and create their own. In some extreme cases they may even at times invade the therapist's premises, private life, family, and home. Many violate the boundaries of their own bodies, expelling that which is meant to be contained (food, blood) or taking in that which is meant to be kept out (toxins, excessive food). While they need an explicit frame set by the therapist to establish definitive boundaries, they also need the therapist's acceptance of their desire for a lack of boundaries, a "frameless frame." Therapists must be open to the posibility that sometimes certain boundaries hinder the patient's psychological growth. Only the most necessary limits should be set.

There are times when it is detrimental to the patient for the therapist to actively involve himself in preventing acts of self-harm, yet there are also times when the therapist's failure to intervene leaves the patient at the mercy of her own savage aggression. Much of the treatment of these patients is about walking fine lines. Experiences of feeling nurtured and cared for, as well as experiences of limit setting are needed to provide a climate in which ego and superego functions can develop optimally (Druck 1999).

PHYSICAL AND EMOTIONAL SAFETY

Two kinds of safety are essential in treatment, the patient's physical safety and a beginning sense of emotional safety in the relationship with the therapist. The patient's physical safety is the most basic.The self-harming patient must experience the therapist's concern about his physical well-being as much as his emotional well-being. Patients should have as much responsibility as they can manage for choosing what behaviors to change and for monitoring their progress. The language we use about this is important, and metaphors implying autonomy and self-control speak to the healthier part of the patient and help him exercise greater autonomy and self-control. This may be the beginning of their being able to feel a positive sense of ownership of their own bodies.

Expecting the patient to make any big immediate change in her self-harm behavior is not realistic and can set the patient up to fail and feel even worse about herself. It is crucial that the therapist not intrude his own agenda on the patient, and this is best done by not having a hidden agenda, by being forthright and transparent about his motivation and values. For example, the therapist might convey that he hopes the patient can arrive at a place in her life where she no longer finds it necessary to harm herself, and he will help her try to do that if and when she is ready. The therapist must convey that he understands that her self-harm has been a precious means of coping and will not try to take it away from her (Burstow 1992). The patient will need to be in control and decide for herself just what changes she wants to make. She may need to feel free in the treatment not to make any changes at all in the behavior, and may begin treatment by starting to explore what happens affectively when she starves, cuts, binges, or purges. The change may need to be not in behavior but in an attitude about her self-harm. It is when she feels free not to change the behavior that she can come to feel free to choose to change it, not to please the therapist but to please herself. In other words, as the toddler needs to be able to say no to the mother (Spitz 1957), she may need to say no to changing the behavior and have that no accepted by the therapist before she can say yes to herself and change the behavior to please herself. She may need to experience success in taking small steps before making more major changes. Sometimes an accumulation of baby steps does amount to a giant step, of which patients need to be reminded.

Whether the patient chooses to try to reduce her self-harm or not, safety issues must be discussed. Medical monitoring of the physical effects of self-harm may be a necessary component of the treatment plan. Although some patients may initially refuse, this should be part of the goal of self-care. The actively bulimic patient may need to be seen regularly and her physician can help her find small but essential ways to start to change her behavior. If her electrolytes are imbalanced, the physician may prescribe certain supplements to be taken after purging to help restore the balance. The anorexic who manages to eat nourishing food, not diet food, with greater frequency than before is making a start. The patient who cuts herself without attention to first aid can get basic instructions on how to use antiseptics, how to bandage her wounds, and how to know if she needs medical attention.

There may be times when symptoms get worse in therapy, posing an increased threat to the patient's safety. If there is a loss or even the threat of loss of a significant relationship in the patient's life, the patient may respond with increased self-harm. This includes those times when the patient expects that she will lose the therapist or there is any disruption to the treatment relationship. A patient whose therapist is anxious or angry, or is on vacation, may experience this as a rupture in the containing relationship and may respond with increased self-harm. When therapy sessions are overly stimulating, the patient may respond with increased self-harm. Another critical time when the self-harm symptoms may increase is when the patient has made some unusual progress. This negative therapeutic reaction may be a sign that the forward movement in treatment poses the threat of losing the deep attachment to abusive or neglectful objects from the past.

Any worsening of the patient's self-harm symptoms in the course of treatment is to be treated as a bodily communication to the therapist that something is going on that disturbs her greatly but about which she cannot readily speak.

Self-harm may increase or even appear for the first time when the patient begins to experience disturbing intrusive thoughts, memories, or images of past trauma. When therapists probe into potentially painful areas and the patient does not have the ability to contain her disturbing thoughts and feelings, she may respond with increased self-harm. Unfortunately, too many clinicians and patients have the notion that simply recovering traumatic memories of sexual or physical abuse provides a catharsis that in itself is healing, and treatment then turns into an overzealous hunt for recovered memories. It has become more common for clinicians to use hypnosis to help the patient recover memories, a process that may result in additional cognitive confusion and regression to self-harm. When the patient's self-harm increases as the result of intrusive emotional flooding, the therapist may need to take extra steps to contain the patient's destructive impulses, providing additional support and perhaps introducing behavioral tools such as relaxation techniques, deep breathing, or soothing visualizations that the patient can use to calm and soothe herself (Davies and Frawley 1994). When this is not enough, a stepped-up period of treatment may be needed, either hospitalization or day-hospital treatment to provide the containment the patient needs and the opportunity to develop a repertoire of behavioral tools so that she can become better able to contain her own destructive impulses.

Because control is a major issue with these patients, feeling more in control is likely to help her to feel safe with the therapist. For the patient who may have been intruded upon or in some way violated, it is of paramount importance that she feel safe. The therapeutic relationship should be a safe haven. The therapist holds and contains the patient, like a "second skin," until the patient's experience of herself is sufficiently intact and cohesive so that she can live within her own skin. This experience, described by Winnicott as the experience of "going on being," fosters the patient's healthy narcissism. A climate is created in which it can feel safe to begin to experience dysphoric affect and to risk forming an attachment to the therapist and to group members. Because symptomatic behavior is likely to increase with the disclosure of painful and shameful secrets (Davies and Frawley 1994, Miller 1994), it is crucial that a "holding environment" of trust and safety be established to contain the symptomatic behavior before such disclosure occurs (Miller 1994). It is also important that the patient have a social support system to expand the holding environment. Miller advises that in the early stages of treatment it may be necessary for the therapist to block the disclosure of abuse and self-harm secrets until the time that the patient feels sufficiently protected and cared for, to ensure that when these secrets are told, the disclosure can be a healing experience. When her story is distorted by the listener, the experience can be devastating as it was when Karen, Miller's patient, tried for the first time in her life to tell a counselor at her nursing school about her confusing experiences with her father.

"So . . . you are an incest survivor? . . . No wonder you seem so scared and angry," she said. . . . "Have you reported this to the police or told your mother?"

"No."

The counselor leaned forward . . . in this really fake attempt at sympathy, "I know how much pain you are in. It's okay to cry. You're safe here." So, like a jerk, I do sort of tear up a little. . . .

"What your father did . . . was terrible. He used you. . . . It's okay to get really angry. Just let it all out. You'll feel better." . . .

"I loved my father, I still do." . . .

"You loved him, because he coerced you and made you dependent on him. You had no choice. . . . But Karen, your father did not love you. Fathers who love their children don't abuse them."

"I'll have to think about that," I said, . . . putting on my coat. I made an appointment to go back, but I never went. That night I binged and drank . . . until I puked my brains out. [Miller 1994, pp. 86–87]

Miller's experience with a different patient illustrates how premature disclosure can potentially be a repetition of earlier trauma dynamics, when those who knew the secret failed to protect her. Her new patient had come straight from an inpatient treatment program and then a twelve-step halfway house and had been told that self-disclosure was the path to recovery. She was extremely anxious at meeting the new therapist to whom she had been referred.

Laura insisted on telling me as much of her childhood incest history as she could squeeze into the session. . . . I was as disconnected from her as any listener would have been if Laura had been telling her story on a talk show. Thus, the tales of sadistic abuse served only to stimulate in Laura feelings of guilt, shame, and violated family loyalty, leading again and again to self-punishing behavior. I was a helpless bystander, witnessing the excruciating reenactment of traumatic abuse, this time by her own hand. [Miller 1994, p. 87]

QUALITIES NEEDED FOR THERAPISTS TREATING
SELF-HARMING PATIENTS

The therapist who chooses to treat such patients needs to enjoy taking on a challenge and needs to know that his efforts might fail, so he must be relatively unafraid of failing. Should failure happen, it is necessary to know that one can continue to "go on being." The therapist must be lively, vital, and interested in the patient (Greif 1989b), projecting an attitude of confidence. His interest must outweigh his fear. At the same time, his fear is a necessary component if it is at the level of signal anxiety, for this is what prompts him to take the necessary steps to safeguard the patient's well-being.

When patients are devitalized and terrified of their own affective experiences, knowing the therapist's vitality, strength, and humor can stimulate their hope for recovery and becoming alive again. A therapist who is not afraid to express humor and sadness, with laughter and even at times with tears, is a therapist who can rekindle affective sparks in the patient. Sometimes a patient, experiencing the therapist's great sadness about the patient's experience, can come to feel far more empathy for himself. Even a therapist's anger, when honestly acknowledged, can move a patient and unlock a stalemated treatment. The therapist's sense of vitality is especially powerful at those treatment impasses when it is necessary to confront the patient with how he is sabotaging or thwarting the treatment. Most important, the therapist's ability to maintain his connectedness to that which is alive will help him to overcome a masochistic surrender to the patient's pathology (Greif 1989b). This fortitude on the part of the therapist is necessary to withstand patients' chaotic regressions. It furthers the treatment and helps the therapist to develop the clinical "muscle" needed for working with such challenging patients.

Many of us in the mental health field have strong rescue fantasies that may have led to our choosing this field. Self-harming patients, especially those closer to primary process thinking, have an uncanny ability to pick up on this and use it to evoke guilt in the therapist. "If I cut myself over the weekend, it will be your fault." The therapist, therefore, must have a clear sense of professional and personal boundaries and must be in touch with his rescue fantasies. The therapist who continues to assume responsibility for the patient's well-being deprives him of the opportunity to develop, finally, a sense of personal responsibility for his own safety and well-being.

An ability to tolerate a great deal of one's own aggression is necessary, as transference storms make major demands upon the therapist's ego strengths and provoke much aggressive feeling in the therapist. The most crucial qualities the therapist should have are a certain unflappable presence, even-temperedness, and the ability to remain solidly in the present with the patient. He must have an abiding ability to continue to "go on being." It is a beacon in the storm for the patient when the therapist maintains a firmness of conviction that the patient can and will get through these terrible times. It signifies hope, a crucial ingredient in the treatment. When the patient has no hope of his own, he may need to borrow some from the therapist to keep himself going. And when the therapist is losing hope, he may need to borrow some from colleagues.

The therapist must be able to use himself flexibly and creatively, unafraid to become passionate at times, while at the same time maintaining professional boundaries. Those boundaries should be firm but at the same time have a certain elasticity. Working with self-harming patients requires a greater level of commitment and emotional availability. Steven Zimmer (1999) wrote about how his boundaries were stretched to the limits by a self-harming patient and how revealing his vulnerability was a turning point in treatment.[2] Patients who feel insignificant often have no idea how deeply they affect us, and knowing can make a big difference.

> Unfortunately, investigation and analysis had not stopped the cutting. Neither had every medication imaginable nor two hospitalizations. Since I have no faith in behavioral contracts and I wasn't going to threaten her with termination, Sara and I were stuck with the cutting.
> One morning when she arrived for our session, Sara had a slightly sheepish expression on her face. . . . When I pushed her for an explanation she admitted she had cut her arm the night before. I knew without even asking that she had cut herself while she was in a dissociative state. She had no memory of actually cutting herself. It wasn't fair to blame her, but the cutting still angered and upset me. I used to ask her to show me the cuts. She would roll up her sleeve and and let me see what she had done to herself with a razor blade. Sometimes they were violent and haphazard marks; sometimes they were neat and tidy. Then there were the "message" cuts that said things like DIE or HATE. I looked at them all until I noticed that I was recalling images of Sara's bloody arms long after she had left. It was getting to be too much for me. That's when I told her I was having my own problems looking at the cuts and stopped asking to see them. But the cutting continued. . . . In calmer moments I could appreciate that she was somehow inoculating me with what it feels like to be her. But now I decided to tell her how I was feeling.
> "Sara, I can't stand the cutting. You have no idea how upset I get when you do this. You've got to stop it." Her eyes opened wide and she looked like a frightened little girl. "I'm really sorry. I don't want to upset you. Honestly. I didn't even know about it until I woke up this morning," she said imploringly. . . . "If I can't stop, what happens then?"
> "Nothing happens, Sara," I told her. "I'm not going anywhere. I hate the cutting. That's all."
> Sara didn't want to upset me. She had learned that bad things happen if you anger the people you rely upon. It was one of the stories of her life. Oftentimes, I spared her this kind of confrontation. I edited it out without giving it a thought, though sometimes I couldn't hide my feelings. . . .
> One of the things I tried to say to Sara is, "You're not cutting yourself in a vacuum. There is an 'us' here. What you do affects me. Your 'self' is bumping up against my 'self.'" . . . I was sure that sharing my upset about Sara's cutting would be an exercise in frustration. It turned out that my being upset was the first thing about her self-mutilation that she could actually care about. [pp. 6–7]

The therapist must consider whether he can make a commitment to a long-term treatment and to the kind of availability the patient might need. Many

---

2. I am appreciative to Steven Zimmer, C.S.W., for our discussion about the need for mutuality in the treatment.

patients may not need to contact the therapist during off hours, but even so may have the need to know that the therapist is available beyond working hours, either by phone or, on occasion, to schedule an extra session. This is especially true at the initial phase of treatment when the patient is uncertain of the therapist's commitment and may need to test it, and in times of emotional crisis. When the patient might otherwise turn to self-harm but instead calls the therapist for help in dealing with the impulse to harm herself, it is a sign that the patient is ready to find out whether a relationship with another human being might possibly be better than the relationship with self-harm, and should be welcomed. As treatment proceeds and the patient comes to trust the therapist more, the need for testing will probably diminish. Also, with time, as the patient comes to internalize the soothing functions of the therapist and develops something of a repertoire of self-soothing mechanisms and behavioral tools to divert herself from the self-harm impulses, she will have less need to use the therapist in that way. If the patient seems to need the therapist continually during off hours, then this will require discussion with the patient of whether she is testing limits or consideration of whether she might be in need of a more structured level of treatment.

The therapist serves as the therapeutic instrument whose most crucial task is that of a container for the patient, with the capacity to tolerate, contain, and ultimately interpret the patient's projective identifications. He must be able to endure and allow the patient her chaotic ego regressions while ensuring her emotional and physical safety, maintaining an optimism that these regressions will ultimately give way to healthier progressions. To do this, the therapist must be able to identify empathically with the patient's regressed states, to tolerate dwelling there for a time himself, confident in his ability to emerge whole from the regression. Treatment can become a corrective emotional experience for the patient by means of an internalization of a secure attachment to the therapist.

13

Diagnosis, Assessment, and Core Features

The diagnostic scheme which we present is consistent with the view that diagnosis is to be made, not from the symptom or symptom cluster, but from appraisal of the structure of the ego in which the symptom is embedded. . . . In adult borderline and psychotic structures, it is always essential to be aware that rarely, if ever, is the situation the stagnant one of simple arrest at a point in development. In addition to modification (usually ego distortion), regression is always to be considered, both ego regression and psychosexual. Therefore, diagnosis includes consideration of degree of modification; of the highest level reached; and of where regression exists at the time of diagnostic evaluation. The more intact egos are better able to reverse regression. The neurotic regresses along psychosexual lines, but not in lasting ego regression. Finally, dictating our diagnostic philosophy is the clinical fact that all sorts of symptoms, even those traditionally regarded as psychotic, are found in normal and neurotic structures as well. . . . If the stress is great enough, one can lose speech, or memory, and the like.

Gertrude and Rubin Blanck, Ego Psychology: Theory and Practice

To treat self-harming patients appropriately, we need to assess the self-harm behavior and other symptoms within the context of a diagnostic appraisal of the patient's ego structure. Eissler (1953), whose views on diagnosis are as relevant today as they were more than four decades ago, said that diagnosis must be made not from the symptom or symptom cluster itself but from the structure of the ego in which the symptom is embedded. Symptoms alone do not tell us much because all kinds of symptoms, even those usually found in psychotic individuals, can be found as well in the neuroses and in character pathology.

Diagnosing according to ego structure differs from diagnosing according to *Diagnostic and Statistical Manual* (DSM) categories. A DSM diagnosis only targets the symptoms and other observable phenomena, and a treatment aimed only at symptom reduction can be more harmful than helpful. When the symptoms serve defensive functions and mask a fragile ego structure, removing them may precipitate a severe ego regression, even into psychosis or attempted suicide, or may result in the patient's clinging to the symptom as if to her life. It is important to understand whether the self-harm is embedded in an essentially neurotic ego, or whether it has become interwoven into the fabric of an ego with characterological defects that may have some neurotic and psychotic features, or whether it exists within an ego that is frankly psychotic. It is also important to understand whether the self-harm is essentially alien to the ego or whether it has become interwoven into the fabric of the personality. We also must consider whether it arose in relation to the earliest body ego experiences such as abuse, neglect, and dissociation or whether it arose in relation to later body ego experiences, such as puberty, illness, rape or abuse.

Assessment of the self-harm and ego psychological diagnosis go hand in hand in dictating the direction treatment should take and the level of care that is needed (i.e., outpatient, inpatient, day hospital). It is an assessment that is pragmatic, holistic, and meaningful. It should consider how the symptomatic behavior relates to the self-care functions of the ego, body image, self cohesion, transitional object development and object relations development, somatization, dissociative processes, and alexithymia.

Diagnostic assessment is an ongoing process as treatment proceeds, so to some extent it creates an artificial distinction to say that diagnostic assessment precedes treatment. An initial diagnostic assessment can be altered as treatment proceeds.

ASSESSMENT OF SELF-HARM

Before self-harm can be assessed, it must be acknowledged. The acknowledgment of the behavior opens the door to further inquiry about it and other self-harm behaviors. The clinician should take an active role in helping the patient to tell more. Sitting and waiting passively for the patient to disclose more about these problems may be experienced by her not only as evidence that the therapist does not have specific knowledge about her problem, but also as quite painful and even traumatizing.

The patient will take her cues from the therapist as to what the therapist is comfortable hearing about, so the therapist must convey familiarity with the various ways that people harm themselves and that he will not be horrified by what the patient reports. This openness helps to engage the patient in the therapeutic relationship. The medical model of the question and answer session during history taking should be avoided as it is likely to be experienced by the patient as an interrogation. The therapist should appear knowledgeable and competent, but also warm, empathic, and, above all, not authoritarian. Therapists who are psychoanalytically trained may be unnecessarily subdued about asking for further information, but once some degree of rapport and comfort is established for the patient, she is likely to appreciate the therapist's taking a more active stance in assessing the self-harm. The patient may feel relief that what she had been secretive about is now out and on the table. But many patients minimize the extent of the self-harming behavior for fear of frightening off the therapist.

Once the patient acknowledges one kind of self-harm behavior, the door has been opened for exploration of other kinds of self-harm. A comfortable way to do this is to use a self-care line of inquiry, because the ways that people care for themselves can range from indifferent to malignant neglect and frank self-abuse. For example, if the patient presents with an eating disorder, a comment from the clinician that the patient seems to have difficulty caring for herself can be a natural transition into asking about other ways in which the patient might also neglect or abuse her body. When the presenting problem is not self-harm, a simple inquiry about the patient's physical health can open the door for further disclosure about self-care or somatic complaints. The therapist should ask when the patient last had a physical examination and what the findings were. Initiating contact with the doctor may be in order. If patients have a chronic illness, it is important to know how well or poorly they control and manage it, or how they care for themselves when they get ordinary maladies such as a cold, flu, or strained muscle. This will say something about the degree to which they take responsibility for their own well-being and recovery. What is their attitude toward illness? Do they ignore their illness and neglect themselves when they are ill? Or do they maintain their illness, relishing the role of patient and finding it a means to obtain object connection? Do they gain some sadistic pleasure in rendering their doctors impotent to help them?

CRITERIA USED IN ASSESSING SELF-HARM

The therapist should obtain as complete and detailed a picture as possible of the extent of the self-harm in order to assess the risk. Self-harm should be assessed according to the following criteria: the potential lethality of the behavior; the frequency or repetitiveness; the chronicity; the directness of the harm; the extent to which the behaviors are compulsive or impulsive, or both; the extent to which the behavior is acceptable to the ego (i.e., how ego-alien or ego-syntonic it is); the level of consciousness or dissociation that accompanies the act; the adaptive functions that are served by the self-harm; the degree to which the intent is suicidal, sadistic, or masochistic; how much pleasure is derived from the self-harm and the degree to which the pleasure is erotized; and the multiple psychic functions served by the behavior. These axes will suggest which points need immediate intervention. Implicit in these criteria is the issue of body image. No assessment of these patients is complete without some explicit inquiry into the patient's feelings and beliefs about his body. These axes will also suggest areas for further exploration at a later date.

While this discussion focuses on a general model of assessment for the different kinds of self-harm, there are various structured interview formats available that can be used as more specific guides for assessing specific kinds of self-harm. They should, however, be used flexibly, so that the consultation feels like a collaborative inquiry and not an interrogation. At times, a patient consultation with a clinician especially knowledgeable about substance abuse, eating disorders, or self-mutilation may be useful in formulating the overall diagnosis, assessment, and treatment plan. Psychotherapeutic and medical contact should also serve a psychoeducational function that can correct patients' distorted thinking about their behavior. Hearing the clinician making connections between behavior, thoughts, and feelings can help the patient start to think differently about what she is doing.

To determine the lethality of the current self-harm behavior, the clinician relies on his powers of observation and on the information he gets from the patient, which may or may not be reliable. A baseline medical evaluation will let the clinician and patient know the extent to which the patient has harmed herself, something patients may minimize. Before the exam, the clinician should report to the physician what is known about the self-harm behavior, such as what the patient does, how long it has been going on, how frequently, and anything else about the patient that will help the doctor structure the exam. In the case of patients with eating disorders, the exam should be done by a physician with special expertise in this area.

Clinicians who evaluate self-harming patients should use the rapidity of weight loss, the number of purging strategies and frequency of purging, the extent of self-mutilation, and alcohol-related medical damage as indicators of severity. To assess the lethality of the behavior, the clinician will need to know how severe and out of control it is. Superficial scratches with fingernails are a less severe kind of mutilation than cuts, and shallow cuts are less severe than deep cuts. In anorexia, the rapidity and amount of weight loss, the extent of exercise, and the degree of determination the patient has to continue her weight loss are crucial factors. The extent to which the self-harm has spiraled upward in frequency and severity is an indication that an addictive-like cycle may be beginning or is already established. If already established, the self-harm is already out of control. For example, episodes of bingeing and purging twice a week in which each binge is followed by a purge is less dangerous than seven or eight episodes a day in which each binge is followed by several purges. The more purging methods used, the more dangerous the behavior is likely to be. Inquiries should be made about vomiting, and the use of laxatives, diuretics, or syrup of ipecac. Do patients consume anything during a binge that could harm them? When the binge is out of control, some people may consume cleaning fluid, lye, Drano, bleach, or poison.

The clinician needs to know if there is a certain occurrence, thought, or sequence of events that serves either to trigger the self-harm or as a ritual leading up to it. Generally the more bizarre the rituals are, the closer the patient may be to primary process thinking or psychosis. The self-harm that occurs in groups can be far more dangerous because of the contagion factor, because substance abuse is more likely to be involved as well, and, in the case of cutting, because cutting instruments might be shared. Most self-harm occurs in solitary but the clinician should never assume it. There are other important questions. Do patients ever mutilate themselves shortly after a bulimic episode? Are the acts of self-harm repetitive and regular, or sporadic? How regular—two, three, six times a day, or once a week? Hair pulling and head banging are usually stereotyped and repetitive once they start, but may occur only sporadically. Not all bulimics binge and purge regularly; there may be periods of no self-harm, followed by periods of extensive bingeing or purging. Each binge may be followed by one purge, by numerous purges, or by none. Specificity is important.

It is important to know whether the patients' thoughts of harming themselves are impulsive, compulsive, or both. With impulsive thoughts, there is an impulse to harm themselves that feels irresistible. With compulsive thoughts, there is the feeling of being compelled to harm themselves, that something terrible will happen if they don't do it. Usually the compulsive thoughts are ego-alien, that is, they are experienced as strange or unwelcome. Sometime there are elements of both combined. The more impulsive the self-harm is, the more dangerous it is likely to be. Using drugs or alcohol is likely to make other self-harm behavior more impulsive. Are they usually drunk or high when they binge, purge, self-mutilate? Some patients can dissociate more readily than others, which enables them to harm themselves more easily. Some who cannot dissociate readily will seek a boost from drugs or alcohol to help them to "numb out" and act on their impulses. Do they use clean instruments straight from the package or do they share cutting instruments? Are their cutting instruments sharp, dull, rusty, or jagged? Do they make shallow or deep cuts? How many? How severe are the burns? Do their injuries require medical attention? Do they seek it? Some bulimics have certain compulsive rituals, and some cutters line up their instruments, their antiseptic, and their bandages ahead of time as they prepare to cut themselves. Some bulimics make certain to eat something high in potassium after purging to compensate for the electrolyte imbalance they have created, and should know that the monitoring physician can provide additional help in this regard. Such rituals may convey a realistic and welcome concern for their own safety, in which they play the maternal role with themselves, or the ritual may be a repetition of past experience. Others may cut much more impulsively, using anything at hand, breaking a glass and using jagged shards or grabbing a rusty scissors. Jagged scars may be a sign of impulsive cutting, and the therapist can get some sense of how patients cut themselves by looking at the scars, which may be covered up. Depending on where the scars are, the therapist might ask to see them. One can tell a lot about whether the self-harm is ego-alien or ego-syntonic (in accordance with the patient's ego) by whether the patient shows them off proudly and defiantly, or exhibits a sense of shame or embarrassment. (For some patients, the therapist's willingness to look becomes an indelible moment.)

The patient's disclosures about her self-harm enable the clinician to inquire more specifically. For example, if the patient says that she has been dieting, "cutting down a little," it would be helpful to inquire about what she had for breakfast this morning, or what her most recent meal consisted of. An anorectic might acknowledge having a cup of coffee in the morning and a muffin. Then the clinician might ask how much of the muffin the patient managed to eat, a question that demonstrates that the therapist understands how hard eating is for her. With patients who drink or use drugs, the tendency is to minimize the extent of their substance abuse. Overdoses should be inquired about and specific information should be sought. Is an overdose five aspirins or a whole bottle, or downing a fifth of vodka? Do patients combine alcohol and drugs in ways that increase lethality, for example consuming alcohol and barbiturates together or smoking marijuana while drinking?

The level of consciousness associated with the act of self-harm must be assessed. Are patients overly conscious or hyperaroused, and do they harm themselves to stop the hyperarousal? Do they dissociate in order to harm themselves, or do they harm themselves in order to end a period of dissociation? Do they depersonalize, experience fugue states or derealization, or is there amnesia about the self-harm? It may be difficult to distinguish amnesia from alcoholic blackouts.

The time of onset and degree of chronicity of the self-harm should be inquired about. How long have they been doing this? Have they ever tried to stop? What was it like and how long did it last? Self-harm behavior that is neither chronic nor severe sometimes can be stopped by patients as long as they have access to their therapist. Sometimes just beginning to talk about it is enough for them to feel less need to enact it. Self-harm that has just begun may be associated with the intrusive memories, images, and somatic symptoms that are indicators of posttraumatic stress disorder (PTSD), and special caution must be taken about exploration of dissociated memories.

All self-harm is not active and direct, and so it must be determined whether patients at times allow or engage others to harm them or engage in activities with others that may be harmful. So, for example, if they cut themselves in the presence of others, the clinician might ask if it has ever happened that they were cut by someone else. Have they ever provoked someone to hurt them because they wanted to be hurt? Have they ever convinced a physician to perform a surgery on them that they did not need medically?

One cannot know the intent of the patient's self-harm without asking about it. Is the self-harm used as anesthesia, as self-medication, or is it used with the intention of ending their life? While all self-harm is sadomasochistic in that the patient is both the sadist in inflicting harm on herself and the masochist in being the object of the sadism, the clinician should determine whether the act is meant primarily to punish the self or some internalized object. It must be understood, too, that what is primarily masochistic in a patient on one day may be sadistic in that same patient the next, or that masochistic and sadistic elements may be part of the same episode. One might ask, "When you were cutting (or purging or picking at) yourself, whom (or what) were you thinking about?"

To introduce the patient to the concept of the behavior serving multiple psychic functions, the therapist might ask, "What does this self-harm do for you? How does it help you?" To begin to explore how the self-harm can serve several adaptive functions that can vary from day to day or episode to episode, the therapist might ask, "How was today's episode different from yesterday's?" To introduce the patient to the concept of the body speaking for the patient, the therapist might say, "Let's try to understand what your body is trying to say for you." When the body speaks, what is it trying to say? When the body speaks, to whom is it speaking?

DIAGNOSIS

The term character, *derived from the Greek* charassein *and* charakter, *refers to the engraving instrument and its product, the sign. Applied to personality, the term denotes those features considered indelibly engraved upon it.*

Ruth F. Lax, Introduction, *Essential Papers on Character Neurosis and Treatment*

To determine the appropriate direction for treatment, we must consider the ego structure in which the symptoms are embedded and the multiple functions of the symptoms. We need to consider how the patient's character, the typical regularities in his unique patterns of thought, attitude, and affect, serve adaptive functions and serve as a source of resistance to treatment. It is essential to assess the different aspects of the self-harm behaviors in each patient in detail, understanding them as symptoms that are the consequences of both ego defect and unconscious psychic conflict arising from contending forces within the individual. It is necessary to think about the nature and origin of the psychic conflict out of which the self-harm symptom emerges (Brenner 1982). These behaviors must be understood as having many possible meanings that can range from presymbolic to more concrete and literal psychophysiological reenactments of past experience.

The psychosomatic focus of the self-harm symptoms must be understood in relation to the patient's ego structure and ego functioning, with emphasis on body image
and on the defensive and adaptive functions of the ego and the punitive superego
aspects. It is equally important to understand how the self-harm behavior serves
to bolster and compensate for a defective ego and a fragmented sense of self.

The patient's ego defenses should be examined in regard to adaptive and
destructive aims and goals, so that the therapist can consider which defenses are
most malignant and likely to obstruct or destroy the treatment. The defenses may
range from primitive defenses that may well have been adaptive earlier in development but prove pathological in adulthood, to more mature, higher-level defenses.
The more primitive defenses include acting out, repetition compulsion, conversion hysteria, physical illness, somatic anxiety, psychophysiological posttraumatic
reenactment, denial, minimizing, repression, projection and projective identification, dissociation, the splitting of the psychic representations of oneself and
others into all-good and all-bad categories, the tendency toward polarized all-or-
nothing thinking, and alexithymia. All of these defenses come with a destructive price, so the more of these defenses the patient uses, the more destructive
his behavior is likely to be. Because the regression to self-harm behavior occurs
when the patient uses dissociation, minimizing, or disavowal as a way of not
allowing herself to know what she is doing, these defenses are especially critical.
Because projection, projective identification, and splitting of self and object representations are very powerful defenses with the potential to destroy the therapeutic relationship, these defenses are also critical.

The higher-level defenses include altruism, humor, sublimation, and suppression. Often patients manifest an uneven constellation of lower- and higher-
level defenses, all of which must be recognized and understood if the patient is
to be known as more than his pathology but as a complex human being in whose
character are interwoven both the deleterious effects of strain or shock trauma
and healthier structure. Neurotic patients can at times regress to the use of primitive self-harm defenses, but their lives and identities are not organized around
it. When neurotic patients use self-harm as a means of defense, the self-harm is
bound to be of a milder and less potentially dangerous kind.

The most severe kinds of self-harm are more prevalent toward the more
severe end of the diagnostic spectrum, in the severe personality disorders and
psychoses. Kernberg (1989, 1992) posits that varying types of psychopathology
are determined by an abnormal development of internalized object relations. He
therefore classifies character pathology on a continuum ranging from less to more
severe in a way that helps to understand the more severe forms, especially borderline character pathology. At the higher level, the character defenses are largely
inhibitory or phobic and excessive defensive operations center around repression,
not splitting or dissociation. The patient's superego is severe and punitive but it
is well integrated. The ego is somewhat constricted, but social adaptation is not
seriously impaired and the ego is well integrated. Ego identity and a stable self

concept are well established. The patient is capable of deep stable object relationships and of experiencing guilt, mourning, and a wide range of affective responses. Patients with severe self-harm problems do not fall in this category but in the intermediate and lower levels of character pathology organization, in which hatred and pathological envy play a major role.

At the intermediate level, the superego is even more punitive but less integrated. Repression is the main defensive operation along with related defenses of intellectualization, rationalization, and undoing, but at the same time there are some dissociative trends such as mutual dissociation of contradictory ego states, and projection and denial. Oral features predominate clinically and the aggressive components are toned down in contrast to the primitive aggression at the lower level. There is a capacity for lasting deep involvements with others and for tolerating the ambivalent and conflictual nature of such relationships. Most oral types of character pathology, sadomasochistic personalities, and many narcissistic personalities are organized at this level (Kernberg 1989). Many people with eating disorders and some of the milder forms of self-mutilation are probably at this level.

At the lower level, there is minimal superego integration but a tremendous propensity for projection of primitive and sadistic superego components and for projective identification, giving rise to paranoid traits. The synthetic or organizing function of the ego that gives the individual the ability to think, feel, and act in an organized manner is seriously impaired, with dissociation, not repression, used as the central defensive operation. The dissociation is reinforced by the use of denial, projective identification, and unconscious fantasies of omnipotence. The character defenses are primarily of an impulsive type, used to discharge unintegrated libidinal and aggressive strivings. Severe ego weakness is reflected in the patient's lack of anxiety tolerance, of impulse control, and of channels for sublimation, as evidenced by chronic failure in work or creative areas. Excessive aggression makes for serious impairment in the capacity to encompass contradictory (good and bad) self and object images, and their inner world is composed of the best and the worst aspects of important persons but in an unintegrated or split way. They can speak of a mother who is loving and devoted and moments later of a cruel and sadistic mother in a way that suggests they are speaking of two separate people. At the same time, their inner view of themselves is a chaotic mix of unintegrated shameful and exalted images. The absence of integrated internalized self and object representations determines the presence of an identity diffusion syndrome, an outstanding characteristic of this level of character pathology. Primary process thinking filters into cognitive functioning, although it is not always evident; it shows up on projective psychological testing. Many narcissistic, impulse-ridden, schizoid and paranoid personalities are at this level (Kernberg 1989). Many of those with the more severe, atypical eating disorders, more severe kinds of self-mutilation, and sexual sadomasochistic perversion are at this lower level. Along this continuum, the next step down is the psychoses, and the differential diagnosis between those in the borderline field and the psychoses centers around the persistence of reality testing in borderlines while reality testing is lost in the psychoses. Underlying this difference is the differentiation between self and object representations and the delimitation of ego boundaries derived from this differentiation. These are present in the lower level organization of character pathology but are lost or absent in the psychoses.

Special attention in these cases must be paid to destructive narcissism (Rosenfeld 1971), the defensive system associated with a narcissistic organization of the personality in which the primitive destructive part of the self comes to dominate the personality, destroying and immobilizing the healthy parts. It is the destructive narcissism that underlies the chaotic intensity and regressiveness of these patients and the perverse flavor of the transference (Rosenfeld 1971).

Many of these patients fit Kroll's (1993) tentative working model of the PTSD/borderline, who suffers first and foremost from a disorder of the stream of consciousness. These are most likely to be those borderline patients who had experienced childhood and adolescent physical or sexual abuse and who fit both the clinical picture of the severe borderline and at the same time manifest the symptoms of PTSD. Some have not suffered horrific abuse but rather cumulative strain trauma; regardless of the kind of trauma, they seem to respond to virtually all of life as a series of traumas. When we can recognize a PTSD syndrome in these patients, we need to consider how much of the response is attributable to the nature of the stress and how much to the nature of the responder. That is, a certain constitutionally inherent temperament or biological changes due to illness may leave a developing child far more likely to develop the PTSD syndrome. However, not all abused, traumatized children develop the adult PTSD/borderline self-harm picture, especially the self-destructive patterns that typically involve ensnaring others into their sadomasochistic scenarios. Individual differences play an important role in determining the form that the response to trauma will take.

14

Using Attachment Theory in Therapy of Self-Harm Patients

I watched it grow around me
fed it anyway and
wallowed in it

Catherine Taormina,
Chalkboard with a Bad Eraser

Self-harming patients demonstrate a broad spectrum of borderline ego organization, and are usually given one or more *DSM-IV* axis I diagnoses, such as mood or anxiety disorder, dissociative disorder, or posttraumatic stress disorder. Their pathological envy and hatred and their wish for intimacy and fear of it are manifested by an impairment of attachment relationships. They are given to destructive repetitions, reenactments of early experience and negative therapeutic reactions, regressing in response to therapeutic progress, especially when they consciously regard the therapist as a good object. All these factors threaten to destroy the treatment and impede or destroy the attachment to the therapist.

The critical process underlying the patients' chaotic intensity, regressiveness, and the perverse flavor of the transference is their destructive narcissism (Rosenfeld 1971), that perverse relationship in which the healthy part of the self colludes and allows itself to be taken over knowingly by the destructive parts of the self (Steiner 1981). This is the most formidable obstacle in the way of the development of the therapeutic alliance. The aim of treatment, therefore, is the reacquisition and reintegration of projected parts of the self (Steiner 1996). This conceptualization does not replace the conflict model, in which the central aim is insight into unconscious processes, but allows us to better understand how such insight is impeded or facilitated. It thus enlarges and deepens the conflict model of treatment by helping the patient use his own mental assets more optimally in order to resolve his conflicts in his own way. The therapist must point out when the patient is sabotaging the therapeutic relationship by confronting the patient's destructive narcissism, which can help the patient identify how and why he destroys and sabotages healthy and trusting relationships with others as well. A process-oriented approach to treatment uses the relationship between the patient and therapist as a means of engaging the patient in the arena of his interpersonal psychopathology.

CORE FEATURES OF THE SELF-HARMING PATIENT

Combining the applied concept of destructive narcissism with Kroll's (1988, 1993) pragmatic approach to treatment of those in the broad borderline range (roughly equivalent to Kernberg's intermediate and lower levels of character pathology) can serve as a schematic guide with practical value for the therapist for organizing thoughts and observations regarding the nature of therapeutic interventions. The schema is presented in terms of core clinical features.

Destructive Narcissism and Secret Truths

Destructive narcissism involves not a simple split between the healthy and destructive parts of the self but a far more complex phenomenon—a perverse relationship in which the healthy part of the self colludes and allows itself to be taken over knowingly by the destructive parts of the self (Steiner 1981), while the patient manages to keep herself from knowing what she is doing. It is like making a "pact with the devil" but without acknowledging having done so. These pathological personality organizations provide a stability that is resistant to change, giving rise to states of mind that are "psychic retreats" (Steiner 1996) because they seem to be experienced spatially as places of safety in which the patient can find a refuge from reality, and thus from guilt and anxiety.

Charlotte was in her early fifties when she came to me for help with her compulsive eating. She was a quiet single woman who lived with her elderly mother and was lonely and socially phobic. She cried through most of the initial session and continued for several weeks. She was depressed in the way of people who have lived with depression for so long that it seems normal. She despaired that she could ever stop her overeating, was sure she was a "food addict" and always would be. She had attended Overeaters Anonymous meetings for awhile, and said she believed that she was helpless to control her overeating. The best she could try to do was stick to the Weight Watchers program, because on it she lost weight and felt good about herself.

The only problem was that she always regained it and then felt even worse about herself. Part of her wanted to go back to Weight Watchers—she loved how she got applause as she was losing weight and it was, at least, some social contact and recognition. But she also hated the applause because she felt that she had to be thin to earn it and she hated the "yo-yo" dieting. But now she had given up, and was not even sure what she was doing in my office, except that she had broken down in her gynecologist's office and told him that she hates herself for being so fat. She appreciated that he had spent a good deal of time talking and listening to her—"I have an HMO plan and most of those doctors rush me out of there so fast my head is spinning but he is very special. He doesn't know it but I kind of think of him as my Dad. So when he suggested that you might be able to help me, I agreed to call and give it a try."

She spoke of how she hates herself for bingeing, that while doing it she knows it will make her feel ill and that she will feel disgusted with herself.

> At work I become distracted from what I'm doing, there's no one to talk to, and I find myself getting up and going down two flights of stairs to the vending machines. I buy a small individual package of Archway chocolate chip cookies—there are three big cookies in the package—thinking that I'm not going to get into trouble with a limited portion. It's better than buying a whole box of cookies. I can even begin to feel virtuous about it, that's the kind of sicko I am. I start to eat them as I go back up the stairs. By the time I get there I am spaced out and the cookies are gone. I turn around and go back down to the machines. By the time the work day is over I've done this several times and I'm bloated and queasy. . . . I have no control. Something comes over me and compels me to do this, over and over again. I know this sounds crazy—it's like a force inside me, some devil or something.

I pick up on her idea of there being a devil inside her and suggest that this devilish force may not be so alien as she thinks, that maybe it is simply a part of herself that exists alongside a healthier part of herself. She looks shocked and tells me that that is a weird idea. "Please don't take offense. I know you're much more educated than I am and must know a lot, but it strikes me as downright weird." I nod and tell her I know it does, but if it is weird, it's no weirder than the destructive part that lives inside all of us along with the healthier part. At this, she looks interested and receptive and asks what I mean. I tell her that we all have a natural inclination toward health and goodness but that sometimes that healthy part of ourselves can be taken over by a very destructive and perverse part of ourselves. This can happen, I explained as she listened raptly, when the healthy part that had been opposing the destructive part, decides to give up and throw in the towel, thus submitting to the strength of the destructive, devil-like part. I also tell her that there is probably a crucial moment when the compulsion shifts to a certain clarity

386 / When the Body Is the Target

of thinking, when she realizes that she has a choice about stopping the binge or continuing it, but that her healthier part knowingly agrees to submit.

At this came a look of recognition and she grinned in a way best described as devilish, and said that what I had told her was amazing because that is exactly how it goes with her. For the longest time she has always known that she has a tiny invisible angel sitting on one shoulder and an equally tiny and invisible devil sitting on the other shoulder, and that they were at war with each other. She never knew how it was that the devil always ended up taking over but it did—the angel may stand up to the devil for a while and defy him but always ends up giving in to the devilish part. I told her that each time she allows her angel to submit to and be taken over by the devil by feeding him all this extra food, the devilish part of herself grows bigger and stronger, requiring and demanding more and more food, at the same time that the healthy part of herself becomes diminished and smaller. No wonder she feels like a big fat disgusting thing. She said in excitement, "Yes, yes, there is this little moment, I never realized I had it, when it's clear that I can stop or continue to stuff myself. And in an instant I make the decision to continue. I never knew before that I had a choice but you're right, I do. But as soon as I give in I tell myself that I am fat and disgusting and always will be, so why try to do anything about it." I asked her why she thought she had not let herself know that she actually *had* a choice and had *made* a choice, and again she started to grin. "If I let myself know what I'm doing, I guess it makes it pretty hard for me to continue to allow myself to do it." When she came in for her next session, she said that she had begun noticing when she made the decision to give in to the devilish part of her, and it made her binges different. She did not like the difference. She could not say what it was but I told her that she seemed sad. She had not realized she was feeling sad, but now that I had mentioned it, yes she was. Something crucial was missing, some part of the bingeing was not the same as it had been. "Maybe you mean that it's losing some of its pizzazz, its power over you?" I asked. Maybe, she reluctantly agreed. The following week she missed her appointment, we discovered together, by her managing not to let herself remember the time of her appointment. Or at least, she remembered it but then promptly got so involved in things at work that it was not until two hours past her appointment that she remembered it again. After discussing this, she began to see that her devil and the angel did not limit themselves to the arena of her eating but were even more pervasive in her personality.

Beliefs in devils and angels are quite common. These dualities are essentially religious beliefs that therapists need to be comfortable in accepting, exploring, and thinking about. Rizzuto (1993) suggests that the formation of private deity representations is a process occurring in a dialectical integration with the formation of self representations. People have their own personal mental representation of a private deity that is "neither everybody's God nor the God of official doctrine but the only God that particular individual is able to have" (p. 18). We need to understand that mental representations of the deity may be male or female, and, like self and object representations, are subject to splitting into good and bad and prey and predator representations. Once religious beliefs are established, says Rizzuto, they require major psychic shifts to be changed. The superstitions about the evil eye, part of many mythologies and known in Italian culture as the *malocchio* and in Jewish culture as the *kein ahora*, is a more primitive form of the devil, a part-object that is really part of the self (Grotstein 1979).

> The Devil in the final analysis is really that aspect of us which originally disavows ourselves in order to become invisible and thus vanish our real body and soulful selves into a nether world of abandonment and exploitation. . . . Following the disavowal and abanishment of the visible self . . . into its perfidious exile, the disavowing self then uses this split-off and alienated image as a refuse heap—much like a scapegoat or sacrificial lamb—upon which to cast all unwanted elements from the psyche [Grotstein 1979, pp. 441–442].

In the treatment of a woman who was a cantor in a synagogue, when the destructive and healthy parts of herself were identified, she immediately named them her *yetzer ra* (evil inclination) and *yetzer tov* (good inclination). Her training had taught her that we each have both within us. By naming them herself, they became more real to her.

I have found that once the processes involved in the destructive narcissism were described to patients in a straightforward nonjudgmental manner, very often they will respond very positively initially, as Charlotte did. There is usually a sense of chagrin that the secret has been exposed as well as relief that someone understands the hidden mental games they play with themselves. It is essential that the therapist repeatedly, consistently, and relentlessly confront the healthier part of the self with its role in allowing the destructive part of the self to take over.

In a group I run for women with compulsive eating problems, Ellie, who weighed over 300 pounds and covered her anger with a sweet facade, was speaking of how she starts a binge but then cannot stop it because some terrible force takes over her. The others were murmuring consoling words— "I know, it's like that for me too. There's nothing I can do about it." I told them that if they can pay very close attention to what really goes on inside them, it's like a war between the healthy and destructive parts of themselves. There are moments of clarity and control when they realize that just because they started to eat does not mean they have to continue, that they *could* choose to stop. The destructive part urges them on, as they think self-loathing thoughts, telling themselves how disgusting and out of control they are, until in a tiny moment the healthy part gives in and submits to the destructive part, making the destructive part bigger and more powerful. "The more you feed the monster in you, the bigger and fatter it grows." As I spoke, Ellie was nodding and the others were listening raptly. Ellie looked at me with a mischievous grin, her eyes gleaming, and said that she's always thought of herself as having an angel sitting on each shoulder. One was her thin angel, the healthy part of her, and the other was her fat angel, the destructive part. I asked her how it happens for her that the fat angel takes over, and she laughed and said that the fat angel just sits on the thin angel and squashes it to death. The room rocked with laughter until I suggested that the thin angel must sit still long enough to allow the fat angel to kill her, that she probably has time to get out of the way if she chooses to. At this, Ellie began to cry and acknowledged that this is true, she's just so tired of trying and she gives in at those moments. Three other women disclosed that they too recognized something of the same process in themselves, with one envisioning a good angel and bad angel, another envisioning an angel and devil, and the third envisioning a good girl and a bad girl.

This same concept of a perverse destructive relationship between parts of the self can be very powerful for confronting the resistance to giving up various kinds of destructive attachments and the ferocity with which they fight and try to destroy healthier attachments. With each refusal to submit to the destructive part, the healthier part of the self grows stronger and more capable of affirming itself, essentially saying "Get thee behind me, Satan."

Key Processes and Themes

Kroll (1988) proposes that we focus attention on several key processes—cognitive style and emotional intensity/lability—and themes—victimization and loneliness or emptiness—that can serve as concepts around which to organize a treatment plan. These two interacting processes consist of a particular cognitive style marked by poorly focused thinking, transient dissociative states, self-rumination, regressive disorganization under stress, and impulsive activity and an overwhelming emotional intensity or lability.

Self-harming patients organize their view of themselves and of the world around the experiences of victimization as well as loneliness and emptiness, themes in their self-harm symptoms and their object relations. Other prominent clinical features are variations on these themes, and include depersonalization and derealization; severe ego regressions; depression, anger, and despair; dependency, narcissistic entitlement, and specialness; and envy and hatred. Some of these patients may be relatively high functioning and may exhibit these processes in relatively subtler ways, while others are low functioning and may present the more flagrant picture of a *DSM-IV* borderline personality disorder. Many higher functioning patients who present a very uneven diagnostic picture may nonetheless suffer severe episodes of "aloneness affect," feelings of emptiness, alterations in consciousness and ego regressions, during which they harm themselves or allow others to harm them, and they experience the world as especially predatory and harmful.

The emotional and cognitive issues and the themes of victimization and loneliness/emptiness are irreducibly inseparable. For example, if we examine two of the responses from my study in which subjects were asked to describe how the act of self-harm usually occurs, we will see the circular interaction between behavior, thought, and feeling in the written sequence. At times they are so intertwined that they cannot really be differentiated.

> I'm usually feeling inadequate (FEELING and THOUGHT).
> Everything and everyone else in my life seems to be in control and I'm not (THOUGHT).
> I have no rational sense of myself (THOUGHT and FEELING).
> I'd like to rip the skin right off me if I could. Just shred myself till I was gone (FEELING and THOUGHT).
> Instead, I pick (BEHAVIOR).
> And I make myself so ugly (BEHAVIOR, THOUGHT, and FEELING).
> Because that's how I feel inside (FEELING and THOUGHT).

> I may look in the mirror (BEHAVIOR),
> see fat (BEHAVIOR, THOUGHT, and FEELING),
> and get mad at myself (FEELING).
> Or I'll eat something (BEHAVIOR),
> then torment myself in my mind that I'll get sick or fat (THOUGHT and FEELING),
> and the guilt (FEELING)
> makes me start itching, reopening scabs (BEHAVIOR),
> self-critical thoughts (THOUGHT and FEELING).

The need to consider these issues and themes in a linear sequence makes it necessary to address them one at a time if the therapist is to make an informed decision on whether to address the issues of cognitive style or emotional dysregulation and the themes of victimization and loneliness/emptiness, and in what order.

Cognitive Disturbances

The cognitive style often has an hysterical quality in which the patient loses significant details and distorts the meaning of an interaction or communication (Kroll 1988). The patient comes to a global but superficial or one-sided interpretation of the significance of perceptions, fantasies, memories, or emotions.

In the midst of a binge Charlotte would regress to all-or-nothing polarized thinking and her "devil" would tell her, "You have no control, you're so disgusting. It's no use trying." By the time her workday had ended and she was on her way home she had already stopped at the store and bought an Entenmann's pound cake, half of which she ate in the car on the way home.

Many other self-harmers buy into the idea that they have no control and say to themselves, "I ate half the cake, so I might as well go to hell with myself completely," and they finish the whole thing, or once they finish the cake, they punish themselves with painful purging or a direct attack on their body with fingernails or razor blades. It is essential that they look at how the cognitive distortions lead to a chain of further distortions and emotions that lead to self-harm behavior. Because the upward spiral of self-harm is experienced as something that happens seamlessly and automatically in a manner that is out of control, it is necessary to break down the chain of events (thoughts, feelings, behavior) to challenge the basic assumptions (thoughts) they make about themselves.

I wanted Charlotte to replace her harsh judgment of her self with a greater appreciation of the self-soothing component of her bingeing, so I pointed out that identifying the feelings that led to the bingeing might be more helpful to her than judging herself so harshly.

Charlotte: Yes, I get antsy sitting at that computer by myself. I want to talk to someone and there's no one there. I don't know what to do with myself so I get up and go to the vending machines.

SF: So you feel lonely, a little anxious? (She nods.) It's not a good way to feel and you want to feel better?

Charlotte: I guess so, and even though the eating makes me miserable, when I first start, it's exciting and it feels good.

SF: What is so bad about wanting to feel better? Which one of us human beings wants to feel bad?

Charlotte: (Her face lights up.) I never thought of it like that. I guess you have a point.

SF: Maybe if you can stop judging what you do as disgusting and think of it instead as a very human attempt to feel better, you would not feel so bad about yourself.

Charlotte: That makes sense. I can see that.

SF: OK, so if you can get yourself to see that when it's happening, then you could think more clearly about whether you want to stop eating or whether you want to continue. You'd feel you had a choice instead of feeling driven.

Charlotte: That's what I want. To feel in control. When I eat like that I am so out of control.

Patients may forget significant recent events or may have a more global amnesia for entire periods of childhood. Depersonalization, derealization, and confusion may occur in the context of painful images, associations, intrusive thoughts, and other stress, escalating to the point of disorientation and disorganization so dramatic that they appear to be transient psychotic episodes. The patient spirals up in an escalating confused cycle in which her worldview escalates as well, and she becomes more and more distraught, convinced that she is the victim and others, often including the therapist, are the victimizers. A few key themes ("I am all alone, everyone hates me, I am no good") or powerful images, often of pain and violence, recur and dominate the person's consciousness. She may try to short-circuit this painful state by inducing a trance state and taking some potentially destructive action: running out alone in the middle of the night to roam around in unsafe neighborhoods, taking an overdose, cutting herself, going into a bar and getting drunk with strangers.

For the therapist it often feels like being caught in a whirlwind or a child's temper tantrum, which discourages the therapist from intervening at all. For the patient this cognitive style can cause her a great deal of emotional pain and despair. For example, if the patient interprets the therapist's announcement that he is taking a week off to mean that the therapist can no longer tolerate her presence, is disgusted, and has to get away from her, she will experience the week's hiatus as a very painful personal rejection, may have further fantasies of other abandonment, may terminate treatment or escalate her bulimic behavior, or make a suicide attempt. The times when the therapist is not available to see the patient are especially important in the treatment of severe self-harming patients because they are so reactive to experiences of loss and separation. The patient may or may not volunteer these thoughts or feelings, but the therapist must always ask, so that there is the opportunity for cognitive restructuring or the correction of cognitive distortions. In the case of June, as with many self-harming patients, cognitive distortions were based on the projected parts of the self that served as retreats from reality.

June had very serious problems with dissociation, projection, and projective identification that made for numerous cognitive difficulties, one of which was her persistent thought that I did not want her there but wanted her to leave, a theme that dominated her sessions for the first year of treatment. If she had to cancel a session she assumed I was glad that she would not be there, and when she was there she assumed I was unhappy about it. She was certain that even though I "acted right" and said all the "right therapeutic" things, she was certain that it was just an act and that ultimately I would be revealed for the cold and rejecting person she knew I really was. She had difficulty beginning her sessions, remaining for her sessions, and ending her sessions. When she came in and sat down, and just as we were settling in to what was starting to feel as if we were working together, the thought would intrude in her mind that I did not want her there and she would get up to leave. This often happened several times in a session. As we were getting close to the end of the session and had several minutes left, she assumed that

I wanted her gone that very instant and would jump up to leave. It would go like this:

> June: (She enters the treatment room and carefully scrutinizes my face for what truths she was certain it would reveal, and scans the room for evidence of something.) Hello. (Her voice is constricted and flat as she carefully seats herself. Her anxiety is palpable.)
>
> SF: Hi.
>
> June: (Looking distracted for a moment, she then looks at me.) What? . . . What?
>
> SF: (I suspect she had "spaced out" for a moment, then thought she had thought I said something that went by her.) Did you think I said something that you didn't quite hear?
>
> June: Yes, you want me leave, don't you? I'll go right now. I knew this was a mistake. (She stands up.)
>
> SF: Please wait a moment. What makes you think I want you to leave?
>
> June: It's all right, you don't have to act as if you want me to stay. I know you don't.
>
> SF: Why do you think I would want you to leave?
>
> June: (still standing) You have better things to do with your time, I'm sure.

I asked if there were anything I had said or done to cause her to think she was unwelcome. She had to acknowledge that there was not, that I was acting quite correctly, but she knew that deep down I did not want her there. These occurrences were very frequent and I had to point out to her numerous times that she seemed oddly determined to see me as someone two-faced, who acted "right" but really did not want her there. Several times in the midst of one of these interactions, I observed the change in her face, especially the eyes, that suggested that she was dissociating. I would ask if she could tell me what she was thinking or remembering, and often it would be an instance of when she felt that her mother, to whom correct appearances were very important, was oblivious to her presence. In fact, for much of her life, she felt that her very depressed mother, who had been in and out of mental hospitals, taken overdoses, and cut herself, was oblivious to her existence.

Almost a year later, although the therapeutic alliance was much improved and the theme of my not wanting her no longer was so predominant, it was far from gone. When June discovered that I was writing a book, she felt competitive with the book for my attention and was certain that I preferred to sit and write than see her. If she had to cancel an appointment, she would say in her sarcastically staccato attacking manner, "I'm sure that's quite all right with you. More time for the book. That's what you *really* want to be doing. Maybe I'll do you a favor and cancel my Thursday session, too." She once asked if I really thought I were capable of writing a book. I had to be aware, of course, of my anger and how I was feeling myself physically becoming tied in knots. These reactions could have easily rendered me impotent to help her, which on some level I was certain she wanted. Although she was projecting onto me the wish that she not exist and, through projective identification, her own feelings of being small and inconsequential, both of which had to be addressed, on the more basic level of reality testing, it was essential to ask her if she really did believe that it was either/or, that I had to want to spend time either writing my book or seeing her twice a week. Could I not want to work with her despite the obstacles she kept putting in my path, and could I not also want to work on my book and have the time and interest for both? As she recovered from her ego regression, she was able to entertain the idea that both might really be true. She could even acknowledge that she was in fact putting obstacles in my way and began to think about why she was doing that.

At times when the patient has spiraled up he can be "talked down," but at other times no intervention helps (Kroll 1988). It is a cognitive style that promotes distancing between the patient and others, tries the therapist's patience to the limit, and defies the therapist to remain connected to the patient.

Emotional Intensity and Lability

Emotions are experienced with an intensity so great that it threatens to overwhelm these patients. Often their self-mutilation, bulimic behavior, and other impulsive behavior are ways not to feel these intense emotions and, simultaneously, to express them. Not surprisingly, their object choices are of people as intense and labile as themselves.

Marisa, 24, had been cutting and burning herself since eighth grade and she knew these acts had nothing to do with a wish to kill herself. Her boyfriend knew about her cutting, too. One evening, when they were talking about it at her house, he demanded to know why she does it. All she could say was "I don't know" to his repeated demand to know why. She felt herself getting very angry and they began to argue about it, as he continued to ask the same question. She ran upstairs to her bedroom with him in pursuit, and began punching out the walls. By now he was screaming "Why? Why? Why? I demand to know," and she quickly pulled out the straight-edge razor she kept under her mattress and began slashing her arms.

Yet at the same time they are intolerant of less labile relationships and drive each relationship to ever greater intensity or abandon the relationship despairingly. "I will never see him again. He couldn't love me the way I needed and no one ever will. I want to die." Often the emotional intensity and lability seem inseparable from the cognitive disturbances. Marisa's difficulties in processing information about mental illness and her own emotions led to developing inaccurate assumptions about herself, further identity confusion, and detachment from herself and others.

When I first saw Marisa, I found out that she had been hospitalized a few years earlier. "I'm a borderline personality disorder and a little bipolar," she said as she looked me dead in the eye awaiting my response. "Pretty scary," I said drolly, and she laughed in surprise. (In that response, I realized in retrospect, I was trying to create something of a transitional space to challenge the rigid categories about which she thought of herself. Not responding as she expected caught her off guard, creating an opportunity for a connection.) I said that it felt as if she had been trying to scare me off with the clinical labels. She thought about it a moment and replied that maybe she was, that there is a lot she does and says that she does not understand.

When I asked her if, in all the numerous times she had cut, burned, starved, purged, and gotten drunk, she had ever wanted to die, she said that one time, and one time only, she had made a suicide attempt. She did not know why, only that of all the times she had cut herself, this was the one that got her hospitalized. She told me about a sexual incident involving her and two men. "I was pretty drunk. It was fun at the time, exciting. We did just about everything except intercourse." Later, when she was home alone and trying to fall asleep, she began to feel a terrible sense of shame. She became agitated, tossing and turning, not knowing what to do with herself but feeling she had to do something. She got up, took her straight-edge blade from under the mattress, and began cutting her arms and wrists. She immediately felt much better, bandaged her arms and fell asleep. The next morning she was shocked and frightened to find her sheets and pajamas drenched in blood. She dressed, drove to her mother's office, and said, "I have something to show you. You have to help me." She took off her bandages and in a dramatic gesture, displayed her cuts. "Why did you do that?" her mother demanded. "I guess I tried to kill myself," she replied. Her mother, frightened more than she had ever been by Marisa's cutting, took her home, called her husband, and both mother and father took turns closely guarding Marisa for four days as she slept and when she was awake. They sat awake by her bed, ready to restrain her if she tried again to "kill" herself. By the time she was admitted to the hospital, Marisa and her parents and the hospital staff all thought she had made a suicide attempt. The medical record and the record from the residential treatment program to which she subsequently was transferred both note that a suicide attempt was the precipitating incident for hospitalization. "Ms. Green is a 20-year-old female who was hospitalized recently for lacerating her left wrist in an attempt to kill herself."

It was not until I asked her to tell me about her "suicide attempt" that, in the telling, Marisa made the connection for the first time between her sense of shame, subsequent agitation, and the wish to do something to stop the bad feeling. For the first time she realized that she had never really had the intention of dying, only ending the pain, and cutting had always worked for her. She had never really made a suicide attempt. What she and her family had known about her for several years was a cognitive distortion made during a time of extreme emotional intensity. Unfortunately "suicide attempt" had become part of her identity. Discussing it in detail began a process of altering that sense of identity.

She could not remember how she first started cutting herself, but recalled an incident in college when she was smoking a cigarette and deliberately burned her arm with it. When I asked how it happened she said matter-of-factly that she did not have an ashtray. (Momentarily stunned, I thought how extraordinarily disconnected she was.) "You didn't have an ashtray, so you used your arm instead?" I asked. "I guess," she said, then after thinking about it a moment said she thought that sounded pretty weird. I said, "You must have been feeling pretty disconnected from your body to treat your arm as if it were a thing to be used that way." She thought about it, then said that that made her think about the way she would have sex with different men, that she let them use her as if she were a thing. She became interested in the connection she had made, that she did to her body what she let others do to her body.

Interestingly, her medical record stated that she had been raped at age 14 by a stranger in the woods, that she had used marijuana, cocaine, heroin, and crack, and had psychotic symptoms as a result of drug use. When I asked her about this, she said that although she had abused alcohol and marijuana, the rest of the information was not true. She readily acknowledged having lied in the past about her history, saying that she was raped at 14 and again in college because she thought that the severity of her self-harm symptoms could only be justified by an abuse history. In the psychiatric hospital, the only patients she met who did things like that to themselves had been beaten, raped, or otherwise sexually abused. And the extent of the substance abuse and psychotic symptoms? Marisa thought she needed to make herself more interesting and dramatic for people there to be interested in her. Otherwise she would just be another pissed-off kid who fought with her parents. She enjoyed the drama and felt herself to be much more interesting and glamorous this way. After a while she started to believe in her own lies and in her own identity as a chronic mental patient, a "really fucked-up head case."

Themes of Victimization and Predation

The sense of being a victim at the hands of one's parents retains affective power and centrality and can be considered a primary unit of mental life (Pine 1994). The victimization theme is pervasive and unifying. It is reenacted in the patient's preying upon her body and in unstable interpersonal relationships, and underlies many seemingly unrelated behaviors. In the largest sense, victimization includes getting others to act upon oneself usually in an openly negative, rejecting or aggressive way, but sometimes even in a caregiving way that can become destructive if it is excessive or infantilizing. Victimization, then, is seen in patients' ability to get others to do things to them or upon them, or to tell them what to do or to take over ordinary adult functions and decision making for them (Kroll 1988). Usually the patient presents herself in a characteristic mode of provocativeness or incompetence that ultimately renders her a victim. She may present a sense of narcissistic entitlement, expecting or demanding that others rescue her from real or perceived victimization, or she may insist that others who could rescue or protect her instead stand by callously and allow her to be victimized. She may become the victimizer in her relations with others, or may see in others who try to help her the intent to victimize her.

These scenarios are powerful enough to render the therapist ineffective, or may evoke such an aggressive or erotic response in the therapist that he or she does victimize or reject the patient, thus reenacting the patient's earlier experiences. Therapists must carefully monitor their own sexual responses. (Transference and countertransference issues and enactments are discussed in Chapter 15.) Patients who have a history of childhood sexual abuse often report having been sexually abused by doctors, therapists, or hospital staff, while those with a history of physical abuse may invite further abuse of this sort. Incest victims may present themselves seductively and make themselves vulnerable to further victimization by caregivers.

I had a consultation with a young woman who reported a history of sexual abuse by multiple family members. She reported that when she was hospitalized in a state facility, she was sexually abused by two guards, and when she sought help from a psychiatrist for her eating disorder, he molested her. She had been starving herself and was at a very low weight and was bulimic as well. She agreed to have a baseline medical evaluation. At that time I did not know a suitable female physician with experience in evaluating people with eating disorders, and she objected to a male physician for fear that he would want to do a pelvic exam. Despite my telling her that usually was not done, she nonetheless was terrified, explaining that when she has to have a pelvic, she invariably has flashbacks and "freaks out." I suggested that it might be more comfortable if she brought a friend with her and offered to call the doctor to explain how fearful she was so that he could be sensitive to her concerns. She agreed to this and called me after the exam to say that the doctor had explained everything he needed to do, that she felt so comfortable that she left her friend in the waiting room and did even not need to bring her into the examining room. "I trusted him completely." It sounded as if she had become overly trusting. I soon received a call from the physician confirming that the exam had gone well, but adding that she had presented herself as so vulnerable and unable to take care of herself that "it was as if she were serving herself up on a silver platter."

Some patients are adept at eliciting the excessive need to take care of patients that many clinicians have, at the same time that they can also bring out the worst in us. With Carrie I had to struggle with both. Themes of victimization, competence, hatred, and fears of being left alone were paramount

Carrie, married and in her late thirties, had never developed a sense of competence about herself as a person, although she had an advanced degree and a responsible job in her chosen profession, and was a devoted and caring mother to her son and daughter. She presented herself as disorganized—she bounced checks, overcharged her credit cards, and canceled appointments at the last minute because she had neglected to make the necessary babysitting arrangements. Much later I learned secrets that were precious to her— she shoplifted at times, sneaked out of work to go grocery shopping in the middle of the day, and drove recklessly at high speeds. Even her therapy was a secret from her husband, as she knew he would demand she stop. He said she did not need therapy and she thought maybe he was right. On the days she was daring, she paid me with a check from the household account, and on days when she feared discovery, she paid in cash. Much of her disorganization was a function of her dissociation, as she would know what she was doing at the same time that she would disavow the knowledge of what she was doing. She lived with secrets and lies—the fear that the check would bounce, the fear of being found to be incompetent at work, the fear of being apprehended as she shoplifted, the fear of her husband finding out she was in treatment.

She had grown up emotionally neglected by a mentally ill mother and remote father and was at a loss as to how to manage her life. After college, she got involved with a man who structured and organized her life, writing out daily lists of things for her to do, for which she was very grateful. If she did not do as she was supposed to, however, he would berate her and she would become frightened that he would abandon her. She always felt that he was trying to take her over, to dominate her and she even broke off the relationship once but resumed it because she felt she could not manage her life without him. It had become clear to her that she was the incompetent and he was the epitome of competence. He gave orders and she tried to follow them. Everything she did was wrong, according to him. When with him, she could not think for herself or access her own ability to think critically.

She had trouble shopping for clothes because she had never developed her own taste or style. She frequently pointed out some new article of clothing she was wearing, wanting to know if I thought it was all right, fearful of dressing or grooming herself in the "off" way that some mentally ill people have. I often felt like the mother hen, wanting to take her under my wing and take care of her. I often had to straddle the line between giving her the kind of information about navigating in the world that she genuinely seemed to need, and taking over and directing her life, which she often seemed to invite.

Yet she often criticized my clothing and my office. Knowing that social workers were low in the mental health hierarchy, she attacked me with this numerous times and numerous ways with sadistic glee. Although she had found my name, listed with my degree, on a list of social workers affiliated with her managed care plan, she insisted that I had deliberately tricked her into thinking I was a psychologist with a Ph.D. because I had an inferior degree in an inferior profession for which other mental health professionals had no respect. She had found a sore spot, because I had struggled against more prejudicial and discriminatory treatment by psychologists, psychiatrists, and other physicians in the course of my professional life than I wanted to be reminded of, and I found her attacks particularly difficult to bear.

On the days of her sessions, I sometimes found myself anticipating what nasty remark she might make about what I was wearing. "You actually *bought* that outfit?" (I refrained from saying what popped into my mind, that at least I had paid for it and not stolen it.) I felt preyed upon in and out of sessions, and enjoyed fantasies about revenge; I had to struggle not to act on them. The treatment had the potential for deteriorating into a sadomasochistic scenario if I allowed myself to rise to her bait, which was hard not to do as she was baiting me much of the time.

On numerous occasions I confronted her with the observation that she seemed to enjoy belittling and degrading me. Doing this helped me to feel strong and competent and less angry, and even resulted in my finding something comical in her verbal assaults. I came to regard her less as a victimizer and felt even more empathy for her. My being able to confront her resulted in her trying to inhibit her sadism, and she expressed the fear that I would stop seeing her. Her worldview seemed to be that one was either preyed upon or was a predator, but in either event one ended up alone.

Carrie did, fortunately, have much more of an observing ego than one might think initially, although far too often she disavowed what she had observed of herself and allowed her observing ego to be overtaken by her destructive narcissism. I interpreted this in a way that was palatable to her. Trying to align myself with her observing ego, I told her that the choice was not necessarily an either-or one—either to act on her sadism or to disavow her sadistic wishes—but that she could, when feeling the impulse to say something hateful to me, observe it out loud in the session and tell me that that is what she was feeling and thinking and that we could talk about it together. She doubted that she could do that, but was quite intrigued with the idea. In time, when once again I had to confront her on her sadistic pleasure in demeaning me, this elicited from her a surprising insight about what she seemed intuitively to know was her projective identification: "He [her husband] puts his venom in me and I have no choice but to spew it out onto you." That is, she knew on a preconscious level that she could not contain her rage and sadistic wishes and so virtually automatically projected her venom into me; my ego would become the container for her aggression. She could persecute me and at the same time identify with the despised person she tried to make me. She could identify with her husband as the aggressor and at the same time displace her rage from him to me. She was able to look at how much her hateful behavior encompassed that she had not been aware of.

This discussion and interpretation furthered my being able to be heard a bit more about how she plays a major part in her own victimization, and how she uses her sharp tongue to prey on others. It furthered exploration of her wish to hurt and demean people. She told me she has always done this to people and can never be spontaneous at meetings at work or in other interpersonal interactions for fear she would say something terrible to someone.

It was fortunate for her that I could be a container for her aggression, but I felt that I was reaching my limit and informed her of this so that she might begin to assume greater responsibility for maintaining the treatment. I said, "You treat me as if you can continue to degrade and chip away at me indefinitely, as if I have no limit." She was startled by the confrontation (which was also an interpretation) but was glad that I had told her this. No one had ever called her on this, she said, with the exception of a high school teacher who once took her aside and told her that she was very cruel to others in her class and if she continued to treat people in this way, she would drive everyone away and she would end up all alone. She had been moved to tears that he cared enough to tell her. Her vicious tongue had always been a problem, she said, and had ruined potential friendships before they had a chance. She was glad I had confronted her and in fact even said that she had been wondering if I ever was going to say or do anything to stop it. Despite her devaluation of the treatment, she said, it was valuable to her and she did not want to jeopardize it and drive me away. Some time later, when she developed the courage to stand up to her husband and draw a line between what was and was not acceptable behavior from him, it seemed that my having drawn the line with her had enabled her to do the same with him.

Whatever the multiple psychic functions of their self-harm, these patients know that it has a very powerful effect on others. This is not necessarily to say that they are being overtly manipulative. The persistence with which they harm themselves in proximity to others or bring their ravaged bodies to the attention of others has, invariably, an interpersonal meaning, and often patients know on some level that their self-harm preys upon and victimizes others. These behaviors challenge the efficacy of the treatment and the therapist. The therapist's failure to confront the more overt interpersonal incentives and consequences of their self-harm is to lose the most important therapeutic leverage that the therapist has (Kroll 1988).

Kelly, in her early thirties, was referred to me by a man in her profession who had become her mentor and friend. She had risen quickly up the ladder and was regarded as something of a star. She claimed to have been sexually abused as a child by her alcoholic father, while her alcoholic mother claimed not to know anything about what was going on. In adolescence she began starving and dehydrating herself, a punishment because she never felt she deserved to have anything good. Each mouthful had to be earned by exercising until her bones ached and her feet bled. She suffered from colitis.

For most of her life, a very impressive false self development and high functioning in her professional life masked a primitive and fragile ego structure, and she lived a socially isolated existence that enabled her to keep her eating disorder a secret. Yet in the past year her self-harm behavior had worsened significantly (starving, severe vomiting and laxative abuse, punching her hand through windows, burning her hand, excessive exercise) and had become so life threatening so quickly that she had lost her job. Her life was like a house of cards that had come tumbling down.

She was so well regarded at work that she was virtually guaranteed that she might have her job back when she was well. In fact, her company invested very large sums of money above and beyond what her medical insurance would cover for her care, and was ready to do whatever it took to get her healthy again. She looked like a starving waif that one could knock over with a feather; she had an endearing helpless quality that made people want to go out on a limb for her. One couple she knew professionally even opened their home to her indefinitely when it was too unsafe for her to live alone.

Her mentor had assumed a major caregiving role, arranging for numerous treatments, including outpatient individual and group therapy, two hospitalizations, and day hospital treatment in an eating-disorder facility, none of which helped. She seemed to be no better than before. The initial individual and group therapy had been with a psychiatrist whom she liked very much who specialized in issues of sexual abuse. She hated listening in group to the others' "horror stories" and could not bring herself to tell her own. In fact, her self-harm got worse during this treatment, requiring several acute medical and psychiatric hospitalizations. Her mentor realized that this treatment was not helpful and referred her to an inpatient eating-disorder facility. Although upset at the loss of her psychiatrist, she formed an immediate trusting relationship with her inpatient therapist, with whom she met four times a week. She had made symptomatic improvement in the controlled environment of the facility when she did not have to make decisions about whether or what to eat—she was expected to eat what was served—and when purging after meals was deliberately prevented. The self-mutilation stopped entirely.

Yet she could not tolerate any discussion of her abuse history in her group therapy sessions and could barely acknowledge it. Once she made symptomatic improvement and she was "stepped down" to a less closely supervised level of care where she was allowed to choose her food from a small buffet and bathrooms were not off limits immediately after meals, she began purging with ipecac, laxatives, and diuretics, burning herself and punching her hand through windows. At the same time that she was "stepped down," she lost the relationship with the inpatient therapist. Her behavior seemed to shriek, " I need someone to take care of me. I am incompetent to care for myself." Although she had been starving herself since puberty without anyone really noticing, the current symptom picture she presented began a year before, when she began having severe dissociative episodes and intrusive memories and flashbacks about childhood sexual abuse that she claimed had gone on from early childhood until early adolescence.

Given the clinical picture, I was virtually certain that outpatient treatment would not work, but when her mentor called me I agreed to see her for consultation. She was well on her way to developing a career as a mental patient, already involved in a revolving door cycle of admissions and discharges. I hoped to intervene in this cycle in some way, and so when Kelly called me herself and asked rather desperately, without having met or spoken to me before, if I could be her therapist, I told her that I did not know but that we could meet and talk and I could see how I might be able to be of some help to her.

We met four times in two weeks, during which I felt tender, caring feelings and empathy for Kelly, but came very quickly to feel victimized and preyed upon. In the first session she spoke of the monster in her that makes her starve herself so that she will disappear. She spoke of terrifying dissociative episodes when she thinks her father is next to her and she burns or cuts herself. She denied that she was currently purging but complained of not feeling well and called her gastroenterologist from my office to arrange to see him immediately. She said it must be her colitis. Or maybe it was her heart. I later discovered that only hours later she had been rushed to the emergency room where intravenous fluids and electrolytes had to be administered. Her gastroenterologist was fed up with her lying about her purging and her self-destructiveness, as the staff at the eating-disorder facility seemed to be. People who had cared about for her had come to feel great anger. I began to rein in my rescue fantasies, realizing that she was a master of deception. In session two I discovered that even while being treated in the emergency room and starting to feel stronger, she felt she did not deserve the infusions and did not deserve to live. Sometimes she wants to hurt herself and sometimes she wants to kill herself. She wanted to continue seeing me and thought she would enroll in another intensive outpatient treatment program at the same time. Then suddenly she had a dissociative episode, standing up abruptly, glassy-eyed, insisting her father was standing behind her. I had to talk her down, grounding her in where she was in time and space, which ended the dissociative episode. If I had not been able to do that, she might have put her fist through the window behind her.

In fact, when I asked her what would she have wanted to do or say if her father had really been standing there behind her, she immediately and passionately said she'd want to kill him or "at least cut his balls off." A devout Christian, she was shocked to hear herself say that and immediately expressed guilt about having such terrible thoughts and feelings. Punching her hand through the window would have been an expression of her wish to kill him and punish herself. Instead of cutting his testicles off, she cut herself instead, thus punishing herself at the same time for the gratification of her aggressive wishes and participation in sexual acts with her father. She was preying upon herself as he had preyed upon her and her destructiveness was frighteningly out of control.

Between sessions two and three I explored and considered other options for Kelly. In the third session I told her that I was very concerned for her life, that her destructive impulses were so out of control that she needed a very different kind of treatment than she had ever had—a long-term treatment in an open psychoanalytic hospital where she could develop a greater autonomous ability to care for herself and could confront the demons that ruled her. The open hospital presents a unique opportunity for very troubled destructive patients who have not improved elsewhere. There are no locked wards or seclusion rooms, no privileges to be earned; all patients have the same rights and privileges, come and go as they like, participate as equal members in a democratic patient-run community, and meet with their therapists four times a week. The hospital offers a potential safe space, a true holding environment for examined living, the chance to find a balance between freedom and responsibility. If patients cannot maintain a minimal level of self-care, they may be transferred to a medical facility for medical treatment or a closed psychiatric hospital setting. This opportunity provided the only way I knew that Kelly could begin to assume greater responsibility for her physical well-being and could begin to develop some ability to live reflectively. Without this opportunity, I could see no future for Kelly other than a lifetime career as a mental patient, and said this to her and her mentor.

She was disturbed by the degree of freedom she would be allowed but she listened. She asked if she could visit the hospital before applying for admission, if she would have her own therapist there, and, if she did become a patient there, if I would be her therapist when she was discharged. She agreed that her life was out of control, and if she did not kill herself she was sure she did not want a career as a mental patient. Just the night before while lying in bed she observed herself in her dissociated state jump up, grab a hammer, and smash her hand with it. (The hand she persisted in hurting was the one that had committed unspeakable sexual acts with her father.) At that moment in my office she did not want to die and she consented for me to talk with the facility's admissions office about her. Although she agreed that she would keep herself safe so that she could go visit the hospital, she also told me that she could not promise me anything. I asked her to call me if she was feeling as if she might hurt herself, but she could not even be sure she could do that. I was worried about her remaining alive and called her mentor, collaborating with him on a contingency plan in the event of another acute crisis. My sleep was troubled that night as she preyed on my mind. I wished I had never agreed to see her. The title of Winnicott's (1958b) paper, "Hate in the Countertransference," came to mind several times.

The following day the admissions office invited her to visit, tour the facility, and talk with other patients, a visit quickly arranged between her, her mentor, and the couple she was living with. We had one session the day before her visit, in which she was preparing herself for the possibility of a second trip for an admissions interview and admission several days later. She asked again if I would be her therapist after discharge. I agreed that when she was discharged, which was undoubtedly not in the near future, if she could take the responsibility of keeping herself safe enough so that I did not have to stay up at night worrying about whether she would live or die during the night, then I would be glad to talk with her seriously about this. "You were awake worrying about me?" she asked incredulously. "Yes," I said, "and that is not a good way to conduct therapy—not good for you and not good for me." For any therapist to remain contained enough to help you, inpatient or outpatient, you will need to take much greater responsibility than you have for not giving in to your self-destructive impulses. If not, you will die."

She visited the open hospital the next day, Friday, and her mentor called me that evening with the news that she was returning Monday morning for her admissions interview. I advised him that the intervening weekend was of great concern as we could expect an upsurge of the dissociative and self-harm symptoms in anticipation of hospitalization. We pieced together a con-

404 / *When the Body Is the Target*

tingency plan. By Sunday I had not heard from Kelly directly and called her. I found out that she had been vomiting terribly, and by very early Monday morning, she was in the E.R. once again, and then directly from there, on her way to her admissions interview.

Once admitted, she succeeded in inducing in her therapist and other staff at the hospital the same feelings she induced in me and in others who had cared for her. She waved her self-destructiveness in front of all of us as the matador waves the flag in front of the bull. She was transferred numerous times to an acute medical facility when her physical condition was grave. Finally, staff at the open hospital agreed that they could no longer treat her under current conditions and she was discharged. Several days later she sought and gained readmission, promising to take greater responsibility for herself. As of this writing, she has been there over a year, with only minimal improvement despite intensive psychotherapy with a committed and talented therapist, expert supervision and consultation, deep involvement of the nurses, and family therapy. When staff expressed their anger and frustration, she could not understand her role in this and felt that the staff was picking on her. When she began cutting her hand and dropping weights on it nightly, her therapist found treating her to be intolerable and finally took the position that this was unbearable, and if she continued to do this, she would no longer be her therapist. As if by magic, this intervention resulted in the behavior stopping.

Themes of Loneliness and Emptiness

The sense of loneliness and inner emptiness that dominates the clinical picture is linked to a fear of abandonment in some patients, while in others, destructive thoughts and behaviors reflecting past abuses occur when the patient is alone or is feeling a sense of aloneness. If memories of past abuse are triggered, the patient may respond by depersonalizing, which can ultimately make her feel all the more alone. Sometimes the sense of aloneness is tied to the ways the patient victimizes and drives others away.

June, the patient who got a sense of power from demeaning and insulting me, also at times felt very much alone when she feared being abandoned. In adolescence, when her mother's depression and self-cutting worsened and required hospitalizations, June felt herself all alone. With each cut her mother made, which she did not hesitate to show June, June felt that her mother had cut her away in the same way that one cuts away and discards the outer layer of fat from meat. Feeling abandoned and discarded, June came to rely upon her own body all the more for self-regulation. She had an anorexic period, denying herself food and she began to scratch her arms and abdomen. In college, she saved bits of skin picked from her cuticles and put them in a little box. When she felt very lonely, she would open the box to look at them, which helped her to feel better. When she was out, she always checked the little box upon returning to make sure its contents were still there.

She noticed a small painted wooden box on my bookcase and wanted to know what it contained. I opened it and showed her the six tiny "worry dolls" from Guatemala and when she asked, explained their purpose. According to the legend, if a child has a problem, he should share it with a worry doll. Before going to bed, he is to tell one worry to each doll and then place them all beneath his pillow. When he awakens, his worries will be gone. She liked the worry dolls and acknowledged that she had had a favorite stuffed animal when she was a child but that her mother threw it out. She could see that saving bits of her skin had something of a transitional soothing function as did the stuffed animals and the worry dolls. For a while each time she came into my office she would look for the box of worry dolls, laugh anxiously, and ask if they were all all right. Once it was established that they were where they were supposed to be, she would relax. Soon she brought in her daughter's transitional object to show me, a very endearing looking stuffed animal, and not surprisingly, I found that she was as attached to it as her daughter was. She began to call me sometimes when she felt very anxious, and those times when I was not directly available, hearing my voice on the answering machine helped her to maintain a sense of object constancy about me and also served as a soothing mechanism for her. Around a year later, a fierce thunderstorm broke as she was leaving my office. An unclaimed umbrella was in my umbrella stand and I offered that she could use it if she wanted and could return it next time. Sheepishly she brought back a different umbrella, asking if she could exchange it for the one I had lent her. Having what she thought of as my umbrella provided a sense of comfort. Many months later by chance and to her delight, she came upon the worry dolls in a museum gift shop, and bought them for herself. She showed me them in her session, wanting to compare them to mine, and again asked, this time playfully, if we could trade a few—having a few of mine helped her and trading was fun.

At other times she thought she saw or heard violence when with me—a lawnmower outside or her eye drawn to a pointy memo spindle on my bookcase. She would become suddenly and acutely aware of it, asking anxiously what I was going to do with it. It was associated with violent impulses, which more often than not, she projected onto me. Sometimes, after she had attacked me verbally, she would become fearful that I would not want to see her any more, that she would lose me and then she would be all alone.

Depersonalization, Derealization, and Hyperarousal

Self-harm is an all too efficient means of both ending and reinforcing dissociation (depersonalization and/or derealization) and hyperarousal. The depersonalization is often experienced by patients as a terrible state of aloneness, and an attack on the body is a way of feeling connected to somebody, even if the body they are connected to is their own. The atavistic aggression associated with hyperarousal pushes for immediate discharge, and the attack upon their bodies is experienced as soothing and calming. Breaking the addiction to the trauma response requires that the relationship with the therapist provides the feeling of connection to somebody and the soothing that is desperately needed. The therapist must be available to be used as a transitional object if patients are to internalize the positive object representations that will help them to calm and soothe themselves. At the same time patients will need to acquire behavioral and cognitive tools for regulating these states that they can use independently. Helping patients to anticipate and develop strategies for dealing with these regressive states promotes the development of the ego functions of anticipation and signal anxiety and promotes a sense of autonomy and competence. *Understanding Self-Injury: A Workbook for Adults* (Trautmann and Connors 1994)[1] is an excellent resource that therapists and patients alike can use to promote affect identification, toleration, and regulation. Although it is a self-help manual developed specifically for self-mutilators, the tools, which are much like the ones I use with a variety of self-harming patients, can readily be adapted for use with other impulsive behaviors.

Marisa's cutting or burning usually occurred when she was in an angry, agitated state. While in residential treatment, she had formed trusting relationships with two clinical staff members who taught her how to use simple cognitive and behavioral tools to identify when she was starting to get angry and to calm herself down before her anger reached the point of no return. She counted slowly and as she did, the slow pace slowed the anger down so it felt less and less to her that she needed to do something about it immediately. If she was already at the point of feeling the impulse to cut or burn herself, she managed to intervene into this state by doing deep-breathing exercises, which calmed her. A family therapist had worked with her and her parents, which resulted in a much better relationship, and when Marisa was discharged, she was able to turn to them for comfort and support as well when she was feeling bad, instead of turning to her body.

---

1. *Understanding Self-Injury: A Workbook for Adults* can be purchased directly from the publisher, Pittsburgh Action Against Rape, telephone (412) 431-5665.

Severe Ego Regressions

Severe ego regressions may happen in and out of treatment and may include a brief but reversible descent into psychosis, which includes severe cognitive disorganization and flooding with intrusive memories, images, and hallucinations, and may include an episode of self-harm behavior. The rapidity with which some patients can regress in the therapist's presence is dramatic and can be quite unnerving; the therapist must intervene to reverse the destructive process. When Kelly dissociated and became terrified that her father was standing behind her in my office, I could intervene to talk her down. With some "provocation and crash tantrums" (M. Stone 1988), as described below, there is no intervening by the therapist to end it, as it has a powerful life of its own, and the therapist can only wait for it to peak and then subside before intervening. Severe ego regressions may also be in the nature of an enactment, a powerful two-person phenomenon in which both patient and therapist participate (see Chapter 15).

In some ego regressions there may be somatic manifestations, depersonalization, derealization, hyperarousal, and splitting. Patients may allude to hearing voices, which may or may not be true hallucinations, a reference to the polarized bad and good (demon and angel) aspects of the self that have been projected. Patients tend to be harsh and judgmental about these regressions, which promotes the need to punish the self, which leads to more such ego regressions, and so on. The patient's thinking about these regressions must be changed, which can be done through a psychoeducational approach in which the patient is introduced to the concept of a perverse relationship between parts of the self. It is also important for patients to develop some empathy for themselves and to understand that one ego regression is not the same as a relapse. In fact, such an attitude can go a long way toward preventing relapses to ongoing self-harm. While some patients may not immediately be able to consider realistically some alternative to self-harm, it is important to talk about these possibilities very early on in treatment, so that such alternatives can become short-range goals to be strived for, a more optimistic look toward the future.

Depression, Anger, and Despair

Moods in which anger predominates assume dimensions of depression and demoralization, while repeated interpersonal, vocational, or academic failures lead to demoralized states tinged with anger, which inevitably become indistinguishable from chronic depression (Kroll 1988). There may be endogenous biological factors that make self-harming patients prone to emotional intensity, especially to states of anger and depression. That is, they may have particular difficulty in regulating their angry feelings because constitutionally they may have been born with more than their share of aggression or because their hyperirritability was traumatically induced. Hyperirritability is the "neurophysiological red thread" that runs through this group of patients (M. Stone 1988), playing a part in differentiating between those who turn their anger against themselves in the form of a depressed mood, sleep and appetite disturbances, anhedonia, and feelings of guilt and blame, and those who turn their anger against themselves in the form of an attack on the body. M. Stone (1988) discusses "provocation and crash: the borderline tantrum" from the point of view of chaos theory, a concept that has important clinical implications for those times when the patient turns his unremitting rage on the therapist.

> The unpredictability of mood shift appears to be an expression of the same phenomenon that underlies the predictability of climatic shifts; namely, sensitive dependence on initial conditions. . . . By this is meant the inherent instability of the system, such that tiny . . . unpredictable perturbations set in motion cause huge shifts in the system's state. . . .
>
> In the tantrum or provocation-and-crash behavior, . . . the response to certain stimuli is not only exaggerated but seems incapable of dying out back to the baseline or relaxed level unless spiked still further to the peak. . . . Once stimulated to near-orgasm, . . . one tends to remain in an uncomfortable state, unable to relax, until pushed further to the peak/orgastic level. Borderline patients, caught in situations that arouse in them moderately intense anger, often provoke the person engendering this emotion until a state of maximal fury (*borderline rage*) is reached. There is usually an outbreak of impulsive behavior at this moment ("Flash point"), in the form of hitting, hurling, screaming, etc., followed by rapid relaxation and abrupt recovery of more rational thinking. [M. Stone 1988, pp. 7–8]

When anger and depression are central to the clinical picture, treatment with medication may be indicated. The combination of intense anger and impulsivity is a particularly dangerous one that often responds well to antidepressant medications other than Prozac, which may exacerbate and energize the anger (Breggin and Breggin 1994). The anger is still experienced but not nearly so intensely as in states of hyperarousal, providing greater opportunity for the patient to begin to regulate a level of anger that is more manageable.

This was the case for Marty, the patient discussed in Chapter 10, who, when cut off on the highway by another driver, gunned the engine in a mad chase to crash into him. I referred him to a psychopharmacologist who prescribed an antidepressant, which toned down the degree of anger and hyperarousal. He still got angry, but had a window of opportunity within which to think, and so instead of shouting, "Don't fuck with me!" and gunning the accelerator, he muttered curses under his breath and thought of terrible things he wanted to do to the other driver, but did not do them. The medication helped him to contain his rage, making it possible for him to be treated on an outpatient basis. Marty's envy of my education and status evoked a great deal of narcissistic rage directed at me. "Who the hell are you? What makes you think you're so much better than me?" A continual barrage of such comments evoked a great deal of anger on my part; I thought to myself that there are some people who can provoke their own murder and Marty was one of them.

Marisa was someone who I suspected may have been born with a larger-than-usual share of aggression.

> "It's like I'm in a battered wife's relationship with myself—I hit myself and then tell myself I'm sorry." As Marisa became more comfortable in discussing her anger, she very gingerly revealed that her anger is something that both frightens and fascinates her. She had never really talked with anyone about this because she thought of it as so crazy, but she is fascinated to know how far out of control she is capable of going, how far her destructiveness will go. What evil is she capable of? In the past she had hit and scratched her mother. Sometimes when she is having sex, as she becomes more excited, she gets what she calls "an adrenaline rush" of animal rage that scares her. She told me about a little boy for whom she babysat; he was so cute, sweet, and cuddly; she really loved him, and yet, there were moments that terrified her when she felt such visceral rage toward him that she felt capable of tearing him limb from limb. Terrified of being near him, she would walk away from him in order to protect him. We began to understand her impulses toward self-harm as a displacement of her fury, a means of protecting others from her rage, which helped her to regard both the impulses toward self-harm and her ego regressions as more understandable.
>
> Why would she have such a store of anger, she wondered. She gets along so much better with her parents now than in the past, when she would storm and rage at them, especially her father. She had good reason to be angry then, she thought, but now? It did not make sense to her. This led in time to exploration of her attraction to very angry people like her drug-abusing boyfriend with whom she was always fighting. I also wondered if perhaps she had not been born constitutionally endowed with an unusually large aggressive instinct or whether the lack of attention to her learning problems had produced a deep anger.

The ability to express anger is more a problem for women in general and is expressed more through depression and depressive equivalents. It was unusually problematic for Jane, who needed to develop the ability to tolerate and regulate mood and affect states, expand her very limited range of affect, and move from the language of the body to expressive language (Farber 1998a,b).

> Jane came from a long line of women who were expected to tolerate their men's alcoholism and from an Irish-American culture that expected people to be stoic and not express their feelings. She believed what she had learned from her Roman Catholic indoctrination, that it is as sinful to wish the terrible wish as it is to commit the terrible deed. Because she never

developed a voice with which to express her feelings, her body became the vehicle for enacting her angry destructive wishes and speaking of the trauma of family violence and secret shame, and of lack of secure human attachments.

At 26, Jane was a college graduate with a good job, who lived at home with her raging alcoholic father and frightened, submissive mother. She was depressed, obese, and extremely isolated socially. Her father had been a problem drinker for a long time, and Jane had been a compulsive overeater since early childhood, but in her sophomore year of high school her father's drinking and then her eating had become even more out of control. Jane had became more socially withdrawn, coming home after school feeling ashamed and depressed. She managed to complete her college education while living at home and then went to work. When she would come home she would try not to witness or hear her father's frightening alcoholic rages every night. Ever since sophomore year in high school, the evening routine was that she would stay in her room and "go away" in her mind into a dissociated state. When her father's rampage was over and the house had become quiet, Jane would sneak into the kitchen. She would load up on food, bringing it to her room to feed to herself, her behavior conveying that she needed no one, that she was the comforting mother feeding the hurting child.

Jane was a somatizer, expressing emotion through her body. Her fair Irish skin would get red and hot, her body overheating. She was chronically constipated and would sit on the toilet straining until she felt dizzy and would almost pass out and fall off the seat. "It wants to come out but it can't." She would lose her sense of time on the toilet; it felt like she was in a trance sometimes as she moved her bowels. I noticed some bruises on her arms and legs and patches of irritated skin, but she could not account for any of these, shrugging them off saying she must bruise easily because her skin is so fair. I noticed that there were times in the session when she would rub her arm or leg hard, or pinch it or pick at it. But Jane did not know it. When I told her what I observed her doing in the session, she was shocked.

The progression of her treatment is capsulized here, a greatly simplified version of a complex treatment that did not go nearly as smoothly as this version might suggest. Over time, as I gently pointed out her dissociation in sessions, she became more able to identify those moments immediately before that triggered the dissociation. She was able to develop more ability to observe herself picking and pinching herself in the session, and became able to avert dissociating. She observed that sometimes while straining on the toilet she'd think of her mother placating her father, and would pick at her skin. In time she came to feel angry at the mother who had gotten under her skin instead. Sometimes she'd think of her father, drunk again, and the next thing she knew, she was pinching herself so hard it was a wonder she did not scream. In time she came to experience the anger at him. We began to work on trying to identify what feelings were stirring in her right before she pinched or picked at herself. This was difficult because she did not know what feelings were, except for the feeling of being depressed. I had to educate her about a range of affects. All she knew about was feeling bad, and so I acquainted her with the varieties of bad feelings one could have: shame, guilt, annoyance, fury, anxiety, terror, sadness, depression. She was amazed. No one had ever done this before. On the one hand, she was poignantly grateful, but on the other hand, she was very angry at me for helping her to examine the pain to which she had become so attached. There were numerous negative therapeutic reactions, stormy times when I was sure she would quit therapy, but I found that the two of us were able to hang on for the ride.

In time she came to understand that no one had ever helped her to know what she felt, and she stopped blaming herself for these lacks. She was becoming more attached to me and less to self-harm. She experienced different kinds of bad feelings and even occasionally, to her surprise, different kinds of good feelings. It was like having all the Baskin-Robbins flavors to choose from when she thought there was only vanilla or chocolate.[2] As the affect array was expanding, we worked on affect tolerance, both analytically and using cognitive-behavioral methods, with the aim of becoming able to tolerate affect without having to resort to dissociation, compulsive eating, and self-injury. Verbal expression of affect, especially anger, conflicted with both her religious beliefs and cultural style, which had to be explored. She came up with the idea of playing music when her father was yelling, and enjoyed a sense of power in shutting him out in this way. In time she realized that she did not have to stay at home so much, and she joined an Adult Children of Alcoholics group, which got her out of the house with some regularity and provided opportunities for other new attachments. Over two years' time the overeating was reduced, the picking and pinching diminished, she was able to move out into her own apartment, and opened up her life to new friends and dating. As her life became more regular and self-regulated, so did her eating and bowel functioning. Out of a safe and secure attachment to her therapist that helped to regulate her, Jane had become more capable of regulating herself.

Dependency, Entitlement, Envy, and Specialness

Based on their life experiences, self-harming patients often present themselves with the sense that there is something special about them. This sense of specialness is not normal egocentricity, the sense of our unique humanness, which

---

2. I am grateful to James Sacksteder, M.D., for this metaphor, used in a presentation at the Center for the Study of Anorexia and Bulimia, June 18, 1997, "Treatment of the Hospitalized Eating-Disordered Patient."

provides us with the sense of our specialness that we all have (Kroll 1988). Their sense of specialness is different; it is intensely felt but not understood by them or their therapists. It may even be a core part of their identity, founded upon a series of childhood abuses or rejections. It is a sense of specialness that has a duality about it based on polarities of entitlement and evil. They recognize that often others do treat them in a special way, although they may claim to fight this and feel undeserving of such special treatment while enjoying the benefit of it. They recognize some special ability to get others to do things to them, such as getting others to abuse them, or for them, such as extending themselves in a way that often fosters the patients' dependency. They are not at all sure of how they do this and are often frightened or unhappy about it. They may fear there is something special about them that is evil and brings out the evil in others, that they turn relationships into something bad.

As Kroll (1988) states, the sense of specialness is often based on magical thinking, while sometimes a component is a realistic appraisal of how they have observed others behaving toward them. That is, they perpetuate a dual myth about themselves: that they are deserving of special consideration and treatment and that they are so inherently evil and worthless that they barely deserve to be alive. This dual concept of specialness (Kroll 1988, Grotstein 1993) is invaluable to the therapist working with self-harming patients. Entitlement is the feeling that certain things are owed or due to them, because they have suffered or been deprived, and they now simply expect it as their due that others will give them special treatment. They may feel this so intensely that they may become very resourceful, demanding, manipulative, and frantic in regard to getting their wishes met. Often they are regarded by others as manipulative, which has a large kernel of truth in it, but they respond with hurt feelings and counteraccusations that no one understands them, which also has a large kernel of truth in it.

Their pathological envy often fuels their sense of entitlement. Envying what others have in the way of personal qualities or possessions, there are underlying assumptions that there is only a limited quantity of what is envied and that the only way they can have it is to take it or demand it for themselves. Sometimes the envy is overt, as in Marty's case, but often it is more subtle. June could not let herself know that she envied what she perceived as my sense of containment and confidence. Eventually I understood that her continual devaluation of me also served the unconscious purpose of rattling me and taking the containment and confidence from me for herself so that she could sit back and enjoy a few moments of smug, contained pleasure. It was necessary to begin to confront her envy and her assumptions about it. First, she had to look at whether it was really possible to appropriate my qualities for herself, and second, she had to question whether the only way to have a true sense of containment and confidence was to take it from someone else, that maybe there was another way. This discussion introduced a new sense of possibility in relationships as I explained that it might be possible for her to feel better about herself and more contained without having to chip away at me, but this could not occur so long as she allowed herself to indulge so readily in the pleasure of dissociation. The price for this psychic retreat from reality was a chronic feeling of not being able to live in her own skin, a lack of containment and sense of herself that only promoted the envy and devaluation of others that ultimately left her feeling alone and isolated. This discussion helped to make her dissociation less acceptable to her ego and became a source of motivation for change.

A very concrete attitude of entitlement fuels the desire of many of these patients to transgress their therapists' boundaries. They often feel very needy and experience a sense of imminent danger if their wishes are not immediately met (Grotstein 1993), and may become enraged when they are thwarted or someone behaves in a way that does not conform to their myth of entitlement. Their sense of entitlement may well even extend to the expectation that the therapist simply "be there for them" to tolerate their abuse. In their narcissistic entitlement, they either lose perspective about the needs and rights of others or may never have developed any at all. While many therapists stretch the usual boundaries of the treatment frame when it seems indicated, it can be quite infuriating when a patient demands as his due that the therapist reduce the treatment fee when he is having financial trouble, or that the therapist be glad to take his phone calls at all hours, or provide makeup sessions for missed appointments or not charge for them. The therapist may harbor the thought, "Who the hell does he think he is?" when in fact, despite the feeling of entitlement, the patient may feel as if he is nothing much at all.

When Marty's managed care program refused to authorize further sessions despite his very real need, he was very angry and saw this as another way that the world was abusing him as his wealthy money-worshiping father did. Despite my considerable effort in appealing the decision and taking other action, he believed I owed it to him to accept as payment in full the very small amount of his copayment. When I wanted to discuss it further, he thundered that this was not fair, that he didn't need discussion, just a reduced fee, and that I was just another money-hungry vulture who did not give a damn about him. What was so startling about this was that he could not see at all that he was experiencing me as if I were his father, but demonstrated a literalness and concreteness in his expectations of me. He thought I was abandoning him, that he was entitled to make this demand of me, and that I owed him "big time." He succeeded in getting me to feel guilty and to think that perhaps he was right, at least for a few minutes.

It is indisputable that Kelly, discussed above, was treated as someone very special. Not only did she manage to get her friend and mentor overly involved in her treatment, she got him and acquaintances to assume major caregiving and housing functions for her, and she got her company to hold her job for her indefinitely and to invest an extraordinary sum of money in her treatment. The way she presented herself over the phone got me to agree to see her for consultation, spend a tremendous amount of time on collateral telephone consultations, feel responsible for her, and stay awake worrying about whether she would kill herself. She managed to enrage her therapist and the clinical staff at the open hospital through her expectations that she could continue to behave in the most flagrantly life-threatening way and they would have to stick around, watch, and assume responsibility for her and get her stitched up and hydrated again and again. On some level she felt entitled to torment people in this way indefinitely.

It is important that the therapist acknowledge the real ways in which the patient *is* special in getting others to hurt her or do for her. The therapist must take seriously the patient's fears of her specialness, recognizing that she is saying something vitally important about how she feels about herself, how she perceives the world, and what drives her toward self-harm.

ATTACHMENTS: DIFFERENT ROADS LEAD TO ROME

So many treatment options are available for self-harming patients that it can be confusing to know which to use and how to integrate them. The most crucial question is whether the patient is in serious physical danger and requires hospitalization. When hospitalization is being considered, particular attention should be paid to exercising control and providing containment in a way that minimizes for the patient the experience of retraumatization (Shapiro and Dominiak 1992). Decisions need to be made about hospitalization or day hospital treatment versus outpatient treatment, the use of psychopharmacology, medical management (for chronic eating-disordered or alcoholic patients), nutritional counseling, self-help or psychoeducational programs, family therapy, group therapy, individual psychotherapy, twelve-step programs, and expressive therapies. All are means for the patient to form safer and healthier attachments. For example, many self-help groups are open-ended and informal, and people can attend anonymously, making it easier even for fearful, schizoid patients to begin to connect with and trust others. Psychoeducational treatment efforts that can lead to direct treatment can be made within professionally led self-help groups. Although it is within the dyadic relationship of individual treatment that the patient can understand the role of the past and his own role in the nature of past and present attachments, not every patient is ready to risk the intimacy of individual psychotherapy. At times, less intimate means of connection can open the door for beginning individual psychotherapy.

POWER OF THE FAMILY

In the treatment of the most severely psychosomatically ill children, Melitta Sperling (1978) found it was often necessary to treat both mother and child. When psychopathology within the individual is maintained by the dysfunctional nature of the family system, therapeutic efforts may be addressed to modifying the pathology within the family to create healthier attachments, to help the individual to separate and individuate from his family, and, in the most malignant family systems, to effect the physical removal of the child from the destructive influence of the family. Both of these aims may involve working directly with the family as a system, seeing only the individual, or involving parents in treatment through seeing parents together and the child separately as is often the case in child therapy. This is also true with parents and adult children. The decision about whether the same therapist or two different therapists should work with the individual and the parents is best made on a case-by-case basis, as is the decision about one or two therapists to do individual psychotherapy and conduct family therapy. Sometimes the decision is made simply because the therapist who is skilled at individual psychotherapy is less able to do family therapy, and vice versa.

Chaos theory provides a strong scientific basis for the effectiveness of techniques that deliberately unbalance family systems (Chamberlain and Butz 1998). The therapist may have to be a "chaotician," injecting chaos into the most recalcitrant of family systems through techniques of reframing, paradoxical interventions, and symptom prescription in order to increase the confusion, uncertainty, and disequilibrium in the family that can force it to search for different solutions.

At times, parents of children with specific problems can be seen together in a parents' group, such as the group I ran for parents living with adult children with eating disorders. These parents' groups have much the same benefit as groups for individuals with self-harm problems. The focus can be psychoeducational, supportive, psychodynamic, or an integrated focus, depending on the makeup of the group and the skills of the therapist.

POWER OF THE GROUP

Just as the group can have an enormous power for destruction, chaos theory is instructive in illuminating how the same energy can be used within the group for growth, health, and a sense of community. Formed groups, most typically closed therapy groups or open self-help groups, and unformed groups, such as are worked with in social group work, are valuable for the flexibility afforded in addressing the issues in the life of someone addicted to drugs or alcohol or other addictive-like relationships. Twelve-step recovery groups serve for many as a bridge to the world of healthier relationships and offer a transitional space for personal exploration of spiritual needs. When used in conjunction with individual treatment, the group greatly expands the holding environment.

Researchers and clinicians have reported on the successful group treatment of borderline patients with self-harming behaviors (Linehan 1993a, Sansone et al. 1994). Through the group, patients can be helped to integrate dialectically two seemingly paradoxical needs—to accept themselves as they are and to change. That is, the treatment must be both supportive and mutative. For example, the women in my therapy group for compulsive eaters all want to stop eating compulsively so that they can lose weight. At the same time, if they are to become able to change their relationship to food so that it is no longer adversarial, they must accept both their bodies and their current relationship with food. This dialectic is central to dialectical behavior therapy (DBT), an approach to the treatment of borderline and self-destructive patients that can be used in individual or group therapy (Linehan 1993a,b). DBT combines supportive techniques derived from Zen Buddhism—self-acceptance and mindfulness of the present moment—with cognitive behavioral therapy that promotes behavioral change.

What makes group therapy powerful in terms of symptom management is that the frank discussion helps demystify the uniqueness of the behavior and lessens its shamefulness, allowing patients to appreciate its adaptive aspects. Psychoeducational efforts can help members to recognize and identify certain destructive relationships, behaviors, and patterns and can provide links between different kinds of self-harm behavior and emotions (Sansone et al. 1994). Simple explanations about what an obsession is and how and why it functions to displace the locus of anxiety onto weight can be a very useful way to get women with body image issues to begin to think differently about how and why weight is so meaningful to them. The concept of the body speaking for the self that cannot speak is one that many self-harming patients can resonate with even if they cannot articulate why. Psychoeducational efforts offer hope that if there can be a different way of viewing their behavior, they might become more able to live within their own skin. Patients who are harsh and judgmental with themselves often find themselves developing a sense of empathy for others in the group, which can help them ultimately develop a greater sense of empathy for themselves. The very nature of the group experience eases the "aloneness affect," allowing trust to develop over the lifetime of the group, and providing an opportunity for members to begin to risk making human connections to group members and the leader.

Group cohesion is promoted through identification and the common goal of developing a capacity to regulate moods and affects without the use of self-harm behavior. The group promotes an active problem-solving approach through the therapist's introduction of various cognitive-behavioral interventions. Simple behavioral diversion and delay techniques (Conterio and Vaughan 1989, Wooley and Wooley 1985) can be used to demonstrate to self-harmers that they can divert themselves from their impulse, can postpone acting on the impulse, and by "gutting it out" find that the impulse does in fact pass and that they can survive it without going mad. Body image exercises, guided imagery, and other gestalt exercises can be done. I suggest in my group for women with compulsive eating problems that members tape record many of the exercises so that they will have them available for their private use at home. Typically, there is great resistance to doing this and to monitoring their eating episodes through written journal entries. Often members will re-create a "strict parent–bad child" scenario by passive aggressive noncompliance. When this occurs and it can be identified as such, members can usually be engaged in acknowledging it and beginning to explore its etiology, while they often continue the working it through in their individual treatment. The journal monitoring requires the willingness to be alone with oneself long enough to pay attention to what one was feeling and thinking when the eating occurred, which many fear they cannot do. The anxiety about getting in touch with something so terrifying about themselves is enormous. Being able to hear from other resistant members who finally broke down and wrote about it and lived not only to survive it but to learn something useful about themselves in the process is an invaluable experience.

The group can be used to integrate some of the aspects of psychoanalytic psychotherapy with the focused group treatment of compulsive eating in order to more fully exploit the properties of each. Group members have the opportunity to track their own symptoms over time in terms of how they have changed in terms of their multiple functions, noting, often with considerable sorrow, that the symptom has come to lose much of its emotional power. They have the opportunity to mourn the loss with the group and, at the same time, to celebrate their achievement. Group members form a common history together, knowing how and where each one has started, and how far each one has come. They identify with the therapist, whose superego is not as harsh and punitive as their own, and they continue to see themselves in the others, a powerful means for altering their superego. They become an alternate family as they struggle to become better mothers to each other and themselves. When the leader's stance is engaged and spontaneous, it leaves room not only for serious discussion but for play and laughter. When the therapist maintains a playful spirit in herself and the group, she can deliver communications to the group members that otherwise would not be readily received. When tormented human beings can look at and laugh at themselves, healing can begin and the beginning of a reflective self can emerge.

The serious problems these patients have in the identification of, tolerance for, and expression of aggressive affect can be addressed in an environment of safety in the dyadic as well as in the group relationship, where strategies for tolerating and managing aggression can be developed. For many group members the opportunity to express anger at the therapist within the safety of the group setting provides an experience so meaningful that it can allow those who have never been in individual treatment to consider it as something good that they might allow themselves to have. When combined with individual treatment, the holding environment is greatly expanded. For example, one sexual abuse survivor group has created an unusual means of expression, a safe vehicle for feeling and expressing a lifetime accumulation of anger and sadness. They call themselves "The Lizzie Borden Rage Society," in reference to the infamous nineteenth-century Lizzie Borden, who allegedly murdered her mother and father in Fall River, Massachusetts. They meet at a secluded beach in winter on Saturday mornings, creating a safe place and sense of community in which to express their feelings toward their abusers.

> I build large sand effigies of my perpetrators and destroy them with a plastic bat. I can scream whatever I want. . . . At first I was afraid . . . but once I started there was a lot of anger and grief to let out. The other members of the group witness my pain and anger, as I do for them.
>
> I make images in the sand of my father's face. . . . My heart pounds when I approach this old menace even though it's made of sand. . . . My survivor "sisters" hold my hands until the old fear subsides. A new clarity and strength flow into my body.
>
> The ocean plays a big part in my healing. . . . I take stones that represent the penises that hurt me and throw them into the waves. I write messages in huge letters in the sand, spelling out my rage. The ocean's power seems to cheer and cleanse me. . . . It is a comfort to know there is a place and time to release my overwhelming emotions each week with supportive survivors. [Holliday 1993, p. 4]

Combing group with individual psychotherapy can be a very powerful tool for change. There is the opportunity for the therapist, using judicious care and creativity, to offer a certain interpretation to a member of the group using the knowledge of the patient gained in individual treatment. Or at times certain interpretations can be offered to the members of the group, which, like the offerings of a smorgasbord, they can take or leave. In the other direction, there is the opportunity for issues that have been identified in the group to be worked through in individual treatment, or aspects of the group experience serving much as day residue does for the dream, to be worked on in individual sessions.

As the self-harming symptoms diminish and take up less of the group's attention and as members develop a greater ability for self-reflection, the focus of the group can shift to one that is more interpersonal and psychodynamic, or members can be integrated into traditional interpersonal psychoanalytic groups, where their attachments are no longer defined by their self-harm but by their humanity.

In the many worlds of psychotherapy, we are too often convinced that ours is the one and only true way. The longer I practice the more convinced I become that we adhere to our theoretical orientation often because its clinical application simply suits our personality, is what we most enjoy doing, and is probably what we do best. Marisa's treatment history illustrates the variety of ways that attachments can be formed in treatment and how the course of treatment, not only for self-harm patients but for all patients, is often idiosyncratic, dictated by the nature of the patient's resistance, treatment funding, managed care restrictions, the theoretical orientation of the therapist, and the availability of or lack of treatment options in certain geographic areas. It is what the therapist does with the opportunity for attachment that matters.

Since childhood, Marisa had picked at her nails and cuticles, pulled off scabs, and scratched herself until she bled. She had been cutting and burning herself since eighth grade, and to add to the bad girl image, had acquired four tattoos and a tongue piercing. There was no history of physical or sexual abuse in her life to explain her symptoms, to explain why she spent a year in college drinking and having sex with more men than she could remember, to explain her not finishing various vocational programs. Being inherently bad explained everything.

She had never really tried to cover the scars on her arms. "This is me. What you see is what you get." Her cutting first came to her parents' attention in ninth grade, as a teacher noticed her sleeve was soaked in blood and sent her to the nurse, who saw through Marisa's not very convincing explanations that she had scratched herself on a locker. Her parents were contacted and that began a succession of visits to therapists' offices that succeeded only in confirming in Marisa's mind what she already believed, that she was the sick one, the bad one. The self-injury continued and worsened, as did the fighting with her parents. In despair, her parents finally consulted a therapist about how to help their daughter who would not accept help. The therapist worked with the parents as a couple for a while, which resulted in an improved relationship with Marisa. So when the therapist suggested that Marisa join her parents in treatment, she was guardedly receptive. Through family sculpting techniques, Marisa was able to identify family patterns that troubled her, and the therapist helped her to communicate her inner feelings to her parents in a way they could accept and understand. The family system, which had already begun to change, changed further for the better, and with it, Marisa's view of herself as inherently bad had begun to undergo a subtle shift. When she made her "suicide attempt," it frightened her and her family terribly, and with the help of the therapist they became ready three months later for Marisa's hospitalization.

The hospitalization lasted ten days. Although her record indicates that she was treated with individual, group, and family therapy, medication, substance abuse group, educational groups, recreation therapy and psychodrama, Marisa remembered the hospitalization as a time of not much treatment, but testing and interviews. It was recommended that she enter a residential treatment program for borderline patients.

She was diagnosed with an agitated major depression and a personality disorder marked by self-defeating patterns and borderline traits. She was treated as an inpatient for three months, during which time a behavior profile analysis indicated that there was a 46 percent reduction of symptoms, including her cutting, burning, and self-induced vomiting. Her primary therapist was a young man with a bachelor's degree. Her parents participated in family sessions and their relationship continued to improve. She continued as an outpatient for another two and a half months, and was discharged to continue family therapy with the referring therapist. The residential treatment was a major factor for Marisa in helping her to develop an attachment to two key staff members and a sense that at least some people could be trusted. The other very important factor for Marisa what that she had to participate, not like the hospital where she could sleep all day. She was expected to participate and expected to practice the skills she was being taught for resisting the impulses to harm herself. She learned how to start breathing deeply to reduce her anxiety level and she practiced relaxation techniques. She learned to count slowly when feeling very angry, and in the time it took to count to 100 she found that the intensity of her rage had diminished enough to be manageable. She found these behavioral tools to be invaluable in keeping herself from cutting and burning herself and creating chaos around her.

Marisa and her parents continued family therapy for a while, and then Marisa continued to work individually with the therapist. However, her drinking became more problematic and the therapist refused to continue treatment unless she stopped drinking. She refused and so treatment stopped around two years before she came into treatment with me. Marisa had one episode of cutting since then, but she continued to be troubled by recurrent impulses to cut herself, and was referred to me.

She had been having dramatic mood swings. The day before the consultation she had been a "raging bitch," yelling, then crying, and having to leave work several times. She was afraid she'd be fired; the firm was unusually tolerant of her moods but she was afraid she had gone too far. Nonetheless, she awakened that morning feeling hopeful and looking forward to the consultation. She was feeling so good, in fact, that she had little to tell me and so told her mother maybe she should not come. Her idea of treatment, of which she was not aware at the time, is that very dramatic symptoms entitled her to be seen by a therapist. On the morning of our first meeting, she felt good and so felt not entitled to the appointment. Right from the beginning, we began to talk about her need for dramatic symptoms, that she could not feel entitled to have this kind of attention without the requisite drama. She does not deliberately hide her scars, and while she would not acknowledge it, it seemed that she liked the disturbing message her scars communicated. She had not felt entitled to ask directly for psychotherapy; her bleeding body had to speak for her. And she did not feel entitled to have these dramatic symptoms without having invented a false history of childhood sexual abuse.

In the prior week she had had numerous impulses to hurt herself but had resisted them. If she's in the kitchen and notices a sharp knife on the counter, she'll walk out and eat her meal elsewhere to avoid seeing knives. She was helping her boyfriend's mother clean up after workmen left, and found the straight-edge razors they used buried under the debris. She felt tingly sensations and had to cover up the blades so she did not see them. One of the best results of the family therapy was that when she gets the impulses to hurt herself, she could call her mother or her father and they will talk to her and help her feel better. This helped her to feel not so alone, but on the negative side it also made her feel incompetent to deal with her impulses on her own. A sense of her own incompetence loomed large. She had not completed college, this was her first job, and she was screwing it up. She could not do what other people seem to do easily.

She felt bad that she depends so much on her parents and bad that she has caused them such suffering. She wondered how she would ever be able to live on her own and support herself. She felt entirely dependent on others. She confided in a recent session that she has great difficulty going to public places alone. She feels acutely self-conscious, feels that people are looking at her and disapproving. For example, Mother's Day was coming and she wanted to send her mother a floral arrangement. There are several florists in her neighborhood but she will go only to one, where she is known. But with her friend Beth, who is very gregarious and confident, she feels great, can go anywhere and do anything. Beth is used like a prosthesis, a desperately needed selfobject. I suggested to her that she deliberately go to a florist where she had never been before and order the flowers there. "But I'll feel anxious." "And?" I asked. "I don't want to feel that," she replied. I told her that I thought she had convinced herself that she was so incompetent that she could not even go to a new florist. I thought she could. If she felt very anxious, she had tools for dealing with the anxiety. I told her that sometimes you have to let yourself feel the fear and do the thing anyway in order to figure out what was so scary. I suggested she go there on her way home, and call me later to tell me how it went. That evening Marisa called to say she had gone to the new florist and ordered the flowers: "No sweat, no big deal." The people there were even very nice. She had thought of calling Beth to go with her but decided to see if she really could do it on her own and was glad she did. Two weeks later, she came to her session carrying a book titled *Feel the Fear and Do It Anyway*, which she said was pretty good.

In this current round of treatment, in order to begin to look at how it was that Marisa had come to regard herself as so bad, incompetent, and undeserving of attention, numerous past efforts must be honored and acknowledged. I was grateful to Marisa's parents who tried to get help for her for so long and who did not give up. I was grateful to the staff at the residential treatment program for helping her to begin to develop a sense of trust and hope and for equipping her with necessary behavioral tools to protect herself from her own destructive impulses. I was grateful to the psychiatrist to whom I referred her for medication, for his persistence in struggling with thorny psychopharmacological and medical difficulties. (Marisa did stop drinking when she understood that alcohol was a depressant that would interfere with the action of the antidepressant prescribed for her.) I was especially grateful to the previous therapist, for the work in family therapy that had made such a difference in Marisa's life. All of this had to come before Marisa could begin to tackle her question: "If I wasn't abused physically or sexually, if there was no big trauma in my life, why did I hurt myself the way I did for so long? Why do I feel like such a jerk-off?"

I explained that some of the things that may seem like ordinary events in a child's life, things that are no big drama to others, may in fact have been far more important and disturbing to a child than one might think. Immediately she said, "I wanted a dog so badly and they said no. Do you think that could have done it? Lots of kids want pets and don't get them." Had you had a pet before? I asked. Yes, she said, she had Nick, whom she loved more than anything, but Nick was dead. When I asked her to tell me about Nick, this opened the door to an unfolding of grief and sadness connected with a series of childhood losses. She had come home from school one day to find that her beloved dog Nick had been "put to sleep." Initially raging at her parents because they had done this without talking with her, she tried to accept their explanation that it was all for the best because he was so sick. She convinced herself that she had no right to be angry at them and so carried her anger around still. Like a little girl, she did a Nick imitation for me, a sad "woof woof." When I asked if she had a picture of him, she offered to bring pictures next time.

The next time she arrived with a large framed collage of photographs, looking very sad. In fact, she had been crying as she sat in the waiting room, not knowing why. She had been angry the whole day before and awoke feeling very sad. She did not know what to do with the feeling. It became intolerable while she was taking a shower and she struggled not to take the blade out of the razor to cut herself. I told her that if she could tell me about the sadness, it might not make it go away but it might help her feel less alone with it. "But I don't know why I'm feeling so sad," she replied. I suggested that perhaps it has something to do with what we talked about last time, about Nick, and perhaps other losses that she had not talked about. She took the photo collage, which she had wrapped in a towel for protection from the rain, and moved her chair close to mine so we could look together. I told her Nick was beautiful. She sobbed that she had loved him so much, he was the family dog but he was really hers, hers, hers. Always, when she came home from school, she knew Nick would be there on the other side of the door waiting for her. When she was feeling bad, he just knew and would come and lie down with her and lick her hand. I told her that I suspected that Nick had filled a spot in her heart that no one else filled, not her somewhat depressed submissive mother and not her dynamo of a father. "Yes," she nodded, tears streaming down.

She showed me pictures of her parents, herself with Nick, and herself with her brother, in which she looked angry. "That's characteristic," she said. She was 4 when he was born. She had wanted a sister and was very disappointed. I suggested that maybe it was hard with so much of her mother's time and attention going to her infant brother. Maybe, she said. She had no memory. There was so much she could not remember. Until recently, she hated her brother and beat him up, while all he wanted was to be with his big sister. Shortly after his birth, the family moved, a traumatic experience for Marisa. They had lived in a community with their large, extended family nearby, all their lives intertwined. Her cousins were her best friends, and her grandmother doted on her. She had adored her paternal grandfather, Poppy, who used to take her for walks to the candy store. Suddenly she remembered a song he sang: "Skip, skip to the barbershop/ To buy a penny candy/ One for you/ And one for me/ and one for sister Annie." She had not known she remembered it. She showed me the picture of herself with Poppy, then told me of his death from cancer two years earlier. When the phone call came, she knew. She had talked with him just an hour before, told him she loved him, and he said good-bye. Her father picked up the phone and got the news that he had just died. As he turned to tell Marisa, she simply said, "I know. He's dead. I have to go to work," left the house and went to work. Business as usual. Her boss knew something was wrong and Marisa told her what had happened. She wanted to stay at work but her boss sent her home. She went to a bar, and the bartender, sensing something was wrong, asked and she told him her grandfather had just died. He told her she belonged at home, not sitting in a bar with a beer. In beginning to tell me about the photographs, Marisa began to understand what she had had and lost and what she had never had. How far this therapy will go is not known, but so far, Marisa is coming to feel her sadness and anger and understand it. It is beginning to make sense and have meaning.

15

Transference, Countertransference, and Enactments

No event is unique, nothing is enacted but once . . . ;
every event has been enacted, is enacted, and will be
enacted perpetually; the same individuals have appeared,
appear, and will appear at every turn of the circle.

Henri-Charles Puech, Man and Time

The process of change is inextricably linked to disruption, disorder,
confusion, and irregularity: chaos. Only when there is sufficient unrest
in a system is it likely to be amenable to transformation. . . . It is
during periods of chaos, when the old "structure" or approach to
solving problems and coping with life no longer works, that people are able
to make significant leaps out of previous patterns into new behaviors.

Linda Chamberlain, "An Introduction to Chaos and Nonlinear Dynamics,"
in Clinical Chaos: A Therapist's Guide to Nonlinear Dynamics
and Therapeutic Change

Because the treatment of self-harming patients is often marked by intense and stormy transference regressions, they frequently evoke correspondingly disturbing countertransferences in the therapist (Grotstein 1993). It is in the arena of the transference–countertransference matrix or in the arena of the body that enactments can occur that can result in self-harm episodes or can cause the destruction of the treatment. As Jill Montgomery (1989a) has succinctly put it, "The question in these cases is always how to gain entry into a masochistically constructed subjectivity without being caught up in the aggressivity of the struggle of the master–slave relationship" (pp. xiv–xv). How the therapist responds to his own powerful countertransference feelings can make the difference between a destructive enactment or the furthering of the treatment.

PROJECTIVE IDENTIFICATION AND SPLITTING

Melanie Klein's theories of splitting and projective identification have radically altered our view of mental structure and deepened the theory of mental conflict by allowing us to reformulate the aims of psychoanalysis in terms of the reacquisition and reintegration of projected parts of the self (Steiner 1996). Although Freud spoke of splitting of the ego, he used the idea in a specific way to account for the coexistence of contradictory beliefs, particularly in fetishism and psychosis. Freud (1927) suggested that in fetishism reality is simultaneously acknowledged and disavowed, while in psychosis it is as if a sane person were present alongside the madness, watching it (Freud 1940). To Steiner, the split was quite like that which Bion postulated between the psychotic and non-psychotic parts of the personality, a rather different usage of the term *splitting* from that introduced by Klein. Although Freud (1924) described how the ego could avoid a rupture in relation to the superego and the id by "deforming" itself (1924),

> for the most part he considered it as unitary, . . . not split or fragmented and certainly not partitioned off, with aspects disowned and attributed to others. . . . Ego weakness arose from conflict rather than from depletion through loss of parts of the self, and repression rather than splitting was seen as the mechanism by which access to elements in the self was denied. The individual, even though driven by different mental agencies, was thought of as a whole person having to negotiate a path through the dangers and conflicts of life. [Steiner 1996, p. 1074]

When Klein introduced the idea of splitting of the object to account for the alternation of idealized and persecutory states, she believed from the beginning that the split in the object was accompanied by a split in the ego. That is, a good part of the self in relation to a good object was split off from a bad part of the self in relation to a bad object (Steiner 1996).

Growing out of the concept of splitting was the more radical concept of projective identification in which after splitting, the split-off fragments are disavowed, projected, and attributed to someone else (Klein 1964). Whatever the motive for projective identification, it always results in a denial of separateness between self and the object, and a consequent depletion of personal resources as well as a distortion of the object, which is then experienced as if it contained the disowned attributes (Rosenfeld 1971). Unlike Freud's theory, the self is no longer seen as a unitary structure, so that a coherent sense of self has to be achieved through the regaining and integration of lost and dispersed elements. At the same time, however, objects in the external world are imbued with the person's personal attributes, which have been projected on to them so that a relationship that may appear to be with a separate person is actually more significantly with the self or with an object controlled by the self. Klein's discoveries illuminated the underlying structure of this type of narcissistic relationship and its basis in the mechanism of projective identification, ideas which were synthesized by Rosenfeld (1971, 1987) in his work on narcissistic states and destructive narcissism (Steiner 1996).

THERAPIST AS NEW OBJECT AND CONTAINER

Originally the concept of the corrective emotional experience held that the discrepancy between the real person of the therapist and the patient's expectations of him, based on expectations transferred from the past, could provide an emotional experience that was corrective (Alexander 1958). Loewald (1960) put forth the concept of the therapist as a new and real object in the patient's life, representing a higher level of ego functioning and a higher level of being and relating. When treatment is effective, it frees the patient to reach toward that differential, to develop levels of integration higher than those already reached. More recent understandings of the concept include understanding transference–countertransference relations in terms of the container and the contained (Bion 1962). That is, the therapist is understood to be a container, with the capacity to contain and tolerate and ultimately to interpret the patient's projective identifications (Rosenfeld 1987). This can be an extremely difficult, sometimes impossible thing to do, taxing the limits of the therapist's emotional resources.

For the therapist to function as a container, he must be able to allow the patient his chaotic regressions, while maintaining an optimism that these regressions will ultimately give way to healthier progressions (Boyer 1999). He must be able to tolerate the introjection of whatever the patient is projecting into him while observing it without reacting badly. At the same time the patient is introjecting the therapist's acceptance, kindness, and equanimity. This is the essential element, the therapist's capacity to view himself and the patient, each as subject and object, watching and evaluting what goes on between him and the patient, assessing his own somatic sensations and overt thoughts. Both patient and therapist enter into various degrees of reverie and intersubjective play, generating a potential space in which creativity can occur (Boyer 1997, 1999).

THERAPIST AS INTERPRETER

Containment, difficult and remarkable as it is, however, is not enough, says Steiner. Containment relieves anxiety by providing a sense of being understood by the therapist but containment itself does not permit a true separateness to be achieved (Steiner 1996). Being understood relies too much upon the therapist's authority, while understanding, which must arise from within the patient and depends on a capacity to think and judge for himself, involves relinquishing the dependence on the views and containing functions of the therapist and other authority figures. For the patient to go from being understood to understanding means he must become able to reverse his projective identification, and this depends on his capacity to face psychic reality, in particular to confront the reality of loss and to go through the mourning process that results from this confrontation. It is precisely through the mourning process that projections are removed from the object and returned to the self so that the lost object is seen more realistically and the previously disowned parts of the self are gradually acknowledged as belonging to the self (Steiner 1996). This shift toward the depressive position has a profound effect upon all aspects of mental life, including thinking and symbol formation (Steiner 1996), which will be elaborated in Chapter 16.

THE PATIENT'S PERSONA AND TRANSFERENCE

There are two different transference-like manifestations operating in the treatment, one in the background and one in the foreground (Grotstein 1993). The background one is the most important, a supportive presence that has been described in terms of concepts such as the holding environment (Winnicott 1963); the container and the contained (Bion 1962); attachment (Bowlby 1969); the mirroring, idealizing, and twinship selfobjects (Kohut 1971); the background presence (Grotstein 1993); and the matrix of the mind (Ogden 1989). This background presence fosters the development of a positive transference, in which the therapist supplies certain transitional functions (Modell 1963). At the same time, the key processes and clinical features as elaborated in the previous chapter all make for very intense, negative transference reactions in the foreground. The term *transference-like* suggests that the search to replicate early experiences with the primary objects occurs before true separation-individuation has taken place, and that transference per se is possible only after separation-individuation processes have been largely completed (Blanck and Blanck 1979). These transference-like manifestations have also been called transference replications (Blanck and Blanck 1974) or transitional object transferences (Modell 1963).

Envy (Moore and Fine 1990), the desire to have what another has, can generate hostility toward the other. It is a critical issue in the treatment—the patient's envy of the therapist and the therapist's envy of the patient. Pathological envy of the therapist, especially envy of the therapist's ability to use his mind to think productively and critically, is usually unconscious, but it may be manifested by the provocation of destructive enactments that momentarily destroy the therapist's ability to think. When the patient destroys the therapist's attempts to create meaning, this, more than anything else, can bring the treatment to ruin. The patient's narcissism is a major stumbling block for therapists because it tends to evoke strong feelings of anger and unconscious envy, something that is rarely acknowledged but which can be as destructive as the patient's envy. Patients who create chaos and destroy meaning are oblivious and confused about the effect they have on others, encased in their narcissistic bubble as they are. Therapists for the most part are an introspective, reflective lot, struggling to contain our own and our patients' emotions, and so it is easy to envy those who simply blast others with their emotions. The therapist is like the mother of a toddler—after the toddler has had one or two tantrums too many, the mother is filled to bursting with having to contain so much, and may let herself be seduced into appropriating the child's narcissism and having a tantrum herself.

The patient's narcissism may be of this overinflated type, but can also present the subtler picture of the deflated type (Bach 1994). The overinflated narcissist's sense of his internal objects seems to fade away, and so he compensates by puffing himself up and presenting himself as so grandiose and powerful that he does not need others. He insists that the therapist reflect or mirror his grandiose wishes. The deflated narcissist is the other side of the same coin, demonstrating a sense of inferiority and hypersensitivity. His sense of himself is fading and he compensates by overinflating an object such as the therapist, insisting that the therapist embody his grandiose wishes and clinging to him for stability. Finally and inevitably he becomes disillusioned with the object.

These narcissistic types are not necessarily two different kinds of people. They can be the overt or covert selves of the same person, so a crucial part of the therapeutic task is accessing the sense of depletion and inferiority in the grandiose narcissist and in accessing the hidden sense of grandiosity and entitlement in the deflated narcissist (Bach 1994). A similar concept is Herbert Rosenfeld's (1987) "thick-skinned" narcissism (corresponding to the overinflated type), when the patient is inaccessible and defensively aggressive, while "thin-skinned" narcissism (corresponding to deflated narcissism) finds the patient fragile and vulnerable. The thick-skinned position corresponds more or less to the coarse hide of the predator, while the thin-skinned position corresponds to the sensitive skin of the preyed-upon innocent. Like Bach, Anthony Bateman (1998) finds that the transference-like manifestations may oscillate between the thick-skinned and thin-skinned positions. Take, for example, the thick-skinned position of Elizabeth Wurtzel's (1994) ferocious projective identification, and then imagine the overwhelming anger and anguish her parents, teachers, and psychiatrist must have experienced.

> They have no idea what a bottomless pit of misery I am. They will have to do more and more and more. . . . They still don't know that they need to do more and more and more, they need to try to get through to me until they haven't slept or eaten or breathed fresh air for days, they need to try until they've died for me. They have to suffer as I have. And even after they've done that, there will still be more. . . . They will have to do more than they ever thought they could if they want me to stay alive. They have no idea how much energy and exasperation I am willing to suck out of them until I feel better. I will drain them and drown them until they know how little of me there is left even after I've taken everything they've got to give me because I hate them for not knowing. [p. 45]

Within these thick- and thin-skinned, predator and prey dichotomies, there are specific transference-like manifestations that are especially pronounced in survivors of severe abuse that reflect the childhood relational patterns that have become internalized as fragmented parts of the personality (Davies and Frawley 1994, Farber 1997, Miller 1994). There is the uninvolved but present parent who failed to protect the child; the sadistic abuser and the helpless victim; the omnipotent rescuer and the entitled child who demands to be rescued; and the seducer and the seduced. These manifestations can alternate in what may feel to the therapist like a dizzying sequence in which the patient tries on various dramatic roles and assigns corresponding roles to the therapist. That is, the patient may cast the therapist in the role of her abuser while clinging to her role as victim, then cast the therapist in the role of the parent who failed to protect her while demonstrating her need for protection, then cast the therapist in the role of the helpless victim while she traumatizes the therapist as she had been traumatized, and then cast the therapist in the role of seducer while clinging to her role as the seduced.

When therapists are themselves abuse survivors, the extent to which they have worked through their own trauma issues will determine how effective they can be in treating these patients. Clinicians who have been abused can empathize with the terror, rage, and loss that abused patients experience in a way that clinicians who have not been abused cannot, but at the same time, they are susceptible to particular countertransference complications (Davies and Frawley 1994). If they do not remember their own abuse, the clinical work may evoke the recall of traumatic memories that may require that they enter or reenter treatment themselves. Therapists who are survivors may tend to assume a persistently masochistic position with patients, provoking sadistic attacks through their patients' self-destructive or abusive acting out. Or they may feel a special need for their patients to see them as a good object, and thus defuse their patients' aggressive transference reactions.

While the therapist may become a transitional transference object or a new and better object, the treatment is predisposed to be marked by negative therapeutic reactions in which the patient cannot tolerate such benevolence because he remains attached to painful affects (Valenstein 1973) and persecutory internal objects (Seinfeld 1990). The benign therapist then is cause for alarm in the patient because he threatens the patient's attachment to painful affects and harsh punitive internal objects.

> Meryl sought treatment at age 27 when her usual defenses (dissociation, denial, intellectualization, projection, projective identification, obsessional thinking, smoking marijuana, drinking, and binge eating) were no longer successful in warding off her psychotic regressions. In very constricted, intellectualized manner, she said, "I want to explore the didactics of my personality." This translated into the fact that she was planning to continue

her counseling studies on the graduate level and wanted to be sure she was not going into this field to satisfy neurotic needs of her own. In addition she was very angry at her husband, who was impotent with her but sexually attracted to her friend. Her jealousy and anger alarmed her because her spiritual leader, S'ai Baba Muktananda, taught love and transcendence of such negative emotions.

I learned that she had been born in the midst of her mother's psychotic depression, when she was very regressed and both the mother and the patient had to be cared for by the patient's father, a man with a history of numerous psychiatric hospitalizations and suicide attempts. She recalled witnessing her mother's violent rages at her father, hitting and kicking him, and she remembered the beatings she received from her father. "They took turns being mentally ill." In adolescence she read sadomasochistic pornography and had a sexual relationship in which she enjoyed being tied up and insulted by her boyfriend. Once the insults went too far and she tried to kill him, then set off on a campaign of enraged promiscuity, her "four F's" ("Find 'em, feel 'em, fuck 'em, forget 'em").

The above-mentioned defenses, as well as her yoga, fasting, chanting, and vegetarianism, had managed for some years to keep her from psychosis, but were now failing. Terrified, she had experienced an overwhelming ego regression to psychosis, with cold sweats and shivering, heart palpitations, visual distortions, and visual hallucinations of her facial features changing grotesquely when she looked in the mirror. She sat naked on the floor, rocking herself and drooling, chanting in rhyme and in her words, "acting like a real crazy," enjoying the whole thing too much to stop it, although aware at the time that she could have stopped it if she had wanted to. She physically attacked her husband repeatedly for several hours. It was her ability to construct her new defense that enabled her to emerge from this extraordinary ego regression. She actively and consciously constructed her "filing cabinet," filing away intolerable affects and memories into psychic drawers labeled "Do not open *ever*," "Open only at own risk," or "Do not open until you see therapist." It was her "holding operation," but at the same time she was as drawn to the symbiotic merger of psychosis as much as she was terrified of it.

Even before beginning treatment, there were positive transference-like manifestations. She wanted to experience her new therapist as omnipotent and curative so that she could voluntarily dismantle the filing cabinet and "just flow with the feelings." I was to be her omnipotent "holding operation" at the same time that she wanted to merge with me. I accepted her wishes to merge while using opportunities to affirm our separateness, often by answering her questions having to do with our differences and asking her what my answer meant to her.

She wore her identifications on her sleeve (feminism, vegetarianism, follower of S'ai Baba Muktananda) to compensate for her identity diffusion.

She did not use her husband's last name and had difficulty with the fact that I used my married name. "How can you give in to these sexist patriarchal customs?" It disturbed her that I was different from her, but she was intrigued when I asked if it was not possible for each of us to think differently about the same issue. One question was very important to her and demonstrated something of her view of the world: "Are you a meat eater?" The question, in its concreteness and primitiveness, was startling. I answered it and asked what it meant to her that I was a "meat-eater." It meant that she might have to find another therapist, she said. She did not know if she could continue in treatment with a meat-eater; she should have asked me this over the phone before even coming in to see me. Apparently her world was divided into meat-eating predators and plant-eating prey. How could she reconcile her positive transference with this discordant information?

Because she had some ability to tolerate these differences, treatment continued and went well. She quickly found ways to incorporate some of my thinking, my words, and even part of my functions of observation and synthesis. Dramatic and intense manifestations of a transference psychosis occurred that I found frightening initially, given her history of violence, until I found some success in helping her to emerge from them. She spoke of her religious quest and cult involvement, especially a profound experience at the S'ai Baba ashram. One of S'ai Baba's priests was a man named Freedom who could read her mind, and could, with one electrifying look, unite his soul with hers. He could purge her of all her evil thoughts so that they became reflected in his face, changing and contorting as he absorbed her ugliness. Her whole body was jolted with electricity, and Freedom glowed with golden rays, and she and he were one—one body, one mind, one soul. It was a remarkable experience, she said, and nothing like this had happened since this episode four years earlier because the ashram disbanded. If only she could go to India and meet S'ai Baba himself, she would be content to sit at his feet forever.

She was beaming with pleasure in having told me this and liked how interested I was in her religion, and wanted to bring me religious literature to read. Understanding that she wanted me to join her in this oceanic experience, I told her that I was interested in knowing about her religion so I could better understand what she found in it that provided so much of what she wanted. She seemed not to hear me, was smiling and said I had started to glow. I looked very soft, she said and had a golden aura. She was feeling "spacey"; it was lovely, she said. I said she seemed to see me as having the special powers that Freedom had, which seemed to help bring her back to reality a bit, at which I relaxed. We were each back in our own separate skins. At another time, rather than settling into the regression, she was alarmed by it and had an anxiety attack, a more positive sign. She announced that she was feeling very peculiar: she was having trouble breathing, the room was starting to glow and I too was glowing, her heart was beating very hard, she was in a cold sweat, and she didn't feel too sure she was still in her chair. I told her to feel the arms of her chair, feel the seat under her supporting her weight, touch her legs with her hands. She did. Soon the glow began to fade and she was feeling better.

THE THERAPIST'S PERSONA
AND COUNTERTRANSFERENCE

Each therapist brings his personality, strengths, vulnerabilities, values, beliefs, needs for approval, and personal preoccupations to the treatment of any patient. When these personal factors inevitably interact with the special difficulties that the self-harming patient brings to treatment, the therapist must to be prepared to struggle with how his own history and past traumas intrude into the intersubjective arena of the therapeutic process, increasing his vulnerability to disorganizing and potentially fragmenting dissociative processes within the countertransference (Davies 1999). Because they are so much closer to primary process, patients with primitive psychopathology have very sensitive radar systems for detecting and exploiting clinicians' hidden and not so hidden vulnerabilities and for bringing out their worst features. The therapeutic process forces the therapist to struggle with his own personal issues at the same time that he must struggle with keeping the patient's needs central.

We often do not appreciate to what extent body-based transferences and countertransferences are part of the clinical picture. Patients may be focused on their own body or the therapist's in the session more than we are aware. Women patients in treatment with a female therapist often comment easily on the therapist's appearance in paying a compliment and may look to her for feedback on their own appearance. At times men in treatment with a female therapist may have emotional or physiological responses to the body of the therapist. Yet we rarely hear from the patient when the therapist's body is a source of unconscious fantasy and transference, probably because we unwittingly thwart these disclosures. Sensing that the size and shape of her overweight body was a source of unconscious musing to some of her patients, Jane Burka (1996) explicitly invited them to share these with her. Her own feelings about her body varied with different patients at different times in their treatment, according to transference phenomena, "sometimes feeling dumpy and self-conscious, sometimes feeling voluptuous and racy, sometimes feeling motherly and nurturing, sometimes feeling shriveled and empty. My same body can seem frail in relation to a large man or monumental in relation to a petite woman. With two bodies present and two unconsciouses at play, any experience is possible" (p. 263). The attractive body of a patient may evoke erotic countertransference responses, while clinicians treating eating-disordered patients may envy the anorectic or bulimic patient's thinness. The way the body (the patient's or therapist's) is subjectively experienced in the session can be what brings the patient or therapist into the immediate experience of the other. The therapist's awareness that he has stopped breathing for a moment may be a signal that he is containing the patient's anxiety, or a pain or tension in some part of the therapist's body may suggest that he is trying very hard not to feel what he is feeling emotionally, or a limb going numb may suggest feeling disconnected from the patient. One evening, when I was leading my compulsive eaters' group in a guided imagery exercise and began with a deep-breathing relaxation exercise, a woman who was new to the group broke down in tears. Everyone present was very moved when she said that the experience of someone paying attention to how she breathed was new, and she realized that it made her cry because she was so used to feeling invisible and uncared for.

When the therapist uses the patient to meet his or her own needs (for flattery, caregiving, feeling sexually desirable, being in control, or being correct), or when he uses the patient to protect himself from his fears (of criticism, engulfment, being seduced, passivity, or being wrong), the treatment will be adversely affected (Kroll 1988). Certain characteristics of patients in the borderline range play into these problems of the therapist. Their proclivity to idealization plays into the therapist's need for flattery, their ability to evoke nurturing feelings plays into the therapist's caregiving wishes, and their extreme neediness plays into the therapist's fear of being swallowed up by the patient. When the patient's idealization of the therapist or neediness is eroticized, this can play into the therapist's need to be found sexually desirable or his fear of being seduced. Testing the boundaries of the therapeutic frame by requests for extra sessions, special telephone time, and frequent appointment changes can play into the therapist's need to be in control and can stir up fear of losing control of the treatment.

Understanding and using the countertransference is crucial. Optimally the transference–countertransference communication involves the therapist's introjection and reworking of the patient's projective identifications and the patient's similar use of the therapist's projections (Boyer 1999). Whatever the therapist experiences during the session is influenced by his idiosyncratic introjection and reformulation of the patient's verbal and nonverbal communications and vice versa. The therapist's prevailing emotional state and individual conflicts will determine his degree of openness to the patient's communications. In the countertransference, projective identification functions as a means of communication by which the therapist learns from the patient that which the patient cannot think consciously. The way that he reworks his introjections will be influenced by his own idiosyncratic life experiences. The therapist must develop the ability to be aware of the patient's transference and his own countertransference reactions (psychic, sensory, somatic, verbal, nonverbal).

So when the therapist feels overwhelmed by love, hate, dizziness, or visual or spatial distortions, he has probably introjected the patient's psychotic core. For example, just when Meryl said that I had started to glow, I suddenly had an unsettling spatial experience of her seeming to be further away from me by several feet, and she seemed gray, depleted of color, quite the opposite of the glow she saw in me. I felt anxious, thin-skinned, and vulnerable, which I came to understand as my countertransference response to her projective identification. It was as if our separate skins, the physical boundaries that separated us, had merged as Meryl split off the good parts of herself and projected them into me, her container.

The therapist must allow the intersubjective arena to be elaborated and eventually interpreted (Boyer 1999). This is possible when the therapist, within a reverie state, can adapt himself to the work of attending to both his own and the patient's separate subjective experiences and to the intersubjective experience. When the therapist has the ability to contain and reflect upon his own powerful countertransference responses, he can struggle to find the words to bridge his own subjective state and that of the patient, and then to elaborate them. This potential space, says Winnicott (1958a), is where creativity can occur, and sometimes that creativity is fostered by the therapist entering into a state of reverie (Bion 1962). The therapist must be able to allow the existence of the potential space (Boyer 1997). When the therapist struggles in this way to understand, it is equivalent to holding a hand out to the patient to bridge their experiences and an invitation to the patient to join the therapist in this reverie space. "Accurate interpretation through the countertransference gives lease to a play-space through which [patients] newly and creatively express their experience" (Boyer 1997, p. 76). During episodes of play, the dissociated aspects of the patient's experience can become linked and further integrated. Paradoxically, the psychological space that separates patient and therapist is the potentially powerful link that connects the patient's dissociated states (Bion 1962, Boyer 1999). It is the play-work that goes on in this space that can build ego functions in the patient and further and deepen the treatment. And it is not coincidental that it is the play-work that can also build ego functions in the therapist and greater clinical acumen.

ENACTMENTS

Although there is no universally agreed-upon definition of enactment, the one used here is that of Anthony Bateman (1998), who has defined enactment as any mutual action within the analyst–patient relationship that arises in the context of difficulties in countertransference work. Enactments may be either to the detriment or to the benefit of the therapeutic process, with the patient and therapist either bringing out the worst in each other or the best. In enactments, patients get stuck in repeating and repeating the same experience, like dreaming the same dream over and over again. They are unproductive enactments; like dry coughs, they yield nothing, they open up nothing new for the patient. Like the autistic child, the self-harming patient cannot tell you how he feels or what his psyche is made of; he can only show you, and this he does quite well if the clinician is willing to be used as an object and to be guided via his own internal world through the subject's memory of his object relations. . . . An autistic child may utter not a word, but his cries, dense preoccupied silence and his mimetic use of people is his language. He lodges himself inside the other, compelling the other to experience the breakdown of language (and hope and desire). [Bollas 1987, p. 3]

When a therapist can help the patient to decode the enactment, either through understanding what it communicates via his own countertransference response or through understanding the language of the body or perhaps both, then the enactment can become something productive, communicative, and meaningful.

Enactment is most likely when a patient moves transferentially from thick-skinned to thin-skinned narcissistic positions or vice versa, in an unstable clinical balance. The scales can be tipped in a way that can be a danger to the treatment or an opportunity for deepening it and strengthening the therapeutic alliance (Bateman 1998). On the one hand, the movement increases the likelihood of enactment in the form of violence to others or in the form of self-destructive acts, depending on whether thick- or thin-skinned elements, respectively, are to the fore. The therapist can trigger the enactment simply by trying to engage the patient in thinking about his omnipotence, narcissism, or envy rather than by complying with the patient's hidden omnipotent demands (Anderson 1999).

Yet, on the other hand, it is only when a patient is moving between narcissistic positions that an interpretation of what has occurred in the transference–countertransference space can become effective and move the treatment to a higher level of object relatedness. Enactments can occur in all kinds of treatment, not only psychoanalysis or psychoanalytically oriented psychotherapy, so understanding the concept of enactment can be an extremely useful tool for all therapists.

Enactment as a Transference–Countertransference Creation

The literature on enactment deals essentially with enactments in the transference–countertransference relationship, and contains two main themes: enactment as a powerful two-person phenomenon occurring between patient and therapist, and enactment as a positive force in treatment, perhaps even a corrective emotional experience. In the first theme, enactment is powered by projective identification, a primitive defense to which we all can regress in certain situations, but a prominent defense in those with borderline personalities or dissociative disorders. It is an unconscious process by which the patient, unable to contain within himself an unacceptable affect or quality, splits it off from himself and projects it, like a projectile missile whistling across the boundaries separating his own ego organization from the therapist's, to land directly in the therapist's ego. This missile can contain aggressive or sexual wishes, anything the patient cannot contain and tolerate in himself. The therapist finds himself reacting intensely to the patient as if he were being controlled from within, like a puppet whose strings are being pulled by some powerful coercive force. There is an abrupt rupture in the working alliance, which both patient and therapist experience as being the consequence of the other's behavior; the therapist may experience it as the patient's "provocation and crash tantrum" (M. Stone 1988) while the patient may regard it as the therapist's inexplicably "losing it." If the therapist cannot successfully contain the aggressive or sexual wishes and treats his patient like a thing, then his fury, or rejection or sexual involvement with the patient can destroy the treatment frame and the treatment. In considering how easy it is to treat patients like things, Sheldon Bach's (1994) words are instructive:

> In one of the more philosophical passages of the Marquis de Sade's *The 120 Days of Sodom*, the Duke reflects with sadness and resignation that people are generally so difficult to comprehend. "Yes," replies his friend, "most people are indeed an enigma. And perhaps that is why it is *easier* every time to fuck a man than to try to understand him."
> This aphorism . . . speaks to the regressive nature of perversion and thus to the sadomasochist in each of us. No doubt it is easier to exploit a person than to relate to him, for relationships require a dialogue, whereas usage can be simple or unilateral, requiring only force, intimidation, or cunning. [p. 3]

Patients with a history of incest are at high risk for exploitation by psychotherapists. The transgression of childhood boundaries can be reenacted (Gabbard 1996) when the patient conveys consciously or unconsciously that nothing short of repetition of the original incestuous relationship will allow him to feel loved and cared for, and the therapist joins the patient to meet his own needs.

I have had several patients whose emotional hunger and need to react negatively to progressive movement in their treatment led them to try to take money from me. An anorectic patient did it directly by depositing insurance checks incorrectly made out to her which were meant for me, after we had worked long and hard together for several years. When I discovered it and brought it up, she denied realizing that the money was meant for me, then balked at returning it. A bulimic patient with whom I had worked almost a year, who had made considerable improvement, did it less directly. But both, I am certain, were attempted enactments of the wish to take from me that which they had never gotten earlier in life. Both occurred at a point when they had made significant gains in treatment, enough so that they could begin to believe that it might be possible to begin to live a life in which pleasure could be enjoyed without masochistic suffering. Neither patient could begin to acknowledge what she had done, and responded with narcissistic rage to my trying to discuss with them what happened. Both treatments were destroyed.

Boyer (1971) distinguishes between two kinds of reenactments: "living out" reenactments, repetitions of earlier behavior that are not connected directly with the therapeutic situation, and "acting out" reenactments, behaviors that attempt to solve transference problems through action. The therapist's contribution to the enactment is what distinguishes enactment from what we usually call acting out per se. Enactment involves the therapist as a participant, vulnerable to his own transferences, susceptible to blind spots and intensely caught up in the relationship rather than observing it. When the therapist is not attuned to the shifts from the thick-skinned to thin-skinned narcissistic position and back again, but instead responds from his own thick- or thin-skinned position, a destructive enactment is most likely to occur.

The second theme is that of enactment as a positive force in treatment, perhaps even part of a corrective emotional experience. To work through the enactment is a collaborative venture of interactive repair between patient and therapist, which depends very much on the therapist's ability to recognize and regulate the negative affect within himself. If the therapist can contain these feelings that have been induced in him by the patient without succumbing to the wish simply to project the missile back into the patient, a shift in the relationship can occur that leads to psychological growth for the patient. It can also lead to psychological growth for the therapist as well. It requires that the therapist be able to contain powerful affect, listen to his own inner state, and take responsibility for his own feelings, without reflexively accepting the role the patient is thrusting on him. If the therapist can pay attention to his own unconscious, he can understand what the patient's unconscious is communicating by means of the projective identification. If he can find a way to communicate to the patient the patient's own unconscious communication, this can further the patient's understanding of what he was feeling and can further his ability to contain his feelings and express them verbally. It is through these affect-laden interpersonal processes that real psychological change can occur.

When the patient's transference is very provocative and hateful, it is so much easier to strike back and obtain immediate sadistic pleasure than to contain one's hateful feelings. "The analyst must be able to step back from the patient's pathology and to tolerate the patient's resistances without feeling defeated, emptied, or castrated and without detaching emotionally from the patient" (Greif 1989b, p. 176). Containing one's hateful countertransference requires that the therapist adopt, only temporarily, a masochistic stance against the patient's sadism in order not to respond in kind (Greif 1989b).

> The analyst should be ready to withstand the onslaught of the patient's rage, as the past is relived in the therapy. Lucia Tower . . . describes how she temporarily adopted a masochistic stance vis-à-vis the patient's sadism. She writes: "There developed in me, on a transient basis, an amount of masochism sufficient to absorb the sadism which he was now unloading, and which had terrified him throughout his life. . . . The other

ingredient of my affective response was, I believe, a joining with him and a supporting of him, through identification, in a true unconscious grief reaction" (p. 248). . . .

This is another element in the analyst's successfully dealing with the patient's masochism, namely, tolerating first the unconscious reaction of the grief and sadness the patient is still defending against. By both absorbing the patient's rage and being available to experience the hidden grief, the analyst moves out from under the struggle with the patient over who will change and who will feel, and accepts temporary submission at the hands of the patient's pathology in the service of ultimate conflict resolution and working through. [p. 176]

Temporarily adopting a "one down" masochistic stance may be especially important for disarming the patient from his self-destructive urges and for restoring him to a sense of "one up," a sense of efficacy and control. However, there are times when the therapist must be ready to confront and challenge the transference distortions and refuse to participate in the patient's pathology. There are times when the patient must be confronted with the fact that he has the power to destroy the treatment and that there is absolutely nothing the therapist can do about it. The patient is likely to have been feeling so utterly powerless and vulnerable that such a confrontation can restore him to feeling a sense of control sufficient for him to relinquish his destructiveness and promote the therapeutic alliance. If the patient still persists in destroying the treatment there is nothing for the therapist to do but resign from it.

Winnicott (1958b) states that the therapist must be able to bear hating her patient without doing anything about it, in much the same way a mother must be able to bear hating her child without doing anything about it:

> The analyst must be prepared to bear strain without expecting the patient to know anything about what he is doing. . . . He must be easily aware of his own fear and hate. . . . Eventually, he ought to be able to tell his patient what he has been through on the patient's behalf, but an analysis may never get as far as this. . . .
>
> In analysis of psychotics the analyst is under greater strain to keep his hate latent, and he can only do this by being thoroughly aware of it. I want to add that in certain stages of certain analyses the analyst's hate is actually sought by the patient, and what is then needed is hate that is objective. If the patient seeks objective or justified hate he must be able to reach it, else he cannot feel he can reach objective love. . . . It seems that he can believe in being loved only after reaching being hated. . . .
>
> A mother has to be able to tolerate hating her baby without doing anything about it. She cannot express it to him. If, for fear of what she may do, she cannot hate appropriately when hurt by her child she must fall back on masochism. . . . The most remarkable thing about a mother is her ability to be hurt so much by her baby and to hate so much without paying the child out, and her ability to wait for rewards that may or may not come at a later date. . . .
>
> If all this is accepted there remains for discussion the question of the interpretation of the analyst's hate to the patient. This is obviously a matter fraught with danger,

and it needs the most careful timing. But I believe an analysis is incomplete if even towards the end it has not been possible for the analyst to tell the patient what he, the analyst, did unbeknown for the patient whilst he was ill, in the early stages. Until this interpretation is made the patient is kept to some extent in the position of infant—one who cannot understand what he owes to his mother. [pp. 198–202]

Enactments on the Body

The tendency toward sadomasochistic object relations not only fuels transference–countertransference enactments but fuels enactments on the body, the violent expression of that which cannot be expressed in words. Enactments on the body are different in that they are even more intense and out-of-control ego regressions in which the body is used very concretely in the present in the service of repeating real sadomasochistic scenarios from the past as if they were happening in the present (reenactments) and to fulfill current sadomasochistic wishes (enactments), including transference wishes. That is, the patient has a sadomasochistic object relationship with the self that is used to reenact past sadomasochistic scenarios or enact current sadomasochistic wishes. It is difficult much of the time to know whether a bodily enactment has occurred because the therapist can know this only in retrospect by the patient's verbal associations to the self-harm. That is, the enactment must be present in the clinical situation.

In the case of Kelly, the patient described in the previous chapter whose self-harm was wildly dangerous and out of control, a distinction can be made in at least some of the self-harm between some episodes that are enactments and reenactments and others that may be presymbolic expressions of mood, affect, or ideas about the self. Her self-starvation, which began at around age 13, had become a way of life for her that seemed to be an ongoing expression of her notion that she did not deserve to have anything good inside her. When she would pass out from dehydration and would be infused with the fluids her body desperately needed, she would think to herself, "No, I don't deserve to have this." Many of the episodes of punching her hand through windows and otherwise injuring her hand seem to have served as enactments and reenactments that were triggered by an intrusive image or memory. These were sudden and impulsive episodes that enacted several wishes. In the one that was averted in my office, when she had a dissociative episode and was sure her father was behind her, the wishes that were not enacted were the wish to punish the hand that had been party to the sexual involvement with her father, and the wish to mutilate and kill her father.

The way the therapist responds to the bodily enactments may determine whether he becomes drawn in to what becomes a transference–countertransference enactment. When he can contain his countertransference feelings, he is in a position to better help the patient understand the nature of the bodily enactment. A special circumstance is when the patient does something potentially harmful to his body in the presence of the therapist. For example, during a session, it is not unusual to find a patient absentmindedly picking at or scratching herself. Such a common and undramatic act is less likely to provoke strong countertransference feelings in the therapist and should be easier to deal with. The patient may not even be aware that he was doing it and so the therapist should note it out loud in order to engage the patient in discussion of it. For example, "I noticed that when you were telling me about your sister's illness, you made your right hand into a fist and started pounding on your leg." Helping the patient to link the behavior with repressed or dissociated feelings can help the patient not only to become more aware of the behavior but to begin to speak of the feelings, and when she speaks of them, she is then less likely to need to enact them physically.

Bulimics may at times feel nauseated in the session. Helping them to speak of what feelings or thoughts they were having before feeling nauseated may help to transform a potential enactment into an opportunity for verbal expression. Thus, intervening into a potential enactment may help to create meaning from the somatic distress. If the patient still feels the need to vomit, being with her physically at this time may help to transform a lonely reenactment of past experience into something more positive. The simple act of getting the patient a glass of water afterward or placing a hand on her shoulder while she is heaving can be a very powerful corrective experience for the patient. As Winnicott (1958a) said, "In psychology it must be said that the infant falls to pieces unless held together, and physical care is psychological care at these stages."

Dr. Fayek Nakhla and his patient, Grace Jackson (a pseudonym), collaborated in a compelling account of the patient's treatment (Nakhla and Jackson 1993). After 18 months of near silence in her sessions, Ms. Jackson, a writer, began cutting herself with razor blades and glass, even at times cutting herself in the session. Although both doctor and patient were terrified, her doctor did not stop her. "The doctor says, 'You have to keep cutting yourself; you have to remain in touch with your body, with yourself, in whatever way you can'" (p. 55). Although Ms. Jackson worked and functioned in the outside world, the two things that made her feel real and made her really feel were cutting herself and writing in a journal. Dr. Nakhla understood that she needed to enact on her body that which she could not express verbally so that she could become able to relinquish these acts and express the feelings in words. He told her that if she had to cut, to save it for when they were together. Treatment was a long, circular, interactive process in which, eventually, verbal expression came to the foreground and self-inflicted violence receded to the background. During this process Dr. Nakhla had arrangements with a cosmetic surgeon who repaired the damage and with a hospital that served as an extension of the holding environment, where he hospitalized her temporarily when necessary. Dr. Nakhla's treatment of his patient is very controversial and risky.

Early in my career, when I was not at all equipped to treat people who harm themselves, I found myself in a very disturbing clinical situation that required me to decide quickly about whether to intervene to stop the patient's self-harm:

My first clinical experience with self-mutilation came with 8-year-old Tommy when I worked at a physical rehabilitation center. He had lived with his mother, an apparently devoted and caring woman. Tommy had been a physically normal child who had quite suddenly become paralyzed from the waist down, the result, it was believed but never known for certain, of contracting a viral infection from contaminated stagnant water when he fell off his bicycle into a puddle. Tommy drove the medical and nursing staff to distraction by regularly digging into his legs with any sharp object he could find, continuously infecting and reinfecting himself despite treatment with oral antibiotics and ointments. Nothing they did could stop him, and they tried desperately. As soon as cotton mittens were put on his hands, he removed them. He looked for safety pins, paper clips, scissors, any sharp object he could find, and used his fingernails when nothing else was at hand. As soon as an infection would start to clear, a new pus-filled infection would appear. Out of desperation, the staff had begun to talk of using physical restraints.

I usually met with Tommy in his room or we went downstairs to the coffee shop together. If he ever came to my office, it was to ask me to go somewhere else with him. But one day, surprisingly, he wheeled himself into my office to stay for awhile. He positioned his wheelchair in front of my desk where I usually sat, and soon began fiddling with the top drawer. He opened it and removed a compass, that device with a sharp pointed end best known to geometry students for drawing circles and arcs. Immediately I knew what he was going to do. I was filled with confusion, anxiety, and conflict. I *should* stop him, I thought. *Should* I try to stop him, even though it is to no avail? Do I let him do this? What shall I do? Deciding to do nothing was equivalent to deciding to do something. I did not know then what I know now, but in retrospect, on some unconscious level I knew he wanted to make someone listen to what his body had to say. So I sat there with him, sometimes in silence and sometimes I spoke to him while he dug at his leg. I kept my eyes on his face even though he was not looking at me, because I could not bear to look at what he was doing. When the silence bore nothing other than my anxiety, I would speak, as much to him as for myself. "What are you digging for, Tommy? What might you find in there? . . . Some people dig for gold, or buried treasure. What about you?" He would at times stop what he was doing and look up at me, and then my anxiety would diminish—I had been able to make contact with him through this strange state that he was in. We sat together for close to a half hour and in bits and pieces, stops and starts, he became able to say that he was searching for a place in his leg where it would hurt. If he could feel pain in his leg, then he would know that it was alive. What he did not say was that if he knew his leg was alive, then the rest of him, deadened by depression as it was, would come alive too. Tommy was enacting the desperate wish to have his leg back they way he had known it, alive and vital, the way he had been.

This was the first and last time that this occurred. I do not know what I would have done then had Tommy come back to see me in my office again to sit at my desk and dig. But I knew that he needed to tell a story about himself, and I knew that attempts to control his behavior were useless.

How Enactments in the Treatment and on the Body Almost Destroyed the Treatment[1]

> *What each of us needs from the other . . . is at depth pretty much the same. We need to find in the other an affirming witness to the best that we hope we are, as well as an accepting and durable respondent to those worst aspects of ourselves that we fear we are.*
> James McLaughlin, "Touching Limits in the Psychoanalytic Dyad"

There are various lenses through which any case can be viewed—transference, defense, resistance, the real relationship, ego needs, id desires, therapeutic alliance. This case is presented through the overarching lens of attachment, the vicissitudes of which can promote or destroy the treatment. Thus, the nature of the therapeutic alliance, the transference and countertransference difficulties, projective identifications, and enactments in the treatment will be highlighted. The case provides a firsthand sense of how personal issues in my life and my own countertransference issues contributed to enactments in the treatment of a woman who was chronically prone to destructive enactments in her relationships and on her body. It also demonstrates how, even when destructive enactments may be virtually inevitable in some treatments, the treatment can be salvaged and in doing so, the patient can be helped to move up to a higher level of thinking and symbolic thought. To those of us who struggle with omnipotent wishes to rescue our patients, it can be of some consolation that even though we cannot rescue our patients, some of the time we can rescue the treatment.

The Patient and the Therapist

Loretta, a single woman in her late fifties from a working-class background, has been in treatment with me on a once a week basis for four years. Shortly before she was referred, her boss had informed her that he would soon be leaving the company, and she felt devastated. She loved him, she said, but not in a romantic way. She had worked at the company, a major corporation, for over thirty years and took enormous pride in being his executive secretary, his "right

---

1. This case was originally presented to the Westchester Chapter of the New York State Society of Clinical Social Workers in September 1998.

hand," his "gal Friday," just as she had with his predecessor. When his predecessor left, her weight, somewhere in the 240 to 250 pound range, ballooned up over 300 pounds. She was frightened that the same thing would happen again. She would have to interview for a position elsewhere in the company, not knowing whom she would end up working for but desperately hoping it would not be a woman. "Women are bitches . . . I say what's on my mind and not everyone likes that. Sometimes I say it too loud and too much." (At this, I imagined myself putting on an imaginary pith helmet and chest protector, and buckling myself in for what I knew was going to be a rocky road ahead. I had to remind myself that I had a good sense of humor that would come in handy.) She came to me wanting me to help her to keep her weight from increasing, knowing I had treated other people with eating problems. She also came with expectations of magic.

At the initial consultation I went to greet her in the waiting room and was struck by her appearance: her obesity and by what looked like stained, dirty white bandages that wrapped around her legs from her arches to her knees. This was just the tip of the medical iceberg. She had arthritis in her legs and cardiovascular problems that required her to wear these, she told me, and there are some ulcerations that would not heal. She could not bathe or shower because she had to keep the bandages dry, so she took sponge baths but they may not have been frequent or thorough enough because she emitted an odor bad enough to require spraying the room with air deodorizer after she left. She had a cardiac arrhythmia that had brought her to the emergency room and intensive care unit five years before, and she knows that at some time in the future she might need a pacemaker. She was on cholesterol-lowering and blood pressure medications. She was supposed to have vascular surgery but her doctor would not perform the surgery while she was so overweight because it was too risky. Similarly, she had terrible visual problems that required a corneal transplant in each eye, also quite risky at her current weight. Her ability to read and drive was compromised, and she required a special computer monitor and special car mirrors.

She moved slowly and the few downward steps that led from the waiting room to the consultation room gave her some trouble. After she seated herself she had to rest a moment to catch her breath. In this first session I learned that she had a compulsive eating and weight problem since early childhood. Her mother, who had died of heart failure when Loretta was 11, was always after her to lose weight and would get angry at her for eating so much. She also had been a bed wetter and continued to wet until she was 14 or 15. "Don't tell me it was psychological," she warned, "my life was awful at that time." I told her that I wanted to hear about how awful things were for her then, but that it also seemed that she wanted to be in control of what we talked about. She replied that she did not want to waste her time discussing that crap about problems with your mother or father causing bed-wetting. I agreed that we could forgo talking about her bed-wetting at this time, but hoped that she could at least try to tolerate some exploration of matters that she might not think worth exploring. She conceded that she thought she could do that as long as I did not ram some dumb theory down her throat. (I reminded myself to breathe deeply.) She proceeded to tell me that what made her life so awful was that her father had remarried one-and-a-half years after her mother's death, and she and her stepmother fought constantly. Loretta described a controlled domineering woman who fit the stereotype of the wicked stepmother, speaking of her with an intensity and fury that suggested that she was still reliving whatever had occurred between them. I was to witness and experience this angry hyperarousal a lot.

Loretta lived with her father and stepmother until her stepmother's death two years before Loretta began treatment. Since then, she lived with her father, a quiet unexpressive man in his mid-eighties, in an apartment "stuffed to the gills" with things she had accumulated throughout her life and could not get rid of, including all of her stepmother's clothing. Every surface is covered, including all the chairs, but usually she does not even notice it. (Emotional hunger can drive people to take possession of objects uncritically so that they barely notice that these processes have happened.) The mess made her father "crazy" and he begged her repeatedly to do something about it before he dies. "Do I have to live in this pig sty until I die?" He worried about her and was anxious about how she would fare when he was gone.

She felt hopeless about her hoarding and her weight and begged me to help her to keep her weight from going up again. Taking a weight history, I discovered that when she was 18 and desperate to lose weight, she had gone from 220 to 135 pounds in three months with the help of a diet doctor and amphetamines. She loved how she looked but hated how she felt, hearing her heartbeat and feeling "wired" all the time, and when she stopped the medication, her weight soared again. Since then, she found that she could lose a great deal of weight on her own, as much as 150 pounds, on the Weight Watchers program. She had lost and regained tremendous amounts of weight several times. I was impressed that she had the impulse control and determination to do this, unlike many overeaters who cannot adhere to any diet for any period of time, but was concerned about the obsessiveness with which she dieted. Even though she came to me for help with her eating problem, she did not want to hear anything about it or my "fancy theories." When she was ready, she would go back to Weight Watchers.

She was quite anxious and depressed and was having trouble sleeping. She was so tired at work that occasionally she fell asleep sitting up at her desk. I thought that she might need to be evaluated for sleep apnea, explaining to her that it might be a factor in her sleep problems and could be treated. It was important to know if her sleep problems were caused by her depression, sleep apnea, or both. She dismissed my suggestion and refused to allow me to speak to her primary physician; she was sure all her symptoms were because her boss was leaving and did not want me "monkeying around" with her medical care. She could not allow herself to think that her emotional problems had something to do with her eating problems and her numerous medical problems. Her efforts to control me and the treatment spoke of an enormous need to experience herself as omnipotent and a paranoid sense that others were trying to take away something from her. From the outset she was determined to maintain the treatment in an encapsulated pocket of her life, where it would in no way become integrated in her mind with her life and medical care. The treatment was to be split off in the same way she split off the destructive parts of herself.

I discovered that her binge eating had been an unconscious act of defiance against her stepmother and had become equated with fighting for her life, for psychic survival. Through it she could at times enact her murderous wishes. All of her significant memories were remembered through food. She remembered what she ate when she and her father visited her mother in the hospital shortly before she died. Her guilt about eating in a restaurant with her father when it should have been her mother and father eating together was remembered through what she ate. She remembered what she ate when everyone came to the house for the wake. Eating had always been a problem for her, but got much worse after her mother's death. She had never mourned that loss and all the losses associated with it. She and her father had moved in with her paternal grandparents after her mother died. Her father sold the house she had grown up in, and many of her favorite toys were lost in the move. She was supposed to be strong, not cry, and not supposed to "want sympathy" from others. She grew up "fat and furious," in a chronic rage, trying to stuff her anger down with food.

Her father remarried a little over a year later and bought a house quite distant from her extended family. She and her stepmother seemed to bring out the worst in each other. Loretta, desperately in need of mothering, would have hated any woman who took her mother's place in the family, but she virtually ensured that she could never get what she needed from her stepmother. At the same time, her stepmother had her notions of what the household should be like and was a stickler for order and neatness. She and Loretta locked horns over Loretta's accumulations of junk that were spread all over the house, and they vied with each other for first place in the father's heart. Loretta's father, always an emotionally detached man, became even more so. When she needed a ride to a friend's house, or when a group of friends needed a parent to drive them to the movies or a dance in their suburban town, neither Loretta's father nor stepmother ever pitched in. Loretta felt embarrassed with her friends and their parents, whose homes were far more welcoming to her than her own. She spent much time at school, involved in clubs and social events, talking with her friends about which boys they liked. She contented herself with being on the prom committee, denying to herself how bad she felt that she never went to the prom.

Loretta felt devastated that her father did not step in to help her in her struggles with her stepmother, feeling entirely shut out, motherless and fatherless, an orphan. When they made plans to visit relatives, they never included Loretta, further cutting her off from her extended family. When they moved further north, Loretta became even more isolated, lonely, and enraged. By this time she had a car and she came home late from school to avoid dinner with her father and stepmother. On the way, she often stopped to buy Chinese food or a whole pizza, gorging herself in a frenzy in her car at the side of the road. She recalled thoughts as she bit and chewed: "Susan, you bitch, I can't even eat dinner in my own house because of you. . . . You took my father from me. . . . Goddamn bitch, you keep me from my family, you took everything from me." Bite bite, chew chew, rip to bits.

After high school graduation, it got even worse when her friends scattered in different directions. Loretta was a bridesmaid at several weddings, "Always a bridesmaid, never the bride." She found an office job and felt even more isolated and lonely amidst other women who were married or engaged or dating. She missed the high school camaraderie and felt that her life was at a dead end. Her secret eating rituals continued out of the house and at home, where Susan would find food wrappers in secret places in Loretta's bedroom. Loretta was getting fatter and fatter and angrier and angrier. She consumed food and books, imagining her life transformed into the romantic, exciting life of a woman in a novel. Loretta and Susan had terrible screaming matches, sometimes about her weight, usually battles for control. Susan would scream that she was eating herself into an early grave and Loretta would scream back that she'd eat what she wanted and no one could stop her. Loretta was not aware that these struggles with Susan resonated with struggles she had had with her mother around her eating.

Life was miserable for Loretta, but as so many women do, she saw in weight loss the possibility of a magical transformation—dates, romance, marriage. A diet doctor supplied her with the amphetamines that enabled her to lose eighty-five pounds in three months. It was like magic, initially, but she barely recognized her 135-pound shapely body and contoured face in the mirror. One summer night on her way home from work, she had stopped her car at a stoplight and was startled when a handsome young man in an adjacent car called to her, then honked his horn to get her attention. She could barely believe he wanted to talk to her, but he did. It was the most exciting thing that had ever happened to her. Against her better judgment, she pulled her car over to a side street and allowed him to join her. They talked awhile, then he began to kiss her and to her surprise, she responded until her excitement, confusion, and anxiety mounted so much that she abruptly yelled at him to get out of her car and leave her alone. She drove away in a daze, stopping at her favorite pizzeria, and pulled over at the side of the road with a pizza and a large bottle of soda. Sad and sorry as this was, this was safer than a relationship with a man, and so, inevitably, her weight began to climb. At least she knew who she was when she looked in the mirror—a fat girl. All her bad feelings got chewed up and pushed down under huge amounts of food, "shit food," as she called the cakes, chips, and pastries with which she tried to fill her emptiness. She stuffed herself with "shit" until she fell into a stupor, her body becoming a container for shit, a toilet.

When both her eating and self-esteem had reached rock bottom, she became desperate to feel better, and once again weight loss held out the promise of a new beginning and a transformation. She decided to try Weight Watchers and approached it with ferocious determination. She was quite successful at losing weight this way, but once she had lost a significant amount of weight she began her binge eating once again. When she would hit bottom again and was repelled by the image in the mirror, she would return to obsessional dieting and Weight Watchers once again. She sought the applause and special recognition of her achievement in the meetings, and wore her merit pins proudly. And so it went that her weight yo-yo'ed up and down and up again numerous times.

In treatment, although much of the time she actively thwarted any attempt of mine to help her find any meaning in her feelings or behavior, she seemed to find my interest in her narcissistically gratifying and she responded quite positively to that and to the little bit of analytic work that was managed. Her mood lifted and she did not gain the weight she had expected she might. Her evaluations began to improve and she began to develop a sense of tact in her dealings with co-workers that had been entirely lacking. Her narcissism oscillated from thin- to thick-skinned positions, as she presented at times a sense of vulnerability and barely disguised wish that I like her, and at other times was hardened and determined to keep me at a distance and not allow me to have any impact on her. At times she brought me little "gifts," for example, retelling discussions with supervisors or co-workers verbatim so that I could see how well she was doing. She could in this way acknowledge that our work together was having a real effect on her life and that I was having an effect on her.

Yet when I moved away from being her supportive selfobject and reminded her of a reality she did not want to look at, she could shift in an instant into her thick-skinned mode, shooting out verbal porcupine quills. Attempts to get her to look at the interpersonal processes between us were meet with ferocious resistance. She was prone to narcissistic injury and responded with narcissistic rages and vicious attacks. For example, she expected to take unlimited time off from treatment for vacations and expected me to hold her hour for her and not charge her. I told her that if she expected me to commit myself to holding the time, I would expect her to commit herself to paying for it; if it were possible I would be glad to offer her a makeup session upon her return. If the time were not paid for, I would feel free to fill it and could not assure her that the hour would be there for her upon her return. It was her choice. She responded that she was going with her father on a cruise and I wanted to punish her for it. How come I could take a vacation but if she did, she was punished? There could be no discussion of her transferential expectations or her cognitive distortions, of anything that acknowledged me as a separate person not subject to her control. She began to shout, "I'll pay you when hell freezes over, when hair grows on the palm of my hand, that's when I'll pay you!"

She could not tolerate looking at her wish to be special, my special child who would be loved unconditionally. It simply seemed a given to her that she was entitled to special treatment and was entitled to treat me any way she wanted. If anything interfered with her illusion of complete omnipotence, I could expect terrible affect storms. There were times when I stretched the boundaries of treatment and times when I stuck to established boundaries and managed to contain the angry affect she projected into me.

Despite her insistence that she wanted to be able to eat normally, she had no wish to look at her eating problem as a problem, and seemed pleased that at least she was not gaining weight. However, her weight and visual problems were obstacles in finding another position within the company and this, along with her personality problems and lack of technological proficiency, had prevented her from achieving promotions. Given a "floater" position until a permanent position could be found, Loretta had difficulty with this because it required a degree of physical mobility she did not have. The company physician, a woman who had taken an interest in helping her, thought that if she did not lose weight, she might ultimately lose her job, as the company was downsizing. Loretta was furious that once again her weight was an issue. She saw injustice all around her, and refused to lose weight to satisfy "them." She had the omnipotent fantasy that her weight would be no problem at work, that the company physician would somehow protect her in the company. The company had become her life, and the co-workers and managers she quarreled with had become like family to her. It was home and it was her identity and sense of self.

She seemed to hold onto her weight as if her life depended on it, as if others were determined to take it from her. Having lost so much already, it seemed that she could not bear to lose this, too. And yet at the same time, she was afraid not to lose weight, and so after six months of treatment she decided to return to Weight Watchers in the hope that she could lose enough weight to keep her managers off her back. The thrill of losing weight this way took hold, and she refused to let me help her find another way. She became angry at my reminders that big rapid weight losses for her were always followed by big rapid weight gains, that alternating bingeing and strict dieting did not constitute eating normally. She did not want to think of the unpleasant reality when she could think of the exhilarating state of mind experienced by losing weight—the sense of power and omnipotence that vanquished depression and anxiety, serving as it does for so many chronic dieters as a psychic retreat from reality. As we came to discover much later on, her attempts at permanent weight loss were bound to fail because the real motives for losing weight, split off from her awareness as they were, were conflictual. In her persistence, she managed to lose 90 pounds in ten months, and was quick to tell me that she did it all herself—without any help from me.

I discovered that although she did not allow herself her affect storms with her physicians, she nonetheless used her relationship with them to defeat them in trying to help her, unconsciously relishing her pyrrhic victory over parental figures. Yet I could find no way for her to look at her relationship with them as she clung to the masochistic pleasure of defeating them with her illness. I found it difficult to listen to her complain that they had begun to give up on her, to write her off in their minds. She simply voiced the expectation that they should be eternally strong and steadfast and provide encouragement and hope for her. She could tolerate no exploration of how she defeats and drives away those she hires to help her, of how she envies them their power and tries to strip them of it, blaming them when she fails to get better. She did the same with me when she stopped dieting and began bingeing again: "You're supposed to be this eating-disorder expert and what good does it do me? Nothing—I'm still as big as a house." When I asked her how she expected me to help her when she refuses to consider anything I might have to offer, she simply escalated her attack. At moments like these, when feeling that I wanted to attack back, I would call upon a joke I had made about another patient who could make me feel powerless and incompetent at times, and I would say it silently to myself like a soothing mantra: "This woman could provoke her own murder." It helped me to acknowledge my own murderous wishes toward her while providing some containing distance from them.

It was in treating Loretta that I was inspired to formulate a theory of a particular kind of projective identification, "the therapist as toilet." (I credit Loretta for unwittingly serving as my muse.) That is, in the unconscious mind of the patient who "feels like shit," the therapist is simply a container in which to "drop a load," a toilet into which she projects or purges the bad parts of herself. The patient comes to her sessions to make her fecal deposits, thus degrading and diminishing the therapist. The patient feels relieved and the therapist is stuffed up with anger.

The Stage Is Set for the Enactment

Events in Loretta's life and concurrent events in my life and each of our responses to these events and to each other joined together to create an enactment that almost destroyed the treatment. There were enactments with Loretta before, to be sure, but I was able to acknowledge my role in them in ways that helped Loretta begin to acknowledge hers. In retrospect, I came to consider them the "little enactments" that she and I survived, the ones we cut our teeth on to create a history together in which we were able to survive a far bigger and more destructive storm, the one I remember as the "big enactment." These little ones built up some scar tissue in each of us, evidence of mutual wounding and healing and growing trust. But this one, this enactment was different and threatened the future of her treatment. What happened was a drama, a scenario that set the stage for what could very easily have become a tragedy for Loretta. In tragedy, the protagonist, like Oedipus, has a tragic flaw in his character that brings him to ruin. Loretta bore more than a passing semblance to Oedipus.

I will describe the events leading up to the big enactment and how they were subjectively experienced by each of us in order to set the stage for the scenario that unfolded. Rather personal self-disclosures have been made with the intention of facilitating the exploration of the role of the therapist's countertransference issues, issues in his personal life, and personality traits in contributing to the creation of enactments.

As described, Loretta had lost ninety pounds on Weight Watchers in ten months, with no help from me. She would come in and report how much she had lost in the past week, and tell me of her struggles with temptation. The pleasure of being in control was one of the two real pleasures she had in her life. The other was that a few months before, she had found a temporary position within the company as executive secretary to another man she had grown quite fond of. She loved being in control of his calendar and loved his needing her as he did. "The man could not function without me. He said so himself." She was not just "another girl" in the typing pool, as she had been years before. She felt herself to be invulnerable to the corporate upheaval going on all around her, about which she had ample warning. She felt that she had been rescued from all that, that she was special and exempt. Life was better for her, and the treatment had moved to a somewhat different level. It was less stormy, and she and I had settled into an easier way of working together. Her rage and fury at all those who had let her down and hurt her was tempered somewhat, and she began to become a bit more reflective, expressing some sadness about her losses.

But nine months later, a pivotal event occurred in Loretta's life. Her boss had decided to take another position within the company but at a different location, and had offered Loretta the opportunity to join him there as his executive secretary. Despite the fact that her future at the company was jeopardized, he was willing to go out on a limb for her and insist to those in power that he wanted her to join him. This might have been a welcome opportunity for a younger, healthier person who had the stamina to work the twelve-hour days that came with the new position, but it was a terribly difficult decision for Loretta to make. She was giddy with excitement at the chance to work even more closely with her boss, and kept repeating the phrase "He wants to take me with him" in a way that suggested that she was having fantasies of being taken sexually. Here was a man willing to go out on a limb for her, so unlike her own father. The pressure for her to respond forced her to consider the offer realistically, and so with a great sense of loss she had to acknowledge that she could not accept it.

She became more depressed and her weight began to climb. She became aware that she was using food as an antidepressant and could acknowledge that it was not working because all it did was divert herself from the depressed feelings temporarily, but she refused to have a psychopharmacological evaluation. Her evaluations at work, which had improved since starting therapy, began to get worse. As Loretta got angrier and angrier and ate more and more, she was able to turn to me more for help. All the time that elapsed in which I had been able to contain my countertransference feelings was finally paying off. Rather than continuing to rant against all those who had hurt her and refusing to use her mind to think, she began to participate at times in the treatment in a new collaborative way and began to reflect in a way that had been previously impossible. She began to think more realistically about the possibility of losing her job. We began tracking her feelings in the sessions in relation to times of overeating or binge eating, and exploring this further. She discovered that her supervisor, "the bitch," reminded her of Susan, her stepmother, even to the point that at times when she was eating she would think of her supervisor or Susan and she would bite into the food with rage. Difficult times in her life that she had told me about could now be explored in a different way and reconstructed in such a way that helped her to begin to have some empathy for the poor self who knew only how to fight and stuff herself with food to feel better. It was quite a relief to me that just as I had been feeling more and more discouraged, I could once again feel competent as her therapist.

She even allowed me to introduce her to the healthy and destructive parts of herself, and could acknowledge that the destructive part was something that seemed to take over her and was beyond her control. She did not like being so out of control with her temper and her eating. What offered some hope that she might be able to take control was understanding how these two parts of herself could join forces for destructive purposes, and so I explained to her how these two parts of the self could have an unhealthy relationship that led to destructiveness or could have a healthier relationship in which the healthy part refuses to submit to the unhealthy part. What made this more tolerable for her to think about was that I had experienced both the destructive part of her and a more likable part and had accepted both. Once again, the treatment focused on the loss of a significant man in her life, and began to resonate with memories of other losses.

The thick-skinned narcissism that had served as a defense for the thin-skinned self began to lessen. When it appeared in relation to other objects in her life, she could, some of the time at least, tolerate my interpretations about the healthy part allowing the destructive part to take over. When she showed me her thick-skinned and obnoxious side by attacking me or thwarting my efforts to reach her, I could often, if I were patient enough and tried several times, interpret how she was trying to make me feel the sense of helplessness she was feeling, and she would think about and respond to it in a productive way. Despite the climate at work becoming more oppressive, Loretta was dealing with this very difficult situation. At tough times, she would think of things I had said and found them helpful. However, employees were being laid off and Loretta was feeling more hopeless.

She knew I was taking a two-week vacation shortly before Christmas and was very angry. This was not a good time for her for me to be away, she said. She was eating more, and confronted me with her six-pound weight gain, which she insisted was clearly my fault. I expressed my regret that the timing of my vacation was indeed so unfortunate for her. She retreated into her thick-skinned position and decided to take a short cruise with her father and an old high school friend the week before I left. I questioned the timing of her cruise, and suggested that she was angry and wanted to leave me before I could leave her. She would hear nothing of this and insisted that I was not so important to her as to influence her this way. Did I have "delusions of grandeur or whatever they are called?" She simply needed a break from the environment at work and she loved being near the water and loved being around people on a cruise. Simple as that.

The Big Enactment: Is This Really Happening?

I returned from my vacation in mid-December to an even angrier Loretta who maintained that it was very unprofessional of me to take a vacation when a patient is having such a hard time. Couldn't I have waited? I recognized once again that it was indeed unfortunate timing for her and I was sorry that she was having such a hard time. I told her that in fact I took the two weeks when I did because I very much needed the time off. She seemed incredulous that I had needs, acknowledging that she has always seen me as strong and invulnerable.

Less than two weeks later my mother died. It was a shock but not a surprise. My vacation had been so necessary then because I was exhausted and depleted from the unrelenting past three years of her illness. I called my patients and told them that my mother had died and that I would not be seeing patients during the week but expected to return the following Monday. Loretta was not home, and so I left a message on her answering machine.

Based on past experience, I had expected that when I returned, patients would offer condolences, and some might be concerned about my well-being. I expected too that many would feel constrained about telling me about their difficulties, not wanting to add to my burden. I knew that the best thing to do was to assure them that working with them in the ways that they were accustomed to could only be helpful to me in getting back to the world of the living.

It was the patients who could be concerned about my well-being whom I wanted to return to. "We are who we are, most of us would now agree, in order to repair our ailing internal objects and heal ourselves and keep healing ourselves, over and over again. . . . We seek ways of reaching and touching each other, of nurturing, exciting, soothing, arousing, and ultimately healing the places that hurt. Within this intersubjective space, the analyst, too, wants to be reached, known, and recognized" (Davies 1999, pp. 187–188). I wanted to feel their care and at the same time know I could continue to do my work, keeping the patient's unconscious process central to the endeavor. How impossible a task this was when Loretta was the first patient I saw. When she entered the room she told me how sorry she was about my loss. It was my mother who had died, wasn't it, she asked. "Thank you," I told her. "Yes, my mother died." OK so far. Then she asked a simple question in a kindly voice: "Had she been sick?" Her question triggered an immediate return to the vulnerable, anxious self state that had been part of how I had lived for the past three years, catapulting me back to the pain of that time, and so her kind inquiry felt instead like a knife in my heart. I feared being completely overcome by grief right then and there and just sobbing. Gathering the pieces of my destabilized self together, I took the only way I knew at that moment to fend her off. "Yes, she was quite ill for some time [I felt my voice quiver, then heard it break], but I wonder [now in a firm but cold voice] in what way your knowing about this will be helpful to you."

No sooner had the words come out of my mouth than I wished I could take them back. Loretta's violent response remains with me, although I do not remember exactly what she said because I was stunned. But her words started out with a thunderous "Who the hell do you think you are?" I had experienced some of her rages, but this was something different. She attacked me verbally for what seemed like forever to me. Could this really be happening? I figured that the only way to survive it was to wait it out, and so I sat there, saying to myself in my mind, like a little girl cowering before her raging mother, "Let it be over, just let it be over," a survivor's mantra. I had some personal knowledge of what it was to cower before a raging mother, and here I was, back there again. I was stunned into muteness and reduced to helplessness but my mind was working. I wanted to get her out of there, I just wanted to be left alone. I considered telling her in my best professional manner, "I'm sorry but you have to leave now. I cannot tolerate this." Yet I knew that if I did that, she would experience it as a repetition of past rejections and it would be the end of the treatment. It would only affirm her belief that women are bitches who can hurt and reject her. I was not going to let this treatment that I had worked so hard at be ruined, for her and for me, at least not without a struggle. I would not join her in destroying the treatment, so I waited it out and managed to hang on until the wave of rage subsided. When it did she showed no awareness of what she had said or done to me, and I certainly was in no condition to discuss it with her. I was just quiet, telling myself to say little for fear of what I might say, and waiting for the clock to tell me I could end the session so I could fall apart privately. By the following week, although still feeling fragile, I had pulled myself back together enough that I was not so concerned about becoming overwhelmed by my feelings.

I replayed that session over and over again in my mind, looking at what had come before it and what was occurring presently in the treatment. This was an ongoing process that still continues, more than four years later. In the following session after Loretta made no mention of what had occurred, I acknowledged that she had given me quite a knockout punch. She insisted that her behavior was justified because I had given her such a terrible answer to her question, that it was my fault for provoking it. "I was being nice and you treated me like I didn't even deserve to live." I apologized for being so insensitive to her and acknowledged that her question, kind as it was, was going in a direction in which I could not go then. She listened intently and offered that she was glad to hear that, but wanted to know why I had been so awful. I was able to tell her then what I could not tell her at the time of the question, that it reached me so deeply that I was not capable of acknowledging it at that time.

I told her that if I allowed myself to be so moved by her words, I was afraid that I might feel my raw grief and become overwhelmed by it in her presence. I did not want to do that, I told her, for two reasons: first, my grief was a deeply private thing; and second, I was afraid that her seeing me in the throes of grief would frighten or overwhelm her and I wanted to protect her from that. She listened with rapt attention, then told me that when I began to say that my mother had been sick for a while, she *thought* she had heard grief in my voice. She seemed incredulous that I could feel that way. I interpreted that perhaps she sees my strength as a barrier to vulnerability and so was surprised to hear the vulnerability in my voice. Yes, that was right, she told me, and told me that even now as we were speaking, she heard it a bit again. Yes, I said, my eyes welling up, grief can be so strong; when you lose someone, it can just come upon you in a wave. She knew that, she said, because she had seen others in the throes of grief so she knew what it could look like, but it was something she had never felt herself. I suggested that maybe her knockout punch was a way of knocking me out the same way she felt knocked out when her mother died and she wasn't supposed to want sympathy, when she was left alone to feel helpless and her life went spiraling out of control. Maybe it was a way of communicating how she felt. She listened intently.

In retrospect, I understood that because I had been so involved in my own pain and in protecting myself, I could not realize until later that her question, even though it felt like a knife in me, was not at all a knife but came from the vulnerable part of her that knew all too well the pain of having a mother who was ill, of visiting in hospitals, and then, despite all the medical care, losing her to death. She knew what it was like to feel like an orphan and was connecting empathically with my thin-skinned self. But I could not tolerate that connection then, experiencing it as an assault to my fragile defenses, and shifted to a thick-skinned narcissistic position and responded coldly. This must have felt like a knife to her, a hostile attack on her thin-skinned self and so she retreated in defense to her most monstrous thick-skinned position to attack me. She knew I was bleeding emotionally, and, smelling the blood, she went for an easy kill.[2] She would have succeeded in destroying the treatment if I had accepted the rejecting role she had projected into me. Because I did not accept this role in this potentially tragic scenario, I was able to preserve the integrity of her therapy.

---

2. My thanks to Rosemary Sacken, M.S.W., for offering her clinical understanding of this case when it was presented in September 1998.

After the Enactment

*Hate that is justified in the present setting has to be sorted out and kept in
storage and available for eventual interpretation.*
    Donald W. Winnicott, "Hate in the Countertransference"

From this point on, the treatment took a different direction and finally, after
many years a slow painful process of grieving began for Loretta. She was able to
visit in memory the time of her mother's death and began to get in touch with
the anger she felt at the grave site. Everyone else was crying and she had been
angry and remained angry ever since. She had always known that she had been
angry but had never known why. She began to know how angry she was at her
mother for dying and leaving her. She began to know that her mother had not
been the idealized mother that she had wanted to remember. Good times and
bad times were recalled. Her becoming able to connect with my grief made her
more able to begin to connect with her own encapsulated grief. Losing her mother
was the beginning of a series of devastating losses. As I struggled with my own
grief, it helped me to help Loretta begin to claim hers, and as I helped Loretta,
this helped me to struggle through another layer of my own. I had to tolerate my
own grief processes if I was to be able to help her with hers. This experience caused
me to think of Therese Benedek's (1959) paper, "Parenthood as a Developmental Phase," in which she points out that developmental processes continue beyond
adolescence and are repeated in reversed fashion in the parent (therapist). That
is, parenthood is not just one phase in the psychic evolution of the parent (therapist) but "is a dominant factor in the emotional life of the parent (therapist),
requiring a continual adaptation from the parent to the child" (p. 378). As the
symbiosis between the mother and infant is a reciprocal interaction that, through
processes of introjection and identification, creates structural change in each of
the participants, so can the reciprocal interaction between patient and therapist
create structural change in each.

Even Loretta's relationship with her stepmother was revisited, and she began to look at it somewhat differently. As an adult she could begin to think about
how difficult it must have been for Susan, newly married to a man who had a
daughter who hated her. She could even acknowledge how "crazy" she got with
Susan, and how often she became a monster with her. She began to recall a few
times when Susan tried to reach out to her. She had forgotten the time Susan
took her shopping and out to lunch because the memory had become submerged
under the memory of the fight they had in the restaurant. And there were others.
The mental representations of her stepmother began to shift. She was not entirely
a monster but they both seemed to bring out the monster in each other. Loretta
could begin to acknowledge the wishes she had kept a secret from herself, that
Susan would love her and be a mother to her. And we discovered together that

Loretta was still holding on to Susan's clothing because even a not-so-good step-mother is better than no mother at all. She looked back with regret and sorrow about how terrible they had been to each other.

As she could acknowledge the monstrous part of herself in relation to Susan, I could get her to look at the monstrous part of herself in relation to me. As Winnicott (1958b) said, "In certain stages of certain analyses the analyst's hate is actually sought by the patient, and what is then needed is hate that is objective. If the patient seeks objective or justified hate he must be able to reach it, else he cannot feel he can reach objective love. . . . It seems that he can believe in being loved only after reaching being hated" (p. 199). Loretta had certainly sought and reached my hatred. When I thought she could tolerate hearing this, I told her that the way she had treated me made me want to throw her out. With passion in harness, I had even told her, "You know, you really can make somebody want to kill you." It was the first time anyone had ever told her this, but she knew it. We continued to reconstruct together what had contributed to the big enactment. She was able to tolerate exploring what happens when the monster in her suddenly emerges and takes over. She wanted to tame the monster because she did not like herself like this. We were able to identify together Loretta's smoldering resentments of her remote and unattuned father and less than perfect mother.

By no means was it smooth sailing, far from it. It was back and forth between progress and regressive resistance, and I had to muster my determination and consistency in relentlessly interpreting the perverse relationship between parts of her self. I had to struggle not to allow Loretta to terrorize me into submission. At times I felt worn away, eroded, tired. It was easier for me to become readily co-opted by Loretta's perversity, and at times I was, the healthier part of myself giving in by allowing these perverse processes in the patient to slip by. Occasionally I would rationalize, "So what if you don't confront every little perverse thing. Who can be so vigilant? She's going to fight you tooth and nail anyway. Give yourself a break. What could it hurt?" I had to monitor my readiness to give in and give up in helplessness.

It came to anger me more than I realized that she had never shown any remorse for what she had done to me. Without realizing just how much I wanted it, I wanted an apology, a verbal acknowledgment from her of how she had hurt me and how sorry she was. (Had she been able to do this, she would have been far more object related than she was.) It was not forthcoming but I kept trying to get her to give in and give it to me, to submit. I was like the mother who wants her child to be openly grateful for all she has done for her and tries to extract gratitude from the child. I told Loretta, quite prematurely, that if it were not for my being able to contain my anger at her, she would have destroyed the treatment. None of her numerous doctors would have tolerated that behavior. All of this was true and I fooled myself that I was doing what Winnicott (1958b) proposed good mothers and good therapists do—bearing the strain of containing my hatred, sometimes over a long period of time, without expecting the patient to know anything about what he is doing.

Winnicott suggests that the therapist eventually ought to be able to tell his patient what he has been through on his behalf, but that unfortunately sometimes the treatment may not get that far. That was where I was with Loretta; the treatment had not gotten there and I was trying to force the issue, to get blood from a stone. In time I became aware that I was getting a little too much pleasure in referring to the monstrous part of Loretta, and in carefully pronouncing the word *monster* slowly and deliberately. I was angrily calling her a monster, in a way that was transparent but not to me. I thought I was being brave and clever with my interpretations. She tolerated it but complained that I was always referring back to that incident and asked why couldn't I just leave it alone. Without realizing what was happening, I had become the sadist and she the masochist now that I was feeling strong enough to get back at her. In fact, I had come to think of her as a monster. How dare she treat me so badly, I ruminated. What an awful person she is, I thought, not realizing that my own countertransference wishes to be cared for and understood by her had brought some of my least favorite personality traits to the fore: a high-horse moralism and a judgmental quality that came disguised as interpretations. A bit of the monster in me had emerged. I have had to struggle with the countertransference issue of why obtaining Loretta's recognition was so important, why I needed her to "pin a medal of gratitude" on me.

Several months after the big enactment, Loretta lost her job. The farewell luncheon her co-workers made for her became the high point in her life, when all the attention was on her. Her depression worsened and her very constricted life became even more so, and on some days she never left the house. I had to take a very supportive stance for quite a while. And then several months later, there was a pivotal session that occurred immediately after I returned from a two-week summer vacation. She came in eager to see me and tell me about some new thoughts she had had while I was gone. "You know how you've said sometimes that there's a part of me that's like a monster? And how sometimes when we wish something bad on someone, we get worried that our wishing it will make it come true? Well, I was thinking about this. Sometimes I don't think about things you say at the time, but I sometimes do later. Well, I was thinking about this girl who came to my good-bye luncheon. I never liked her and I remember thinking at the luncheon, 'I hope your daughter miscarries in her first pregnancy.' I began to feel terrible about wishing that and worried that it might come true because of me. I couldn't live with myself. Now I know it really wouldn't happen just because I wished it, but I decided to change it anyway. I still can't stand her, but now I think 'I hope it rains on the day of your daughter's wedding.' That's not so bad, is it?" Then to my surprise she went on to tell me she was thinking of memories and how they are made. "How is a memory made?"

she asked. "Why do we remember some things, and not others? Why did I re-member only what a bitch Susan was but not the other part of her? Why are all my memories connected with food? Why don't I allow myself any pleasure in my life? Ever since you said that I've been thinking about it and you're right." Then somehow the subject of her sponge baths came up. It was August and quite hot. Her sponge baths were quick and efficient, no source of pleasure, not like the baths she had as a little girl. She recalled how in the summertime, her mother would give her a bath and pat her with baby powder. She recalled ly-ing on her bed in her pajamas, clean and smelling of soap. How nice it was hear-ing her mother and grandmother downstairs talking as they cooked and smell-ing the good smells that came wafting up. "Why haven't I ever cried for my mother?"

She went on to say that she thinks of that 11-year-old girl whose mother died and feels for her but cannot cry for her. It is as if she is someone else. She remembered looking at her mother's body at the wake and leaning down toward her face and breathing a long slow breath directly at her. She was trying to breathe life into her, and was thinking, Breathe, Mommy, breathe. Then hold-ing her breath, she looked at her mother for signs that she was breathing but there were none. "How can a body be colder even than metal?" We could begin to reconstruct why she was so angry at the funeral. Her mother's cold body meant that she had rejected Loretta's omnipotent gift of life, the worst narcis-sistic injury.

Toward the end of the session, she spoke of her stepmother, then asked, "How is it when you don't use someone's name, they're not a person to you?" (She and her stepmother never called each other by their names.) She spoke of how the Nazis made nonpersons out of the Jews. They lost their names and became just tattooed numbers. She spoke of photos of American young men who died fighting the Nazis. She was starting to cry (it was the first time I had ever seen her cry) but trying to hold it back, wondering aloud why she was crying. I replied that maybe it's easier to cry for the Jews in the Holocaust and the soldiers who died than to cry for that little girl who wanted to breathe life into her mother. As I said it, an image flashed into my mind. I was entering my mother's hospital room, but was confused to find her lying there, disconnected from the respirator and all the other tubes and wires. Was she dead? No one had told me. As I touched her still warm face, I held my breath while looking for signs of her breathing but there were none. I could feel the tears rolling down my face. Loretta saw. "Look at this," she said, "you're the one crying and I can't." "No," I said. "You can if you only let yourself. I think you're getting ready to." At this, she spoke of how guilty she came to feel when she and her father left her mother in the hospital far from home and how she enjoyed having her father all to herself. They stayed in a hotel overnight together and had a delicious meal in Howard Johnson's on the way home. All this thinking and reflection followed on the heels of a separation, one that was not only tolerable but enormously productive for her. I had gone away on vacation and I had come back.

The next week, she told me that she had had such a wonderful experience and couldn't wait to tell me. Thinking about what we had talked about, she had a sponge bath, but it was different—she took her time, using a new soap that smelled good. Afterward, she put powder all over herself and lay down on her bed naked. Her father was out so she could leave the door open to feel the lovely summer breeze. As she lay there, she thought of her mother downstairs with her grandmother, enjoying the memory of their voices and the cooking smells. As she spoke, an image formed in my mind of a fat pink cherub, sweet-smelling from soap and powder, a child who was loved.

Then a month later, still complaining of feeling sleepy all the time, she was referred by her cardiologist to a hospital sleep disorders unit for possible sleep apnea. In fact, she did have sleep apnea and was equipped with a special sleep mask to wear while sleeping, which she would not wear because it was uncomfortable and did not fit properly. No, she would not call the technician and ask him to return so she could show him what was wrong. (I had suggested this.) That was that. No, she would not allow me to speak with her doctor about her problem. She saw no reason for me to get so involved in this. It was her business, not mine. How galling it was that when I wanted to refer her to be assessed for sleep apnea, she would not go. Now, she spent a night in the sleep-disorder unit but refused to take the last step toward resolving her sleep problem. That was it. No more. I told Loretta that after all this, if she insists on this self-destructive course of action when medical help is available to her, it *was* my business because she was wasting her time and mine, and I would not see her anymore under those circumstances. I reminded her that what she was doing was within the context of a working relationship we had struggled long and hard to build together and I had very definite feelings about what she was doing to herself. "I have my limits as to what I can tolerate. If you want to continue to destroy yourself, you can do that but I do not have to sit here and watch it any longer. So you decide what you want to do."

Loretta was shocked. I had shattered her illusion of omnipotence by emphasizing that we were separate people, each with our own needs and minds, and that I would not be slave to her destructive omnipotence. This was a wake-up call to which she responded immediately and positively; she called the technician who came and discovered what the problem was and corrected it. She let me speak with her doctor. And so our work together continued, but it was still a rocky road.

Only recently she said, "You know, I wasn't always like this, hard-boiled and angry. There was a time when I had friends, I was loved, and I was happier." In time she was even able to say that she likes it that I talk with her doctors about her. It makes her feel well cared for and makes her want to take care of herself better.

THE POWER OF AFFECTIVE EXPERIENCE

In thinking about my work with Loretta and other difficult patients, the words "love," "hate," and "passion" come to mind. Passion is what a mother feels when she slaps her child after he runs into the street, and yells: "I hit you because I love you and I don't want you to get hurt." Passion is what a mother feels when she wishes to hurt her child and make him pay for her suffering. Like a mother who can both love and sometimes hate her child with a passion, we must let ourselves know and not fear the depth of passion we feel for our patients. When we can know and feel it, we can then harness and redirect it and transform it into something greater. "Sublimation is passion transformed" (Loewald 1988, p. 9) into the realm of the higher emotions. It is in those indelible moments when the patient is moved or shaken by the therapist's passion and discovers that the therapist can weather the storm, that the patient can begin to know that he can find safety, trust, and love in another person.

16

From Self-Harm to Self-Reflection

Play is the exultation of the possible.
Martin Buber, *"Brother Body,"*
Pointing the Way

Before there can be a mind, there is a body. Before there can be a representational world there is the world of eating and excreting, rocking, hair twirling, foot tapping, rhythm, skin against skin. Four decades ago Felix Deutsch tried to demystify the regressive leap from the mind to the body. This chapter discusses what occurs when the self-harming patient makes the progressive leap from the body to the mind.

To relinquish self-harm and move into a symbolic and reflective mode of experience, the paranoid-schizoid and autistic-contiguous modes of experiencing emotion that had been in the foreground must recede to the background, giving way to the depressive mode. This means that the patient must begin to relinquish his reliance on omnipotent defenses and become more rooted in his own history, created by interpreting the past (Ogden 1989). The patient must grieve what he never had in his life, what he once had but lost, what might have been but was not and was never to be, and what happened to him that should not have happened. But before there can be grief, there has to be anger, and so the anger that had been directed against himself must be metabolized and refocused. Once such internal change has occurred and the patient's self-harm poses little danger, the focus of treatment can become increasingly intrapsychic. If the therapist has not had sufficient training to conduct such a treatment, the case should be referred to one who does, adding another significant loss to be metabolized.

The therapist must accomplish several very difficult tasks (Kroll 1993). He must ascertain the patient's old patterns and help him become aware of the various ways these patterns and intrusive streams of consciousness operate in his life and their destructive consequences. Another possible task is to trace the old patterns back to the hurts, deprivations, and losses of childhood. It is still not clear to what extent the past can be reconstructed or even how necessary it is to do so for the patient to relinquish old patterns. The therapist must be willing to struggle with the patient and with himself in treatment, resisting the patient's attempts to make the therapist a source of unreasonable gratifications and a participant in playing out old traumatic issues. Finally, the therapist must provide affirmation of the patient's intrinsic worth as a human being, and as a new object must provide permission for healthy emotional growth. The therapist must maintain a real and vital presence in the therapy without gratifying the patient's regressive wishes or exploiting him.

Psychoanalytic therapy re-creates the childhood situation of being alone in the presence of the mother. The therapist must create an attachment in which the patient can play with ideas, fantasies, and symbols in the presence of the therapist, in much the same way that the child plays in the presence of the mother. When this experience becomes internalized, the patient will be able to play with ideas and fantasies in solitude, oblivious of his body. "In states of absorption, in the solitude of concentration, the other object that disappears is the body. The good-enough environment of the body can be taken for granted; it is most reliably present by virtue of its absence. It does not, as in states of desire or illness, insist on its importance. . . . A fertile solitude is a benign forgetting of the body that takes care of itself" (Phillips 1994, p. 40).

The process of helping the patient achieve the ability to reflect and be alone in solitude and separate in relation to others should be based on the therapist's understanding of the patient's personality structure combined with the therapist's creative use of himself. Freud saw psychoanalysis not only as a procedure for investigating mental processes and a method of treatment but as a collection of information leading to a new scientific discipline. Martin Bergmann (1999) said, "If we follow this line of thought, we can say that any method of treatment that is based on the data collected by the analytic method deserves to be called psychoanalysis" (p. 282).

HOW THE STORY IS TOLD

Give sorrow words; the grief that does not speak
Whispers the o'erfraught heart, and bids it break.

Shakespeare, *Macbeth*, IV:4

The circumstances under which the patient begins to tell his story are crucial. Sometimes patients feel driven to disclose memories of trauma prematurely to strangers, as the Ancient Mariner did in Samuel Taylor Coleridge's (1798) "The Rime of the Ancient Mariner." In the poem, an albatross, a seabird, had been guiding a ship safely through the frigid winds and ice storms as it approached the South Pole. In an apparent act of sin and perversity, the ancient mariner shot the albatross. Without the bird's guidance the ship lost its direction and became stuck in the ice floes. Many of the sailors lay freezing and dying of thirst. The hardier ones hung the dead albatross around the Mariner's neck to torment him with guilt and then one by one they all died, leaving the Mariner alone with the dead. Miraculously, he was rescued and returned to his native land but he was never the same man. Traumatized and haunted, the emaciated Mariner was compelled to go endlessly from land to land to tell his terrible story of anxiety, guilt, and aloneness to anyone he could capture to listen. One by one he would stop strangers in the street. Holding them emotional hostage with his feverish look, he forced them to listen to his story.

> Forwith this frame of mine was wrenched
> With a woful agony.
> Which forced me to begin my tale:
> And then it left me free.

> Since then, at an uncertain hour,
> That agony returns:
> And till my ghastly tale is told,
> This heart within me burns. [p. 23]

One could speculate that the Ancient Mariner had become addicted to the trauma response and the retelling of the story. When one is driven to tell a personal story to a person with whom there is no relationship and no trust, the story has no meaning and there is no gratification in being heard. The storyteller remains alone with his terror. It is not a story told and heard but one that is repetitively reenacted with each telling. The story thus must be told again and again, like a record stuck in the same groove. When one has suffered trauma, psychotherapy provides a way of telling the story in which the teller can find some meaning in his experience. It is a creative piecing together of the dissociated fragments of personal history. These fragments emerge initially as traumatic scenarios that are reenacted within the therapeutic relationship, the patient and therapist alternating roles as prey and predator, victim and victimizer, the neglected child and the neglectful parent. When the therapist can use words to bridge his own subjective state and that of the patient, he is verbally symbolizing and encoding overwhelming chaotic experiences for the patient. As a new object, the therapist represents a higher level of ego functioning and a higher level of being. The verbal bridge created by the therapist is like a hand extended to the patient, inviting her to cross over and develop levels of integration higher than those already reached. Using the Siamese twin paradigm, Grotstein (1981) describes the bonding between the patient and the therapist as part of the therapeutic alliance that allows for an umbilical-like "exchange transfusion" (footnote, p. 134).

When the patient can begin to use words to symbolize experiences for which symbols previously had not been possible, words can be used to form meaningful connections between events in treatment and events in the patient's past. The therapist hears the emergence of past traumatic memories, bearing witness to and validating their essential truth. This is not the same as confirming that the events of the past as the patient remembers them are true. We cannot know what did or did not occur in the past, and we cannot distinguish what actually happened from the patient's fantasied elaborations of what happened. We can, however, validate that the patient endured horrific experiences without knowing precisely what they were. We can validate that they did not deserve to get what they got in childhood and that they deserved better. We can validate their need to grieve and we can validate their anger. Working through the enactments and understanding them enables both patient and therapist to know through experience that each can be very angry with the other without destruction, abandonment, or annihilation occurring. Emotion, even very intense emotion, can be contained.

This process makes possible a communication within the patient of dissociated aspects of her inner world, thus strengthening her tenuous sense of reality by seaming together various parts of her personality to form a fabric. The patient understands not only what happened in the past but how events from the past have become a template for organizing internally all subsequent experiences and self and object representations. In this way, meaning is constructed out of overwhelming chaos and words become the means for expressing and regulating affect. Treatment can take on an increasingly intrapsychic focus as words can be used symbolically.

PLAYING AND THE CREATIVE

The creation of something new is not accomplished by the intellect but by the play instinct acting from inner necessity. The creative mind plays with the objects it loves.

Carl J. Jung, *Mysterium Coniunctionis*

In psychotherapy words can be used as playthings for patient and therapist to bat back and forth like balloons. Those who have done psychotherapy with children know that the play that goes on in the playroom is quite serious and can even be reparative. "The child's best-loved and most intense occupation is with his play or games. Might we not say that every child at play behaves like a creative writer, in that he creates a world of his own, or, rather, re-arranges the things of his world in a new way which pleases him? It would be wrong to think he does not take that world seriously; on the contrary, he takes his play very seriously and he expends large amounts of emotion on it" (Freud 1908, pp. 143–144). When a fearful child sits in my playroom and cannot begin to play, I know that if I gently tap a balloon or toss a ball toward him and he returns it, there is some ability to play, but if he cannot respond playfully the immediate therapeutic task is to help him become able to play. Similarly, in psychoanalytic psychotherapy the consulting room serves as the therapeutic playground, in which the therapist's playful engagement of the patient and the patient's emerging ability to embrace playfully the freeing possibilities of treatment are significant turning points (Sanville 1991). Playing is a form of symbolic communication in which there exists the dialectic of reality and fantasy (Ogden 1994). Play is the ability to invest chosen external phenomena with dream meaning and feeling; this is what the world of transference, the world of literature, music, the arts, and other creativity, and the world of the child have in common. Play is a way of escaping momentarily from reality or changing reality to something better. Freud (1908) stated:

> The opposite of play is not what is serious but what is real. In spite of all the emotion with which he cathects his world of play, the child distinguishes it quite well from reality; and he likes to link his imagined objects and situations to the tangible and visible things of the real world. This linking is all that differentiates the child's "play" from "phantasying."
>
> As people grow up, then, they cease to play, and they seem to give up the yield of pleasure which they gained from playing. . . . What appears to be a renunciation is really the formation of a substitute or surrogate. In the same way, the growing child, when he stops playing, gives up nothing but the link with real objects; instead of playing, he now phantasies. He builds castles in the air and creates what are called daydreams. [pp. 144–145]

Winnicott (1971), a pediatrician and psychoanalyst, took Freud's (1914a) idea of "the transference as a playground" and developed it further, based on his observations of many children and their mothers. He defined psychoanalysis and psychotherapy as a kind of play used in the service of communication with oneself and others, with psychotherapy conducted in the overlap of the two play areas, that of the patient and that of the therapist. "If the therapist cannot play, then he is not suitable for the work. If the patient cannot play, then something needs to be done to enable the patient to become able to play, after which psychotherapy may begin. . . . It is in playing and only in playing that the individual child or adult is able to be creative and to use the whole personality, and it is only in being creative that the individual discovers the self" (Winnicott 1971, p. 54). Playing occurs in the potential space, the intermediate area that lies between reality and fantasy in which self experience is created and recognized. It is a metaphor for the state of mind in which the baby "begins to be" (Winnicott 1971). Much of the work of treatment consists of building this potential space, the "space in which we are creative in the most ordinary sense of the word . . . the space in which we experience ourselves as alive and as the authors of our bodily sensations, thoughts, feelings, and perceptions" (Ogden 1989, p. 200). In treatment, reverie is simultaneously a personal and private creative event and an intersubjective one (Ogden 1997). Reverie is

> an experience that takes the most mundane and most personal of shapes. These shapes, especially early on in the process of moving toward verbal symbolization of reverie experience (and we are most of the time early on in the process), are the stuff of ordinary life—the day-to-day concerns that accrue in the process of being alive as a human being.
>
> Reveries "are things made out of lives and the world that the lives inhabit. . . . [They are about] people: people working, thinking about things, falling in love, taking naps . . . [about] the habit of the world, its strange ordinariness, its ordinary strangeness" (Randall Jarrell speaking about Frost's poetry). They are our ruminations, daydreams, fantasies, bodily sensations, fleeting perceptions, images emerging from states of half-sleep, tunes and phrases that run through our minds, and so on. [p. 568]

When the patient and therapist can tolerate the experience of being adrift, of playing with words and meaning without feeling pressured to make immediate use of them (Ogden 1997), unconscious constructions are generated in the interplay of each of their unconscious lives. It is in the potential space where the therapist can make use of his own and his patient's "overlapping states of reverie," knowing when to be silent to receive the patient's communications as he free associates and knowing when to communicate what is in his own mind to the patient. This communication is a variant of Winnicott's written squiggle game, but this one is primarily verbal, allowing for easy communication between patient and therapist as they each quickly shift among autistic-contiguous, paranoid-schizoid, and depressive positions (Boyer 1997). Whether the patient is a child playing on the floor with toys or an adult sitting or lying down, he must be allowed the freedom to relax and rest in order to communicate a flow of ideas, thoughts, impulses, sensations, and images, and the therapist must relax enough not to intrude with premature interpretations. As Winnicott (1971) said,

> There is room for the idea of unrelated thought sequences which the analyst will do well to accept as such. . . . Perhaps it is to be accepted that there are patients who at times need the therapist to note the nonsense that belongs to the mental

state of the individual at rest without the need even for the patient to communicate this nonsense, that is to say, without the need for the patient to organize nonsense. . . . The therapist who cannot take this communication becomes engaged in a futile attempt to find some organization in the nonsense, as a result of which the patient leaves the nonsense area because of hopelessess about communicating nonsense. . . . The therapist has, without knowing it, abandoned the professional role . . . by bending over backwards to be a clever analyst, and to see order in chaos. . . . My description amounts to a plea to every therapist to allow for the patient's capacity to play, that is, to be creative in the analytic work. The patient's creativity can be only too easily stolen by a therapist who knows too much. It does not really matter, of course, how much the therapist knows provided he can hide this knowledge, or refrain from advertising what he knows. [pp. 55–57]

During these moments of such supreme understanding, early pathological experiences can be relived, understood, and repaired. It is in the potential space where the patient becomes able to tell his story in a way that creates meaning, to construct his history, the intertwining of "the consciously symbolized past and the unconscious living past" (Ogden 1989, p. 193). It is in the process of playing that the patient becomes acquainted with his true self and feels the most alive. That is, the creativity is in the process of creating the self and not in the finished product.

Creativity does not require inherent talent or artistic giftedness. It is a process, not unlike sculpting, of carving away at solid matter to find the real self that has been embedded within. It is when the creative self appears in this unintegrated state of the personality that the therapist can reflect it back to the patient, and through the process of working through (Freud 1914b), the patient integrates it into his personality, which eventually "makes the individual to be, to be found; and . . . enables himself . . . to postulate the existence of the self" (Winnicott 1971, p. 64). This transitional space is a paradoxical shared skin (McDougall 1989) or permeable membrane between patient and therapist. The therapist, both by fostering the patient's ability to play with ideas and fantasies and reflecting this creative part of him back to him, fosters the patient's sense of health, aliveness, and separateness.

The self-harming patient has a lot in common with the child who cannot play. He does not communicate his feelings or intentions; he suffers a failure of relatedness, and may engage in repetitive, often rhythmic behaviors (rocking, hair twirling and pulling, foot tapping) that are self-perpetuating (Sanville 1994). Like the child who cannot play, the self-harming patient must be lured away from this mad fixation in whatever way we can imagine—with music, rhythmic activity, or other activities that can stimulate the senses pleasurably (Mahler 1952). Playing with poetry, art, drama therapy, dance, jokes and humor all are ways through which the beginning of a reflective self can emerge. The patient may begin to discover who he is.

PLAYING WITH SECRETS

Where is your Self to be found? Always in the deepest enchantment that you have experienced.

Hugo von Hofmannsthal

A life of secret self-harm may be precious, a valuable alternative to suicide or homicide and a means of survival. Even in the most extreme case of false self compliance, says Winnicott (1971), "Hidden away somewhere there exists a secret life that is satisfactory because of its being creative or original to that human being" (p. 68).

Secrets can be embedded in the mind or under the skin. In her novel *Stones from the River*, Ursula Hegi (1994) wrote about the secrets of numerous German citizens in a small town in the years before and during the Holocaust: a married woman's clandestine rendezvous, the sexual secrets of others, what people would not let themselves know or ask about their role in the Holocaust. These secrets allowed them to live with themselves, but with secret guilt and shame.

> Her mother pushed her skirt aside and exposed her left knee. Here," she said and guided Trudi's hand across her kneecap. "Feel this." . . . "Harder." . . .
>
> Deep below the warm skin she did feel something—like uncooked kernels of rice—shifting under her fingers. She glanced up into her mother's eyes; they revealed such anguish that she thought she should look away, but she couldn't. "It's gravel, " her mother whispered. "From when I fell. . . . Emil Hesping's motorcycle."
>
> Carefully, the girl skimmed her fingers across her mother's knee. It was smooth; the skin had closed across the tiny wounds like the surface of the river after you toss stones into the waves. Only you knew they were there. [pp. 30–31] . . .
>
> Some people had sins attached to them like second skins, even the sins of their parents. Like Anton Immers, the butcher. . . . Everyone in town knew that he had been born three months after his parents' wedding. That meant sin. . . . That skin of sin—the town wouldn't let the people take it off entirely even though everyone pretended it was not there. The town knew. Except for those sins that penetrated the skin and remained secrets—then the town didn't exactly know what had happened except that whatever had happened had changed that person. Like the bits of gravel under Gertrud Montag's left knee. They had stayed there, a reminder to no one else unless she gripped your hand and guided your fingertips across the raised bumps below her skin, saying, "There, feel this?" [pp. 86–87] . . .
>
> Her mother had initiated her into the power of secrets. By taking Trudi's hand and pressing it against her knee, she'd transfused her with the addiction to the unspoken stories that lay beneath people's skins. [p. 153]

Keeping a secret from oneself can be a way of coming to recognize some things. As Adam Phillips (1994) said, "The profoundest way of recognizing something, or the only way of recognizing some things . . . is through hiding them from oneself" (pp. 16–17). Masud Khan (1978) proposed that having a secret or secret life sometimes provides a potential space in which the threatened ongoing life of a child can be sustained intact. Allowing a patient the privacy to have a secret in the treatment can create an atmosphere of mutuality that can ultimately enable the patient to share the secret with the therapist. The secret may be in the form of private jokes, secret dissociated thoughts and memories, or secret rituals. Ritual is about remembering. "The whole point of ritual is remembering. . . . [Rituals] fix things in time; they work like primitive record-keeping, tying knots in strings. . . . Time is the string, rituals the knots" (Prose 1997, p. 114). To communicate secret rituals is to begin to communicate secret memories, often leading to memories of loss, neglect, or abuse. What helps the patient begin to disclose secrets is for the therapist to be open and forthright.

June was the previously discussed patient who had serious problems with dissociation, projection, and projective identification. She had the persistent thought I did not want her in the office with me, traced back to feeling that her depressed mother, who had cut herself, had been cutting June out of her life. Her mother would show June the cuts, but June felt she could not say or feel anything about it; only her mother was allowed to have feelings. There were lots of secrets at home, many having to do with her mother's illness and hospitalizations. June never knew when she came home from school if her mother would be there or if she might have been taken away to a hospital. June was told little about her mother's illness and knew not to ask. At times June's treatment reminded me of the aboriginal dreamtime, as depicted in the film *Walkabout*. A walkabout is the aboriginal ritual of self-discovery in which time and space are bent, and reality is malleable as the person walks about. Sometimes metaphorically and sometimes literally, June walked about disconnected and dissociated in the treatment room, and I tried metaphorically to walk about, following her route and finding ways to connect with her. I will try to convey something of the feeling of what it was like to work with June in this way.

Walking from the waiting room to my office, June peeked in the door to my playroom, which had been left ajar. A quick secret look. "That's where I work with young children," I told her. Not a secret. At this, she let her gaze linger on the toys, dollhouse, crayons. I said, "It looks like you would like to play." (Retrospectively, I remembered that she had enjoyed playing with her mother before her mother became so ill, but I was not conscious of that during the session.) She entered the office, eyes darting about, up, down, sideways, like a bird, looking for what had changed the slightest bit about the room or me since last time. (Later on, when June could reflect about her dissociation and its defensive functions, she supplied the bird metaphor. "I had this nervous birdy way, hopping around from one thing to another.") A bird walkabout or hop-about.

Secret looks, my desk, envelopes, mail, from whom, what what what? Secret information. Eyes dart to my feet, then up. I saw. She knows, she laughs anxiously. A secret exposed. "My feet," I say. "Your shoes," she responds. "My shoes?" "They're new. I haven't seen them before." "Yes, they're new." "You take care of yourself. You went shopping." "Yes." "They're nice. Maybe I'll get a pair like that, too." "OK." More laughter, not so anxious. "We'll be like the Bobbsey twins. . . . You do remember the Bobbsey twins, don't you?" I nod. Then, a secret sideways look to sneak a peek at the title of the book sitting next to me. I held the book up, cover facing her. "Here, take a look," I said, showing it to her. She laughs (secret exposed again!), reads the title aloud, asks if it is good, and says, "Maybe I'll read it too." I say that she seems to like us doing the same thing and seems to think my way is the way she should be. She replies that if I'm reading something it must be good to read; if I'm wearing something it must be the right thing to wear. Her eyes go to the wall. "You need a paint job." "Yes," I say. "So why don't you get it painted?" "In time." "You said that three months ago." "I guess so. You want me to paint my office?" "Yes, of course. What will people think?" "I don't know. What do *you* think about it?" "I think that you don't care enough about what things look like. If the walls look shabby, people will think you're a shabby therapist." (She's becoming indignant.) "And what's more, your plants are withering outside. They look terrible; you don't take care of them. If you take care of your patients the way you take care of your plants, people will think you're a terrible therapist." I say: "If you need a gardener, you don't look for a therapist." She laughs, pauses, and tosses back, "If you need a therapist, you don't look for a gardener. . . . [laughing] Is this one of those Zen poems, you know, the sound of one hand clapping or whatever it is?" We both enjoy the laugh.

She is quiet, relaxed, as I am, too. Then, suddenly, her eyes dart to the memo spindle, voice shrill: "That thing should not be here. Why do you have it? What do you do with it?" "What might I do with it?", I ask. She does not know but says it's not safe. "It seems dangerous to you?" I ask. "Of course, get rid of it. I don't like it here." "Maybe I might stick myself with it? Or you?" "Who knows what you might do!" "You're frightened I might hurt myself all of a sudden the way your mother did, or maybe hurt you." "Yes, that's what I think. You can never know what someone might do. Never!" I ask, "Do you really think I might do either of those things?" She is very anxious, leaning forward, "You could; you might; it's possible. How can I know what to expect?" I say that of course anything is within the realm of possibility, but please, think for a minute—did she really think I would? Silence a moment, then no, she did not think I would. She relaxed visibly, then asked if I wanted her to leave. "Always sure I want to get rid of you. Maybe you're having a nasty thought about me?" A moment later, she stood up, saying she had to go to the bathroom. "Before you leave the room, can you tell me what you're thinking or feeling, what's making you feel you have to go this very moment?" "No, I'm on a diet, I'm drinking a lot of water, I have to pee a lot. And I have to go right now. I'm not lying." She darted out to the bathroom and returned moments later. "I'm back. Surprised?" "No, I'm used to you running away for a bit and then returning. It seems to make you feel better." "Yes, sometimes I just have to get away from you. It's too much. When I can get away, then I can come back." "I'm glad you did. And I'm glad you told me how you need to do this. I think I'm understanding better how you need to get away from me, and I wonder if also maybe you wanted to get rid of me by peeing me away down the toilet?" "What an absolutely disgusting thing to say! [Long pause] Do you really think so?" I shrug: "It's a thought." A moment or two of silence passes before a slow smile inches across her face, and she says, "Now, wouldn't it be wonderful if we *could* pee people away?" And so we could begin to explore the many ways she has invented to keep herself from knowing what she really knows, how her dissociation allows her to disavow what she knows to be true.

PLAYING WITH WRITING, DRAWING, MUSIC

Writing and other creative activity is a way of being one with one's mother and repairs the experience of the infant who has lost touch with his mother (Freud 1930). In the creative act, one feels held and contained in the world. "We cannot fall out of this world. That is to say, it [the 'oceanic feeling'] is a feeling of an indissoluble bond, of being one with the external world as a whole" (Freud 1930, p. 65). "Writing was in its origin the voice of an absent person; and the dwelling house was the substitute for the mother's womb, the first lodging, for which in all likelihood man still longs, and in which he was safe and felt at ease" (p. 90). It is writing or other creativity that keeps many people from succumbing to depression.

Getting patients to write about their feelings is a very helpful adjunct to treatment, as it promotes access to their inner life and free association. But just as in free association, it is difficult for them to get over their self-consciousness and self-censorship. Many are afraid the journal or notebook will be read by someone else, or they obsess about grammar, spelling, and writing style, worrying that it will not be good enough. Yet when patients do get beyond this thin-skinned narcissism, often when pushed to do so by very painful affect that they are motivated to contain, and they finally write, they often are surprised to find it enormously helpful. Things start to become clearer and make sense; connections are made. Many alexithymic patients have great difficulty in writing about their emotional states because they do not have the words to use to identify them. Using a chart that depicts various emotional states in cartoon form can be a most useful aid in acquainting them with a range of emotional states. For some, nonverbal forms of expression like art, dance, or music may serve as precursors to using words expressively.

Many an adolescent girl has come to journal writing or diary keeping on her own as a means of being with herself, keeping herself company when alone, and finding out who she is. Today "writing a life" workshops for women have become popular for good reason. Writing helps one to know oneself and to know that one has a self. In a memoir essay, writer Cynthia Ozick (1996) wrote: "I am incognito. No one knows who I truly am. The teachers in P.S. 71 don't know. . . . A writer is dreamed and transfigured into being by spells, wishes, goldfish, silhouettes of trees. . . . A writer is buffeted into being by school hurts . . . but after awhile other ambushes begin: sorrows, deaths, disappointments, subtle diseases, delays, guilts, . . . and then one day you find yourself . . . writing this, an impossibility, a summary of how you came to be where you are now" (pp. 112–115). Writers, often struggling with mood disorders and other emotional problems, know that to write one's thoughts and feelings can create one's own holding environment (Jamison 1994). Keeping a journal of behavior, moods, life experiences, and thoughts can be a powerful adjunct to psychotherapy. It can help to contain impulses and emotions, and make thoughts and feelings more real to the writer. In *The Courage to Heal: A Guide for Women Survivors of Child Sexual Abuse* (Bass and Davis 1988), women are asked to write about their experiences as a tool for healing. Writing can become a better and more reliable "friend" than eating, purging, cutting, or drinking:

> Writing is an important avenue for healing because it gives you the opportunity to define your own reality. You can say: This did happen to me. It was that bad. . . .
>
> One handy thing about writing is that it's almost always available. At three in the morning, when you're alone or you don't want to wake your partner, when your friends are out of town, when your counselor's answering machine is on and even the cat is out prowling, your journal is there. It's quiet, cheap, and portable. A journal can help you figure out how you feel, what you think, what you need, what you want to say, how you want to handle a situation, just by writing it through. [p. 27]

Many of the newsletters for abuse survivors advise their readers to write or draw or paint their experiences, and the newsletters publish journal excerpts, letters, and drawings. Writing exercises are an integral part of *Understanding Self-Injury: A Workbook for Adults* (Trautmann and Connors 1994), *Self Abuse Finally Ends* (Conterio and Vaughan 1989), *Why Weight? A Guide to Ending Compulsive Eating* (Roth 1989), *Transforming Body Image* (Hutchinson 1983), and *Bodylove* (Freedman 1988). It is of no importance whether what is written or drawn has any artistic or aesthetic value; what matters is the transformation of hidden destructive thoughts and feelings into creative symbolic expression.

One patient, in both individual psychotherapy and in my therapy group for compulsive eaters, was struggling to write but resisted it terribly. Motivated to change this, she asked during her individual session if she could write with me present. The idea came from her; it had not occurred to me. She thought it might help her for me to be there; it might feel safer in my presence than writing alone and being all alone with the feelings she was so frightened of feeling. It brought to my mind that the child who can play in the presence of the mother can then go on to play by herself. She felt free enough to improvise and seemed to know what she needed from me. I suggested she write about the particular issue in which she was stuck, and sat there with her while she wrote. There was no hesitation, and five minutes of writing unleashed grief and facilitated the working through of unresolved mourning. Seeing the words on the page made the feelings real to her, and once they were written, then they could be spoken. Since then I have felt freer to improvise and use writing in the session in this way with some patients who resist it. Sometimes I may need to begin a sentence about a particular issue and the patient will go on to complete the sentence, adding others. One patient said of writing in the session, "Sometimes when the words won't come out of my mouth, they just can glide off my pen. And when they do that, then they *can* come out of my mouth." Patients who can do that, I have found, often can then write when alone. They imagine my presence or remember writing in my presence and it enables them to proceed.

To Freud and his followers, improvisation was more the domain of artists than scientists, and they worked very hard for psychoanalysis to be considered a science. But we must remember that psychoanalysis is also an art, which, at the beginning, "had no texts, no institutions, and no rhetoric. . . . The first practitioners of psychoanalysis were making it up as they went along. Psychoanalysis, that is to say, was improvised . . . [it] began then, as a kind of virtuoso improvisation within the science of medicine; and free association—the heart of psychoanalytic treatment—is itself ritualized improvisation . . ." (Phillips 1994, pp. 3–4).

PLAYING WITH THE DARK SIDE

Robert Crumb, the underground cartoonist who created the "Keep on Truckin'" logo, the cover of Janis Joplin's "Cheap Thrills" record album, and Fritz the Cat, is known for his ugly, violent, and sadistic images of women and racial minorities. In *Crumb*, a feature-length documentary about his life and work by Terry Zwigoff, we get a glimpse into his psyche and hear revelations about his dark sexual obsessions and the creative process. What is so striking about these revelations is that as disturbing as they are, there is something comforting about them, because we realize that if Crumb were not creating these ugly symbols of his violent and sadistic wishes, he might be enacting them. His work seems to function as a sublimation (Freud 1905a), in which his sexual and aggressive drives become deflected from their original aims or objects to more socially valuable ones. Called "the Breughel of the twentieth century," critics have recognized Crumb as an extraordinary and iconoclastic talent. His work has found its way into New York's Museum of Modern Art and other museums and has been reprinted in costly fine art editions.

The film is also the story of the remarkably pathological Crumb family. There is a tyrannical father and a mother living, in Robert's words, in a house "out of *Whatever Happened to Baby Jane?*" His elder brother Charles, a witty, smart, and talented artist, was a depressive who killed himself a year after the film was completed. And younger brother Maxon, also an artist and a self-admitted molester, meditates on a bed of nails while consuming a lengthy string he has to pass through his gastrointestinal tract every few weeks. Crumb described himself as a "nerd": "As a teenager, there was no place where I fit in at all. I saw no hope of ever connecting with anything. The instant I realized I was an outcast, I became a critic, and I've been disgusted with American culture from the time I was a kid. I started out by rejecting all the things that the people who rejected me liked, then over the years I developed a deeper analysis of these things. . . . At least I hate myself as much as I hate anybody else." He could have followed in the path of the boys responsible for the massacres at Littleton, Colorado, or Jonesboro, Arkansas. What seemed to be Robert's saving grace were his creativity and humor.

The act of creating these images seemed to gratify destructive and self-destructive wishes and impulses. When confronted about his artistic and social responsibility in creating such grotesque images of women (headless female sex objects or a woman whose head is stuffed into a toilet), Crumb responded, "I have this hostility toward women, I admit it. It's out in the open. I have to put it out there. Sometimes I think it's a mistake . . . but somehow revealing that truth about myself is somehow helpful. I hope it is. Maybe I shouldn't be allowed to do it, maybe I should be locked up and my pencils taken away from me." When asked about how it happens that he creates such disturbing images, Crumb said that he is constantly drawing, that it is something that he needs to do. "If I don't draw for awhile, I get crazy and suicidal. . . . I don't work in terms of conscious messages. It has to be something I'm revealing to myself while I'm doing it." In other words, he seems to go into a state of reverie, and ends up drawing what he needs to draw to the attention of his self. His drawing pen is his voice. His wife said that when she met him he did not speak and was virtually autistic: "The only voice he had was his pen."

Interestingly enough, his pen and how he used it served as a displaced display of phallic power. He explained how this came about, stating "When I was five or six I was sexually attracted to Bugs Bunny. I cut out this Bugs Bunny from the cover of a comic book and carried it around with me. I'd take it out and look at it periodically and it got all wrinkled up from handling it so much that I asked my mother to iron it." As he matured, women regarded him as the quintessential nerd and wouldn't talk to him. But when he became a celebrity artist, women suddenly started pursuing him. As Crumb observed: "I thought that if I was sensitive, girls would like me more and be impressed by the fact that I could draw. But they liked these cruel, aggressive guys and not me. Later I learned they do want you to be sensitive and tender toward them, but a real bastard out there in the world. . . . Women are susceptible to power, any display of power and 'Oh, who's that man over there who's being so obnoxious and arrogant? He's so interesting.' . . . So art became my method, you know, 'I'll show them, I'll become famous.'"

PLAYING WITH HUMOR

At the height of laughter, the universe is flung into a kaleidoscope of new possibilities.

Jean Houston

Playing with what is comical is a wonderful way to lessen some of the resistance to treatment. When the patient can make a joke or laugh at something humorous, he is beginning to overcome an obstacle to enjoying healthy pleasures and to remembering. The joke, said Freud (1905b), is the most ingeniously efficient way of rescuing our pleasure from the unconscious obstacles that stand in the way of pleasure. Jokes allow us to say what we might otherwise not be able to say, to express forbidden aggressive or sexual thoughts or feelings. Through humor, the patient can make his enemy, who looms large in his mind, a smaller, more inferior being and thus have the pleasure of overcoming him. Playing with humor can weave even greater webs of attachment between patient and therapist, as one enjoys the joke of the other. Expressing forbidden thoughts or wishes toward the therapist in the form of a joke or witticism is often the precursor to the ability to own them and to state them directly.

PLAYING WITH DREAMS

Dreams, by their very nature, invite a certain playfulness since their meanings are not inherent but have to be attributed by the dreamer, with or without the help of interpreters.

Jean Sanville, *The Playground of*
Psychoanalytic Therapy

Dreams are "private playthings" (Sanville 1994, p. 167), existing as potential space. Dreams can be kept a secret from others and even from the self, or can be secrets the patient can choose to unlock with the help of a therapist. In dreaming we think in pictures, very incomplete ways of becoming conscious (Freud 1923). Images are the language of dreams but a language that is private to the dreamer. Not only the visual sense but the senses of smell, hearing, touch, and kinesthesia can be incorporated into the dream in a private language constructed by the patient. When the patient shares the images from the dream with the therapist, he must use a very different kind of language, using words that are accepted by his culture. The patient can begin to convey the contents of his inner world, individually constructed images, using socially determined words and language proper, to represent what is signified by the dream images (Sanville 1994).

PLAYING WITH THE BODY

With the emergence of a sense of self, the psyche develops by the "imaginative elaboration of somatic parts, feelings and functions" (Winnicott 1958a, p. 244), and in time the body is felt by the individual to form the center of the imaginative self. Just as the infant plays with his body to experience it as separate and different from that of the mother, the patient who is coming to find himself an integrated self will need to play with the adult body to experience it as his or her own and to form a positive body image.

Playing with oneself is a colloquialism for masturbation, and masturbation certainly can be a way of playing with one's body to experience ownership of the body. For patients who have had a history of sexual abuse or who fear sexual pleasure as something potentially dangerously out of control, the experience of controlling their own sexual pleasure through masturbation can be a safe way to begin to enjoy their sexuality without fear or humiliation. Other ways of playing with the body include dance, yoga, sports, exercise, and physical games, all of which help the person experience the body as strong, competent, and a source of pleasure. Being touched and touching are fundamental modes of human interaction, and increasingly, many people are seeking out their own "professional touchers" and body work teachers—chiropractors, physical therapists, Gestalt therapists, Rolfers, the Alexander technique and Feldenkrais practitioners, massage therapists, and martial arts and T'ai Chi Ch'uan instructors—to aid in their healing process. These are somatopsychic approaches to human change, using movement and touch to affect psychological functioning (e.g., body image). The body-oriented approaches are based on a principle that is becoming more obvious to researchers: "For every mental 'problem' or 'knot', there is a corresponding bodily 'knot', and vice versa since, in fact, the body and the mind are not two" (Pruzinsky 1990, p. 303, quoting K. Wilbur, *The Spectrum of Consciousness*). That is, psychic conflict, guilt, shame, unresolved grief all can be lodged in the body as body memories, and when the site of the psychic difficulty is deeply touched through massage or other manipulation, it can not only release the physical pain but also make the psychic pain accessible.

There has always been controversy over the use of touch in psychotherapy, primarily over the question of whose needs is the touch serving, the patient's or the therapist's. In today's litigious climate in which therapists and teachers have been accused of sexual molestation, clinicians have become virtually phobic about touch and any body-oriented work in treatment, inadvertently reinforcing the mind–body dichotomy that is exaggerated in self-harming patients. There may be times in psychotherapy when restrained forms of physical contact are needed to sustain the treatment (McLaughlin 1995). For example, self-cutters bear the scars of their pain, which often evoke painful responses from others. When a patient feels ugly and repulsive, it can be remarkably healing when another looks at and touches those scars with compassion. Cindy (1995) wrote about the effect on her of her therapist touching her scars. She said that after 21 years of self-injury, mainly cutting, her body is incredibly scarred. She has explored plastic surgery and found that her only option is skin grafts, which would improve her appearance only minimally. Nonetheless, she decided it was time to join the real world, and began wearing short sleeves but has gotten hurtful looks and comments from friends, family, and strangers that make her despair of being anything other than a freak.

> People stop on the street to get a better look. . . . store owners . . . stare, throw my change at me so they don't have to touch me and ask me to leave because I'm making the other clients "uncomfortable" . . . . My therapist touches me. She hugs me and she will actually touch my scars and I see compassion and understanding, not revulsion and disgust. . . . I think I made the right decision about skin grafts. I'm not going to have them done. I think my therapist is right and the work for me is internal. I need to feel better about myself, and with the love and respect that I get from my therapist I find myself healing and becoming more of a whole person. . . . That is my goal. To be with anyone . . . and not feel like a freak. [Cindy 1995, pp. 8–9]

If we want to help our patients become connected to what is going on inside them, we need to help them become connected not only to emotional states but to somatic states as well. Somatopsychic treatment that uses direct touch can have a depth and potency that can have a great therapeutic impact. When the patient is assured that this kind of work is free from infringement, that sexual contact is clearly out of bounds, and that the patient can say no to any intervention the body-work practitioner proposes, then the patient can have the experience of trust and physical touch in the context of a controlled respectful relationship.

At the same time, there is much that can be done of a physical nature in psychotherapy by verbally directing the patient's consciousness to body processes, such as breathing, posture, hunger, or movement. The mind and body of the patient can be touched very deeply by the therapist without using physical touch; the heart can soften, breathing can slow and deepen, cold hands can warm up. And especially, when the therapist can acknowledge and try to repair the destructive consequences of his countertransferential responses, there is a power in this that touches both patient and therapist very deeply in body and mind.

PLAYING WITH IMAGES OF THE BODY

In the scenery of spring
There is nothing superior
Nothing inferior;
Flowering branches
Are by nature
Some short
Some long.

Zen Proverb

If positive experiences with grooming or shopping for clothing have not been part of the patient's experience, playing with hair, skin, and dress, much as adolescent girls do, can help the patient experience her body as a positive source of pleasure. Getting a professional haircut, facial, manicure, or pedicure involves being touched in a nonintrusive way that the patient can control. Experimenting with hair styles, clothing, or cosmetics can promote a sense of individuation. For those who have neglected their medical and dental care, selecting a physician or dentist and arranging for checkups and treatment also contribute to the sense of their bodies being worth caring for. Such experiences are more important than we might think for those whose experiences have been touch deprived or involved intrusive touching.

The most difficult and crucial aspect of treating self-harming patients is altering the negative body image. Even when there has been much significant change in terms of ego structure and symptom reduction, the remaining body image difficulties leave these patients especially vulnerable to recurrences of illness or to maintenance of the illness at a subclinical level. The treatment of body image disturbance involves more than the working through of historical material related to body hatred and understanding the projections of negative feelings onto the body. It requires developing and strengthening alternative, more adaptive body schemas by effecting real changes in the negative internalized representations of the physical self and in the projections of chaotic or overwhelming feelings onto their bodies. Guided imagery and cognitive-behavioral techniques are ways of playing with internalized representations of the body that can be used to help patients develop alternative positive body schemas. Guided imagery can be a most powerful tool in altering body image because it can arouse an affective response easily and quickly. Through the induction of a light trance state, the patient can circumvent his defensiveness and resistance to gain access to preverbal material. Through this process, newer, kinder mental patterns can be created (Hutchinson 1983) that serve to override old "tapes" or rewrite old scripts. Through cognitive-behavioral methods, the new body schemas can be charted by the patient on a continuum, which can help shift dichotomous absolute beliefs to more balanced differentiated beliefs about the body. They can also look for positive ideas about their bodies and record them in logs.

For example, in my treatment group for women with compulsive eating problems, a powerful guided imagery is the Fat/Thin Fantasy (Ohrbach 1982), in which the patients are guided to imagine themselves at a party. They are instructed to pay attention to how they are behaving, noting their behavior with men and then with women; whether they are on-lookers or participants at the party; whether they approach people or wait for others to approach them; what they are wearing; how they have done their hair and makeup, whether they move freely or self-consciously; how they feel inside; and what kinds of thoughts run through their minds. Then they are asked to imagine themselves fatter than they have ever been in their lives, and to note all the above aspects of their experience of being at the party. Then they are asked to imagine themselves as being at their ideal size at the party, and once again, to note all the above aspects of their experience of being at the party. They have the opportunity to see not only how being fat hinders them from enjoying themselves at the party, which most of them already know, but also how being fat serves defensive functions. Some are able to voice for the first time that their fat serves as a protective buffer from unwanted sexual attention because men don't want fat women. When I challenge this distorted cognition by noting that many fat women do get and enjoy sexual attention, and then ask why they could not simply say no to a man, then they become relatively open to receiving my interpretation that perhaps the fat protects them, not from the man's sexuality but from experiencing their own sexuality, which might become aroused. At that point, one or two might say that they have been using their weight so long to keep men away that they never developed a sense of their own sexuality and were afraid that it might become out of control, that they might have sex with any man who wanted them. This was especially the case with a woman who had been the victim of childhood incestuous abuse. Similarly, many found that when they imagined themselves at their ideal size, they were dressed in sexier clothing, flirted, and danced, in general behaving with less inhibition than when they were at their present size or even fatter. Although some could enjoy this projected image of themselves, others found that they felt anxious about being this way because they felt sexually vulnerable and unprotected. They also noted in the visualization that other women at the party were envious, and although initially they enjoyed being the object of envy, this too contributed to their anxiety as they feared that they might lose their friends. Most of the women are in a combined individual and group psychotherapy and use their individual treatment to further explore and work through these conflicts.

Patients will need to practice guided imagery, and use the cognitive-behavioral tools repetitively in a sustained effort. Women especially are exposed to information that confirms their self-critical views of their bodies, and will need to focus a good deal of energy on the hard work of countering the powerful messages of popular culture.

RESONATING WITH PATIENTS' LANGUAGE
AND METAPHORS

A subterranean passage between mind and body underlies all analogy.
Ella Sharpe

The use of metaphor performs a particular function in the treatment of self-harming patients. Ella Sharpe, a psychoanalyst and former teacher of English literature, related the achievement of sphincter and urethral control to the contemporaneous acquisition of speech. Linguistic discharge substitutes for physical discharge and "words themselves become the very substitutes for the bodily substances" (Shahly 1987, p. 404, quoting Sharpe). For example, bulimics often swallow their anger with food, or may chew up large amounts of food to keep themselves from knowing how much they want to chew someone out. Self-mutilators may cut themselves to avoid using a rapier tongue to cut someone else. *The Cutting Edge* newsletter for self-mutilators is a play on the double meaning of "cutting" and a reference to the way these individuals live on the edge of crisis, of arousal, of the borders between life and death. A newsletter for abuse survivors is called *For Crying Out Loud*; as children they may well have been told, "What are you crying about? For crying out loud, *I'll* give you something to cry about."

The concrete referents of food and body metaphors can be used in therapy as a transitional bridge from physical discharge to symbolic understanding (Shahly 1987). Speaking to patients in a way that resonates with their own language and metaphors spins webs of attachment, linking patient and therapist in the transitional space between inner and outer reality, self and other, childhood and adult experience (Shahly 1987). The patient's metaphors are ambiguous, and the therapist's ability to resonate with them makes "psychoanalysis . . . essentially a metaphorical enterprise. The patient addresses the analyst metaphorically, the analyst listens and understands in a corresponding manner" (Shahly 1987, p. 408, quoting Arlow 1979). Davies and Frawley (1994) state, "The words chosen [for symbolic use] must be the patient's own—carefully selected, always subject to change and reformulation. The therapeutic process, like a piece of sculpture, brings the patient ever closer to a final construction with which she can feel satisfied; but the work remains 'in process' for some time. . . . Each word spoken between patient and therapist captures a piece of the patient's . . . world" (pp. 212–213).

Lillian is a 45-year-old literary-minded woman whose presenting problem on beginning treatment was her moodiness. She prided herself on her knowledge of world literature and her distinguished use of language, and disdained others less literary. She was quite heavy, and although it was clear that she used food for emotional reasons, this was something she did not want to examine. She liked to think of herself as a gourmet, and enjoyed believing that she savored food in the same way she savored language.

She began one session by talking quite animatedly of the superb food she had eaten at a wedding buffet. She had visited the buffet table several times to refill her plate, but confided that she had been careful to approach it at a different spot each time and to leave "respectable" intervals of time between each trip so as not to call attention to how much she was eating. "Had I been alone, I would have just slurped it off the table like a pig at the trough." (She pronounced it correctly, "troff".) "I had a splendid time! All my favorites were there." I was surprised at how matter-of-factly she seemed to be starting to acknowledge her overeating. She spoke of the bridal couple with biting sarcasm: "She looks like a bleached blonde anorexic without a brain in her head, and he reminded me of the Neanderthal man. What a pair!" Then she remarked equally sarcastically about a young couple who got up from their table to dance: "They were all over each other like animals." My comment that she sounded angry at the two couples was met with flat denial.

About ten minutes later her lively sarcasm had disappeared and was replaced by a slowness and dullness in her speech, and she had begun to slump in her chair. Speculating (silently) that she had fallen into a depressed mood, I asked if she had noticed that her lively mood had been replaced by something slower and duller in her speech and posture. She conceded that I was right, but could not say why. Moments later she was able to discern that she was in fact feeling depressed but did not want to speak of it; it was hard for her to speak of it, as she was feeling so tired all of a sudden. Slowly, she said in a rather dramatic literary manner, "I am in a slough of despair," but oddly enough, she mispronounced it "sloff." I pointed out that she had said she was in a "sloff" of despair. She felt embarrassed at my noting her mispronunciation and insisted that she did not know why in the world she could have so mispronounced a word she had used many times before. She did listen with interest, however, when I said that the "sloff" of despair rhymed with the "troff" she would have slurped from if others had not been present. As I expected, her interest in her misuse of language was piqued. I asked her what came to mind about "troff" and "sloff" and she recalled that she had been stuffing herself while watching couple after couple get up from their tables to dance and watching single men ask single women to dance. "Mostly thin ones but some fat ones, too." She had been feeling like a wallflower, alone and unwanted. How many weddings had she attended, burying her sorrows in mounds of food while others danced and had a good time? The question was rhetorical, she pointed out to me. She looked like a pig and ate like one and it was never going to be any different; she would always be alone stuffing herself and that's what links "troff" and "sloff" together: the pig eating from the "troff" fell into a "sloff" of despair. She has her "troff" while other women have husbands or at least the hope of having a husband. She also realized that her biting remarks about the bridal couple and the young couple dancing were her verbal expression of wanting to bite and chew up those who had what she wanted. I suggested that perhaps all the food she bit into was her body expressing angry wishes to bite. She thought about it and had the insight that so much of what she really likes are foods for biting and crunching. Why should other women have what she does not?

Mimi, age 35, came into treatment after being married a year. She was considerably overweight, wore unisex clothing, and had her hair cut as short as possible in a very unflattering style. (Later on, she told me how it bothered her that sometimes people mistook her for a man.) She wanted to stop eating in the way she was accustomed to: "inhaling" food just because it was there. She joked that she wished she could be like Bill Clinton in one specific way, and that is, not inhale (referring to Clinton's famous admission that he had smoked marijuana but did not inhale). But otherwise, she said, Clinton was a slimebucket who can't control his sexual appetite. When I said that "inhaling" was an unusual way to describe eating a lot, she told me that she also has real difficulty in inhaling sometimes because she has asthma. She also suffered from various allergies and had unusual skin sensitivities. She sometimes gets rashes that come and go, and for some reason the left side of her neck is ultrasensitive; when her husband kisses her there, she gets so excited she can't stand it. My thoughts were that one ingests food and air as an infant sucks at the mother's breast. The need for so much food, the difficulty in getting enough air, and the rashes all suggested that they were psychosomatic expressions of emotional hunger.

Mimi told me that she had always been heavy. Her mother, not much of a "touchy-feely" person, always tried to curb Mimi's eating because she told her that no man wanted a fat bride. Nonetheless, she had a boyfriend when she was 15 and recalled an incident that made her certain that this boy, whom she had trusted, must have slipped some drug into her soda to knock her out so he could rape her. Nothing else could explain how it happened that her underpants were down around her ankles and there was semen between her legs. She remembered they had been making out but had no memory at all of having intercourse with him. She never talked with him about what had occurred, and simply refused to see or speak to him. There had been an incident three years earlier in which a janitor cornered and molested her at age 12 in the vestibule of an apartment building, while her mother waited outside in the car for her. He told her she was beautiful, then pushed her into the corner, groping her breasts. She did not remember if he did anything else but remembers breaking away and running out of the building and into the car. Anxious and tearful, she told her mother what had happened. Her mother said she must be mistaken, she knew the janitor; he was a nice man and would never do such a thing. Mimi never spoke of this incident again until she began therapy. Several months after telling me about it, she returned to it to fill in the blanks, remembering it quite differently. What had really happened was that she was so happy when he told her she was beautiful that she opened her coat like a little girl to show off her pretty dress. He continued to tell her she was beautiful as he fondled her breasts and the rest of it remained a blur in her mind. But she remembered in retrospect that she had loved the feeling of someone holding her, until it started to feel different and scary and that's when she stopped remembering. She realized that she must have done the same thing with her boyfriend after going further sexually than she could acknowledge to herself. She grew up afraid of her sexuality and denying much of it until she got married. It is no wonder that sometimes when her husband kisses her neck, she becomes hyperaroused. Even now, although she enjoys her sex life, at times she will stop in the middle because the face of the janitor intrudes into her consciousness. Her conflicts about her sexuality and her hunger for love and touching had become split off and disavowed in order to keep her sexuality under control.

FROM THE LANGUAGE OF THE BODY TO SYMBOLIZATION

The world of silence without speech is the world before creation, the world of unfinished creation. In silence truth is passive and slumbering, but in language it is wide-awake. Silence is fulfilled only when speech comes forth from silence and gives it meaning and honor.

Picard

Repressed, projected, or split-off fragments of thoughts and feelings cannot be reflected upon (Bion 1962). The aim of treatment with the self-harming patient is to help her to go from using destructive activity to using her mind as a tool for self-regulation. When she can begin to use words as symbols of her experiences and memories, she feels more real in the world. Dorothy Allison (1988) wrote about the role her writing played in making her traumatic experiences real and in her transition from courting self-destruction to wanting to live. Her writing, like Robert Crumb's drawings, served as a sublimation.

There was a day in my life when I decided to live . . . but I did not know if I could. . . . I began by looking to . . . how I had become the woman I was. . . .
Every evening I sat down with a yellow legal-size pad, writing out the story of my life. I wrote it all: everything I could remember. . . .

Writing it all down was purging. Putting those stories on paper took them out of the nightmare realm and made me almost love myself for being able to finally face them. . . . I was writing for myself, trying to shape my life outside my terrors and helplessness, to make it visible and real in a tangible way, in the way other people's lives seemed real. [pp. 7–9]

REENACTMENTS AND HEALING: A PARADOXICAL CIRCULAR PROCESS

Giving up self-harm behavior is a complex circular process. When the individual can use symbolic language to understand the need for the reenactment and the functions it serves, the nature of the behavior changes from a reenactment to something else. Loewald (1960) has said that new spurts of self-development may be intimately connected with the regressive rediscoveries of oneself that occur in the controlled regressions in psychoanalysis:

Ego development is a process of increasingly higher integration and differentiation of the psychic apparatus and does not stop at any given point except in neurosis and psychosis; even though it is true that there is normally a marked consolidation of ego-organization around the period of the Oedipus complex. Another consolidation normally takes place toward the end of adolescence, and further, often less marked and less visible, consolidations occur at various other life stages. These later consolidations—and this is important—follow periods of relative ego-disorganization and reorganization, characterized by ego-regression. [p. 17]

This is important because similarly, new and progressive spurts of self-development may be intimately connected with the regressive rediscoveries of oneself that occur in the regression to self-harm. That is, the patient may continue to enact past trauma on her body, and yet in the process may discover something about herself with each episode. And so, with increasing healing, each regression to self-harm becomes more controlled, a regression in the service of self-discovery rather than a reenactment. Such is the paradoxical creativity of self-harm.

In each act of self-harm the three modes of generating experience (Ogden 1989) (depressive, paranoid-schizoid, and autistic-contiguous) exist in a dialectical relationship to each other, each creating, preserving, and negating the others. With the interaction of symbolic thought with each act of self-harm, the more primitive paranoid-schizoid and autistic-contiguous modes shift to the background and lose power as the depressive mode comes to the foreground and gains ascendance. This makes the tempo of treatment irregular, like the child's game of giant steps, in which the child may take a very large step forward, to be followed by several small steps backward. The therapist must be able to accept the patient's regressions to self-harm as temporary and inevitable, and hold the view that the journey to healing is nonlinear and circular, involving interacting progressions and regressions. This attitude, transmitted to the patient, will help to prevent relapses, which are regressions from which they do not recover. Lapses or slips are not the same as relapses. Everyone regresses to earlier patterns if there is sufficient stress, and therapists must not only be tolerant of these regressions but also help patients to accept them without judging themselves harshly for having them. When they can accept that they have slipped, this attitude serves to prevent relapse. Once they have fallen "out of the saddle," they can get past it and get back in the saddle. Without this acceptance of themselves, their destructive narcissism is likely to take control, convincing them that they are bad, unworthy and unlovable, thus fueling a true relapse to ongoing self-harm.

Developing the capacity for creating true symbols and creating meaning is not a linear process, going from the atavistic to the evolved, in a straight line from point A to point B, but a circular interacting process that transforms the self-harm from an atavistic act to an act in which the individual's body communicates to an evolving mind. The reenactment speaks to the self, and while the self-harm behavior may continue, it is experienced differently, becoming less driven, less urgent, and less necessary. It becomes less a reenactment and more a repetition about which the individual has conscious choice and control. Intense feeling, once impossible to be contained within the self, is contained. The act of self-harm becomes transformed into something less driven and more deliberate and symbolic. Giving it up can occur after a conscious decision is made to give it up, or it can simply seem to fall by the wayside. It is no longer necessary as a tool for surviving trauma and can be retired. Like the teddy bear that is not discarded but is retired to a shelf, it is there to be retrieved if and when needed. It is a slow, gradual transformation to a new way of living, quite different from the dramatic but short-lived sense of rebirth experienced after the act of self-harm. A most articulate description of this complex circular process comes from Ruta Mazelis, the founder and publisher of *The Cutting Edge*, who wrote to her readers of her own experience in giving up self-inflicted violence (SIV).

> I believe that to heal from the pain of past trauma, as well as the pain of SIV, we must first acknowledge its existence. Then, little by little, we can learn to sit with it for awhile, so that some of it may flow out and away. I do not believe that the pain of childhood trauma can be quickly nor easily transformed. The effort requires courage and perseverance, and at least some measure of self-respect and hope. I believe that, by the sheer fact that one has managed to survive, these elements are present or available to us. I hope that in sharing the pain it becomes more tolerable. I also hope that each time we bear witness to each other, including the reading of the tremendous amount of pain within the writings in this newsletter, we grow stronger by acknowledging that we are not alone in the experience of surviving. I have learned to cry and channel my outrage, rather than cut, over the despair and cruelty we have experienced. It has been a privilege to have you share your pain. Sitting with it has

been a difficult experience, and yet profoundly worthwhile. Pain can be transformed. I wish us all well on the journey in doing so. [Mazelis 1995, p. 3]

On occasion I receive requests to publish an issue of this newsletter on the topic of "how to stop SIV." I wish I could do so in the way that there are step by step directions for repairing appliances. I recognize the popularity of self-help books on the market. Some of these are useful, some not, in providing directives and lists of actions to change the particular aspects of people's lives. Certainly something of this nature can be done for SIV. I have refrained from doing so, however, because every attempt I've seen to do this leaves the topic addressed too shallowly. . . .

It is so very tempting to want to focus on stopping self-injury before understanding it. Yet there are many questions to be asked when discussing the topic. One of these is the simple but powerful, "why?" Not only "why stop?" but also "why SIV?" The importance of having at least a basic sense of why we self-injure is clear when we recognize that it is most difficult to stop something we don't understand. It is for this reason that I have declined to previously present any sort of simplified "how to stop the hurting" list. I understand the deep desire to stop the SIV—my own as well as others'. SIV brings out painful emotions and responses. It is tempting to try to eliminate them all by stopping the self-injury. My belief is, however, that even stopping the act of self-injury will not be truly healing until we attend to the reasons SIV was important in our lives to begin with.

Stopping SIV is a process, even if it occasionally appears to be an impulsive action. There are often multiple changes that lead to stopping SIV. A woman needs to expand her options and abilities for managing the reasons that led to her self-injury. Oftentimes we want to stop SIV but, regardless of how intense the desire, we cannot because there are no other outlets yet available.

As trauma survivors, many of us turn to familiar means of coping with discomfort, methods we created to manage initial traumatic experiences. Most of us did not have a varied assortment of coping skills to choose from. Many adults, traumatized as children, have not expanded their coping abilities to a great extent, but remain busy with survival. It is not uncommon to have the consequences of trauma survival be very impacting on how we manage daily life in the present. Fears, internalized shame, inexplicable guilt and/or rage are a common base from which we experience life. These are the repercussions of the past. They carry with them all the different methods we created to survive difficult times.

Trauma in the past profoundly impacts relationships on the present. If I am motivated to stop self-injury for someone else's relief, then it is important that I am aware of that intention. . . . There are times when I stopped SIV as an act of self-preservation. Perhaps the most intense of these times was when I was faced with psychiatric commitment when my SIV became known. I was told I would be forcibly hospitalized and/or medicated if I did not stop SIV. Like many other psychiatric inmates I had to feign wellness according to the standards determined by the institution and its employees to obtain my release. Mental health, in this context, was often determined by the absence of the supposed markers of the different labels I was "diagnosed" with. I readily learned to stop, or at least hide SIV to show "progress." I also altered other symptoms to facilitate my departure from an environment I found cold and often brutal as well as ignorant of my needs. I needed help to understand my SIV so that I could begin to heal those aspects of my self that were in such pain that I cut and burned and beat myself. I knew this would be a process. What the professionals needed was for me to "stop hurting myself." While behavior modification may lead to modified behavior, it does not touch the human heart and soul from which behaviors such as SIV are born. True healing of SIV did not occur for me in the context of traditional psychiatric care, but in the slowly growing understanding and respect for myself that has taken a long time to nurture. [Mazelis 1996, pp. 1–2]

This perspective really stands out to me because, time and again, what I've heard from women who live with SIV is the benefit of experiencing a healing relationship. As this newsletter has been published over the past eight years, I've come to know quite a few readers who have written to say that they no longer find it necessary or comforting to turn to SIV to manage their lives. They do not often give much credit for their healing, especially in the long term, to drugs nor other biological psychiatric interventions. The most predominant reason I'm given for healing from SIV is a supportive and freeing relationship which allows the woman to explore her SIV while accepting its existence, and then helping heal the psychic wounds from which the need for SIV stems. Once the source of the emotional pain, dissociation, self-hatred, and other reasons for SIV is acknowledged and at least begun to be healed, the need for SIV decreases. Eventually most of us no longer need it. Our lives become different enough in the present that the wounds of past traumas do not need to be managed by the physical wounds of SIV. This, of course, is a lengthy and nonlinear process. It is a process of empowerment rather than management.

Certainly very few, if any, of us desire to have SIV in our lives. Yet SIV is a crucial, although oftentimes secret tool of survival for many women. I have yet to meet a woman living with SIV whose life was emotionally secure. SIV appears in the lives of persons who are living with the repercussions of past traumas that have severely narrowed their lives. It is an option, and often a necessity, for those who have deep and open wounds from the past. Unbearable psychic injuries are not managed by normal tools. SIV serves as a tool of survival until growth can evolve the person to a new personal universe that is free from the intense sequelae of past traumas. This freedom brings with it a much greater variety of options from which to choose to manage life's difficulties.

What allows for the transition from survivor to being a person actively alive is often the presence of a guiding helper. That person is oftentimes a compassionate and knowledgeable therapist. A healing relationship can serve as a model for health, an example of the possibilities for living one's life differently. A person who can guide another from the depths of a despairing life is important indeed. This is especially crucial for those who did not experience any, or many, loving relationships in childhood, a scenario that is not uncommon in the lives of those who later turn to SIV. Of course a relationship which is powerful enough to provide for profound personal changes requires a leap of faith to enter into and considerable time and effort to develop. These are the factors that are currently being limited for many survivors who have turned to therapists to assist them in healing. Rather than an evolving spiral of growth, many people are limited to brief interactions and/or drug therapies. Survivors are being challenged to find creative ways to heal themselves outside the traditional mental health community. Certainly one can heal without interaction with mental health providers. It is, however, that those who turn to the psychiatric/psychological industry for help are finding their choices increasingly limited to treatments that do not provide long term healing.

The past fifteen months have been a time of great personal struggle for me. I have lost six family members and friends to death, and helped several others through serious illness. One beloved family member died in my arms. My scarred, but not bloody arms. As I sat down to write this editorial, I realized that despite the incredible stresses of the past year, I have not cut, burned, nor bruised myself. I have not even considered doing so. In the midst of profound grief, shock, outrage, and fear, I did not consider SIV. I did not need to. I had not made a promise to anyone, including myself, to avoid SIV. I have always believed that if I need to cut, then I need to cut. Survival always comes first. But I can also attest to the possibility of living without SIV, even in immensely difficult times. One after another, unexpectedly for most, I lost many I loved. My own healing had evolved to a place, however, wherein I did not consider SIV to help me cope with very deep and raw emotions and extremely difficult decisions. Through my own experiences of a healing relationship, by learning empathy, respect for, and trust in myself, I had arrived in this strong and powerful place. Without question, life without SIV is preferable to that with it. It was not controlling SIV that led me to the freedom that I now have, but outgrowing the need for it. I am truly grateful for all the healing relationships I have had, including that with myself, which have brought me to this new place. To say that the journey has been worth the effort is truly an understatement. [Mazelis 1998, pp. 1–2]

Along similar lines, a reader of The Cutting Edge wrote how much the newsletter has helped her by connecting her to others who harm themselves, and how the attachment to a therapist who has not insisted she relinquish her self-harm behavior has allowed her the freedom to choose a different way of living.

It's not that I want to give up cutting. . . . I want better for myself. Sometimes, I believe better is possible. As I thought this over today, I sort of grieved what I would be giving up. And I'm not sure I can do it. Is there anything else that can make me feel so alive, if even for a moment? My previous therapist, who handled many things well, put me in a hospital. . . . It wasn't my first hospitalization; it was the most pointless, the least productive. My new therapist seems to understand and he has made it my choice. It's one of the reasons I'm cutting again, yet it's been a time of tremendous growth. . . . I don't have to stop, fearing I'll be hospitalized if I don't or if I tell. (I'm always so damned honest in therapy.) This has left me free to explore, really understand the role cutting plays in coping with my life [Carla 1996, p. 8]

Another valuable description of this process comes from Catherine Taormina, whose "Song of the Brufiliac" poem (Chapter 2) elaborates on her various self-harm behaviors.

Catherine became anorectic in early adolescence and still struggles with anorexia. At age 14 she was 5'4" and weighed 90 pounds; her alarmed parents sent her to a psychotherapist and a nutritionist. As part of her treatment, her therapist suggested she keep a log of her thoughts and feelings about her various ways of harming herself. Each time she picked at or chewed her skin, she was to write down the date, time, location, whom she was with, what she was doing, what she felt and thought. She was unusually diligent and motivated to give up self-injury and did after she had completed around thirty entries. She discontinued the log but the writing, a new-found pastime continued, and as she became used to writing words on the page, she began to play with them. This resulted in her collection of dark, disturbing poems, *Chalkboard with a Bad Eraser* (Taormina 1996). She wrote:

> In a style I called warped confessionalism, this work is a portrait from and of my late adolescence. The basis of these writings are how I perceived the world as it presented itself to me and my struggle to plow through my obvious unpleasant experiences. . . . My writings functioned as therapy. My search for clarity and explanations was quenched with the appearance of Jesus Christ whose words found in the New Testament have convinced me that art is to heighten. My creepy, crawly thoughts and feelings are still present, but they have minimized. I strive, as always, for peace and harmony only now I have a foundation and an answer. I still write warped confessionally, but with a new vision.

I asked Catherine if there is something she could tell the readers of this book about this part of her healing process. She replied:

> Dear Dr. Farber,
>   I'm sorry I didn't write sooner and I should have written down the thoughts we discussed that night because maybe they would have been better. But here we are.
>   Now, I did some writing about what you wanted me to expand upon. So here it is: I think a lot. And I analyze a lot. To make sense of where and how my obsessions began I guess I'll explain it in the order in which it all happened. First, I came from a dysfunctional family. My father was physically and mentally abusive to me. He and my mother did not have a good relationship and I witnessed a lot of mental abuse between the two of them. I think and feel I internalized a lot of what was going on and I think it also forced me to think about a lot of things a child really shouldn't or normally think about. Thinking and thinking and thinking and thinking.
>   OK, next, like I explain in my Brufiliac poem, I went to the dentist for my first cavity and just as I explain, I bit my cheek (by accident) when it was numbed with Novocain, and when it wore off, I had this piece of flesh that was annoying to me and I bit that off. This did not help the healing but created a larger area that felt "uneven" inside my mouth. It sounds strange, but I would periodically continue to try to "smooth"[1] things out on

---

1. The obsessive smoothing or evening things off is typical behavior of many compulsive eaters, who use the obsession to explain how and why they consumed a great amount: "The cake had a jagged edge and I was just taking the knife to even it off. Then the other side looked funny so I had to even that off, too."

my cheek by continuing to bite off the uneven flesh. Of course it would never heal because I would never give it a chance to heal, because just when it might be almost healed, I would bite my cheek again because the uneven- ness would be annoying.

I realized and knew I would do this more often when I was given opportu- nities to think or internalize. When I was nervous, annoyed, frustrated, bored, reading, etc. Especially when my hands were not occupied, because I would use my hand to push my cheek into my teeth to bite it, and any other time my mind was not preoccupied enough and allowed me to think, "Hey, let me run my tongue over my cheek to check out the condition of it to see if any thing else is worthy of being bitten off."

After a while, I developed other "Hey, this isn't smooth, let me just smooth it out by picking it off" habits. A perpetual scab on my ear, one on my leg (the leg one went away after a year of picking, I finally picked off the scar tissue bump so "well" it was virtually smooth and I guess I was satisfied because I never picked it again, but the other habits continued), scratching my head, etc.

I also knew I didn't mind any of the pain and blood that went along with these habits. It actually at times felt good or didn't bother me. And the blood tasted OK or good coming out of my cheek. (I know it sounds kind of sick.)

All this stuff, my eating disorder, etc., made sense to me after going to a psychologist.

In fact, my therapy to rid myself of "playing with my body" involved writ- ing down every instance I went to bite or pick myself. I wanted to get rid of these habits so badly that I even forced myself to write down even when I felt the thought that I wanted to bite or pick, if my hand moved up to my cheek, or if my tongue made its way across my cheek to feel its condition and if it was good for biting. (It is very bizarre writing about this, like this for you.)

It wasn't until I had spoken with you that I actually put two and two to- gether and kind of hypothesized about the fact that the writing could have given birth to my actual creative writing. In a sense my playing with my body turned into my playing with words because just as I internalized my thoughts, and thought and bit or thought and picked at the same time, later on, I thought and wrote and thought and wrote what I was thinking about. I even started to be creative and play with words and try to create a feeling so precise with the fewest words possible. So, my habits were displaced from my body to the paper. But now it wasn't a habit, it was a healthy pleasure.

This is how I feel my writings functioned as therapy. They helped me sort out the information, my questions, my wonders, figure things out and if they didn't help me figure things out, that was OK too because I felt better about myself that I created something creative and creativity always made me feel good, and even superior. They helped me get somewhere or progress mentally, whereas my self generated therapy, that is, is picking on my body, got me just that, picking on my body.

I know you wanted something short but I think I could explain it better detailed like this.

I hope to hear from you again soon.

HOW THERAPY HEALS

To understand how therapy heals for self-harming patients as well as for all patients, we need to understand the significant interactions between patient and therapist that ultimately lead to structural change in the patient's personality. Both intrapsychic and intersubjective dimensions must be encompassed. Freud himself thought that the crucial factors in achieving treatment benefits are first, understanding and attachment, and second, integration, which bridges the gap between the two (Friedman 1978). That is, it is not understanding alone, whether intellectual understanding or emotional understanding, or the attachment to the therapist alone that is the basis for the therapeutic action of treatment, but the integration of both as seen in the transference (Friedman 1978). It is in the transference interpretation that understanding and attachment are integrated, that aspects of the therapist are introjected piecemeal. Combining the interpretation of conflict with attention to the patient's structural difficulties, or deficits, can lead to structural change (Druck 1999).

My own ideas about how therapy heals, repairs and builds ego structure have been greatly influenced by Loewald's (1960) landmark paper, "On the Therapeutic Action of Psychoanalysis." Through the therapist's empathic communication and uncovering, the patient is guided toward a new synthesis, and in the process his interest in the therapist as a separate person is elicited. A psychoanalytic psychotherapy or psychoanalysis can set ego development in motion through the therapist's making himself available as a new object. Despite the tendency of the patient to make this potentially new relationship into an old one via the transference, the extent to which a positive transference develops keeps the potential of a new object relationship alive during stages of resistance. The patient becomes interested in the therapist's mind and his thinking, and it is this interest that fuels his struggle to understand the therapist's nontransference interpretations as well, leading to ever higher levels of integration and synthesis. According to Loewald (1960), the therapeutic action comes about through the patient's wish to bridge the gap between his own ego organization and that of the therapist. Loewald suggests that the patient's struggle to bridge the gap is itself internalized and serves as a model to bridge the gap from unconscious to preconscious, the place where the "unthought known" (Bollas 1987) lives. In Joanie's case, healing and ego building began immediately, surprising both of us with the dramatic but profound shifts.

Joanie, age 30, came into treatment because she kept having impulses to cut herself. She had been hospitalized in college and had had several psychotherapies in which her therapists had tried to get her to contract that she would not cut herself. Despite the contracts she always cut herself anyway. She had not cut herself, however, in the past few years even though she very much wanted to. Her husband had told her that he could not tolerate it; because that attachment was very important to her and she feared he might leave her, she resisted her impulses. But in the past year the impulses had become more insistent. She did extremely well in therapy from the outset, so well that treatment felt like magic to her. After the first session, the impulse to cut receded and so did her schizoid quality. She began to do better at socializing at work and began questioning her own previously automatic assumption that no one could be trusted. She had a fine mind, which I challenged her to use in a new and different way. As a scientist she immediately became fascinated by the connections I helped her make and that she began making herself through journal writing. It seemed that no one had listened to her thoughts and feelings as a child, they were negated, ignored, or demeaned. The regular and reliable experience of being listened to, taken seriously, and coming to understand the connections between her thoughts, feelings, behavior, and relationships were for her the ingredients that made magic. As a child she had the ability to use language to express herself and tried to use it to communicate to her parents, but through no fault of her own, did not succeed. Having then turned to her body to express what she needed to say, she became convinced that she *had* to turn to her body this way, that there was no other way to live. When I pointed out to her that she did, in fact, have the ability to withstand the impulse, she was astounded, because she had not realized that this willingness to gut it out was both an ability she had and a choice she had made, and that she could get even better at it. She took to journal writing like a duck to water because it held the promise of making tolerating her feelings and impulses less painful and more understandable. Her writing quickly became an extension of the treatment holding environment and to her surprise, her thinking began to shift from dichotomous thinking to a tolerance for ambiguity.

Language, when it is not defensively used, says Loewald (1960), is used by the patient for communication and creative growth. "By an interpretation, both the unconscious experience and a higher organizational level of that experience are made available to the patient. . . . Language, in its most specific function in analysis, as interpretation, is thus a creative act similar to that in poetry, where language is found for phenomena, contexts, connexions, experiences not previously known and speakable" (p. 26). An interpretation can promote understanding as well as attachment. As Winnicott said, "A correct and well-timed interpretation in an analytic treatment gives a sense of being held physically that is more real (to the non-psychotic) than if a real holding or nursing had taken place" (Phillips 1994, p. 107, citing Winnicott, *Human Nature*). It is through this dialogic experience that the patient becomes attached to the therapist and can see the possibility of a new, differentiated, more real kind of satisfaction in his life and he can allow himself to want it (Friedman 1991). As Shengold (1979) said, "With successful therapy, the false identity and the as-if facade, as the emotional relationship to the analyst is allowed, can give way to a feeling of authenticity. The destructive and self-destructive robot is able to become a human being with an ability to tolerate contradictions and maintain emotional ambiguity that is so necessary for full humanity. The analyst has the privilege of assisting in the psychological rebirth of a soul" (p. 556).

Loewald's (1960) concept of the therapist as a new object echoed Freud, who referred to the analyst as a teacher, educator, and substitute parent. As a parental figure, the therapist must continually adapt himself to the patient's needs just as Benedek (1959) states the parent must continually adapt himself to the child. The therapist must use himself creatively as an analyzing and synthesizing instrument, weaving together his subjective experiences—associations, thoughts, emotions, bodily experience—with those of the patient to form a fabric, to improvise an intersubjective riff together. This is the play work, "the to-and-fro of work and play, of reflecting and experiencing that take place between the two participants" (Bollas 1992, p. 46). The analyst "must turn his own unconscious like a receptive organ towards the transmitting unconscious of his patient. He must adjust himself to the patient as a telephone receiver is adjusted to the transmitting microphone" (Freud 1912, pp. 115–116). To do this the therapist must have the ability to identify with the regressed patient in order to help free the patient's growth potential by means of understanding, empathy and interpretation. The "patient and analyst . . . become both artist and medium for each other. For the analyst as artist his medium is the patient . . . ; for the patient as artist the analyst becomes his medium. . . . As living human media they have their own creative capabilities, so that they are both creators themselves and upon each other" (Loewald 1988, p. 75).

I would suggest that just as the reciprocal interaction between mother and infant, by means of processes of introjection and identification, is a symbiotic process that creates structural change in each of the participants, so too is the reciprocal interaction between patient and therapist a symbiotic process that creates structural change in both patient and therapist. The process is fueled by the symbiotic yearnings of patient and therapist, each wanting to understand the other and to be understood by the other. The origin of the wish to understand another can be traced to the infantile yearning to get inside another human being, to be one with the mother as in utero, the oceanic experience. The less structure there is to the patient's ego and the greater his pathological narcissism, the further must the therapist bend his unconscious to the patient in empathy, and the more he must utter empathic utterances to create the holding environment. The therapist must do the bulk of the work. Over time, and as structure is built, the therapist bends his unconscious to that of the patient, but need not exert himself so much in bending, as the patient is bending his unconscious and his developing capacity for synthesis toward the therapist. It becomes more of an equal division of labor, in which the therapist listens empathically and provides empathic interpretations that the patient struggles to understand. As the integrative and synthetic functions of the patient are strengthened by the exercise of function, so too are the therapist's integrative and synthetic functions strengthened. As this occurs, the attachment bond is strengthened, resulting in greater object relatedness and empathy in both patient and therapist. Each is more real and more separate than before.

BECOMING REAL

Nowadays, more and more people come in and actually say that they don't feel alive. . . .

I remember certain people I've met in my life, like Winnicott, Allen Ginsberg, or the rebbe Menachem Schneerson. When I was with them, I felt it was okay to be the sort of person I am. With them it was okay for me to be somehow off the map, beyond the map; it was okay for there to be in life such a person as I was. In that passage [about patients feeling an endless sense of aloneness], *then, I was trying to encode, for whomever it might reach, something like a message in a bottle. Floating on the sea, it might then reach some people, who would hear the message that it's okay for them to be the sort of alone person they are. And by some miracle, by making room for such a message, some of these people, through the course of years, have tapestried out. They've found themselves situated in a larger tapestry that makes room for the sorts of being they were and are, whereas earlier there didn't seem to be any place for them.*

Michael Eigen, interviewed in Freely Associated:Encounters in Psychoanalysis with Christopher Bollas, Joyce McDougall, Michael Eigen, Adam Phillips, Nina Coltart

When the patient has nobody to whom he can turn for soothing, it feels as if he has no body. So to attack his own body means that there is a body there, that there is somebody for him. To be somebody without having to attack the body means using words with someone who can listen, so that meaning can be created. It is a way of making real a life that had seemed unreal and was lived in an unreal or dissociated way. The patient becomes real in the relationship with the therapist in the same way that a toy becomes real to a child.

"What is REAL?" asked the Rabbit one day, when they were lying side by side near the nursery fender, before Nana came to tidy the room. "Does it mean having things that buzz inside you and a stick-out handle?"

"Real isn't how you are made," said the Skin Horse. "It's a thing that happens to you when a child loves you for a long, long time, not just to play with but REALLY loves you, then you become Real."

"Does it hurt?" asked the Rabbit.

"Sometimes," said the Skin Horse, for he was always truthful. "When you are Real you don't mind being hurt."

"Does it happen all at once, like being wound up," he asked, "or bit by bit?"

"It doesn't happen all at once," said the Skin Horse. "You become. It takes a long time. That's why it doesn't happen to people who break easily, or have sharp edges or have to be carefully kept. Generally, by the time you are Real, most of your hair has been loved off, and your eyes drop out and you get loose in the joints and very shabby. But these things don't matter at all, because once you are Real you can't be ugly, except to people who don't understand. [Beresin et al. 1989, pp. 103–104, quoting from Margery Williams' *The Skin-Horse and the Velveteen Rabbit or How Toys Become Real*]

Appendix: The Study and Transitional Space

Although some of the findings of the study and their implications have been interwoven throughout the book and are at its foundation, the purpose of the Appendix is twofold: first, to present the critical research aspects (methods and design, analysis of data, hypotheses, empirical findings, implications) for those with an interest in research, and second, to elaborate how the design of the data collection instrument facilitated the creation of a transitional space for subjects that allowed their voices to emerge as openly as they did. The second purpose has implications for the creation of a transitional space for patients in treatment, and should be of interest to clinicians who ordinarily do not have an interest in research.

The study involved an exploration of the mind–body relationship and the role of the body in self-organization. It invited participants to struggle to answer personal, often painful questions about the past and the present, and was the source of many of the voices that told so candidly how the body speaks. I offered them only my wish to understand them better. For the subjects, there was the risk that participating in the study might evoke disturbing memories, images, flashbacks, and somatic sensations that might cause symptomatic regression, including, of course, an increase in self-harm behavior. Yet apparently what I offered was enough because people responded, providing an amazing wealth of personal information, including a great deal of expressive material that was most saddening, heartening, and moving to read. This appendix discusses how it happened that some of the individuals who speak with their bodies came to speak to me, a stranger, through the transitional space of the study.

Why would anyone want to participate in the study? For subjects to invest the time and emotional energy in participating, they needed to know and believe two crucial things: first, that how they thought about and subjectively experienced their self-harm was very important to the researcher, and secondly, that the researcher was concerned about their safety and well-being during and after their participation in the study. To tell me what I wanted to know, they needed to experience the space between themselves and me as a safe one with the potential to provide them with something good.

THE STUDY

The relationship between binge-purging and self-mutilation was explored in a study done in partial requirement for my Ph.D. in clinical social work at New York University. It was an exploratory cross-sectional study meant to further the development of concepts around bodily self-harm, and compared these two categories of self-harm behaviors for similarities and differences. Of the 158 questionnaires that were requested, 110 were returned, a very good return rate. Of these 110 people, eleven, including the three men who responded, did not meet selection criteria and so were not included in the final sample. The ninety-nine subjects in the final sample comprised a group of chronically eating-disordered women with a median age of 28.5, whose bingeing and purging endured, on average, almost 13 years, and whose childhood and adult self-injury endured for around 21.5 years. Although I originally planned to compare and contrast the responses of adults who binge and purge but who do not self-mutilate with those of adults who binge and purge and also self-mutilate, the design had to be revised because, to my great surprise, 89 of the 99 subjects (89.9%) who reported binge–purge behavior also reported current self-mutilating behavior ranging from mild to severe. This is consistent with Heller's findings (1990) in her dissertation study at Smith School of Social Work, comparing bulimics and self-mutilators in terms of object relations and symptom choice. Heller was surprised at how quickly her subgroup of bulimic self-mutilators filled. Typically, a subject was identified as bulimic and placed in the bulimic subgroup, yet revealed in the course of the study a history of self-mutilation that required that she be reassigned to the bulimic mutilator subgroup.

Flexible Inclusion Criteria for Exploring the Borderland

The sample (N = 99) was divided into two comparison groups different from those originally planned: a group of purging bulimics who self-mutilated severely (N = 75), and a group of purging bulimics who self-mutilated mildly or not at all

(N = 24), to be referred to from now on as the Severe and the Mild groups. It should be noted that of those who self-mutilated severely, usually by cutting and burning themselves, most also employed a number of milder forms of self-mutilation, a mean number of 7.3.

Any exploratory study must allow for considerable flexibility in method and can exclude no potential subject from the outset, and so the word "bulimic" was not meant to refer to a *DSM* diagnosis of Bulimia Nervosa but simply to bingeing and purging behavior. Although current treatment trials for individuals with eating disorders use specific inclusion and exclusion criteria out of the wish to select a relatively homogeneous sample, the disadvantage is that such homogeneity may select the more resilient patients who have the best prognoses (Mitchell et al. 1997). Strict *DSM* selection criteria were not utilized in this study because they would exclude the individuals who usually fell through the cracks on research in eating disorders—the most severely ill and most difficult to treat individuals—who were most likely to provide the invaluable data that could inform us about those who live on the borders between *DSM* diagnostic categories. The final sample included many individuals who would have been excluded from Bulimia Nervosa treatment studies because they did not meet the strict *DSM* inclusion criteria (Mitchell et al. 1997, Niego et al. 1997).

A few potential subjects who did not meet the initial objective selection criteria were included as long as they reported some bulimic behavior, not necessarily the full binge/purge syndrome. In a few cases, the subjects did not satisfy the usual objective criteria for bulimic behavior, that is, they did not necessarily eat large quantities of food within a discrete period of time and then try to get rid of it by inducing a purge. They did, however, satisfy subjective criteria for binge eating, a criteria that warrants further investigative effort (Niego et al. 1997). For example, several subjects indicated that they did not eat large quantities by other people's standards, but according to their own subjective standard, even a minute portion was much too much, requiring that they purge themselves. These individuals were included. Another binged on large quantities of food but did not purge, and also mutilated herself in various ways. She was included. Interestingly, she wrote about the blood she shed and the ooze from burns as bad fluid that she needed to rid herself of, suggesting that there may need to be a consideration of the subjective factor in defining purging behavior, that is, that blood-letting is a form of purging.

Several potential subjects who only mutilated themselves but did not binge or purge were not included. The criterion for the Mild group was the current absence of severe self-mutilating behaviors. These respondents indicated that they did not self-mutilate at all or if they did, their self-mutilation included head-banging, severe nail or cuticle biting (causing soreness or bleeding), hair-pulling, or skin-picking. This group roughly corresponded to the category conceptualized as compulsive self-mutilation by other researchers (Favaro and Santonastoso 1999, Favazza and Simeon 1995). If, however, these behaviors resulted in serious infection or abnormal appearance, they were put in the category of severe self-mutilation. While adult subjects of both sexes were recruited, the final sample was entirely female.

Recruitment and Selection of Subjects

Sampling was purposive—that is, I looked for subjects where I expected I might find them. While I expected that I might find many in inpatient treatment facilities, access to potential subjects in these places was problematic. Subjects were self-selected from recruitment notices distributed at the State University of New York at Purchase; publications for people with eating disorders, obsessive-compulsive disorder, trichotillomania, and dissociative disorders; and newsletters for survivors of sexual abuse. Notices were distributed through self-help groups for people with eating disorders, for self-mutilators, and for obsessive-compulsives, through clinicians known to serve these populations; through body piercing and tattoo studios; and through a body modification magazine. The largest number were recruited from newsletters for abuse survivors. Subjects were given the choice to write for the questionnaire at a postal box number or to call a voice-mail number. When the questionnaire was mailed to them, a hand-written stick-on note thanking them for their help and wishing them health, hope, and healing was attached. The recruitment notice was as follows:

I am a doctoral candidate at New York University School of Social Work studying binge–purging and other body-focused behavior. Your participation in the study may be valuable in helping to promote further understanding of these behaviors.

The questionnaire is meant for people over eighteen who currently or within the past year at least twice a month have binged on large quantities of food and then used vomiting, laxatives, enemas, or diuretics to "undo" the binge or get rid of the food. In addition, if you have also deliberately cut, scratched, burned or picked at yourself, or pulled out your hair, severely chewed your skin or nails, hit yourself, or if you have allowed someone else to tattoo, pierce, brand or scar you, I am very interested in understanding these experiences as well.

HOWEVER YOU DO NOT NEED TO HAVE DONE BOTH (binge–purging behavior and other behavior resulting in altered body tissue) TO PARTICIPATE IN THE STUDY; THE BINGE-PURGING IS SUFFICIENT.

Most of the questions concern how you experience the binge-purging and other body-focused behavior. Also included are some questions about your childhood and adult experiences, including physical or sexual abuse, and physical illness. If such questions are likely to upset you, it may be better for you if you do not participate. If you are in therapy, you may want to discuss the decision about participation with your therapist.

If you decide to participate, you may nonetheless choose to withdraw from the study at any time. To participate, please fill out the questionnaire as best you can, and mail it to me in the attached addressed and stamped envelope. To protect your privacy your name is not asked for on the questionnaire or the return envelope. Your name and address will not be kept after it has been used to mail you the questionnaire. Feel free to add extra pages to write anything that might help me to understand your experiences. Anything you can add that I have not thought to ask about in the questionnaire will be especially valuable.

If you would like me to send you a summary of my findings when the study is complete, please enclose a self-addressed stamped envelope (29¢ U.S. postage) with your questionnaire.

If filling out the questionnaire raises concerns about your relationship with food or other body-focused behaviors and you would like to speak privately and confidentially with a knowledgeable professional, you may call any of the resources listed below for information about this and about self-help groups that meet across the country.

The majority of subjects were single women, most never having been married, employed in diverse positions ranging from waitress and cleaning jobs to physician, intensive care nurse, director of women's athletics at a large university, and owner of a body modifications studio. A number identified themselves as professionally trained social workers and psychologists and as psychiatric aides in treatment programs. The geographic distribution included the United States and Canada, with the northeast representing the largest portion.

Data Collection and Analysis

Data was collected by means of a sixteen page self-report questionnaire, using closed as well as open-ended questions to allow for greater elaboration of experiential or subjective information. The directions for filling out the questionnaire were:

Please answer each item as best you can. There are no right or wrong answers. The best answer is what is true for you. Your answers regarding your own experiences with binge–purging and other body-focused behavior are what I am interested in understanding. Feel free to tell me anything else about your experience that might help me to understand it better, adding extra pages if needed.

At the end of the questionnaire was the following statement:

This is the end of the questionnaire. Thank you so much for your time and effort. If there is anything else that has not been included about your experiences with bingeing and purging and other body-focused behaviors that you would like to tell me about so that I can understand it better, please do so here. Feel free to include comments about the experience of filling out this questionnaire as well. You may add additional paper if needed. When you are finished, please return the completed questionnaire to me in the enclosed stamped envelope.

Scales for eliciting and organizing data were created by the researcher, who adapted the Self-Harm Behavior Survey (Favazza and Conterio 1988),[1] the Revised Diagnostic Survey for Eating Disorders (Johnson and Connors 1987), and an unpublished scale created by the researcher and fellow doctoral candidates to measure anxiety and depersonalization in self-cutters (Camper et al. 1988). Scores were a combination of nominal, ordinal, and rank ordered. The rates and proportions of pertinent scales and/or items were assessed by analyses of means, and techniques for analyzing the contrasts between the Mild and Severe subgroups on the various independent variables included *t* tests and simple one-way analysis of variance techniques.[2]

Because it was expected that certain small subgroups of the total sample would vary from the comparison subgroups in their mean scores on some or many scales, a comparison of mean scores on these scales was done to detect that variation. First, the total sample was divided into three groups according to which part of the binge–purge episode they experienced as being the apex of intensity: the binge, the purge, or both binge and purge equally intense, and their mean scores on the number of purging behaviors used and on the severity of the purge were compared. To measure covariation, a multiple regression analysis was done to determine the effect of the chronicity of binge–purging behavior and the severity of the purge on the severity of self-mutilating behavior. Other post hoc analysis included obtaining the mean strengths of each of the self-medicating behaviors and ranking ranging from relatively weak to relatively strong. Similarly, mean numbers were obtained for all the variables on the binge–purge symptom substitution scale, which also were ranked. The mean scores on all scales were obtained and compared for several self-identified subgroups within the Severe group.

---

1. I am grateful to Dr. Armando Favazza for sending me a copy of his self-harm survey.

2. It is important that statistical significance not be confused with theoretical or practical significance. A test of significance gives us really minimal information. Is a difference or association worth taking seriously? Tests of significance can best be seen as providing rough criteria that help us separate findings to be taken seriously from those that may be considered unstable, aberrant, unreliable and so on (Reid and Smith 1981). When $p \leq .05$, this means that findings are significant if there is only a 5 percent probability that the findings could be explained by chance. Findings of $p \leq .10$, however, were accepted as trend findings, or tendencies, meaning that there is reason to accept the .10 level as meaningful. That is, applying very stringent tests of significance can prevent the researcher from detecting possible clues to be pursued further, especially in an exploratory study and with small samples. With small samples, the results must be more extreme to rule out a chance finding.

Hypotheses and Findings

The hypotheses, which were supported by the findings, were as follows.

- Compared to the bulimic who does not self-mutilate or does so mildly, the binge-purger who self-mutilates severely will tend to engage in the more severe binge–purge behavior.

  There was a trend finding ($p \leq .10$) (see n. 2, this chapter) for the Severe group reporting engaging in significantly more severe purge behavior than the Mild group. They utilized more forms of purging ($p \leq .05$) and purged more frequently than the Mild group. Some did not even require a binge to purge, purging after every mouthful, while others followed any ingestion of food with a series of several violent purges.

- Compared to the bulimic who does not self-mutilate or does so mildly, the binge-purger who self-mutilates severely will tend to experience the purge as the apex of the binge–purge episode.

  There was a trend finding ($p \leq .10$) (see n. 2, this chapter) for the Severe group reporting that they experienced the purge as the apex of the binge–purge episode, in comparison to the Mild group for whom the binge was the apex.

- Compared to the bulimic who does not self-mutilate or does so mildly, the binge-purger who self-mutilates severely will tend to have other, more severe emotional and physical symptoms.

  Both groups had unusually high scores in somatization and childhood onset dissociation. The Severe group reported significantly higher scores on dissociation ($p \leq .05$), suicidality ($p \leq .001$), and number of somatic illnesses ($p \leq .05$) than the Mild group.

- Compared to the bulimic who does not self-mutilate or does so mildly, the binge-purger who self-mutilates severely will tend to have had more severely traumatic childhood and adolescent experiences.

  The Severe group reported having experienced significantly more traumatic experiences in childhood and adolescence, specifically more non-medical trauma ($p \leq .05$), family violence ($p \leq .001$), and physical abuse ($p \leq .05$), as well as greater numbers of childhood severe or chronic illnesses ($p \leq .05$). The Severe group also reported greater numbers of adolescent non-medical trauma in general ($p \leq .001$), specifically family violence ($p \leq .05$), physical abuse ($p \leq .05$), and sexual abuse ($p \leq .05$), as well as greater numbers of adolescent medically-related trauma in general ($p \leq .01$), surgical procedures ($p \leq .01$), and chronic or severe physical illnesses ($p \leq .05$).

- Compared to the bulimic who does not self-mutilate or does so mildly, the binge-purger who self-mutilates severely will tend to have had more severe childhood self-injurious and disturbed eating/feeding habits.

The Severe group tended to report significantly more childhood self-injurious (mean = 2.60, t = 4.12, p ≤ .01) and disordered feeding habits (mean = 1.71, t = 2.97, p ≤ .01), as well as significantly more numerous adolescent self-mutilating (mean = 4.21, t = 4.64, p = ≤ .001) and disordered eating behavior than the Mild group. The Severe group reported more disordered eating behavior than the Mild group but not at a greater level of significance.

• Compared to the bulimic who does not self-mutilate, the binge-purger who does self-mutilate will tend to have a more negative body image.

While both groups were found to have very negative body image, the Severe group reported a significantly more negative body image than the Mild group. The Severe group reported significantly lower scores measuring satisfaction with their appearance (p ≤ .05), satisfaction with specific body parts (p ≤ .001), and total body image (p ≤ .001).

Other Findings

Both groups were chronic in terms of their self-harm behavior, the Mild group reporting that they had engaged in the binge–purge behavior syndrome for 10.82 years, compared with a mean of 13.61 years for the Severe group. The Mild group reported that they had engaged in self-mutilating behavior for 19.06 years, compared with a mean of 22.03 years for the Severe group.

Of the total sample, the subgroup reporting the binge as the experiential apex of the binge-purge episode (N = 20) had the lowest mean score on the total number of purging behaviors used (4.20), representing a trend finding (t = 1.97, p ≤ .10). The subgroup reporting that the experiences of the binge and purge were equally intense (N = 28) had a mean score of 4.43 on the total number of purging behaviors used (t = 2.8, p ≤ .01). The largest subgroup was the one reporting that the purge was the most intense part of the binge-purge experience (N = 46). This group also had the highest mean score on the total number of purging behaviors used (4.71), suggesting that they utilized greater numbers of purging behaviors in order to heighten the purging experience.

There was a trend finding (p ≤ .10) (see n. 2, this chapter) for the chronicity of binge–purge behavior as predictive of the development of severe self-mutilation. It is believed that the severity of purging behavior functions as an intervening variable, that with the increase in the chronicity of binge–purge behavior, there is a corresponding increase in the severity of purging that is a significant factor in the production of severe self-mutilation. There is a positive but not significant correlation between the chronicity of binge–purge behavior and the severity of purging. For each one point increase in the chronicity of binge-purge behavior, the severity of self-mutilating behavior increases by .016. However, it is believed that there would be a far more significant correlation if the sample size were larger or if the study were done using the original comparison group categories.

There are findings regarding the phenomenon of symptom substitution, when self-mutilating behavior and other self-medicating behaviors cropped up to substitute for or alternate with binge-purge behavior when that behavior stopped or decreased. The severely self-mutilating group reported a significantly higher number of behavioral symptoms appearing after stopping or decreasing the binge–purge behavior. When mean frequencies for each of the behaviors on the binge–purge Symptom Substitution scale were ranked in a spectrum ranging from high to low in the total sample, shopping had the highest mean score (.64), followed in this order by drinking (.51), self-mutilation (.44) and suicide attempts (.44) equally, reckless driving (.34), drug use (.33), sex (.30), shoplifting (.23), allowing others to cut, brand, pierce, or tattoo them (.17), and unnecessary surgery (.07).

The findings supported the hypothesis that both purging and self-mutilating behavior were particularly powerful forms of self-medication. When the mean scores on the scale measuring the strength of each of the self-medicating behaviors were ranked, ranging from relatively strong to relatively weak, purging was ranked the highest (3.74), followed by cutting, burning, or hitting oneself (3.60); hair pulling, severe nail/cuticle biting, or piercing (3.51); exercise (3.22); bingeing (2.95); shopping (2.79); drug use (1.99); drinking (1.96); sex (1.68) ; and shoplifting (1.16). In the whole sample, 61 out of 99 subjects reported mutilating themselves shortly after a bulimic episode; two subjects reported that this occurred once, 31 reported that this occurred a few times, 24 reported that this occurred numerous times, and 4 reported that this occurred every time.

THE CONCEPT OF TRANSITIONAL SPACE

Although the subjects provided the data that supported my hypotheses in much the way I had expected, what I could not have anticipated was the total response to my effort, both positive and negative. The men and women who responded to my recruitment efforts often responded in ways I never would have imagined, most of which was very gratifying and moving. Although it was expected that many in the body modification subculture would oppose the study, I never would have anticipated how powerfully they would oppose the study and attack me. In retrospect, however, it made sense, as will be explained. Many who contacted me were women who became subjects in the study but I learned something from all who contacted me, and learned about the power of the study as a potential transitional space. As will be demonstrated, the subjects responded in a way that conveyed that they wanted, above all, to be understood. In addition, they seemed to want their suffering to have some meaning, which was expressed through the idea that their participation in a study might prove helpful for others suffering from similar problems. That some of them valued meaning—these people whose self-harm behavior so often seems to be a destruction of meaning—was exciting, a bridge to be used for engaging individuals who might seek treatment.

The questionnaire items were extremely personal and potentially quite painful. The study was the work of a clinician who wants to understand her patients. Of course, the people who participated were not my patients but virtually everything about this study was driven by the wish to understand and explain the human experience of these two different kinds of self-harm behaviors.

My clinical thinking was that patients who abuse themselves need the treatment relationship to serve the transitional and containing functions that they themselves lack. Although I could not articulate it at the time, in retrospect I understood that in order to engage these subjects in the study I had to engage them with me in the intermediate area of experience that the study could serve. All too often, scientific empiricism limits an understanding of human behavior and the human mind. I wanted the experience of participating in this study to be different, as much like a good clinical interview as it could be—humane, engaging, empathic, interested, and reciprocal—like two adults speaking directly to each other in a human relationship. I wanted to learn from them and I wanted them to want to teach me. Although I did not conceptualize it at the time as an effort to create an attachment, that is just what I wanted to do. It was a symbiotic wish on both parts: to understand on my part, and to be understood on theirs.

Wanting so much to be understood, the subjects found the study to be an opportunity and they took it. They were invited to tell me anything they thought might help me understand how they subjectively experience the self-harming episodes. Although my object, of course, was obtaining the needed data, there was a therapeutic agenda as well. While I obtained the data I needed, I hoped at the same time to provide an experience that could be therapeutic. Subjects who found filling out the questionnaire to be something of a therapeutic experience would be more likely to be thoughtful in completing it. The more thoughtful they were in completing it, the more they would be using thought processes rather than (destructive) action-oriented behavior. It was necessary for the subjects to feel accepted and believed. Whatever their actual experiences of abuse and trauma were, I could not know. There was no way to know if what they reported was based on memories of real events, on fantasies, or on fantasied elaborations of real events, but I did regard whatever they reported as being true for them. It was their psychic reality, and had to be accepted as such in the study, just as such reports must be accepted in psychotherapy.

It was the wish to engage them in the study that impelled me to design a data collection instrument that would be experienced as much as possible as an invitation to engage in an authentic dialogue, what theologian Martin Buber (1970) called an I–Thou relationship. Buber bids us to make the secular sacred. "God is present when I confront You. But if I look away from You, I ignore him. As long as I merely experience or use you, [sic] I deny God. But when I encounter You I encounter him (p. 28)." I wanted the subjects to feel personally and directly addressed, as if the study were a poem or painting, inviting a response.

THE TRANSITIONAL AREA OF EXPERIENCE
AS A SAFE SPACE

I knew that the study had to feel like a safe transitional space in much the same way some patients use the telephone or letters as a transitional space between themselves and the therapist, feeling held and contained at a distance. Sometimes, before even permitting a face-to-face encounter, some potential patients look for a safe transitional space outside the office. It can be through a telephone call of inquiry. How the therapist speaks to a potential patient often determines whether the individual does or does not come to meet the therapist in person. Sometimes the transitional space of several telephone calls may be necessary, and even the outgoing messages on answering machines may be listened to several times before an appointment is made. Before becoming or allowing their children to become patients, some individuals might take advantage of the chance to hear the therapist speak publicly. Others might venture an initial consultation based on the transitional space of a letter or article the therapist has published in a newspaper or magazine.

The creation of a transitional space is a creative act for the patient, done out of need, requiring that the therapist be sufficiently accepting of that need and flexible enough to tolerate a stretching of the usual boundaries of the therapeutic relationship. The following case is illuminating in elaborating how transitional space is created, and can inform our understanding of how each of the subjects in my study seem to have used it to create a transitional space.

Joyce Aronson (1996) described how it was necessary for her to accept the creation of such a transitional space by a very masochistic psychotic patient if the treatment were to proceed at all. Ms. K., her 26-year-old anorexic patient, began treatment after discharge from a psychiatric hospital, but found the face-to-face contact intolerable because it brought her in touch with her need for the therapist, something that was terrifying. A definite appointment that started and ended at a specific time imposed an unbearable sense of separateness. Looking at the therapist meant that at some time she would have to stop looking at her, which was equally unbearable. Living an autistic sensory dominated existence, she was frightened of human contact. She was 4'10" and weighed 80 pounds, although in the past she had been at a low weight of 54 pounds. She lived an isolated life with her cat in a dirty, rat-infested apartment and looked like a bag lady, with bloody scabs visible on her scalp. She starved herself and tortured herself with hours of painful exercise and by pulling her hair out and scratching at her scalp. Initially she came to some sessions but was very late, then refused to come to the office for her three-times-a-week treatment. Instead she created a transitional space out of her need for a more intermediate area of experience in the therapeutic relationship. She used the telephone and the answering machine as that intermediate area, phoning the therapist at the end of her appointed hour to talk briefly, to leave messages asking that the therapist call her back, and to make contact on an as-needed basis. At times she left very lengthy messages to which the therapist listened at her convenience.

Ms. K. needed the illusion of omnipotence, of having the therapist at any time or all times, and she did that by talking to the therapist's answering machine as if she were speaking to her directly. She could be provocative and abusive toward the machine/therapist without destroying the relationship. The treatment was conducted like this for three years, although the therapist insisted they meet in person once a week because she needed to see if in fact, her patient's weight was decreasing or if her appearance were better or worse. Ms. K. agreed to this but often missed these meetings. When she did show up it was for the last fifteen minutes of the session, and she spent the first five minutes in the bathroom. Even when the therapist was on vacation, the patient needed telephone contact if she were to avoid a psychotic withdrawal. This went on for three years before the patient could "graduate" to tolerating the lack of direct telephone contact during vacations and could endure leaving messages for the therapist with the assurance that the therapist would call in to receive them every few days. Finally, she began having face-to-face sessions in the office, experiencing both her need for the therapist and her loss when the session was over. As the child can eventually give up the teddy bear at bedtime, the patient could relinquish the telephone as a transitional space and experience a greater sense of herself and the therapist as separate beings.

THE STUDY AS A SAFE SPACE

I came to understand that the process of engaging people to complete a questionnaire itself functioned as a transitional process. The subjects had no relationship with me that could give them a reason to trust me, and from what they wrote, their past experiences had created a template of distrust through which they experienced new relationships. We were not engaged face-to-face but through words on paper. The subjects lived at a distance from me. It was somewhat like the Internet, where the distance and sense of anonymity helps people feel freer to "play" with strangers. Just as there are predators awaiting their prey in cyberspace, the subjects were left to determine if I were one or if I might be trusted. The study served as a transitional bridge between each subject and me and I served as a bridge between each subject and the object world.

The recruitment notices contained the customary statement that must be approved by the university Human Subjects Committee: who is conducting the study and under what auspices, what the study is about, selection criteria, and what the possible risks and benefits involved in participation are. This information was repeated on the cover page of the questionnaire. Sufficient information was given about the nature of the study to allow prospective subjects to screen themselves out, and an explicit statement was included about their being able to drop out of the study at any time for any reason. The comment that it might be better for some that they *not* participate was made because I felt protective of the subjects and wanted them to know that.

Confirming the anxiety many potential subjects had about participating in the study was the note one woman enclosed with her completed questionnaire, saying that she had had several bad experiences with mental health professionals and that my concern for her well-being helped her to feel more comfortable about participating in the study. "When you said that if I thought I'd get too upset it might be better for me not to be in the study, I knew that my welfare was more important to you than just getting another guinea pig to look at." The publishers of some self-help newsletters were cautious about serving as a connection for researchers and potential subjects and took a protective stance toward their readers. At the same time they were interested in the study and wanted to be helpful. For example, after I discovered the existence of *The Cutting Edge*, the newsletter for women who live with self-inflicted violence, I wrote to the publisher requesting that she publish my recruitment notice, and at the same time began a subscription.

> I have been preparing this study for several years, and could not believe my good fortune to have discovered your newsletter. I particularly appreciate the focus on the experiential aspect of self-mutilation, which my study explores. While I have developed my own ideas about the many functions that self-mutilation and bulimia can serve for those who do these things, I expect I will learn even more about this from the people who participate in my study. I have read the professional literature exhaustively but nothing can take the place of accounts of their experience by those who have had the experience.

As I was to learn, the publisher of this newsletter has herself lived for many years using self-mutilation as a survival tool, and has written eloquently for her readers about the wisdom she has acquired through her experiences. (Her words on giving up her self-inflicted violence are quoted in Chapter 16.) In response to my letter, I received the following letter, beginning a "snail mail" and e-mail correspondence.

Dear Sharon,
I received your letter, and hope this one finds you well. I have looked up some of the addresses of newsletters, to at least give you a start on contacting other publications dealing with abuse survival and /or MPD. Obviously this is not a complete list but I hope that you find it useful.
I neglected to inform you that I do not publish requests to obtain research subjects in *The Cutting Edge*. This is partially because I do not have the room, but mostly

because I do not have the time nor energy to screen the requests I receive. Without doing so, I will not subject the readers to any professional inquiries. Most have experienced significant psychiatric abuse.

I did, however, see your research request published in another newsletter recently (I do not remember which one right now). I read that you consider receiving tattoos as a form of self-injury and was surprised by that. Maybe you could explain that to me? Regardless, I hope that your work goes well, and that the information I am providing is helpful.

Sincerely,

Ruta

THE RESEARCHER AS IDEALIZED READER

Even before obtaining the questionnaire, some used the initial contact as an opportunity to tell quite a lot of very personal material. They expressed what seemed to be an immediate idealizing transference, writing in much the same way that the diarist, in addressing his "Dear Diary," writes to an imaginary reader, an imaginary "You" who resides in his unconscious (Mallon 1986).

> Is that the only person I'm writing for—myself . . . ? Or is there someone else? Who is this "you" that's made its way more and more often onto these pages. . . , this odd pronoun I sometimes find myself talking to like a person at the other end of a letter? . . .
>
> I can say without a trace of coyness that I have no idea who "you" is. I don't know if "you" is male or female, met or unmet, born or unborn, tied to me by blood or accident.
>
> Whether or not they admit it, I think all the purchasers of the five million blank diaries sold each year in country have a "you" in mind as well. Perhaps in the backs of their minds, or hidden in the subconscious strata, but there. [Mallon 1986, p. xvi]

Many of those who wrote letters in response to my recruitment notice were writing to an unknown, yet idealized reader, someone to whom they could risk baring their souls, someone who might know them as they really were. To record one's words on paper reflects a wish to be remembered, a sense of future in which one's memory remains in the mind and heart of another. These women, reporting histories of severe loss and the most egregious childhood abuse of their bodies, minds, and trust, expressed themselves in ways that demonstrated a reciprocal relationship between their hope to be understood and their listener's (reader's) wish to understand, and between their risking their trust in the listener (reader) and the listener's (reader's) concern for their well-being.

Many wrote at length of their experiences with self-harming behavior, childhood abuse, abusive relationships, medication, hospitalization, psychotherapy, concerns about the effect of their illness on their children, their subjective experience of filling out the questionnaire, their hopes and despair, their thoughts about the etiology of their self-harm, their gratitude to the researcher for wanting to know so much, and their hope that knowledge of their suffering might be helpful to others with similar problems.

WANTING TO FIND MEANING IN THEIR SUFFERING

Even in the request that a questionnaire be sent to them, some individuals expressed gratitude and wished me well. For some it was a simple "thank you," for others a more articulated expression of thanks for the chance to be listened to, for the study itself, and for the opportunity for an understanding of their suffering to help others. There was evidence in some of a positive idealizing transference.

Some hoped their participation might help them to discover something new about their illness that might be helpful in overcoming it and ending the intergenerational cycle of abuse. Through the transitional space, they seemed to find some satisfaction of narcissistic as well as altruistic wishes. Some sought out participation in the desperate hope that it might help, while some made themselves available for further contact by telephone or mail.

I would really like to help out your study in any way that I can. If by doing your study and research on the whole binge–purge cycle and other body behaviors can help find out why these things happen, or how they can be helped, I would gladly help. Maybe it won't help me personally, but maybe it can help some other women down the road.

My name is _____ _____ and I am twenty years old. I have been bulimic for two years now and have suffered a great deal. I have also been through a lot of self destructive behaviors. I have burnt, cut, scratched myself, pulled out hair, hit myself, bruised myself, put my hands through windows. I have also tried to commit suicide twice already, and was placed in the psychiatric ward of _____ Hospital after an attempted suicide.

I have also had two separate therapists to help me through the bulimia and depression. I am very frustrated at the fact that nothing is working. If by doing this questionnaire I could find out something more about my problem and understand it better, that would be great.

I look forward to receiving it. Thank you.

I believe I read in either *KINESIS* or *OFF OUR BACKS* about your study. I'm enclosing a S.A.S.E. (self-addressed stamped envelope) so you can send me a questionnaire.

My sisters and I were raised in a dysfunctional home with two alcoholic parents. I was beaten & we were all picked off emotionally. It's a long story. Dad's been dead 5 yrs. this Dec. & we all talked to him before he died to resolve our issues. Nothing was perfect. Mom is still a functioning-in-the -work force lush. All my sisters (2) &

I have distanced ourselves from her & told her why. . . . Well, these last 5 yrs. I've begun to deal with my issues. My eating disorder, starve and binge has really almost ceased. I haven't had a bad day in almost a year. I discovered why that began—the core issue of why I starve myself—or used to.

I've had a lot of problems or symptoms, co-dependency, eating disorder, abandonment fears, promiscuity & my self-mutilating tactics. All, obviously, have sprung from childhood difficulties. One by one I have uncovered the source or core issue & some are gone /completely resolved. One—no, two are in remission, I call it, because so far I haven't had something trigger me to begin my eating disorder & promiscuity (although I really feel the latter is finally ended.) And the last—self-mutilation is one I have not begun to really work on. All these actually have different core issues that helped them begin & yet they're still very much connected/ tied together. So as I handle one, the weft & weave of my life pulls on others & the fabric won't lie flat until all is completed peacefully. I'm finally content.

My sisters & I have decided that in this generation—with we 3—this is where the abusive cycle ends.

Well, I've spoken to each sister & they want to look over the questionnaire also. So, I've enclosed a S.A.S.E. for each one of us! Thanks!

This letter is being written after I had seen a note on the bulletin board at My Sister's Words bookstore in Syracuse, N.Y. . . . I am 34 years old, white, female. In June 1990 I was hospitalized for 7 weeks following 103 lb. weight loss. . . . Diagnosis: Generalized eating disorder with conditioned response to food/purging. I was in an extremely weakened state. At this time, 3 years later, I still use laxatives & suppositories & natural remedies as a means of purging. I have undergone therapy with an MSW for 2 yrs. In addition to seeing a psychiatrist for medication: Prozac.

If filling out a questionnaire will eventually lead to a new understanding of eating disorders & help others, I would like to participate.

For further information, please contact me at. . . .

I saw a flier asking for survey volunteers on the bulletin board at *Lommas*, Washington D.C.'s finest (and only) women's bookstore.

I am a 32 year old lesbian. I've been bulimic since the age of 15 or so. I've engaged in therapies of varying modalities to treat this disease. Although this disease has been getting more attention in recent years, I believe that only a glimmering of understanding has shown through regarding its etiology.

I would be willing to fill out your survey and assist you in any way I can.

At the end of her completed questionnaire, a woman wrote: "Dear Dr. Farber, I'm glad and relieved someone cares enough to do a study like this. Maybe it will help others. You are a very kind person to be interested in and collect data in this area. Bless you." Another wrote: I really hope my personal information will help you understand more about eating disorders and how powerful these are. ☺ Please continue to research eating disorders. Best wishes in your future . . . I know I can have one now too. Please excuse errors in my writing. ☺ I'm still working on communicating my feelings clearly so others can understand."

PAIN, ATTACHMENTS, AND TEDDY BEARS

There was a striking abundance of material that spoke of the need for transitional objects. Some wrote on children's stationery or applied stickers of dolls, cuddly kittens, smiling faces, flowers, rainbows, and hearts to their writing paper. They seemed to know that they needed the soothing transitional experiences that were so lacking in their childhoods. Several included poems and photographs with their completed questionnaires, and seemed to be reaching for such a transitional experience with me.

Just as transitional objects are sometimes the targets of their owner's anger and get beaten up and worn out, I, too, was the target of anger. In response to the query about her experience in filling out the questionnaire, one woman wrote: "CONDESCENDING, PATRONIZING, PURPOSE UNCLEAR." At the end of her questionnaire another wrote angrily about my having listed only one hotline number for self-mutilators, which turned out to be unavailable, in my resource list. I replied with a brief note of apology.

The comments about the experience of filling out the questionnaire were quite informative. For some it seemed to be an organizing experience, helping them to put together their thoughts or access their emotions, and gain a new perspective. One woman wrote, "Thanks for the opportunity—it was helpful to put facts/info into an orderly manner," while another said, "I found your questionnaire to be comprehensive. . . . Looking back on what I'd done to myself frightens me now—I feel blessed to be alive." One wrote, "I've learned from completing this questionnaire." Another wrote, "It was sad to fill it out. I do hope I am getting better."

One woman returned the questionnaire unmarked, enclosing a note that said that after reading it, she realized that filling it out would have been more painful than she could bear. Several found filling out the questionnaire to be very difficult and took a month or two to complete it, doing it in spurts. "Filling this out: Harder than I thought. When I just read thru it I didn't think it would be too bad. But thinking about some of the questions brings back memories." Yet some of those who found it difficult also found it helpful in gaining greater understanding about the nature of their self-harm behavior and placing themselves within the spectrum of human behavior. "After going over the questionnaire I immediately became afraid, scared to see my pain in black and white. Well, I got through it & found it to be a release. . . . It has helped me to let some of this shame out to you and I thank you." "The questions that asked about feelings: I am not sure how well I could really answer them. I am not very in touch with my feelings." "After filling out the questionnaire, I found myself in a space that felt very lonely, very unsafe. I removed myself & went somewhere else. I also stopped at the store to buy food. I was not hungry. I had just eaten dinner. This questionnaire gave me a reference point from which to place my behaviors within the continuum of possible responses."

One subject thought that the specific methods of self-harm listed in the questionnaire might give suggestible people dangerous ideas that they never had before:

> I could see one possible side effect of filling out the questionnaire. Some of the questions are about methods or how things are done. The danger is providing information/ideas about *new dangerous things you can do to yourself* (if you were looking for more!) For example—I never knew about these things:
> —what do nutshells do?
> —why would anyone drink Drano?
> —Scarification is something that has its own name?

Others told of finding wonderful therapists or partners who stuck with them through terrible times, and held out hope. They told me how their attachments to spouses, partners, friends, therapists, and pets sustained them. "A good therapist, a safe place, & a willingness to stop any self-destructive behaviors is what's needed." A few wrote that they brought the questionnaire into their psychotherapy, and that it was a helpful addition to their treatment. One such therapist wrote requesting several questionnaires for her patients.

Some told of their considerable contact with the mental health system, much of it experienced as negative or even frankly abusive. One subject wrote about the attachments that she has in her life and expressed a very moving concern that my emotional well-being might be jeopardized by reading so much potentially painful material.

> Thank you for wanting to hear about it and understand it more. I can't understand not wanting to hurt the body. It's not about weight, it's about hate—hating myself, hating being alive, hating what happened to me and I get really tired of the struggle. I was anorexic at one time to the point where I got fuzzy and lost my period for over a year. Then I left "home" and slowly am making progress through therapy. Maybe someday this will all be behind me but I don't see that right now. I'm slowly losing my hips and the pain I feel because of that makes me hate myself more so I hurt myself more. But I have: a pen pal, wonderful therapist, nice husband, faithful pets (1 dog, 2 bunnies).
> This study seems like it's got the potential to be overwhelming. Please take care of yourself and read them (the questionnaires) slowly. Pace yourself. Do deep breathing exercises. If I can be of further help my address is _____. Thank you for the enclosed phone numbers. Once I tried to get to the Eating Disorder part of a hospital & the doctor sexually assaulted me! So I will not try that again!

One woman wrote about how her concern for her children is what keeps her from mutilating herself. At the same time she expresses a chilling fear that her self-harm may have already damaged her children.

> It was weird filling out the questionnaire, especially addressing the self-mutilation so much. I feel so alone—the feeling I got from your choice of answers is that

there are others out there like me. I self-mutilated from '86 to '90, purging etc from about 87–88 to 90, when I had my first baby. I've been in & out of many mental hospitals from '86 to 89, for depression and suicide, but no one really addressed my self-mutilation except to make me stop—(would take away privileges, etc). No one worked with me to see why I did it. Same with purging—no one addressed it. I was very anorexic, then turned to purging also. I now have two children, I had a miscarriage first. Brian is 3, Joshua is 16 months. I'm pregnant and due in October. For some reason, while I'm pregnant, I'm able to stop the self-mutilation & purging & anorexic behaviors. Also since I had the children I haven't self-mutilated—I know they'd put me back in the hospital & I couldn't do that to my children. But I haven't been able to control the anorexia/bulimia. I know after I deliver I'll at some time resort back.

What really bothers me about all this—all three children have special needs. Brian is developmentally delayed and has sensory integration dysfunction. Joshua is blind—he has septo-optic dysplasia & ty-neg albinism. He also has a kidney disorder and pituitary problems. The baby I'm carrying has a severe cardiac condition—hypoplastic left heart syndrome & isn't expected to live more than a few days. We've been thru genetic counseling—my husband & I & the boys—so far everything has come back normal. Nothing is hereditary except the albinism. It's always been in the back of my head—am I responsible—for my damage to my body for years of abuse—with the laxatives, diuretics, self-starvation etc? Could this have affected or caused my children's conditions? I'm leaving my name and address—only if you have any insight into this for me.

Similarly, another woman wrote about her illness and the effect of it on her children. She too hoped her participation in the study would help others.

I would like you to know that I began pulling out my hair sometime between the ages of 9 and 11. . . . I was taken to a number of mental health professionals who basically told my parents I would outgrow it. My parents also began beating me physically to get me to stop. . . . At age 14 I was sent away to boarding school. I have had small periods of time when growing up that I didn't pull out my hair, but they never lasted very long and it was always when I was away from home for a period of time.

I began treatment for depression when I was 37 years old and after therapy for a couple of years I began exploring why I pulled out my hair. My therapist thought the stroking was a source of comfort but that I needed to follow it up with a punitive action—the pulling out. We worked for some time on why I developed the need for this and I began having memories of my father molesting me when I was around 9 or so.

I believe this behavior is directly related to the trauma of molestation. I have since discovered there were multiple abuses at a much younger age, but am unable to have clear visual memories of those molestations. I do, however, have body memories.

Last October my psychiatrist discovered an article on trichotillomania being successfully treated with Lithium. . . . Within one week of beginning the Lithium . . . I literally stopped pulling out my hair. I was very nearly bald, but chose not to wear a wig. Now most of my hair has grown in.

I still pull out my hair. I never completely stopped. I think the part that stopped was probably neurochemical and the part that hasn't stopped is habit. I've been doing this behavior for well over 30 years. I also think the parts of me that have not completely resolved the sexual abuse still responds by hair-pulling.

I could write a book on this subject, from waking up as a little girl realizing I was pulling out my hair and eating it to being hit with a belt (sometimes with clothes, sometimes without) and banished from family outings. I was sent out of my home, screamed at, hurt, humiliated, had my fingers taped together, and being "inspected" by my father as a nightly ritual to see if I'd pulled out any eyelashes or eyebrows that day, all of this in view of my four younger siblings. I could never answer the why's. "Why do you do that? It makes you look so dumb."

The behavior is just that, a behavior. The why is severe trauma. My trauma began as sexual and extended to emotional, verbal, and physical. My understanding right now is that trichotillomania is caused by neurological change in the brain caused by severe trauma. Sexual abuse is severe trauma.

Maybe you are curious as to why this behavior didn't begin earlier if I have strong feelings that there was sexual abuse at an earlier age. I believe the earlier sexual abuse was preverbal. I think I am probably very fragmented as a result of that early abuse. I don't know how I coped as an infant. Perhaps I dissociated, perhaps part of me split off and there are other personalities. My therapy hasn't gone that far and I'm not sure I want to know until my boys are out of school. They've already been through a lot with a mom being in various stages of depression for the past six years or so, uncovering the horror of childhood sexual abuse, voluntary admittance to a psychiatric hospital twice (once for attempted suicide), and walking around nearly bald because she pulls her hair out so much.

Someday somebody should do a study about the repercussions of family members whose parents began having memories of sexual abuse during their formative years.

Anyway, I hope your study accomplishes what you want it to. I'm at a point in my therapy and development through this horror that I really want to be able to offer something to someone else whether it be information or hope or a listening ear.

My best to you.

BODY MODIFICATIONS AND TRANSITIONAL SPACE

Through the study, I invited replies from people actively involved in piercing, tattooing, and sadomasochism, and got quite a different response than I could have anticipated. I had thought that my recruitment efforts would be met with some resistance and hostility, but was surprised at the degree of anger my study engendered and at active attempts to thwart it. I quickly learned that to conceptualize tattooing, body piercing, and other body modifications as forms of self-mutilation without other qualifying information was the equivalent of waving a red flag in front of a bull and inviting an angry, sadistic attack. (The owner of a tattoo/piercing studio almost threw me out.)

I was accused of "pathologizing" behavior they wanted to consider simply part of an "alternate" lifestyle, without examining or truly seeking to understand it. Despite these attacks, several people who heard of the study through the *PFIQ* requested questionnaires, participated in the study, and were the source of valuable information. Sara, a 37-year-old divorced woman, was one of them. A victim of childhood physical and sexual abuse, she spent much of her adolescence in group care. She has several skeletons tattooed on her abdomen, a signifier of her suicidal inclinations, as well as 11 earlobe piercings, 3 piercings on the upper ear, 3 nostril piercings, 2 nipple piercings, and a genital piercing. She binges and purges very violently, using vomiting, laxative pills and suppositories, enemas, syrup of Ipecac, and diuretics. She has consumed poisonous cleaning agents during binges to try to kill herself, and has deliberately overdosed on opium and heroin. Despite the pain she inflicts on herself she finds her flirtation with death renewing and energizing.

> I am trying to kill myself but in an inconspicuous way—I cannot slit my wrists because I just can't bring myself to do it that way but I have a great desire to harm myself in other ways that will end my life.
>
> I get a new "renewal" in positive spirit when I live through each suicide attempt, although I would like each to be the last. . . . I purposely O.D. on drugs (to try to kill myself).
>
> . . . I hate myself & the hate actually builds up to a point that I want to kill myself and end the mental pain. . . . Physical pain is renewing "life."

Another who responded to the recruitment notice in the *PFIQ* but who did not satisfy selection criteria was a prison inmate who seemed to be looking for ways to make sense of his potentially lethal behavior. He seemed eager to participate in the study and wanted to make a good impression, using words for his self-harm behavior so technical that I did not know to which behavior he was referring and neither did two dictionaries on hand to which I referred before resorting to the *Oxford English Dictionary*. The bracketed material in his letter is mine.

> I am writing in response to your study on binge/purge and self-mutilating that I read about in my February issue of *Piercing Fans International Quarterly*. I would be very interested in participating in your study.
>
> For quite a few years I have considered myself a self-mutilator but have yet to discuss this topic with anybody. I am into hypoxyphilia [erotic strangulation] and infibulation [sewing closed the foreskin of the penis to make erection or masturbation very painful] and believe I could make a great contribution to your study and future research.

A subscriber to *Piercing Fans International Quarterly* wrote a lengthy and articulate letter communicating how offended he and his wife were by my recruitment notice and what personal meaning their piercing has for them. He did, however, allow that perhaps they have misunderstood my intentions and conveyed that they wanted their unconventional behavior not to be judged but to be understood.

I am a subscriber to *Piercing Fans International Quarterly* and an enthusiastic participant in the world of piercing. . . . I read your notice regarding your study and I immediately took offense. . . .

Both my wife and I are pierced. We consider our piercings synonymous to our wedding rings. There is by far a greater symbolism in our mutual experience and commitment to a unique marriage ritualized by our piercings.

The act of piercing, the reenactment of the pain and struggle in one's life, is not an aberration you can identify with binge–purging and self-mutilation . . . I read in your request an intolerance to perversion. Paradoxically you succumb to the perverse need to dehumanize. I cannot imagine that you have studied primitive societies and their rituals, the meaning of symbolism and its importance to any society, shamanism, alchemy and mythology and still proceed with your study.

There seems to be a populace within the United States of America which dehumanizes every aspect of our modern society which differs with traditional ways of life. They fear the unknown. They make laws displacing the rights of those who differ from their sense of morality. . . .

If by chance we have jumped to a wrong conclusion about your potential research, we offer our apology.

Included with the letter was a reading list to help in the research endeavor, quite a good one that included several psychoanalytic references and references from mythology and anthropology. He urged me to acquaint myself with *Modern Primitives* and even provided the address and telephone number of a bookstore which carried it.

As I continued to mail recruitment notices, I reworded those sent to body modification studios, emphasizing that I wanted to understand how the tattooing and piercing was subjectively experienced. I referred to "body-focused behaviors" rather than using the word "self-mutilation," and expressed interest in wanting to understand how body-modifications associated with binge–purging were used as efforts toward healing or transcending past experiences. The response to the revised notice was less antagonistic, with one owner of a tattoo and piercing studio requesting three additional questionnaires for friends who also owned studios. The response to the revised notice and to some extent, to the original one, suggested that the study did to some degree serve as transitional space with this subculture.

References

Abel, J. (1996). Modern docs deal with ancient rites. *New York Post*, November 12, p. 47.

Abraham, S., and Beaumont, P. (1982). How patients describe bulimia or binge eating. *Psychological Medicine* 12:625–635.

Ackerman, D. (1990). *A Natural History of the Senses*. New York: Vintage.

Ainsworth, M., Blehar, M., Waters, E., and Wall, S. (1978). *Patterns of Attachment*. Hillsdale, NJ: Lawrence Erlbaum.

Alexander, F. (1958). Unexplored areas in psychoanalytic theory and treatment—Part II. In *The Scope of Psychoanalysis*, pp. 319–335. New York: Basic Books.

Allison, D. (1988). *Trash: Stories by Dorothy Allison*. Ithaca, NY: Firebrand.

———. (1992). *Bastard Out of Carolina*. New York: Dutton.

American Psychiatric Association. (1994). *Diagnostic and Statistical Manual of Mental Disorders*, 4th ed. Washington, DC: APA.

Ammon, G. (1979). *Psychoanalysis and Psychosomatics*. New York: Springer.

Anderson, C. (1986). Predation and primate evolution. *Primates* 27(1):15–39.

Anderson, M. (1999). The pressure toward enactment and the hatred of reality. *Journal of the American Psychoanalytic Association* 47(2):503–518.

Angier, N. (1994). Mother's milk found to be potent cocktail of hormones. *The New York Times*, May 24, p. C1.
————. (1998). A gallery of human oddities who are, after all, human. *The New York Times*, August 23, pp. 29–33.
Anzieu, D. (1980). Skin ego. In *Psychoanalysis in France*, ed. S. Lebovici and D. Widlocher, pp. 17–32. New York: International Universities Press.
————. (1990). *Psychic Envelopes*. New York: Brunner/Mazel.
Armstrong, J., and Roth, D. (1989). Attachment and separation difficulties in eating disorders: a preliminary investigation. *International Journal of Eating Disorders* 8(2):141–155.
Armstrong, M. (1991). Career-oriented women with tattoos. *IMAGE: Journal of Nursing Scholarship* 23(4):215–220.
Armstrong, M., McConnell, C. (1994). Tattooing in adolescents: more common than you think—the phenomenon and risks. *Journal of Student Nursing* 10(1):26–33.
Aronson, J. (1986). The level of object relations and severity of symptoms in the normal weight bulimic patient. *International Journal of Eating Disorders* 5:669–681.
————. ed. (1993). *Insights in the Dynamic Psychotherapy of Anorexia and Bulimia*. Northvale, NJ: Jason Aronson.
————. (1996). The use of the telephone as a transitional space in the treatment of a severely masochistic anorexic patient. In *Fostering Healing and Growth: A Psychoanalytic Social Work Approach*, ed. J. Edward and J. Sanville, pp. 163–178. Northvale, NJ: Jason Aronson.
Asch, S. (1971). Wrist-scratching as a symptom of anhedonia. *Psychoanalytic Quarterly* 40:603–617.
Atlas, J. (1997). The sandwich generation. *The New Yorker*, October 13, pp. 54–60.
Atwood, M. (1989). *Cat's Eye*. New York: Doubleday.
Bach, S. (1985). *Narcissistic States and the Therapeutic Process*. New York: Jason Aronson.
————. (1994). *The Language of Perversion and the Language of Love*. New York: Jason Aronson.
Bach-Y-Rita, G. (1974). Habitual violence and self-mutilation. *American Journal of Psychiatry* 131:1018–1020.
Baker, A., Brisbane, M., and Burke, M. (1996). *Self Injury: A Resource Pack*. Liverpool, England: Ashworth Hospital Authority.
Barkin, L. (1978). The concept of the transitional object. In *Between Reality and Fantasy: Winnicott's Concepts of Transitional Objects and Phenomena*, ed. S. Grolnick and L. Barkin, pp. 513–536. Northvale, NJ: Jason Aronson.
Bass, A. (1994). Aspects of urethrality in women. *Psychoanalytic Quarterly* 63(3):491–517.

Bass, E., and Davis, L. (1988). *The Courage to Heal: A Guide for Women Survivors of Child Sexual Abuse*. New York: Harper & Row.

Bateman, A. (1998). Thick-and thin-skinned organisations and enactment in borderline and narcissistic disorders. *International Journal of Psycho-Analysis* 79:13–25.

Battegay, R. (1991). *Hunger Diseases*. Lewiston, NY: Hogrefe and Huber.

Bear. (1993). Body piercing: self-adornment or self-abuse? *Piercing Fans International Quarterly* 41:14–35.

Becvar, R., and Becvar, D. (1982). *Systems Theory and Family Therapy*. New York: University Press of America.

Bell, R. (1985). *Holy Anorexia*. Chicago: University of Chicago Press.

Bemporad, J. R., and Herzog, D. B., eds. (1989). *Psychoanalysis and Eating Disorders*. New York: Guilford.

Benedek, T. (1949). The psychosomatic implications of the primary unit: Mother–child. In *Psychoanalytic Investigations: Selected Papers, 1973*, pp. 255–275. New York: Quadrangle.

———. (1959). Parenthood as a developmental phase. In *Psychoanalytic Investigations: Selected Papers, 1973*, pp. 377–407. New York: Quadrangle.

Benedict, R. (1934). *Patterns of culture*. Boston: Houghton Mifflin.

Benson, A., ed. (2000). *I Shop, Therefore I Am: Compulsive Buying and the Search for Self*. Northvale, NJ: Jason Aronson.

Benson, A., and Futterman, L. (1985). Psychotherapeutic partnering: an approach to the treatment of anorexia nervosa and bulimia. In *Theory and Treatment of Anorexia Nervosa and Bulimia*. ed. S. Emmet, pp. 154–173. New York: Brunner/Mazel.

Beres, D. (1952). Clinical notes on aggression in children. *Psychoanalytic Study of the Child* 7:241–263. New York: International Universities Press.

Beresin, E., Gordon, C., and Herzog, D. (1989). The process of recovering from anorexia nervosa. *Journal of the American Academy of Psychoanalysis* 17(1): 103–130.

Berger, J. (1972). *Ways of Seeing*. New York: Penguin.

Bergh, C., Eklund, T., Sodersten, P., and Nordin, C. (1997). Altered dopamine function in pathological gambling. *Psychological Medicine* 27:473–475.

Bergmann, M. S. (1992). *In the Shadow of Moloch: The Sacrifice of Children and Its Impact on Western Religions*. New York: Columbia University Press.

———. (1999). Asking for Freud's blessing. In *The Modern Freudians: Contemporary Psychoanalytic Technique*, ed. C. Ellman, S. Grand, M. Silvan, and S. Ellman, pp. 269–298. Northvale, NJ: Jason Aronson.

Bergmann, M. S., and Jucovy, M. (1982). *Generations of the Holocaust*. New York: Basic Books.

Bergmann, M. V. (1988). On eating disorders and work inhibition. In *Bulimia: Psychoanalytic Treatment and Theory*, ed. H. Schwartz, pp. 347–397. Madison, CT: International Universities Press.

Berliner, L., and Williams, L. (1994). Memories of child sexual abuse: a response to Lindsay and Read. *Applied Cognitive Psychology* 8:379–387.

Bettelheim, B. (1943). Individual and mass behavior in extreme situations. *Journal of Abnormal Psychology* 38:417–452.

Bick, E. (1968). The experience of the skin in early object relations. *International Journal of Psychoanalysis* 49:484–486.

Bion, W. (1962). *Learning from Experience*. London: Heinemann.

Blanck, G. (1998). Lay analysis in the postwar years. *Journal of the American Psychoanalytic Association* 46(4):1243–1245.

Blanck, G., and Blanck, R. (1974). *Ego Psychology: Theory and Practice*. New York: Columbia University Press.

———. (1979). *Ego Psychology II: Psychoanalytic Developmental Psychology*. New York: Columbia University Press.

———. (1986). *Beyond Ego Psychology: Developmental Object Relations Theory*. New York: Columbia University Press.

Blanck, R. (1998). *Structural considerations in transference*. Paper delivered posthumously by Dr. Gertrude Blanck, Society of the New York School for Psychoanalytic Psychotherapy and Psychoanalysis, New York, October.

Blau, M. (1994). Ordinary people: S&M is suddenly everywhere, in movies, in fashion, and in the bedroom next door. *New York Magazine*, pp. 37–46, November 28.

Bliss, E. (1980). Multiple personalities: a report of 14 cases with implications for schizophrenia. *Archives of General Psychiatry* 37:1388–1397.

Bloch, D. (1994). *"So the Witch Won't Eat Me": Fantasy and the Child's Fear of Infanticide*. Northvale, NJ: Jason Aronson.

Blos, P. (1962). *On Adolescence: A Psychoanalytic Interpretation*. New York: Free Press.

Bollas, C. (1987). *The Shadow of the Object: Psychoanalysis of the Unthought Known*. New York: Columbia University Press.

———. (1992). *Being a Character: Psychoanalysis and Self Experience*. New York: Hill and Wang.

———. (1997). *Freely Associated: Encounters in Psychoanalysis with Christopher Bollas, Joyce McDougall, Michael Eigen, Adam Phillips, Nina Coltart*. London/New York: Free Association.

Bordo, S. (1997). The body and the reproduction of femininity. In *Writing on the Body: Female Embodiment and Feminist Theory*, ed. K. Conboy, N. Medina, and S. Stanbury, pp. 90–110. New York: Columbia University Press.

Bornstein, B. (1953). Masturbation in the latency period. *Psychoanalytic Study of the Child* 8:65–78. New York: International Universities Press.

Bowlby, J. (1969). *Attachment and Loss, vol. 1: Attachment*. New York: Basic Books.

———. (1974). Attachment theory, separation anxiety, and mourning. In *American Handbook of Psychiatry, Volume VI*, ed. D. Hamburg and H. Brodie, pp. 385–408. Westbury, NY: PJD Publications Limited.

————. (1979). *The Making and Breaking of Affectional Bonds*. New York: Routledge.

Boyer, B. (1956). On maternal overstimulation and ego defects. *Psychoanalytic Study of the Child* 11:236–256. New York: International Universities Press.

————. (1971). Psychoanalytic technique in the treatment of certain characterological and schizophrenic disorders. *International Journal of Psycho-Analysis* 52:67–85.

————. (1997). The verbal squiggle game in treating the seriously disturbed patient. *Psychoanalytic Quarterly* 66(1):62–81.

———— (1999). *Counter-Transference and Regression*. Northvale, NJ: Jason Aronson.

Bray, G. (1986). Effects of obesity on health and happiness. In *Handbook of Eating Disorders: Physiology, Psychology, and Treatment of Obesity, Anorexia, and Bulimia*, ed. K. Brownell and J. Foreyt, pp. 3–44. New York: Basic Books.

Brazelton, T. B. (1972). *Infants and Mothers: Differences in Development*. New York: Dell.

————. (1974). *Toddlers and Parents: A Declaration of Independence*. New York: Delacorte.

————. (1981). *On Becoming a Family: The Growth of Attachment*. New York: Delacorte.

Brazelton, T. B., and Cramer, B. (1990). *The Earliest Relationship: Parents, Infants, and the Trauma of Early Attachment*. Reading, MA: Addison-Wesley.

Bredvold, L., McKillop, A., and Whitney, L., eds. (1973). William Blake. In *Eighteenth Century Poetry and Prose*, pp. 1450–1458. New York: Ronald.

Breggin, P., and Breggin, G. (1994). *Talking Back to Prozac*. New York: St. Martin's Press.

Brenner, C. (1982). *The Mind in Conflict*. Madison, CT: International Universities Press.

Brenner, D. (1983). Self-regulatory functions in bulimia. *Contemporary Psychotherapy Review* 1(1):79–96.

Brenner, I. (1994). The dissociative character: a reconsideration of "multiple personality." *Journal of the American Psychoanalytic Association* 42(3):819–846.

Breuer, J., and Freud, S. (1893). On the psychical mechanism of hysterical phenomena: a preliminary communication. *Standard Edition* 2:1–17.

Briere, J. (1992). *Child Abuse Trauma: Theory and Treatment of the Lasting Effects*. Newbury Park, CA: Sage.

Brisman, J., and Siegel, M. (1984). Bulimia and alcoholism: two sides of the same coin. *Journal of Substance Abuse Treatment* 1:113–118.

Browne, A., and Finkelhor, D. (1986). Impact of child sexual abuse: review of the research. *Psychological Bulletin* 99:66–77.

Bruch, H. (1973). *Eating Disorders: Obesity, Anorexia Nervosa and the Person Within.* New York: Basic Books.

———. (1978). *The Golden Cage: The Enigma of Anorexia Nervosa.* Cambridge, MA: Harvard University Press.

———. (1985). Four decades of eating disorders. In *Handbook of Psychotherapy for Anorexia Nervosa and Bulimia*, ed. D. Garner and P. Garfinkel, pp. 7–18. New York: Guilford.

Brumberg, J. (1988). *Fasting Girls: The Emergence of Anorexia Nervosa as a Modern Disease.* Cambridge: Harvard University Press.

———. (1997). *The Body Project: An Intimate History of American Girls.* New York: Random House.

Buber, M. (1970). *I and Thou*, transl. Walter Kaufman. New York: Scribner.

Buchholz, E. (1997). *The Call of Solitude: Alonetime in a World of Attachments.* New York: Simon and Schuster.

Bullitt-Jonas, M. (1999). *Holy Hunger.* New York: Alfred A. Knopf.

Burka, J. (1996). The therapist's body in reality and fantasy: a perspective from an overweight therapist. In *The Therapist as a Person: Life Crises, Life Choices, Life Experiences, and Their Effects on Treatment*, ed. B. Gerson, pp. 255–275. Hillsdale, NJ: Analytic Press.

Burstow, B. (1992). *Radical Feminist Therapy: Working in the Context of Violence.* Newbury Park, CA: Sage.

Bushnell, J., Wells, J., McKenzie, J., and Hornblow, A. (1994). Bulimia comorbidity in the general population and in the clinic. *Psychological Medicine* 24(3):605–611.

Buxbaum, E. (1960). Hair-pulling and fetishism. *Psychoanalytic Study of the Child* 15(243):260. New York: International Universities Press.

Camper, F., Farber, S., and Gerson, S. (1988). *A study of anxiety and depersonalization in delicate self-cutters.* Unpublished research paper, New York University School of Social Work.

Camper, F., Farber, S., Gerson, S., and Murphy, J. (1988). *Self-mutilating behavior in female victims of sexual abuse.* Unpublished research paper, New York University School of Social Work.

Candland, D. (1993). *Feral Children and Clever Animals: Reflections on Human Nature.* New York: Oxford University Press.

Carla. (1996). Untitled. *The Cutting Edge* 7(4):8.

Carmen, E., Crane, B., Dunnicliff, M., et al. (1996). *Task force on the restraint and seclusion of persons who have been physically or sexually abused: report and recommendations*, pp. 1–18. Brockton, MA: Massachusetts Department of Mental Health.

Carmen, E., Rieker, P., and Mills, T. (1984). Victims of violence and psychiatric illness. *American Journal of Psychiatry* 141:378–383.

Carrasquillo-Ramirez, A. (1998). *Tattooing the name of the mother: inscriptions in the body of juvenile delinquents.* Paper presented at the Ninth Annual Conference of the International Federation on Psychoanalytic Education, *How Will the Body Speak in the 21st Century?*, New York, November.

Carroll, K., and Leon, G. (1981). *The bulimic-vomiting disorder within a generalized substance abuse pattern.* Paper presented at the annual meeting of the Association for the Advancement of Behavior Therapy. Toronto, Canada.

Chamberlain, L. (1998). An introduction to chaos and nonlinear dynamics. In *Clinical Chaos: A Therapist's Guide to Nonlinear Dynamics and Therapeutic Change*, ed. L. Chamberlain and M. Butz, pp. 3–14. New York: Brunner/Mazel.

Chamberlain, L., and Butz, M., eds. (1998). *Clinical Chaos: A Therapist's Guide to Nonlinear Dynamics and Therapeutic Change.* Philadelphia: Brunner/Mazel.

Chandler, S., Abood, D., Lee, D., et al. (1994). Pathogenic eating attitudes and behaviors and body dissatisfaction differences among black and white college students. *Eating Disorders: The Journal of Treatment and Prevention* 2(4):319–328.

Chasseguet-Smirgel, J. (1984). *Creativity and Perversion.* New York: W. W. Norton.

———. (1995). Auto-sadism, eating disorders, and femininity: reflections based on case studies of adult women who experienced eating disorders as adolescents. In *Essential papers on Masochism*, ed. M. Hanly, pp. 453–470. New York: New York University Press.

Chassler, L. (1997). Understanding anorexia nervosa and bulimia nervosa from an attachment perspective. *Clinical Social Work Journal* 25(4):407–423.

Chatoor, I. (1989). Infantile anorexia nervosa: a developmental disorder of separation and individuation. *Journal of the American Academy of Psychoanalysis* 17(1):43–64.

Cheever, S. (1999). *Note Found in a Bottle: My Life as a Drinker.* New York: Simon and Schuster.

Cindy. (1995). Untitled. *The Cutting Edge* 6(4):8–9.

Claude-Pierre, P. (1997). *The Secret Language of Eating Disorders.* New York: Times Books.

Clendenin, W. and Murphy, G. (1971). Wrist cutting; new epidemiological findings. *Archives of General Psychiatry* 25:465–469.

Cochrane, C., Brewerton, T., Wilson, D., and Hodges, E. (1993). Alexithymia in the eating disorders. *International Journal of Eating Disorders* 14(2):219–222.

Coid, J., Allolio, B., and Rees, C. (1983). Raised plasma metenkephalin in patients who habitually mutilate themselves. *Lancet*, September 3, pp. 545–546.

Coleridge, S. (1798). *Selected Poetry and Prose of Coleridge*, ed. D. Stauffer. New York: The Modern Library, 1951.

Colt, G. (1997). The magic of touch. *Life*, August, pp. 52–62.

Conboy, K., Medina, N., and Stanbury, S., eds. (1997). *Writing on the Body: Female Embodiment and Feminist Theory.* New York: Columbia University Press.

Connors, R. (1996a). Self-injury in trauma survivors: 1. Functions and meanings. *American Journal of Orthopsychiatry* 66(2):197–206.

————. (1996b). Self-injury in trauma survivors: 2. Levels of clinical response. *American Journal of Orthopsychiatry* 66(2):207–216.

Conterio, K., and Vaughan, J. (1989). *S.A.F.E. (Self Abuse Finally Ends). Manual for a Structured Therapy Group for Those Who Self-Injure and Who Are Motivated to Stop Their Self-Injurious Behavior.* Chicago: Hartgrove Hospital.

Conway, F., and Siegelman, J. (1995). *Snapping: America's Epidemic of Sudden Personality Change.* New York: Stillpoint.

Cooper, J. (1993). *Eat and Be Satisfied: A Social History of Jewish Food.* Northvale, NJ: Jason Aronson.

Coric, M., and Murstein, B. (1993). Bulimia nervosa: prevalence and psychological correlates in a college community. *Eating Disorders: The Journal of Treatment and Prevention* 1(1):38–51.

Crabtree, L. (1967). A psychotherapeutic encounter with a self-mutilating patient. *Psychiatry* 30:91–100.

Crabtree, L., and Grossman, W. (1974). Administrative clarity and redefinition for an open adolescent unit. *Psychiatry* 37:350–359.

Crisp, A., Burns, T., and Bhat, A. (1986). Primary anorexia nervosa in the male and female: a comparison of clinical features and prognosis. *British Journal of Medical Psychology* 59:123–132.

Cross, L. (1993). Body and self in feminine development: implications for eating disorders and delicate self-mutilation. *Bulletin of the Menninger Clinic* 57(1):41–68.

Daldin, H. (1988a). A contribution to the understanding of self-mutilating behavior in adolescence. *Journal of Child Psychotherapy* 14:61–66.

————. (1988b). The fate of the sexually abused child. *Clinical Social Work Journal* 16(1):22–32.

Davies, J. (1999). Getting cold feet, defining safe enough borders: dissociation, multiplicity, and integration in the analyst's experience. *Psychoanalytic Quarterly* 78:184–208.

Davies, J., and Frawley, M. (1994). *Treating the Adult Survivor of Childhood Sexual Abuse: A Psychoanalytic Perspective.* New York: Basic Books.

de Beauvoir, S. (1949). *The Second Sex.* New York: Vintage.

Deutsch, F. (1959). *On the Mysterious Leap from the Mind to the Body.* New York: International Universities Press.

deYoung, M. (1982). Self-injurious behavior in incest victims: a research note. *Child Welfare* 61(8):577–584.

de Zulueta, F. (1994). *From Pain to Violence: The Traumatic Roots of Destructiveness.* Northvale, NJ: Jason Aronson.

DiClemente, R., Ponton, L., and Hartley, D. (1990). Prevalence and correlates of cutting behavior: risk for HIV transmission. *Journal of the American Academy of Child and Adolescent Psychiatry* 30(5):735–739.

Doctors, S. (1981). The symptom of delicate self-cutting in adolescent females: a developmental view. *Adolescent Psychiatry* 9:443–450.

Dossey, L. (1993). *Healing Words: The Power of Prayer and the Practice of Medicine.* New York: HarperCollins.

Drewnowski, A., Yee, D., and Krahn, D. (1988). Bulimia in college women: incidence and recovery rates. *American Journal of Psychiatry* 145:753–755.

Druck, A. (1999). Deficit and conflict: an attempt at integration. In *The Modern Freudians: Contemporary Psychoanalytic Technique,* ed. C. Ellman, S. Grand, M. Silvan, and S. Ellman, pp. 209–233. Northvale, NJ: Jason Aronson.

Dulit, R., Fyer, M., Leon, A., et al. (1995). Clinical correlates of self-mutilation in borderline personality disorder. *American Journal of Psychiatry* 151(9):1305–1311.

Dunbar, F. (1954). *Emotions and Bodily Functions.* New York: Columbia University Press.

Dunbar, R. (1997). *Grooming, Gossip, and the Evolution of Language.* Cambridge, MA: Harvard University Press.

Easton, D. and Liszt, C. (1995). *The Topping Book: Getting Good at Being Bad.* San Francisco: Greenery Press.

———. (1996). *The Bottoming Book: How to Get Terrible Things Done to You by Wonderful People.* San Francisco: Greenery Press.

Egan, J. (1997). The thin red line. *The New York Times,* July 27, pp. 21–48.

Ehrenreich, B. (1997). *Blood Rites: Origins and History of the Passions of War.* New York: Holt.

Eigen, M. (1997). *Freely Associated: Encounters in Psychoanalysis with Christopher Bollas, Joyce McDougall, Michael Eigen, Adam Phillips, Nina Coltart.* London: Free Association.

Eissler, K. (1953). The effect of the structure of the ego on psychoanalytic technique. *Journal of the American Psychoanalytic Association* 1:104–143.

Eliade, M. (1958). *Rites and Symbols of Initiation: The Mysteries of Birth and Rebirth.* New York: Harper and Row.

Ellman, S., and Monk, C. (1997). The significance of the first few months of life for self-regulation: a reply to Schore. In *The Neurobiological and Developmental Basis for Psychotherapeutic Intervention,* ed. M. Moskowitz, C. Monk, C. Kaye, and S. Ellman, pp. 73–89. Northvale, NJ: Jason Aronson.

Emerson, L. (1914). A preliminary report of psychoanalytic study and treatment of a case of self-mutilation. *Psychoanalytic Review* 1:41–52.

Engel, G., and Schmale, A. (1967). Psychoanalytic theory of somatic disorder: conversion, specificity and the disease onset situation. *Journal of the American Psychoanalytic Association* 15:344–365.

Epling, W., and Pierce, W. (1996). *Activity Anorexia: Theory, Research, and Treatment.* Mahwah, NJ: Lawrence Erlbaum.

Etheart, M., and Perkins, H. (1998). From "expert" supervision to collaborative consultation: Meeting the developmental need of the therapist. *The Renfrew Perspective* 4(2):10–11.

Faber, R. (1992). Money changes everything: compulsive buying from a bio-psychosocial perspective. *American Behavioral Scientist* 35(6):809–819.

Faber, R., Christenson, G., de Zwaan, M., and Mitchell, J. (1995). Two forms of compulsive consumption: Comorbidity of compulsive buying and binge eating. *Journal of Consumer Research* 22:296–304.

Fairbairn, R. (1952). *Psychoanalytic Studies of the Personality*. London: Routledge & Kegan Paul.

Fairburn, C. (1985). Cognitive–behavioral treatment for bulimia. In *Handbook of Psychotherapy for Anorexia Nervosa and Bulimia*, ed. D. Garner and P. Garfinkel, pp. 160–192. New York: Guilford.

Fairburn, C., and Wilson, G.T. (1993). *Binge Eating: Nature, Assessment, and Treatment*. New York: Guilford.

Fallon, A. (1990). Culture in the mirror: sociocultural determinants of body image. In *Body Images: Development, Deviance, and Change*, ed. T. Cash and T. Pruzinsky, pp. 80–109. New York: Guilford.

Farber, S. (1990). Eating disorders, self-mutilation and other primitive symptoms: attempts to regulate and medicate the self. Paper presented at a seminar sponsored by The New York School for Psychoanalytic Psychotherapy, New York, November.

———. (1991). A response to "The Emotional Consequences of Physical Child Abuse" by Annaclare Van Dalen. *Clinical Social Work Journal* 19(1):95–98.

———. (1992). *A failure-to-thrive child grows old and begins treatment: a psycho-analytically oriented treatment of a 67 year old woman with a chronic atypical eating disorder*. Paper presented to the Society for the New York School for Psychoanalytic Psychotherapy, New York, April.

———. (1995a). *A psychoanalytically informed understanding of the association be-tween binge-purge behavior and self-mutilating behavior: a study comparing binge-purgers who self-mutilate severely with binge-purgers who self-mutilate less severely or not at all*. Doctoral Dissertation, New York University School of Social Work. Published by UMI Dissertation Services, telephone 1-800-521-3042.

———. (1995b). *Women and self-harm: a psychoanalytic understanding of the re-lationship between binge-purging behavior and self-mutilating behavior*. Paper presented to the Fifth National Conference of National Membership Com-mittee on Psychoanalysis in Clinical Social Work, New York, October.

———. (1996a). Eating problems and self-mutilation in survivors of sexual abuse: self-destructiveness or survival tools? Paper presented at N.Y. State Men-tal Health Association Conference, Sexual Abuse Survivors Diagnosed with Serious Mental Illnesses, Albany, April.

———. (1996b). *Bulimic behavior and self-mutilating behavior as self-regulatory attempts in trauma survivors: a study comparing binge-purgers who self mutilate severely with binge-purgers who self mutilate mildly or not at all*. Paper presented at Trauma and Memory: An International Research Conference, Family Research Laboratory, University of New Hampshire, Durham, NH, July.

————. (1997). The mystery of addictive self-harm: eating disorders, self-mutilation, and symptom substitution. *Cortland Medical Addiction Services Newsletter* Spring 1997.

————. (1998a). The body speaks, the body weeps: eating disorders, self-mutilation and body modifications. *The Renfrew Perspective* 4(2[Fall]):8–9.

————. (1998b). *The body speaks: the language of disordered eating, self-mutilation, body modifications and other self-harm.* Paper presented at the annual conference of the NY State Society of Clinical Social Workers, and at the 9th Annual Interdisciplinary conference of the International Federation on Psychoanalytic Education, "How Will the Body Speak in the 21st Century?", Fordham University, New York, November.

Farberow, N., and Shneidman, E. (1957). *Clues to Suicide.* New York: McGraw-Hill.

Favaro, A., and Santonastoso, P. (1999). Different types of self-injurious behavior in bulimia nervosa. *Comprehensive Psychiatry* 40(1):57–60.

Favazza, A. (1987). *Bodies Under Siege: Self-Mutilation in Culture and Psychiatry.* Baltimore: Johns Hopkins University Press.

————. (1994). *Why patients harm themselves.* New York Psychiatric Center Grand Rounds Telecast, April.

————. (1996). *Bodies Under Siege: Self-Mutilation and Body Modification in Culture and Psychiatry.* Baltimore: Johns Hopkins University Press.

Favazza, A., and Conterio, K. (1988). The plight of chronic self-mutilators. *Community Mental Health Journal* 24:22–30.

Favazza, A., DeRosear, L., and Conterio, K. (1989). Self-mutilation and eating disorders. *Suicide and Life Threatening Behavior* 19(4):352–361.

Favazza, A., and Rosenthal, R. (1990). Varieties of pathological self-mutilation. *Behavioral Neurology* 3:77–88.

Favazza, A., and Simeon, D. (1995). Self-mutilation. In *Impulsivity and Aggression*, ed. E. Hollander and D. Stein, pp. 185–200. Sussex, England: Wiley.

Fenichel, O. (1954). Anorexia. In *Collected Papers of Otto Fenichel*, ed. O. Fenichel, pp. 288–292. New York: W. W. Norton.

Ferenczi, S. (1949). Confusion of tongues between the adult and child. The language of tenderness and the language of passion. *International Journal of Psychoanalysis* 30: 225–230.

Fichter, M., Daser, M., and Postpischil, F. (1985). Anorexic syndromes in the male. *Journal of Psychiatric Research* 19:305–313.

Finkelhor, D. (1994). The international epidemiology of child sexual abuse. *Child Abuse and Neglect* 18(5):409–417.

Fonagy, P. (1997). *When cure is inconceivable: the aims of psychoanalysis with borderline patients.* Paper presented at the New York Freudian Society, New York, April.

Fonagy, P., Steele, M., Steele, H., et al. (1995). Attachment, the reflective self, and borderline states. In *Attachment Theory: Social, Developmental, and Clini-*

cal Perspectives, ed. S. Goldberg, R. Muir, and J. Kerr, pp. 233–278. Hillsdale, NJ: Analytic Press.

Fonagy, P., and Target, M. (1995). Understanding the violent patient: The use of the body and the role of the father. International Journal of Psycho-Analysis 76:487–501.

Foucault, M. (1977). The History of Sexuality, vol. 1: An Introduction. New York: Vintage.

Freedman, R. (1988). Bodylove. New York: Harper and Row.

Freud, A. (1946). The psychoanalytic study of infantile feeding disturbances. Psychoanalytic Study of the Child 2:119–132. New York: International Universities Press.

———. (1949). Aggression in relation to emotional development: normal and pathological. Psychoanalytic Study of the Child. 3/4:37–48. New York: International Universities Press.

———. (1966). The Writings of Anna Freud, Vol. 2: The Ego and the Mechanisms of Defense. New York: International Universities Press.

Freud, S. (1896). The aetiology of hysteria. Standard Edition 3:191–221.

———. (1905a). Three essays on the theory of sexuality. Standard Edition 7:135–243.

———. (1905b). Jokes and their relation to the unconscious. Standard Edition 8:9–236.

———. (1908). Creative writers and daydreaming. Standard Edition 9:141–153.

———. (1909). Notes upon a case of obsessional neurosis. Standard Edition 10:158–318.

———. (1911). Formulations on the two principles of mental functioning. Standard Edition 12:215–226.

———. (1912). Recommendations to physicians practicing psychoanalysis. Standard Edition 12:109–120.

———. (1913a). Theme of the three caskets. Standard Edition 12:289–301.

———. (1913b). Totem and taboo. Standard Edition 13:1–162.

———. (1914a). On narcissism: an introduction. Standard Edition 14:73–104.

———. (1914b). Remembering, repeating, and working through. Standard Edition 12: 143–153.

———. (1915a). Instincts and their vicissitudes. Standard Edition 14:117–140.

———. (1915b). Thoughts for the times on war and death. Standard Edition 14:273–300.

———. (1916). Introductory lectures on psychoanalysis, Part III. Standard Edition 16:243–463.

———. (1917). Mourning and melancholia. In Standard Edition 14:243–258.

———. (1918). From the history of an infantile neurosis. Standard Edition 17:7–122.

————. (1919). A child is being beaten. *Standard Edition* 17:175–204.

————. (1920a). Beyond the pleasure principle. *Standard Edition* 18:7–64.

————. (1920b). Two encyclopaedia articles. *Standard Edition* 18:235–259.

————. (1921). Group psychology and the analysis of the ego. *Standard Edition* 18:67–143.

————. (1923a). The ego and the id. *Standard Edition* 19:3–66.

————. (1923b). A seventeenth century demonological neurosis. *Standard Edition* 19:69–105.

————. (1927). Fetishism. *Standard Edition* 21:149–157.

————. (1930). Civilization and its discontents. *Standard Edition* 21:64–145.

————. (1933). New introductory lectures on psychoanalysis. *Standard Edition* 22:7–182.

————. (1937). Analysis terminable and interminable. *Standard Edition* 23:209–253.

————. (1938). An outline of psychoanalysis. *Standard Edition* 23:139–207.

————. (1940). Splitting of the ego in the process of defense. *Standard Edition* 23:271–278.

Friedman, L. (1978). Trends in the psychoanalytic theory of treatment. *Psychoanalytic Quarterly* 47(4):524–567.

————. (1991). On the therapeutic action of Loewald's theory. In *The Work of Hans Loewald: An Introduction and Commentary*, ed. G. Fogel, pp. 91–104. Northvale, NJ: Jason Aronson.

Friedman, M., Glasser, M., Laufer, E., et al. (1972). Attempted suicide and self-mutilation in adolescence. *International Journal of Psychoanalysis* 53:179–183.

Fromm, M., and Smith, B. (1989). *The Facilitating Environment: Clinical Application of Winnicott's Theory*. Madison, CT: International Universities Press.

Gabbard, G. (1996). *Love and Hate in the Analytic Setting*. Northvale, NJ: Jason Aronson.

Gaddini, R. (1975). The concept of transitional object. *Journal of the American Academy of Child Psychiatry* 14:731–736.

————. (1978). Transitional object origins and the psychosomatic symptom. In *Between Reality and Fantasy: Winnicott's Concepts of Transitional Objects and Phenomena*, ed. S. Grolnick and L. Barkin, pp. 109–131. Northvale, NJ: Jason Aronson.

Galenson, E., and Roiphe, H. (1971). The impact of early sexual discovery on mood, defensive organization and symbolization. *Psychoanalytic Study of the Child* 26:195–216. New Haven: Yale University Press.

Gardner, A. R., and Gardner, A. J. (1975). Self-mutilation, obsessionality, and narcissism. *International Journal of Psycho-Analysis* 127:127–132.

Gardner, D., and Cowdry, R. (1985). Alprazolam-induced dyscontrol in borderline personality disorder. *American Journal of Psychiatry* 142:98–100.

Garfinkel, P., Moldofsky, H., and Garner, D. (1980). The heterogeneity of anorexia nervosa. *Archives of General Psychiatry* 37:1036–1040.

Garma, A. (1953). The internalized mother as harmful food. *International Journal of Psycho-Analysis* 34:102–110.

Garner, D. (1993). Binge eating in anorexia nervosa. In *Binge Eating: Nature, Assessment, and Treatment*, ed. C. Fairburn and G. Wilson, pp. 50–76. New York: Guilford.

Garner, D., Garner, M., and Rosen, L. (1993). Anorexia nervosa "restrictors" who purge: implications for subtyping anorexia nervosa. *International Journal of Eating Disorders* 13:171–185.

Gaylin, W., and Person, E., eds. (1988). *Passionate Attachments: Thinking about Love*. New York: Free Press.

Ghadirian, A. (1997). Bulimic purging through blood donation. *American Journal of Psychiatry* 153:435–436.

Gilbert, S. (1997). Early puberty onset seems prevalent. *The New York Times*, April 9, p. C10.

Gilligan, C. (1982). *In a Different Voice: Psychological Theory and Women's Development*. Cambridge, MA: Harvard University Press.

Gilmore, K. (1998). Cloacal anxiety in female development. *Journal of the American Psychoanalytic Association* 46(2):443–470.

Giovacchini, P. (1993). The regressed patient and the psychosomatic focus. In *Master Clinicians on Treating the Regressed Patient*, ed. L. B. Boyer and P. Giovacchini, pp. 85–106. Northvale, NJ: Jason Aronson.

Girard, R. (1977). *Violence and the Sacred*. Baltimore: Johns Hopkins University Press.

Golden, B., and Walker-O'Keefe, J. (1988). Self-Injury: hidden pain in the workplace. *EAP Digest*, November/December, 13–69.

Goldhagen, D. (1997). *Hitler's Willing Executioners: Ordinary Germans and the Holocaust*. New York: Vintage.

Goldstein, E. (1990). *Borderline Disorders: Clinical Models and Techniques*. New York: Guilford.

Goode, E. (1999). With help, climbing back from schizophrenia's isolation. *The New York Times*, January 30, pp. A1–A8.

Goodsitt, A. (1985). Self psychology and the treatment of anorexia nervosa. In *Handbook of Psychotherapy for Anorexia Nervosa and Bulimia*, ed. D. Garner and P. Garfinkel, pp. 55–82. New York: Guilford.

Graff, H., and Mallin, R. (1967). The syndrome of the wrist cutter. *American Journal of Psychiatry* 124:74–80.

Green, A. (1975). The analyst, symbolization and absence in the analytic setting. *International Journal of Psycho-Analysis* 56:1–22.

———. (1978). Self-destructive behavior in battered children. *American Journal of Psychiatry* 135:579–582.

Greenacre, P. (1957). The childhood of the artist: libidinal phase development and giftedness. *Psychoanalytic Study of the Child* 12:27–72. New York: International Universities Press.

———. (1969). The fetish and the transitional object. *Psychoanalytic Study of the Child* 24:144–164.

Greenberg, H., and Sarner, C. (1965). Trichotillomania: symptom and syndrome. *Archives of General Psychiatry* 12:482–489.

Greenson, R. (1960). Empathy and its vicissitudes. In *Explorations in Psychoanalysis*, pp. 147–161. New York: International Universities Press, 1978.

Greenson, R., and Wexler, M. (1969). The nontransference relationship in the psychoanalytic situation. In *Explorations in Psychoanalysis*, ed. R. Greenson, pp. 359–386. New York: International Universities Press.

Greenspan, S. (1979). *Intelligence and Adaptation*. New York: International Universities Press.

Greif, A. (1989a). Introduction: historical synthesis. In *Masochism: The Treatment of Self-Inflicted Suffering*, ed. J. Montgomery and A. Greif, pp. 1–15. Madison, CT: International Universities Press.

———. (1989b). Masochism in the Analyst. In *Masochism: The Treatment of Self-Inflicted Suffering*, ed. J. Montgomery, pp. 169–178. Madison, CT: International Universities Press.

Greif, J., and Hewitt, W. (1996). *First International Collegiate Body Art Project*. Paper presented at Barnard College, New York, October.

Grinker, G. (1953). *Psychosomatic Concepts*. New York: W. W. Norton.

Groddeck, G. (1923). *The Book of the It*. New York: New American Library.

Grossman, C., and Grossman, S. (1965). *The Wild Analyst: The Life and Work of George Groddeck*. New York: Dell.

Grossman, W. (1991). Pain, aggression, fantasy, and concepts of sadomasochism. *Psychoanalytic Quarterly* 60(1):22–52.

Grotstein, J. (1979). Demoniacal possession, splitting, and the torment of joy: a psychoanalytic inquiry into the negative therapeutic reaction, unanalyzability, and psychotic states. *Contemporary Psychoanalysis* 15(3):407–453.

———. (1981). *Splitting and Projective Identification*. New York: Jason Aronson.

———. (1986). The psychology of powerlessness: disorders of self regulation and interactional regulation as a newer paradigm of psychopathology. *Psychoanalytic Inquiry* 6:93–118.

———. (1990). Invariants in primitive emotional disorders. In *Master Clinicians on Treating the Regressed Patient*, ed. B. Boyer and P. Giovacchini, pp. 139–163. Northvale, NJ: Jason Aronson.

———. (1993). Boundary difficulties in borderline patients. In *Master Clinicians on Treating the Regressed Patient*, vol. 2, ed. L. B. Boyer and P. Giovacchini, pp. 107–141. New York: Jason Aronson.

———. (1997). Why Oedipus and not Christ?: A psychoanalytic inquiry into innocence, human sacrifice, and the sacred. Part I: innocence, spirituality and human sacrifice. *American Journal of Psychoanalysis* 57(3):193–218.

536 / References

Grunberger, B. (1979). *Narcissism: Psychoanalytic Essays*. Madison, CT: International Universities Press.

Grunebaum, H., and Klerman, G. (1967). Wrist slashing. *American Journal of Psychiatry* 124:527–534.

Gull, W. (1874). Anorexia nervosa (apepsia hysterica, anorexia hysterica). *Transactions of the Clinical Society of London* 7:22–28.

Haines, J., Williams, C., Brain, K., and Wilson, G. (1995). The psychophysiology of self-mutilation. *Journal of Abnormal Psychology* 104(3):471–485.

Hall, R., and Beresford, T. (1989). Bulimia nervosa: diagnostic criteria, clinical features, and discrete clinical sub-syndromes. *Psychiatric Medicine* 7(3):13–25.

Hall, R., Hoffman, R., Beresford, T., et al. (1989). Physical illness encountered in patients with eating disorders. *Psychosomatics* 30(2):174–191.

Hall, R., Quinones, J., Graves, S., and Hall, A. (1990). *Bulimic sub-types: a review of 500 patients*. Paper presented at the 143rd annual meeting, American Psychiatric Association, New York, May.

Hall, S. (1999). Fear itself: what we know about how it works, how it can be treated and what it tells us about our unconscious. *The New York Times*, February 28, pp. 42–91.

Halmi, K., Falk, J., and Schwartz, E. (1981). Binge-eating and vomiting: a survey of a college population. *Journal of Psychological Medicine* 11:697–706.

Hamburg, P. (1989). Bulimia: the construction of a symptom. In *Psychoanalysis and Eating Disorders*, ed. J. Bemporad and D. Herzog, pp. 131–150. New York: Guilford.

Hamill, P. (1997). *Snow in August*. New York: Warner.

Hansburg, H. (1976). Detection of self-destructive tendencies in early adolescence. In *Researches in Separation Anxiety: A Third Volume on the Separation Anxiety Test*, pp. 225–256. Malabar, FL: Robert E. Krieger, 1986.

———. (1980). *Adolescent Separation Anxiety*, volumes 1 and 2. Huntington, NY: Robert E. Krieger.

———. (1986). *Researches in Separation Anxiety*. Malabar, FL: Robert E. Krieger.

Harrison, B. (1996). *An Accidental Autobiography*. New York: Houghton Mifflin.

Harrison, K. (1991). *Thicker Than Water*. New York: Random House.

———. (1997). *The Kiss*. New York: Avon.

Hartmann, H. (1939). *Ego Psychology and the Problem of Adaptation*. New York: International Universities Press.

Hedges, L. (1994). *In Search of the Lost Mother of Infancy*. Northvale, NJ: Jason Aronson.

Hegi, U. (1994). *Stones from the River*. New York: Simon & Schuster.

Heller, N. (1990). *Object relations and symptom choice in bulimics and self-mutilators*. Doctoral dissertation, Smith College School for Social Work. (Published by UMI Dissertation Services, telephone 1-800-521-3042.)

Henk, D. (1997). Women now comprise 12% of nation's 20 million hunters. *Herald Statesman*, November 28, p. 11.

Herman, J. (1986). Histories of violence in an outpatient population: an exploratory study. *American Journal of Orthopsychiatry* 56:137–141.

——— (1992). *Trauma and Recovery: The Aftermath of Violence, from Domestic Abuse to Political Terror*. New York: Basic Books.

Herman, J., Perry, J., and van der Kolk, B. (1989). Childhood trauma in borderline personality disorder. *American Journal of Psychiatry* 146:490–495.

Herzog, D., Bradburn, I., and Newman, K. (1990). Sexuality in males with eating disorders. In *Males with Eating Disorders*, ed. A. Andersen, pp.40–53. New York: Brunner/Mazel.

Herzog, D., Norman, D., Gordon, C., and Pepose, M. (1984). Sexual conflict and eating disorders in 27 males. *American Journal of Psychiatry* 141:989–990.

Hirsch, S., Walsh, C., and Draper, R. (1982). Parasuicide: a review of treatment interventions. *Journal of Affective Disorders* 4(4):299–311.

Hofer, M. (1995). Hidden regulators: implications for a new understanding of attachment, separation, and loss. In *Attachment Theory: Social, Developmental, and Clinical Perspectives*, S. Goldberg, R. Muir, and J. Kerr, pp. 203–230. Hillsdale, NJ: Analytic Press.

Hogan, C. (1992). The adolescent crisis in anorexia nervosa. In *Psychodynamic Technique in the Treatment of the Eating Disorders*, ed. C. Wilson, C. Hogan, and I. Mintz, pp. 111–127. Northvale, NJ: Jason Aronson.

Holderness, C., Brooks-Gunn, J., and Warren, M. (1994). Co-morbidity of eating disorders and substance abuse: Review of the literature. *International Journal of Eating Disorders* 16(1):1–34.

Hollander, E. (1993). Obsessive-compulsive spectrum disorders: an overview. *Psychiatric Annals* 23(7):355–358.

Holliday, P. (1993). The Lizzie Borden Rage Society. *The Healing Woman* 2(2):4.

Holmes, J. (1996). *Attachment, Intimacy, Autonomy: Using Attachment Theory in Adult Psychotherapy*. Northvale, NJ: Jason Aronson.

Hornbacher, M. (1998). *Wasted: A Memoir of Anorexia and Bulimia*. New York: HarperFlamingo.

Howard, M. (1996). Facts in life. In *Modern American Memoirs*, ed. A. Dillard and C. Conley, pp. 68–79. New York: Harper.

Hsu, J. (1990). *Eating Disorders*. New York: Guilford.

Hsu, J., Kaye, W., and Weltzin, T. (1993). Are the eating disorders related to obsessive compulsive disorder? *International Journal of Eating Disorders* 14(3):305–318.

Hsu, L., and Zimmer, B. (1988). Eating disorders in old age. *International Journal of Eating Disorders* 7(7):133–138.

Hunter, M. (1990). *Abused Boys: The Neglected Victims of Sexual Abuse*. New York: Fawcett Columbine.

Hutchinson, M. (1983). *Transforming Body Image: Learning to Love the Body You Have*. Freedom, CA: Crossing Press.

Ivanoff, A. (1991). Suicide and suicidal behavior. In *Handbook of Social Work Practice with Vulnerable Populations*, ed. A. Gitterman, pp. 677–709. New York: Columbia University Press.

Jacobson, E. (1964). *The Self and the Object World*. New York: International Universities Press.

Jamison, K. (1994). *Touched with Fire: Manic Depressive Illness and the Artistic Temperament*. New York: Free Press.

Jellinek, E. (1994). Alcoholism as a progressive disease. In *The Dynamics and Treatment of Alcoholism*, ed. J. Levin and R. Weiss, pp. 35–47. Northvale, NJ: Jason Aronson.

Johnson, C. (1991). Treatment of eating disorder patients with borderline and false self/narcissistic disorders. In *Psychodynamic Treatment of Anorexia Nervosa and Bulimia*, ed. C. Johnson, pp. 165–193. New York: Guilford.

Johnson, C. and Connors, M. (1987). *The Etiology and Treatment of Bulimia Nervosa*. New York: Basic Books.

Johnson, C., and Larson, R. (1982). Bulimia: an analysis of moods and behavior. *Psychological Medicine* 44:333–345.

Jones, J. (1997). *Alfred C. Kinsey: A Public/Private Life*. New York: W. W. Norton.

Joseph, B. (1982). Addiction to near-death. *International Journal of Psychoanalysis* 63:449–456.

Jung, C. (1957). *Mysterium Coniunctionis*, transl. R. F. C. Hull. Princeton: Princeton University Press, 1970.

Juno, A., and Vale, V. (1993). *Bob Flanagan: Super-Masochist*. San Francisco: Re/Search.

Kaesuk-Yoon, C. (1996). Within nests, egret chicks are natural born killers. *The New York Times*, August 6, pp. C1–C4.

Kafka, F. (1948). *In the Penal Colony: Stories and Short Pieces*. New York: Schocken.

Kafka, J. (1969). The body as transitional object: a psychoanalytic study of a self-mutilating patient. *British Journal of Medical Psychology* 42:207–211.

Kahan, J., and Pattison, E. (1984). Proposal for a distinctive diagnosis: the deliberate self-harm syndrome. *Suicide and Life Threatening Behavior* 14:17–35.

Kakar, S. (1982). *Shamans, Mystics, and Doctors: A Psychological Inquiry into India and Its Healing Traditions*. New York: Alfred A. Knopf.

Kaminer, W. (1993). *I'm Dysfunctional, You're Dysfunctional*. New York: Vintage.

Kaplan, L. (1991). *Female Perversions: The Temptations of Emma Bovary*. New York: Doubleday.

Kardiner, A. (1941). *The Traumatic Neuroses of War*. New York: P. Hoeber.

Karon, B. (1992). The fear of understanding schizophrenia. *Psychoanalytic Psychology* 9(2):191–211.

Katzman, M., Wolchik, S., and Braver, S. (1984). The prevalence of frequent binge-eating and bulimia in a nonclinical college sample. *International Journal of Eating Disorders* 3:440–445.

Kaufman, M., and Heiman, M. (1964). *Evolution of Psychosomatic Concepts—Anorexia Nervosa: A Paradigm.* New York: International Universities Press.

Kearney-Cooke, A., and Steichen-Asch, P. (1990). Men, body image, and eating disorders. In *Males with Eating Disorders*, ed. A. Andersen, pp. 54–74. New York: Brunner/Mazel.

Keesey, R. (1986). A set point theory of obesity. In *Handbook of Eating Disorders: Physiology, Psychology, and Treatment of Obesity, Anorexia, and Bulimia*, ed. K. Brownell and J. Foreyt, pp. 63–87. New York: Basic Books.

Kernberg, O. (1975). *Borderline Conditions and Pathological Narcissism.* New York: Jason Aronson.

———. (1987). A psychodynamic approach to self-mutilation. *Journal of Personality Disorders* 1:344–346.

———. (1989). A psychoanalytic classification of character pathology. In *Essential Papers on Character Neurosis and Treatment*, ed. R. Lax, pp. 191–210. New York: New York University Press.

———. (1992). *Aggression in Personality Disorders and Perversions.* New Haven, CT: Yale University Press.

Kestenberg, J. (1975). *Children and Parents: Psychoanalytic Studies in Development.* New York: Jason Aronson.

Keys, A., Brozek, J., Henschel, A., et al. (1950). *The Biology of Human Starvation.* Minneapolis: University of Minnesota Press.

Khan, M. (1963). The concept of cumulative trauma. *Psychoanalytic Study of the Child* 18:286–306. New York: International Universities Press.

———. (1978). Secret as potential space. In *Between Reality and Fantasy: Winnicott's Concepts of Transitional Objects and Phenomena*, ed. S. Grolnick, L. Barkin, in collaboration with W. Muensterberger, pp. 259–270. Northvale, NJ: Jason Aronson.

———. (1989). *The Long Wait and Other Psychoanalytic Narratives.* New York: Summit.

Khantzian, E. (1985). The self-medication hypothesis of addictive disorders: focus on heroin and cocaine dependence. *American Journal of Psychiatry* 142(11):1259–1264.

———. (1989). Addiction: self-destruction or self-repair? (Editorial). *Journal of Substance Abuse Treatment* 6:75–75.

Khantzian, E., and Mack, J. (1983). Self-preservation and the care of the self: ego instincts reconsidered. *Psychoanalytic Study of the Child* 38:209–232. New Haven, CT: Yale University Press.

Kim. (1993). Untitled. *The Cutting Edge* 4(3):3–4.

Klein, M. (1964). *Contributions to Psychoanalysis.* New York: McGraw-Hill.

Kluft, R. (1993). Multiple personality disorder. In *Dissociative Disorders: A Clinical Review*, ed. D. Spiegel, R. Kluft, and R. Loewenstein, pp. 17–44. Lutherville, MD: Sidran.

Knapp, C. (1996). *Drinking: A Love Story.* New York: Dial.

Kohut, H. (1971). *The Analysis of the Self*. New York: International Universities Press.

———. (1972). Narcissism and narcissistic rage. *Psychoanalytic Study of the Child* 27:360–400. New Haven, CT: Yale University Press.

———. (1977). *The Restoration of the Self*. New York: International Universities Press.

Krakow, A. (1994). *The Total Tattoo Book*. New York: Warner.

Kramer, P. (1993). *Listening to Prozac*. New York: Viking.

Kreitman, N. (1977). *Parasuicide*. London: Wiley.

Kris, E. (1956). The recovery of childhood memories in psychoanalysis. *Psychoanalytic Study of the Child* 11:54–88. New York: International Universities Press.

Kriss, G. (1998). Lessons at the end of a paintgun barrel. *The New York Times*, December 6, Westchester Edition 1–19.

Kroll, J. (1988). *The Challenge of the Borderline Patient: Competency in Diagnosis and Treatment*. New York: W. W. Norton.

———. (1993). *PTSD/Borderlines in Therapy: Finding the Balance*. New York: W. W. Norton.

Kron, J. (1998). *Lift: Wanting, Fearing and Having a Facelift*. New York: Viking.

Krueger, D. (1984). *Success and the Fear of Success in Women*. New York: Free Press.

———. (1988). On compulsive shopping and spending: a psychodynamic inquiry. *American Journal of Psychotherapy* 22(4):574–584.

———. (1989). *Body Self and Psychological Self: Developmental and Clinical Integration in Disorders of the Self*. New York: Brunner/Mazel.

———. (1997). Food as selfobject in eating disorder patients. *Psychoanalytic Review* 84(4):617–630.

Krystal, H. (1978). Trauma and affects. *Psychoanalytic Study of the Child* 33:81–116. New Haven, CT: Yale University Press.

Kuczynski, A. (1998). Anti-aging potion or poison? *The New York Times*, April 12, pp. 1–2.

Kuhn, T. (1962). *The Structure of Scientific Revolutions*. Chicago: University of Chicago Press.

Kupfermann, K. (1996). Modification of the psychoanalytic technique with a severely abused borderline patient and the meaning and purpose of the development of a factitious disorder, Munchausen syndrome (cancer). Unpublished paper.

———. (1998). Cancer as a factitious disorder (Munchausen syndrome) related to body self-image and object relations in a borderline patient. In *Relational Perspectives on the Body*, ed. L. Aron and F. Anderson, pp. 139–171. Mahwah, NJ: Analytic Press.

Kwawer, J. (1980). Some interpersonal aspects of self-mutilation in a borderline patient. *Journal of the American Academy of Psychoanalysis* 8(2):203–216.

Lacan, J. (1977). *Ecrits: A Selection*. New York: W. W. Norton.

Lacey, J. H. (1993). Self-damaging and addictive behaviour in bulimia nervosa: a catchment area study. *British Journal of Psychiatry* 163:190–194.

Lacey, J.H. and Evans, C. (1986). The impulsivist: A multi-impulse personality disorder. *British Journal of Addiction* 81:641–649.

Lachmann, F., and Beebe, B. (1997). The contribution of self- and mutual regulation to therapeutic action: a case illustration. In *The Neurobiological and Developmental Basis for Psychotherapeutic Intervention*, ed. M. Moskowitz, C. Monk, C. Kaye, and S. Ellman, pp. 91–121. Northvale, NJ: Jason Aronson.

Lahr, J. (1998). Skeleton of the new: the story behind the scenes of "Ragtime." *The New Yorker*, January 5, pp. 56–60.

Langone, M., and Eisenberg, G. (1993). Children and cults. In *Recovery from Cults: Help for Victims of Psychological or Spiritual Abuse*, ed. M. Langone, pp. 327–324. New York: W. W. Norton.

Lappe, M. (1996). *The Body's Edge: Our Cultural Obsession with Skin*. New York: Henry Holt.

Lasegue, E. (1873). On hysterical anorexia. *Medical Times and Gazette* 2:265–266.

Lawrence, L. (1990). The psychodynamics of the compulsive shopper. *American Journal of Psychoanalysis* 50(1):67–70.

Lax, R. (1989). Introduction. In *Essential Papers on Character Neurosis and Treatment*, p. 1, New York: New York University Press.

———. (1994). Aspects of primary and secondary genital feelings and anxieties in girls during the preoedipal and early oedipal phase. *Psychoanalytic Quarterly* 63(2):271–296.

Le Blanc, A. (1994). Gang girl: while Manny's locked up. *The New York Times*, August 14, p. 26.

Lerner, H. (1991). Masochism in subclinical eating disorders. In *Psychodynamic Treatment of Anorexia Nervosa and Bulimia*, ed. C. Johnson, pp. 109–127. New York: Guilford.

Lesser, W. (1995). An anthropologist on Mars: seven paradoxical tales. *The New York Times Book Review*, February 19, pp. 1–31.

Levenkron, S. (1981). *The Best Little Girl in the World*. New York: Warner.

Levin, J., and Weiss, R., eds. (1994). *The Dynamics and Treatment of Alcoholism*. Northvale, NJ: Jason Aronson.

Levine, D. (1974). "Needle freaks": compulsive self-injection by drug users. *American Journal of Psychiatry* 131(3):297–300.

Levine, G. (1990). Anorexia stalks the moors. Book review of *A Chainless Soul: A Life of Emily Bronte* by Katherine Frank. *The New York Times*, November 11, p. 13.

Levi-Strauss, C. (1964). *The Raw and the Cooked: Introduction to a Science of Mythology*. New York: Harper & Row.

Levitan, H. (1989). Failure of the defensive function of the ego in psychosomatic patients. In *Psychosomatic Medicine, Vol. I*, ed. S. Cheren, pp. 135–157. Madison, CT: International Universities Press.

Levy-Warren, M. (1996). *The Adolescent Journey*. Northvale, NJ: Jason Aronson.

Levy, A., and Dixon, K. (1985). The relationship between anorexia nervosa and depression: a reevaluation. *International Journal of Eating Disorders* 4(4):389–405.

Lichtenberg, J. (1983). *Psychoanalysis and Infant Research*. Hillsdale, NJ: Analytic Press.

Lifton, R. (1986). *The Nazi Doctors: A Study in the Psychology of Evil*. London: Papermac.

Lindemann, E. (1944). Symptomatology and management of acute grief. *American Journal of Psychiatry* 101:141–148.

Linehan, M. (1993a). *Cognitive-Behavioral Treatment of Borderline Personality Disorder*. New York: Guilford.

―――. (1993b). *Skills Training Manual for Treating Borderline Personality Disorder*. New York: Guilford.

Litman, R., and Swearingen, C. (1996). Bondage and suicide. In *Essential Papers on Suicide*, ed. J. Maltsberger and M. Goldblatt, pp. 243–258. New York: New York University Press.

Litsky, F. (1997). Collegiate wrestling deaths raise fears about training. *The New York Times*, December 19, pp. A1, C8.

Loewald, H. (1960). On the therapeutic action of psychoanalysis. *International Journal of Psycho-Analysis* 41:16–33.

―――. (1988). *Sublimation: Inquiries into Theoretical Psychoanalysis*. New Haven, CT: Yale University Press.

Logue, A. (1986). *The Psychology of Eating and Drinking: An Introduction*. New York: W. H. Freeman.

Lourie, R. (1949). The role of rhythmic patterns in childhood. *American Journal of Psychiatry* 105:653–660.

Lowy, F. (1983). Forward: anorexia nervosa: a paradigm for mind-body interdependence? In *Anorexia nervosa: Recent Developments in Research*, ed. P. L. Darby, pp. xii–xv. New York: Alan R. Liss.

Mack, J., and Hickler, H. (1981). Vivienne: *The Life and Suicide of an Adolescent Girl*. Boston/Toronto: Little, Brown.

Mahler, M. (1952). On child psychosis and schizophrenia: autistic and symbiotic infantile psychosis. *Psychoanalytic Study of the Child* 7(286):305. New York: International Universities Press.

―――. (1968). *On Human Symbiosis and the Vicissitudes of Individuation*. New York: International Universities Press.

Mahler, M., and McDevitt, J. (1982). Thoughts on the emergence of the sense of self, with particular emphasis on the body self. *Journal of the American Psychoanalytic Association* 30(4):827–848.

Mahler, M., Pine, F., and Bergmann, A. (1975b). *The Psychological Birth of the Human Infant*. New York: Basic Books.

Maine, M. (1991). *Father Hunger: Fathers, Daughters, and Food*. Carlsbad, CA: Gurze.

Malcove, L. (1933). Bodily mutilation and learning to eat. *Psychoanalytic Quarterly* 2:557–561.

Mallon, T. (1986). *A Book of One's Own: People and Their Diaries.* New York: Penguin.

Mannino, F., and Delgado, R. (1969). Trichotillomania in children: a review. *American Journal of Psychiatry* 126(4):505–511.

Marks, I. (1987). *Fears, Phobias, and Rituals: Panic, Anxiety, and Their Disorders.* New York and London: Oxford University Press.

Marks, I., and Nesse, R. (1994). Fear and fitness: an evolutionary analysis of anxiety disorders. *Ethology and Sociobiology* 15:247–261.

Martin, A. (1997). On teenagers and tattoos. *Journal of American Academy of Child and Adolescent Psychiatry* 36(6):860–861.

Martin, J. (1989). *Miss Manners' Guide for the Turn-of-the-Millennium.* New York: Pharose.

Marty, P., and Debray, R. (1989). Current concepts of character disturbance. In *Psychosomatic Medicine*, Vol. I, ed. S. Cheren, pp. 159–188. Madison, CT: International Universities Press.

Marty, P., and de M'Uzan, M. (1963). La pensée operatoire. *Revue Francaise de Psychanalyse* 27:1345–1356.

Masson, J. (1984). *The Assault on Truth: Freud's Suppression of the Seduction Theory.* Harmondsworth, England: Penguin.

Masterson, J. (1972). *Treatment of the Borderline Adolescent.* New York: Wiley.

Masterson, J., and Rinsley, D. (1975). The borderline syndrome: the role of the mother in the genesis and psychic structure of the borderline personality. *International Journal of Psycho-Analysis* 56:163–177.

May, R. (1969). *Love and Will.* New York: Norton.

Mazelis, R. (1995). SIV: Transforming the pain. *The Cutting Edge* 6(4):1–3.
———. (1996). SIV: Expanding our options. *The Cutting Edge* 7(1):1–2.
———. (1998). SIV: Reflections on healing. *The Cutting Edge* 8(4):1–2.

McCann, L., and Pearlman, L. (1990). Vicarious traumatization: a framework for understanding the psychological effects of working with victims. *Journal of Traumatic Stress* 3:131–149.

McDevitt, J. (1985). The emergence of hostile aggression and its defensive and adaptive modifications during the separation-individuation process. In *Defenses and Resistance*, ed. H. Blum, pp. 273–298. New York: International Universities Press.

McDougall, J. (1989). *Theaters of the Body: A Psychoanalytic Approach to Psychosomatic Illness.* New York: Norton.

McGlashan, T. (1986). The Chestnut Lodge follow-up study: long-term outcome of borderline personalities. *Archives of General Psychiatry* 43:20–30.

McLane, J. (1996). The voice on the skin: self-mutilation and Merleau-Ponty's theory of language. *Hypatia* 11(4):107–118.

McLaughlin, J. (1995). Touching limits in the psychoanalytic dyad. *Psychoanalytic Quarterly* 64:433–465.

Meloy, R. (1992). *Violent Attachments*. Northvale, NJ: Jason Aronson.

Menninger, K. (1935). A psychoanalytic study of the significance of self-mutilations. *Psychoanalytic Quarterly* 4:408–466.

Merkin, D. (1997). *Dreaming of Hitler*. New York: Crown.

Merleau-Ponty, M. (1962). *The Phenomenology of Perception*. New York: Routledge and Kegan Paul.

Michelman, J., Eicher, J., and Michelman, S. (1991). Adolescent dress, part 1: dress and body markings of psychiatric outpatients and inpatients. *Adolescence* 26(102):375–385.

Michels, R. (1988). Passionate attachments: the essential but fragile nature of love. In *Passionate Attachments: Thinking About Love*, ed. W. Gaylin and E. Person, pp. 115–121. New York: Free Press.

Mickalide, A. (1990). Sociocultural factors influencing weight among males. In *Males with Eating Disorders*, ed. A. Anderson, pp. 30–39. New York: Brunner/Mazel.

Mifflin, M. (1997). *Bodies of Subversion: A Secret History of Women and Tattoo*. San Francisco: Re/Search.

Milkman, H., and Sunderwirth, S. (1987). *Craving for Ecstasy: The Consciousness and Chemistry of Escape*. New York: Lexington.

Miller, A. (1983). *For Your Own Good: Hidden Cruelty in Child Rearing and the Roots of Violence*. New York: Farrar, Straus, Giroux.

Miller, C. (1988). *My Name Is Caroline*. New York: Doubleday.

Miller, D. (1994). *Women Who Hurt Themselves: A Book of Hope and Understanding*. New York: Basic Books.

Mintz, I. (1988). Self-destructive behavior in anorexia and bulimia. In *Bulimia: Psychoanalytic Treatment and Theory*, ed. H. Schwartz, pp. 127–171. Madison, CT: International Universities Press.

———. (1989). Treatment of a case of asthma and severe asthma. In *Psychosomatic Symptoms: Psychodynamic Treatment of the Underlying Personality Disorder*, ed. C. Wilson and I. Mintz, pp. 251–307. Northvale, NJ: Jason Aronson.

———. (1992a). The unconscious role of teeth in anorexia and bulimia: the lizard phenomenon. In *Psychodynamic Technique in the Treatment of the Eating Disorders*. ed. C. Wilson, C. Hogan, and I. Mintz, pp. 311–353. Northvale, N.J.: Jason Aronson.

———. (1992b). Clinical vignettes. In *Psychodynamic Technique in the Treatment of the Eating Disorders*, ed. C. Wilson, C. Hogan, and I. Mintz, pp. 355–378. Northvale, NJ: Jason Aronson.

Minuchin, S., Rosman, B., and Baker, L. (1978). *Psychosomatic Families: Anorexia Nervosa in Context*. Cambridge, MA: Harvard University Press.

Mitchell, J., Boutacoff, L., Hatsukami, O., et al. (1986). Laxative abuse as a variant of bulimia. *Journal of Nervous and Mental Disease* 174:174–176.

Mitchell, J., Hatsukami, D., Eckert, E., and Pyle, R. (1985). Characteristics of 275 patients with bulimia. *British Journal of Psychiatry* 142:482–485.

Mitchell, J., Maki, D., Adson, D., et al. (1997). The selectivity of inclusion and exclusion criteria in bulimia nervosa treatment studies. *International Journal of Eating Disorders* 22(3):242–252.

Modell, A. (1963). Primitive object relationships and the predisposition to schizophrenia. *International Journal of Psychoanalysis* 44:282–292.

Monette, P. (1992). *Becoming a Man*. New York: Harcourt, Brace, Jovanovich.

Monroe, J., and Abse, D. (1963). The psychopathology of trichotillomania and trichophagy. *Psychiatry* 26: 95–103.

Montagu, A. (1971). *Touching: The Human Significance of the Skin*. New York: Harper & Row.

Montgomery, J. (1989a). Preface. In *Masochism: The Treatment of Self-Inflicted Suffering*, ed. J. Montgomery and A. Greif, pp. ix–xv. Madison, CT: International Universities Press.

———. (1989b). Chronic patienthood as an iatrogenic false self. In *The Facilitating Environment: Clinical Applications of Winnicott's Theory*, ed. M. Fromm and B. Smith, pp. 345–364. Madison, CT: International Universities Press.

———. (1989c). The return of masochistic behavior in the absence of the analyst. In *Masochism: The Treatment of Self-Inflicted Suffering*, ed. J. Montgomery and A. Greif, pp. 29–36. Madison, CT: International Universities Press.

Montgomery, S. (1995). *Spell of the Tiger: The Man-Eaters of Sundarbans*. Boston: Houghton-Mifflin.

Moore, B., and Fine, B., eds. (1990). *Psychoanalytic Terms and Concepts*. New Haven: The American Psychoanalytic Association and Yale University Press.

Morris, D. (1971). *Intimate Behavior*. New York: Random House.

Morris, D. B. (1991). *The Culture of Pain*. Berkeley: University of California Press.

Morton, R. (1694). *Phthisoiologia: Or a Treatise on Consumption*. London: Smith and Walford.

Muensterberger, W. (1994). *Collecting: An Unruly Passion*. New York: Harcourt Brace.

Musafar, F. (1992). *Body Play and Modern Primitives Quarterly* 1(1):31.

Mushatt, C. (1992). Anorexia nervosa as an expression of defective ego functioning. In *Psychodynamic Technique in the Treatment of the Eating Disorders*, ed. C. Wilson, C. Hogan, and I. Mintz, pp. 301–309. Northvale, NJ: Jason Aronson.

Myers, J. (1995). Nonmainstream body modification: genital piercing, branding, burning, and cutting. In *S & M: Studies in Dominance and Submission*, ed. T. Weinberg, pp. 151—193. Amherst, NY: Prometheus.

Nacht, S. (1995). *Le masochisme*, introduction. In *Essential Papers on Masochism*, ed. M. Hanly, pp. 18–34. New York: New York University Press.

Nagata, T., McConaha, C., Rao, R., et al. (1997). A comparison of subgroups of inpatients with anorexia nervosa. *International Journal of Eating Disorders* 22(3):309–314.

Nakhla, F., and Jackson, G. (1993). *Picking Up the Pieces: Two Accounts of a Psychoanalytic Journey*. New Haven, CT: Yale University Press.

Nemiah, J., Freyberger, H., and Sifneos, P. (1976). Alexithymia: a view of the psychosomatic process. In *Modern Trends in Psychosomatic Medicine*, vol. 3, ed. O. Hill, pp. 430–439. London: Butterworths.

Newcombe, N., and Lerner, J. (1982). Britain between the two wars: the historical context of Bowlby's theory of attachment. *Psychiatry* 45:1–12.

Ney, T. (1995). *True and False Allegations of Child Sexual Abuse*. New York: Brunner/Mazel.

Niego, S., Pratt, E., and Agras, W. (1997). Subjective or objective binge: is the distinction valid? *International Journal of Eating Disorders* 22(3):291–298.

Novick, J., and Novick, K. (1996). *Fearful Symmetry: The Development and Treatment of Sadomasochism*. Northvale, NJ: Jason Aronson.

———. (1998). An application of the concept of the therapeutic alliance to sadomasochistic pathology. *Journal of the American Psychoanalytic Association* 46(3):813–846.

Novotny, P. (1972). Self-cutting. *Bulletin of the Menninger Clinic* 36:505–514.

Oates, J. (1992). *Heat and Other Stories*. New York: Plume.

Ogden, T. (1989). *The Primitive Edge of Experience*. Northvale, NJ: Jason Aronson.

———. (1990). On the structure of experience. In *Master Clinicians on Treating the Regressed Patient*, ed. B. Boyer and P. Giovacchini, pp. 69–95. New York: Jason Aronson.

———. (1994). Playing, dreaming, and interpreting experience. In *The Facilitating Environment: Clinical Applications of Winnicott's Theory*, ed. M. G. Fromm and B. Smith, pp. 255–278. Madison, CT: International Universities Press.

———. (1996). *Subjects of Analysis*. Northvale, NJ: Jason Aronson.

———. (1997). Reverie and interpretation. *Psychoanalytic Quarterly* 66(4):567–595.

Ohrbach, S. (1982). *Fat is a Feminist Issue II: A Program to Conquer Compulsive Eating*. New York: Berkley.

Oliner, M. (1988). Anal components in overeating. In *Bulimia: Psychoanalytic Treatment and Theory*, ed. H. Schwartz, pp. 227–253. Madison, CT: International Universities Press.

Orwell, G. (1949). *1984*. London, Harmondsworth: Penguin.

Ozick, C. (1996). A drugstore in winter. In *Modern American Memoirs*, ed. A. Dillard and C. Conley, pp. 108–115. New York: HarperCollins.

Pao, P. (1969). The syndrome of delicate self-cutting. *British Journal of Medical Psychology* 42:195–206.

Parens, H. (1979). *The Development of Aggression in Early Childhood*. New York: Jason Aronson.

Parkin, J., and Eagles, J. (1993). Blood-letting in bulimia nervosa. *British Journal of Psychiatry* 162:246–248.

parrish, g. (1993). Tear down that wall. *Body Memories: Radical Perspectives on Childhood Sexual Abuse* 5/6:18–20.

Parry-Jones, B., and Parry-Jones, W. (1993). Self-mutilation in four historical cases of bulimia. *British Journal of Psychiatry* 163:394–402.

Parry, A. (1934). Tatooing among prostitutes and perverts. *Psychoanalytic Quarterly* 3:476–482.

Pattison, E., and Kahan, J. (1983). The deliberate self-harm syndrome. *American Journal of Psychiatry* 140:867–872.

Phillips, A. (1994). *On Kissing Tickling and Being Bored: Psychoanalytic Essays on the Unexamined Life.* Cambridge, MA: Harvard University Press.

Phillips, D. (1996). The influence of suggestion on suicide: substantive and theoretical implications of the Werther effect. In *Essential Papers on Suicide,* pp. 290–313. New York: New York University Press.

Piaget, J., and Inhelder, B. (1969). *The Psychology of the Child.* New York: Basic Books.

Pine, F. (1980). On the expansion of the affect array: a developmental description. In *Rapprochement: The Critical Subphase of Separation-Individuation,* ed. R. Lax, S. Bach, and J. Burland, pp. 217–233. New York: Jason Aronson.

———. (1994). Conflict, defect, and deficit. *Psychoanalytic Study of the Child* 49:222–240. New Haven, CT: Yale University Press.

Pines, D. (1980). Skin communication: early skin disorders and their effects on the transference and counter-transference. *International Journal of Psycho-Analysis* 61:315–323.

Pinker, S. (1997a). Why they kill their newborns. *The New York Times,* November 2, pp. 52–54.

———. (1997b). *How the Mind Works.* New York: W. W. Norton.

Pipher, M. (1994). *Reviving Ophelia: Saving the Selves of Adolescent Girls.* New York: Ballantine.

Podvoll, E. (1969). Self-mutilation within a hospital setting: a study of identity and social compliance. *British Journal of Medical Psychology* 42:213–221.

Polhemus, T. (1988). *Body Styles.* Luton, England: Lennard.

Polivy, J., and Herman, C. (1993). Etiology of binge eating: psychological mechanisms. In *Binge Eating: Nature, Assessment, And Treatment,* ed. C. Fairburn and G. Wilson, pp. 173–205. New York: Guilford.

Pope, H., Hudson, J., Yurgelon-Todd, D., and Hudson, M. (1984). Prevalence of anorexia nervosa and bulimia in three student populations. *International Journal of Eating Disorders* 3:45–51.

Prager, E. (1996). A legend confronts its ultimate challenge: taking Manhattan. *The New York Times,* November 3, pp. 53–56.

Prose, F. (1997). Imaginary problems. In *On the Couch: Great American Stories about Therapy,* ed. E. Kates, pp. 103–117. New York: Atlantic Monthly Press.

Pruzinsky, T. (1990). *Body Images: Development, Deviance, and Change.* New York: Guilford.

Pumariega, A., Gustavson, C., Gustavson, J., et al. (1994). Eating attitudes in African-American women: the *Essence* eating disorders survey. *Eating Disorders: The Journal of Treatment and Prevention* 2(1):5–16.

Putnam, F., Guroff, J., Silberman, B., et al. (1986). The clinical phenomenology of multiple personality disorder: review of 100 recent cases. *Journal of Clinical Psychology* 47:285–293.

Pyle, R., Halvorson, P., Neuman, P., and Mitchell, J. (1986). The increasing prevalence of bulimia in freshman college students. *International Journal of Eating Disorders* 5:631–647.

Pyle, R., Mitchell, J., Eckert, E., et al. (1983). The incidence of bulimia in freshman college students. *International Journal of Eating Disorders* 2:75–78.

Rada, R., and James, W. (1982). Urethral insertion of foreign bodies: a report of contagious self-mutilation in a maximum security hospital. *Archives of General Psychiatry* 39:423–429.

Ramsland, K. (1998). *Piercing the Darkness: Undercover with Vampires in America Today.* New York: HarperPrism.

Real, T. (1997). *I Don't Want to Talk About It: Overcoming the Secret Legacy of Male Depression.* New York: Scribner.

Reid, W., and Smith, A. (1981). *Research in Social Work.* New York: Columbia University Press.

Reiser, M. (1966). Toward an integrated psychoanalytic-physiological theory of psychosomatic disorders. In *Psychoanalysis: A General Psychology: Essays in Honor of Heinz Hartmann,* ed. R. Loewenstein, L. Newman, M. Schur, and A. Solnit, pp. 570–582. New York: International Universities Press.

Resnick, P. (1999). Maternal infanticide. Paper presented at The American Psychiatric Association 152nd Annual Meeting. Washington, DC, May.

Reto, C., Dalenberg, C., and Coe, M. (1993). Dissociation and physical abuse as predictors of bulimic symptomatology and impulse dysregulation. *Eating Disorders: The Journal of Treatment and Prevention* 1(3&4):226–239.

Reus, V. (1984). Affective disorders. In *Review of General Psychiatry,* ed. H. Goldman, pp. 346–361. Los Altos, CA: Lange Medical Publications.

Rich, A. (1977). Foreword. In *Working It Out: 23 Women Writers, Artists, Scientists, and Scholars Talk about Their Lives and Work,* ed. S. Ruddick and P. Daniels, pp. xiii–xxiv, New York: Pantheon.

Richards, A. D. (1988). Self-mutilation and father–daughter incest: a psychoanalytic case report. In *Fantasy, Myth, and Reality: Essays in Honor of Jacob Arlow,* ed. H. Blum, Y. Kramer, and A. K. Richards, pp. 435–478. Madison, CT: International Universities Press.

Richards, A. K. (1992). The influence of sphincter control and genital sensation on body image and gender identity in women. *Psychoanalytic Quarterly* 61:331–351.

———. (1996). Ladies of fashion: pleasure, perversion, or paraphilia. *International Journal of Psycho-Analysis* 77:337–351.

Ritvo, S. (1988). Mothers, daughters, and eating disorders. In *Fantasy, Myth, and Reality*, ed. H. Blum, A. K. Richards, and A. D. Richards, pp. 423–434. Madison, CT: International Universities Press.

Rizzuto, A. (1985). Eating and monsters: a psychodynamic view of bulimarexia. In *Theory and Treatment of Anorexia Nervosa and Bulimia: Biomedical, Sociocultural, and Psychological Perspectives*, ed. S. Emmett, pp. 194–210. New York: Brunner/Mazel.

——. (1993). Exploring sacred landscapes. In *Exploring Sacred Landscapes*, ed. M. Randour, pp. 16–33. New York: Columbia University Press.

Rodin, J. (1992). *Body Traps: Breaking the Binds that Keep You from Feeling Good About Your Body*. New York: William Morrow.

Root, M., Fallon, P., and Friedrich, W. (1986). *Bulimia: A Systems Approach to Treatment*. New York: W. W. Norton.

Rose, L. (1988). Freud and fetishism: previously unpublished minutes of the Vienna Psychoanalytic Society. *Psychoanalytic Quarterly* 57:147–160.

Rosen, P., Walsh, B., and Rode, S. (1990). Interpersonal loss and self-mutilation. *Suicide and Life Threatening Behavior* 20(2):177–184.

Rosenbaum, M. (1979). The changing body image of the adolescent girl. In *Female Adolescent Development*, ed. M. Sugar, pp. 234–252. New York: Brunner/Mazel.

Rosenfeld, D. (1990). Psychotic body image. In *Master Clinicians on Treating the Regressed Patient*, ed. B. Boyer and P. Giovacchini, pp. 165–188. Northvale, NJ: Jason Aronson.

Rosenfeld, H. (1971). A clinical approach to the psychoanalytic theory of the life and death instincts: an investigation into the aggressive aspects of narcissism. *International Journal of Psycho-Analysis* 52:169–178.

——. (1987). *Impasse and Interpretation*. London: Tavistock.

Rosenthal, R., Rinzler, C., Walsh, R., and Klausner, E. (1972). Wrist-cutting syndrome: the meaning of a gesture. *American Journal of Psychiatry* 128(11):47–52.

Rosenzweig, M., and Spruill, J. (1987). Twenty years after Twiggy: a retrospective investigation of bulimic-like behaviors. *International Journal of Eating Disorders* 6(1):59–65.

Ross, C. (1989). *Multiple Personality Disorder*. New York: Wiley.

Ross, R., and McKay, H. (1979). *Self-Mutilation*. Lexington, MA: Lexington.

Roth, G. (1989). *Why Weight? A Guide to Ending Compulsive Eating*. New York: Plume.

——. (1996). *Appetites: On the Search for True Nourishment*. New York: Penguin.

Russ, M. (1992). Self-injurious behavior in patients with borderline personality disorder. *Journal of Personality Disorder* 6:64–81.

Ryan, P. (1993). A personal account: Eastern meditation group. In *Recovery from Cults: Help for Victims of Psychological or Spiritual Abuse*, ed. M. Langone, pp. 129–139. New York: W. W. Norton.

Sacksteder, J. (1988). Sadomasochistic relatedness to the body in anorexia nervosa. In *Masochism: The Treatment of Self-Inflicted Suffering*, ed. J. Montgomery, pp. 37–49. Madison, CT: International Universities Press.

———. (1989a). Psychosomatic dissociation and false self development in anorexia nervosa. In *The Facilitating Environment: Clinical Applications of Winnicott's Theory*, ed. M. Fromm and B. Smith, pp. 365–393. Madison, CT: International Universities Press.

———. (1989b). Personalization as an aspect of the process of change in anorexia nervosa. In *The Facilitating Environment: Clinical Applications of Winnicott's Theory*, ed. M. Fromm and B. Smith, pp. 394–423. Madison, CT: International Universities Press.

Sanders, C. (1989). *Customizing Your Body: The Art and Culture of Tattooing*. Philadelphia: Temple University Press.

Sandler, J., and Sandler, A. (1978). On the development of object relationships and affect. *International Journal of Psychoanalysis* 59:285–296.

Sansone, R., Fine, M., and Sansone, L. (1994). An integrated psychotherapy approach to the management of self-destructive behavior in eating disorder patients with borderline personality disorder. *Eating Disorders; The Journal of Treatment and Prevention* 2(3):251–260.

Sanville, J. (1994). *The Playground of Psychoanalytic Therapy*. Hillsdale, NJ: Analytic Press.

Satter, E. M. (1986). Childhood eating disorders. *Journal of the American Dietetic Association* 86(3):357–361.

———. (1990). The feeding relationship: problems and interventions. *Journal of Pediatrics* 117(2):181–189.

Savage, D. (1996). Savage love. *The Village Voice*, November 12, p. 121.

Schemo, D. (1996). Recife journal: the decorated veterans of Brazil's stark streets. *The New York Times*, May 21, p. A4.

Schilder, P., and Wechsler, D. (1935). What do children know about the interior of the body? *International Journal of Psycho-Analysis* 16:355–360.

Schneider, J., and Agras, W. (1987). Bulimia in males: a matched comparison with females. *International Journal of Eating Disorders* 6:235–242.

Schore, A. (1997). Interdisciplinary developmental research as a source of clinical models. In *The Neurobiological and Developmental Basis for Psychotherapeutic Intervention*, ed. M. Moskowitz, C. Monk, C. Kaye, and S. Ellman, pp. 1–71. Northvale, NJ: Jason Aronson.

Schotte, D., and Stunkard, A. (1987). Bulimia versus bulimic behaviors on a college campus. *Journal of the American Medical Association* 258:1213–1217.

Schupak-Neuberg, E., and Nemeroff, C. (1993). Disturbances and identity and self-regulation in bulimia nervosa: implications for a metaphorical perspective of "body as self." *International Journal of Eating Disorders* 13(4):335–347.

Schur, M. (1955). Comments on the metapsychology of somatization. *Psycho-*

analytic Study of the Child 10:119–164. New York: International Universities Press.

———. (1972). Freud, Living and Dying. New York: International Universities Press.

Seinfeld, J. (1990). The Bad Object: Handling the Negative Therapeutic Reaction in Psychotherapy. Northvale, NJ: Jason Aronson.

Selvini Palazzoli, M. (1974). Self-Starvation: From Individual to Family Therapy in the Treatment of Anorexia Nervosa, transl. Arnold Pomerans. Northvale, NJ: Jason Aronson.

Shahly, V. (1987). Eating her words: food metaphor as transitional symptom in the recovery of a bulimic patient. Psychoanalytic Study of the Child 42:403–421. New Haven, CT: Yale University Press.

Shapiro, S. (1987). Self-mutilation and self-blame in incest victims. American Journal of Psychotherapy 41(1):46–54.

Shapiro, S., and Dominiak, G. (1992). Sexual Trauma and Psychopathology. New York: Free Press.

Sharp, C., and Freeman, C. (1993). The medical complications of anorexia nervosa (review article). British Journal of Psychiatry 162:452–462.

Shengold, L. (1979). Child abuse and deprivation: soul murder. Journal of the American Psychoanalytic Association 27(3):533–559.

———. (1989). Soul Murder: The Effects of Childhood Abuse and Deprivation. New Haven, CT: Yale University Press.

Shneidman, E. (1976). The components of suicide. Psychiatric Annals 6:51–66.

———. (1993). Suicide as Psychache: A Clinical Approach to Self-Destructive Behavior. Northvale, NJ: Jason Aronson.

Shneidman, E., Farberow, N., and Litman, N. (1994). The Psychology of Suicide: A Clinician's Guide to Evaluation and Treatment. Northvale, NJ: Jason Aronson.

Shorter, E. (1992). From Paralysis to Fatigue: A History of Psychosomatic Illness in the Modern Era. New York: Free Press.

———. (1994). From the Mind into the Body: The Cultural Origins of Psychosomatic Symptoms. New York: Free Press.

———. (1997). A History of Psychiatry: From the Era of the Asylum to the Age of Prozac. New York: Wiley.

Silberstein, R., Blackman, S., and Mandell, W. (1966). Autoerotic head-banging: a reflection on the opportunism of infants. Journal of Clinical Psychology 5:235–243.

Silverman, M. (1989). Power, control, and the threat to die in a case of anorexia nervosa. In Psychosomatic Symptoms: Psychodynamic Treatment of the Underlying Personality Disorder, ed. C. Wilson and I. Mintz, pp. 351–364. Northvale, NJ: Jason Aronson.

Silverman, S. (1970). Psychologic Cues in Forecasting Physical Illness. New York: Appleton-Century-Crofts.

Simeon, D., and Hollander, E. (1993). Self-mutilation and the relationship to OCD. OCD Newsletter 7,1 6–6.

Simeon, D., Stanley, B., Frances, A., et al. (1992). Self-mutilation in personality disorders: psychological and biological correlates. American Journal of Psychiatry 149:221–226.

Simpson, C., and Porter, G. (1981). Self-mutilation in children and adults. Bulletin of the Menninger Clinic 45(5):428–438.

Simpson, M. A. (1980). Self-mutilation as indirect self-destructive behavior: "Nothing to get so cut up about. . ." In The Many Faces of Suicide, ed. N. Farberow, pp. 257–283. New York: McGraw-Hill.

Siomopoulos, V. (1974). Repeated self-cutting: an impulse neurosis. American Journal of Psychotherapy 28:85–94.

Slater, L. (1998). Prozac Diary. New York: Random House.

Smith, F. (1980). Nail Biting: The Beatable Habit. Provo, UT: Brigham Young University Press.

Smith, J., and Krejci, J. (1991). Minorities join the majority: eating disturbances among Hispanic and Native American youth. International Journal of Eating Disorders 10(2):179–186.

Sours, J. (1980). Starving to Death in a Sea of Objects: The Anorexia Nervosa Syndrome. Northvale, NJ: Jason Aronson.

Sperling, M. (1953). Food allergies and conversion hypteria. Psychoanalytic Quarterly 22:525–538.

———. (1968). Trichotillomania, trichophagy, and cyclic vomiting: a contribution to the psychopathology of female sexuality. International Journal of Psycho-Analysis 49:682–690.

———. (1978). Psychosomatic Disorders in Childhood. New York: Jason Aronson.

Spitz, R. (1945). Hospitalism: an inquiry into the genesis of psychiatric conditions in early childhood. Psychoanalytic Study of the Child 1:53–74. New York: International Universities Press.

———. (1946). Hospitalism: a followup report. Psychoanalytic Study of the Child 2:113–117. New York: International Universities Press.

———. (1957). No and Yes: On the Genesis of Human Communication. New York: International Universities Press.

———. (1958). On the genesis of superego components. Psychoanalytic Study of the Child 13:375–404.

———. (1965). The First Year of Life: A Psychoanalytic Study of Normal and Deviant Development of Object Relations. New York: International Universities Press.

Sprince, M. (1988). Experiencing and recovering transitional space in the analytic treatment of anorexia nervosa and bulimia. In Bulimia: Psychoanalytic Treatment and Theory, ed. H. Schwartz, pp. 73–88. Madison, CT: International Universities Press.

Steele, V. (1996). Fetish: Fashion, Sex, and Power. New York: Oxford University Press.

Steinberg, S., Tobin, D., and Johnson, C. (1990). The role of bulimic behaviors in affect regulation: different functions for different patient subgroups? *International Journal of Eating Disorders* 9(1):51–55.

Steiner-Adair, C. (1991). New maps of development, new models of therapy: the psychology of women and the treatment of eating disorders. In *Psychodynamic Treatment of Anorexia Nervosa*, ed. C. Johnson, pp. 225–244. New York: Guilford.

Steiner, J. (1981). Perverse relationships between parts of the self: A clinical illustration. *International Journal of Psycho-Analysis* 62:241–251.

———. (1996). The aim of psychoanalysis in theory and practice. *International Journal of Psycho-Analysis* 77(6):1073–1082.

Stern, C., ed. (1978). *Gates of Repentance: The New Union Prayerbook for the Days of Awe*. New York: Central Conference of American Rabbis.

Stern, D. (1985). *The Interpersonal World of the Infant*. Cambridge: Harvard University Press.

Stoller, R. (1985). *Observing the Erotic Imagination*. New Haven, CT: Yale University Press.

———. (1991). *Pain & Passion: A Psychoanalyst Explores the World of S & M*. New York: Plenum.

Stolorow, R. (1986). Critical reflections on the theory of self psychology: an inside view. *Psychoanalytic Inquiry* 6(3):387–402.

Stone, L. (1988). Passionate attachments in the west in historical perspective. In *Passionate Attachments*, ed. W. Gaylin and E. Person, pp. 15–26. New York: Free Press.

Stone, M. (1988). Toward a psychobiological theory on borderline personality disorder: Is irritability the red thread that runs through borderline conditions? *Dissociation* 1:2–15.

———. (1990). *The Fate of Borderline Patients*. New York: Guilford.

Stone, M., Stone, D., and Hurt, S. (1987). Natural history of borderline patients treated by intensive hospitalization. *Psychiatric Clinics of North America* 10:185–206.

Striegel-Moore, R., Tucker, N., and Hsu, J. (1990). Body image dissatisfaction and disordered eating in lesbian college students. *International Journal of Eating Disorders* 9(5):493–500.

Strong, M. (1998). *A Bright Red Scream*. New York: Viking.

Sugarman, A., and Jaffe, L. (1989). A developmental line of transitional phenomena. In *The Facilitating Environment: Clinical Applications of Winnicott's Theory*, ed. M. Fromm and B. Smith, pp. 88–129. Madison, CT: International Universities Press.

Sugarman, A., and Kurash, C. (1982). The body as transitional object in bulimia. *International Journal of Eating Disorders* 1(4):57–67.

Sugarman, A., Quinlan, D., and DeVenis, L. (1981). Anorexia nervosa as a defense against anaclitic depression. *International Journal of Eating Disorders* 1:44–61.

Sylvester, E. (1945). Analysis of psychogenic anorexia and vomiting in a four year old child. Psychoanalytic Study of the Child 1:167–184.

Talbot, M. (1998). Attachment theory: the ultimate experiment. The New York Times, May 24, Section 6, p. 24.

Tamburrino, M., Campbell, N., Franco, K., and Evans, C. (1995). Rumination in adults: two case histories. International Journal of Eating Disorders 17(1):101–104.

Taormina, C. (1996). Chalkboard with a Bad Eraser. Asbury Park, NJ: Broken Star.

Taylor, G. (1987). Psychosomatic Medicine and Contemporary Psychoanalysis. Madison, CT: International Universities Press.

Taylor, G., Bagby, R., and Parker, J. (1991). The alexithymia construct: a potential paradigm for psychosomatic medicine. Psychosomatics 32(2):153–164.

Terr, L. (1973). Children of Chowchilla: a study of psychic trauma. Psychoanalytic Study of the Child 34:547–623. New Haven, CT: Yale University Press.

———. (1990). Too Scared to Cry. New York: Harper & Row.

———. (1994). Unchained Memories: True Stories of Traumatic Memories Lost and Found. New York: Basic Books.

Teusch, R. (1988). Level of ego development and bulimics' conceptualizations of their disorder. International Journal of Eating Disorders 7:17–36.

Theroux, P. (1998). Nurse Wolf: For a dominatrix who sees herself as a healer, can a dungeon be a clinic? The New Yorker, June 15, pp. 50–63.

Thompson, B. (1994). Food, bodies and growing up female: childhood lessons about culture, race, and class. In Feminist Perspectives on Eating Disorders, ed. P. Fallon, M. Katzman, and S. Wooley, pp. 355–378. New York: Guilford.

Tobin, D., Johnson, C., and Dennis, A. (1992). Divergent forms of purging behavior in bulimia nervosa patients. International Journal of Eating Disorders 11(1):17–24.

Tolpin, M. (1972). On the beginning of a cohesive self: an application of the concept of transmuting internalization to the study of the transitional object and signal anxiety. Psychoanalytic Study of the Child 26:316–353. New Haven, CT: Yale University Press.

Tomkins, S. S. (1962). Affects, Imagery, Consciousness, vol. 1. New York: Springer.

Torem, M. (1986). Dissociative states presenting as an eating disorder. American Journal of Clinical Hypnosis 29:137–142.

Trautmann, K., and Connors, R. (1994). Understanding Self-Injury: A Workbook for Adults. Pittsburgh: Pittsburgh Action Against Rape.

Treasure, J., and Owen, J. (1997). Intrigung links between animal behavior and anorexia nervosa. International Journal of Eating Disorders 21(4):307–311.

Turnbull, J., Freeman, C., Barry, F., and Henderson, A. (1989). The clinical characteristics of bulimic women. International Journal of Eating Disorders 8(4):399–409.

Tustin, F. (1981). Autistic States in Children. London: Routledge and Kegan Paul.

———. (1990). The Protective Shell in Children and Adults. London: Karnac.

Vale, V., and Juno, A. (1989). *Modern Primitives: An Investigation of Contemporary Adornment and Ritual—Tattoo, Piercing, Scarification*. San Francisco: Re/ Search.

Valenstein, A. (1973). On attachment to painful feelings and the negative therapeutic reaction. *Psychoanalytic Study of the Child* 28:365–392. New Haven, CT: Yale University Press.

van der Kolk, B. (1987). *Psychological Trauma*. Washington, DC: American Psychiatric Press.

———. (1988). The trauma spectrum: the interaction of biological and social events in the genesis of the trauma response. *Journal of Traumatic Stress* 1(3):273–290.

———. (1989). The compulsion to repeat the trauma: re-enactment, revictimization, and masochism. *Psychiatric Clinics of North America* 12(2):389–411.

———. (1994). The body keeps the score: memory and the evolving psychobiology of posttraumatic stress. *Harvard Review of Psychiatry* 1:253–265.

van der Kolk, B., and Fisler, R. (1994). Childhood abuse and neglect and loss of self-regulation. *Bulletin of the Menninger Clinic* 58(2):145–168.

van der Kolk, B., Perry, J., and Herman, J. (1991). Childhood origins of self-destructive behavior. *American Journal of Psychiatry* 149:1665–1671.

Vanderlinden, J., and Vandereycken, W. (1997). *Trauma, Dissociation, and Impulse Dyscontrol in Eating Disorders*. New York: Brunner/Mazel.

Verny, T. (1981). *The Secret Life of the Unborn Child*. New York: Summit.

Viederman, M. (1988). The nature of passionate love. In *Passionate Attachments: Thinking About Love*, ed. W. Gaylin and E. Person, pp. 1–14. New York: Free Press.

Vogel, V. (1970). *American Indian Medicine*. Norman, OK: University of Oklahoma Press.

Waelder, R. (1936). The principle of multiple function: observations on overdetermination. *Psychoanalytic Quarterly* 5:45–62.

Walant, K. (1995). *Creating the Capacity for Attachment: Treating Addictions and the Alienated Self*. Northvale, NJ: Jason Aronson.

Walker, A. (1992). *Possessing the Secret of Joy*. New York: Washington Square Press.

Walsh, B. (1987). *Adolescent self-mutilation: an empirical study*. Doctoral dissertation, Boston College Graduate School of Social Work.

Walsh, B., and Rosen, P. (1985). Self-mutilation and contagion: an empirical test. *American Journal of Psychiatry* 142:119–120.

———. (1988). *Self-Mutilation: Theory, Research, Treatment*. New York: Guilford.

Wechsler, D. (1931). Incidence and significance of fingernail biting in children. *Psychoanalytic Review* 18:201–209.

Weiner, H., and Fawzy, F. (1989). An integrative model of health, disease, and illness. In *Psychosomatic Medicine*, ed. S. Cheren, Vol. I, pp. 9–44. Madison, CT: International Universities Press.

556 / References

Weissman, M. (1975). Wrist cutting. *Archives of General Psychiatry* 32:1166–1171.

Weissman, M., Bland, R., Canino, G., et al. (1996). Cross-national epidemiology of major depression and bipolar disorder. *Journal of the American Medical Association* 276(4):293–299.

Welbourne, J., and Purgold, J. (1984). *The Eating Sickness.* Bristol, England: Harvester.

Wickwire, J., and Bullitt, D. (1998). *Addicted to Danger: A Memoir About Affirming Life in the Face of Death.* New York: Pocket Books.

Willard, S., Winstead, D., Anding, R., and Dudley, P. (1989). Laxative abuse in eating disorders. *Psychiatric Medicine* 7(3):75–87.

Williams, L. (1995). Recovered memories of abuse in women with documented child sexual victimization histories. *Journal of Traumatic Stress* 8(4):649–673.

Wilson, C. (1983). The family psychological profile and its therapeutic implications. In *Fear of Being Fat: The Treatment of Anorexia Nervosa and Bulimia*, ed. C. Wilson, C. Hogan, and I. Mintz, pp. 29–47. Northvale, NJ: Jason Aronson.

———. (1986). The psychoanalytic psychotherapy of bulimic anorexia nervosa. *Adolescent Psychiatry* 13:274–314.

———. (1988). Bulimic equivalents. In *Bulimia: Psychoanalytic Theory and Treatment*, ed. H. Schwartz, pp. 489–522. Madison, CT: International Universities Press.

———. (1989). Ego functioning in psychosomatic disorders. In *Psychosomatic Symptoms: Psychodynamic Treatment of the Underlying Personality Disorder*, ed. C. Wilson and I. Mintz, pp. 13–32. New York: Jason Aronson.

Wilson, C., Hogan, C., and Mintz, I., eds. (1983). *Fear of Being Fat: The Treatment of Anorexia Nervosa and Bulimia.* New York: Jason Aronson.

Wilson, C., and Mintz, I., eds. (1989). *Psychosomatic Symptoms: Psychodynamic Treatment of the Underlying Personality Disorder.* Northvale, NJ: Jason Aronson.

Winchel, R. (1991). Self-mutilation and aloneness. *Academy Forum of American Academy of Psychoanalysis* 35:10–12.

Winchel, R., and Stanley, M. (1991). Self-injurious behavior: a review of the behavior and biology of self-mutilation. *American Journal of Psychiatry* 148(3):307–317.

Winnicott, D. (1949). Mind and its relation to the psyche-soma. In *Collected Papers: Through Paediatrics to Psychoanalysis*, pp. 243–254. New York: Basic Books, 1975.

———. (1953). Transitional objects and transitional phenomena. *International Journal of Psycho-Analysis* 34:(47):510–516.

———. (1958a). Mind and its relation to the psyche-soma. In *Collected Papers: Through Paediatrics to Psychoanalysis*, pp. 243–254. New York: Basic Books, 1975.

———. (1958b). Hate in the countertransference. In *Collected Papers: Through Paediatrics to Psychoanalysis*, pp. 194–203. New York: Basic Books, 1975.

―――. (1958c). The capacity to be alone. In *The Maturational Processes and the Facilitating Environment*, pp. 29–36. New York: International Universities Press, 1965.

―――. (1963). Dependence in infant-care, child-care, and in the psychoanalytic setting. In *The Maturational Processes and the Facilitating Environment*, pp. 249–259. New York: International Universities Press, 1965.

―――. (1965). *The Maturational Processes and the Facilitating Environment*. New York: International Universities Press.

―――. (1971). *Playing and Reality*. New York: Basic Books.

Witherspoon, T. (1990). Self-destruction. *Employee Assistance* 2(8):11–14.

Witkin, G. (1988). *Quick Fixes and Small Comforts: How Every Woman Can Resist Those Irresistible Urges (Eating, Shopping, Yelling, Napping, Smoking, Drinking, Redecorating, Cleaning, and Other Compulsions)*. New York: Villard Books.

Wolf, E. (1988). *Treating the Self: Elements of Clinical Self Psychology*. New York: Guilford.

Wolf, N. (1991). *The Beauty Myth: How Images of Beauty Are Used Against Women*. New York: Morrow.

Woodruff, M. (1998). Flesh made word: cutting in search of the mother. Paper presented at American Psychological Association meeting, Division 39, Boston, Spring.

Woodside, B., Garner, D., Rockert, W., and Garfinkel, P. E. (1990). Eating disorders in males: Insights from a clinical and psychometric comparison with female patients. In *Males with Eating Disorders*, ed. A. Andersen, pp. 100–115. New York: Brunner/Mazel.

Wooley, S., and Wooley, O. (1985). Intensive outpatient and residential treatment for bulimia. In *Handbook of Psychotherapy for Anorexia Nervosa and Bulimia*, ed. D. Garner and P. Garfinkel, pp. 391–430. New York: Guilford.

Wurtman, J., Wurtman, R., Growdon, J., et al. (1981). Carbohydrate craving in obese people: suppression by treatments affecting serotonergic transmission. *International Journal of Eating Disorders* 1:2–15.

Wurtzel, E. (1994). *Prozac Nation: Young and Depressed in America*. Boston: Houghton Mifflin.

Yablonsky, L. (1997). *The Story of Junk*. New York: Farrar, Straus, Giroux.

Yaryura-Tobias, J., and Neziroglu, F. (1978). Compulsions, aggression and self-mutilation: a hypothalamic disorder. *Orthomolecular Psychiatry* 7:114–117.

Yaryura-Tobias, J., Neziroglu, F., and Kaplan, S. (1995). Self-mutilation, anorexia, and dysmenorrhea in obsessive-compulsive disorder. *International Journal of Eating Disorders* 17(1):33–38.

Yates, A. (1991). *Compulsive Exercise and the Eating Disorders: Toward an Integrated Theory of Activity*. New York: Brunner/Mazel.

Yellowlees, A. (1985). Anorexia and bulimia in anorexia nervosa. *British Journal of Psychiatry* 146:648–652.

Zakin, D. (1989). Eating disturbance, emotional separation, and body image. *International Journal of Eating Disorders* 8(4):411–416.

Zeeman, C. (1976). Catastrophe theory. *Scientific American* 234(4):341–353.

Zetzel, E. (1956). Current concepts of transference. *International Journal of Psycho-Analysis* 37:369–376.

———. (1965). The theory of therapy in relation to a developmental model of the psychic apparatus. *International Journal of Psycho-Analysis* 46:39–52.

Zetzel, E., and Meissner, W. (1973). *Basic Concepts of Psychoanalytic Psychiatry.* New York: Basic Books.

Zimmer, S. (1999). Self-care through mutuality. *The Renfrew Perspective* 5(1):5–7.

Zimmerman, J., and Reavill, G. (1998). *Raising Our Athletic Daughters: How Sports Can Build Self-Esteem and Save Girls' Lives.* New York: Doubleday.

Credits

"Savage Love," by Dan Savage, in *The Village Voice*, November 12, 1996. Used by permission of the author.

Standard Edition of the Complete Psychological Works of Sigmund Freud, translated and edited by James Strachey. Used by permission of Sigmund Freud Copyrights, The Institute of Psycho-Analysis, and The Hogarth Press.

The Collected Papers, Volume 4, by Sigmund Freud. Authorized translation under the supervision of Joan Riviere. Published by Basic Books, Inc. by arrangement with The Hogarth Press, Ltd. and The Institute of Psycho-Analysis, London. Reprinted by permission of Basic Books, a member of Perseus Books, L.L.C.

"The Voice on the Skin: Self-Mutilation and Merleau-Ponty's Theory of Language," by Janice McLane, in *Hypatia* 11(4):107–118. Copyright © 1996 by Janice McLane and used with permission.

Vivienne: A Book on Adolescent Suicide, by John E. Mack and Holly Hickler. Copyright © 1981 by John E. Mack and Holly Hickler. Reprinted by permission of Russell & Volkening as agents for the authors. Poetry, letters, school compositions, and journal entries by Vivienne Loomis copyright © 1981 by David Loomis and Paulette Loomis.

The author expresses her gratitude to those whose names appear above for permission to use the passages indicated. Every effort has been made to ascertain the owner of copyrights for the selections used in this volume and to obtain permission to reprint copyrighted passages. The author will be pleased, in subsequent editions, to correct any inadvertent error or omission that may be pointed out.

Index

566 / *Index*

574 / *Index*